HISTORY OF THE LITERATURE

OF

ANCIENT GREECE.

VOLUME I.

KARL OTFRIED MULLER.

A

HISTORY OF THE LITERATURE

OF

ANCIENT GREECE.

By K. O. MÜLLER

CONTINUED AFTER THE AUTHOR'S DEATH BY

JOHN WILLIAM DONALDSON, D.D.

IN THREE VOLUMES.

VOL. I.

KENNIKAT PRESS
Port Washington, N. Y./London

HISTORY OF THE LITERATURE OF ANCIENT GREECE

First published in 1858
Reissued in 1971 by Kennikat Press
Library of Congress Catalog Card No: 70-113282
ISBN 0-8046-1201-3

Manufactured by Taylor Publishing Company   Dallas, Texas

KENNIKAT CLASSICS SERIES

MY DEAR SIR,

In inscribing this work with your name, I discharge
at once a public and a private duty : a public duty, because the book,
which I have attempted to complete, owes its commencement to your
suggestion, and its first appearance in an English form to your labours
as translator and editor; a private duty, because I have been associated
in this labour only through you and as your substitute. If, however,
you had been unconnected with this publication, I could hardly have
found an English scholar to whom a history of Greek Literature would
be more appropriately dedicated. Your important contributions to
Classical Learning, from which your political engagements have not
altogether withdrawn your attention, have placed you by general
consent in the foremost rank of English philologers, and I should seem
to be guilty of flattery if I attempted to give expression to the universal estimate of your exact and comprehensive erudition.

Believe me,

My dear Sir,

Very truly yours,

J. W. DONALDSON.

PREFACE.

WHEN K. O. Müller died in 1840, the Society for the Diffusion of Useful Knowledge, for which I was translating the History of Greek Literature from the author's manuscript, commissioned me to complete the work, and a few pages of my continuation had been published, when the Society came to an end. From that time until rather less than three years ago, I heard no more of the book; but the present publishers, having become possessed of the copyright, have requested me to complete my original undertaking, and the following pages are the result.

In thus accepting a task, perhaps the most laborious, in proportion to its extent, that I could have undertaken, I have been induced by two motives: first, a wish to fulfil an obligation to the public, and to perform a promised duty to the memory of a distinguished scholar; secondly, a conviction that this book, if completed with tolerable success, would furnish an aid to the classical student which has not been and is not likely to be superseded.

With regard to the first of these motives, I am quite aware that there are many who feel a respect for the memory of K. O. Müller, and who wish that his last and not least important work should be completed according to his plan, and that among these there are some who are at least as competent as I can pretend to be to write a history of Greek literature. But, on the other hand, I have every reason to believe that the public announcement of the fact, that one of the translators had been appointed to continue the work by the Society, for which Müller himself was writing it, must have deterred his friends in Germany and England from attempting to perform the same good office. In point of fact, the work is still a fragment; and though two editions have been published in

Germany, no one has essayed to take up the broken thread of
Müller's narrative. Among his colleagues and successors at
Göttingen, Schneidewin, who at one time wished to finish the
history, and K. F. Hermann, who was as well qualified to write
on the subject as any German professor, have both been removed by death within the last year. And it really seems that,
if I had not been willing or able to redeem my promise, this
debt due to the public and to Müller would never have been
paid.

In asserting the great importance of Müller's work as an
aid to the classical student, and in saying that it is without any
rival, present or prospective, I hope I shall not be understood
as wishing to reflect on any history of Greek literature, either
published or in the course of publication. I merely desire to
intimate my opinion that, besides being now complete, Müller's
is the only book on this subject which is concise without
sinking to the level of a mere compendium, and which is
sufficiently popular, while it possesses all the attributes of exact
scholarship. A diffuse and voluminous work, whatever may be
its merits, cannot serve the same purpose 'in the hands of
persons commencing or pursuing the study of the Greek
authors.'* A history of Greek literature should stimulate the
curiosity of the classical student without attempting to satisfy
it. It must not even pretend to say all that is known about
the Greek authors themselves : for this is best left to dictionaries
and encyclopædias. Its work is accomplished, as far as the
student is concerned, if it tells him how literature rose, grew,
and declined among the Greeks ; if it indicates how the different
writers contributed to its development or decadence, and if it
links together their separate biographies by the proper chain of
cause and effect. A history of Greek literature for the use of
students is not a collection of unconnected notices ; it is not a
catalogue of all the works written in the Greek language, like
that which we owe to the diligence of Fabricius ; it is not an
elaborate review of the separate writings of eminent Greeks,
like those which find their place in the Prolegomena of critical
editions ; it is not a history of philosophy, except so far as

---

* See the translators' preface to the first volume of this work ; below, p. xxxi.

philosophy is a development of literature. It should serve as a
guide to those who are engaged in reading the Greek authors
themselves; it should be a sort of index map to connect the
detailed surveys of particular districts; and for all beyond this
it must refer the student to the original texts or special treatises.
Such a book was Müller's as far as it went, and I know no
other of precisely the same kind, either in English or in any
foreign language, either already published or in the course of
publication.

For my own part, I have endeavoured, to the best of my
ability, to carry out the plan on which Müller commenced this
work. Besides the general principles laid down in his introduction, I have had before me the following list of the chapters
which he had intended to write, with the numbers which he
originally attached to them :—

XXXIV.
Xenophon.

XXXVI.
Plato's Sokratische Dialogen.

XXXVII.
Demosthenes' Beredtsamkeit.

XXXVIII.
Demosthenes' Zeitgenossen unter den Rednern.

XXXIX.
Historiker aus Isokrates' Schule.

XL.
Aristoteles.

DRITTE PERIODE, GELEHRTE LITERATUR.

XLI.
*Alexandrinische Epopöen: Kallimachos, Apollonios, Rhianos,
Euphorion.*

LIV.

Historiker in der Zeit der Antoninen.

LV.

Wissenschaftliche Gelehrte. Ptolemœos, &c.

LVI.

Literarische Sammler. Athenœos, &c.

LVII.

Letzte Zeiten des Heidenthums. Heidnische Rhetoren und Philosophen.

LVIII.

Antagonismus der Christlichen. Schriftsteller gegen die Heidnischen.

LIX.

Nachklänge der alten Literatur. Romane. Epos des Nonnus.

LX.

Überblick des Betriebs der Literatur in Byzanz.

It will be observed that, in filling up this brief outline, or rather in writing on this series of themes, I have closely followed Müller in all that relates to the plan and arrangement of the book. While I have completed the history in the sixty chapters which he originally assigned to it, I have added two to those which are given in this list—namely, those 'on the Socratic schools' and 'on the writings of Hippocrates.' But I have arranged the four chapters assigned to Alexandrian literature in two; I have also combined Müller's forty-ninth and fiftieth chapters, and his fifty-fifth and fifty-sixth chapters, in one chapter for each pair; and have thus, as I conceive, given greater distinctness to his classification of the subject.

The period which is comprised in these narrow limits is more than eighteen centuries; and I need hardly say that I do not pretend to give new or original information on all parts of this extensive survey. There are several subjects which I have made my own by special study, but an equal attention to all the authors would have involved the unprofitable labour of a *Chalcenterus* or *Bibliolathas.* I have therefore considered it my duty to avail myself of recent as well as ancient learning, and for this reason I have referred more frequently than Müller did to modern authorities. Every special obligation has been carefully acknowledged in the notes. But I have been constantly indebted for suggestions, guidance, references, and other assistance more or less valuable, to the *Bibliotheca* of Fabricius, to the literary histories of Schöll, Westermann, and Bernhardy, to the philosophical researches of H. Ritter, Hegel, and Schleiermacher, to the *Fasti* of the late Mr. Clinton, and to the dictionaries of Drs. A. Pauly and W. Smith. It has often been of great advantage to me to be able to refer to the learned volumes of Dr. Thirlwall and Mr. Grote; and I have much regretted that the latter scholar has not yet published his promised discussions on Greek philosophy. The greater part of Mr. Mure's valuable work treats of the authors who had been previously reviewed by Müller: and my own chapters on Xenophon and the minor historians were written before I had an opportunity of seeing his fifth volume, in which alone he has traversed some of the ground surveyed in my continuation.

In conclusion, I have only to express my hope that this supplementary labour will contribute, at least in some degree, to realize the intended usefulness of Müller's unfinished work, and thus to fulfil the wishes of the excellent Society, by which it was so far advanced during the lifetime of its lamented author, and to which I owe my first connexion with the undertaking.

J. W. D.

Cambridge, 25th June, 1858.

THE LIFE AND WRITINGS

OF

K. O. MÜLLER.

BY DR. DONALDSON.

THE LIFE AND WRITINGS

OF

KARL OTFRIED MÜLLER.

KARL OTFRIED MÜLLER was born at Brieg in Silesia on the 28th of August, 1797. The only name, which was given to him at baptism, was *Karl*, and he assumed the second name *Otfried*, as a literary prænomen to distinguish him from many other *Karl Müllers*, on the publication of his first important work in 1819. He received the rudiments of his education from his father, at that time a young Lutheran pastor. At Easter 1810 he was entered in the fourth class of the gymnasium at Brieg, and remained there until he had reached the head of the school, with a great reputation for classical scholarship, especially Latin verse composition, at Easter 1814, when he was removed to the University of Breslau. Here he enjoyed the great advantage of receiving instruction in classical philology from J. G. Schneider, the editor of Xenophon and Theophrastus, and the father of improved Greek lexicography in Germany, and from L. F. Heindorf, who had been an eminent member of Niebuhr's coterie at Berlin, and who is well known by his commentaries on Plato and Horace. For the latter scholar, who showed a very early appreciation of his talents, and gave him encouragement at a time when such a stimulus to his exertions was most efficacious, Müller formed a strong attachment, which contributed, when he went to Berlin, to increase his prejudice against the celebrated F. A. Wolf, who had been Heindorf's teacher, but had yielded to the feelings of jealousy, which tutors of a certain temper entertain towards their successful pupils, and had endeavoured, in a very unhandsome manner, to disparage

Heindorf's merit as a critical interpreter. Although philology was the main pursuit of Müller at Breslau, especially after he had become well acquainted with Heindorf, he engaged in almost all the other studies of the University. Philosophy, which he learned in the lecture-rooms of Steffens, Kayssler, and Thilo, seemed likely at one time to withdraw him from classical scholarship. Another of his favourite studies was botany, in which he found an admirable teacher in Link. He read mathematics up to a certain point under Jungnitz, attended the theological lectures of Augusti and Gass, heard Raumer on the French Revolution, and made some progress in Hebrew and Syriac under Middeldorpf. But with all this diversity of reading he was growing more and more devoted to that which became the special study of his life—classical antiquity in its widest range and compass. And in order to gratify his increasing love for this branch of learning he removed in the spring of 1816 to Berlin, which enjoyed at that time the highest reputation among the Universities of Germany. Although he studied only for a year at the Prussian capital, for he passed as Doctor in Philosophy at Easter 1817, this short residence at Berlin produced an important influence on his career. His exertions were indefatigable, and at no period during his laborious life did he spend a greater number of hours in intense study. In a letter written to his brother Edward on the eighteenth of February 1817,* he describes himself as surrounded by books : fifteen to twenty folios mostly open were lying on chairs, on the sofa, or on the ground, intermixed with countless borrowed books, which in spite of threatened fines he could not return to the public libraries. His excellent constitution sustained his bodily health in the midst of these efforts to amass learning, the more so, as he did not neglect to take exercise in the open air, to which his love for botany furnished a constant inducement, and he left Berlin a taller and stronger man than when he commenced his studies there. The fruits of his reading were shown in the inaugural dissertation ' on the history and antiquities of Ægina' which he drew up as an exercise for his Doctor's

---

* Eduard Müller, *Biographische Erinnerungen an K. O. Müller*, p. xviii.

degree and published shortly afterwards in an expanded form with the following title:

> ' Ægineticorum liber. Scripsit C. Müller, Silesius, Dr.
> Phil. Berolini. 1817. E. librariâ Reimarianâ.'

This little book was dedicated to Augustus Böckh, in whose school of classical philology Müller had finally enlisted himself, and who, recognizing in him a congenial spirit, became his firm friend to the end of his life. There are many indications in Müller's writings of the high esteem in which he held this great Berlin Professor, and on the other hand Böckh contributed more than any one to the early reputation and professional success of his admiring pupil, by writing a friendly review of the *Æginetica* and taking every opportunity of recommending him for educational appointments.

Müller's career as a teacher commenced in January 1818, when he was appointed assistant-master in the Magdalenæum, a public school at Breslau, then under the management of Manso, the well-known author of a book on Sparta. In this office, with no higher promotion than from the seventh to the sixth mastership in the school, he remained until June 1819, when Heeren, influenced chiefly, as it seems, by Müller's *Æginetica*, and Böckh's laudatory review of that book, wrote to invite him to Göttingen as adjunct professor (*Professor extraordinarius*) of ancient literature, and joint director of the Philological Seminary, a vacancy having been occasioned by Welcker's removal to Bonn. He accepted the flattering proposal with undisguised satisfaction. ' Göttingen,' he wrote to his parents, ' is the place of places for me !' And his gratification was increased by the liberality of the Hanoverian government, which, in addition to his promised salary of 600 dollars, allowed him 400 dollars to defray the expenses of a stay of eight weeks at Dresden, where he had long wished to study the monuments of ancient art. This opportunity, of which he diligently availed himself, not only gave fixity to his views on the archæology of the fine arts, which to the end of his life was one of his favourite subjects, but also cultivated his natural taste for the fine arts in general ; and he speaks with as much enthu-siasm of the great masters of the Italian schools, who are represented by masterpieces in the Dresden Gallery, as of the candelabra and bas-reliefs which he saw in the Museum there. In a letter to his mother he says :* ' I often stand by the half-hour together before that painting of paintings, the Madonna of Raphael, and come continually back to it, in spite of my wish to go on to other pictures. The majesty of the head of the infant Christ, who seems to be teeming with the work of redemption, is beyond all description. He has in truth ten Jupiters in his head.' Notwithstanding his youth, Müller was treated with great distinction at Dresden, and formed a lasting acquaintance with Böttiger and other eminent men in the Saxon capital.

On his arrival at Göttingen he was warmly received by Dissen and the other philological professors, and soon became one of the most active and popular lecturers at that seat of learning. The special and immediate subject of his lectures was ' the archæology and history of ancient art ;' but his various courses branched over nearly all the topics of classical erudition. During the first winter he discoursed on ancient oracles and prophecies, a subject not unconnected with his literary labours at this time. For in January 1820 he published a Latin essay :

' De Tripode Delphico. Gotting. 1820.'

And more elaborate investigations into the mythological lore of early Greece appeared soon after in the first volume of his great work :

' Geschichte Hellenischer Stämme und Städte,'

' Histories of Greek races and cities,' which bore the special title :

' Orchomenos und die Minyer. Breslau. 1820.'

In the same year appeared his essay :

' Minervæ Poliadis sacra et ædem in arce Athenarum illustravit C. O. Müller, Prof. in univers. lit. Götting. extraordinarius. Gottingæ. 1820.'

About the same time he contributed to Böttiger's *Amalthea* an article ' on the Tripods,' and prepared an elaborate paper ' on Athens and Attica,' for the general cyclopædia of Ersch and Gruber. In the midst of all these labours he retained his

---

* Eduard Müller, *Biographische Erinnerungen an K. O. Müller*, p. xlii.

overflowing spirits and a cheerfulness which no book-learning could damp. Many stories are told of the ebullitions of innocent gaiety with which he amused his friends. In fact liveliness was his distinguishing characteristic. In writing to his sister Gottliebe, he would go on rhyming every two or three words to the end of the letter. The following specimen is given* from an epistle dated Easter, 1819 : ' Liebchen, komm zum Bübchen, in mein Stübchen, Herzensspitzbübchen. Wir sind selig und wählig (*i. e.* he and his brother Julius), mitunter geht's kunterbunter, ein Bischen knurrig und schnurrig. Mit meinem Sehnen und Wähnen und allen Plänen ist's ein langsames Drucksen und Mucksen. Wird nichts draus, mach mir nichts draus.' In the same spirit of innocent pleasantry we are told how he and his immediate intimates at Göttingen acted charades of the most ludicrous ingenuity. For example, in representing the word ' Iphigenie,' the tallest of the party would appear holding his hat over his head to indicate the capital ' I,' with its dot; another on all fours would exhibit a ' Vieh,' (*phi*); and a third with fantastic gestures would imitate the *genie* of the last syllables.† The excitability of Müller's temperament often relieved itself with exclamations, and a ludicrous story is told of a mistake occasioned by his frequent ejaculation ' Himmel, O Himmel,' when he was much delighted. A Silesian lady of his acquaintance invited him to hear her daughter's splendid performance on the pianoforte. ' Himmel, O Himmel!' cried the enraptured listener. ' No,' interposed the gratified parent; ' it is not Himmel but Hummel, who composed that piece.' The strength of Müller's imaginative powers was shown not only by poems of a somewhat higher aim, but by dramatic talents of no inconsiderable order. While quite a child he delighted in all the details of a little puppet theatre, and as a young man, when he visited his parents during the Göttingen vacations, he would occasionally organize family gatherings after the fashion of an ancient Greek festival.‡

In the summer and autumn of 1822 the liberality of the Hanoverian government enabled Müller to undertake a journey to Holland, England, and France, chiefly for the purpose of in-

---

* E. Müller. *Biograph. Erinn.* p. xxxii.   † *Ibid.* p. xlix.   ‡ *Ibid.* p. xlvi.

specting museums, and so increasing his knowledge as a teacher
of archæology. The eminent persons whose acquaintance he
made during this tour, and who received the young philologer
with kindness and forwarded his studies with friendly interest,
were, in Holland, Reuvens, professor of archæology at Leyden;
in England, Dr. Herbert Marsh, Bishop of Peterborough, Mr.
Payne Knight, and Colonel Leake ; and in Paris, Letronne and
Raoul-Rochette.

On his return to Göttingen, he applied himself with increased diligence to the continuation of his ' Histories of Greek
races and cities,' and the fruits of his labours appeared in 1824,
in two further volumes of that work which bore the separate
title :

' Die Dorier.'

Of all Müller's works, there is no one which has produced a
greater influence on the studies of his contemporaries, or more
largely contributed to the establishment of his European
reputation.   Perhaps, indeed, there is no one product of
German learning which exhibits a greater mass of well-digested
erudition.   In combination with Niebuhr's ' History of Rome,'
which in its improved form first appeared in English in 1828,
Müller's ' Dorians ' gave a new direction to the classical studies
of the country.   With the author's sanction, and with many
additions from his pen, which made it equivalent to a new
edition of the original,* this work was published in England as :

> ' The History and Antiquities of the Doric race, by C. O.
> Müller, translated from the German by Henry
> Tufnell, Esq., and George Cornewall Lewis, Esq.
> Oxford, 1830.' 2 vols. 8vo.

This translation also contained, in the form of an appendix,
Müller's essay on the settlements, origin, and early history of
the Macedonian nation, which had appeared at Berlin in 1825,
as a separate treatise, with the title :

> ' Ueber die Makedonier. Eine ethnographische Unter-
> suchung, von K. O. Müller.'

---

* See the Translators' Preface, p. ii.

The great work on the Dorians was republished in German four years after the author's death, under the superintendence of Schneidewin, and with additions from Müller's papers.

In the year 1823, Müller declined a very complimentary invitation to join the University of Berlin, and he was this year raised to the rank of Professor Ordinarius. Thoroughly established at Göttingen, and with a sufficient income to meet the humble demands of German housekeeping, he was enabled to marry the daughter of the celebrated jurist Hugo, a young lady for whom he had conceived a warm affection. The wedding took place on the 8th September, 1824, and the newly married couple, with the bride's father, set out on a tour to the Rhine-land to visit the family of the Hugo's, in Baden. On this occasion, Müller made the acquaintance of Niebuhr and A. W. Schlegel at Bonn, and of Umbreit, Voss, and Creuzer at Heidelberg; on his way back to Göttingen, he paid a visit to Platner. His establishment as a married man at Göttingen is described by his friends as a model of elegance and comfort, especially after he got into his new house. 'It always gave me the greatest pleasure,' says Lücke,* 'to visit at his house, especially the new one, with its beautiful garden, which he had arranged himself, with a view to hospitality, with the best practical judgment and with refined taste, in a style which, as we used to say by way of banter, was not that of Göttingen, but Græco-Silesian. The cheerful happiness which reigned there, without any pride, the managing and kindly wife, the lustre shed upon them by the reputation of her father, Hugo, the loveable children, the tasteful but solid comfort, the elegance without any false adornment, in short, the whole had in my eyes always a classical tone.'

The year 1825 witnessed the publication of one of Müller's most original and important works: his 'introduction to a scientific system of mythology,' or in its German title:

'Prolegomena zu einer wissenschaftlichen Mythologie.'

Like 'The Dorians' this work has been translated into English, the author of the version being Mr. John Leitch.

---

* *Erinnerungen an K. O. Müller, von Dr. Friedrich Lücke.* Göttingen. 1841. p. 35.

The book takes a sober view of the subject, and endeavours to mediate between the extreme theories of Creuzer and Lobeck. About the same time, the Royal Academy of Sciences at Berlin proposed the following subject for a prize essay : ' To explain and exhibit critically the nature and constitution of the training of the Etruscan nation, both generally and in reference to the several branches of the activity of a cultivated nation, in order as far as possible to ascertain which of them really, and in what degree each of them, flourished in this celebrated people.' Müller competed for this prize, which was awarded to him on the 3rd July, 1826. In preparing for the press the work which obtained this distinction, he considered himself entitled to give it a greater extension than this programme seemed to presume, and it appeared two years afterwards as a complete treatise on Etruscan antiquities with the title:

' Die Etrusker. Vier Bücher von K. O. Müller. Breslau. 1828.' 2 vols. 8vo.

In this work he showed that his knowledge of Italian antiquities was not inferior to his Greek learning, and the book will always occupy a high place in the department of research, which Thomas Dempster opened, and which is not yet closed to the inquisitiveness of scholars. Just before he obtained the Berlin prize on the 11th June, 1826, Müller's domestic affections were gratified by the birth of a daughter, and he seemed to have realized every wish which his affectionate heart or his literary ambition could have prompted. While the two volumes on the Etruscans were preparing for the press, Müller published his excellent essay :

' De Phidiæ vita et operibus. Gotting. 1827.'

His popular ' Manual of Ancient Art' was published about the same time as the English translation of ' The Dorians,' with the title :

' Handbuch der Archæologie der Kunst. Breslau. 1830.'

The second edition appeared in 1835, and the third was edited by Welcker in 1847. This work has been translated into English by Mr. Leitch, whose version has been reprinted. An Italian translation has appeared at Naples, and a French version was published by Nicard in 1841. For methodical learning and completeness, there is no better book on the subject of ancient art. The outline illustrations to this treatise have appeared in a series of parts commencing in the year 1832, with the title:

> 'Denkmäler der alten Kunst nach der Auswahl und Anordnung von K. O. Müller, gezeichnet und radirt von K. Oesterley.'

In 1831 he drew up a geographical supplement to his work on 'The Dorians' with the title:

> 'Zur Karte des nördlichen Griechenlands. Beilage zu dem Werke dess. Verf.: die Dorier.'

And he has shown his familiarity with the land of Hellas in his

> 'Bemerkungen zu Rienacker's Bearbeitung der Leake-schen Topographie. Halle. 1829.'

In 1833 his studies in Latin philology, which had been stimulated by his Etruscan researches, bore their first fruits in a critical edition of Varro's essay on his mother-tongue. The title is:

> 'M. Terentî Varronis de Lingua Latina Librorum quæ supersunt emendata et annotata a C. O. Muellero.'

Thus far his numerous writings had been received with general applause or with fair and moderate criticism. But his edition and translation of the *Eumenides* of Æschylus involved him in a bitter controversy, which was a source of great discomfort to him during the year which followed its publication. He had commenced this book and announced it in the winter of 1826-27, and had read the translation to his brothers in the summer of 1828, but for some reason he kept the work in his desk, and he did not give it to the public till 1833, when it came out with a complete apparatus of explanatory essays, as:

> 'Æschylos Eumeniden griechisch und deutsch mit erläuternden Abhandlungen über die äussere Darstellung und über den Inhalt und die Composition dieser Tragödie.'

Müller had formed a warm attachment to Dissen, who was at this time a great invalid, and had shared in his friend's indig-

nation at the manner in which the renowned Godfrey Hermann
of Leipsig had attacked Dissen's *Pindar*, (see his *Opuscula*,
vol. VI. pp. 3—69). It seemed to Müller and to other
philologers of Böckh's school, that Hermann had usurped
the position of a literary dictator, and was unwilling to allow
to others a free expression of opinion on questions of
Greek scholarship. With the frankness, then, of his noble
nature, and with a due sense of his own position in the literary
world, Müller could not enter on a field especially appropriated
by the Leipsig scholar, without proclaiming his own independence, and anticipating an attack which perhaps a humbler
mode of proceeding would not have averted. He concludes his
preface to the *Eumenides* with the following words : ' Unfortunately I cannot indulge in the hope of successfully recommending a renewed consideration of many points to the distinguished
philologer from whom we have long been expecting a new
edition of Æschylus, because this scholar seems to be determined
beforehand to break his stick over that which modern researches
produce in certain directions, which are out of the reach of his
own studies, and especially when they concern Æschylus. I
do not cherish the imagination that I shall form an exception
to this general rule. But I must enter my most decided
protest beforehand against Hermann's setting me right before
the public with a dictatorial sentence, like a judge who has
been asked his opinion, before he has as yet convinced us in the
slightest degree that he really possesses a clear conception of the
connexion of thought and of the plan of one tragedy of Æschylus,
or in general of any one work of ancient poetry—a conception
to the attainment of which, in our opinion, the efforts of philology at the present day ought principally to be directed.' These
remarks were regarded as a sort of challenge by Hermann and
his adherents ; and Müller's book on the *Eumenides* was sharply
attacked by Hermann himself in the *Wiener Jahrbücher*, vol.
LXIV. (reprinted in his *Opuscula*, vol. VI. pars II. pp. 9—
215), and by his pupil F. W. Fritzche in a tract entitled :
' Recension des Buches Æschylos Eumeniden von K. O.
Müller, von einem Philologen. Leipsig. 1834-35.' To
these criticisms Müller replied in a spirited and vigorous
manner ('Anhang z. d. B. Æsch. Eumenid. Göttingen. 1834.'

'Erklärung.' 1855); and it must be allowed at any rate that the Göttingen professor came forth from the conflict with undiminished reputation.

In the mean time Müller was receiving from the government of Hanover those distinctions which generally fall to the lot of distinguished literary men in Germany. In 1830 he had been appointed member of the ' Scientific Committee of Inquiry ;' in 1831 he became 'Member of the Academical Senate,' and chairman of the committee just mentioned ; in 1832 he received the title of ' Aulic Councillor' (*Hofrath*) ; in 1834 he was made Knight of the Guelphic order by William IV.; and in 1837 his salary was largely increased. As a general rule Müller took but little interest in politics, and although he was director of the news rooms, he was often a fortnight behind the date in his acquaintance with the public journals.* He was intimately connected with the seven eminent professors who protested against the subversion of the Constitution of 1834 by an edict of King Ernest (our Duke of Cumberland), and he did not conceal his general agreement with them. But he took no public steps in opposition to the Government, and retained his place in the University, when Grimm and Dahlmann and Ewald felt it to be their duty to seek another home.

It was soon after the termination of his controversy with Hermann that Müller was induced to engage in the work which we have undertaken to complete. The Society for the Diffusion of Useful Knowledge had been for some few years established in London by a number of eminent men, who combined liberal sentiments in politics with an earnest desire to promote the literary culture of the country. Although the works, which they issued in parts, were intended to be for the most part of a general and popular character, as far as the execution was concerned, they entered from the first upon some of the highest domains of literature and science. And in some of their books no attempt was made to refrain from displaying the apparatus of classical learning. Thus although Mr. F. Malkin's *History of Greece* contained no marginal references, in compliance no doubt with what was the original intention of the Society, the elaborate

---

* Lücke, *Erinnerungen*, p. 37.

History of Rome undertaken in different departments by Mr. Malden, Mr. Donne, and Mr. C. Merivale, in the few parts to which it is unfortunately limited, exhibited an array of erudition which is not surpassed by the most learned productions of the University Press at Oxford or at Cambridge. It was not therefore at all surprising that a History of the Literature of Greece should occur to the Committee, including as it did some of the best scholars in England, as a work which might be published under their auspices. The credit of having first suggested this undertaking is due to Mr. (now Sir) George Cornewall Lewis, who proposed to the Committee to employ Professor Müller to write the history, and, having obtained their consent, was enabled by his previous acquaintance with the author of 'The Dorians,' to engage him in this important work. Besides these good offices, Mr. Lewis took upon himself all the trouble of making the arrangements with Müller; the manuscript of the successive numbers of the work was transmitted to him by Müller, and he made the translation and carried it through the press, exercising, with the author's consent, a discretionary power as editor, up to the spring of 1839, when, having received a public appointment which engrossed all his time, he transferred his task to the present writer.

Müller was given to understand that a work of popular character, specially designed for English readers, was expected from him. In accepting the undertaking, he expressed some diffidence as to his powers of treating such a subject in a popular manner, which he had never attempted, all his previous works having been written exclusively for learned readers. It is to be regretted that he was induced by this consideration to withhold a full display of his exhaustless learning, but the consequence of the limitations which he imposed on himself, and of his efforts to write popularly, especially assisted as he was by the editorial labours of his translator, has been the production of a work which, while thoroughly scholarlike, is infinitely more readable than any similar production from the pen of a German philologer.* Müller bestowed great pains

---

* Bernhardy, in his remarks on Müller's History (*Grundriss der Griechischen Literatur*, vol. II. pp. x. xi.), indicates sufficiently the contrast between his own work and that of its immediate predecessor.

upon this work, which, though undertaken for a foreign public, interested his literary ambition, and was in itself a labour of love to him. He told his translators, to mention one instance, that he had re-perused the whole of Euripides before he wrote his chapter on that poet; and any competent reader may see that he prepared himself by similar study for his examination of every considerable author. If he had been spared to complete the work, there can be little doubt that it would have been accepted by the learned world as one of the happiest efforts of his genius and learning, and that it would have obtained for him in this country an established place among those who teach by their writings the classical students of our great schools and universities.

The ' History of the Literature of Greece' was published in German, after the author's death, by his brother Edward, with the title,

> ' K. O. Müller's Geschichte der griechischen Literatur bis auf das Zeitalter Alexanders. Nach der Handschrift des Verfassers herausgegeben von Dr. Edward Müller. 2 Bde. Breslau. 1841.'

More than one edition of this form of the work has already appeared. In his memoir of his brother,* Edward Müller states briefly that Karl Otfried ' laboured since 1835 at his History of Greek Literature, in the first instance for England, (*zunächst für England*).' But in his list of K. O. Müller's works,† he does not mention the English edition of this history. It is difficult to see how this is in accordance with any strict sense of propriety. Edward Müller must have been aware of the relations between his brother and the Society for the Diffusion of Useful Knowledge; he could hardly have been ignorant that the history was written for the ' exclusive use ' of that Society, and that its author had received a very liberal remuneration on the appearance of each successive number. In suppressing these facts his conduct has been, to say the least, unhandsome. And he has not consulted his brother's literary reputation in publishing the book from the rough drafts; for the transcribed

---

* p. LXII.   † pp. LXXVI—LXXVIII.

and corrected manuscript is in England, a considerable portion
of it being in the possession of the present writer—to say
nothing of the editorial labour bestowed upon the book, in correspondence with the author, and with his express sanction and
approbation.

The only other separate publications of K. O. Müller were
the following :—

> ' Antiquitates Antiochenæ. Commentationes duæ. Got-
> tingæ. 1839. (Comment. prior ab auct. recitata in
> consessu soc. reg. d. XIV. Junii a. 1834. Comment.
> altera d. VIII. Junii a. 1839).'
> ' Sexti Pompei Festi de verborum significatione quæ
> supersunt cum Pauli epitome emendata et annotata.
> Lipsiæ. 1839.'

He also, in 1836, lent his name and contributed a preface to
the architect R. Wiegmann's interesting little book : ' Die
Malerei der alten in ihrer Anwendung und Technik insbesondere
als Decorationsmalerei.'

The edition of Festus, which he undertook at the solicitation
of Böcking, and which is dedicated to his father-in-law Hugo,
' antiquorum Muciorum et Sulpiciorum in explanando
Romanorum jure civili alumno et æmulo,' makes an epoch in
this department of learning, not only from the soundness of
the criticisms of which it is the vehicle, but also because it
gives for the first time a comparative view of the original
Vocabulary of Festus, as far as it has survived, and its epitome
by Paulus Diaconus.

It only remains to narrate Müller's journey to Italy and
Greece, and its unfortunate conclusion. A visit to the homes
of classical antiquity had long been an object of hope to Müller
himself, and had been desired for him by those who thought
that one who was so familiar with ancient life might bring back
much to instruct the world, if he had an opportunity of
travelling to these countries, and especially to Greece. Speaking of the Bavarian mission of Professor Thiersch, Dr.
Thirlwall remarked, in 1832 :* ' Much as this intelligence

---

* *Philological Museum,* I. p. 309.

promises, it would have been a still more agreeable piece of news if we had heard that K. O. Müller had been enabled to spend a year or two in ocular inspection of the country where he has lived in spirit so long, and with which he is already more familiar than most men are with their own. Should it ever happen that a person possessing in an equal degree all the qualities and requisites of an accomplished traveller in Greece, has the means of visiting it, and of pursuing his researches with all the assistance that a liberal government can afford to such undertakings, what hopes of the result could be deemed too sanguine?' The long desired opportunity of undertaking such a tour presented itself in the summer of 1839. Arrangements were made for the performance of his academical duties in his absence, and though he took upon himself the expenses of his journey, the government furnished him with a draftsman at their cost. Accompanied by this artist and two friends, he started from Munich, the place of rendezvous, spent three months in Italy, attended the Winckelmann festival on the 9th December, then travelled through southern Italy and Sicily, and finally sailed for the Piræus. He spent some time at Athens, travelled for forty days in the Peloponnesus, and after a second stay at Athens, set out for an exploration of northern Greece, in the heat of the summer of 1840. Exposure to the sun, while copying inscriptions at Delphi, liability during the night to the unhealthy exhalations of the Copaic fens, and excessive fatigue of body and mind, overcame the vigour of his constitution. He was seized with a nervous bilious fever, affecting both his secretions and his brain, was brought back to Athens senseless, and died there on the 1st August, 1840, at four o'clock in the afternoon. The place of his interment is a hill near the Academus, where a monument has been erected to his memory. The funeral oration was spoken in Greek by Philippus Joannes, professor in the University of Athens, and his funeral was attended by a large assembly.

Müller left behind him a wife and five young children. The manner in which the tidings of his death reached his friends has been described in a touching manner by his friend Lücke.*

---

* *Erinnerungen*, pp. 45, 46.

They had heard that his return might be expected. His wife and children had gone to Silesia to meet him there. Hugo was preparing for the reception of the re-united pair at Göttingen. Lücke himself, who had sustained a severe domestic affliction, was longing for the comfort which he hoped to find in Müller's society. On the 27th of August, Müller's birth-day, the tidings came like a thunder-stroke to Göttingen, that the great scholar was no more! Hugo himself was the first to read the intelligence. Lücke hastened to him and found him overwhelmed with distress. The old man, bowed down with sorrow, silently referred his visitor to the words of Schiller's *Wallenstein :**

> 'I shall grieve down this blow—of that I'm conscious :
> For what does not man grieve down ? From the highest,
> As from the vilest thing of every day,
> He learns to wean himself: for the strong hours
> Conquer him. Yet I feel what I have lost
> In him. The bloom has vanished from my life.
> For O ! he stood beside me, like my youth,
> Transformed for me the real to a dream,
> Clothing the palpable and familiar
> With golden exhalations of the dawn.
> Whatever fortunes wait my future toils,
> The beautiful is vanished—and returns not.'

Of the character of Karl Otfried Müller, it is no exaggeration to say that, as far as human judgment is concerned, it was blameless. In all the relations of life he showed himself ' a man four-square, and wrought without reproach.' As a son, a brother, a husband, and a father, he merited and obtained the love of his nearest connexions. His other friends felt for him that attachment which his frank and noble nature could not fail to conciliate. His religious sentiments did not exhibit themselves in connexion with any dogmatic system of theology, but many traits have been preserved which show that he was a sincere and earnest Christian ; and his younger brother, Julius, who is still living, and has attained the very highest place among the profound divines of Germany, is well able to answer for the speculative orthodoxy of the whole family.† As a

---

* Act V. Sc. 1.

† It may perhaps be said that *Die christliche Lehre von der Sünde,* by Julius Müller, is at once the ablest and soundest product of modern German theology.

classical scholar, we are inclined to prefer K. O. Müller, on the whole, to all the German philologers of the nineteenth century. He had not Niebuhr's grasp of original combination; he was hardly equal to his teacher Böckh in some branches of Greek philosophy, antiquities, and palæography; he was inferior to Hermann in Greek verbal criticism; he was not a comparative philologer, like Grimm and Bopp and A. W. Schlegel, nor a collector of facts and forms like Lobeck. But in all the distinctive characteristics of these eminent men, he approached them more nearly than most of his contemporaries, and he had some qualifications to which none of them attained. In liveliness of fancy, in power of style, in elegance of taste, in artistic knowledge, he far surpassed most if not all of them. Ancient mythology and classical geography were more his subjects than those of any German of his time; he will long be the chief authority on ancient art; and he laid the foundations for a new school of Latin criticism. He was always ready to recognize the truth, when discovered by processes with which he was less familiar; and did not, like too many of his countrymen, surround himself with a wall of national prejudice beyond which he could see nothing excellent or admirable. Both for the great qualities which he possessed, and for the faults which he avoided, we would concede to K. O. Müller the place of honour among those who, in the German universities, have promoted the study of ancient literature since the commencement of the present century.

A

HISTORY OF THE LITERATURE

OF

ANCIENT GREECE;

DOWN TO THE DEATH OF ISOCRATES.

TRANSLATED FROM THE GERMAN MANUSCRIPT OF

K. O. MÜLLER,

LATE PROFESSOR IN THE UNIVERSITY OF GÖTTINGEN;

BY

SIR GEORGE CORNEWALL LEWIS, Bart., M.P.,

LATE STUDENT OF CHRIST CHURCH, OXFORD;

AND

JOHN WILLIAM DONALDSON, D.D.,

LATE FELLOW OF TRINITY COLLEGE, CAMBRIDGE.

THE TRANSLATORS' PREFACE

TO THE FIRST VOLUME.

THE following History of Greek Literature has been composed by Professor K. O. Müller of Göttingen, at the suggestion of the Society for the Diffusion of Useful Knowledge, and for its exclusive use. The work has been written in German, and has been translated under the superintendence of the Society, but the German text has never been published, so that the present translation appears as an original work.

Before the publication of the present work, no History of Greek Literature had been published in the English language. The Society thought that, since the Greek Literature is the source from which the literature of the civilized world almost exclusively derives its origin; and since it still contains the finest productions of the human mind in Poetry, History, Oratory, and Philosophy; a History of Greek Literature would be properly introduced into the series of works published under their superintendence. The present work is intended to be within the compass of the general reader; but at the same time to be useful to scholars, and particularly to persons commencing or pursuing the study of the Greek authors. Agreeably with this view the chief authorities for the statements in the text are mentioned in the notes ; but few references have been given to the works of modern critics, either foreign or native.

The translation has been executed in correspondence with the author, who has read and approved of the larger part of it. Mr. Lewis was the translator of the first twenty-two chapters ; and the remainder of the version was executed by Mr. Donaldson.

January, 1840.

CONTENTS

OF

THE FIRST VOLUME.

CHAPTER IV.

ORIGIN OF THE EPIC POETRY.

CHAPTER V.

HOMER.

CHAPTER VI.

THE CYCLIC POETS.

CHAPTER VII.

THE HOMERIC HYMNS.

CHAPTER VIII.

HESIOD.

CHAPTER IX.

OTHER EPIC POETS.

CHAPTER X.

THE ELEGY AND THE EPIGRAM.

CHAPTER XI.

IAMBIC POETRY.

CHAPTER XII.

PROGRESS OF THE GREEK MUSIC.

CHAPTER XIII.

THE ÆOLIC SCHOOL OF LYRIC POETRY.

CHAPTER XIV.

CHORAL LYRIC POETRY.

CHAPTER XV.

PINDAR.

CHAPTER XVI.

THEOLOGICAL AND PHILOSOPHICAL POETRY.

CHAPTER XVII.

THE EARLY GREEK PHILOSOPHERS.

CHAPTER XVIII.

THE EARLY GREEK HISTORIANS.

CHAPTER XIX.

HERODOTUS.

SECOND PERIOD OF GREEK LITERATURE.

CHAPTER XX.

LITERARY PREDOMINANCE OF ATHENS.

CHAPTER XXI.

ORIGIN OF THE GREEK DRAMA.

CHAPTER XXIV.

SOPHOCLES.

CHAPTER XXV.

EURIPIDES.

CHAPTER XXVI.

THE OTHER TRAGIC POETS.

HISTORY

OF THE

LITERATURE OF ANCIENT GREECE.

INTRODUCTION.

IN undertaking to write a history of Grecian literature, it is not our intention to enumerate the names of those many hundred authors whose works, accumulated in the Alexandrine Library, are reported, after passing through many other perils, to have finally been burnt by the Khalif Omar—an event from which the cause of civilization has not, perhaps, suffered so much as many have thought; inasmuch as the inheritance of so vast a collection of writings from antiquity would, by engrossing all the leisure and attention of the moderns, have diminished their zeal and their opportunities for original productions. Nor will it be necessary to carry our younger readers (for whose use this work is chiefly designed) into the controversies of the philosophical schools, the theories of grammarians and critics, or the successive hypotheses of natural philosophy among the Greeks—in short, into those departments of literature which are the province of the learned by profession, and whose influence is confined to them alone. Our object is to consider Grecian literature as a main constituent of the character of the Grecian people, and to show how those illustrious compositions, which we still justly admire as the *classical* writings of the Greeks, naturally sprang from the taste and genius of the Greek races, and the constitution of civil and domestic society as established among them. For this purpose our inquiries may be divided into three principal heads :—

1. The development of Grecian poetry and prose before the

rise of the Athenian literature; 2. The flourishing era of poetry
and eloquence at Athens; and, 3. The history of Greek literature in the long period after Alexander; which last, although
it produced a much larger number of writings than the former
periods, need not, consistently with the object of the present
work, be treated at great length, as literature had in this age
fallen into the hands of the learned few, and had lost its living
influence on the general mass of the community.

In attempting to trace the gradual development of the
literature of ancient Greece from its earliest origin, it would
be easy to make a beginning, by treating of the extant works
of Grecian writers in their chronological order. We might
then commence at once with Homer and Hesiod: but if we
were to adopt this course, we should, like an epic poet, place
our beginning in the middle of the history; for, like the Pallas
of Grecian poetry, who sprang full-armed from the head of
Jupiter, the literature of Greece wears the perfection of beauty
in those works which Herodotus and Aristotle, and all critical
and trustworthy inquirers among the Greeks, recognized as
being the most ancient that had descended to their times.
Although both in the *Iliad* and *Odyssey* we can clearly discern
traces of the infancy of the nation to which they belong, and
although a spirit of simplicity pervades them, peculiar to the
childhood of the human race, yet the class of poetry under
which they fall, appears in them at its full maturity; all the
laws which reflection and experience can suggest for the epic
form are observed with the most refined taste; all the means
are employed by which the general effect can be heightened;
nowhere does the poetry bear the character of a first essay or
an unsuccessful attempt at some higher poetical flight; indeed,
as no subsequent poem, either of ancient or modern times, has
so completely caught the genuine epic tone, there seems good
reason to doubt whether any future poet will again be able to
strike the same chord. It seems, however, manifest, that there
must have been many attempts and experiments before epic
poetry could reach this elevation; and it was, doubtless, the
perfection of the *Iliad* and *Odyssey*, to which these prior essays
had led, that buried the productions of former bards in oblivion.
Hence the first dawn of Grecian literature is without any per-

fect memorial; but we must be content to remain in ignorance of the connexion of literature with the character of the Greek races at the outset of their national existence, if we renounce all attempt at forming a conception of the times anterior to the Homeric poems. In order, therefore, to throw some light on this obscure period, we shall first consider those creations of the human intellect which in general are prior to poetry, and which naturally precede poetical composition, as poetry in its turn is followed by regular composition in prose. These are *language* and *religion*. When these two important subjects have been examined, we shall proceed, by means of allusions in the Homeric poems themselves, and the most credible testimonies of later times, to inquire into the progress and character of the Greek poetry before the time of Homer.

CHAPTER I.

CHARACTERISTICS OF THE GREEK LANGUAGE.

§ 1. General account of the languages of the Indo-Teutonic family. § 2. Origin and formation of the Indo-Teutonic languages—multiplicity of their grammatical forms. § 3. Characteristics of the Greek language, as compared with the other languages of the Indo-Teutonic family. § 4. Variety of forms, inflexions, and dialects in the Greek language. § 5. The tribes of Greece, and their several dialects—characteristics of each dialect.

§ 1. LANGUAGE, the earliest product of the human mind, and the origin of all other intellectual energies, is at the same time the clearest evidence of the descent of a nation and of its affinity with other races. Hence the comparison of languages enables us to judge of the history of nations at periods to which no other kind of memorial, no tradition or record, can ascend. In modern times, this subject has been studied with more comprehensive views and more systematic methods than formerly : and from these researches it appears that a large part of the nations of the ancient world formed a family, whose languages (besides a large number of radical words, to which we need not here particularly advert) had on the whole the same grammatical structure and the same forms of derivation and inflexion. The nations between which this affinity subsisted are—the *Indians*, whose language, in its earliest and purest form, is preserved in the Sanscrit; the *Persians*, whose primitive language, the Zend, is closely allied with the Sanscrit; the *Armenians* and *Phrygians*, kindred races, of whose language the modern Armenian is a very mutilated remnant, though a few ancient features preserved in it still show its original resemblance; the *Greek* nation, of which the Latin people is a branch; the *Sclavonian races*, who, notwithstanding their intellectual inferiority, appear from their language to be nearly allied with the Persians and other cognate nations; the *Lettic*

tribes, among which the Lithuanian has preserved the fundamental forms of this class of languages with remarkable fidelity ;
the *Teutonic,* and, lastly, the *Celtic* races, whose language (so
far as we can judge from the very degenerate remains of it now
extant), though deviating widely in some respects from the
general character perceptible in the other languages, yet unquestionably belongs to the same family. It is remarkable
that this family of languages, which possess the highest perfection of grammatical structure, also includes a larger number of
nations, and has spread over a wider extent of surface, than any
other : the Semitic family (to which the Hebrew, Syrian, Phœnician, Arabian, and other languages belong), though in many
respects it can compete with the Indo-Germanic, is inferior to
it in the perfection of its structure and its capacity for literary
development ; in respect of its diffusion likewise it approaches
the Indian class of languages, without being equal to it ; while,
again, the rude and meagre languages of the American aborigines are often confined to a very narrow district, and appear
to have no affinity with those of the other tribes in the immediate vicinity.[1]   Hence, perhaps, it may be inferred, that the
higher capacity for the formation and development of language
was at this early period combined with a greater physical and
mental energy—in short, with all those qualities on which the
ulterior improvement and increase of the nations by which it
was spoken depended.

While the Semitic branch occupies the south-west of Asia,
the Indo-Germanic languages run in a straight line from south-
east to north-west, through Asia and Europe : a slight interruption, which occurs in the country between the Euphrates
and Asia Minor, appears to have been occasioned by the pres-
sure of Semitic or Syrian races from the south ; for it seems
probable that originally the members of this national family
succeeded one another in a continuous line, although we are
not now able to trace the source from which this mighty stream
originally flowed.   Equally uncertain is it whether these languages were spoken by the earliest inhabitants of the countries

---

[1] Some of the American languages are rather cumbersome than meagre in their
grammatical forms; and some are much more widely spread than others.—*Note by
Editor.*

to which they belonged, or were introduced by subsequent im-
migrations ; in which latter case the rude aborigines would
have adopted the principal features of the language spoken by
the more highly endowed race, retaining at the same time much
of their original dialect—an hypothesis which appears highly probable as regards those languages which show a general affinity
with the others, but nevertheless differ from them widely in
their grammatical structure and the number of their radical
forms.

§ 2. On the other hand, this comparison of languages leads
to many results, with respect to the *intellectual state* of the
Greek people, which throw an unexpected light into quarters
where the eye of the historian has hitherto been able to discover nothing but darkness. We reject as utterly untenable
the notion that the savages of Greece, from the inarticulate
cries by which they expressed their animal wants, and from the
sounds by which they sought to imitate the impressions of outward objects, gradually arrived at the harmonious and magnificent language which we admire in the poems of Homer. So
far is this hypothesis from the truth, that language evidently is
connected with the power of abstracting or of forming general
notions, and is inconsistent with the absence of this faculty. It
is plain that the most abstract parts of speech, those least likely
to arise from the imitation of any outward impression, were the
first which obtained a permanent form ; and hence those parts
of speech appear most clearly in all the languages of the Indo-
Teutonic family. Among these are the verb ' to be,' the forms
of which seem to alternate in the Sanscrit, the Lithuanian, and
the Greek ; the pronouns, which denote the most general relations of persons and things to the speaker ; the numerals, also
abstract terms, altogether independent of impressions from
single objects ; and, lastly, the grammatical forms, by which
the actions expressed by verbs are referred to the speaker, and
the objects expressed by nouns are placed in the most various
relations to one another. The luxuriance of grammatical forms
which we perceive in the Greek cannot have been of late introduction, but must be referred to the earliest period of the language ; for we find traces of nearly all of them in the cognate
tongues, which could not have been the case unless the lan-

guages before they diverged had possessed these forms in
common : thus the distinction between aorist tenses, which
represent an action as a moment, as a single point, and others,
which represent it as continuous, like a prolonged line, occurs
in Sanscrit as well as in Greek.

In general it may be observed, that in the lapse of ages, from
the time that the progress of language can be observed, grammatical forms, such as the signs of cases, moods, and tenses,
have never been increased in number, but have been constantly
diminishing. The history of the Romance, as well as of the Ger-
manic languages, shows in the clearest manner how a grammar,
once powerful and copious, has been gradually weakened and
impoverished, until at last it preserves only a few fragments of
its ancient inflections. The ancient languages, especially the
Greek, fortunately still retained the chief part of their grammatical forms at the time of their literary development; thus,
for example, little was lost in the progress of the Greek language from Homer to the Athenian orators. Now there is no
doubt that this luxuriance of grammatical forms is not an
essential part of a language, considered merely as a vehicle of
thought. It is well known that the Chinese language, which
is merely a collection of radical words destitute of grammatical
forms, can express even philosophical ideas with tolerable precision; and the English, which, from the mode of its formation
by a mixture of different tongues, has been stripped of its
grammatical inflections more completely than any other European language, seems nevertheless, even to a foreigner, to be
distinguished by its energetic eloquence. All this must be
admitted by every unprejudiced inquirer ; but yet it cannot be
overlooked, that this copiousness of grammatical forms, and the
fine shades of meaning which they express, evince a nicety of
observation and a faculty of distinguishing, which unquestionably prove that the race of mankind among whom these languages arose was characterized by a remarkable correctness and
subtlety of thought. Nor can any modern European, who
forms in his mind a lively image of the classical languages in
their ancient grammatical luxuriance, and compares them with
his mother tongue, conceal from himself that in the ancient
languages the words, with their inflections, clothed as it were

with muscles and sinews, come forward like living bodies, full
of expression and character; while in the modern tongues the
words seem shrunk up into mere skeletons. Another advantage
which belongs to the fulness of grammatical forms is, that words
of similar signification make likewise a similar impression on
the ear; whence each sentence obtains a certain symmetry and,
even where the collocation of the words is involved, a clearness
and regularity, which may be compared with the effect produced
on the eye by the parts of a well-proportioned building; whereas,
in the languages which have lost their grammatical forms,
either the lively expression of the feeling is hindered by an
unvarying and monotonous collocation of the words, or the
hearer is compelled to strain his attention, in order to comprehend the mutual relation of the several parts of the sentence.
Modern languages seem to attempt to win their way at once to
the understanding without dwelling in the ear; while the
classical languages of antiquity seek at the same time to produce a corresponding effect on the outward sense, and to assist
the mind by previously filling the ear, as it were, with an imperfect consciousness of the meaning sought to be conveyed by
the words.

§ 3. These remarks apply generally to the languages of the
Indo-Germanic family, so far as they have been preserved in a
state of integrity by literary works and have been cultivated by
poets and orators. We shall now limit our regards to the
Greek language alone, and shall attempt to exhibit its more
prominent and characteristic features as compared with those of
its sister tongues. In the sounds which were formed by the
various articulation of the voice, the Greek language hits that
happy medium which characterizes all the mental productions
of this people, in being equally removed, on the one hand, from
the superabundant fulness, and, on the other, from the meagre-
ness and tenuity of sound, by which other languages are
variously deformed. If we compare the Greek with that language which comes next to it in fitness for a lofty and flowing
style of poetry, viz., the Sanscrit, this latter certainly has some
classes of consonants not to be found in the Greek, the sounds
of which it is almost impossible for an European mouth to
imitate and distinguish : on the other hand, the Greek is much

richer in short vowels than the Sanscrit, whose most harmonious poetry would weary our ears by the monotonous repetition of the A sound; and it possesses an astonishing abundance of diphthongs, and tones produced by the contraction of vowels, which a Greek mouth could alone distinguish with the requisite nicety, and which, therefore, are necessarily confounded by the modern European pronunciation. We may likewise perceive in the Greek the influence of the laws of *harmony*, which, in different nations, have caused the rejection of different combinations of vowels and consonants, and which have increased the softness and beauty of languages, though sometimes at the expense of their terminations and characteristic features. By the operation of the latter cause, the Greek has, in many places, lost its resemblance to the original type, which, although not now preserved in any one of the extant languages, may be restored by conjecture from all of them; even here, however, it cannot be denied that the correct taste and feeling of the Greeks led them to a happy mixture of the consonant and vowel sounds, by which strength has been reconciled with softness, and harmony with strongly marked peculiarities; while the language has, at the same time, in its multifarious dialects, preserved a variety of sound and character, which fit it for the most discordant kinds of poetical and prose composition.

§ 4. We must not pass over one important characteristic of the Greek language, which is closely connected with the early condition of the Greek nation, and which may be considered as, in some degree, prefiguring the subsequent character of its civilization. In order to convey an adequate idea of our meaning, we will ask any person who is acquainted with Greek, to recal to his mind the toils and fatigue which he underwent in mastering the forms of the language, and the difficulty which he found to impress them on his memory; when his mind, vainly attempting to discover a reason for such anomalies, was almost in despair at finding that so large a number of verbs derive their tenses from the most various roots; that one verb uses only the first, another only the second, aorist, and that even the individual persons of the aorist are sometimes compounded of the forms of the first and second aorists respectively; and that many verbs and substantives have retained only single or a few forms, which have been left standing by themselves, like the remains of a past age. The convulsions and catastrophes of which we see so many traces around us in the frame-work of the world have not been confined to external nature alone. The structure of languages also has evidently, in ages prior to the existence of any literature, suffered some violent shocks, which may, perhaps, have received their impulse from migrations or internal discord ; and the elements of the language, having been thrown in confusion together, were afterwards re-arranged, and combined into a new whole. Above all is this true of the Greek language, which bears strong marks of having originally formed part of a great and regular plan, and of having been reconstructed on a new system from the fragments of the former edifice. The same is doubtless also the cause of the great variety of dialects which existed both among the Greeks and the neighbouring nations ;—a variety, of which mention is made at so early a date as the Homeric poems.[1] As the country inhabited by the Greeks is intersected to a remarkable degree by mountains and sea, and thus was unfitted by Nature to serve as the habitation of a uniform population, collected in large states, like the plains of the Euphrates and Ganges; and as, for this reason, the Greek *people* was divided into a number of separate tribes, some of which attract our attention in the early fabulous age, others in the later historical period ; so likewise the Greek *language* was divided, to an unexampled extent, into various dialects, which differed from each other according to the several tribes and territories. In what relation the dialects of the Pelasgians, Dryopes, Abantes, Leleges, Epeans, and other races widely diffused in the earliest periods of Grecian history, may have stood to one another, is indeed a question which it would be vain to attempt to answer ; but thus much is evident, that the number of these tribes, and their frequent migrations, by mixing and confounding the different races, contributed powerfully to produce that irregularity of structure which characterizes the Greek language in its very earliest monuments.

---

[1] In *Iliad* II. 804, and IV. 437, there is mention of the variety of dialects among the allies of the Trojans; and in *Odyssey* XIX. 175, among the Greek tribes in Crete.

§ 5. The primitive tribes just mentioned, which were the earliest occupants of Greece known to tradition, and of which the PELASGIANS, and after them the LELEGES, were the most extended, unquestionably did much for the first cultivation of the soil, the foundation of institutions for divine worship, and the first establishment of a regular order of society. The *Pelasgians*, widely scattered over Greece, and having their settlements in the most fertile regions (as the vale of the Peneus in Thessaly, the lower districts of Bœotia, and the plains of Argos and Sicyon), appear, before the time when they wandered through Greece in isolated bodies, as a nation attached to their own dwelling-places, fond of building towns, which they fortified with walls of a colossal size, and zealously worshipping the powers of heaven and earth, which made their fields fruitful and their cattle prosperous. The mythical genealogies of Argos competed as it were with those of Sicyon; and both these cities, by a long chain of patriarchal princes (most of whom are merely personifications of the country, its mountains and rivers), were able to place their origin at a period of the remotest antiquity. The *Leleges* also (with whom were connected the Locrians in Northern Greece and the Epeans in Peloponnesus), although they had fewer fixed settlements, and appear to have led a rougher and more warlike life—such as still prevailed in the mountainous districts of Northern Greece at the time of the historian Thucydides—yet celebrated their national heroes, especially Deucalion and his descendants, as founders of cities and temples. But there is no trace of any peculiar creation of the intellect having developed itself among these races, or of any poems in which they displayed any peculiar character; and whether it may be possible to discover any characteristic and distinct features in the legends of the gods and heroes who belong to the territories occupied by these different tribes is a question which must be deferred until we come to treat of the origin of the Grecian mythology. It is however much to be lamented that, with our sources of information, it seems impossible to form a well-grounded opinion on the *dialects* of these ancient tribes of Greece, by which they were doubtless precisely distinguished from one another; and any such attempt appears the more hopeless, as even of the dialects which were spoken in

the several territories of Greece within the historical period we
have only a scanty knowledge, by means of a few inscriptions
and the statements of grammarians, wherever they had not
obtained a literary cultivation and celebrity by the labours of
poets and prose writers.

Of more influence, however, on the development of the intellectual faculties of the Greeks was the distinction of the tribes
and their dialects, established at a period which, from the domi-
nation of warlike and conquering races and the consequent
prevalence of a bold spirit of enterprise, was called the *heroic
age*. It is at this time, before the migration of the Dorians into
Peloponnesus and the settlements in Asia Minor, that the seeds
must have been sown of an opposition between the races and
dialects of Greece, which exercised the most important influence
on the state of civil society, and thus on the direction of the
mental energies of the people, of their poetry, art, and literature.
If we consider the dialects of the Greek language, with which
we are acquainted by means of its literary monuments, they
appear to fall into two great classes, which are distinguished
from each other by characteristic marks. The one class is
formed by the *Æolic* dialect ; a name, indeed, under which the
Greek grammarians included dialects very different from one
another, as in later times everything was comprehended under
the term Æolic, which was not Ionic, Attic, or Doric. According to this acceptation of the term about three-fourths of the
Greek nation consisted of Æolians, and dialects were classed
together as Æolic which (as is evident from the more ancient inscriptions) differed more from one another than from the Doric ; as,
for example, the Thessalian and Ætolian, the Bœotian and Elean
dialects. The Æolians, however, *properly so called* (who occur
in mythology under this appellation), lived at this early period
in the plain of Thessaly, south of the Peneus, which was afterwards called Thessaliotis, and from thence as far as the Paga-
setic Bay. We also find in the same mythical age a branch of
the Æolian race, in southern Ætolia, in possession of Calydon ;
this fragment of the Æolians, however, afterwards disappears
from history, while the Æolians of Thessaly, who also bore the
name of Bœotians, two generations after the Trojan war, migrated into the country which was called after them Bœotia,

and from thence, soon afterwards, mixed with other races, to the maritime districts and islands of Asia Minor, which from that time forward received the name of Æolis in Asia Minor.[1] It is in this latter Æolis that we become acquainted with the Æolian dialect, through the lyric poets of the Lesbian school, the origin and character of which will be explained in a subsequent chapter. On the whole it may be said of this dialect, as of the Bœotian in its earlier form, that it bears an archaic character, and approaches nearest to the source of the Greek language; hence the Latin, as being connected with the most ancient form of the Greek, has a close affinity with it, and in general the agreement with the other languages of the Indo-Germanic family is always most perceptible in the Æolic. A mere variety of the Æolic was the dialect of the *Doric* race, which originally was confined to a narrow district in Northern Greece, but was afterwards spread over the Peloponnesus and other regions by that important movement of population which was called the Return of the Heracleids. It is characterized by strength and breadth, as shown in its fondness for simple open vowel sounds, and its aversion for sibilants. Much more different from the original type is the other leading dialect of the Greek language, the *Ionic*, which took its origin in the mother-country, and was by the Ionic colonies, which sailed from Athens, carried over to Asia Minor, where it underwent still further changes. Its characteristics are softness and liquidness of sound, arising chiefly from the concurrence of vowels, among which, not the broad *a* and *o*, but the thinner sounds of *e* and *u*, were most prevalent; among the consonants the tendency to the use of *s* is most discernible. It may be observed, that wherever the Ionic dialect differs either in vowels or consonants from the Æolic, it also differs from the original type, as may be disco-

---

[1] We here only reckon those Æolians who were in fact considered as belonging to the Æolian race, and not all the tribes which were ruled by heroes, whom Hesiod, in the fragment of the ἠοῖαι, calls sons of Æolus; although this genealogy justifies us in assuming a close affinity between those races, which is also confirmed by other testimonies. In *this* sense the Minyans of Orchomenus and Iolcus, ruled by the Æolids Athamas and Cretheus, were of Æolian origin; a nation which, by the stability of its political institutions, its spirit of enterprise, even for maritime expeditions, and its colossal buildings, holds a pre-eminent rank among the tribes of the mythical age of Greece. (See Hesiod, *Fragm.* 28, ed. Gaisford.)

vered by a comparison of the cognate languages; it must therefore be considered as a peculiar form of the Greek, which was
developed within the limits of the Grecian territory.   It is probable that this dialect was spoken not only by the Ionians, but
also, at least one very similar, by the ancient Achæans; since
the Achæans in the genealogical legends concerning the descendants of Hellen are represented as the brothers of the Ionians :
this hypothesis would also explain how the ancient epic poems,
in which the Ionians are scarcely mentioned, but the Achæan
race plays the principal part, were written in a dialect which,
though differing in many respects from the genuine Ionic, has
yet the closest resemblance to it.

Even from these first outlines of the history of the Greek
dialects we might be led to expect that those features would be
developed in the institutions and literature of the several races
which we find in their actual history.   In the *Æolic* and *Doric*
tribes we should be prepared to find the order of society regulated by those ancient customs and principles which had been
early established among the Greeks ; their dialects at least show
a strong disposition to retain the archaic forms, without
much tendency to refinement.   Among the Dorians, however,
everything is more strongly expressed, and comes forward
in a more prominent light than among the Æolians; and as
their dialect everywhere prefers the broad, strong, and rough
tones, and introduces them throughout with unbending regularity, so we might naturally look among them for a disposition
to carry a spirit of austerity and of reverence for ancient
custom through the entire frame of civil and private society.
The *Ionians*, on the other hand, show even in their dialect a strong
tendency to modify ancient forms according to their taste and
humour, together with a constant endeavour to polish and refine,
which was doubtless the cause why this dialect, although of later
date and of secondary origin, was first employed in finished
poetical compositions.

CHAPTER II.[1]

RELIGION OF THE GREEKS.

§ 1. The earliest form of the Greek religion not portrayed in the Homeric poems. § 2. The Olympic deities, as described by Homer. § 3. Earlier form of worship in Greece directed to the outward objects of Nature. § 4. Character and attributes of the several Greek deities, as personifications of the powers and objects of Nature. § 5. Subsequent modification of these ideas, as displayed in the Homeric description of the same deities.

§ 1. NEXT to the formation of language, religion is the earliest object of attention to mankind, and therefore exercises a most important influence on all the productions of the human intellect. Although poetry has arisen at a very early date among many nations, and ages which were as yet quite unskilled in the other fine arts have been distinguished for their poetical enthusiasm, yet the development of religious notions and usages is always prior, in point of time, to poetry. No nation has ever been found entirely destitute of notions of a superior race of beings exercising an influence on mankind; but tribes have existed without songs, or compositions of any kind which could be considered as poetry. Providence has evidently first given mankind that knowledge of which they are most in need; and has, from the beginning, scattered among the nations of the entire world a glimmering of that light which was, at a later period, to be manifested in brighter effulgence.

This consideration must make it evident that, although the

---

[1] We have thought it absolutely essential, for the sake of accuracy, in treating of the deities of the ancient Greek religion, to use the names by which they were known to the Greeks. As these, however, may sound strange to persons not acquainted with the Greek language, we subjoin a list of the gods of the Romans with which they were in later times severally identified, and by whose names they are commonly known:—*Zeus*, Jupiter; *Hera*, Juno; *Athena*, Minerva; *Ares*, Mars; *Artemis*, Diana; *Hermes*, Mercury; *Demeter*, Ceres; *Cora*, Proserpine; *Hephæstus* Vulcan; *Poseidon*, Neptune; *Aphrodite*, Venus; *Dionysus*, Bacchus.

Homeric poems belong to the first age of the *Greek poetry*, they nevertheless cannot be viewed as monuments of the first period of the development of the *Greek religion*. Indeed, it is plain that the notions concerning the gods must have undergone many changes before (partly, indeed, by means of the poets themselves) they assumed that form under which they appear in the Homeric poems. The description given by Homer of the life of the gods in the palace of Zeus on Olympus is doubtless as different from the feeling and the conception with which the ancient Pelasgian lifted up his hands and voice to the Zeus of Dodona, whose dwelling was in the oak of the forest, as the palace of a Priam or Agamemnon from the hut which one of the original settlers constructed of unhewn trunks in a solitary pasture, in the midst of his flocks and herds.

§ 2. The conceptions of the gods, as manifested in the Homeric poems, are perfectly suited to a time when the most distinguished and prominent part of the people devoted their lives to the occupation of arms and to the transaction of public business in common; which time was the period in which the heroic spirit was developed. On Olympus, lying near the northern boundary of Greece, the highest mountain of this country, whose summit seems to touch the heavens, there rules an assembly or family of gods; the chief of which, Zeus, summons at his pleasure the other gods to council, as Agamemnon summons the other princes. He is acquainted with the decrees of fate, and is able to guide them; and, as being himself king among the gods, he gives the kings of the earth their power and dignity. By his side is a wife, whose station entitles her to a large share of his rank and dominion; and a daughter of a masculine complexion, a leader of battles, and a protectress of citadels, who by her wise counsels deserves the confidence which her father bestows on her; besides these a number of gods, with various degrees of kindred, who have each their proper place and allotted duty in the divine palace. On the whole, however, the attention of this divine council is chiefly turned to the fortunes of nations and cities, and especially to the adventures and enterprises of the heroes, who, being themselves for the most part sprung from the blood of the gods, form the connecting link between them and the ordinary herd of mankind.

§ 3. Doubtless such a notion of the gods as we have just described was entirely satisfactory to the princes of Ithaca, or any other Greek territory, who assembled in the hall of the chief king at the common meal, and to whom some bard sang the newest song of the bold adventures of heroes. But how could this religion satisfy the mere countryman, who wished to believe that in seed-time and in harvest, in winter and in summer, the divine protection was thrown over him ; who anxiously sought to offer his thanks to the gods for all kinds of rural prosperity, for the warding off of all danger from the seed and from the cattle? As the heroic age of the Greek nation was preceded by another, in which the cultivation of the land, and the nature of the different districts, occupied the chief attention of the inhabitants (which may be called the *Pelasgian period*), so likewise there are sufficient traces and remnants of a state of the Grecian religion, in which the gods were considered as exhibiting their power chiefly in the operations of outward nature, in the changes of the seasons, and the phenomena of the year. Imagination—whose operations are most active, and whose expressions are most simple and natural in the childhood both of nations and individuals—led these early inhabitants to discover, not only in the general phenomena of vegetation, the unfolding and death of the leaf and flower, and in the moist and dry seasons of the year, but also in the peculiar physical character of certain districts, a sign of the alternately hostile or peaceful, happy or ill-omened coincidence of certain deities. There are still preserved in the Greek mythology many legends of a charming, and at the same time touching simplicity, which had their origin at this period, when the Greek religion bore the character of a worship of the powers of Nature. It sometimes also occurs that those parts of mythology which refer to the origin of civil society, to the alliances of princes, and to military expeditions, are closely interwoven with mythical narratives, which when minutely examined are found to contain nothing definite on the acts of particular heroes, but only describe physical phenomena, and other circumstances of a general character, and which have been

combined with the heroic fables only through a forgetfulness of
their original form; a confusion which naturally arose, when in
later times the original connexion of the gods with the agencies
of Nature was more and more forgotten, and those of their attributes and acts which had reference to the conduct of human
life, the government of states, or moral principles, were perpetually brought into more prominent notice. It often happens
that the original meaning of narratives of this kind may be
deciphered when it had been completely hidden from the most
learned mythologists of antiquity. But though this process of
investigation is often laborious, and may, after all, lead only to
uncertain results, yet it is to be remembered that the mutilation and obscuring of the ancient mythological legends by the
poets of later times affords the strongest proof of their high
antiquity; as the most ancient buildings are most discoloured
and impaired by time.

§ 4. An inquiry, of which the object should be to select
and unite all the parts of the Greek mythology which have
reference to natural phenomena and the changes of the seasons,
although it has never been regularly undertaken, would doubtless show that the earliest religion of the Greeks was founded
on the same notions as the chief part of the religions of the
East, particularly of that part of the East which was nearest to
Greece, Asia Minor. The Greek mind, however, even in this
the earliest of its productions, appears richer and more various
in its forms, and at the same time to take a loftier and a wider
range, than is the case in the religion of the oriental neighbours
of the Greeks, the Phrygians, Lydians, and Syrians. In the
religion of these nations, the combination and contrast of two
beings (Baal and Astarte), the one male, representing the productive, and the other female, representing the passive and
nutritive powers of Nature, and the alternation of two states,
viz., the strength and vigour, and the weakness and death of
the male personification of Nature, of which the first was celebrated with vehement joy, the latter with excessive lamentation,
recur in a perpetual cycle, which must in the end have wearied
and stupified the mind. The Grecian worship of Nature, on
the other hand, in all the various forms which it assumed in
different places, places *one* deity, as the highest of all, at the

head of the entire system, the God of *heaven* and *light ;* for that this is the meaning of the name *Zeus* is shown by the occurrence of the same root (*Diu*) with the same signification, even in the Sanscrit,[1] and by the preservation of several of its derivatives which remained in common use both in Greek and Latin, all containing the notion of *heaven* and *day*. With this god of the heavens, who dwells in the pure expanse of ether, is associated, though not as a being of the same rank, the goddess of the Earth, who in different temples (which may be considered as the mother-churches of the Grecian religion) was worshipped under different names, *Hera, Demeter, Dione,* and some others of less celebrity. The marriage of Zeus with this goddess (which signified the union of heaven and earth in the fertilizing rains) was a sacred solemnity in the worship of these deities. Besides this goddess, other beings are associated on one side with the Supreme God, who are personifications of certain of his energies; powerful deities who carry the influence of light over the earth, and destroy the opposing powers of darkness and confusion : as *Athena,* born from the head of her father, in the height of the heavens ; and *Apollo,* the pure and shining god of a worship belonging to other races, but who even in his original form was a god of light. On the other side are deities, allied with the earth and dwelling in her dark recesses ; and as all life appears not only to spring from the earth, but to return to that whence it sprung, these deities are for the most part also connected with death : as *Hermes,* who brings up the treasures of fruitfulness from the depth of the earth, and the child, now lost and now recovered by her mother Demeter, *Cora,* the goddess both of flourishing and of decay-ing Nature. It was natural to expect that the element of water (*Poseidon*) should also be introduced into this assemblage of the personified powers of Nature, and should be peculiarly combined with the goddess of the Earth : and that fire (*Hephæstus*) should be represented as a powerful principle de-

---

[1] The root DIU is most clearly seen in the oblique cases of Zeus, ΔιϜός ΔιϜί, in which the U has passed into the consonant form Ϝ : whereas in Ζεὺς, as in other Greek words, the sound DI has passed into Z, and the vowel has been lengthened. In the Latin *Iovis* (*Iuve* in Umbrian) the D has been lost before I, which, however, is preserved in many other derivatives of the same root, as *dies, dium.*

rived from heaven and having dominion on the earth, and be closely allied with the goddess who sprang from the head of the god of the heavens.   Other deities are less important and necessary parts of this system, as *Aphrodite,* whose worship was evidently for the most part propagated over Greece from Cyprus and Cythera[1] by the influence of Syrophœnician tribes. As a singular being, however, in the assembly of the Greek deities, stands the changeable god of flourishing, decaying, and renovated Nature, *Dionysus,* whose alternate joys and sufferings, and marvellous adventures, show a strong resemblance to the form which religious notions assumed in Asia Minor.   Introduced by the Thracians (a tribe which spread from the north of Greece into the interior of the country), and not, like the gods of Olympus, recognized by all the races of the Greeks, Dionysus always remained to a certain degree estranged from the rest of the gods, although his attributes had evidently most affinity with those of Demeter and Cora.   But in this isolated position, Dionysus exercises an important influence on the spirit of the Greek nation, and both in sculpture and poetry gives rise to a class of feelings which agree in displaying more powerful emotions of the mind, a bolder flight of the imagination, and more acute sensations of pain and pleasure, than were exhibited on occasions where this influence did not operate.

§ 5.   In like manner the Homeric poems (which instruct us not merely by their direct statements, but also by their indirect allusions, not only by what they *say,* but also by what they do *not* say), when attentively considered, clearly show how this ancient religion of nature sank into the shade as compared with the salient and conspicuous forms of the deities of the heroic age.   The gods who dwell on Olympus scarcely appear at all in connexion with natural phenomena.   Zeus chiefly exercises his powers as a ruler and a king; although he is still designated (by epithets doubtless of high antiquity) as the god of the ether and the storms;[2] as in much later times the old picturesque expression was used, 'What is Zeus doing?' for 'What kind of weather is it?'   In the Homeric conception of Hera, Athena,

---

[1] See Herod. I. 105; and *Hist. of Rome,* pp. 121, 122.
[2] αἰθέρι ναίων· νεφεληγερέτης.

and Apollo, there is no trace of any reference of these deities to
the fertility of the earth, the clearness of the atmosphere, the
arrival of the serene spring, and the like ; which, however, can
be discovered in other mythical legends concerning them, and
still more in the ceremonies practised at their festivals, which
generally contain the most ancient ideas.   Hephæstus has passed
from the powerful god of fire in heaven and in earth into a
laborious smith and worker of metals, who performs his duty by
making armour and arms for the other gods and their favourite
heroes.   As to Hermes, there are some stories in which he is
represented as giving fruitfulness to cattle, in his capacity of the
rural god of Arcadia; from which, by means of various metamorphoses, he is transmuted into the messenger of Zeus, and
the servant of the gods.

Those deities, however, which stood at a greater distance from
the relations of human life, and especially from the military and
political actions of the princes, and could not easily be brought
into connexion with them, are for that reason rarely mentioned
by Homer, and never take any part in the events described by
him ; in general they keep aloof from the circle of the Olympic
gods.   Demeter is never mentioned as assisting any hero, or
rescuing him from danger, or stimulating him to the battle ;
but if any one were thence to infer that this goddess was not
known as early as Homer's time, he would be refuted by the
incidental allusions to her which frequently occur in connexion
with agriculture and corn.   Doubtless Demeter (whose name
denotes the earth as the mother and author of life[1]) was in the
ancient Pelasgic time honoured with a general and public worship beyond any other deity ; but the notions and feelings excited by the worship of this goddess and her daughter (whom
she beheld, with deep lamentation, torn from her every autumn,
and recovered with excessive joy every spring) constantly became more and more unlike those which were connected with
the other gods of Olympus.   Hence her worship gradually obtained a peculiar form, and chiefly from this cause assumed the
character of *mysteries :* that is, religious solemnities, in which
no one could participate without having undergone a previous

---

[1] Δῆ μήτηρ, that is, γῆ μήτηρ.

ceremony of admission and initiation. In this manner Homer was, by a just and correct taste, led to perceive that Demeter, together with the other divine beings belonging to her, had nothing in common with the gods whom the epic muse assembled about the throne of Zeus; and it was the same feeling which also prevented him from mixing up Dionysus, the other leading deity of the mystic worship of the Greeks, with the subject of his poem, although this god is mentioned by him as a divine being, of a marvellous nature, stimulating the mind to joy and enthusiasm.

CHAPTER III.

§ 1. MANY centuries must have elapsed before the poetical
language of the Greeks could have attained the splendour, the copiousness, and the fluency which so strongly excite
our admiration in the poems of Homer. The service of the
gods, to which all the highest energies of the mind were first
directed, and from which the first beginnings of sculpture, architecture, music, and poetry proceeded, must for a long time have
consisted chiefly in mute motions of the body, in symbolical
gestures, in prayers muttered in a low tone, and, lastly, in loud
broken ejaculations (ὀλολυγμός), such as were in later times
uttered at the death of the victim, in token of an inward feeling;
before the winged word issued clearly from the mouth, and
raised the feelings of the multitude to religious enthusiasm—in
short, before the first hymn was heard.

The first outpourings of poetical enthusiasm were doubtless
songs, describing, in few and simple verses, events which powerfully affected the feelings of the hearers. From what has been
said in the last chapter it is probable that the earliest date may
be assigned to the songs which referred to the seasons and
their phenomena, and expressed with simplicity the notions and
feelings to which these events gave birth: as they were sung by

peasants at the corn and wine harvest, they had their origin in
times of ancient rural simplicity.   It is remarkable that songs
of this kind often had a plaintive and melancholy character ;
which circumstance is however explained when we remember
that the ancient worship of outward nature (which was preserved in the rites of Demeter and Cora, and also of Dionysus)
contained festivals of wailing and lamentation as well as of rejoicing and mirth.   It is not, however, to be supposed that this
was the only cause of the mournful ditties in question, for the
human heart has a natural disposition to break out from time
to time into lamentation, and to seek an occasion for grief even
where it does not present itself—as Lucretius says, that ' in
the pathless woods, among the lonely dwellings of the shepherds, the sweet laments were sounded on the pipe.' [1]

§ 2. To the number of these plaintive ditties belongs the
song *Linus* mentioned by Homer,[2] the melancholy character of
which is shown by its fuller names, Αἴλινος and Οἰτόλινος
(literally, ' Alas, Linus !' and ' Death of Linus.')   It was frequently sung in Greece, according to Homer, at the grape-
picking.   According to a fragment of Hesiod,[3] all singers and
players on the cithara lament at feasts and dances Linus, the
beloved son of Urania, and call on Linus at the beginning and the
end ; which probably means that the song of lamentation began
and ended with the exclamation Αἲ Λίνε.   Linus was originally
the subject of the song, the person whose fate was bewailed in
it; and there were many districts in Greece (for example,
Thebes, Chalcis, and Argos) in which tombs of Linus were
shown.   This Linus evidently belongs to a class of deities
or demigods, of which many instances occur in the religions of Greece and Asia Minor ; boys of extraordinary beauty,
and in the flower of youth, who are supposed to have
been drowned, or devoured by raging dogs, or destroyed by
wild beasts, and whose death is lamented in the harvest or

---

[1] Inde minutatim *dulceis didicere querelas,*
   Tibia quas fundit digitis pulsata canentum,
   Avia per nemora ac sylvas saltusque reperta,
   Per loca pastorum deserta atque otia dia.—Lucretius, v. 1383—1386.
[2] *Iliad* XVIII. 570.
[3] Cited in Eustathius, p. 1163 (*Fragm.* 1, ed. Gaisford).

other periods of the hot season. It is obvious that these cannot have been real persons, whose death excited so general a
sympathy, although the fables which were offered in explanation
of these customs often speak of youths of royal blood, who
were carried off in the prime of their life. The real object of
lamentation was the tender beauty of spring destroyed by the
summer heat, and other phenomena of the same kind, which
the imagination of these early times invested with a personal
form, and represented as gods or beings of a divine nature.
According to the very remarkable and explicit tradition of the
Argives, Linus was a youth, who, having sprung from a divine
origin, grew up with the shepherds among the lambs, and was
torn in pieces by wild dogs ; whence arose the ' festival of the
lambs,' at which many dogs were slain. Doubtless this festival
was celebrated during the greatest heat, at the time of the constellation Sirius ; the emblem of which, among the Greeks, was,
from the earliest times, a raging dog. It was a natural confusion of the tradition that Linus should afterwards become a
minstrel, one of the earliest bards of Greece, who begins a
contest with Apollo himself, and overcomes Hercules in playing
on the cithara ; even, however, in this character Linus meets
his death, and we must probably assume that his fate was mentioned in the ancient song. In Homer the Linus is represented
as sung by a boy, who plays at the same time on the harp, an
accompaniment usually mentioned with this song ; the young
men and women who bear the grapes from the vineyard follow
him, moving onward with a measured step, and uttering a shrill
cry,[1] in which probably the chief stress was laid on the exclamation αἲ λίνε. That this shrill cry (called by Homer ἰυγμὸς)
was not necessarily a joyful strain will be admitted by any one
who has heard the ἰυγμὸς of the Swiss peasants, with its sad
and plaintive notes, resounding from hill to hill.

§ 3. Plaintive songs of this kind, in which not the misfortunes of a single individual, but an universal and perpetually

---

[1] τοῖσιν δ' ἐν μέσσοισι πάϊς φόρμιγγι λιγείῃ
ἱμερόεν κιθάριζε, Λίνον δ' ὑπὸ καλὸν ἄειδε
λεπταλέῃ φωνῇ· τοὶ δὲ ῥήσσοντες ἁμαρτῇ
μολπῇ τ' ἰυγμῷ τε, ποσὶ σκαίροντες ἕποντο.—Iliad XVIII. 569—572 ;
on the meaning of μολπή in this passage, see below, § 6.

recurring cause of grief was expressed, abounded in ancient Greece, and especially in Asia Minor, the inhabitants of which country had a peculiar fondness for mournful tunes. The *Ialemus* seems to have been nearly identical with the Linus, as, to a certain extent, the same mythological narrations are applied to both.   At Tegea, in Arcadia, there was a plaintive song, called *Scephrus*, which appears, from the fabulous relation in Pausanias,[1] to have been sung at the time of the summer heat. In Phrygia, a melancholy song, called *Lityerses*, was sung at the cutting of the corn.   At the same season of the year, the Mariandynians, on the shores of the Black Sea, played the mournful ditty *Bormus* on the native flute.   The subject of their lamentation may be easily conjectured from the story that Bormus was a beautiful boy, who, having gone to fetch water for the reapers in the heat of the day, was, while drawing it, borne down by the nymphs of the stream.   Of similar meaning are the cries for the youth *Hylas*, swallowed up by the waters of the fountain, which, in the neighbouring country of the Bithynians, re-echoed from mountain to mountain.   In the southern parts of Asia Minor we find, in connexion with the Syrian worship, a similar lament for *Adonis*,[2] whose untimely death was celebrated by Sappho, together with Linus; and the *Maneros*, a song current in Egypt, especially at Pelusium, in which likewise a youth, the only son of a king, who died in early youth, was bewailed; a resemblance sufficiently strong to induce Herodotus,[3] who is always ready to find a connexion between Greece and Egypt, to consider the Maneros and the Linus as the same song.[4]

---

[1] VIII. 53, 2.

[2] Beautifully described in the well-known verses of Milton :—
> 'Thammuz came next behind,
> Whose annual wound in Lebanon allured
> The Syrian damsels to lament his fate
> In amorous ditties, all a summer's day,
> While smooth Adonis from his native rock
> Ran purple to the sea, supposed with blood
> Of Thammuz yearly wounded.'—*Paradise Lost*, I. 446.

[3] II. 79.

[4] On the subject of these plaintive songs generally, see Müller's *Dorians*, book II. ch. 8, § 12 (vol. I. p. 366, English translation), and Thirlwall in the *Philological Museum*, vol. I. p. 119.

§ 4. A very different class of feelings is expressed in another kind of songs, which originally were dedicated only to Apollo, and were closely connected with the ideas relating to the attributes and actions of this god, viz., the *pæans* (παιήονες in Homer). The pæans were songs, of which the tune and words expressed courage and confidence. 'All sounds of lamentation' (αἴλινα), says Callimachus, 'cease when the Ie Pæan, Ie Pæan, is heard.'[1] As with the Linus the interjection αἴ, so with the Pæan the cry of ἰή was connected; exclamations, unmeaning in themselves, but made expressive by the tone with which they were uttered, and which, as has been already mentioned, dated back from the earliest periods of the Greek worship, they were different for different deities, and formed as it were the first rudiments of the hymns which began and ended with them. Pæans were sung, not only when there was a hope of being able, by the help of the gods, to overcome a great and imminent danger, but when the danger was happily past; they were songs of hope and confidence as well as of thanksgiving for victory and safety. The custom, at the termination of the winter, when the year again assumes a mild and serene aspect, and every heart is filled with hope and confidence, of singing *vernal pæans* (εἰαρινοὶ παιᾶνες), recommended by the Delphic oracle to the cities of Lower Italy, is probably of very high antiquity. Among the Pythagoreans likewise the solemn purification (κάθαρσις), which they performed in spring, consisted in singing pæans and other hymns sacred to Apollo. In Homer,[2] the Achæans, who have restored Chryseis to the priest her father, are represented as singing, at the end of the sacrificial feast, over their cups, a pæan in honour of the far-darting god, whose wrath they thus endeavour completely to appease. And in the same poet, Achilles, after the slaughter of Hector, calls on his companions to return to the ships, singing a pæan, the spirit and tone of which he expresses in the following words: 'We have gained great glory; we have slain the divine Hector, to whom the Trojans throughout the city prayed as to a god.'[3] From these passages it is evident that the pæan

---

[1] οὐδὲ Θέτις Ἀχιλῆα κινύρεται αἴλινα μήτηρ,

ὅππστ' ἰὴ Παιῆον ἀκούσῃ. ν, η.—*Hymn. Apoll.* 20.

[2] *Iliad* I. 473.   [3] *Iliad* XXII. 391.

was sung by several persons, one of whom probably led the others (ἐξάρχων), and that the singers of the pæan either sat together at table (which was still customary at Athens in Plato's time), or moved onwards in a body. Of the latter mode of singing a pæan the hymn to the Pythian Apollo furnishes an example, where the Cretans, who have been called by the god as priests of his sanctuary at Pytho, and have happily performed a miraculous voyage from their own island after the sacrificial feast which they celebrate on the shores of Crissa, afterwards ascend to Pytho, in the narrow valley of Parnassus. 'Apollo leads them, holding his harp (φόρμιγξ) in his hand, playing beautifully, with a noble and lofty step. The Cretans follow him in a measured pace, and sing, after the Cretan fashion, an Iepæan, which sweet song the muse had placed in their breasts.'[1] From this pæan, which was sung by a moving body of persons, arose the use of the pæan (παιωνίζειν) in war, before the attack on the enemy, which seems to have prevailed chiefly among the Doric nations, and does not occur in Homer.

If it was our purpose to seek merely probable conclusions, or if the nature of the present work admitted a detailed investigation, in which we might collect and combine a variety of minute particles of evidence, we could perhaps show that many of the later descriptions of hymns belonging to the separate worships of Artemis, Demeter, Dionysus, and other gods, originated in the earliest period of Greek literature. As, however, it seems advisable in this work to avoid merely conjectural inquiries, we will proceed to follow up the traces which occur in the Homeric poems, and to postpone the other matters until we come to the history of lyric poetry.

§ 5. Not only the common and public worship of the gods, but also those events of private life which strongly excited the feelings, called forth the gift of poetry. The *lamentation for the dead*, which was chiefly sung by women with vehement expressions of grief, had, at the time described by Homer, already been so far systematized, that singers by profession stood near the bed where the body was laid out, and began the lament ; and while they sang it, the women accompanied them with cries and

---

[1] Hom. *Hymn. Apoll.* 514.

groans.[1] These singers of the *threnos* were at the burial of Achilles represented by the Muses themselves, who sang the lament, while the sisters of Thetis, the Nereids, uttered the same cries of grief.[2]

Opposed to the threnos is the *Hymenæos*, the joyful and merry bridal song, of which there are descriptions by Homer[3] in the account of the designs on the shield of Achilles, and by Hesiod in that of the shield of Hercules.[4] Homer speaks of a city, represented as the seat of bridal rejoicing, in which the bride is led from the virgin's apartment through the streets by the light of torches. A loud hymenæos arises: young men dance around; while flutes and harps (φόρμιγγες) resound. The passage of Hesiod gives a more finished and indeed a well-grouped picture, if the parts of it are properly distinguished, which does not appear to have been hitherto done with sufficient exactness. According to this passage, the scene is laid in a fortified city, in which men can abandon themselves without fear to pleasure and rejoicing: 'Some bear the bride to the husband on the well-formed chariot; while a loud hymenæos arises. Burning torches, carried by boys, cast from afar their light: the damsels (viz., those who raise the hymenæos) move forwards beaming with beauty. Both (*i. e.* both the youths who accompany the car and the damsels) are followed by joyful choruses. The one chorus, consisting of youths (who accompanied the car), sings to the clear sound of the pipe (σύριγξ) with tender mouths, and causes the echoes to resound: the other, composed of damsels (forming the hymenæos, properly so called), dance to the notes of the harp (φόρμιγξ).' In this passage of Hesiod we have also the first description of a *comos*, by which word the Greeks designate the last part of a feast or any other banquet which is enlivened and prolonged with music, singing, and other amusements, until the order of the table is completely deranged, and the half-intoxicated guests go in irregular bodies through the town, often to the doors of beloved damsels: 'On another side again comes, accompanied by flutes,

---

[1] ἀοιδοὶ θρήνων ἔξαρχοι.—*Iliad* XXIV. 720—722.
[2] *Odyssey* XXIV. 59—61.   [3] *Iliad* XVIII. 492—495.
[4] *Scut.* 274—280.

a joyous band (κῶμος) of youths, some amusing themselves with
the song and the dance, others with laughter.   Each of these
youths moves onwards, attended by a player on the flute (precisely as may be seen so often represented on vases of a much
later age, belonging to southern Italy).   The whole city is
filled with joy, and dancing, and festivity.'[1]   The circumstances
connected with the comos afforded (as we shall hereafter point
out) many opportunities for the productions of the lyric muse,
both of a lofty and serious and of a comic and erotic description.

§ 6. Although in the above description, and in other passages
of the ancient epic poets, choruses are frequently mentioned,
yet we are not to suppose that the choruses of this early period
were like those which sang the odes of Pindar and the choral
songs of the tragedians, and accompanied them with dancing
and appropriate action.   Originally the *chorus* had chiefly to
do with dancing : the most ancient sense of the word *chorus* is
a *place for dancing* : hence in the *Iliad* and *Odyssey* expressions
occur, such as levelling the chorus (λειαίνειν χορόν), that is,
making the place ready for dancing ; going to the chorus
(χορόνδε ἔρχεσθαι), &c. : hence the choruses and dwellings of
the gods are mentioned together ; and cities which had spacious
squares are said to have wide choruses (εὐρύχοροι).   To these
choruses young persons of both sexes, the daughters as well as the
sons of the princes and nobles, are represented in Homer as going:
at these the Trojan and Phæacian princes are described as being
present in newly-washed garments and in well-made armour.
There were also, at least in Crete, choruses in which young men
and women danced together in rows, holding one another by
the hands :[2] a custom which was in later times unknown among
the Ionians and Athenians, but which was retained among the
Dorians of Crete and Sparta, as well as in Arcadia.   The
arrangement of a chorus of this description is as follows :—a
citharist sits in the midst of the dancers, who surround him in
a circle, and plays on the phorminx, a kind of cithara : in the
place of which (according to the Homeric hymn to Hermes)
another stringed instrument, the lyre, which differed in some
respects, was sometimes used ; whereas the flute, a foreign,

---

[1] *Scut.* 281—285.   [2] *Iliad* XVIII. 593.

originally Phrygian, instrument, never in these early times was used at the chorus, but only at the comos, with whose boisterous and unrestrained character its tones were more in harmony. This citharist also accompanies the sound of his instrument with songs, which appear to have scarcely differed from such as were sung by individual minstrels, without the presence of a chorus; as, for example, Demodocus, in the palace of the Phæacian king, sings the loves of Ares and Aphrodite during the dances of the youths.[1] Hence he is said to begin the song and the dance.[2] The other persons, who form the chorus, take no part in this song; except so far as they allow their movements to be guided by it: an accompaniment of the voice by the dancers, such as has been already remarked with respect to the singers of the pæan, does not occur among the chorus-dancers of these early times: and Ulysses, in looking at the Phæacian youths who form the chorus to the song of Demodocus, admires not the sweetness of their voices, or the excellence of their singing, but the rapid motions of their feet.[3] At the same time, the reader must guard against a misapprehension of the terms μολπή and μέλπεσθαι, which, although they are sometimes applied to persons dancing, as to the chorus of Artemis,[4] and to Artemis herself,[5] nevertheless are not always connected with singing, but express any measured and graceful movement of the body, as for instance even a game at ball.[6] When, however, the Muses are described as singing in a chorus,[7] they are to be considered only as standing in a circle, with Apollo in the centre as citharist, but not as also dancing: in the prœmium to the *Theogony* of Hesiod, they are described as first dancing in chorus on the top of Helicon, and afterwards as moving through the dark, and singing the race of the immortal gods.

---

[1] *Odyssey* VIII. 266.   [2] ἡγούμενος ὀρχηθμοῖο.—*Od.* XXIII. 134, compare 144.

[3] μαρμαρυγαὶ ποδῶν.—*Odyssey* VIII. 265.

[4] *Iliad* XVI. 182.   [5] *Hymn. Pyth. Apoll.* 19.

[6] αὐτὰρ ἐπεὶ σίτου τάρφθεν δμωαί τε καὶ αὐτὴ,

σφαίρῃ ταί τ' ἀρ'ἔπαιζον ἀπὸ κρήδεμνα βαλοῦσαι.

τῇσι δὲ Ναυσικάα λευκώλενος ἥρχετο μολπῆς.—*Odyssey* VI. 101.

Compare *Iliad* XVIII. 604: δοιὼ δὲ κυβιστητῆρε κατ' αὐτοὺς

μολπῆς ἐξάρχοντες ἐδίνευον κατὰ μέσσους.

[7] Hesiod. *Scut.* 201—205.

In the dances of the choruses there appears, from the descriptions of the earliest poets, to have been much variety and art, as in the choral dance which Vulcan represented on the shield of Achilles:[1]—'At one time the youths and maidens dance around nimbly, with measured steps, as when a potter tries his wheel whether it will run ; at another, they dance in rows opposite to one another (a dance in a ring alternately with one in rows). Within this chorus sits a singer with the phorminx, and two tumblers ($\kappa\nu\beta\iota\sigma\tau\eta\tau\tilde{\eta}\rho\epsilon$, the name being derived from the violent motions of the body practised by them) turn about in the middle, in accordance with the song.' In a chorus celebrated by the gods, as described in one of the Homeric hymns,[2] this latter part is performed by Ares and Hermes, who gesticulate ($\pi\alpha\iota\zeta\text{ov}\sigma\iota$) in the middle of a chorus formed by ten goddesses as dancers, while Apollo plays on the cithara, and the Muses stand around and sing. It cannot be doubted that these $\kappa\nu\beta\iota\sigma\tau\eta\tau\tilde{\eta}\rho\epsilon\varsigma$, or tumblers (who occurred chiefly in Crete, where a lively, and even wild and enthusiastic style of dancing had prevailed from early times), in some measure regulated their gestures and motions according to the subject of the song to which they danced, and that a choral dance of this kind was, in fact, a variety of *hyporcheme* ($\dot{\nu}\pi\acute{o}\rho\chi\eta\mu\alpha$), as a species of choral dances and songs was called, in which the action described by the song was at the same time represented with mimic gestures by certain individuals who came forward from the chorus. This description of choral dances always, in later times, occurs in connexion with the worship of Apollo, which prevailed to a great extent in Crete ; in Delos likewise, the birth-place of Apollo, there were several dances of this description, one of which represented the wanderings of Latona before the birth of that god. This circumstance appears to be referred to in a passage of the ancient Homeric hymn to the Delian Apollo,[3] where the Delian damsels in the service of Apollo are described as first celebrating the gods and heroes, and afterwards singing a peculiar kind of hymn, which pleases the

---

[1] *Iliad* XVIII. 591—606. Compare *Odyssey* IV. 17—19. It is doubtful whether the latter part of the description in the *Iliad* has not been improperly introduced into the text from the passage in the *Odyssey*.—*Editor*.

[2] *Hymn*, Hom. ad *Apoll. Pyth.* 10—26.   [3] v. 161—164.

assembled multitude, and which consists in the imitation of the voices and languages of various nations, and in the production of certain sounds by some instruments like the Spanish castanets (κρεμβαλιαστύς), according to the manner of the different nations, so that every one might imagine that he heard his own voice—for what is more natural than to suppose that this was a mimic and orchestic representation of the wandering Latona, and all the islands and countries, in which she attempted in vain to find a refuge, until she at length reached the hospitable Delos ?

§ 7. Having now in this manner derived from the earliest records a distinct notion of the kinds of poetry, and its various accompaniments, which existed in Greece before the Homeric time, with the exception of epic poetry, it will be easier for us to select from the confused mass of statements respecting the early composers of hymns which are contained in later writers, that which is most consonant to the character of remote antiquity. The best accounts of these early bards were those which had been preserved at the temples, at the places where hymns were sung under their names : hence it appears that most of these names are in constant connexion with the worship of peculiar deities; and it will thus be easy to distribute them into certain classes, formed by the resemblance of their character and their reference to the same worship.

I. Singers, who belong to the worship of *Apollo* in Delphi, Delos, and Crete. Among these is Olen, according to the legend, a Lycian or Hyperborean, that is to say, sprung from a country where Apollo loved to dwell. Many ancient hymns, attributed to him, were preserved at Delos, which are mentioned by Herodotus,[1] and which contained remarkable mythological traditions and significant appellatives of the gods ; also *nomes*, that is, simple and antique songs, combined with certain fixed tunes, and fitted to be sung for the circular dance of a chorus. The Delphian poetess Boeo called him the first prophet of Phoebus, and the first who, in early times, founded the style of singing in epic metre (ἐπέων ἀοιδά).[2] Another of these bards is Philammon, whose name was celebrated at Parnassus, in the

---

[1] IV. 35.   [2] Pausan. X. 5, 8.

territory of Delphi. To him was referred the formation of
Delphian choruses of virgins, which sung the birth of Latona
and of her children. It is plain, from what has been already
observed, that so far as these songs really originated in the
ancient mythical period, they were intended to be sung, not by
a dancing chorus, but by an individual to the choral dance.
Lastly, Chrysothemis, a Cretan, who is said to have sung the
first chorus to the Pythian Apollo, clothed in the solemn dress
of ceremony, which the citharodi in later times wore at the
Pythian games.

II. Singers in connexion with the cognate worships of *Demeter*
and *Dionysus*. Among these were the Eumolpids in Eleusis of
Attica—a race which, from early times, took part in the
worship of Demeter, and in the historical age exercised the
chief sacerdotal function connected with it, the office of Hiero-
phant. These Eumolpids evidently derived their name of
' beautiful singers' from their character (from εὖ μέλπεσθαι),
and their original employment was the singing of sacred hymns ;
it will be afterwards shown that this function agrees well with
the fact, that their progenitor, the original Eumolpus, is called
a Thracian. Also another Attic house, the Lycomids (which
likewise had in later times a part in the Eleusinian worship of
Demeter), were in the habit of singing hymns, and, moreover,
hymns ascribed to Orpheus, Musæus, and Pamphus. Of the
songs which were attributed to Pamphus we may form a general
idea, by remembering that he is said to have first sung the
strain of lamentation at the tomb of Linus. The name of
Musæus (which in fact only signified a singer inspired by the
Muses) is in Attica generally connected with songs for the
initiations of Demeter. Among the numerous works ascribed
to him, a hymn to Demeter is alone considered by Pausanias
as genuine ;[1] but however obscure may be the circumstances
belonging to this name, thus much at least is clear, that music
and poetry were combined at an early period with this worship.
Musæus is in tradition commonly called a Thracian ; he is also
reckoned as one of the race of Eumolpids, and stated to be the
disciple of Orpheus. The Thracian singer, Orpheus, is unques-

---

[1] I. 22, 7. Compare IV. 1, 5.

tionably the darkest point in the entire history of the early Grecian poetry, on account of the scantiness of the accounts respecting him, which have been preserved in the more ancient writers—the lyric poets, Ibycus[1] and Pindar,[2] the historians Hellanicus[3] and Pherecydes,[4] and the Athenian tragedians, containing the first express testimonies of his name. This deficiency is ill supplied by the multitude of marvellous stories concerning him, which occur in later writers, and by the poem and poetical fragments which are extant under the name of Orpheus. These spurious productions of later times will be treated in that part of our history to which they may with the greatest probability be referred : here we will only state our opinion that the name of Orpheus, and the legends respecting him, are intimately connected with the idea and the worship of a Dionysus dwelling in the infernal regions (Ζαγρεύς), and that the foundation of this worship (which was connected with the Eleusinian mysteries), together with the composition of Hymns and songs for its initiations (τελεταί), was the earliest function ascribed to him. Nevertheless, under the influence of various causes, the fame of Orpheus grew so much, that he was considered as the first minstrel of the heroic age, was made the companion of the Argonauts,[5] and the marvels which music and poetry wrought on a rude and simple generation were chiefly described under his name.

III. Singers and musicians, who belonged to the *Phrygian worship of the great mother of the gods, of the Corybantes,* and other similar beings. The Phrygians, allied indeed to the Greeks, yet a separate and distinct nation, differed from their neighbours in their strong disposition to an orgiastic worship— that is, a worship which was connected with a tumult and excitement produced by loud music and violent bodily movements, such as occurred in Greece at the Bacchanalian rejoicings ;

---

[1] Ibycus in Priscian, VI. 18, 92, tom. I. p. 283, ed. Krehl.(*Fragm.* 22, ed. Schneidewin), who calls him ὀνομάκλυτὸς 'Ορφής. Ibycus flourished 560—40, B.C.

[2] *Pyth.* IV. 3, 5.

[3] Hellanicus in Proclus on Hesiod's *Works and Days,* 631 (*Fragm.* 75, ed. Sturz), and in Proclus περὶ 'Ομήρου in Gaisford's *Hephæstion,* p. 466 (*Fragm.* 145, ed. Sturz).

[4] Pherecydes in *Schol. Apollon.* I. 23 (*Fragm.* 18, ed. Sturz).

[5] Pindar, *Pyth.* IV. 315.

where, however, it never, as in Phrygia, gave its character to every variety of divine worship. With this worship was connected the development of a peculiar kind of music, especially on the flute, which instrument was always considered in Greece to possess a stimulating and passion-stirring force. This, in the Phrygian tradition, was ascribed to the demi-god *Marsyas,* who is known as the inventor of the flute, and the unsuccessful opponent of Apollo, to his disciple *Olympus,* and, lastly, to *Hyagnis,* to whom also, the composition of nomes to the Phrygian gods in a native melody was attributed. A branch of this worship, and of the style of music and dancing belonging to it, spread at an early date to Crete, the earliest inhabitants of which island appear to have been allied to the Phrygians.

§ 8. By far the most remarkable circumstance in these accounts of the earliest minstrels of Greece is, that several of them (especially from the *second* of the three classes just described) are called *Thracians.* It is utterly inconceivable that, in the later historic times, when the Thracians were contemned as a barbarian race,[1] a notion should have sprung up, that the first civilisation of Greece was due to them; consequently we cannot doubt that this was a tradition handed down from a very early period. Now, if we are to understand it to mean that Eumolpus, Orpheus, Musæus, and Thamyris, were the fellow-countrymen of those Edonians, Odrysians, and Odomantians, who in the historical age occupied the Thracian territory, and who spoke a barbarian language, that is, one unintelligible to the Greeks, we must despair of being able to comprehend these accounts of the ancient Thracian minstrels, and of assigning them a place in the history of Grecian civilisation; since it is manifest that at this early period, when there was scarcely any intercourse between different nations, or knowledge of foreign tongues, poets who sang in an unintelligible language could not have had more influence on the mental development of the people than the twittering of birds. Nothing but the dumb language of mimicry and dancing, and musical strains independent of articulate speech, can at such a period pass from nation to nation, as, for example, the Phrygian music passed over to

---

[1] See, for example, Thucyd. VII. 29.

Greece; whereas the Thracian minstrels are constantly represented as the fathers of *poetry*, which of course is necessarily
combined with language. When we come to trace more precisely the country of these Thracian bards, we find that the
traditions refer to *Pieria*, the district to the east of the
Olympus range, to the north of Thessaly and the south of
Emathia or Macedonia; in Pieria likewise was Leibethra, where
the Muses are said to have sung the lament over the tomb of
Orpheus: the ancient poets, moreover, always make Pieria, not
Thrace, the native place of the Muses, which last Homer clearly
distinguishes from Pieria.[1] It was not until the Pierians were
pressed in their own territory by the early Macedonian princes
that some of them crossed the Strymon into Thrace Proper,
where Herodotus mentions the castles of the Pierians at
the expedition of Xerxes.[2] It is, however, quite conceivable,
that in early times, either on account of their close vicinity, or
because all the north was comprehended under one name, the
Pierians might, in Southern Greece, have been called Thracians.
These Pierians, from the intellectual relations which they maintained with the Greeks, appear to be a Grecian race; which
supposition is also confirmed by the Greek names of their
places, rivers, fountains, &c., although it is probable that,
situated on the limits of the Greek nation, they may have
borrowed largely from neighbouring tribes.[3] A branch of the
Phrygian nation, so devoted to an enthusiastic worship, once
dwelt close to Pieria, at the foot of Mount Bermius, where
King Midas was said to have taken the drunken Silenus in his
rose-gardens. In the whole of this region a wild and enthusiastic
worship of Bacchus was diffused among both men and women.
It may be easily conceived that the excitement which the mind
thus received contributed to prepare it for poetical enthusiasm.
These same Thracians or Pierians lived, up to the time of the
Doric and Æolic migrations, in certain districts of Bœotia and
Phocis. That they had dwelt about the Bœotian mountain of
Helicon, in the district of Thespiæ and Ascra, was evident to
the ancient historians, as well from the traditions of the cities

---

[1] *Iliad* XIV. 226.   [2] VII. 112.
[3] See Müller's *Dorians*, vol. I. p. 472, 488, 501.

as from the agreement of many names of places in the country
near Olympus (Leibethrion, Pimpleis, Helicon, &c.).　At the
foot of Parnassus, however, in Phocis, was said to have been
situated the city of Daulis, the seat of the Thracian king
Tereus, who is known by his connexion with the Athenian king
Pandion, and by the fable of the metamorphosis of his wife
Procne into a nightingale.　The story (which occurs under
other forms in several parts of Greece) is one of those simple
fables which, among the early inhabitants of Greece easily grew
from a contemplation of the phenomena of Nature and the
still life of animals : the nightingale, with her sad nocturnal
song, seemed to them to lament a lost child, whose name *Itys*,
or *Itylus*, they imagined that they could hear in her notes ; the
reason why the nightingale, when a human being, was supposed
to have dwelt in this district was, that it had the fame of being
the native country of the art of singing, where the Muses
would be most likely to impart their gifts to animals; as in
other parts of Greece it was said that the nightingales sang
sweetly over the grave of the ancient minstrel, Orpheus.　From
what has been said, it appears sufficiently clear that these
Pierians or Thracians, dwelling about Helicon and Parnassus
in the vicinity of Attica, are chiefly signified when a Thracian
origin is ascribed to the mythical bards of Attica.

　§ 9. It is an obvious remark, that with these movements of
the Pierians was also connected the extension of the temples of
the *Muses* in Greece, who alone among the gods are represented
by the ancient poets as presiding over poetry, since Apollo, in
strictness, is only concerned with the music of the cithara.
Homer calls the Muses the *Olympian ;* in Hesiod, at the beginning of the *Theogony,* they are called the *Heliconian,* although,
according to the notion of the Bœotian poet, they were born on
Olympus, and dwelt at a short distance from the highest pinnacle
of this mountain, where Zeus was enthroned ; whence they only
go at times to Helicon, bathe in Hippocrene, and celebrate their
choral dances around the altar of Zeus on the top of the mountain.　Now, when it is borne in mind that the same mountain
on which the *worship of the Muses* originally flourished was

---

[1] Apollodorus, I. 3. 3.

also represented in the earliest Greek poetry as *the common abode of the Gods;* in which, whatever country they might singly prefer, they jointly assembled about the throne of the chief god, it seems highly probable that it was the poets of this region, the ancient Pierian minstrels, whose imagination had created this council of the gods and had distributed and arranged its parts. Those things which the epic poetry of Homer must have derived from earlier compositions (such as the first notions concerning the structure of the world, the dominions of the Olympian gods and the Titans, the established epithets which are applied to the gods, without reference to the peculiar circumstances under which they appear, and which often disagree with the rest of the epic mythology) probably must, in great measure, be referred to these Pierian bards. Moreover, their poetry was doubtless not concerned merely with the gods, but contained the first germs of the epic or heroic style; more especially should Thamyris, who in Homer is called a Thracian,[1] and in other writers a son of Philammon (by which the neighbourhood of Daulis is designated as his abode), be considered as an epic poet, although some hymns were ascribed to him : for in the account of Homer, that Thamyris, while going from one prince to another, and having just returned from Eurytus of Oechalia, was deprived both of his eyesight and of his power of singing and playing on the cithara by the Muses, with whom he had undertaken to contend,[1] it is much more natural to understand a poet, such as Phemius and Demodocus, who entertained kings and nobles at meals by the narration of heroic adventures, than a singer devoted to the pious service of the gods and the celebration of their praises in hymns.

These remarks naturally lead us to the consideration of the *epic style of poetry,* of which we shall at once proceed to treat.

---

[1] *Iliad* II. 594—600.

CHAPTER IV.

ORIGIN OF THE EPIC POETRY.

§ 1. Social position of the minstrels or poets in the heroic age. § 2. Epic poems sung at the feasts of princes and nobles, and at public festivals. § 3. Manner of reciting epic poems; explanation of *rhapsodists* and *rhapsodising*. § 4. Metrical form, and poetical character of the epic poetry. § 5. Perpetuation of the early epic poems by memory and not by writing. § 6. Subjects and extent of the ante-Homeric epic poetry.

§ 1. IT is our intention in this chapter to trace the Greek Poetry, as far as we have the means of following its steps, on its migration from the lonely valleys of Olympus and Helicon to all the nations which ruled over Greece in the heroic age, and from the sacred groves of the gods to the banquets of the numerous princes who then reigned in the different states of Greece. At the same time we propose, as far as the nature of our information permits, to investigate the gradual development of the heroic or epic style of poetry, until it reached the high station which it occupies in the poems of Homer.

In this inquiry the Homeric poems themselves will form the chief sources of information; since to them we are especially indebted for a clear, and, in the main, doubtless, a correct picture of the age which we term the heroic. The most important feature in this picture is, that among the three classes of nobles,[1] common freemen,[2] and serfs,[3] the first alone enjoyed consideration both in war and peace; they alone performed exploits in battle, whilst the people appear to be there only that these exploits may be performed upon them. In the assembly of the people, as in the courts of justice, the nobles alone speak, advise, and decide, whilst the people merely listen to their ordinances and decisions, in order to regulate their own con-

---

[1] Called ἄριστοι, ἀριστῆες, ἄνακτες, βασιλῆες, μέδοντες, and many other names.
[2] δῆμος (both as a collective and a singular name), δήμου ἄνδρες.
[3] δμῶες.

duct accordingly; being suffered, indeed, to follow the natural impulse of evincing, to a certain extent, their approbation or disapprobation of their superiors, but still without any legal means of giving validity to their opinion.

Yet amidst this nobility, distinguished by its warlike prowess, its great landed possessions and numerous slaves, various persons and classes found the means of attaining respect and station by means of intellectual influence, knowledge, and acquirements, viz., *priests*, who were honoured by the people as gods ;[1] *seers*, who announced the destinies of nations and men, sometimes in accordance with superstitious notions, but not unfrequently with a deep foresight of an eternal and superintending Providence ; *heralds*, who by their manifold knowledge and readiness of address were the mediators in all intercourse between persons of different states; *artisans*, who were invited from one country to another, so much were their rare qualifications in request ;[2] and, lastly, *minstrels*, or *bards* ; who, although possessing less influence and authority than the priests, and placed on a level with the travelling artisans, still, as servants of the Muses,[3] dedicated to the pure and innocent worship of these deities, thought themselves entitled to a peculiar degree of estimation, as well as a friendly and considerate treatment. Thus Ulysses, at the massacre of the suitors, respects Phemius their bard ;[4] and we find the same class enjoying a dignified position in royal families ; as, for instance, the faithful minstrel to whose protection Agamemnon entrusted his wife during his expedition against Troy.[5]

§ 2. Above all, we find the bards in the heroic age described by Homer as always holding an important post in every festal banquet; as the Muses in the Olympian palace of Zeus himself, who sing to Apollo's accompaniment on the cithara ;

---

[1] θεὸς δ' ὡς τίετο δήμῳ. *Odyss.* XIV. 205.

[2] τίς γὰρ δὴ ξεῖνον καλεῖ ἄλλοθεν αὐτὸς ἐπέλθων
ἄλλον γ', εἰ μὴ τῶν οἳ δημιόεργοι ἔασιν ;
μάντιν ἢ ἰητῆρα κακῶν ἢ τέκτονα δούρων,
ἢ καὶ θέσπιν ἀοιδόν, ὅ κεν τέρπῃσιν ἀείδων ;
οὗτοι γὰρ κλητοί γε βροτῶν ἐπ' ἀπείρονα γαῖαν.
Odyssey XVII. 383 *et seq.*

[3] Μουσάων θεράποντες.

[4] *Odyss.* XXII. 344; see particularly VIII. 479.   [5] *Odyss.* III. 267.

amongst the Phæacians, Demodocus, who is represented as possessing a numerous choice of songs, both of a serious and lively cast ; Phemius, in the house of Ulysses, whom the twelve suitors of Penelope had brought with them from their palaces in Ithaca.[1] The song and dance are the chief ornaments of the banquet,[2] and by the men of that age were reckoned as the highest pleasure.[3]

This connexion of epic poetry with the banquets of princes had, perhaps, been of considerable duration in Greece. Even the first sketch of the *Iliad* and *Odyssey* may have been intended to be sung on these occasions, as Demodocus sang the celebrated poem on the contest between Achilles and Ulysses,[4] or the taking of Troy by means of the wooden horse.[5] It is clear also that the Homeric poems were intended for the especial gratification of princes, not of republican communities, for whom the adage ' The government of many is not good ; let there be one lord, one king,'[6] could not possibly have been composed : and although Homer flourished some centuries later than the heroic age, which appeared to him like some distant and marvellous world, from which the race of man had degenerated both in bodily strength and courage ; yet the constitutions of the different states had not undergone any essential alteration, and the royal families, which are celebrated in the *Iliad* and *Odyssey*, still ruled in Greece and the colonies of Asia Minor.[7] To these the minstrels naturally turned for the

---

[1] *Od.* XVI. 252. [2] ἀναθήματα δαιτός. [3] *Od.* XVII. 518.
[4] *Od.* VIII. 74. [5] *Od.* VIII. 500. [6] *Iliad* II. 204.

[7] The supposed descendants of *Hercules* ruled in Sparta, and for a long time also in Messenia and Argos (Müller's *Dorians*, book III. chap. 6, §. 10) as Bacchiads in Corinth, as Aleuads in Thessaly. The *Pelopids* were kings of Achaia until Oxylus, probably for several centuries, and ruled as Penthilids in Lesbos as well as in Cyme. The *Nelids* governed Athens as archons for life until the seventh Olympiad, and the cities of the Ionians as kings for several generations (at Miletus, for example, the succession was Nileus, Phobius, Phrygius). Besides these the descendants of the Lycian hero *Glaucus* ruled in Ionia : Herod. I. 147—a circumstance which doubtless influenced the poet in assigning so important a part to the Lycians in the Trojan war, and in celebrating Glaucus (*Iliad* VI.). The *Æacids* ruled over the Molossians, the *Æneads* over the remnant of the Teucrians, which maintained itself at Gergis, in the range of Ida and in the neighbourhood. (*Classical Journal*, vol. XXVI. p. 308, *seq.*) In *Arcadia* kings of the race of *Æpytus* (*Iliad* II. 604) reigned till about Olympiad 30. Pausan. VIII. 5. *Bœotia* was, in Hesiod's time, governed by kings with extensive powers ; and *Amphidamas of Chalcis*, at whose funeral

purpose of making them acquainted with the renown of their forefathers, and whilst the pride of these descendants of heroes was flattered, and the highest enjoyment secured to them, poetry became the instrument of the most various instruction, and was adapted exclusively for the nobles of that age; so that Hesiod rightly esteems the power of deciding law-suits with justice, and influencing a popular assembly, as a gift of the Muses, and especially of Calliope, to kings.[1]

But even before Homer's time heroic poetry was not only employed to give an additional zest to the banquets of princes, but for other purposes to which, in the later republican age, it was almost exclusively applied, viz., the contests of poets at public festivals and games. A contest of this nature is alluded to in the Homeric description of the Thracian bard Thamyris, who, on his road from Eurytus, the powerful ruler of Œchalia, was struck blind at Dorium by the Muses, and deprived of his entire art, because he had boasted of his ability to contend even with the Muses.[2] The Bœotian minstrel of the *Works and Days* gives an account of his own voyage to the games at Chalcis, which the sons of Amphidamas had celebrated at the funeral of their father; and says, that among the prizes which were there held out, he carried off a tripod, and consecrated it to the Muses on Mount Helicon.[3] Later authors converted this into a contest between Hesiod and Homer. Finally, the author of the Delian Hymn to Apollo, which stands the first amongst those attributed to Homer, entreats the Delian virgins (who were themselves well versed in the song, and probably obeyed him with pleasure), that when a stranger should inquire what bard had pleased them most, they would answer the blind man of Chios, whose poetry everywhere held the first rank. It is beyond doubt that at the festivals, with which the Ionians

---

games the Ascræan bard was victorious ("Εργα, v. 652), was probably a king in Eubœa (see Proclus, Γένος 'Ησιόδου, and the 'Αγών); although Plutarch (*Conviv. sept. sap.* c. 10) only calls him an ἀνὴρ πολεμικός. The Homeric epigram, 13, in the *Life of Homer*, c. 31, calls the γεραροὶ βασιλῆες ἥμενοι εἰν ἀγορῇ, the ornament of the market-place; the later recension of the same epigram in 'Ησιόδου καὶ 'Ομήρου ἀγών mentions instead the λαὸς εἰν ἀγορῇσι καθήμενος, in a republican sense, the *people* having taken the place of *kings*.

[1] *Theogony*, v. 84.
[2] *Iliad* II. 594, *seq.*   [3] v. 654, *seq.*, compare above p. 42, note 7.

celebrated the birth of Apollo at Delos, contests of rhapsodists
were also introduced, just as we find them spread throughout
Greece, at a time when Grecian history assumes a more connected form;[1] and, as may be inferred with respect to the
earlier period, from numerous allusions in the Homeric hymns.

§ 3. The mention of *rhapsodists* leads us to consider the
circumstance from whence that name is derived, and from which
alone we can collect a clear and lively idea of epic poetry, viz.,
the manner in which these compositions were delivered.   Homer
everywhere applies the term ἀοιδή to the delivery of poems,
whilst ἔπη merely denotes the every-day conversation of common life; on the other hand, later authors, from Pindar downwards, use the term ἔπη frequently to designate poetry, and
especially epic, in contradistinction to lyric.   Indeed, in that
primitive and simple age, a great deal passed under the name
of Ἀοιδή, or song, which in later times would not have been
considered as such; for instance, any high-pitched sonorous
recitation, with certain simple modulations of the voice.

The Homeric minstrel makes use of a stringed instrument,
which is called a *cithara,* or, more precisely, *phorminx,*[2] an instrument by which dances were also accompanied.   When the
phorminx was used to lead a dancing-chorus, its music was of

---

[1] Contests of rhapsodists at *Sicyon*, in the time of the tyrant Clisthenes, Herod.
V. 77 ; at the same time at the *Panathenæa*, according to well known accounts ; in
Syracuse, about Olymp. 69, Schol. Pind. *Nem.* II. 1 ; at the *Asclepiea* in Epidaurus,
Plato, *Ion*, p. 530 ; in Attica also, at the festival of the *Brauronian Artemis*,
Hesych. in Βραυρωνίοις; at the festival of the Charites in *Orchomenos ;* that of the
Muses at *Thespiæ*, and that of Apollo Ptous at *Acræphia*, Boeckh. *Corp. Inscript.
Gr.*, Nos. 1583—1587, vol. I. p. 762—770 ; in *Chios*, in later times, but doubtless
from ancient custom, *Corp. Inscript. Gr.* No. 2214, vol. II. p. 201 ; in *Teos*, under
the name ὑποβολῆς ἀνταποδόσεως, according to Boeckh. *Prœm. Lect. Berol. æstiv.*
1834.   Poems were likewise sometimes rhapsodised in *Olympia,* Diog. Laert. VIII.
6, 63 ; Diod. XIV. 109.   Contests of rhapsodists also suited the festivals of *Dionysus,*
Athenæus, VII. p. 275 ; and those of *all* gods, which it is right to remark for the
proper comprehension of the Homeric hymns.

[2] That the phorminx and cithara were nearly the same instrument appears not
only from the expression φόρμιγγι κιθαρίζειν, which often occurs, but from the converse expression, κιθάρει φορμίζειν, which is used in the *Odyssey :*—

κῆρυξ δ' ἐν χερσὶν κίθαριν περικάλλεα θῆκεν
Φημίῳ, ὅς ῥ' ἤειδε περὰ μνηστῆρσιν ἀνάγκῃ.
ἤτοι ὁ φορμίζων ἀνεβάλλετο καλὸν ἀείδειν.—*Od.* I. 153—5.

course continued as long as the dancing lasted;[1] whilst, at the recitation of epic poetry, it was only employed in the introduction (ἀναβολή), and merely served to give the voice the necessary pitch.[2] A simple accompaniment of this description is very well adapted to the delivery of epic poetry ; and in the present day the heroic lays of the Servians, which have most faithfully retained their original character, are delivered in an elevated tone of voice by wandering minstrels, after a few introductory notes, for which the *gurla*, a stringed instrument of the simplest construction, is employed.   That a musical instrument of this nature was not necessary for the recital of epic poetry is proved by the fact, that Hesiod did not make use of the cithara, and on that account is said to have been excluded from the musical contests at Delphi, where this instrument was held in the highest estimation, as the favourite of Apollo himself. On the other hand, the poets of this Bœotian school merely carried a laurel staff,[3] as a token of the dignity bestowed by Apollo and the Muses, as the sceptre was the badge of judges and heralds.

In later times, as music was more highly cultivated, the delivery of the two species of poetry became more clearly defined.   The rhapsodists, or chaunters of epic poetry, are distinguished from the citharodi, or singers to the cithara.[4] The expression ῥαψῳδὸς, ῥαψῳδεῖν, signifies nothing more than the peculiar *method of epic recitation;* and it is an error which has

---

[1] See, for example, *Od.* IV. 17 :--

μετὰ δέ σφιν ἐμέλπετο θεῖος ἀοιδὸς

φορμίζων· δοιὼ δὲ κυβιστητῆρε κατ᾽ αὐτοὺς

μολπῆς ἐξάρχοντες ἐδίνευον κατὰ μέσσους.

[2] Hence the expression, φορμίζων ἀνεβάλλετ᾽ ἀείδειν, *Od.* I. 155 ; VIII. 266 ; XVII. 262 ; *Hymn to Hermes,* v. 426.

τάχα δὲ λιγέως κιθαρίζων

Γηρύετ᾽ ἀμβολάδην, ἐρατὴ δέ οἱ ἕσπετο φωνή.

On ἀμβολὰ, in the sense of *prelude,* see Pindar, *Pyth.* I. 7 ; compare Aristoph. *Pac.* 830 ; Theocrit. VI. 20.   I pass over the testimonies of the grammarians.

[3] ῥάβδος, αἴσακος, also called σκῆπτρον. See Hesiod, *Theogon.* 30 ; Pindar, *Isthm.* III. 55 ; where, according to Dissen, ῥάβδος, as the symbolical sign of the poetical office, is also ascribed to Homer, *Pausan.* IX. 30 ; X. 7 ; Götling *ad Hesiod.* p. 13.

[4] See, for example, Plato, *Leg.* II. p. 658, and the inscriptions quoted above, p. 44, note 1.

been the occasion of much perplexity in researches respecting Homer, and which has moreover found its way into ordinary language, to endeavour to found upon this word conclusions with respect to the composition and connexion of the epic lays, and to infer from it that they consisted of scattered fragments subsequently joined together. The term *rhapsodising* applies equally well to the bard who recites his own poem (as to Homer, as the poet of the *Iliad* and *Odyssey*[1]), and to the declaimer who recites anew the song that has been heard a thousand times before. Every poem can be rhapsodised which is composed in an epic tone, and in which the verses are of equal length, without being distributed into corresponding parts of a larger whole, strophes, or similar systems. Thus we find this term applied to philosophical songs of purification by Empedocles ($\kappa\alpha\theta\alpha\rho\mu\omicron\iota$), and to iambics by Archilochus and Simonides, which were strung together in the manner of hexameters;[2] it was, indeed, only lyric poetry, like Pindar's odes, which could not be rhapsodised. Rhapsodists were also not improperly called $\sigma\tau\iota\chi\psi\delta\omicron\iota$,[3] because all the poems which they recited were composed in single lines independent of each other ($\sigma\tau\iota\chi\omicron\iota$). This also is evidently the meaning of the name *rhapsodist*, which, according to the laws of the language, as well as the best authorities,[4] ought to be derived from $\dot\rho\dot\alpha\pi\tau\epsilon\iota\nu$ $\dot\alpha\omicron\iota\delta\dot\eta\nu$, and denotes the coupling together of verses without any considerable divisions or pauses—in other words, the even, unbroken, and continuous flow of the epic poem. As the ancients in general show great steadiness and consistency, both in art and literature, and adhered, without any feeling of satiety or craving after novelty, to those models and styles of composition, which had been once recognised as the most perfect; so epic poems, amongst the Greeks, continued to be rhapsodised for upwards of a thousand years. It is true,

---

[1] Homer, $\dot\rho\alpha\psi\omega\delta\epsilon\hat\iota$ $\pi\epsilon\rho\iota\dot\omega\nu$, the *Iliad* and *Odyssey*, according to Plato, *Rep.* X. p. 600 D. Concerning Hesiod as a rhapsodist, Nicocles ap. Schol. Pindar., *Nem.* II. 1.

[2] See Athenæus, XIV. p. 620 C. Compare Plato, *Ion*, p. 531.

[3] Menæchmus in Schol. Pind., *Nem.* II. 1.

[4] The Homerids are called by Pindar, *Nem.* II. 2, $\dot\rho\alpha\pi\tau\hat\omega\nu$ $\dot\epsilon\pi\dot\epsilon\omega\nu$ $\dot\alpha\omicron\iota\delta\omicron\iota$, that is, *carminum perpetua oratione recitatorum*, Dissen, ed. min. p. 371. In the scholia to this passage a verse is cited under the name of Hesiod, in which he ascribes the $\dot\rho\dot\alpha\pi\tau\epsilon\iota\nu$ $\dot\alpha\omicron\iota\delta\dot\eta\nu$ to himself and Homer, and, moreover, in reference to a hymn, not an epic poem consisting of several parts.

indeed, that at a later period the Homeric poems, like those of Hesiod, were connected with a musical accompaniment,[1] and it is said that even Terpander the Lesbian adapted the hexameters of Homer, as well as his own, to tunes made according to certain fixed nomes or styles of music, and to have thus sung them at the contests,[2] and that Stesander the Samian appeared at the Pythian games as the first who sung the Homeric poems to the cithara.[3] This assimilation between the delivery of epic and lyric poetry was however very far from being generally adopted throughout Greece, as the epic recitation or *rhapsodia* is always clearly distinguished from the poems sung to the cithara at the musical contests; and how great an effect an exhibition of this kind, delivered in a dress of solemn ceremony,[4] with suitable tones and expression,[5] produced upon the listeners, and how much it excited their sympathy, is most plainly described by Ion, the Ephesian rhapsodist, whom Plato, in one of his lesser Dialogues, has brought forward as a butt for the irony of Socrates.

§ 4. The *form* which epic poetry preserved for more than a thousand years among the Greeks agrees remarkably well with this composed and even style of chaunting recitation which we have just described. Indeed, the ancient minstrels of the Homeric and ante-Homeric age had probably no choice, since for a long period the hexameter verse was the only regular and cultivated form of poetry, and even in the time of Terpander (about Olymp. 30) was still almost exclusively used for lyric poetry; although we are not on that account to suppose, that all popular songs, hymeneals, dirges, and ditties (such as those which Homer represents Calypso and Circe as singing at the

---

[1] Athenæus, XIV. p. 620 B, after Chamæleon. But the argument of Athenæus, ib. p. 632 D. Ὅμηρον μεμελοποιηκέναι πᾶσαν ἑαυτοῦ τὴν ποίησιν rests on erroneous hypotheses.

[2] Plutarch *de Musicâ*, 3.   [3] Athen. XIV. p. 638. A.

[4] Plato, *Ion* p. 530. The sumptuous dress of the rhapsodist Magnes of Smyrna, in the time of Gyges, is described by Nicolaus Damasc. *Fragm.* p. 268, ed. Tauchnitz. In later times, when the Homeric poetry was delivered in a more dramatic style (ὑπεκρίνετο δραματικώτερον), the *Iliad* was sung by the rhapsodists in a red, the *Odyssey* in a violet, dress, Eustath. *ad Iliad* A. p. 6, 9, ed. Rom.

[5] Plato, *Ion* p. 535. From this, in later days, a regular dramatic style of acting (ὑπόκρισις) for the rhapsodists or Homerists was developed. See Aristot. *Poet.* 26. *Rhetor.* III. 1, 8 ; Achill. Tat. II. 1.

loom), were composed in the same rhythm. But the circumstance of the dactylic verse, the hexameter, having been the first and, for a long time, the only metre which was regularly cultivated in Greece, is an important evidence with respect to the tone and character of the ancient Grecian poetry, the Homeric and ante-Homeric epic. The character of the different rhythms, which, among the Greeks, was always in exact accordance with that of the poetry, consists in the first place in the relation of the *arsis* and *thesis*, of the strong or weak cadence—in other words, of the greater or less exertion of the voice. Now in the *dactyl* these two elements are evenly balanced,[1] which therefore belongs to the class of *equal rhythms;*[2] and hence a regular *equipoise*, with its natural accompaniment, an even and steady tone, is the character of the dactylic measure. This tone is constantly preserved in the epic hexameter; but there were other dactylic metres, which, by the shortening of the long element, or the *arsis*, acquired a different character, which will be more closely examined when we come to treat of the Æolian lyric poetry. According to Aristotle,[3] the epic verse was the most dignified and composed of all measures; its entire form and composition appears indeed peculiarly fitted to produce this effect. The length of the verse, which consists of six feet,[4] the break which is obtained by a pause at the end,[5] the close connexion of the parts into an entire whole, which results from the dovetailing of the feet into one another, the alternation of dactyls with the heavy spondees, all contribute to give repose and majesty and a lofty solemn tone to the metre, and render it equally adapted to the pythoness who announces the decrees of the deity,[6] and to the rhapsodist who recites the battles and adventures of heroes.

Not only the metre, but the *poetical tone and style* of the ancient epic, was fixed and settled in a manner which occurs in no other kind of poetry in Greece. This uniformity in style is the first thing that strikes us in comparing the Homeric poems

---

[1] For in $\perp$ *υυ*, $\perp$ is equal to two times, as well as *υυ*.   [2] γένος ἴσον.

[3] *Poet.* 24, τὸ ἡρωικὸν στασιμώτατον καὶ ὀγκωδέστατον τῶν μέτρων ἐστίν.

[4] Hence *versus longi* among the Romans.   [5] κατάληξις.

[6] Hence called *Pythium metrum*, and stated to be an invention of the priestess Phemonoë, *Dorians*, II. ch. 8, § 13.

with other remains of the more ancient epic poetry—the differences between them being apparent only to the careful and critical observer. It is scarcely possible to account satisfactorily for this uniformity—this invariableness of character—except upon the supposition of a certain tradition handed down from generation to generation in families of minstrels, of an hereditary poetical school. We recognise in the Homeric poems many traces of a style of poetry which, sprung originally from the muse-inspired enthusiasm of the Pierians of Olympus or Helicon, was received and improved by the bards of the heroic ages, and some centuries later arrived at the matured excellence which is still the object of our admiration, though without losing all connexion with its first source. We shall not indeed undertake to defend the genealogies constructed by Pherecydes, Damastes, and other collectors of legends from all the various names of primitive poets and minstrels extant in their time—genealogies, in which Homer and Hesiod are derived from Orpheus, Musæus, and other Pierian bards;[1] but the fundamental notion of these derivations, viz., the connexion of the epic poets with the early minstrels, receives much confirmation from the form of the epic poetry itself.

In no other species of poetry besides the epic do we find generally prevalent certain traditional forms, and an invariable type, to which every poet, however original and inventive his genius, submits; and it is evident that the getting by heart of these poems, as well as their extemporaneous effusion on particular occasions and at the inspiration of the moment, must have been by these means greatly facilitated. To the same cause, or to the style which had been consecrated by its origin and tradition, we attribute the numerous and fixed epithets of the gods and heroes which are added to their names without any reference to their actions or the circumstances of the persons who may be described. The great attention paid to external dignity in the appellations which the heroes bestow on each other, and which, from the elevation of their tone, are in strange contrast with the reproaches with which they at the same time load each other—the frequently-recurring expres-

---

[1] These genealogies have been most accurately compared and examined with critical acuteness by Lobeck, in his learned work, *Aglaophamus*, vol. I. p. 322, *seq.*

sions, particularly in the description of the ordinary events of heroic life, their assemblies, sacrifices, banquets, &c.—the proverbial expressions and sentences derived from an earlier age, to which class may be referred most of the verses which belong in common to Homer and Hesiod—and, finally, the uniform construction of the sentences, and their connexion with each other, are also attributable to the same origin.

This, too, is another proof of the happy tact and natural genius of the Greeks of that period; since no style can be conceived which would be better suited than this to epic narrative and description. In general, short phrases, consisting of two or three hexameters, and usually terminating with the end of a verse; periods of greater length, occurring chiefly in impassioned speeches and elaborate similes; the phrases carefully joined and strung together with conjunctions; the collocation simple and uniform, without any of the words being torn from their connexion, and placed in a prominent position by a rhetorical artifice; all this appears the natural language of a mind which contemplates the actions of heroic life with an energetic but tranquil feeling, and passes them successively in review with conscious delight and complacency.

§ 5. The tone and style of epic poetry is also evidently connected with the manner in which these poems were perpetuated. After the researches of various scholars, especially of Wood and Wolf, no one can doubt that it was universally preserved by the memory alone, and handed down from one rhapsodist to another by oral tradition. The Greeks (who, in poetry, laid an astonishing stress on the manner of delivery, the observance of the rhythm, and the proper intonation and inflection of the voice) always, even in later times, considered it necessary that persons, who were publicly to deliver poetical compositions, should previously practise and rehearse their part. The oral instruction of the chorus was the chief employment of the lyric and tragic poets, who were hence called *chorodidascali*. Amongst the rhapsodists also, to whom the correctness and grace of delivery was of much importance, this method of tradition was the most natural, and at the same time the only one possible, at a time in which the art of writing was either not known at all to the Greeks or used only by a few, and by them to a very slight extent. The correctness of this supposition is proved, in the first place, by *the silence of Homer*, which has great weight in matters which he had so frequently occasion to describe ; but particularly by the ' fatal tokens ' (σήματα λυγρά), commanding the destruction of Bellerophon, which Proetus sends to Iobates : these being clearly a species of symbolical figures, which must have speedily disappeared from use when alphabetical writing was once generally introduced.

Besides this we have *no credible account of written memorials* of that period ; and it is distinctly stated that the laws of Zaleucus (about Olymp. 30) were the first committed to writing : those of Lycurgus, of earlier date, having been at first preserved only by oral tradition. Additional confirmation is afforded by the *rarity and worthlessness of any historical data* founded upon written documents, of the period before the commencement of the Olympiads. The same circumstance also explains the *late introduction of prose composition* among the Greeks, viz., during the time of the seven wise men. The frequent employment of writing for detailed records would of itself have introduced the use of prose. Another proof is afforded by the *existing inscriptions*, very few of which are of earlier date than the time of Solon ; also by the coins which were struck in Greece from the reign of Phidon, king of Argos (about Olymp. 8), and which continued for some time without any inscription, and only gradually obtained a few letters. Again, the very shape of the letters may be adduced in evidence, as in all monuments until about the time of the Persian war, they exhibit a great uncouthness in their form, and a great variety of character in different districts ; so much so, that we can almost trace their gradual development from the Phœnician character (which the Greeks adopted as the foundation of their alphabet) until they obtained at last a true Hellenic stamp. Even in the time of Herodotus, the term ' Phœnician characters'[1] was still used for writing. If now we return to Homer, it will be found that *the form of the text* itself, particularly as it appears in the citations of ancient authors,

---

[1] Φοινικήια in Herod. V. 58. Likewise in the inscription known by the name of *Diræ Teiorum*.

disproves the idea of its having been originally committed to writing, since we find a great variety of different readings and discrepancies, which are much more reconcilable with oral than written tradition. Finally, the *language of the Homeric poems* (as it still appears after the numerous revisions of the text), if considered closely and without prejudice, is of itself a proof that they were not committed to writing till many centuries after their composition. We allude more particularly to the omission of the *vau*, or (as it is termed) the Æolic digamma, a sound which was pronounced even by Homer strongly or faintly according to circumstances, but was never admitted by the Ionians into written composition, they having entirely got rid of this sound before the introduction of writing : and hence it was not received in the most ancient copies of Homer, which were, without doubt, made by the Ionians. The licence as to the use of the digamma is, however, only one instance of the freedom which so strongly characterizes the language of Homer ; but it could never have attained that softness and flexibility which render it so well adapted for versification—that variety of longer and shorter forms which existed together—that freedom in contracting and resolving vowels, and of forming the contractions into two syllables—if the practice of writing had at that time exercised the power, which it necessarily possesses, of fixing the forms of a language. Lastly, to return to the point, for the sake of which we have entered into this explanation, the poetical style of the ancient epic poems shows the great use it made of those aids of which poetry, preserved and transmitted by means of memory alone, will always gladly avail itself. The Greek epic, like heroic poems of other nations which were preserved by oral tradition, as well as our own popular songs, furnishes us with many instances, where, by the mere repetition of former passages or a few customary flowing phrases, the mind is allowed an interval of repose, which it gladly makes use of in order to recal the verses which immediately follow. These epic expletives have the same convenience as the constantly-recurring burdens of the stanzas in the popular poetry of other nations, and contribute essentially towards rendering comprehensible the marvel (which, however, could only be accounted as such in times when the powers of memory have

been weakened by the use of writing) involved in the composition and preservation of such poems by the means of memory
alone.[1]

§ 6. In this chapter our inquiries have hitherto been directed
to the delivery, form, and character of the ancient epic, as we
must suppose it to have existed before the age of Homer.
With regard, however, to any particular production of this
ante-Homeric poetry, no historical testimony of any is extant,
much less any fragment or account of the subject of the poem.
And yet it is in general quite certain that at the period when
Homer and Hesiod arose, a large number of songs must have
existed respecting the actions both of gods and heroes. The
compositions of these poets, if taken by themselves, do not
bear the character of a complete and all-sufficient body, but
rest on a broad foundation of other poems, by means of which
their entire scope and application were developed to a contemporary audience. In the *Theogony*, Hesiod only aims at bringing the families of gods and heroes into an unbroken genealogical connexion; the gods and heroes themselves he always
supposes to be well known. Homer speaks of Achilles, Nestor,
Diomed, even the first time their names are introduced, as persons with whose race, family, preceding history, and actions,
every person was acquainted, and which require to be only
occasionally touched upon so far as may be connected with the
actual subject. Besides this, we find a crowd of secondary
personages, who, as if well known from particular traditions,
are very slightly alluded to; persons whose existence was
doubtless a matter of notoriety to the poet, and who were interesting from a variety of circumstances, but who are altogether
unknown to us, as they were to the Greeks of later days.
That the Olympian council of the gods, as represented in
Homer, must have been previously arranged by earlier poets,
has been already remarked; and poetry of a similar nature to

---

[1] The author has here given a summary of all the arguments which contradict
the opinion that the ancient epics of the Greeks were originally reduced to writing;
principally because, in the course of the critical examination to which Wolf's inquiries have been recently submitted in Germany, this point has been differently
handled by several persons, and it has been again maintained that these poems were
preserved in writing from the beginning.

one part of Hesiod's *Theogony*, though in some respects essentially different, must have been composed upon Cronus and Japetus, the expelled deities languishing in Tartarus.[1]

In the heroic age, however, every thing great and distinguished must have been celebrated in song, since, according to Homer's notions, glorious actions or destinies naturally became the subjects of poetry.[2] Penelope by her virtues, and Clytæmnestra by her crimes, became respectively a tender and a dismal strain for posterity;[3] the enduring opinion of mankind being identical with the poetry. The existence of epic poems descriptive of the deeds of Hercules, is in particular established by the peculiarity of the circumstances mentioned in Homer with respect to this hero, which seem to have been taken singly from some full and detailed account of his adventures;[4] nor would the ship Argo have been distinguished in the *Odyssey* by the epithet of 'interesting to all,' had it not been generally well known through the medium of poetry.[5] Many events, moreover, of the Trojan war were known to Homer as the subjects of epic poems, especially those which occurred at a late period of the siege, as the contest between Achilles and Ulysses, evidently a real poem, which was not perhaps without influence upon the *Iliad*,[6] and the poem of the Wooden Horse.[7] Poems are also mentioned concerning the return of the Achæans,[8] and the revenge of Orestes.[9] And since the newest song, even at that time, always pleased the audience most,[10] we must picture to ourselves a flowing stream of various strains, and a revival of the olden time in song, such as never occurred at any other period. All the Homeric allusions, however, leave the impression that these songs, originally intended to enliven a few hours

---

[1] That is to say, it does not, from the intimations given in Homer, seem probable that he reckoned the deities of the water, as Oceanus and Tethys, and those of the light, as Hyperion and Theia, among the Titans, as Hesiod does.

[2] See *Iliad* VI. 358; *Od.* III. 204.   [3] *Od.* XXIV. 197, 200.

[4] See Müller's *Dorians*, Appendix V. § 14, vol. I. p. 543.

[5] *Od.* XII. 70: Ἀργὼ πασιμέλουσα.

[6] The words are very remarkable :—

> Μοῦσ' ἄρ' ἀοιδὸν ἀνῆκεν ἀειδέμεναι κλέα ἀνδρῶν,
> οἴμης, τῆς τότ' ἄρα κλέος οὐρανὸν εὐρὺν ἵκανεν,
> νεῖκος Ὀδυσσῆος καὶ Πηλείδεω Ἀχιλῆος.—*Od.* VIII. 73, *seq.*

[7] *Od.* VIII. 492.   [8] *Od.* I. 326.   [9] *Od.* III. 204.   [10] *Od.* I. 351.

of a prince's banquet, were confined to the narration of a single
event of small compass, or (to borrow an expression from the
German epopees) to a single *adventure,* for the connexion of
which they entirely relied upon the general notoriety of the
story and on other existing poems.

Such was the state of poetry in Greece when the genius of
Homer arose.

CHAPTER V.

HOMER.

§ 1. Opinions on the birthplace and country of Homer. § 2. Homer probably a Smyrnæan : early history of Smyrna. § 3. Union of Æolian and Ionian characteristics in Homer. § 4. Novelty of Homer's choice of subjects for his two poems. § 5. Subject of the *Iliad :* the anger of Achilles. § 6. Enlargement of the subject by introducing the events of the entire war. § 7. and by dwelling on the exploits of the Grecian heroes. § 8. Change of tone in the *Iliad* in its progress. § 9. The Catalogue of Ships. § 10. The later books, and the conclusion of the *Iliad.* § 11. Subject of the *Odyssey :* the return of Ulysses. § 12. Interpolations in the *Odyssey.* § 13. The *Odyssey* posterior to the *Iliad ;* but both poems composed by the same person. § 14. Preservation of the Homeric poems by rhapsodists, and manner of their recitation.

§ 1. THE only accounts which have been preserved respecting the life of Homer are a few popular traditions, together with conjectures of the grammarians founded on inferences from different passages of his poems; yet even these, if examined with patience and candour, furnish some materials for arriving at probable results. With regard to the native country of Homer, the traditions do not differ so much as might at first sight appear to be the case. Although seven cities contended for the honour of having given birth to the great poet, the claims of many of them were only *indirect.* Thus the *Athenians* only laid claim to Homer, as having been the founders of Smyrna,[1] and the opinion of Aristarchus, the Alexandrine critic, which admitted their claim, was probably

---

[1] This is clearly expressed in the epigram on Pisistratus, in Bekker's *Anecdota,* vol. II. p. 768.

τρίς με τυραννήσαντα τοσαυτάκις ἐξεδίωξεν
δῆμος Ἀθηναίων, καὶ τρὶς ἐπηγάγετο,
τὸν μέγαν ἐν βουλῇ Πεισίστρατον, ὃς τὸν Ὅμηρον
ἤθροισα, σποράδην τὸ πρὶν ἀειδόμενον.
ἡμέτερος γὰρ κεῖνος ὁ χρύσεος ἦν πολιήτης,
εἴπερ Ἀθηναῖοι Σμύρναν ἀπῳκίσαμεν.

qualified with the same explanation.[1] Even *Chios* cannot establish its right to be considered as the *original source* of the Homeric poetry, although the claims of this Ionic island are supported by the high authority of the lyric poet Simonides.[2] It is true that in Chios lived the race of the Homerids;[3] who, from the analogy of other γένη, are to be considered not as a family, but as a society of persons, who followed the same art, and therefore worshipped the same gods, and placed at their head a hero, from whom they derived their name.[4] A member of this house of Homerids was, probably, 'the blind poet,' who, in the Homeric hymn to Apollo, relates of himself, that he dwelt on the rocky Chios, whence he crossed to Delos for the festival of the Ionians and the contests of the poets, and whom Thucydides[5] took for Homer himself; a supposition, which at least shows that this great historian considered Chios as the dwelling-place of Homer. A later Homerid of Chios was the well-known Cinæthus, who, as we know from his victory at Syracuse, flourished about the 69th Olympiad. At what time the Homerid Parthenius of Chios lived is unknown.[6] But notwithstanding the ascertained existence of this clan of Homerids at Chios, nay, if we even, with Thucydides, take the blind man of the hymn for Homer himself, it would not follow that Chios was the *birthplace* of Homer : indeed, the ancient writers have reconciled these accounts by representing Homer as having, in his wanderings, touched at Chios, and afterwards fixed his residence there. A notion of this kind is evidently

---

[1] The opinion of Aristarchus is briefly stated by Pseudo-Plutarch, *Vita Homeri*, II. 2. Its foundation may be seen by comparing, for example, the *Schol. Venet. on Iliad* XIII. 197, e cod. A, which, according to recent investigations, contain extracts from Aristarchus.

[2] Simonides in Pseudo-Plutarch, II. 2, and others. Compare Theocritus, VII. 17.

[3] Concerning this γένος, see the statements in Harpocration in Ὁμηρίδαι, and Bekker's *Anecdota*, p. 288, which in part are derived from the logographers. Another and different use of the word Ὁμηρίδαι occurs in Plato, Isocrates, and other writers, according to which it means the *admirers of Homer*.

[4] Niebuhr, *Hist. of Rome*, vol. I. note 747 (801). Compare the Preface to Müller's *Dorians*, p. xii. *seq.* English Translation.

[5] Thucyd. III. 104.

[6] Suidas in Παρθένιος. It may be conjectured that this υἱὸς Θεστορος, ἀπόγονος Ὁμήρου, is connected with the ancient epic poet, Thestorides of Phocæa and Chios mentioned in Pseudo-Herodot. *Vit. Hom.*

implied in Pindar's statements, who in one place called Homer a Smyrnæan by origin, in another, a Chian and Smyrnæan.[1] The same idea is also indicated in the passage of an orator, incidentally cited by Aristotle; which says that ' the Chians greatly honoured Homer, although he was not a citizen.'[2] With the Chian race of Homerids may be aptly compared the *Samian* family; although this is not joined immediately to the name of Homer, but to that of Creophylus, who is described as the contemporary and host of Homer. This house also flourished for several centuries; since, in the first place, a descendant of Creophylus is said to have given the Homeric poems to Lycurgus the Spartan,[3] (which statement may be so far true, that the Lacedæmonians derived their knowledge of these poems from rhapsodists of the race of Creophylus); and, secondly, a later Creophylid, named Hermodamas, is said to have been heard by Pythagoras.[4]

§ 2. On the other hand, the opinion that Homer was a Smyrnæan not only appears to have been the prevalent belief in the flourishing times of Greece,[5] but is supported by the two following considerations :—first, the important fact, that it appears in the form of a popular legend, a *mythus*, the divine poet being called son of a nymph, Critheis, and the Smyrnæan river Meles;[6] secondly, that by assuming Smyrna as the central point of Homer's life and celebrity, the claims of all the other cities which rest on good authority (as of the Athenians, already mentioned, of the Cumæans, attested by Ephorus, himself a Cumæan,[7] or the Colophonians, supported by Antimachus of Colophon[8]), may be explained and reconciled

---

[1] See Boeckh. Pindar. *Fragm. inc.* 86.

[2] Aristot. *Rhet.* II. 23. Comp. Pseudo-Herod. *Vit. Hom.*, near the end.

[3] See particularly Heraclid. Pont. πολιτειῶν, *Fragm.* 2.

[4] Suidas in Πυθαγόρας Σάμιος, p. 231, ed. Kuster.

[5] Besides the testimony of Pindar, the incidental statement of Scylax is the most remarkable. Σμύρνα ἐν ᾗ Ὅμηρος ἦν, p. 35, ed. Is. Voss.

[6] Mentioned in all the different lives of Homer. The name or epithet of Homer, *Melesigenes*, can hardly be of late date, but must have descended from the early epic poets.

[7] See Pseudo-Plutarch, II. 2. Ephorus was likewise, evidently, the chief authority followed by the author of the life of Homer, which goes by the name of Herodotus.

[8] Pseudo-Plutarch, II. 2. The connexion between the Smyrnæan and Colophonian

in a simple and natural manner. With this view, the history of Smyrna is of great importance in connexion with Homer, but from the conflicting interests of different tribes and the partial accounts of native authorities, is doubtful and obscure: the following account is, at least, the result of careful investigation. There were *two* traditions and opinions with respect to the foundation or first occupation of Smyrna by a Greek people: the one was the *Ionic;* according to which it was founded from Ephesus, or from an Ephesian village called Smyrna, which really existed under that name;[1] this colony was also called an Athenian one, the Ionians having settled Ephesus under the command of Androclus, the son of Codrus.[2] According to the other, the *Æolian* account, the Æolians of Cyme, eighteen years after their own city was founded, took possession of Smyrna,[3] and, in connexion with this event, accounts of the leaders of the colony are given, which agree well with other mythical statements.[4] As the Ionic settlement was fixed by the Alexandrine chronologists at the year 140 after the destruction of Troy, and the foundation of Cyme is placed at the year 150 after the same epoch (which is in perfect harmony with the succession of the Æolic colonies), the two races met at about the same time in Smyrna, although, perhaps, it may be allowed that the Ionians had somewhat the precedence in point of time, as the name of the town was derived from them. It is credible, although it is not distinctly

---

origin of Homer is intimated in the epigram, ibid. I. 4, which calls Homer the son of Meles, and at the same time makes Colophon his native country.

Τιὲ Μέλητος, Ὅμηρε, σὺ γὰρ κλέος Ἑλλάδι πάσῃ
Καὶ Κολοφῶνι πάτρῃ θῆκας ἐν ἀἴδιον.

[1] See Strabo's detailed explanation, XIV. p. p. 633—4.

[2] Strabo, XIV. p. 632—3. Doubtless, likewise the Smyrnæan worship of Nemesis was derived from Rhamnus in Attica. The rhetorician Aristides gives many fabulous accounts of the Athenian colony at Smyrna in several places.

[3] Pseudo-Herodot. *Vit. Hom.* c. 2, 38.

[4] The οἰκιστὴς was, according to Pseudo-Herod. c. 2, a certain Theseus, the descendant of Eumelus of Pheræ ; according to Parthenius, 5, the same family of Admetus the Pheræan founded Magnesia on the Mæander ; and Cyme, the mother-city of Smyrna, had also received inhabitants from Magnesia. Pseudo-Herod. c. 2. The Homeric epigram 4, in Pseudo-Herod. c. 14, mentions λαοὶ Φρίκωνος as the founders of Smyrna ; thereby meaning the Locrian tribe, which, deriving its origin from Phricion, near Thermopylæ, founded Cyme Phriconis, and also Larissa Phriconis.

stated, that for a long time the two populations occupied Smyrna jointly. The Æolians, however, appear to have predominated, Smyrna, according to Herodotus, being one of the twelve cities of the Æolians, while the Ionic league includes twelve cities, exclusive of Smyrna;[1] for the same reason Herodotus is entirely ignorant of the Ephesian settlement in Smyrna. Hence it came to pass, that the Ionians—we know not exactly at what time—were expelled by the Æolians; upon which they withdrew to Colophon, and were mixed with the other Colophonians, always, however, retaining the wish of recovering Smyrna to the Ionic race. In later times the Colophonians, in fact, succeeded in conquering Smyrna, and in expelling the Æolians from it;[2] from which time Smyrna remained a purely Ionian city. Concerning the time when this change took place, no express testimony has been preserved: all that we know for certain is, that it happened before the time of Gyges, king of Lydia, that is, before about the 20th Olympiad, or 700 B.C., since Gyges made war on Smyrna, together with Miletus and Colophon,[3] which proves the connexion of these cities. We also know of an Olympic victor, in Olymp. 23 (688 B.C.), who was an Ionian of Smyrna.[4] Mimnermus, the elegiac poet, who flourished about Olymp. 37 (630 B.C.), was descended from these Colophonians who had settled at Smyrna.[5]

It cannot be doubted that the meeting of these different tribes in this corner of the coast of Asia Minor contributed by the various elements which it put in motion to produce the active and stirring spirit which would give birth to such works as the Homeric poems. On the one side there were the *Ionians* from Athens, with their notions of their noble-minded, wise, and prudent goddess Athena, and of their brave and philanthropic heroes, among whom Nestor, as the ancestor of the Ephesian and Milesian kings, is also to be reckoned. On the other side were the *Achæans*, the chief race among the

---

[1] I. 149.   [2] Herod. I. 150, comp. I. 16. Pausan. VII. 5, 1.

[3] Herod. I. 14; Pausanias, IV. 21, 3, also states distinctly that the Smyrnæans were at that time Ionians. Nor would Mimnermus have sung the exploits of the Smyrnæans in this war if they had not been Ionians.

[4] Pausan. V. 8, 3.   [5] Mimnermus in Strabo, XIV. p. 634.

Æolians of Cyme, with the princes of Agamemnon's family at their head,[1] with all the claims which were bound up with the name of the king of men, and a large body of legends which referred to the exploits of the Pelopids, particularly the taking of Troy. United with them were various warlike bands from Locris, Thessaly, and Eubœa; but, especially colonists from Bœotia, with their Heliconian worship of the Muses and their hereditary love for poetry.[2]

§ 3. If this conflux and intermixture of different races contributed powerfully to stimulate the mental energies of the people, and to develop the traditionary accounts of former times, as well as to create and modify the epic dialect; yet it would be satisfactory if we could advance a step further, and determine to which race Homer himself belonged. There does not appear to be sufficient reason, either in the name or the accounts of Homer, to dissolve him into a mere fabulous and ideal being: we see Hesiod, with all his minutest family relations, standing before our eyes; and if Homer was by an admiring posterity represented as the son of a nymph, on the other hand, Hesiod relates how he was visited by the Muses. Now, the tradition which called Homer a Smyrnæan, evidently (against the opinion of Antimachus) placed him in the Æolic time; and the Homeric epigram,[3] in which Smyrna is called the Æolian, although considerably later than Homer himself, in whose mouth it is placed, is yet of much importance, as being the testimony of a Homerid who lived before the conquest of Smyrna by the Colophonians. Another argument to the same effect is, that Melanopus, an ancient Cymæan composer of hymns, who, among the early bards, has the best claim to historical reality, the supposed author of a hymn referring to the Delian worship,[4] in various genealogies collected by the logographers and other mythologists is called the grandfather of Homer;[5] whence it appears, that when these genealogies

---

[1] Strabo, XIII. p. 582. An Agamemnon, king of Cyme, is mentioned by Pollux, IX. 83.

[2] On the connexion of Cyme with Bœotia, see below, ch. 8 § 1.

[3] *Epigr.* Homer, 4; in Pseudo-Herod. 14.

[4] Pausan. V. 7, 4, according to Bekker's edition. From this it appears that Pausanias makes Melanopus later than Olen, and earlier than Aristeas.

[5] See Hellanicus and others in Proclus *Vita Homeri*, and Pseudo-Herod. c. 1.

were fabricated, the Smyrnæan poet was connected with the
Cymæan colony. The critics of antiquity have also remarked
some traits of manners and usages described in Homer, which
were borrowed from the Æolians : the most remarkable is that
Bubrostis,[1] mentioned by Homer as a personification of un-
appeased hunger, had a temple in Smyrna which was referred
to the Æolian time.[2]

Notwithstanding these indications, every one who carefully
notes in the Homeric poems all the symptoms of national
feelings and recollections of home, will find himself drawn to
the other side, and will, with Aristarchus, recognise the beat
of an Ionic heart in the breast of Homer. One proof of this
is the reverence which the poet shows for the chief gods of the
Ionians, and, moreover, in their character of Ionic deities.
For Pallas Athenæa is described by him as the Athenian goddess, who loves to dwell in the temple on the Acropolis of
Athens, and also hastens from the land of the Phæacians to
Marathon and Athens :[3] Poseidon likewise is known to Homer
as peculiarly the Heliconian god, that is the deity of the Ionian
league, to whom the Ionians celebrated national festivals both
in Peloponnesus and in Asia Minor :[4] in describing Nestor's
sacrifice to Poseidon, moreover, the poet doubtless was mindful
of those which his successors, the Nelids, were wont to solemnize,
as kings of the Ionians. Among the heroes, Ajax, the son of
Telamon, is not represented by Homer, as he was by the
Dorians of Ægina and most of the Greeks, as being an Æacid
and the kinsman of Achilles (otherwise some mention of this
relationship must have occurred), but he is considered merely as a
hero of Salamis, and is placed in conjunction with Menestheus
the Athenian : hence it must be supposed that he, as well as
the Attic logographer Pherecydes,[5] considered Ajax as being by
origin an Attic Salaminian hero. The detailed statement of
the Hellenic descent of the Lycian hero Glaucus in his famous

---

[1] *Il.* XXIV. 532 ; and compare the Venetian Scholia.
[2] According to the Ionica of Metrodorus in Plutarch *Quæst. Symp.* VI. 8, 1.
Eustathius, on the other hand, ascribes the worship to the Ionians.
[3] *Od.* VII. 80. Compare *Il.* II. 547.
[4] *Iliad* VIII. 203; XX. 404 ; with the Scholia *Epigr.* Hom. VI. in Pseudo-
Herod. 17.   [5] Apollod. III. 12, 6.

encounter with Diomed, gains a fresh interest, when we bear in mind the Ionic kings of the race of Glaucus mentioned above.[1] Moreover, with respect to political institutions and political phraseology, there are many symptoms of Ionic usage in Homer: thus the *Phratrias*, mentioned in the Iliad, occur elsewhere only in Ionic states; the *Thetes*, as labourers for hire without land, are the same in Homer as in Solon's time at Athens; *Demos*, also, in the sense both of ' flat country ' and of ' common people,' appears to be an Ionic expression. A Spartan remarks in Plato,[2] that Homer represents an Ionic more than a Lacedæmonian mode of life; and, in truth, many customs and usages may be mentioned, which were spread among the Greeks by the Dorians, and of which no trace appears in Homer. Lastly, besides the proper localities of the two poems, the local knowledge of the poet appears peculiarly accurate and distinct in northern Ionia and the neighbouring Mæonia, where the Asian meadow and the river Cayster with its swans, the Gygæan lake,[3] and Mount Tmolus, where Sipylon with its Achelous[4] appears to be known to him, as it were, from youthful recollections.

If one may venture, in this dawn of tradition, to follow the faint light of these memorials, and to bring their probable result into connexion with the history of Smyrna, the following may be considered as the sum of the above inquiries. Homer was an Ionian belonging to one of the families which went from Ephesus to Smyrna, at a time when Æolians and Achæans composed the chief part of the population of the city, and when, moreover, their hereditary traditions respecting the expedition of the Greeks against Troy excited the greatest interest; whence he reconciles in his poetical capacity the conflict of the contending races, inasmuch as he treats an Achæan subject with the elegance and geniality of an Ionian. But when Smyrna drove out the Ionians, it deprived itself of this

---

[1] Above, p. 42, note 7. No use has here been made of the suspicious passages, which might have been interpolated in the age of Pisistratus. Concerning Homer's Attic tendency in mythical points, see also Pseudo-Herod. c. 28.

[2] *Leg.* III. p. 680.   [3] *Iliad* II. 865; XX. 392.

[4] *Iliad* XXIV. 615. It is evident from the Scholia that the Homeric Achelous is the brook Achelous which runs from Sipylon to Smyrna.

poetical renown ; and the settlement of the Homerids in Chios was, in all probability, a consequence of the expulsion of the Ionians from Smyrna.

It may, moreover, be observed that according to this account, founded on the history of the colonies of Asia Minor, the time of Homer would fall a few generations after the Ionic migration to Asia : and with this determination the best testimonies of antiquity agree. Such are the computation of Herodotus, who places Homer with Hesiod 400 years before his time,[1] and that of the Alexandrine chronologists, who place him 100 years after the Ionic migration, 60 years before the legislation of Lycurgus :[2] although the variety of opinions on this subject which prevailed among the learned writers of antiquity cannot be reduced within these limits.

§ 4. This Homer, then (of the circumstances of whose life we at least know the little just stated), was the person who gave epic poetry its first great impulse ; into the causes of which we shall now proceed to inquire. Before Homer, as we have already seen, in general only single actions and adventures were celebrated in short lays. The heroic mythology had prepared the way for the poets by grouping the deeds of the principal heroes into large masses, so that they had a natural connexion with each other, and referred to some common fundamental notion. Now, as the general features of the more considerable legendary collections were known, the poet had the advantage of being able to narrate any one action of Hercules, or one of the Argive champions against Thebes, or of the Achæans against Troy; and at the same time of being certain that the scope and purport of the action (viz., the elevation of Hercules to the gods, and the fated destruction of Thebes and Troy) would be present to the minds of his hearers, and that the individual adventure would thus be viewed in its proper connexion. Thus doubtless for a long time the bards were satisfied with illustrating single points of the heroic mythology with brief epic lays ; such as in later times were produced by several poets of the school of Hesiod. It was also possible, if it was desired, to form from them longer series of adventures of the

---

[1] Herod. II. 53.   [2] Apollod. *Fragm.* I. p. 410, ed. Heyne.

same hero; but they always remained a collection of independent poems on the same subject, and never attained to that unity of character and composition which constitutes one poem. It was an entirely *new* phenomenon, which could not fail to make the greatest impression, when a poet selected a subject of the heroic tradition, which (besides its connexion with the other parts of the same legendary cycle) had in itself the means of awakening a lively interest, and of satisfying the mind, and at the same time admitted of such a development that the principal personages could be represented as acting each with a peculiar and individual character, without obscuring the chief hero and the main action of the poem.

One legendary subject, of this extent and interest, Homer found in the *anger of Achilles;* and another in the *return of Ulysses.*

§ 5. The first is an event which did not long precede the final destruction of Troy; inasmuch as it produced the death of Hector, who was the defender of the city. It was doubtless the ancient tradition, established long before Homer's time, that Hector had been slain by Achilles, in revenge for the slaughter of his friend Patroclus: whose fall in battle, unprotected by the son of Thetis, was explained by the tradition to have arisen from the anger of Achilles against the other Greeks for an affront offered to him, and his consequent retirement from the contest. Now the poet seizes, as the most critical and momentous period of the action, the conversion of Achilles from the foe of the Greeks into that of the Trojans; for as, on the one hand, the sudden revolution in the fortunes of war, thus occasioned, places the prowess of Achilles in the strongest light, so, on the other hand, the change of his firm and resolute mind must have been the more touching to the feelings of the hearers. From this centre of interest there springs a long preparation and gradual development, since not only the cause of the anger of Achilles, but also the defeats of the Greeks occasioned by that anger, were to be narrated; and the display of the insufficiency of all the other heroes at the same time offered the best opportunity for exhibiting their several excellencies. It is in the arrangement of this preparatory part and its connexion with the catastrophe that the poet displays his perfect

acquaintance with all the mysteries of poetical composition;
and in his continued postponement of the crisis of the action,
and his scanty revelations with respect to the plan of the entire
work, he shows a maturity of knowledge, which is astonishing
for so early an age. To all appearance the poet, after certain
obstacles have been first overcome, tends only to one point, viz.,
to increase perpetually the disasters of the Greeks, which they
have drawn on themselves by the injury offered to Achilles:
and Zeus himself, at the beginning, is made to pronounce, as
coming from himself, the vengeance and consequent exaltation
of the son of Thetis. At the same time, however, the poet
plainly shows his wish to excite in the feelings of an attentive
hearer an anxious and perpetually increasing desire, not only
to see the Greeks saved from destruction, but also that the un-
bearable and more than human haughtiness and pride of Achilles
should be broken. Both these ends are attained through the
fulfilment of the *secret counsel of Zeus,* which he did not com-
municate to Thetis, and through her to Achilles (who, if he had
known it, would have given up all enmity against the Achæans),
but only to Hera, and to her not till the middle of the poem;[1]
and Achilles, through the loss of his dearest friend, whom he
had sent to battle, not to save the Greeks, but *for his own glory,*[2]
suddenly changes his hostile attitude towards the Greeks, and
is overpowered by entirely opposite feelings. In this manner
the exaltation of the son of Thetis is united to that almost im-
perceptible operation of destiny, which the Greeks were required
to observe in all human affairs.

It is evident that the *Iliad* does not so much aim at the individual exaltation of Achilles, as at that of the hero before
whom all the other Grecian heroes humble themselves, and

---

[1] Thetis had said nothing to Achilles of the loss of Patroclus (*Il.* XVII. 411), for
she herself did not know of it. *Il.* XVIII. 63. Zeus also long conceals his plans
from Hera and the other gods, notwithstanding their anger on account of the sufferings of the Achæans : he does not reveal them to Hera till after his sleep upon
Ida. *Il.* XV. 65. The spuriousness of the verses (*Il.* VIII. 475—6) was recognised
by the ancients, although the principal objection to them is not mentioned. See
Schol. Ven. A.

[2] Homer does not wish that the going forth of Patroclus should be considered as
a sign that Achilles' wrath is appeased : Achilles, on this very occasion, expresses a
wish that no Greek may escape death, but that they two alone, Achilles and Patroclus, may mount the walls of Ilion. *Il.* XVI. 97.

through whom alone the Trojans were to be subdued. The
Grecian poetry has never shown itself favourable to the absolute
elevation of a *single individual,* not even if he was reckoned the
greatest of their heroes; and hence a character like that of
Achilles could not excite the *entire* sympathy of the poet. It
is clear that the poet conceives his hero as striving after something super-human and inhuman. Hence he falls from one
excess of passion into another, as we see in his insatiable hatred
to the Greeks, his desperate grief for Patroclus, and his vehement anger against Hector; but still it is impossible to deny
that Achilles is the first, greatest, and most elevated character
of the *Iliad;* we find in him, quite distinct from his heroic
strength, which far eclipses that of all the others, a god-like
loftiness of soul. Compared with the melancholy which Hector,
however determined, carries with him to the field of battle, anticipating the dark destiny that awaits him, how lofty is the
feeling of Achilles, who sees his early death before his eyes,
and, knowing how close it must follow upon the slaughter of
Hector,[1] yet, in spite of this, shows the most determined resolution before, and the most dignified calmness after the deed.
Achilles appears greatest at the funeral games and at the inter-
view with Priam,—a scene to be compared with no other in
ancient poetry; in which, both with the heroes of the event
and with the hearers national hatred and personal ambition, and
all the hostile and most opposite feelings, dissolve themselves
into the gentlest and most humane, just as the human countenance beams with some new expression after long-concealed and
passionate grief; and thus the purifying and elevating process
which the character of Achilles undergoes, and by which the
divine part of his nature is freed from all obscurities, is one
continued idea running through the whole of the poem; and
the manner in which this process is at the same time communicated to the mind of a hearer, absorbed with the subject,
makes it the most beautiful and powerful charm of the *Iliad.*

§ 6. To remove from this collection of various actions, conditions, and feelings any substantial part, as not necessarily
belonging to it, would in fact be to dismember a living whole,

---

[1] *Iliad* XVIII. 95; XIX. 417.

the parts of which would necessarily lose their vitality. As in an organic body life does not dwell in one single point, but requires a union of certain systems and members, so the internal connexion of the *Iliad* rests on the union of certain parts ; and neither the interesting introduction describing the defeat of the Greeks up to the burning of the ship of Protesilaus, nor the turn of affairs brought about by the death of Patroclus, nor the final pacification of the anger of Achilles, could be spared from the *Iliad,* when the fruitful seed of such a poem had once been sown in the soul of Homer, and had begun to develop its growth. But the plan of the *Iliad* is certainly very much extended beyond what was actually necessary ; and, in particular, the preparatory part consisting of the attempts of the other heroes to compensate the Greeks for the absence of Achilles, has, it must be said, been drawn out to a disproportionate length ; so that the suspicion that there were later insertions of important passages, on the whole applies with far more probability to the first than to the last books, in which, however, modern critics have found most traces of interpolation. For this extension there were two principal motives, which (if we may carry our conjectures so far) exercised an influence even on the mind of Homer himself, but had still more powerful effects upon his successors, the later Homerids. In the first place, it is clear that a design manifested itself at an early period to make this poem complete in itself, so that all the subjects, descriptions, and actions, which could alone give an interest to a poem *on the entire war,* might find a place within the limits of this composition. For this purpose it is not improbable that many lays of earlier bards, who had sung single adventures of the Trojan war, were laid under contribution, and that the finest parts of them were adopted into the new poem ; it being the natural course of popular poetry propagated by oral tradition, to treat the best thoughts of previous poets as common property, and to give them a new life by working them up in a different context.

If in this manner much extraneous matter has been introduced into the poem, which, in common probability, does not agree with the definite event which forms the subject of it, but would more properly find its place at an earlier stage of the

Trojan war ; and if, by this means, from a poem on the *Anger of Achilles*, it grew into an *Iliad*, as it is significantly called, yet the poet had his justification, in the manner in which he conceived the situation of the contending nations, and their *mode of warfare*, until the separation of Achilles from the rest of the army, in which he, doubtless, mainly followed the pre-valent legends of his time. According to the accounts of the cyclic and later poets (in whose time, although the heroic tra-ditions may have become more meagre and scanty than they had been in that of Homer, yet the chief occurrences must have been still preserved in memory), the Trojans, after the Battle at the Landing, where Hector killed Protesilaus, but was soon put to flight by Achilles, made no attempt to drive the Greeks from their country, up to the time of the separation of Achilles from the rest of the army, and the Greeks had had time (for the wall of Troy still resisted them) to lay waste, under the conduct of Achilles, the surrounding cities and islands ; of which Homer mentions particularly Pedasus, the city of the Leleges; theCilician Thebe, at the foot of Mount Placus ; the neighbouring city of Lyrnessus ; and also the Islands of Lesbos and Tenedos.[1] The poet, in various places, shows plainly his notion of the state of the war at this time, viz., that the Trojans, so long as Achilles took part in the war, did not venture beyond the gates ; and if Hector was, perchance, willing to venture a sally, the general fear of Achilles and the anxiety of the Trojan elders held him back.[2] By this view of the contest, the poet is sufficiently justified in bringing within the compass of the *Iliad* events which would otherwise have been more fitted for the beginning of the war. The Greeks now arrange themselves for the first time, by the advice of Nestor, into tribes and phratrias, which affords an occasion for the enumeration of the several nations,

---

[1] The question why the Trojans did not attack the Greeks when Achilles was engaged in these maritime expeditions must be answered by history, not by the mythical tradition. It is also remarkable that Homer knows of no Achæan hero who had fallen in battle with the Trojans *after* Protesilaus, and *before* the time of the *Iliad*. See particularly *Od.* III. 105 *seq.* Nor is any Trojan mentioned who had fallen in battle. Æneas and Lycaon were surprised when engaged in peace-able occupations, and a similar supposition must be made with regard to Mestor and Troilus. *Il.* XXIV. 257.

[2] *Il.* V. 788 ; IX. 352 ; XV. 721.

or the Catalogue of Ships (as it is called), in the second book; and when this has made us acquainted with the general arrangement of the army, then the view of Helen and Priam from the walls, in the third book, and Agamemnon's mustering of the troops, in the fourth, are intended to give a more distinct notion of the *individual* character of the chief heroes. Further on, the Greeks and Trojans are, for the first time, struck by an idea which might have occurred in the previous nine years, if the Greeks, when assisted by Achilles, had not, from their confidence of their superior strength, considered every compromise as unworthy of them; namely, to decide the war by a single combat between the authors of it; which plan is frustrated by the cowardly flight of Paris and the treachery of Pandarus. Nor is it until they are taught by the experience of the first day's fighting that the Trojans can resist them in open battle, that they build the walls round their ships, in which the omission of the proper sacrifices to the gods is given as a new reason for not fulfilling their intentions. This appeared to Thucydides so little conformable to historical probability, that, without regarding the authority of Homer, he placed the building of these walls immediately after the landing.[1] This endeavour to comprehend everything in one poem also shows itself in another circumstance,—that some of the events of the war lying within this poem are copied from others not included in it. Thus the wounding of Diomed by Paris, in the heel,[2] is taken from the story of the death of Achilles, and the same event furnishes the general outlines of the death of Patroclus; as in both, a god and a man together bring about the accomplishment of the will of fate.[3]

§ 7. The other motive for the great extension of the preparatory part of the catastrophe may, it appears, be traced to a certain conflict between the *plan* of the poet and his own patriotic feelings. An attentive reader cannot fail to observe that while Homer intends that the Greeks should be made to suffer severely from the anger of Achilles, he is yet, as it were,

---

[1] Thuc. I. 11. The attempt of the scholiast to remove the difficulty, by supposing a smaller and a larger bulwark, is absurd.

[2] *Il.* XI. 377.

[3] *Il.* XIX. 417; XXI. 359. It was the fate o Achilles, θεῷ τε καὶ ἀνέρι ἶφι δαμῆναι.

retarded in his progress towards that end by a natural endeavour to avenge the death of each Greek by that of a yet more
illustrious Trojan, and thus to increase the glory of the numerous Achæan heroes; so that, even on the days in which the
Greeks are defeated, more Trojans than Greeks are described
as being slain. Admitting that the poet, living among the
descendants of these Achæan heroes, found more legends about
them than about the Trojans in circulation, still the introduction of them into a poem, in which these very Achæans
were described as one of the parties in a war, could not fail to
impart to it a national character. How short is the narration
of the second day's battle in the eighth book, where the incidents
follow their direct course, under the superintendence of Zeus,
and the poet is forced to allow the Greeks to be driven back
to their camp (yet even then not without severe loss to the
Trojans), in comparison with the narrative of the first day's
battle, which, besides many others, celebrates the exploits of
Diomed, and extends from the second to the seventh book; in
which Zeus appears, as it were, to have forgotten his resolution
and his promise to Thetis. The exploits of Diomed[1] are indeed
closely connected with the violation of the treaty, inasmuch as
the death of Pandarus, which became necessary in order that
his treachery might be avenged, is the work of Tydides;[2] but
they have been greatly extended, particularly by the battles
with the gods, which form the characteristic feature of the
legend of Diomed:[3] hence in this part of the Iliad particularly,
slight inconsistencies of different passages and interruptions in
the connexion have arisen. We may mention especially the
contradictory expressions of Diomed and his counsellor Athena,

---

[1] Διομήδους ἀριστεία.

[2] *Il.* V. 290. Homer does not make on this occasion the reflection which one
expects; but it is his practice rather to leave the requisite *moral impression* to be
made by the simple combination of the events, without adding any comment of his
own.

[3] Diomed, in the Argive mythology, which referred to Pallas, was a being closely
connected with this goddess, her shield-bearer and defender of the Palladium.
Hence he is, in Homer, placed in a closer relation with the Olympic gods than any
other hero: Pallas driving his chariot, and giving him courage to encounter Ares,
Aphrodite, and even Apollo, in battle. It is particularly observable that Diomed
never fights with Hector, but with Ares, who enables Hector to conquer.

as to whether · a contest with the gods was advisable or not.[1]
Another inconsistency is that remarked by the ancients with
respect to the breastplate of Diomed ;[2] this, however, is removed,
if we consider the scene between Diomed and Glaucus as an
interpolation added by an Homerid of Chios ; perhaps, with
the view of doing honour to some king of the race of Glaucus.[3]
With regard to the night-scenes, which take up the tenth book,[4]
a remarkable statement has been preserved, that they were originally a separate book, and were first inserted in the *Iliad* by
Pisistratus.[5] This account is so far supported, that not the
slightest reference is made, either before or after, to the contents
of this book, especially to the arrival of Rhesus in the Trojan
camp, and of his horses taken by Diomed and Ulysses ; and the
whole book may be omitted without leaving any perceptible
chasm. But it is evident that this book was written for the
particular place in which we find it, in order to fill up the
remainder of the night, and to add another to the achievements
of the Grecian heroes; for it could neither stand by itself nor
form a part of any other poem.

§ 8. That the first part of the *Iliad*, up to the Battle at the
Ships, has, as compared with the remaining part, a more cheerful, sometimes even a jocose character, while the latter has a
grave and tragic cast, which extends its influence even over the
choice of expressions, naturally arises from the nature of the
subject itself. The ill-treatment of Thersites, the cowardly
flight of Paris into the arms of Helen, the credulous folly of
Pandarus, the bellowing of Mars, and the feminine tears of
Aphrodite when wounded by Diomed, are so many amusing
and even sportive passages from the first books of the *Iliad*,
such as cannot be found in any of the latter books. The

---

[1] *Il.* V. 130, 434, 827 ; VI. 128.

[2] *Il.* VI. 230; and VIII. 194. The inconsistency with regard to Pylæmenes is also
removed, if we sacrifice V. 579, and retain XIII. 658. Of less importance, as it seems
to me, is the oblivion of the message to Achilles, which is laid to the charge of
Patroclus. *Il.* XI. 839 ; XV. 390. May not Patroclus have sent a messenger to
inform Achilles of what he wished to know ? The non-observance by Polydamas of
the advice which he himself gives to Hector (*Il.* XII. 75 ; XV. 354, 447 ; XVI.
367) is easily excused by the natural weakness of humanity.

[3] Above, p. 42, note 7.   [4] Νυκτεγερσία and Δολωνεία.

[5] Schol. Ven. ad *Il.* X. 1 ; Eustath. p. 785, 41, ed. Rom.

countenance of the ancient bard, which in the beginning assumed a serene character, and is sometimes brightened with an ironical smile, obtains by degrees an excited tragic expression. Although there are good grounds in the plan of the *Iliad* for this difference, yet there is reason to doubt whether the beginning of the second book, in which this humorous tone is most apparent, was written by the ancient Homer or by one of the later Homerids. Zeus undertakes to *deceive* Agamemnon, for, by means of a dream, he gives him great courage for the battle. Agamemnon himself adopts a second deceit against the Achæans, for he, though full of the hopes of victory, yet persuades the Achæans that he has determined on the return home; in this, however, his expectations are again deceived in a ludicrous manner by the Greeks, whom he had only wished to try, in order to stimulate them to the battle, but who now are determined to fly in the utmost haste, and, contrary to the decree of fate, to leave Troy uninjured, if Ulysses, at the suggestion of the gods, had not held them back. Here is matter for an entire mythical *comedy*, full of fine irony, and with an amusing plot, in which the deceiving and deceived Agamemnon is the chief character; who, with the words, 'Zeus has played me a pretty trick,'[1] at the same time that he means to invent an ingenious falsehood, unconsciously utters an unpleasant truth. But this Homeric comedy, which is extended through the greater part of the second book, cannot possibly belong to the original plan of the *Iliad;* for Agamemnon, two days later, complaining to the Greeks of being deceived by former signs of victory which Zeus had shown him, uses in *earnest* the same words which he had here used in *joke*.[2] But it is not conceivable that Agamemnon (if the laws of probability were respected) should be represented as able seriously to repeat the complaint which he had before feigned, without, at the same time, dwelling on the inconsistency between his present and his former opinion. It is, moreover, evident, that the graver and shorter passage did not grow out of the more comic and longer one; but that the latter is a copious parody of the former, composed by a later

---

[1] *Il.* II. 114, νῦν δὲ κακὴν ἀπάτην βουλεύσατο.

[2] *Il.* II. 111—18 and 139—41 correspond to *Il.* IX. 18—28.

Homerid, and inserted in the room of an original shorter account of the arming of the Greeks.

§ 9. But of all the parts of the *Iliad*, there is none of which the discrepancies with the rest of the poem are so manifest as the *Catalogue of the Ships*, already alluded to. Even the ancients had critical doubts on some *passages;* as, for instance, the manifestly intentional association of the ships of Ajax with those of the Athenians, which appears to have been made solely for the interest of the Athenian houses (the Eurysacids and Philaids), which deduced their origin from Ajax; and the mention of the *Panhellenians,* whom (contrary to Homer's invariable usage) the Locrian Ajax surpasses in the use of the spear. But still more important are the mythico-historical discrepancies between the Catalogue and the *Iliad* itself. *Meges,* the son of Phyleus, is in the Catalogue King of Dulichium; in the *Iliad*,[1] King of the Epeans, dwelling in Elis. The Catalogue here follows the tradition, which was also known in later times,[2] that Phyleus, the father of Meges, quarrelled with his father Augeas, and left his home on this account. *Medon,* a natural son of Oileus, is described in the Catalogue as commanding the troops of Philoctetes, which come from Methone; but in the *Iliad* as leading the Phthians,[3] inhabiting Phylace, who, in the Catalogue, form quite a different kingdom, and are led by Podarces instead of Protesilaus. With such manifest contradictions as these one may venture to attach some weight to the less obvious marks of a fundamental difference of views of a more general kind. Agamemnon, according to the *Iliad*, governs from Mycenæ the whole of Argos (that is, the neighbouring part of Peloponnesus), and many islands;[4] according to the Catalogue, he governs no islands whatever; but, on the other hand, his kingdom comprises Ægialeia, which did not become Achæan till after the expulsion of the Ionians.[5] With respect to the Bœotians, the poets of the Catalogue have en-

---

[1] *Il.* XIII. 692; XV. 519.

[2] Callimachus ap. Schol. *Il.* II. 629.   Comp. Theocrit. XXI.

[3] *Il.* XIII. 693; XV. 334.   [4] *Il.* II. 108.

[5] Here, in particular, the verse (*Il.* II. 572), in which Adrastus is named as first king of Sicyon, compared with Herod. V. 67—8, clearly shows the objects of the Argive rhapsodist.

tirely forgotten that they dwelt in Thessaly at the time of the Trojan war; for they describe the *whole* nation as already settled in the country afterwards called Bœotia.[1] That heroes and troops of men joined the Achæan army from the eastern side of the Ægean Sea and the islands on the coast of Asia Minor, is a notion of which the *Iliad* offers no trace; it knows nothing of the heroes of *Cos*, Phidippus and Antiphus, nor anything of the beautiful Nireus from Syme; and as it is not said of Tlepolemus that he came from Rhodes, but only that he was a son of Hercules, it is most natural to understand that the poet of the *Iliad* conceived him as a Tirynthian hero. The mention in the Catalogue of a whole line of islands on the coast of Asia Minor destroys the beauty and unity of the picture of the belligerent nations contained in the *Iliad*, which makes the allies of the Trojans come only from the east and north of the Ægean Sea, and Achæan warriors come only from the west.[2] The poets of the *Catalogue* have also made the Arcadians under Agapenor, as well as the Perrhæbians and the Magnetes, fight before Troy. The purer tradition of the *Iliad* does not mix up these Pelasgic tribes (for, among all the Greeks, the Arcadians and Perrhæbians remained most Pelasgic) in the ranks of the Achæan army.

If the enumeration of the Achæan bands is too detailed, and goes beyond the intention of the original poet of the *Iliad*, on the other hand, the *Catalogue of the Trojans and their allies* is much below the notion which the *Iliad* itself gives of the forces of the Trojans: this altogether omits the important allies, the Caucones and the Leleges, both of whom often occur in the *Iliad*, and the latter inhabited the celebrated city of Pedasus, on the Satnioëis.[3] Among the princes unmentioned in this Catalogue, Asteropæus, the leader and hero of the Pæonians, is particularly observable, who arrived eleven days before the battle with

---

[1] There is, likewise, in the *Iliad* a passage (not, indeed, of much importance) which speaks of *Bœotians in Bœotia*. *Il.* V. 709. For this reason Thucydides assumed that an ἀποδασμὸς of the Bœotians had at this time settled in Bœotia ; which, however, is not sufficient for the Catalogue.

[2] The account of the *Rhodians* in the Catalogue also, by its great length, betrays the intention of a rhapsodist to celebrate this island.

[3] For the Caucones, see *Il.* X. 429 ; XX. 329. For the Leleges, *Il.* X. 429: XX. 96 ; XXI. 86. Comp. VI. 35.

Achilles, and, therefore, before the review in the second book,[1] and at least deserved to be named as well as Pyræchmes.[2] On the other hand, this Catalogue has some names, which are wanting in the parts of the *Iliad,* where they would naturally recur.[3] But we have another more decided proof that the Catalogue of the Trojans is of comparatively recent date, and was composed after that of the Achæans. The Cyprian poem, which was intended solely to serve as an introduction to the *Iliad,*[4] gave at its conclusion (that is, immediately before the beginning of the action of the *Iliad*) a list of the Trojan allies;[5] which certainly would not have been the case if, in the second book of the *Iliad,* as it then existed, not the Achæans alone but also the Trojans had been enumerated. Perhaps our present Catalogue in the *Iliad* is only an abridgment of that in the Cyprian poem ; at least, then, the omission of Asteropæus could be explained, for if he came eleven days before the battle just mentioned, he would not (according to Homer's chronology) have arrived till after the beginning of the action of the *Iliad,* that is, the sending of the plague.

But from the observations on these two Catalogues may be drawn other inferences, besides that they are not of genuine Homeric origin : first, that the rhapsodists, who composed these parts, had not the *Iliad* before them *in writing,* so as to be able to refer to it at pleasure ; otherwise, how should they not have discovered that Medon lived at Phylace, and such like particulars ; 2ndly, that these later poets did not retain the *entire Iliad* in their memory, but that in this attempt to give an ethnographical survey of the forces on each side, they allowed themselves to be guided by the parts which they themselves knew by heart and could recite, and by less distinct reminiscences of the rest of the poem.

---

[1] See *Il.* XXI. 155 ; also XII. 102 ; XVIII. 351.

[2] *Il.* II. 848. The author of this Catalogue must have thought only of *Il.* XVI. 287. The scholiast, on *Il.* II. 844, is also quite correct in missing *Iphidamas ;* who, indeed, was a Trojan, the son of Antenor and Theano, but was furnished by his maternal grandfather, a Thracian prince, with a fleet of twelve ships. *Il.* XI. 221.

[3] For example, the soothsayer *Eunomus,* who, according to the Catalogue (*Il.* II. 861), was slain by Achilles in the river, of which there is no mention in the *Iliad.* So likewise *Amphimachus. Il.* II. 871.

[4] See below, chap. VI. § 4.

[5] καὶ κατάλογος τῶν τοῖς Τρῶσι συμμαχησάντων, Proclus in Gaisford's *Hephæstion,* p. 476.

§ 10. A far less valid suspicion than that which has been
raised against the first part of the *Iliad*, principally against the
second, and also against the fifth, sixth, and tenth books, rests
on the *later* ones, and on those which follow the death of
Hector.   A tragedy, which treated its subject dramatically,
might indeed have closed with the death of Hector, but no
epic poem could have been so concluded ; as in that it is necessary that the feeling which has been excited should be allowed to
subside into calm.   This effect is, in the first place, brought
about by means of the games ; by which the greatest honour is
conferred on Patroclus, and also a complete satisfaction is made
to Achilles.   But neither would the *Iliad* at any time have
been complete without the cession of the body of Hector to his
father, and the honourable burial of the Trojan hero.   The
poet, who everywhere else shows so gentle and humane a disposition, and such an endeavour to distribute even-handed
justice throughout his poem, could not allow the threats of
Achilles[1] to be fulfilled on the body of Hector ; but even if
this had been the poet's intention, the subject must have been
mentioned ; for, according to the notions of the Greeks of that
age, the fate of the dead body was almost of more importance
than that of the living ; and instead of our twenty-fourth book,
a description must have followed of the manner in which
Achilles ill-treated the corpse of Hector, and then cast it for
food to the dogs.   Who could conceive such an end to the
Iliad possible ?   It is plain that Homer, from the first,
arranged the plan of the *Iliad* with a full consciousness that the
anger of Achilles against Hector stood in need of some mitiga-
tion—of some kind of atonement—and that a gentle, humane
disposition, awaiting futurity with calm feelings, was requisite
both to the hero and the poet at the end of the poem.

§ 11. The *Odyssey* is indisputably, as well as the *Iliad*, a
poem possessing an unity of subject ; nor can any one of its
chief parts be removed without leaving a chasm in the development of the leading idea ; but it differs from the *Iliad* in being
composed on a more *artificial* and more *complicated* plan.
This is the case partly, because in the first and greater half,
up to the sixteenth book, two *main actions* are carried on side

---

[1] *Il.* XXII. 35 ; XXIII. 183.

by side ; partly because the action, which passes within the
compass of the poem, and as it were beneath our eyes, is
greatly extended by means of an *episodical narration*, by which
the chief action itself is made distinct and complete, and the
most marvellous and strangest part of the story is transferred
from the mouth of the poet to that of the inventive hero
himself.[1]

The subject of the *Odyssey* is the *return* of Ulysses from a
land lying beyond the range of human intercourse or knowledge, to a home invaded by bands of insolent intruders, who
seek to rob him of his wife, and kill his son.   Hence, the
Odyssey begins exactly at that point where the hero is
considered to be farthest from his home, in the island of
Ogygia,[2] at the navel, that is, the central point of the sea;
where the nymph Calypso[3] has kept him hidden from all
mankind for seven years; thence having, by the help of the
gods, who pity his misfortunes, passed through the dangers
prepared for him by his implacable enemy, Poseidon, he gains
the land of the Phæacians, a careless, peaceable, and effeminate
nation on the confines of the earth, to whom war is only
known by means of poetry ; borne by a marvellous Phæacian
vessel, he reaches Ithaca sleeping ; here he is entertained by
the honest swineherd Eumæus, and having been introduced
into his own house as a beggar, he is there made to suffer the
harshest treatment from the suitors, in order that he may afterwards appear with the stronger right as a terrible avenger.
With this simple story a poet might have been satisfied ; and we
should even in this form, notwithstanding its smaller extent,
have placed the poem almost on an equality with the *Iliad*.
But the poet, to whom we are indebted for the *Odyssey* in its
complete form, has interwoven a second story, by which the
poem is rendered much richer and more complete ; although,
indeed, from the union of two actions, some roughnesses have

---

[1] It appears, however, from his soliloquy, *Od.* XX. 18—21, that the poet did not
intend his adventures to be considered as imaginary.

[2] Ὠγυγία from Ὠγύγης, who was originally a deity of the watery expanse which
covers all things.

[3] Καλυψώ, the Concealer.

been produced, which perhaps with a plan of this kind could scarcely be avoided.[1]

For while the poet represents the son of Ulysses, stimulated by Athena, coming forward in Ithaca with newly excited courage, and calling the suitors to account before the people; and then afterwards describes him as travelling to Pylos and Sparta to obtain intelligence of his lost father; he gives us a picture of Ithaca and its anarchical condition, and of the rest of Greece in its state of peace after the return of the princes, which produces the finest contrast; and, at the same time, prepares Telemachus for playing an energetic part in the work of vengeance, which by this means becomes more probable.

Although these remarks show that the arrangement of the *Odyssey* is essentially different from that of the *Iliad*, and bears marks of a more artificial and more fully developed state of the epos, yet there is much that is *common* to the two poems in this respect; particularly that profound comprehension of the means of straining the curiosity, and of keeping up the interest by new and unexpected turns of the narrative. The decree of Zeus is as much delayed in its execution in the *Odyssey* as it is in the *Iliad*: as, in the latter poem, it is not till after the building of the walls that Zeus, at the request of Thetis, takes an active part against the Greeks; so, in the *Odyssey*, he appears at the very beginning willing to acquiesce in the proposal of Athena for the return of Ulysses, but does not in reality despatch Hermes to Calypso till several days later, in the fifth book. It is evident that the poet is impressed with a conception familiar to the Greeks, of a divine destiny, slow in its preparations, and apparently delaying, but on that very account marching with the greater certainty to its end. We also perceive in the *Odyssey* the same artifice as that pointed out in the *Iliad*, of turning the expectation of the reader into a different direction from that which the narrative is afterwards to take; but, from the nature of the sub-

---

[1] There would be nothing abrupt in the transition from Menelaus to the suitors in *Od.* IV. 624, if it fell at the beginning of a new book ; and yet this division into books is a mere contrivance of the Alexandrine grammarians. The four verses 620—4, which are unquestionably spurious, are a mere useless interpolation, as they contribute nothing to the junction of the parts.

ject, chiefly in single scattered passages. The poet plays in the
most agreeable manner with us, by holding out other means by
which the necessary work of vengeance on the suitors may be
accomplished; and also after we have arrived somewhat nearer
the true aim, he still has in store another beautiful invention
with which to surprise us. Thus the exhortation twice addressed to Telemachus in the same words, in the early books of
the *Odyssey*, to imitate the example of Orestes[1] (which strikes
deep root in his heart), produces an undefined expectation that
he himself may attempt something against the suitors; nor is
the true meaning of it perceived, until Telemachus places himself so undauntedly at his father's side. Afterwards, when the
father and son have arranged their plan for taking vengeance,
they think of assaulting the suitors, hand to hand, with lance
and sword, in a combat of very doubtful issue.[2] The bow of
Eurytus, from which Ulysses derives such great advantage, is a
new and unexpected idea. Athena suggests to Penelope the
notion of proposing it to the suitors as a prize,[3] and although
the ancient legend doubtless represented Ulysses overcoming
the suitors with this bow, yet the manner in which it is brought
into his hands is a very ingenious contrivance of the poet.[4] As
in the *Iliad* the deepest interest prevails between the Battle
at the Ships and the Death of Hector, so in the *Odyssey* the
narrative begins, with the fetching of the bow (at the outset of
the twenty-first book), to assume a lofty tone, which is mingled
with an almost painful expectation; and the poet makes use of
everything which the legend offered, as the gloomy forebodings
of Theoclymenus (who is only introduced in order to prepare
for this scene of horror)[5] and the contemporaneous festival of

---

[1] *Od.* I. 302 ; III. 200.

[2] *Od.* XVI. 295. The ἀθέτησις of Zenodotus, as usual, rests on insufficient grounds,
and would deprive the story of an important point of its progress.

[3] *Od.* XXI. 4.

[4] That this part of the poem is founded on ancient tradition appears from the
fact that the Ætolian tribe of the *Eurytanians*, who derived their origin from Eurytus
(probably the Ætolian Œchalia also belonged to this nation, Strabo X. p. 448), possessed an *oracle of Ulysses.* Lycophron V. 799 ; and the Scholia from Aristotle.

[5] Among these the disappearance of the sun (*Od.* XX. 356) is to be observed,
which is connected with the return of Ulysses during the new moon (*Od.* XIV. 162 ;
XIX. 307), when an eclipse of the sun could take place. This also appears to be a
trace of ancient tradition.

Apollo (who fully grants the prayer of Ulysses to secure him glory in the battle with the bow[1]), in order to heighten the marvellous and inspiriting parts of the scene.

§ 12. It is plain that the plan of the *Odyssey*, as well as of the *Iliad*, offered many opportunities for *enlargement*, by the insertion of new passages; and many irregularities in the course of the narration and its occasional diffuseness may be explained in this manner. The latter, for example, is observable in the amusements offered to Ulysses when entertained by the Phæacians; and even some of the ancients questioned the genuineness of the passage about the dance of the Phæacians and the song of Demodocus on the loves of Ares and Aphrodite, although this part of the *Odyssey* appears to have been at least extant in the 50th Olympiad, when the chorus of the Phæacians was represented on the throne of the Amyclæan Apollo.[2] So likewise Ulysses' account of his adventures contains many interpolations, particularly in the *nekyia*, or invocation of the dead, where the ancients had already attributed an important passage (which, in fact, destroys the unity and connexion of the narrative) to the *diaskeuastæ*, or interpolators, among others, to the Orphic Onomacritus, who, in the time of the Pisistratids, was employed in collecting the poems of Homer.[3] Moreover, the Alexandrine critics, Aristophanes and Aristarchus, considered the whole of the last part from the recognition of Penelope, as added at a later period.[4] Nor can it be denied that it has great defects; in particular, the description of the arrival of the suitors in the infernal regions is only a second and feebler *nekyia*, which does not precisely accord with the first, and is introduced in this place without sufficient

---

[1] The festival of Apollo (the νεομήνιος) is alluded to. *Od.* XX. 156, 250, 278; XXI. 258. Comp. XXI. 267; XXII. 7.

[2] Pausan. III. 18, 7.

[3] See Schol. *Od.* XI. 104. The entire passage, from XI. 568-626, was rejected by the ancients, and with good reason. For whereas Ulysses elsewhere is represented as merely, by means of his libation of blood, enticing the shades from their dark abodes to the asphodel-meadow, where he is standing, as it were, at the gate of Hades; in this passage he appears *in the midst of the dead*, who are firmly bound to certain spots in the infernal regions. The same more recent conception prevails in *Od.* XXIV. 13, where the dead *dwell* on the asphodel-meadow.

[4] From *Od.* XXIII. 296, to the end.

reason.   At the same time, the *Odyssey* could never have been considered as concluded, until Ulysses had embraced his father Laertes, who is so often mentioned in the course of the poem, and until a peaceful state of things had been restored, or began to be restored, in Ithaca.   It is not therefore likely that the original *Odyssey* altogether wanted some passage of this kind; but it was probably much altered by the Homerids, until it assumed the form in which we now possess it.

§ 13. That the *Odyssey* was written *after* the *Iliad*, and that many differences are apparent in the character and manners both of men and gods, as well as in the management of the language, is quite clear; but it is difficult and hazardous to raise upon this foundation any definite conclusions as to the person and age of the poet.   With the exception of the anger of Poseidon, who always works unseen in the obscure distance, the gods appear in a milder form; they act in unison, without dissension or contest, for the relief of mankind, not, as is so often the case in the *Iliad*, for their destruction.   It is, however, true, that the subject afforded far less occasion for describing the violent and angry passions and vehement combats of the gods.   At the same time the gods all appear a step higher above the human race; they are not represented as descending in a bodily form from their dwellings on Mount Olympus, and mixing in the tumult of the battle, but they go about in human forms, only discernible by their superior wisdom and prudence, in the company of the adventurous Ulysses and the intelligent Telemachus.   But the chief cause of this difference is to be sought in the nature of the story, and, we may add, in the fine tact of the poet, who knew how to preserve unity of subject and harmony of tone in his picture, and to exclude everything of which the character did not agree.   The attempt of many learned writers to discover a different religion and mythology for the *Iliad* and the *Odyssey* leads to the most arbitrary dissection of the two poems;[1] above all, it ought to have been made clear how the fable of the *Iliad* could have been treated by a professor of this supposed religion of the *Odyssey*, without introducing quarrels, battles, and vehement excitement among

---

[1] Benjamin Constant, in particular, in his celebrated work, *De la Religion*, tom. III. has been forced to go this length, as he distinguishes *trois espèces de mythologie* in the Homeric poems, and determines from them the age of the different parts.

the gods; in which there would have been no difficulty, if the difference of character in the gods of the two poems were introduced by the poet, and did not grow out of the subject. On the other hand, the human race appears in the houses of Nestor, Menelaüs, and especially of Alcinous, in a far more agreeable state, and one of far greater comfort[1] and luxury than in the *Iliad*. But where could the enjoyments, to which the Atridæ, in their native palace, and the peaceable Phæacians could securely abandon themselves, find a place in the rough camp? Granting, however, that a different taste and feeling is shown in the choice of the subject, and in the whole arrangement of the poem, yet there is not a greater difference than is often found in the inclinations of the *same* man in the prime of life and in old age; and, to speak candidly, we know no other argument adduced by the *Chorizontes*,[2] both of ancient and modern times, for attributing the wonderful genius of Homer to two different individuals. It is certain that the *Odyssey*, in respect of its plan and the conception of its chief characters, of Ulysses himself, of Nestor and Menelaüs, stands in the closest affinity with the *Iliad*: that it always presupposes the existence of the earlier poem, and silently refers to it; which also serves to explain the remarkable fact, that the *Odyssey* mentions many occurrences in the life of Ulysses, which lie out of the compass of the action, but not one which is celebrated in the *Iliad*.[3] If the completion of the *Iliad* and the *Odyssey* seems too vast a work for the lifetime of *one* man, we may, perhaps, have recourse to the supposition, that Homer, after

---

[1] The Greek word for this is κομιδή; which, in the *Iliad*, is only used for the care of horses, but in the *Odyssey* signifies human conveniences and luxuries, among which *hot baths* may be particularly mentioned. See *Od.* VIII. 450.

[2] Those Greek grammarians who attributed the *Iliad* and *Odyssey* to different authors were called οἱ χωρίζοντες, 'The Separaters.'

[3] We find Ulysses, in his youth, with Autolycus (*Od.* XIX. 394; XXIV. 333) during the expedition against Troy in Delos, *Od.* VI. 162; in Lesbos, IV. 341; in a contest with Achilles, VIII. 75; near the corpse and at the burial of Achilles, V. 308; XXIV. 39; contending for the arms of Achilles, XI. 544; contending with Philoctetes in shooting with the bow, VIII. 219; secretly in Troy, IV. 242; in the Trojan horse, IV. 270 (comp. VIII. 492; XI. 522); at the beginning of the return, III. 130; and, lastly, going to the men who know not the use of salt, XI. 120. But nothing is said of Ulysses' acts in the *Iliad*: his punishment of Thersites the horses of Rhesus; the battle over the body of Patroclus, &c. In like manner the *Odyssey* intentionally records different exploits and adventures of Agamemnon, Achilles, Menelaus, and Nestor, from those celebrated in the *Iliad*.

having sung the *Iliad* in the vigour of his youthful years, in his old age communicated to some devoted disciple the plan of the *Odyssey*, which had long been working in his mind, and left it to him for completion.

§ 14. It is certain that we are perpetually met with difficulties in endeavouring to form a notion of the manner in which these great epic poems were composed, at a time anterior to the use of writing. But these difficulties arise much more from our ignorance of the period, and our incapability of conceiving a creation of the mind without those appliances of which the use has become to us a second nature, than in the general laws of the human intellect. Who can determine how many thousand verses a person, thoroughly impregnated with his subject, and absorbed in the contemplation of it, might produce in a year, and confide to the faithful memory of disciples, devoted to their master and his art? Wherever a creative genius has appeared it has met with persons of congenial taste, and has found assistance, by whose means it has completed astonishing works in a comparatively short time. Thus the old bard may have been followed by a number of younger minstrels, to whom it was both a pleasure and a duty to collect and diffuse the honey which flowed from his lips. But it is, at least, certain, that it would be unintelligible how these great epics were composed, unless there had been *occasions,* on which they actually appeared in their integrity, and could charm an attentive hearer with the full force and effect of a complete poem. Without a connected and continuous recitation they were not finished works; they were mere disjointed fragments, which might by *possibility* form a whole. But where were there meals or festivals long enough for such recitations? What attention, it has been asked, could be sufficiently sustained, in order to follow so many thousand verses? If, however, the Athenians could at *one* festival hear in succession about nine tragedies, three satyric dramas, and as many comedies, without ever thinking that it might be better to distribute this enjoyment over the whole year, why should not the Greeks of earlier times have been able to listen to the *Iliad* and *Odyssey*, and, perhaps, other poems, at the same festival? At a later date, indeed, when the rhapsodist was rivalled by the player on the lyre, the dithyrambic minstrel, and by many other kinds of poetry and music, these latter necessarily abridged the time allowed to the epic reciter; but in early times, when the epic style reigned without a competitor, it would have obtained an undivided attention.   Let us beware of measuring, by our loose and desultory reading, the intension of mind with which a people enthusiastically devoted to such enjoyments,[1] hung with delight on the flowing strains of the minstrel.   In short, there was a time (and the *Iliad* and *Odyssey* are the records of it) when the Greek people, not indeed at meals, but at festivals, and under the patronage of their hereditary princes, heard and enjoyed these and other less excellent poems, as they were intended to be heard and enjoyed, viz., as *complete wholes*. Whether they were, at this early period, ever recited for a prize, and in competition with others, is doubtful, though there is nothing improbable in the supposition.   But when the conflux of rhapsodists to the contests became perpetually greater ; when, at the same time, more weight was laid on the art of the reciter than on the beauty of the well-known poem which he recited; and when, lastly, in addition to the rhapsodizing, a number of other musical and poetical performances claimed a place, then the rhapsodists were permitted to repeat separate parts of poems, in which they hoped to excel; and the *Iliad* and *Odyssey* (as they had not yet been reduced to writing) existed for a time only as *scattered* and *unconnected fragments*.[2] And we are still indebted to the regulator of the contest of rhapsodists at the Panathenæa (whether it was Solon or Pisistratus), for having compelled the rhapsodists to follow one another, according to the order of the poem,[3] and for having thus restored these great works, which were falling into fragments, to their pristine integrity.   It is indeed true that some arbitrary additions may have been made to them at this period ; which, however, we can only hope to be able to distinguish from the rest of the poem, by first coming to some general agreement as to the original form and subsequent destiny of the Homeric compositions.

---

[1] Above, p. 42, note 3.

[2] διεσπασμένα, διῃρημένα, σποράδην ᾀδόμενα.   See the sure testimonies on this point in Wolf's *Prolegomena*, p. cxliii.

[3] ἐξ ὑπολήψεως (or in Diog. Laërt. ἐξ ὑποβολῆς) ῥαψῳδεῖν.

CHAPTER VI.

THE CYCLIC POETS.

§ 1. General character of the Cyclic poems. § 2. The destruction of Troy and Æthiopis of Arctinus of Miletus. § 3. The little *Iliad* of Lesches. § 4. The *Cypria* of Stasinus. § 5. The *Nostoi* of Agias of Troezen. § 6. The *Telegonia* of Eugammon of Cyrene. § 7. Poems on the War against Thebes.

§ 1. HOMER'S poems, as they became the foundation of all Grecian literature, are likewise the central point of the epic poetry of Greece. All that was most excellent in this line originated from them, and was connected with them in the way of completion or continuation ; so that by closely considering this relation, we arrive· not only at a proper understanding of the subjects of these later epics, but even are able, in return, to throw some light upon the Homeric poems themselves,—the *Iliad* and *Odyssey*. This class of epic poets is called the *Cyclic*, from their constant endeavour to connect their poems with those of Homer, so that the whole should form a great cycle. Hence also originated the custom of comprehending their poems almost collectively under the name of Homer,[1] their connexion with the *Iliad* and *Odyssey* being taken as a proof that the whole was *one* vast conception. More accurate accounts, however, assign almost all these poems to particular authors, who lived after the commencement of the Olympiads, and therefore considerably later than Homer. Indeed, these poems, both in their character and their conception of the mythical events, are very different from the *Iliad* and *Odyssey*. These authors cannot even have been called Homerids, since a race of this name existed only in Chios, and not one of them is called a Chian. Nevertheless it is credible that they were Homeric rhapsodists by profession, to whom the constant

---

[1] Οἱ μέντοι ἀρχαῖοι καὶ τὸν Κύκλον ἀναφέρουσιν εἰς αὐτὸν (Ὅμηρον)—Proclus, *Vita Homeri.*

recitation of the ancient Homeric poems would naturally suggest the notion of continuing them by essays of their own in a similar tone. Hence, too, it would be more likely to occur that these poems, when they were sung by the same rhapsodists, would gradually themselves acquire the name of Homeric epics. From a close comparison of the extracts and fragments of these poems, which we still possess, it is evident that their authors had before them copies of the *Iliad* and *Odyssey* in their complete form, or, to speak more accurately, comprehending the same series of events as those current among the later Greeks and ourselves, and that they merely connected the action of their own poems with the beginning and end of these two epopees. But notwithstanding the close connexion which they made between their own productions and the Homeric poems, notwithstanding that they often built upon particular allusions in Homer, and formed from them long passages of their own poems (a fact which is particularly evident in the excerpt of the *Cypria*) ; still their manner of treating and viewing mythical subjects differs so widely from that of Homer, as of itself to be a sufficient proof that the Homeric poems were no longer in progress of development at the time of the Cyclic poets, but had, on the whole, attained a settled form, to which no addition of importance was afterwards made.[1] Otherwise, we could not fail to recognise the traces of a later age in the interpolated passages of the Homeric poems.

§ 2. We commence with the poems which *continued the Iliad*. ARCTINUS OF MILETUS was confessedly a very ancient poet, nay, he is even termed a disciple of Homer ; the chronological accounts place him immediately after the commencement of the Olympiads. His poem, consisting of 9100 verses[2] (about one-third less than the *Iliad*), opened with the arrival of the Amazons at Troy, which followed immediately after the death of Hector. There existed in antiquity one recension of

---

[1] In these remarks we of course except the Catalogue of the Ships. See chap. V. § 9.

[2] According to the inscription of the tablet in the Museo Borgia (see Heeren, *Bibliothek der alten Literatur und Kunst*, part IV. p. 61), where it is said . . . . Ἄρκτινο]ν τὸν Μιλήσιον λέγουσιν ἐπῶν ὄντα θρ. The plural ὄντα refers to the two poems, according to the explanation in the text.

the *Iliad*, which concluded as follows :—' Thus they performed the funeral rites of Hector ; then came the Amazon, the daughter of the valorous man-destroying Ares.'[1] This, without doubt, was the *cyclic edition* of the Homeric poems, more than once mentioned by the ancient critics : in which they appear to have been connected with the rest of the cyclus so as to form an unbroken series. The same order of events also appears in several works of ancient sculpture, in which on one side Andromache is represented as weeping over Hector's ashes, while, on the other, the female warriors are welcomed by the venerable Priam. The action of the epic of Arctinus was connected with the following principal events. Achilles kills Penthesilea, and then in a fit of anger puts to death Thersites, who had ridiculed him for his love for her. Upon this Memnon, the son of Eos, appears with his Ethiopians, and is slain by the son of Thetis after he himself has killed in battle Antilochus, the Patroclus of Arctinus. Achilles himself falls by the hand of Paris while pursuing the Trojans into the town. His mother rescues his body from the funeral pile, and carries him restored to life to Leucè, an island in the Black Sea, where the mariners believed that they saw his mighty form flitting in the dusk of evening. Ajax and Ulysses contend for his arms ; the defeat of Ajax causes his suicide.[2] Arctinus further related the history of the wooden horse, the careless security of the Trojans, and the destruction of Laocoon, which induces Æneas to flee for safety to Ida before the impending destruction of the town.[3] The sack of Troy by the Greeks returning from Tenedos, and issuing from the Trojan horse, was described so as to display in a conspicuous manner the arrogance and mercilessness of the Greeks, and to occasion the resolution of Athene, already known from the *Odyssey*, to punish them in various ways on their return home. This last part, when divided from

---

[1] Ὡς οἵγ' ἀμφίεπον τάφον Ἕκτορος. ἦλθε δ᾽ Ἀμαζών

Ἄρηος θυγάτηρ μεγαλήτορος ἀνδροφόνοιο.—Schol. Ven. ad *Il.* XXIV. ult. v.

[2] See Schol. Pind. *Isthm.* III. 58, who quotes for this event the *Æthiopis*, and Schol. *Il.* XI. 515, who quotes for it the Ἰλίου πέρσις of Arctinus. I particularly mention this point; since, from the account in the *Chrestomathia* of Proclus, it might be thought that Arctinus had omitted this circumstance.

[3] Quite differently from Virgil, who in other respects has in the second book of the *Æneid* chiefly followed Arctinus.

the preceding, was called the *Destruction of Troy* ('Ιλίου
πέρσις) ; the former, comprising the events up to the death of
Achilles, the *Æthiopis* of Arctinus.

§ 3. LESCHES, or LESCHEUS, from Mitylene, or Pyrrha, in
the island of Lesbos, was considerably later than Arctinus;
the best authorities concur in placing him in the time of
Archilochus, or about Olymp. 18. Hence the account which
we find in ancient authors of a contest between Arctinus
and Lesches can only mean that the later competed with the
earlier poet in treating the same subjects. His poem, which
was attributed by many to Homer, and, besides, to very different authors, was called the *Little Iliad*, and was clearly
intended as a supplement to the great *Iliad*. We learn from
Aristotle[1] that it comprised the events before the fall of Troy,
the fate of Ajax, the exploits of Philoctetes, Neoptolemus, and
Ulysses, which led to the taking of the town, as well as the
account of the destruction of Troy itself : which statement
is confirmed by numerous fragments. The last part of this
(like the first part of the poem of Arctinus) was called the
Destruction of Troy : from which Pausanias makes several
quotations, with reference to the sacking of Troy, and the partition and carrying away of the prisoners. It is evident from
his citations that Lesches, in many important events (*e. g.,* the
death of Priam, the end of the little Astyanax, and the fate of
Æneas, whom he represents Neoptolemus as taking to Phar-
salus), followed quite different traditions from Arctinus. The
connexion of the several events was necessarily loose and
superficial, and without any unity of subject. Hence, according
to Aristotle, whilst the *Iliad* and *Odyssey* only furnish
materials for *one* tragedy each, more than *eight* might be
formed out of the *Little Iliad*.[2] Hence, also, the opening of

---

[1] *Poet.* c. 23, ad fin. ed. Bekker (c. 38, ed. Tyrwhitt).

[2] Ten are mentioned by Aristotle—viz., Ὅπλων κρίσις, Φιλοκτήτης, Νεοπτόλεμος,
Εὐρύπυλος, Πτωχεία (see *Od.* IV. 244), Λάκαιναι, Ἰλίου πέρσις, Ἀπόπλους, Σίνων,
Τρωάδες. Among these tragedies the subject of the Λάκαιναι is not apparent. The
name of course means ' Lacedæmonian women;' who, as the attendants of Helen,
formed the chorus. Helen played a chief part in the adventures of Ulysses as a
spy in Troy: the subject of the Πτωχεία above mentioned. Or perhaps Helen was
represented as the accomplice of the heroes in the wooden horse. See *Od.* IV. 271.
Compare *Æneid* VI. 517. Of Sophocles' tragedy of this name only a few fragments are extant: Nos. 336—9, ed. Dindorf.

the poem, which promises so much, and has been censured as arrogant, ' I sing of Ilion, and Dardania famous for its horses, on whose account the Greeks, the servants of Mars, suffered many evils.'[1]

Before proceeding any further I feel myself bound to justify the above account of the relation between Arctinus and Lesches, since Proclus, the well-known philosopher and grammarian, to whose *Chrestomathia* we are indebted for the fullest account of the epic cycle,[2] represents it in a totally different point of view. Proclus gives us, as an abridgment of the Cyclic poets, a continuous narrative of the events of the Trojan war, in which one poet always precisely takes up another, often in the midst of a closely connected subject. Thus, according to Proclus, Arctinus continued the Homeric *Iliad* up to the contest for the arms of Achilles ; then Lesches relates the result of this contest, and the subsequent enterprises of the heroes against Troy until the introduction of the wooden horse within the walls; at this point Arctinus resumes the thread of the narrative, and describes the issuing forth of the heroes inclosed in the wooden horse; but he too breaks off in the midst of the history of the return of the Greeks at the point where Minerva devises a plan for their punishment : the fulfilment of this plan being related by Agias, in the poem called the *Nostoi*. In order to make such an interlacing of the different poems comprehensible, we must suppose the existence of an academy of poets, dividing their materials amongst each other upon a distinct understanding, and with the most minute precision. It is, however, altogether inconceivable that Arctinus should have twice suddenly broken off in the midst of actions, which the curiosity of his hearers could never have permitted him to leave unfinished, in order that, almost a century after, Lesches, and probably at a still later date Agias, might fill up the gaps and complete the narrative. Moreover, as the extant fragments of Arctinus and Lesches afford sufficient proof that they both sang of the events

---

[1] Ἴλιον ἀείδω καὶ Δαρδανίην εὔπωλον,
   Ἧς περὶ πολλὰ πάθον Δαναοί, θεράποντες Ἄρηος.

[2] This part of the *Chrestomathia* was first published in the Göttingen *Bibliothek für alte Litteratur und Kunst*, part I., inedita, afterwards in Gaisford's *Hephæstion*, p. 378, *seq.*, 472, *seq.*, and elsewhere.

which, according to the abstract of Proclus, formed an hiatus in their poems, it is easy to perceive that his account was not drawn up from these poems according to their original forms, but from a selection made by some grammarian, who had put together a connected poetical description of these events from the works of several Cyclic poets, in which no occurrence was repeated, but nothing of importance was omitted: and this indeed the expressions of Proclus himself appear to indicate.[1] In fact, the Cyclus in this sense included not only the epoch of the Trojan war (where the poems were mutually connected by means of their common reference to Homer), but the whole mythology, from the marriage of Heaven and Earth to the last adventures of Ulysses; for which purpose use must have been made of poems totally distinct from each other, and of whose original connexion, either in their execution or design, no trace whatever is discoverable.[2]

§ 4. The poem which in the Cyclus preceded the *Iliad*, and was clearly intended by its author himself for that purpose, was the *Cypria*, consisting of eleven books, which may be most safely ascribed to STASINUS of the island of Cyprus, who, however, according to the tradition, received it from Homer himself (transformed on that account into a Salaminian from Cyprus), as a portion on the marriage of his daughter. And yet the fundamental ideas of the *Cypria* are so un-Homeric, and contain so much of a rude attempt at philosophizing on mythology, which was altogether foreign to Homer, that Stasinus certainly cannot be considered as of an earlier date than Arctinus. The *Cypria* began with the prayer of the Earth to Zeus, to lessen the burdens of the race of man, already become too heavy; and then related how Zeus, with the view of humbling the pride of mankind, begot Helen upon the goddess Nemesis, and gave her to be educated by Leda. The promise by Venus

---

[1] Καὶ περατοῦται ὁ ἐπικὸς κύκλος ἐκ διαφόρων ποιητῶν συμπληρούμενος μέχρι τῆς ἀποβάσεως Ὀδυσσέως τῆς εἰς Ἰθάκην.—Proclus, ubi sup.

[2] As an additional proof of a point which indeed is almost self-evident, it may be also mentioned that, according to Proclus, there were *five*, and afterwards *two* books of Arctinus in the epic cyclus: according to the *Tabula Borgiana*, however, the poems of Arctinus included 9100 verses, which, according to the standard of the books in Homer, would at least give *twelve* books.

of the woman whose beauty was to cause the destruction of
heroes to the shepherd Paris, as a reward for the decision respecting the apple of discord, her abduction from Sparta during
the absence of her husband Menelaüs in Crete, and while her
brothers, the Dioscuri, are slain in battle by the sons of Aphareus, were all related in conformity with the usual traditions,
and the expedition of the heroes of Greece against Troy was
derived from these events. The Greeks, however, according to
the *Cypria, twice* set out from Aulis against Troy, having the
first time been carried to Teuthrania in Mysia, a district ruled
by Telephus, and in sailing away having been driven back by a
storm; at their second departure from Aulis the sacrifice of
Iphigenia was related. The nine years' contest before Troy,
and in its vicinity, did not occupy near so much space in the
Cypria as the preparations for the war; the full stream of tradition, as it gushes forth from a thousand springs in the Homeric
poems, has even at this period dwindled down to narrow
dimensions: the chief part was connected with the incidental
mentions of earlier events in Homer; as the attack of Achilles
upon Æneas near the herds of cattle,[1] the killing of Troilus,[2]
the selling of Lycaon to Lemnos;[3] Palamedes—the nobler
counterpart of Ulysses—was the only hero either unknown to
or accidentally never mentioned by Homer. Achilles was
throughout represented as the chief hero, created for the purpose of destroying the race of man by manly strength, as Helen
by female beauty; hence also these two beings, who otherwise
coùld not have become personally known to each other, were
brought together in a marvellous manner by Thetis and Am-
phitrite. As, however, the war, conducted in the manner
above described, did not destroy a sufficient number of men,
Zeus at last resolves, for the purpose of effectually granting the
prayer of the Earth, to stir up the strife between Achilles and
Agamemnon, and thus to bring about all the great battles of
the *Iliad.* Thus the *Cypria* referred altogether to the *Iliad*
for the completion of its own subject; and at the same time
added to the motive supposed in the latter poem, the prayer of

---

[1] *Il.* XX. 90, *seq.*

[2] *Il.* XXIV. 257. The more recent poetry combines the death of Troilus with
the last events of Troy.   [3] *Il.* XXI. 35.

Thetis, a more general one, the prayer of the Earth, of which the *Iliad* knows nothing. In the *Cypria* a gloomy destiny hovers over the whole heroic world ; as in Hesiod[1] the Theban and Trojan war is conceived as a general war of extermination between the heroes. The main origin of this fatality is, moreover, the beauty of the woman, as in Hesiod's mythus of Pandora. The unwarlike Aphrodite, who in Homer is so little fitted for mingling in the combats of heroes, is here the conductor of the whole ; on this point the Cyprian poet may have been influenced by the impressions of his native island, where Aphrodite was honoured before all other deities.

§ 5. Between the poems of Arctinus and Lesches and the *Odyssey* came the Epic of AGIAS[2] the Troezenian, divided into five books, the *Nostoi*. A poem of this kind would naturally be called forth by the *Odyssey*, as the author in the very commencement supposes that all the other heroes, except Ulysses, had returned home from Troy. Even in Homer's time there existed songs on the subject of the homeward voyages of the heroes ; but these scattered lays naturally fell into oblivion upon the appearance of Agias's poem, which was composed with almost Homeric skill, and all the intimations to be found in Homer were carefully made use of, and adopted as the outlines of the action.[3] Agias began his poem with describing how Athene executed her plan of vengeance, by exciting a quarrel between the Atridæ themselves, which prevented the joint return of the two princes. The adventures of the Atridæ furnished the main subject of the poem.[4] In the first place the wanderings of Menelaus, who first left the Trojan coast, were narrated almost up to his late arrival at home; then Agamemnon, who did not sail till afterwards, was conducted by a direct course to his native land ; and his murder and the other fortunes of his family were described up to the period when Menelaus arrives after the vengeance of Orestes had been consummated ;[5] with which event the poem properly concluded.

---

[1] Hesiod. *Op. et D.* 160, *seq.*

[2] 'Αγίας is the correct form of his name, in Ionic 'Ηγίας; Αὐγίας is a corruption.

[3] See particularly *Od.* III. 135.

[4] Hence, probably, the same poem is more than once in Athenæus called ἡ τῶν 'Ατρειδῶν κάθοδος.

[5] See *Od.* III. 311 ; IV. 547.

Artfully interwoven with the above narrative were the voyages and wanderings of the other heroes, Diomed, Nestor, Calchas, Leonteus and Polypoetes, Neoptolemus, and the death of the Locrian Ajax on the Capherian rocks, so that the whole formed a connected picture of the Achæan heroes at variance with each other, hastening homewards by different routes, but almost universally contending with misfortunes and difficulties. Ulysses alone was left for the *Odyssey*.[1]

§ 6. The continuation of the *Odyssey* was the *Telegonia*, of which poem only two books were introduced into the collection used by Proclus.[2] EUGAMMON OF CYRENE, who did not live before the 53rd Olympiad, is named as the author. The *Telegonia* opened with the burial of the suitors by their kinsmen. The want of this part renders the *Odyssey* incomplete as a narrative; although, for the internal unity, it is unnecessary, since the suitors are no longer a subject of interest after Ulysses had rid his house of them. The poem then related a voyage of Ulysses to Polyxenus at Elis, the motives for which are not sufficiently known to us; and afterwards the completion of the sacrifices offered by Tiresias; upon which Ulysses (in all probability in compliance with the prophecy of Tiresias, in order to reach the country where the inhabitants were neither acquainted with the sea nor with salt, the product of the sea) goes to Thesprotia, and there rules victoriously and happily, till he

---

[1] In what part of the *Nostoi* the *Nekyia*, or description of the infernal regions, which belonged to it, was introduced, we are not indeed informed; but there can scarcely be any doubt that it was connected with the funeral of Tiresias, which Calchas, in the *Nostoi*, celebrated at Colophon. Tiresias, in the *Odyssey*, is the only shade in the infernal regions who is endowed with memory and understanding, for whose sake Ulysses ventures as far as the entrance of Hades: would not then the poet, whose object it was to make his work an introduction to the *Odyssey*, have seized this opportunity to introduce the spirit of the seer into the realm of shades and by his reception by Hades and Persephone to explain the privileges which, according to the *Odyssey*, he there enjoys? The questioning of Tiresias invites to a preparatory explanation more perhaps than any other part of the *Odyssey*, since, taken by itself, it has something enigmatical.

[2] These two books were evidently only an epitome of the poem; for even all that Proclus states from them has scarcely sufficient space: to say nothing of the poem on the Thesprotians in a mystic tone, which Clemens of Alexandria (*Strom.* VI. 277) attributes to Eugammon, and which was manifestly in its original form a part of the *Telegonia*.

returns a second time to Ithaca, where, not being recognised, he is slain by Telegonus, his son by Circe, who had come to seek his father.

§ 7. With the exception of the events of the Trojan war, and the return of the Greeks, nothing was so closely connected with the *Iliad* and *Odyssey* as the *War of the Argives against Thebes ;* since many of the principal heroes of Greece, particularly Diomed and Sthenelus, were themselves amongst the conquerors of Thebes, and their fathers before them, a bolder and wilder race, had fought on the same spot, in a contest which, although unattended with victory, was still far from inglorious. Hence also reputed Homeric poems on the subject of this war were extant, which perhaps really bore a great affinity to the Homeric time and school. For we do not find, as in the other poems of the cycle, the names of one or several later poets placed in connexion with these compositions, but they are either attributed to Homer, as the earlier Greeks in general appear to have done,[1] or, if the authorship of Homer is doubted, they are usually attributed to no author at all. The *Thebais*, which consisted of seven books, or 5600 verses, originated from Argos, which was also considered by Homer as the centre of the Grecian power : it commenced ' Sing, O Muse, the thirsty Argos, where the princes . . .'[2] Here dwelt Adrastus, to whom Polynices, the banished son of Œdipus, fled, and found with him a reception. The poet then took occasion to enter upon the cause of the banishment of Polynices, and related the fate of Œdipus and his curse twice pronounced against his sons. Amphiaraus was represented as a wise counsellor to Adrastus, and in opposition to Polynices and Tydeus, the heroes eager for battle. Eriphyle was the Helen of this war ; the seductive woman who induced her otherwise prudent husband to rush, conscious of his doom, to meet his unhappy fate.[3] The insolence of the Argive chiefs was pro-

---

[1] In Pausan. IX. 9, 3. Καλλῖνος is certainly the right reading. This ancient elegiac poet, therefore, about the 20th Olympiad, quoted the *Thebaid* as Homeric. The *Epigoni* was still commonly ascribed to Homer in the time of Herodotus, IV. 32.

[2] Ἄργος ἄειδε θεὰ πολυδίψιον, ἔνθα ἄνακτες.

[3] Hence the entire poem is in Pseudo-Herod. *Vit. Hom.* c. 9, called Ἀμφιάρεω ἐξελασίη ἐς Θήβας, in Suidas Ἀμφιαράου ἐξέλευσις.

bably represented as the principal cause of their destruction; Homer in the *Iliad* described it as the crime and curse of these heroes,[1] and Æschylus portrays it in characteristic emblems and words. Adrastus is only saved by his horse Areion, a supernatural being; and a prophecy respecting the Epigoni concluded the whole.

The *Epigoni* was so far a second part of the *Thebais* that it was sometimes comprehended under the same name,[2] though it might also be considered as distinct. It began with an allusion to the first heroic expedition, ' Now, O Muses, let us commence the exploits of the later men;'[3] and related the much less notorious actions of the sons of the heroes, according to all probability under the auspices of the same Adrastus[4] who was destined to conquer Thebes, if his army should be freer from guilt, and thereby become more worthy of glory. Diomed and Sthenelus, the sons of the wild Tydeus and the reckless Capaneus, equalled their fathers in power, while they surpassed them in moderation and respect for the gods.

Even these few, but authentic accounts exhibit glorious materials for genuine poetry; and they were treated in a style which had not degenerated from Homer; the only difference being that an exalted heroic life was not, as in the *Iliad* and *Odyssey*, exhibited in *one* great action, and as accomplishing its appointed purpose: but a longer series of events was developed before the listeners, externally connected by their reference to one enterprise, and internally by means of certain general moral reflections and mythico-philosophical ideas.

---

[1] *Il.* V. 407.

[2] Thus the scholiast on Apoll. Rhod. I. 308, in the account of Manto, cites the *Thebaid* for the *Epigoni*.

[3] Νῦν αὖθ' ὁπλοτέρων ἀνδρῶν ἀρχώμεθα, Μοῦσαι.

[4] See Pindar, *Pyth.* VIII. 48. It can be shown that Pindar, in his mentions of this fable, always keeps near to the *Thebaid*.

CHAPTER VII.

THE HOMERIC HYMNS.

§ 1. General character of the Homeric Hymns, or Procemia. § 2. Occasions on which they were sung : Poets by whom, and times at which, they were composed. § 3. Hymn to the Delian Apollo. § 4. Hymn to the Pythian Apollo. § 5. Hymn to Hermes. § 6. Hymn to Aphrodite. § 7. Hymn to Demeter.

§ 1. ONE essential part of the epic style of poetry consisted of *hymns.* Those hymns which were recited by the epic poets, and which we comprehend under the name of Homeric, were called by the ancients *procemia,* that is *preludes,* or *overtures.* They evidently in part owed this name to their having served the rhapsodists as introductory strains for their recitations : a purpose to which the final verses often clearly refer ; as, ' Beginning with thee I will now sing the race of the demigods, or the exploits of the heroes, which the poets are wont to celebrate.'[1] But the *longer* hymns of this class could hardly have served such a purpose ; as they sometimes are equal in extent to the rhapsodies into which the grammarians divided the *Iliad* and *Odyssey,* and they even contain very detailed narratives of particular legends, which are sufficient to excite an independent interest. These must be considered as preludes to a whole series of epic recitations, in other words, as *introductions to an entire contest of rhapsodists ;* making, as it were, the transition from the preceding festival of the gods, with its sacrifices, prayers, and sacred chants, to the subsequent competition of the singers of heroic poetry. The manner in which it was necessary to shorten one of these long hymns, in order to make it serve as a procemium of a single poem, or part of a

---

[1] See, for example, *Hymn* XXXI. 18. ἐκ σέο δ' ἀρξάμενος κλήσω μερόπων γένος ἀνδρῶν ἡμιθέων, and XXXII. 18. σέο δ' ἀρχόμενος κλέα φώτων ᾄσομαι ἡμιθέων ὧν κλείουσ' ἔργματ' ἀοιδοί. A prayer for victory also sometimes occurs : χαῖρ' ἑλικοβλέφαρε, γλυκυμείλιχε, δὸς δ' ἐν ἀγῶνι νίκην τῷδε φέρεσθαι, *Hymn* VI. 19.

poem, may be seen from the 18th of the Homeric hymns, the short one to Hermes, which has been abridged from the long one for this purpose.

With the *actual ceremonies* of the divine worship these hymns had evidently no immediate connexion. Unlike the lyric and choral songs, they were sung neither on the procession to the temple (πομπή), nor at the sacrifice (θυσία), nor at the libation (σπονδή), with which the public prayers for the people were usually connected ; they had only a general reference to the god as patron of a festival, to which a contest of rhapsodists or poets had been appended. One hymn alone, the eighth to Ares, is not a procemium, but a prayer to the god : in this, however, the entire tone, the numerous invocations and epithets, are so different from the Homeric, that this hymn has been with reason referred to a much later period, and has been classed with the Orphic compositions.[1]

§ 2. But although these procemia were not immediately connected with the service of the gods, and although a poet might have prefixed an invocation of this kind to an epic composition recited by him alone, without a rival, in any meeting of idle persons,[2] yet we may perceive from them how many and different sacred festivals in Greece were attended by rhapsodists. Thus it is quite clear that the two hymns to Apollo were sung, the one at the festival of the nativity of the god in the island of Delos, the other at that of the slaying of the dragon at Pytho ; that the hymn to Demeter was recited at the Eleusinia, where musical contests were also customary ; and that contests of rhapsodists were connected with the festivals of Aphrodite,[3] particularly at Salamis in Cyprus,[4] from which island we have also seen a considerable epic poem proceed. The short hymn to Artemis, which describes her wanderings from the river

---

[1] Ares is in this hymn, VIII. 7, 10, also considered as the *planet* of the same name : the hymn, therefore, belongs to a time when Chaldæan astrology had been diffused in Greece. The contest for which the aid of Ares is implored is a purely *mental* one, with the passions, and the hymn is in fact *philosophical* rather than Orphic.

[2] For example, in a λέσχη, a house of public resort, where strangers found an abode. Homer, according to Pseudo-Herodotus, sang many poetical pieces in places of this description.

[3] *Hymn* VI. 19.   [4] *Hymn* X. 4. Comp. ch. VI. § 4.

Meles at Smyrna to the island of Claros (where her brother Apollo awaits her),[1] appears also to have been recited at a musical contest, which was connected with the festival of these two deities in the renowned sanctuary of Claros, near Colophon. Festivals in honour of the Magna Mater of Phrygia may have likewise been celebrated in the towns of Asia Minor, also accompanied with contests of rhapsodists.

That these procemia were composed by rhapsodists of Asia Minor, nearly the same as those who were concerned in the Homeric cycle, and not by minstrels of the school of Hesiod, is proved by the fact that we find among them no hymn to the Muses, with whom the poet of the *Theogony* as he himself says, began and ended his strains.[2] One short hymn however, formed of verses borrowed from the *Theogony,* has found its way into this miscellaneous collection.[3] By a similar argument we may refute the opinion that these hymns were *exclusively* the work of the Homerids, that is, the house of Chios: these, as we know from the testimony of Pindar, were accustomed to commence with an invocation to Zeus; while our collection only contains one very small and unimportant procemium to this god.[4]

Whether any of the preludes which Terpander, the Lesbian poet and musician, employed in his musical recitation of Homer[5] have been preserved in the present collection, must remain a doubtful question : it seems however probable that those hymns, composed for an accompaniment of the cithara, must have had a different tone and character.

Moreover, these hymns exhibit such a diversity of language and poetical tone, that in all probability they contain fragments from every century between the time of Homer and the Persian war. Several, as for instance that to the Dioscuri, show the transition to the Orphic poetry, and several refer to local worships, which are entirely unknown to us, as the one to

---

[1] *Hymn* IX. 3, *seq.*

[2] *Theogon.* 48. Endings of this kind, called by the grammarians ἐφύμνια, are also mentioned in the Homeric hymns, XXI. 4, and XXXIV. 18, and the short song, *Hymn* XXI. is probably one of them. Comp. Theognis V. I. (925), Apollon. Rhod. *Arg.* IV. 1774.

[3] See *Hymn* XXV. and *Theog.* 94—7.   [4] *Hymn* XXIII.

[5] Plutarch, *de Musicâ,* c. 4, 6 ; and above, chap. IV. § 3 (p. 47).

Selene, which celebrates her daughter by Zeus, the goddess
Pandia, shining forth amongst the immortals; of whom we can
now only conjecture that the Athenian festival of Pandia was
dedicated to her.

§ 3. We will now endeavour to illustrate these general remarks by some special explanations of the five longer hymns.
The hymn to the DELIAN APOLLO is (as has been already stated)[1]
ascribed by Thucydides to Homer himself; and is, doubtless,
the production of a Homerid of Chios, who, at the end of the
poem, calls himself the blind poet who lived on the rocky
Chios.   But the notion that this poet was Cinæthus, who did
not live till the 69th Olympiad,[2] appears only to have originated from the circumstance that he was the most celebrated
of the Homerids.   If any one of these hymns comes near to
the age of Homer, it is this one; and it is much to be lamented
that a large portion of it has been lost,[3] which contained the
beginning of the narration, the true ground of the wanderings
of Latona.   We can only conjecture that this was the announcement, probably made by Here, that Latona would produce a terrible and mighty son: of which a contradiction is
meant to be implied in Apollo's first words, where he calls the
cithara his favourite instrument, as well as the bow, and declares his chief office to be the promulgation of the counsels of
Zeus.[4]   The entire fable of the birth of Apollo is treated so as
to give great honour to the island of Delos, which alone takes
pity on Latona, and dares to offer her an asylum; the fittest
subject of a hymn for the joyful spring festival, to which the
Ionians flocked together from far and wide on their pilgrimage
to the holy island.

§ 4. The hymn to the PYTHIAN APOLLO is a most interesting
record of the ancient mythus of Apollo in the district of Pytho.
It belongs to a time when the Pythian sanctuary was still in
the territory of Crissa: of the hostility between the Pythian
priests and the Crissæans, which afterwards led to the war of
the Amphictyons against the city of Crissa (in Olymp. 47),

---

[1] Above, chap. V. § 1 (p. 57).
[2] Schol. Pind. *Nem.* II. 1.   [3] *Hymn* I. 30.
[4] εἴη μοι κίθαρίς τε φίλη καὶ καμπύλα τόξα,
χρήσω δ' ἀνθρώποισι Διὸς νημερτέα βουλήν.—*Hymn. Del. Ap.* 131—2.

there is no trace; a passage of the hymn also shows that horse-races[1] had not as yet been introduced at the Pythian games, which began immediately after the Crissæan war: the ancient Pythian contests had been confined to music. The following is the connexion of this hymn. Apollo descends from Olympus in order to found a temple for himself; and while he is seeking a site for it in Bœotia, he is recommended by a water-goddess, Tilphussa or Delphussa, to place it in the territory of Crissa in the ravine of Parnassus: her advice being prompted by the malicious hope that a dangerous serpent, which abode there, would destroy the youthful god. Apollo accepts her counsel, but frustrates her intent: he founds his temple in this solitary glen, slays the dragon, and then punishes Tilphussa by stopping up her fountain.[2] Apollo then procures priests for the new sanctuary, Cretan men, whom he, in the form of a dolphin, brings to Crissa, and consecrates as the sacrificers and guardians of his sanctuary.

§ 5. The hymn to HERMES has a character very different from the others; which is the reason why modern critics have taken greater liberties with it in the rejection of verses supposed to be spurious. With that lively simplicity which gives an air of credibility to the most marvellous incidents, it relates how Hermes, begotten by Zeus in secret, is able, when only a new-born child, to leave the cradle in which his mother believed him to be safely concealed, in order to steal Apollo's cattle from the pastures of the gods in Pieria. The miraculous child succeeds in driving them away, using various contrivances for concealing his traces, to a grotto near Pylos, and slays them there, with all the skill of the most experienced slaughterer of victims. At the same time he had made the first lyre out of a tortoise which had fallen in his way on his first going out; and with this he pacifies Apollo, who had at length, by means of his power of divination, succeeded in discovering the thief; so that the two sons of Zeus form at the end the closest intimacy,

---

[1] *Hymn* II. 84, 199, where the noise of horses and chariots is given as a reason why the place is not fitted for a temple of Apollo.

[2] It is not necessary to the right comprehension of this hymn to explain the obscurer connexion of this mythus with the worship of a Demeter Tilphossæa, or Erinnys, hostile to Apollo.

after an interchange of their respective gifts. The story is narrated in a light and pointed style, the poet seems to aim at rapid transitions, and especially at the beginning he indicates the marvellous exploits of Hermes in an enigmatic manner; thus he says that ' Hermes, by finding a tortoise, had gained unspeakable wealth: he had in truth known how to make the tortoise musical.'[1] This style is evidently far removed from the genuine Homeric tone; although some instances of this arch simplicity occur both in the *Iliad* and *Odyssey*, and the story of the loves of Ares and Aphrodite, in the *Odyssey*, appears to belong to nearly the same class of compositions as this hymn. But a considerably later age is indicated by the circumstance that the lyre or the cithara—for the poet treats these two instruments as identical, though distinguished in more precise language— is described as having been at the very first provided with seven strings;[2] yet the words of Terpander are still extant in which he boasts of having introduced the seven-stringed cithara in the place of the four-stringed.[3] Hence it is plain that this poem could not have been composed till some time after the 30th Olympiad, perhaps even by a poet of the Lesbian school, which had at that time spread to Peloponnesus.[4]

§ 6. The hymn to Aphrodite relates how this goddess (who subjects all the gods to her power, three only excepted) is, according to the will of Zeus himself, vanquished by love for Anchises of Troy, and meets him in the form of a Phrygian princess by the herds on Mount Ida. At her departure she appears to him in divine majesty, and announces to him the birth of a son, named Æneas, who will come to reign himself, and after him his family, over the Trojans.[5] It is an obvious conjecture that this hymn (the tone and expression of which have much of the genuine Homer) was sung in honour of princes of the family of Æneas, in some town of the range of Ida, where the same line continued to reign even until the Peloponnesian war.

---

[1] *Hymn* III. v. 24, 25, &c.   [2] v. 51.

[3] Euclides Introduct. Harmon. in Meibomius, *Script. Mus.* p. 19.

[4] We know that the Lesbian lyric poet Alcæus treated the mythus of the birth of Hermes and the robbery of the cattle in a very similar manner, but of course in a lyric form.—See below, chap. XIII. § 25.

[5] *Hymn* IV. 196, *seq.* Compare *Iliad* XX. 307.

§ 7. The hymn to DEMETER is chiefly intended to celebrate the sojourning of this goddess among the Eleusinians. Demeter is seeking for her daughter, who has been carried away by Hades, until she learns from the god of the sun that the god of the infernal regions is the ravisher. She then dwells among the Eleusinians, who have hospitably received her, as the old attendant of Demophoon, until her divinity becomes evident; upon which the Eleusinians build her a temple. In this she conceals herself as a wrathful deity, and withholds her gifts from mankind, until Zeus brings about an agreement that Cora shall be restored to her for two-thirds of the year, and shall only remain one-third of the year with Hades.[1] United again with her daughter, she instructs her hosts, the Eleusinians, in return for their hospitality, in her sacred orgies.

Even if this hymn did not directly invite persons to the celebration of the Eleusinia, and to a participation in its initiatory rites, by calling those blessed who had seen them, and announcing an unhappy lot in the infernal regions to those who had taken no part in them; yet we could not fail to recognise the hand of an Attic bard, well versed in the festival and its ceremonies, even in many expressions which have an Attic and local colour. The ancient sacred legend of the Eleusinians lies here before us in its pure and unadulterated form; so far as it can be clothed with an epic garb in a manner agreeable to a refined taste. We may hence infer the value of this hymn (which was not discovered till the last century, and of which a part is lost) for the history of the Greek religion.

---

[1] This depends on the Athenian festival cycle. At the Thesmophoria, the festival of sowing, Cora is supposed to descend beneath the earth; on the Anthesteria, the festival of the first bloom of spring, exactly four months afterwards, she is supposed to reascend from the infernal regions.

CHAPTER VIII.

HESIOD.

§ 1. Circumstances of Hesiod's Life, and general character of his Poetry. § 2. The *Works and Days*, the *Poem on Divination*, and the *Lessons of Chiron*. § 3. The *Theogony*. § 4. The *Great Eoiæ*, the *Catalogues of Women*, the *Melampodia*, the *Ægimius*. § 5. The *Marriage of Ceyx*, the *Epithalamium of Peleus and Thetis*, the *Descent of Theseus and Pirithous into Hell*, the *Shield of Hercules*.

§ 1. WHILE the fairest growth of the Grecian heroic poetry was flourishing under favourable circumstances upon the coast of Asia Minor in the Æolic and Ionic colonies, the mother-country of Greece, and especially Bœotia, to which we are now to direct our attention, were not so happily situated.   In that country, already thickly peopled with Greek tribes, and divided into numerous small states, the migrations with which the heroic age of Greece terminated necessarily produced a state of lasting confusion and strife, sometimes even reaching into the interior of single families.   It was only on the coast of Asia Minor that the conquerors could find a wide and open field for their enterprises ; this country was still for the most part virgin soil to the Greek settlers, and its native inhabitants of barbarous descent offered no very obstinate resistance to the colonists.   Hence likewise it came to pass that of the Æolic Bœotians, who after the Trojan war emigrated from Thessaliotis, and obtained the sovereignty of Bœotia, a considerable number immediately quitted this narrow territory, and joined the Achæans, who, just at this time, having been driven from Peloponnesus, were sailing to Lesbos, Tenedos, and the opposite shores of Asia Minor, there to found the colonies in which the name of Æolians subsequently preponderated over that of Achæans, and became the collective denomination.   As new cities and states rose up and flourished in these regions of Asia Minor, which were moreover founded and governed by descendants

of the most renowned princes of the heroic age, a free scope
was given to the genius of poetry, and a bright and poetical
view of man's destiny was naturally produced.   But in Bœotia
a comparison of the present with the past gave rise to a different feeling.   In the place of the races celebrated in numerous legends, the Cadmeans and Minyans, who were the early
occupants of Thebes and Orchomenos, had succeeded the Æolic
Bœotians, whose native mythology appears meagre and scanty
as compared with that of the other tribes.   It is true that the
Homeric bards allowed themselves to be so far influenced by
the impressions of the prcsent as to introduce the heroes of
these Bœotians, and not the Cadmeans, as taking a part in the
expedition against Troy.   But how little of real individual character and of poetic truth is there in Peneleus and Leitus, when
compared with the leaders of the Achæan bands from Peloponnesus and Thessaly !   The events of Greek history have,
though not always, yet in most cases, verified the promises of
their early legends ; and thus we find the Bœotians always
remaining a vigorous, hardy race, whose mind can never soar
far above the range of bodily existence, and whose cares are for
the most part limited to the supply of their immediate wants—
equally removed from the proud aspirings of the Doric spirit,
which subjected all things within its reach to the influence of certain deeply implanted notions, and from the liveliness and fine susceptibility of the Ionic character, which received all impressions
with a fond and impassioned interest. But, even in this torpid and
obscure condition of Bœotian existence, some stars of the first
magnitude appear, as brilliant in politics as in art—Pindar,
Epaminondas, and before them HESIOD, with the other distinguished poets who wrote under his name.

But Hesiod, although a poet of very considerable power, was
yet a true child of his nation and his times.   His poetry is
a faithful transcript of the whole condition of Bœotian life ;
and we may, on the other hand, complete our notions of
Bœotian life from his poetry. If, before we proceed to examine each separate poem in detail, we first state our general
impression of the whole, and compare it with that which we
receive from the Homeric poems, we shall find throughout the
writings of Hesiod (as well in the complete ones as in those

which we can only judge by fragments) that we miss the powerful sway of a youthful fancy, which in every part of the poems
of Homer sheds an expression of bright and inexhaustible enjoyment, which lights up the sublime images of a heroic age,
and moulds them into forms of surpassing beauty. That abandonment of the thoughts, with heartfelt joy and satisfaction, to a
flow of poetical images, such as came crowding on the mind of
Homer—how different is this from the manner of Hesiod!
His poetry appears to struggle to emerge out of the narrow
bounds of common life, which he strives to ennoble and to
render more endurable. Regarding with a melancholy feeling
the destiny of the human race, and the corruption of a social
condition which has destroyed all serene enjoyment, the poet
seeks either to disseminate knowledge by which life may be
improved, or to diffuse certain religious notions as to the
influence of a superior destiny, which may tend to produce a
patient resignation to its inevitable evils. At one time he
gives us lessons of civil and domestic wisdom, whereby order
may be restored to a disturbed commonwealth or an ill-regu-
lated household ; at another, he seeks to reduce the bewildering
and endless variety of stories about the gods to a connected
system, in which each deity has his appointed place. Then again
the poet of this school seeks to distribute the heroic legends
into large masses ; and, by finding certain links which bind them
all together, to make them more clear and comprehensible.
Nowhere does the poetry appear as the sole aim of the poet's
mind, to which he devotes himself without reserve, and to
which all his thoughts are directed. Practical interests are,
in a certain sense, everywhere intermixed. It cannot be
denied that the poetry, as such, must thus lose much of its
peculiar merit; but this loss is, to a certain extent, compensated by the beneficent and useful tendency of the composition.

This view of the poetry of Hesiod agrees entirely with the
description which he has given of the manner of his first being
called to the office of a poet. The account of this in the introduction to the *Theogony* (v. 1—35) must be a very ancient
tradition, as it is also alluded to in the *Works and Days*
(v. 659). The Muses, whose dwelling, according to the commonly received belief of the Greeks, was Olympus in Pieria,

are yet accustomed (so says the Bœotian poet) to visit Helicon, which was also sacred to them.   Then, having bathed in one of their holy springs, and having led their dances upon the top of Helicon, they go at night through the adjacent country, singing the great gods of Olympus, as well as the primitive deities of the universe.   In one of these excursions they en-countered Hesiod, who was watching his flocks by night in a valley at the foot of Helicon.   Here they bestowed upon him the gift of poetry, having first addressed him in these words : ' Ye country shepherds, worthless wretches, mere slaves of the belly ! although we often tell falsehoods and pretend that they are true, yet we can tell truth when it pleases us.'

After these words, the Muses immediately consecrated Hesiod to their service by offering him a laurel branch, which the Bœotian minstrels always carried in their hand during the recitation of poetry.   There is something very remarkable in this address of the Muses.   In the first place, it represents poetical genius as a free gift of the Muses, imparted to a rough, unlettered man, and awakening him from his brutish condition to a better life. Secondly, this gift of the Muses is to be dedicated to the dif-fusion of truth ; by which the poet means to indicate the serious object and character of his theogonic and ethical poetry; not without an implied censure of other poems which admitted of an easier and freer play of fancy.

But, beautiful and significant as this story is, it is clear that the poetry of Hesiod can in no wise be regarded as the product of an inspiration which comes like a divine gift from above ; it must have been connected both with earlier and with con-temporary forms of epic composition.   We have seen that the worship of the Muses was of old standing in these districts, whither it had been brought by the Pierian tribes from the neighbourhood of Olympus ; and with this worship the practice of music and poetry was most closely connected.[1]   This poetry consisted chiefly of songs and hymns to the gods, for which Bœotia, so rich in ancient temples, symbolical rites of worship, and festival ceremonies, offered frequent opportunities.

Ascra itself, according to epic poems quoted by Pausanias,

---

[1] Above, chap. III. § 8, 9.

was founded by the Aloids, who were Pierian heroes, and first sacrificed to the Muses upon Mount Helicon. That Hesiod dwelt at Ascra rests upon his own testimony in the *Works and Days* (v. 640); and this statement is confirmed in a remarkable manner by other historical accounts, for which we are indebted to the Bœotian writer, Plutarch. Ascra had, at an early period, been destroyed by the neighbouring and powerful race of Thespians, and the Orchomenians had received the fugitive Ascræans into their city: the oracle then commanded that the bones of Hesiod should be transferred to Orchomenus, and, when what were held to be the remains of the poet were discovered, a monument was erected to him at Orchomenus, upon which was written an inscription, composed by the Bœotian epic poet Chersias, describing him as the wisest of all poets.

On the other hand, the intercourse which subsisted between the Bœotians and their kinsmen on the Æolic coast of Asia Minor, and the flight which poetry had taken in those countries, probably contributed to stimulate the Bœotian poets to new productions. There is no reason to doubt the testimony of the author of the *Works and Days* (v. 636), that his father came from Cyme in Æolis to Ascra: the motive which brought him thither was doubtless the recollection of the ancient affinity between the Æolic settlers and this race of the mother-country; a recollection which was still alive at the time of the Peloponnesian war.[1] The father of the poet is not stated to be a Cymæan bard; but is described as a mariner, who, after repeated voyages from Cyme, had at length taken up his abode at Ascra; yet it must have been by settlers such as this that the fame of the heroic poetry, which at that time was flourishing in the colonies, must have been spread over the mother country. The ancients have eagerly seized upon this point of union in the two schools of poetry, in order to prove that a near relationship existed between Homer and Hesiod. The logographers (or historians before Herodotus) — as Hellanicus, Pherecydes, and Damastes — have combined various names handed down by tradition into comprehensive genealogies, in which it appears that the two poets were descended from a common ancestor: for example, that Apellis (also called Apelles, or

---

[1] See Thucyd. III. 2; VII. 57; VIII. 100.

Apellæus) had two sons—Mæon, the supposed father of Homer,
and Dius, who, according to an ancient but justly rejected interpretation of a verse in the *Works and Days*, was made the
father of Hesiod.[1]

But it is not our intention to support the opinion that the
poetry of Hesiod was merely an offset from the Homeric stock
transplanted to Bœotia, or that it is indebted to the Homeric
poems either for its dialect, versification, or character of style.
On the contrary, the most generally received opinion of antiquity assigns Hesiod and Homer to the same period; thus
Herodotus makes them both about four centuries earlier than
his own time:[2] in such cases, too, Hesiod is commonly named
before Homer, as, for instance, in this passage of Herodotus.
As far as we know, it was first maintained by Xenophanes of
Colophon[3] that Hesiod was later than Homer; on the other
hand, Ephorus, the historian of Cyme, and many others, have
endeavoured to prove the higher antiquity of Hesiod. At any
rate, therefore, the Greeks of those times did not consider that
Homer had formed the epic language in Ionia, and that Hesiod
had borrowed it, and only transferred it to other subjects.
They must have entertained the opinion (which has been confirmed by the researches of our own time), that this epic dialect
had already become the language of refinement and poetry in
the mother-country before the colonies of Asia Minor were
founded. Moreover, this dialect is only identical in the two
schools of poetry so far as its general features are concerned.
Many differences occur in particular points: and it can be
proved that this ancient poetical language among the Bœotian
tribe adopted many features of the native dialect, which was an
Æolism approaching nearly to the Doric.[4] Neither does it

---

[1] v. 299. Ἐργάζευ, Πέρση, Δῖον γένος. [2] II. 53.

[3] In Gellius, *Noct. Att.* III. 17. Xenophanes, the founder of the Eleatic school
of philosophy, who flourished about the 70th Olympiad, was also an epic poet, and
may perhaps, in his κτίσις Κολοφῶνος, have found many opportunities of speaking
of Homer, whom the Colophonians claimed as a countryman. See above, p. 58
(chap. V. § 2).

[4] Thus Hesiod often shortens the ending αs in the accusative plural of the first
declension, like Alcman, Stesichorus, and Epicharmus: it has indeed been observed
hat it only occurs long where the syllable is in the arsis, or where it is lengthened
by position. On the whole, there is in Hesiod a greater tendency to shorter, often
to contracted forms; while Homer's ear appears to have found peculiar delight in
the multiplication of vowel syllables.

appear that the phrases, epithets, and proverbial expressions common to both poets were supposed by the ancient Greeks to have been borrowed by one from the other : in general, too, they have the appearance of being separately derived from the common source of an earlier poetry; and in Hesiod especially, if we may judge from statements of the ancients, and from the tone of his language, sayings and idioms of the highest antiquity are preserved in all their original purity and simplicity.[1]

The opinion that Hesiod received the form of his poetry from Homer cannot, moreover, well be reconciled with the wide difference which appears in the spirit and character of the two styles of epic poetry. Besides what we have already remarked upon this subject, we will notice one point which shows distinctly how little Hesiod allowed himself to be governed by rules derived from Homer. The Homeric poems, among all the forms in which poetry can appear, possess in the greatest degree what in modern times is called *objectivity ;* that is, a complete abandonment of the mind to the *object,* without any intervening consciousness of the situation or circumstances of the *subject,* or the individual himself. Homer's mind moves in a world of lofty thoughts and energetic actions, far removed from the wants and necessities of the present. There can be no doubt that this is the noblest and most perfect style of composition, and the best adapted to epic poetry. Hesiod, however, never soars to this height. He prefers to show us his own domestic life, and to make us feel its wants and privations.

---

[1] Thus the verse of the *Works and Days,* μισθὸς δ' ἀνδρὶ φίλῳ εἰρημένος ἄρκιος εἴη (v. 370), was attributed to Pittheus of Troezen, a sage and prince of the early fabulous times. (See Aristotle in Plutarch, *Theseus,* c. 3.) The meaning, according to Buttmann, is, ' Let the reward be surely agreed on with a friend.' Homer has the shorter expression : μισθὸς δέ οἱ ἄρκιος ἔσται. (See Buttmann's *Lexilogus,* in ἄρκιος, p. 164, Engl. transl.) So likewise the phrase of Hesiod, ἀλλὰ τίη μοι ταῦτα περὶ δρῦν ἢ περὶ πέτρην (*Theog.* 35), is doubtless derived from the highest antiquity; it is connected with the Homeric, Οὐ μέν πως νῦν ἔστιν ἀπὸ δρυὸς οὐδ' ἀπὸ πέτρης τῷ ὀαριζέμεναι, and Οὐ γὰρ ἀπὸ δρυός ἐσσι παλαιφάτου οὐδ' ἀπὸ πέτρης· The oak and the rock here represent the simple country life of the Greek autochthons, who thought that they had sprung from their mountains and woods, and whose thoughts dwelt only upon these ideas, in primitive innocence and familiarity. These words, with which Hesiod breaks off his description of the scene of the shepherds sleeping with their flocks, sound just like a saying of the ancient Pierian bards among the Pelasgians. (Above, p. 37—38.)

It would doubtless be an erroneous transfer of the manners of later poets to this primitive age, if we regarded Hesiod's accounts of his own life as mere fictions used as a vehicle for his poetic conceptions. Moreover, the tone in which he addresses his brother Perses has all the frankness and *naïveté* of reality ; and, indeed, the whole arrangement of the poem of the *Works and Days* is unintelligible, unless we conceive it as founded on a real event, such as the poet describes.

§ 2. This poem (which alone, according to Pausanias, the Bœotians hold to be a genuine work of Hesiod, and with which, therefore, we may properly begin the examination of the several works of this school) is so entirely occupied with the events of common life, that the author would not seem to have been a poet by profession, as Homer was described by the ancients, but some Bœotian husbandman, whose mind had been so forcibly moved by peculiar circumstances as to give a poetical tone to the whole course of his thoughts and feelings. The father of Hesiod, as was before mentioned, had settled at Ascra as a farmer ; and although he found the situation disadvantageous, from its great heat in summer and its storminess in winter, yet he had left a considerable property to his two sons, Hesiod and a younger brother, Perses. The brothers divided the inheritance ; and Perses, by means of bribes to the kings (who at this time alone exercised the office of judge), contrived to defraud his elder brother. But Perses showed a disposition which in later times became more and more common among the Greeks : he chose rather to listen to lawsuits in the market-place, and to contrive legal quibbles by which he might defraud others of their property, than to follow the plough. Hence it came to pass that his inheritance, probably with the help of a foolish wife, was soon dissipated ; and he threatened to commence a new suit against his elder brother, in order to dispute the possession of that small portion of their father's land which had been allotted to him. The peculiar situation in which Hesiod was thus placed called forth the following expression of his thoughts. We give only the principal heads, in order to point out their reference to the circumstances of the poet.[1]

---

[1] I pass over the short procemium to Zeus, as it was rejected by most of the ancient critics, and probably was only one of the introductory strains which the Hesiodean rhapsodists could prefix to the *Works and Days*.

'There are two kinds of contention' (the poet begins by saying), 'the one blameable and hateful, the strife of war and litigation; the other beneficial and praiseworthy, the competition of mechanics and artists. Avoid the first, O Perses; and strive not again through the injustice of the judges to wrest from me my own; keep rather to the works of honest industry. For the gods sent toil and misery among men, when they punished Prometheus for stealing fire from heaven by sending Pandora to Epimetheus, from whose box all evils were spread among mankind. We are now in the fifth age of the world, the age of iron, in which man must perpetually contend with want and trouble. I will now relate to the judges the fable of the hawk which killed the nightingale heedless of her song. The city where justice is practised will alone flourish under the protection of the gods. But to the city where wicked deeds are done, Zeus sends famine and plague. Know, ye judges, that ye are watched by myriads of Jove's immortal spirits, and his own all-seeing eye is upon you. To the brutes have the gods given the law of force—to men the law of justice. Excellence is not to be acquired, O Perses, except by the sweat of thy brow. Labour is pleasing to the gods, and brings no shame : honest industry alone gives lasting satisfaction. Beware of wrongful acts; honour the gods; hold fast good friends and good neighbours; be not misled by an improvident wife; and provide yourself with a plentiful, but not too numerous an offspring, and you will be blessed with prosperity.'

With these and similar rules of economy (of which many are, perhaps, rather adapted to the wants of daily life than noble and elevated) the first part of the poem concludes; its object being to improve the character and habits of Perses, to deter him from seeking riches by litigation, and to incite him to a life of labour as the only source of permanent prosperity. Mythical narratives, fables, descriptions, and moral apophthegms, partly of a proverbial kind, are ingeniously chosen and combined so as to illustrate and enforce the principal idea.

In the second part, Hesiod shows Perses the succession in which his labours must follow if he determines to lead a life of industry. Observing the natural order of the seasons, he begins with the time of ploughing and sowing, and treats of the implements used in these processes, the plough and the beasts which draw it. He then proceeds to show how a prudent husbandman may employ the winter at home, when the labours of the field are at a stand; adding a description of the storms and cold of a Bœotian winter, which several modern critics have (though probably without sufficient ground) considered as exaggerated, and have therefore doubted its genuineness. With the first appearance of spring follows the dressing and cutting of the vines, and, at the rising of the Pleiades (in the first half of our May), the reaping of the grain. The poet then tells us how the hottest season should be employed, when the corn is threshed. The vintage, which immediately precedes the ploughing, concludes the circle of these rural occupations.

But as the poet's object was not to describe the charms of a country life, but to teach all the means of honest gain which were then open to the Ascræan countryman, he next proceeds, after having completed the subject of husbandry, to treat with equal detail that of *navigation*. Here we perceive how, in the time of Hesiod, the Bœotian farmer himself shipped the overplus of his corn and wine, and transported it to countries where these products were less abundant. If the poet had had any other kind of trade in view, he would have been more explicit upon the subject of the goods to be exported, and would have stated how a husbandman like Perses was to procure them. Hesiod recommends for a voyage of this kind the late part of the summer, on the 50th day after the summer solstice, when there was no work to be done in the field, and when the weather in the Greek seas is the most certain.

All these precepts relating to the works of industry interrupt, somewhat suddenly, the succession of economical rules for the management of a family.[1] The poet now speaks of the time of life when a man should take a wife, and how he should look out for her. He then especially recommends to all to bear in mind that the immortal gods watch over the actions of men;

---

[1] It would be a great improvement if the verses relating to marriage (697—705, ed. Göttling) could be placed before Μουνογενὴς δὲ πάϊς εἴη (376). Then all the prudential maxims relating to neighbours, friends, wife, and children, would be explained before the labours of agriculture, and the subsequent rules of domestic economy would all refer to the maxim, εὖ δ' ὄπιν ἀθανάτων μακάρων πεφυλαγμένος εἶναι.

in all intercourse with others to keep the tongue from idle and
provoking words; and to preserve a certain purity and care in
the commonest occurrences of every-day life.   At the same
time he gives many curious precepts, with respect to the de-
corum to be observed in acts of worship, which resemble sacerdotal rules, and, moreover, have much in common with the symbolic rules of the Pythagoreans, which ascribed a deep and
spiritual import to many unimportant acts of common life.

Of a very similar nature is the last part of this poem, which
treats of the days on which it is expedient or inexpedient to
do this or that business.   These precepts, which do not relate
to particular seasons of the year, but to the course of each
lunar month, are exclusively of a superstitious character, and
are in great part connected with the different worships which
were celebrated upon these days: but our knowledge is far too
insufficient to explain them all.[1]

If we regard the connexion of this poem, as indicated by
the heads which we have mentioned, it must be confessed that
the whole is perfectly adapted to the circumstances of the case;
and conformable to the poet's view of turning his brother
Perses from his scheme of enriching himself by unjust lawsuits,
and of stimulating him to a life of laborious husbandry.   On
the other hand, it cannot be denied that the poet has failed in
producing so perfect an agreement of the several members of
his work, that by their combination they form, as it were, one
body.   Indeed, the separate parts have often very little connexion with each other, and are only introduced by announcements such as these, ' Now, if thou wilt, I will tell another
story;' or, ' Now I will relate a fable to the kings,' &c.   This
plainly shows much less art in composition than is displayed in
the Homeric poems; the reason of which was the far greater
difficulty which must have been felt at that time of forming
general reflections upon life into a connected whole, than of
relating a great heroic event.

---

[1] On the seventh day the poet himself remarks the connexion with Apollo.   The
τετράς of the beginning and ending of the month is a day on which evils are to be
feared: it was considered as the birth-day of the toil-worn Hercules.   On the 17th
the corn is to be brought to the threshing-floor: the 17th of Boëdromion was the
sacrificial day of Demeter and Cora at Athens (Boeckh. *Corp. Inscript. Gr.* No. 523),
and a great day of the Eleusinia.

Yet in the general tone of the poem, and in the sentiments which it displays, a sufficient uniformity is not wanting. We feel, as we read it, that we are transported back to an age of primitive simplicity, in which even the wealthy man does not disdain to increase his means by the labour of his own hands; and an attention to economical cares was not considered ignoble, as it was among the later Greeks, who from husbandmen became mere politicians. A coarse vein of homely good sense, nay, even a dash of interested calculating shrewdness, which were deeply rooted in the Greek character, are combined with honourable principles of justice, expressed in nervous apophthegms and striking images. When we consider that the poet was brought up in these hereditary maxims of wisdom, and moreover that he was deeply convinced of the necessity of a life of laborious exertion, we shall easily comprehend how strongly an event such as that in which he was concerned with his brother Perses was calculated to strike his mind; and from the contrast which it offered to his convictions, to induce him to make a connected exposition of them in a poem. This brings us to the true source of the *Didactic Epos,* which never can proceed from a mere desire to *instruct;* a desire which has no connexion with poetry. Genuine didactic poetry always proceeds from some great and powerful idea, which has something so absorbing and attractive that the mind strives to give expression to it. In the *Works and Days* this fundamental idea is distinctly perceptible; the decrees and institutions of the gods protect justice among men, they have made labour the only road to prosperity, and have so ordered the year that every work has its appointed season, the sign of which is discernible by man. In announcing these immutable ordinances and eternal laws, the poet himself is impressed with a lofty and solemn feeling, which manifests itself in a sort of oracular tone, and in the sacerdotal style with which many exhortations and precepts are delivered.[1] We have remarked this priestly character in the concluding part of the poem, and it was not unnatural that

---

[1] We allude particularly to the μέγα νήπιε Πέρση of Hesiod, and the μέγα νήπιε Kροῖσε of the Pythia: and to the truly oracular expressions of the *Works and Days,* as, the 'branch of five,' πέντοζος, for the 'hand;' the 'day-sleeper,' ἡμερόκοιτος ἀνήρ, for the thief, &c. : on which see Göttling's Hesiod, *Praef.* p. xv.

many in antiquity should annex to the last verse, 'Observing the omens of birds, and avoiding transgressions,' another didactic epic poem of the same school of poetry upon *divination.*[1] It is stated that this poem treated chiefly of the flight and cries of birds ; and it agrees with this statement, that Hesiod, according to Pausanias, learned divination among the Acarnanians: the Acarnanian families of diviners deriving their descent from Melampus, whose ears, when a boy, were licked by serpents, whereupon he immediately understood the language of the birds.

A greater loss than this supplement on divination is another poem of the same school, called the *Lessons of Chiron* (Χείρωνος ὑποθῆκαι), as this was in some measure a companion or counterpart to the *Works and Days.* For while the extant poem keeps wholly within the circle of the yearly occupations of a Bœotian husbandman, the lost one represented the wise Centaur, in his grotto upon Mount Pelion, instructing the young Achilles in all the knowledge befitting a young prince and hero. We might not improperly apply to this poem the name of a German poem of the middle ages, and call it a Greek *Ritterspiegel.*

§ 3. We now follow this school of poetry to the great attempt of forming from the Greek legends respecting the gods a connected and regular picture of their origin and powers, and in general of the entire polytheism of the Greeks. The *Theogony* of Hesiod is not, indeed, to be despised as a poem ; besides many singular legends, it contains thoughts and descriptions of a lofty and imposing character; but for the history of the religious faith of Greece it is a production of the highest importance. The notions concerning the gods, their rank, and their affinities, which had arisen in so much greater variety in the different districts of Greece than in any other country of the ancient world, found in the *Theogony* a test of their general acceptance. Every legend which could not be brought into agreement with this poem sank into the obscurity of mere local tradition, and lived only in the limited sphere of the inhabitants of some Arcadian district, or the ministers of some temple, under the form of a strange and marvellous tale, which

---

[1] Τούτοις ἐπάγουσί τινες τὴν ὀρνιθομαντείαν, ἅτινα Ἀπολλώνιος ὁ Ῥόδιος ἀθετεῖ.—Proclus on the *Works and Days*, at the end, v. 824.

was cherished with the greater fondness because its uncon-
formity with the received theogony gave it the charm of mys-
tery.[1] It was through Hesiod that Greece first obtained a
kind of *religious code*, which, although without external sanc-
tions or priestly guardians and interpreters (such as the Vedas
had in the Brahmans, and the Zendavesta in the Magians),
must have produced the greatest influence on the religious condition of the Greeks ; inasmuch as it impressed upon them the
necessity of agreement, and as the notions prevalent among the
most powerful races, and at the most renowned temples, were
embodied by the poet with great skill.   Hence Herodotus was
justified in saying that Hesiod and Homer had *made the theogony* of the Greeks, had assigned the names, offices, and occupations of the gods, and had determined their forms.

According to the religious notions of the Greeks, the deity,
who governs the world with omnipotence, and guides the destinies of man with omniscience, is yet without one attribute,
which is the most essential to our idea of the godhead—*eternity*.
The gods of the Greeks were too closely bound up with the
existence of the world to be exempt from the law by which
large, shapeless masses are developed into more and more perfect forms.   To the Greeks the gods of Olympus were rather
the summit and crowning point of organized and animate life,
than the origin of the universe.   Thus *Zeus*, who must be considered as the peculiar deity of the Greeks, was doubtless, long
before the time of Homer or Hesiod, called Cronion, or Cronides,
which, according to the most probable interpretation, means the
' Son of the Ancient of Days ;'[2] and, as the ruler of the clear
heaven, he was derived from *Uranus*, or heaven itself.   In like
manner all the other gods were, according to their peculiar

---

[1] Numbers of these fables, which cannot be reconciled with the *Theogony*, were,
as we know from Pausanias, in currency, especially in Arcadia ; but how little
should we know of them from writers who addressed themselves to the entire nation.
The Attic tragedians likewise, in their accounts of the affinities of the gods, follow
the Hesiodean *Theogony* far more than the local worships and legends of Attica.

[2] Whatever doubts may exist with regard to the etymology of χρόνος (whether
the name comes from κραίνω, or is allied with κρόνος), yet everything stated of him
agrees with this conception, his dominion during the golden age, the representation
of a simple patriarchal life at the festival of the Κρόνια, Cronus as the ruler of the
departed heroes, &c.

attributes and character, connected with beings and appearances which seemed the most ancient. The relation of the
primitive and the *originating* to the *recent* and the *derived* was
always conceived under the form of *generation* and *birth*—the
universe being considered to have a life, like that of animals ;
and hence even heaven and earth were imagined to have an
animal organization.   The idea of *creation*, of so high antiquity
in the east, and so early known to the Indians, Persians, and
Hebrews, which supposed the Deity to have formed the world
with design, as an earthly artificer executes his work, was foreign
to the ancient Greeks, and could only arise in religions which
ascribed a personal existence and an eternal duration to the
godhead.   Hence it is clear that theogonies, in the widest
sense of the word—that is, accounts of the descent of the gods
—are as old as the Greek religion itself ; and, doubtless, the
most ancient bards would have been induced to adopt and ex-
pand such legends in their poems.   One result of their attempts
to classify the theogonic beings, is the race of *Titans*, who
were known both to Homer and Hesiod, and formed a link
between the general personifications of parts of the universe and
the human forms of the Olympic gods, by whose might they
were supposed to be hurled into the depths of Tartarus.

Surrounded as he was by traditions and ancient poems of
this kind, it would have been impossible for Hesiod (as many
moderns have conceived) to form his entire *Theogony* upon
abstract philosophical principles of his own concerning the
powers of matter and mind : if his system had been invented
by himself, it would not have met with such ready acceptance
from succeeding generations.   But, on the other hand, Hesiod
cannot be considered as a mere collector of scattered traditions
or fragments of earlier poems, which he repeated almost at ran-
dom, without being aware of their hidden connexion : the choice
which he made among different versions of the same fable, and
his skilful arrangement of the several parts, are of themselves a
sufficient proof that he was guided by certain fundamental ideas,
and that he proceeded upon a connected view of the formation
of outward nature.

To make this position more clear, it will perhaps be most
advisable to illustrate the nature of the *primitive beings* which,

according to the *Theogony*, preceded the race of the Titans; with the view of showing the consistency and connexion of Hesiod's notions : for the rest, a more general survey will suffice.

' First of all (the *Theogony*, strictly so called, begins) was *Chaos*,'[1] that is, the abyss, in which all peculiar shape and figure is lost, and of which we arrive at the conception by excluding all idea of definite form. It is evident, however, that, as Hesiod represents other beings as springing out of Chaos, he must have meant by this word not mere empty space, but a confused mixture of material atoms, instinct with the principle of life. ' Afterwards arose (that is from Chaos) the wide-bosomed *Earth*, the firm resting-place of all things; and gloomy *Tartara* in the depth of the earth; and *Eros*, the fairest of the immortal gods.'[2] The Earth, the mother of all living things, according to the notion of the Greeks and many oriental countries, is conceived to arise out of the dark abyss; her foundations are in the depth of night, and her surface is the soil upon which light and life exist. Tartara is, as it were, only the *dark side* of the Earth; by which it still remains connected with Chaos. As the Earth and Tartara represent the brute matter of Chaos in a more perfect form, so in Eros the living spirit appears as the principle of all increase and development. It is a lofty conception of the poet of the *Theogony*, to represent the God of Love as proceeding out of Chaos at the beginning of all things; though probably this thought did not originate with him, and had already been expressed in ancient hymns to Eros, sung at Thespiæ. Doubtless it is not an accidental coincidence that this city, which was 40 stadia from Ascra, should have possessed the most renowned temple of Eros in all Greece ; and that in its immediate neighbourhood Hesiod should have given to this deity a dignity and importance of which the Homeric poems contain no trace.

---

[1] χάος, literally synonymous with χάσμα, chasm.

[2] Plato and Aristotle in their quotations of this passage omit Tartara (also called Tartarus) ; but probably only because it has not so much importance among the *principia mundi* as the others. Tartara could also be considered as included under the Earth, as it is also called Τάρταρα γαίης. But the poet of the *Theogony* must have stated his origin in this place; as lower down he describes Typhœus as the son of the Earth and Tartarus.

But it appears that the poet was satisfied with borrowing this thought from the Thespian hymns without applying it in the subsequent part of his poem. For although it is doubtless implied that all the following marriages and births of the gods spring from the influence of Eros, the poet nevertheless omits expressly to mention its operation. ' Out of Chaos came *Erebus*,' the darkness in the depths of the Earth, ' and black *Night*,' the darkness which passes over the surface of the Earth. ' From the union of Night and Erebus proceeded *Æther* and *Day*.' It may perhaps appear strange that these dark children of Chaos bring forth the ever-shining Æther of the highest heavens, and the bright daylight of the earth ; this, however, is only a consequence of the general law of development observed in the *Theogony*, that the dim and shapeless is the prior in point of time; and that the world is perpetually advancing from obscurity to brightness. Light bursting from the bosom of darkness is a beautiful image, which recurs in the cosmogonies of other ancient nations. ' The Earth then first produced the starry heaven, of equal extent with herself, that it might cover her all round, so as to be for ever a firm resting-place for the gods ; and also the far-ranging mountains, the lovely abodes of the nymphs.' As the hills are elevations of the Earth, so the Heaven is conceived as a firmament spread over the Earth ; which, according to the general notion above stated, would have proceeded, and, as it were, grown out of it. At the same time, on account of the various fertilizing and animating influences which the Earth receives from the Heaven, the Greeks were led to conceive Earth and Heaven as a married pair,[1] whose descendants form in the *Theogony* a second great generation of deities. But another offspring of the Earth is first mentioned. ' The Earth also bore the roaring swelling sea, the *Pontus*, without the joys of marriage.' By expressly remarking of Pontus that the Earth produced him alone without love, although the other beings just enumerated sprung from the Earth singly, the poet meant to indicate his rough and unkindly nature. It is the wild, waste salt sea,

---

[1] The same notion had prevailed, though in a less distinct form, in the early religion of outward nature among the Greeks. See above, ch. II. § 4. (p. 18).

separated at its very origin from the streams and springs of fresh water, which supply nourishment to vegetation and to animal life. These are all made to descend from *Ocean*, who is called the eldest of the *Titans*. These, together with the *Cyclopes* and *Hecatoncheires*, were produced by the union of Earth and Heaven; and it is sufficient here to remark of them that the Titans, according to the notions of Hesiod, represent a system of things in which elementary beings, natural powers, and notions of order and regularity are united into a whole. The Cyclopes denote the transient disturbances of this order by storms, and the Hecatoncheires, or the hundred-handed giants, signify the fearful power of the greater revolutions of nature.

The subsequent arrangement of the poem depends on its mixed genealogical and narrative character. As soon as a new generation of gods is produced, the events are related through which it overcame the earlier race and obtained the supremacy. Thus, after the Titans and their brethren, the Cyclopes and Hecatoncheires, are enumerated, it is related how Cronus deprives his father of the power, by producing new beings, of supplanting those already in existence; whereupon follow the races of the other primitive beings, Night and Pontus. Then succeed the descendants of the Titans. In speaking of Cronus, the poet relates how Zeus was preserved from being devoured by his father, and of Iapetus, how his son Prometheus incensed Zeus by coming forward as the patron of the human race, though not for their benefit. Then follows a detailed account of the battle which Zeus and his kindred, assisted by the Hecatoncheires, waged against the Titans; with the description of the dreadful abode of Tartara, in which the Titans were imprisoned. This part, it must be confessed, appears to be overloaded by additions of rhapsodists. An afterpiece to the battle of the Titans is the rebellion of Typhœus (born of the Earth and Tartara) against Zeus. The descendants of Zeus and the Olympian gods, united with him, formed the last part of the original *Theogony*.

Notwithstanding the great simplicity of this plan, we may yet remark a number of refinements which show a maturely considered design on the part of the poet. For instance, Hesiod might have connected the descendants of Night (born without marriage)[1] with the children which she bore to Erebus, namely Æther and Day.[2] But he relates first the battle of Cronus against Uranus, and the mutilation of the latter; whereby the first interruption of the peaceable order of the world is caused, and anger and curses, personified by the Furies, are introduced into the world. The mutilation, however, of Uranus caused the production of the Meliæ, or Nymphs of the Ash Trees, that is, the mightiest productions of vegetation; the Giants, or most powerful beings of human form; and the Goddess of Love herself. It is not till after this disturbance of the tranquillity of the world that Night produces from her dark bosom those beings, such as Death, and Strife, and Woe, and Blame, which are connected with the sufferings of mankind. Likewise the race of Pontus, so rich in monsters, with which the heroes were to fight their fiercest battles, are properly introduced after the first deed of violence upon Uranus. It is also evidently by design that the two Titans, Cronus and Iapetus, also named together by Homer, are, in the genealogy of their descendants,[3] arranged in a different order than at the first mention of the Titans.[4] In the latter passage Cronus is the youngest of all, just as Zeus is in Hesiod the youngest among his brothers; whilst in Homer he reigns by the right of primogeniture. But Hesiod supposes the world to be in a state of perpetual development; and as the sons overcome the fathers, so also the youngest sons are the most powerful, as standing at the head of a new order of things. On the other hand, the race of Iapetus, which refers exclusively to the attributes and destinies of mankind,[5] is placed after the descendants of Cronus, from whom the Olympic gods proceed; because the actions and

---

[1] v. 211, *seq.*   [2] v. 124.   [3] v. 453, 507.   [4] v. 132, *seq.*

[5] In the genealogy of Iapetus in the *Theogony* are preserved remains of an ancient poem on the *lot of mankind*. Iapetus himself is the ' fallen man' (from ἰάπτω, root ΙΑΠ), the human race deprived of their former happiness. Of his sons, Atlas and Menoetius represent the θυμός of the human soul: Atlas (from τλῆναι, ΤΛΑ), the enduring and obstinate spirit, to whom the gods allot the heaviest burdens; and Menoetius (μένος and οἶτος), the unconquerable and confident spirit, whom Zeus hurls into Erebus. *Prometheus* and *Epimetheus*, on the other hand, personify νοῦς; the former prudent foresight, the latter the worthless knowledge which comes after the deed. And the gods contrive it so that whatever benefits are gained for the human race by the former are lost to it again through his brother.

destinies of those human Titans are entirely determined by their relation to the Olympians, who have reserved to themselves alone a constantly equal measure of prosperity, and act jointly in repelling with equal severity the bold attempts of the Iapetids.

Although therefore this poem is not merely an accumulation of raw materials, but contains many connected thoughts, and is formed on a well-digested plan, yet it cannot be denied that neither in the *Theogony* nor in the *Works and Days* can that perfect art of composition be found which is so conspicuous in the Homeric poems. Hesiod has not only faithfully preserved the ancient tradition, and introduced without alteration into his poetry many time-honoured sayings, and many a verse of earlier songs, but he also seems to have borrowed long passages, and even entire hymns, when they happened to suit the plan of his poem; and without greatly changing their form. Thus it is remarkable that the battle of the Titans does not begin (as it would be natural to expect) with the resolution of Zeus and the other Olympians to wage war against the Titans, but with the chaining of Briareus and the other Hecatoncheires by Uranus; nor is it until the poet has related how Zeus set free these Hecatoncheires, by the advice of the Earth, that we are introduced to the battle with the Titans, which has already been some time going on. And this part of the *Theogony* concludes with the Hecatoncheires being set by the gods to watch over the imprisoned Titans, and Briareus, by his marriage with Cymopoleia, becoming the son-in-law of Poseidon. This Briareus, who in Homer is also called Ægæon, and represents the violent commotions and heavings of the sea, was a being who in many places seems to have been connected with the worship of Poseidon,[1] and it is not improbable that in the temples of this god hymns were sung celebrating him as the vanquisher of the Titans, one of which Hesiod may have taken as the foundation of his narrative of the battle of the Titans.

It seems likewise evident that the *Theogony* has been in many places interpolated by rhapsodists, as was naturally to be

---

[1] Poseidon, from αἶγες, which signifies waves in a state of agitation, was also called Αἰγαῖος and Αἰγαίων.

expected in a poem handed down by oral tradition. Enumerations of names always offered facilities for this insertion of new verses ; as, for example, the list of streams in the *Theogony,* which are called sons of the Ocean.[1] Among these we miss exactly those rivers which we should expect most to find, the Bœotian Asopus and Cephisus; and we find several which at any rate lie beyond the sphere of the Homeric geography, such as the Ister, the Eridanus, and the Nile, no longer the river of Egypt, as in Homer, but under its more modern name. The most remarkable circumstance, however, is that in this brief list of rivers, the passage of Homer[2] which names eight petty streams flowing from the mountains of Ida to the coast, has been so closely followed, that seven of them are named in Hesiod. This seems to prove incontestably that the *Theogony* has been interpolated by rhapsodists who were familiar with the Homeric poems as well as with those of Hesiod.

It has been already stated that the *Theogony* originally terminated with the races of the Olympian gods, that is, at v. 962 ; the part which follows being only added in order to make a transition to another and longer poem, which the rhapsodists appended as a kind of continuation to the *Theogony.* For it seems manifest that a composer of genealogical legends of this kind would not be likely to celebrate the goddesses who, ' joined in love with mortal men, had borne godlike children' (which is the subject of the last part in the extant version), if he had not also intended to sing of the gods who with mortal women had begotten mighty heroes (a far more frequent event in Greek mythology). The god Dionysus, and Hercules, received among the gods (both of whom sprang from an alliance of this kind), are indeed mentioned in a former part of the poem.[3] But there remain many other heroes, whose genealogy is not traced, of far greater importance than Medeius, Phocus, Æneas, and many other sons of goddesses. Moreover, the extant concluding verses of the *Theogony* furnish a complete proof that a poem of this description was annexed to it; inasmuch as the women whom the Muses are in these last verses called on to celebrate[4] can be no other than the mortal beauties to whom

---

[1] v. 388, *seq.*   [2] *Iliad* XII. 20.   [3] v. 940, *seq.*

[4] Νῦν δὲ γυναικῶν φῦλον ἀείσατε ἡδυέπειαι Μοῦσαι, &c.

the gods came down from heaven. As to the nature of this lost poem of Hesiod something will be said hereafter.

Hitherto we have said nothing upon that part of the *Theogony* which has furnished so intricate a problem to the higher department of criticism, viz., the *procemium*, as it is only after having taken a general view of the whole poem that we can hope to succeed in ascertaining the original form of this part. It can scarcely be questioned that this procemium, with its disproportionate length (v. 1—115), its intolerable repetition of the same or very similar thoughts, and the undeniable incoherences of several passages, could not be the original introduction to the *Theogony*; it appears, indeed, to be a collection of all that the Bœotian bards had produced in praise of the Muses. It is not, however, necessary, in order to explain how this confused mass was formed, to have recourse to complicated hypotheses; or to suppose that this long procemium was designedly formed of several shorter ones. It appears, indeed, that a much simpler explanation may be found, if we proceed upon some statements preserved in ancient authors.[1] The genuine procemium contained the beautiful story above mentioned of the visit of the Muses to Helicon, and of the consecration of Hesiod to the office of a poet by the gift of a laurel branch. Next after this must have followed the passage which describes the return of the Muses to Olympus, where they celebrate their father Zeus in his palace as the vanquisher of Cronus, and as the reigning governor of the world; which might be succeeded by the address of the poet to the Muses to reveal to him the descent and genealogies of the gods. Accordingly the verses 1—35, 68—74, 104—115, would form the original procemium, in the connexion of which there is nothing objectionable, except that the last invocation of the Muses is somewhat overloaded by the repetition of the same thought with little alteration. Of the intervening parts one, viz., v. 36—67, is an independent hymn, which celebrates the Muses as Olympian poetesses produced by Zeus in Pieria in the

---

[1] Especially the statement in Plutarch (tom. II. p. 743, C. ed. Francof.) that the account of the birth of the Muses from Hesiod's poems (viz., v. 36—67 in our proem) was sung as a separate hymn; and the statement of Aristophanes, the Alexandrine grammarian (in the scholia to v. 68), that the ascent of the Muses to Olympus followed their dances on Helicon.

neighbourhood of Olympus, and has no particular reference to the *Theogony*.   For the enumeration contained in it of the subjects sung by the Muses in Olympus, namely, first, songs to all the gods, ancient and recent, then hymns to Zeus in particular, and, lastly, songs upon the heroic races and the battle of the Giants, comprehends the entire range of the Bœotian epic poetry; nay, even the poems on divination of the school of Hesiod are incidentally mentioned.[1]   This hymn to the Muses was therefore peculiarly well fitted to serve not only as a separate epic song, but, like the longer Homeric hymns, to open the contest of Bœotian minstrels at any festival.

But the Muses were, according to the statement of this procemium,[2] celebrated at the *end* as well as at the *beginning*; consequently there must have been songs of the Bœotian epic poets, in which they returned to the Muses from the peculiar subject of their composition. For a concluding address of this kind nothing could be more appropriate than that the poet should address himself to the princes, who were pre-eminent among the listening crowd, that he should show them how much they stood in need of the Muses both in the judgment-hall and in the assemblies of the people, and (which was a main point with Hesiod) should impress upon their hearts respect for the deities of poetry and their servants. Precisely of this kind is the other passage inserted in the original procemium, v. 75—103, which would have produced a good effect at the close of the *Theogony*; by bringing back the poetry, which had so long treated exclusively of the genealogies of the gods, to the realities of human life ; whereas, in the introduction, the whole passage is entirely out of place. But this passage could not remain in the place to which it belongs, viz., after v. 962, because the part relating to the goddesses who were joined in love with mortal men was inserted here, in order that the mortal women who had been loved by gods might follow, and thus the *Theogony* be infinitely prolonged. Hence, in making an edition of the *Theogony*, in which the pieces belonging to it were introduced into the series of the poem, nothing remained but to insert the hymn to the Muses as well as the epilogue in the procemium ;

---

[1] v. 38.   ὑμνεῦσαι τά τ᾽ ἐόντα τά τ᾽ ἐσσόμενα πρό τ᾽ ἐόντα.   [2] v. 34.

an adaptation which, however, could only have been made in an age when the true feeling for the ancient epic poetry had nearly passed away.[1]

Lastly, with regard to the relation between the *Theogony* and the *Works and Days,* it cannot be doubted that there is a great resemblance in the style and character of the two poems; but who shall pretend to decide that this resemblance is so great as to warrant an opinion that these poems were composed by an individual, and not by a succession of minstrels? It is, however, certain that the author of the *Theogony* and the author of the *Works and Days* wish to be considered as the same person; viz., as the native of Helicon who had been trained to a country life, and had been endowed by the Muses with the gift of poetry. Nor can it be doubted that the original Hesiod, the ancestor of this family of poets, really rose to poetry from the occupations of common life; although his successors may have pursued it as a regular profession. It is remarkable how the *domestic* and *economical* spirit of the poet of the *Works* appears in the *Theogony,* wherever the wide difference of the subjects permits it; as in the legend of Prometheus and Epimetheus. It is true that this takes a somewhat different turn in the *Theogony* and in the *Works;* as in the latter it is the casket brought by Pandora from which proceed all human ills, while in the former this charming and divinely endowed maiden brings woe into the world by being the progenitress of the female sex. Yet the ancient bard views the evil produced by women not in a *moral* but in an *economical* light. He does not complain of the seductions and passions of which they are the cause, but laments that women, like the drones in a hive, consume the fruits of others' industry instead of adding to the sum.

§ 4. It is remarkable that the same school of poetry which was accustomed to treat the weaker sex in this satiric spirit should have produced epics of the heroic mythology which preeminently sang the praises of *the women of antiquity,* and

---

[1] That there was another and wholly different version of the *Theogony,* which contained at the end a passage deriving the origin of Hephæstus and Athene from a contest of Zeus and Here, appears from the testimony of Chrysippus, in Galen *de Hippocratis et Platonis dogm.* III. 8, p. 349, *seq.*

connected a large part of the heroic legends with renowned names of heroines. Yet the school of Hesiod might probably find a motive in existing relations and political institutions for such laudatory catalogues of the women of early times. The neighbours of the Bœotians, the Locrians, possessed a nobility consisting of a hundred families, all of which (according to Polybius[1]) founded their title to nobility upon their descent from heroines. Pindar, also, in the ninth Olympian ode, celebrates Protogeneia as the ancestress of the kings of Opus. That the poetry of this school was connected with the country of the Locrians also appears from the tradition mentioned by Thucydides[2] that Hesiod died and was buried in the temple of Zeus Nemeius, near Oeneon. The district of Oeneon was bordered by that of Naupactus, which originally belonged to the Locrians; and it cannot be doubted that the grave of Hesiod, mentioned in the territory of Naupactus,[3] is the same burying-place as that near Oeneon. Hence it is the more remarkable that Naupactus was also the birth-place of an epic poem, which took from it the name of *Naupactia*, and in which *women* of the heroic age were celebrated.[4] From all this it would follow that it was a Locrian branch of the Hesiodean school of poets whence proceeded the bard by whom the *Eoiæ* were composed. This large poem, called the *Eoiæ*, or the *Great Eoiæ*, (μεγάλαι Ἡοῖαι), took its name from the circumstance that the several parts of it all began with the words ἢ οἵη, *aut qualis*. Five beginnings of this kind have been preserved which have this in common, that those words refer to some heroine who, beloved by a god, gave birth to a renowned hero.[5] Thence it appears that the whole series began with some such introduction as the

---

[1] XII. 5. [2] III. 95. [3] Pausan. IX. 38. 3.

[4] Pausanias, X. 38, 6, uses of it the expression ἔπη πεποιημένα ἐς γυναῖκας, and elsewhere the Hesiodean poem is called τὰ ἐς γυναῖκας ᾀδόμενα. From single quotations it appears that, in the *Naupactia*, the daughters of Minyas, as well as Medea, were particularly celebrated, and that frequent mention was made of the expedition of the Argonauts.

[5] The extant verses (which can be seen in the collection of fragments in Gaisford's *Poetæ Minores*, and other editions) refer to *Coronis*, the mother of Asclepius by Apollo, to *Antiope*, the mother of Zethus and Amphion by Zeus, to *Mecionice*, the mother of Euphemus by Poseidon, and to *Cyrene*, the mother of Aristæus by Apollo. The longer fragment relating to *Alcmene* is explained in the text.

following : ' Such women never will be seen again as were those of former times, whose beauty and charms induced even the gods to descend from Olympus.' Each separate part then referred to this exordium, being connected with it by the constant repetition of the words ἢ οἵη in the initial verses. The most considerable fragment from which the arrangement of the individual parts can be best learnt is the 56 verses which are prefixed as an introduction to the poem on the shield of Hercules, and which, as is seen from the first verse, belong to the *Eoiæ*. They treat of Alcmene, but without relating her origin and early life. The narrative begins from the flight of Amphitryon (to whom Alcmene was married) from his home, and her residence in Thebes, where the father of gods and men descended nightly from Olympus to visit her, and begot Hercules, the greatest of heroes. Although no complete history of Alcmene is given, the praise of her beauty and grace, her understanding, and her conjugal love is a main point with the poet ; and we may also perceive from extant fragments of the continuation of this section of the *Eoiæ*, that in the relation of the exploits of Hercules, the poet frequently recurred to Alcmene ; and her relations with her son, her admiration of his heroic valour, and her grief at the labours imposed upon him, were depicted with great tenderness.[1] From this specimen we may form a judgment of the general plan which was followed throughout the poem of the *Eoiæ*.

The inquiry into the character and extent of the *Eoiæ* is however rendered more difficult by the obscurity which notwithstanding much examination, rests upon the relation of this poem to the κατάλογοι γυναικῶν, *the Catalogues of Women*. For this latter poem is sometimes stated to be the same as the *Eoiæ* ; and for example, the fragment on Alcmene, which, from its beginning, manifestly belongs to the *Eoiæ*, is in the Scholia to Hesiod placed in the fourth book of the *Catalogue* : sometimes, again, the two poems are distinguished, and the statements of the *Eoiæ* and of the *Catalogue* are opposed to each

---

[1] A beautiful passage, which relates to this point, is the address of Alcmene to her son, ὦ τέκνον, ἦ μάλα δή σε πονηρότατον καὶ ἄριστον Ζεὺς ἐτέκνωσε πατήρ.

On the fragments of this part of the *Eoiæ*, see *Dorians*, vol. I. p. 540, Engl. Transl.

other.[1] The *Catalogues* are described as an historical-genealogical poem, a character quite different from that of the *Eoiæ*, in which only such women could be mentioned as were beloved by the gods : on the other hand, the *Catalogues* resembled the *Eoiæ*, when in the first book it was related that Pandora, the first woman according to the Legend of the *Theogony*, bore Deucalion to Prometheus, from whom the progenitors of the Hellenic nation were then derived. We are, therefore, compelled to suppose that originally the *Eoiæ* and the *Catalogues* were different in plan and subject, only, that both were especially dedicated to the celebration of women of the heroic age, and that this then caused the compilation of a version in which both poems were moulded together into one whole. It is also easy to comprehend how much such poems, by their unconnected form, would admit of constant additions, supposing only that they were strung together by genealogies or other links ; and it need not, therefore seem surprising that the *Eoiæ*, the foundation of which had doubtless been laid at an early period, still received additions about the 40th Olympiad. The part which referred to Cyrene, a Thessalian maid, who was carried off by Apollo into Libya, and there bore Aristæus, was certainly not written before the founding of the city of Cyrene in Libya (Olymp. 37). The entire Mythus could only have originated with the settlement of the Greeks of Thera, among whom were noble families of Thessalian origin.

Of the remaining poems which in antiquity went by the name of Hesiod, it is still less possible to give a complete notion. The *Melampodia* is as it were the heroic representation of that divinatory spirit of the Hesiodean poetry, the didactic forms of which have been already mentioned. It treated of the renowned prince, priest, and prophet of the Argives, Melampus ; and as the greater part of the prophets who were celebrated in mythology were derived from this Melampus, the Hesiodean poet, with his predilection for

---

[1] For example, in the Scholia to Apoll. Rhod. II. 181. Moreover, the part of the Eoiæ in which Coronis was celebrated as the mother of Asclepius, was in contradiction with the Κατάλογος Λευκιππίδων, in which Arsinoe, the daughter of Leucippus, according to the Messenian tradition, was the mother of Asclepius, as appears from Schol. *Theogon.* 142.

genealogical connexion, probably did not fail to embrace the entire race of the Melampodias.

§ 5. The *Ægimius* of Hesiod shows by its name that it treated of the mythical Prince of the Dorians, who, according to the legend, was the friend and ally of Hercules, whose son Hyllus he is supposed to have adopted and brought up with his own two sons Pamphylus and Dyman, a legend which referred to the distribution of the Dorians into three Phylæ or tribes, the Hylleis, Pamphylians, and Dymanes. The fragments of this poem also show that it comprehended the genealogical traditions of the Dorians, and the part of the mythology of Hercules closely allied to it; however difficult it may be to form a well-grounded idea of the plan of this Epos.

An interesting kind of composition attributed to Hesiod are the *smaller epics,* in which not a whole series of legends or a complicated story was described, but some separate event of the Heroic Mythology, which usually consisted more in bright and cheerful descriptions than in actions of a more elevated cast. Of this kind was the *marriage of Ceyx,* the well-known Prince of Trachin, who was also allied in close amity with Hercules; and a kindred subject, *The Epithalamium of Peleus and Thetis.* We might also mention here *the Descent of Theseus and Pirithous into the Infernal Regions,* if this adventure of the two heroes was not merely introductory, and a description of Hades in a religious spirit the principal object of the poem. We shall best illustrate this kind of small epic poems by describing the one which has keen preserved, viz., the *Shield of Hercules.* This poem contains merely *one* adventure of Hercules, his combat with the son of Ares, Cycnus, in the Temple of Apollo at Pagasæ. It is clear to every reader of the poem that the first 56 verses are taken out of the *Eoiæ,* and only inserted because the poem itself had been handed down without an introduction. There is no further connexion between these two parts, than that the first relates the origin of the hero, of whom the short epic then relates a separate adventure. It would have been as well, and perhaps better, to have prefixed a brief hymn to Hercules. The description of the Shield of Hercules is however far the most detailed part of the poem and that for which the whole appears to have been composed; a description which was manifestly occasioned by that of the shield of Achilles in the *Iliad*, but nevertheless quite peculiar, and executed in the genuine spirit of the Hesiodean school. For while the reliefs upon the shield of Achilles are entirely drawn from imagination, and pure poetical imagination, objects are represented upon the shield of Hercules which were in fact the first subjects of the Greek artists who worked reliefs in bronze and other decorative sculptures.[1] We cannot, therefore, suppose the *Shield* of Hesiod to be *anterior to* the period of the Olympiads, because before that time nothing was known of similar works of art among the Greeks. But on the other hand, it cannot be *posterior to* the 40th Olympiad, as Hercules appears in it armed and equipped like any other hero; whereas about this date the poets began to represent him in a different costume, with the club and lion's skin.[2] The entire class of these short epics appears to be a remnant of the style of the primitive bards, that of choosing separate points of heroic history, in order to enliven an hour of the banquet, before longer compositions had

---

[1] The *shield of Achilles* contains, on the prominence in the middle, a representation of earth, heaven, and sea: then in the next circular band two cities, the one engaged in peaceable occupations, the other beleaguered by foes: afterwards, in six departments (which must be considered as lying around concentrically in a third row), rural and joyous scenes—sowing, harvest, vine-picking, a cattle pasture, a flock of sheep, a choral dance: lastly, in the external circle, the ocean. The poet takes a delight in adorning this implement of bloody war with the most pleasing scenes of peace, and pays no regard to what the sculptors of his time were able to execute. The Hesiodean poet, on the other hand, places in the middle of the *shield of Hercules* a terrible dragon (δράκοντος φόβον), surrounded by twelve twisted snakes, exactly as the gorgoneum or head of Medusa is represented: on Tyrrhenian shields of Tarquinii other monstrous heads are similarly introduced in the middle. A battle of wild boars and lions makes a border, as is often the case in early Greek sculptures and vases. It must be conceived as a narrow band or ring round the middle. The first considerable row, which surrounds the centre piece in a circle, consists of four departments, of which two contain warlike and two peaceable subjects. So that the entire shield contains, as it were, a sanguinary and a tranquil side. In these are represented the battle of the Centaurs, a choral dance in Olympus, a harbour and fishermen, Perseus and the Gorgons. Of these the first and last subjects are among those which are known to have earliest exercised the Greek artists. An external row (ὑπὲρ αὐτέων, v. 237) is occupied by a city at war and a city at peace, which the poet borrows from Homer, but describes with greater minuteness, and indeed overloads with too many details. The rim, as in the other shield, is surrounded by the ocean.

[2] See the remarks on Peisander below, ch. IX. § 3.

been formed from them.[1] On the other hand, these short Hesiodean epics are connected with *lyric poetry*, particularly that of Stesichorus, who sometimes composed long choral odes on the same or similar subjects (as for example, Cycnus), and not without reference to Hesiod. This close approximation of the Hesiodean epic poetry and the lyric poetry of Stesichorus doubtless gave occasion to the legend that the latter was the son of Hesiod, although he lived much later than the real founder of the Hesiodean school of poetry.

Of the other names of Hesiodean Poems, which are mentioned by grammarians, some are doubtful, as they do not occur in ancient authors, and others do not by their title give any idea of their plan and subject; so that we can make no use of them in our endeavour to convey a notion of the tone and character of the Hesiodean poetry.

---

[1] See above, p. 54 (ch. IV. § 6).

CHAPTER IX.

OTHER EPIC POETS.

§ 1. General character of other Epic Poets. § 2. Cinæthon of Lacedæmon, Eumelus of Corinth, Asius of Samos, Chersias of Orchomenus. § 3. Epic Poems on
Hercules ; the *Taking of Œchalia ;* the *Heraclea* of Peisander of Rhodes.

§ 1. GREAT as was the number of poems which in ancient
times passed under the name of Homer, and were
connected in the way of supplement or continuation with the
Iliad and *Odyssey,* and also of those which were included under
the all-comprehensive name of Hesiod, yet these formed only
about a half of the entire epic literature of the early Greeks.
The hexameter was, for several centuries, the only perfectly
developed form of poetry, as narratives of events of early times
were the general amusement of the people. The heroic mythology was an inexhaustible mine of subjects, if they were followed
up into the legends of the different races and cities; it was
therefore natural, that in the most various districts of Greece
poets should arise, who, for the gratification of their countrymen, worked up these legends into an epic form, either attempting to rise to an imitation of the Homeric style, or
contenting themselves with the easier task of adopting that of
the school of Hesiod. Most of these poems evidently had
little interest except in their subjects, and even this was lost
when the logographers collected into shorter works the legends
of which they were composed. Hence it happened only occasionally that some learned inquirer into traditional story took
the trouble to look into these epic poems. Even now it is of
great importance, for mythological researches, carefully to collect
all the fragments of these ancient poems ; such, for example, as
the *Phoronis* and *Danais* (the works of unknown authors),
which contained the legends of the earliest times of Argos ;
but, for a history of literature, the principal object of which is
to give a vivid notion of the character of writings, these are

empty and unmeaning names. There are, however, a few epic poets of whom enough is known to enable us to form a general idea of the course which they followed.

§ 2. Of these poets several appear to have made use of the links of *genealogy*, in order, like the poet of the Hesiodean catalogues, to string together fables which were not connected by any main action, but which often extended over many generations. According to Pausanias, the works of Cinæthon the Lacedæmonian, who flourished about the 5th Olympiad, had a genealogical foundation; and from the great pleasure which the Spartans took in the legends of the heroic age, it is probable that he treated of certain mythical subjects to which a patriotic interest was attached. His *Heraclea*, which is very rarely mentioned, may have referred to the descent of the Doric Princes from Hercules; and also his *Œdipodia* may have been occasioned by the first kings of Sparta, Procles and Eurysthenes, being, through their mother, descended from the Cadmean kings of Thebes. It is remarked that the *Little Iliad*, one of the Cyclic poems, which immediately followed Homer, was by many[1] attributed to this Cinæthon; and another Peloponnesian bard, Eumelus the Corinthian, was named as the author of a second Cyclic Epos, the *Nostoi*. Both statements are probably erroneous; at least the authors of these poems must, as members of that school who imitated and extended the Homeric Epopees, have adopted an entirely different style of composition from that required for the genealogical collections of Peloponnesian legends. Eumelus was a Corinthian of the noble and governing house of the Bacchaids, and he lived about the time of the founding of Syracuse (11th Olympiad, according to the commonly received date). There were poems extant under his name, of the genealogical and historical kind; by which, however, is not to be understood the later style of converting the marvels of the mythical period into common history, but only a narrative of the legends of some town or race, arranged in order of time. Of this character (as appears also from fragments) were the *Corinthiaca* of Eumelus, and also, probably,

---

[1] See Schol. Vatic. ad Eurip. *Troad.* 822. Eumelus (corrupted into Eumolpus) is called the author of the νόστοι in Schol. Pind. *Olymp.* XIII. 31.

the *Europia,* in which perhaps a number of ancient legends were joined to the genealogy of Europa. Nevertheless the notion among the ancients of the style of Eumelus was not so fixed and clear as to furnish any certain criterion; for there was extant a *Titanomachia,* as to which Athenæus doubts whether it should be ascribed to Eumelus, the Corinthian, or Aretinus, the Milesian. That there should exist any doubt between these two claimants, the Cyclic poet who had composed the *Æthiopis,* and the author of genealogical epics, only convinces us how uncertain all literary decisions in this period are, and how dangerous a region this is for the inquiries of the higher criticism. Pausanias will not allow anything of Eumelus to be genuine except a *prosodion,* or strain, which he had composed for the Messenians for a sacred mission to the Temple of Delos; and it is certain that this epic hymn, in the Doric dialect, really belonged to those times when Messenia was still independent and flourishing, before the first war with the Lacedæmonians, which began in the 9th Olympiad.[1] Pausanias also ascribes to Eumelus the epic verses in the Doric dialect, which were added to illustrate the reliefs on the chest of Cypselus, the renowned work of ancient art. But it is plain that those verses were contemporaneous with the reliefs themselves, which were not made till a century later, under the Government of the Cypselids at Corinth.[2] Asius of Samos, often mentioned

---

[1] The passage quoted from it by Pausan. IV. 33. 3.

Τῷ γὰρ Ἰθωμάτᾳ καταθύμιος ἔπλετο Μοῖσα,
Ἁ καθαρὰ καὶ ἐλεύθερα ᾷσματ' (?) ἔχουσα,

appears to say that the muse of Eumelus, which had composed the *Prosodion,* had also pleased Zeus Ithomatas; that is, had gained a prize at the musical contests among the Ithomæans in Messenia.

[2] Pausanias proceeds on the supposition that this chest was the very one in which the little Cypselus was concealed from the designs of the Bacchiads by his mother Labda, which was afterwards, in memory of this event, dedicated by the Cypselids at Olympia. But not to say that this whole story is not an historical fact, but probably arose merely from the etymology of the word Κύψελος (from κυψέλη, a chest), it is quite incredible that a box so costly and so richly adorned with sculptures should have been used by Labda as an ordinary piece of furniture. It is far more probable that the Cypselids, at the time of their power and wealth (after Olymp. 30), had this chest made among other costly offerings, in order to be dedicated at Olympia, meaning, at the same time, by the name of the chest (κυψέλη)—quite in the manner of the *emblèmes parlans* on Greek coins—to allude to themselves as donors. Another argument is, that Hercules was distinguished on it by a peculiar costume (σχῆμα); and therefore was not, as in Hesiod's shield, represented in the common heroic accoutrements.

by Pausanias, was a third genealogical epic poet. His poems
referred chiefly to his native country, the Ionian island of
Samos; and he appears to have taken occasion to descend to his
own time; as in the glowing and vivid description of the
luxurious costume of the Samians at a festival procession to
the temple of their guardian goddess, Here. Chersias, the
epic poet of Orchomenus, collected Bœotian legends and
genealogies: he was, according to Plutarch, a contemporary of
the Seven Wise Men, and appears, from the monumental inscription above mentioned, to have been a great admirer and
follower of Hesiod.

§ 3. While by efforts of this kind nearly all the heroes
(whose remembrance had been preserved in popular legends)
obtained a place in this endlessly extensive epic literature, it is
remarkable that the hero on whose name half the heroic
mythology of the Greeks depends, to whose mighty deeds (in a
degree far exceeding those of all the Achaian heroes before
Troy) every race of the Greeks seems to have contributed its
share, that *Hercules* should have been celebrated by no epic
poem corresponding to his greatness. Even the two Homeric
epopees furnish some measure of the extent of these legends, and
at the same time make it probable that it was usual to compose
short epic poems from single adventures of the wandering hero;
and of this kind, probably, was the *Taking of Œchalia* which
Homer, according to a well-known tradition, is supposed to have
left as a present to a person joined to him by ties of hospitality,
Creophylus of Samos, who appears to have been the head of a
Samian family of rhapsodists. The poem narrated how Hercules, in order to avenge an affront early received by him from
Eurytus and his sons, takes Œchalia, the city of this prince,
slays him and his sons, and carries off his daughter Iole, as the
spoil of war. This fable is so far connected with the *Odyssey*
that the bow which Ulysses uses against the suitors is derived
from this Eurytus, the best archer of his time. This may
have been the reason that very early Homerids formed of this
subject a separate epos, the execution of which does not appear
to have been unworthy of the name of Homer.

Other portions of the legends of Hercules had found a place
in the larger poems of Hesiod, the *Eoiæ*, the *Catalogues*, and
the short epics; and Cinæthon the Lacedæmonian may have

brought forward many legends little known before his time. Yet this whole series of legends wanted that main feature which every one would now collect from poets and works of art. This conception of Hercules could not arise before *his contests with animals* were combined from the local tales separately related of him in Peloponnesus, and were embellished with all the ornaments of poetry. Hence, too, he assumed a figure different from that of all other heroes, as he no longer seemed to want the brazen helmet, breast-plate, and shield, or to require the weapons of heroic warfare, but trusting solely to the immense strength of his limbs, and simply armed with a club, and covered with the skin of a lion which he had slain, he exercises a kind of *gymnastic* skill in slaying the various monsters which he encounters, sometimes exhibiting rapidity in running and leaping, sometimes the highest bodily strength in wrestling and striking. The poet who first represented Hercules in this manner, and thus broke through the monotony of the ordinary heroic combats, was Peisander, a Rhodian, from the town of Cameirus, who is placed at the 33rd Olympiad, though he probably flourished somewhat later. Nearly all the allusions in his *Heraclea* may be referred to those combats, which were considered as the tasks imposed on the hero by Eurystheus, and which were properly called Ἡρακλέους ἄθλοι. It is, indeed, very probable that Peisander was the first who fixed the number of these labours at *twelve*, a number constantly observed by later writers, though they do not always name the same exploits, and which had moreover established itself in art at least as early as the time of Phidias (on the temple of Olympia). If the first of these twelve combats have a somewhat rural and Idyllian character, the later ones afforded scope for bold imaginations and marvellous tales, which Peisander doubtless knew how to turn to account; as, for example, the story that Hercules, in his expedition against Geryon, was carried over the ocean in the goblet of the Sun, is first cited from the poem of Peisander. Perhaps he was led to this invention by symbols of the worship of the Sun, which existed from early times in Rhodes. It was most likely the originality, which prevailed with equal power through the whole of this not very long poem, that induced the Alexandrian grammarians to receive Peisander, together with Homer and Hesiod, into the epic canon, an honour which they did not extend to any other of the poets hitherto mentioned.

Thus the Greek Epos, which seemed, from its genealogical tendency, to have acquired a dry and sterile character, now appeared once more animated with new life, and striking out new paths. Nevertheless it may be questioned whether the epic poets would have acquired this spirit if they had never moved out of the beaten track of their ancient heroic song, and if *other kinds of poetry* had not arisen and revealed to the Greeks the latent poetical character of many other feelings and impressions besides those which prevailed in the epos. We now turn to those kinds of poetry which first appear as the rivals of the epic strains.[1]

---

[1] Some epic poems of the early period, as the *Minyis*, *Alcmæonis*, and *Thesprotia*, will be noticed in the chapter on the poetry connected with the Mysteries.

CHAPTER X.

THE ELEGY AND THE EPIGRAM.

§ 1. Exclusive prevalence of Epic Poetry, in connexion with the monarchical period; influence of the change in the forms of Government upon Poetry. § 2. Elegeion, its meaning; origin of Elegos; plaintive songs of Asia Minor, accompanied by the flute; mode of Recitation of the Elegy. § 3. Metre of the Elegy. § 4. Political and military tendency of the Elegy as composed by Callinus; the circumstances of his time. § 5. Tyrtæus, his Life; occasion and subject of his *Elegy of Eunomia.* § 6. Character and mode of recitation of the Elegies of Tyrtæus. § 7. Elegies of Archilochus, their reference to Banquets; mixture of convivial jollity (Asius). § 8. Plaintive Elegies of Archilochus. § 9. Mimnermus; his Elegies; the expression of the impaired strength of the Ionic nation. § 10. Luxury a consolation in this state; the *Nanno* of Mimnermus. § 11. Solon's character; his *Elegy of Salamis.* § 12. Elegies before and after Solon's Legislation; the expression of his political feeling; mixture of Gnomic Passages (Phocylides). § 13. Elegies of Theognis; their original character. § 14. Their origin in the political Revolutions of Megara. § 15. Their personal reference to the Friends of Theognis. § 16. Elegies of Xenophanes; their philosophical tendency. § 17. Elegies of Simonides on the Victories of the Persian War; tender and pathetic spirit of his Poetry; general View of the course of Elegiac Poetry. § 18. Epigrams in elegiac form; their Object and Character; Simonides, as a composer of Epigrams.

§ 1. UNTIL the beginning of the seventh century before our era, or the 20th Olympiad, the epic was the only kind of poetry in Greece, and the hexameter the only metre which had been cultivated by the poets with art and diligence. Doubtless there were, especially in connexion with different worships, strains of other kinds and measures of a lighter movement, according to which dances of a sprightly character could be executed; but these as yet did not form a finished style of poetry, and were only rude essays and undeveloped germs of other varieties, which hitherto had only a local interest, confined to the rites and customs of particular districts. In all musical and poetical contests the solemn and majestic tone of the epopee and the epic hymn alone prevailed; and the soothing placidity which these lays imparted to the mind was the only feeling

which had found its satisfactory poetical expression.   As yet
the heart, agitated by joy and grief, by love and anger, could
not give utterance to its lament for the lost, its longing after the
absent, its care for the present, in appropriate forms of poetical
composition.   These feelings were still without the elevation
which the beauty of art can alone confer.   The epopee kept the
mind fixed in the contemplation of a former generation of
heroes, which it could view with sympathy and interest, but
not with passionate emotion.   And although in the economical
poem of Hesiod the cares and sufferings of the present time
furnished the occasion for an epic work, yet this was only a
partial descent from the lofty career of epic poetry; for it immediately rose again from this lowly region, and taking a survey of things affecting not only the entire Greek nation but the
whole of mankind, celebrated in solemn strains the order of
the universe and of social life, as approved by the Gods.

This exclusive prevalence of epic poetry was also doubtless
connected with the political state of Greece at this time.   It
has been already remarked[1] how acceptable the ordinary subjects of the epic poems must have been to the princes who derived their race from the heroes of the mythical age, as was the
case with all the royal families of early times.   This rule of
hereditary princes was the prevailing form of government in
Greece, at least up to the beginning of the Olympiads, and
from this period it gradually disappeared; at an earlier date
and by more violent revolutions among the Ionians, than among
the nations of Peloponnesus.   The republican movements, by
which the princely families were deprived of their privileges,
could not be otherwise than favourable to a free expression of
the feelings, and in general to a stronger development of each
man's individuality.   Hence the poet, who, in the most perfect
form of the epos, was completely lost in his subject, and was
only the mirror in which the grand and brilliant images of the
past were reflected, now comes before the people as a man with
thoughts and objects of his own; and gives a free vent to the
struggling emotions of his soul in elegiac and iambic strains.
As the elegy and the iambus, those two contemporary and cog-

---

[1] Chap. IV. § 1, 2.

nate species of poetry, originated with Ionic poets, and (as far as we are aware) with citizens of free states; so, again, the remains and accounts of these styles of poetry furnish the best image of the internal condition of the Ionic states of Asia Minor and the Islands in the first period of their republican constitution.

§ 2. The word *elegeion*, as used by the best writers, like the word *epos*, refers not to the *subject* of a poem, but simply to its *form*. In general the Greeks, in dividing their poetry into classes, looked almost exclusively to its metrical shape; but in considering the essence of the Greek poetry we shall not be compelled to depart from these divisions, as the Greek poets always chose their verse with the nicest attention to the feelings to be conveyed by the poem. The perfect harmony, the accurate correspondence of expression between these multifarious metrical forms and the various states of mind required by the poem, is one of the remarkable features of the Grecian poetry, and to which we shall frequently have occasion to advert. The word ἐλεγεῖον, therefore, in its strict sense, means nothing more than the combination of an hexameter and a pentameter, making together a distich; and an elegeia (ἐλεγεία) is a poem made of such verses. The word *elegeion* is, however, itself only a derivative from a simpler word, the use of which brings us nearer to the first origin of this kind of poetry. *Elegos* (ἔλεγος) means properly a strain of lament, without any determinate reference to a metrical form; thus, for example, in Aristophanes, the nightingale sings an elegos for her lost Itys; and in Euripides, the halcyon, or kingfisher, sings an elegos for her husband Ceyx;[1] in both which passages the word has this general sense. The origin of the word can hardly be Grecian, since all the etymologies of it which have been attempted seem very improbable;[2] on the other hand, if it is borne in mind, how celebrated among the Greeks the Carians and Lydians were for laments over the dead, and generally for songs of a

---

[1] Aristoph. *Av.* 218. Eurip. *Iph. Taur.* 1061.

[2] The most favourite is the derivation from ἒ ἒ λέγειν; but λέγειν is here an improper form, and ought in this connexion to be λόγος. The entire composition is, moreover, very strange.

ᴍelancholy cast,[1] it will seem likely that the Ionians, together with ditties and tunes of this kind, also received the word *elegos* from their neighbours of Asia Minor.

However great the interval may have been between these Asiatic dirges and the elegy as embellished and ennobled by Grecian taste, yet it cannot be doubted that they were in fact connected. Those laments of Asia Minor were always accompanied by the flute, which was of great antiquity in Phrygia and the neighbouring parts, but which was unknown to the Greeks in Homer's time, and in Hesiod only occurs as used in the boisterous strain of revellers, called *Comos*.[2] The elegy, on the other hand, is the first regularly cultivated branch of Greek poetry, in the recitation of which the flute alone, and neither the cithara nor lyre, was employed. The elegiac poet Mimnermus (about Olympiad 40, 620 B.C.), according to the testimony of Hipponax,[3] nearly as ancient as himself, played on the flute the κραδίης νόμος; that is, literally, ' the fig-branch strain,' a peculiar tune, which was played at the Ionic festival of Thargelia, when the men appointed to make atonement for the sins of the city were driven out with fig branches. Nanno, the beloved of Mimnermus, was a flute player, and he, according to the expression of a later elegiac poet, himself played on the lotus-wood flute, and wore the mouthpiece (the φορβειὰ) used by the ancient flute players when, together with his mistress, he led a comos.[4] And in entire agreement with this the elegiac poet Theognis says, that his beloved and much praised Cyrnus, carried by him on the wings of poetry over the whole earth,

---

[1] Carian and Lydian laments are often mentioned in antiquity (Franch Callinus, p. 123, *seq*.) ; and the antispastic rhythm ᵛ ⁻ ⁻ ᵛ, in which there is something displeasing and harsh, was called καρικὸς ; which refers to its use in laments of this kind. It is also very probable that the word νηνία came from Asia Minor (Pollux IV. 79), and was brought by the Tyrrhenians from Lydia to Etruria, and thence to Rome.

[2] Above, chap. III. § 5.

[3] In Plutarch *de Musicâ*, c. IX. comp. Hesych. in κραδίης νόμος.

[4] This, according to the most probable reading, is the meaning of the passage of Hermesianax in Athen. XIII. p. 598 A. Καίετο μὲν Ναννοῦς, πολιῷ δ' ἐπὶ πολλάκι λωτῷ κημωθεὶς (according to an emendation in the *Classical Journal*, VII. p. 238); κώμους στείχε συνεξανύων (the latter words according to Schweighæuser's reading).

would be present at all banquets, as young men would sing of him eloquently to the clear tone of little flutes.[1]

Nevertheless, we are not to suppose that elegies were from the beginning intended to be sung, and to be recited like lyric poems in the narrower sense of the word. Elegies, that is distichs, were doubtless accompanied by the flute before varied musical forms were invented for them. This did not take place till some time after Terpander the Lesbian, who set hexameters to music, to be sung to the cithara, that is, probably, not before the 40th Olympiad.[2]

When the Amphictyons, after the conquest of Crissa, celebrated the Pythian games (Olymp. 47, 3. B.C. 590), Echembrotus the Arcadian came forward with elegies, which were intended to be sung to the flute: these were of a gloomy, plaintive character, which appeared to the assembled Greeks so little in harmony with the feeling of the festival, that this kind of musical representations was immediately abandoned.[3] Hence it may be inferred that in early times the elegy was recited rather in the style of the Homeric poems, in a lively tone, though probably with this difference, that where the Homerid used the cithara, the flute was employed, for the purpose of making a short prelude and occasional interludes.[4] The flute, as thus applied, does not appear alien to the warlike elegy of Callinus: among the ancients in general the varied tones of the flute[5] were not considered as necessarily having a peaceful character. Not only did the Lydian armies march to battle, as Herodotus states, to the sound of flutes, masculine and feminine; but the Spartans formed their military music of a large number of flutes, instead of the cithara, which had previously been used. From this however we are not to suppose that the elegy was

---

[1] Theognis, v. 237, *seq.*   [2] Plutarch. *de Musicâ*, III. 4, 8.

[3] Pausan. X. 7, 3. From the statement of Chamæleon in Athen. XIV. p. 620, that the poems of Mimnermus as well as those of Homer were set to music (μελῳδηθῆναι), it may be inferred that they were not so from the beginning.

[4] Archilochus says ᾄδων ὑπ' αὐλητῆρος, probably in reference to an elegy (Schol. Aristoph. *Av.* 1428); and Solon is stated to have recited his *Elegy of Salamis* ᾄδων; but in these passages ᾄδων, as in the case of Homer, probably expresses a measured style of recitation like that of a rhapsodist: above, ch. IV. § 3 (p. 44). Compare also Philochorus ap. Athen. XIV. 630.

[5] Πάμφωνοι αὐλοί, Pindar.

ever sung by an army on its march, or advance to the fight, for which purpose neither the rhythm nor the style of the poetry is at all suited. On the contrary, we shall find in Tyrtæus, Archilochus, Xenophanes, Anacreon, and especially in Theognis, so many instances of the reference of elegiac poetry to *banquets*, that we may safely consider the convivial meeting, and especially the latter part of it, called *Comos*, as the appropriate occasion for the Greek elegy.[1]

§ 3. That the elegy was not originally intended to make a completely different impression from the epic poem, is proved by the slight deviation of the elegiac metre from the epic hexameter. It seems as if the spirit of art, impatient of its narrow limits, made with this metre its first timid step out of the hallowed precinct. It does not venture to invent new metrical forms, or even to give a new turn to the solemn hexameter, by annexing to it a metre of a different character: it is contented simply to remove the third and the last thesis from every second hexameter;[2] and it is thus able, without destroying the rhythm, to vary the form of the metre in a highly agreeable manner. The even and regular march of the hexameter is thus accompanied by the feebler and hesitating gait of the pentameter. At the same time, this alternation produces a close union of two verses, which the hexametrical form of the epos, with its uninterrupted flow of versification, did not admit; and thus gives rise to a kind of small strophes. The influence of this metrical character upon the structure of the sentences, and the entire tone of the language, must evidently have been very great.

§ 4. Into the fair form of this metre the Ionic poets breathed a soul, which was vividly impressed with the passing events, and was driven to and fro by the alternate swelling and flowing of a flood of emotions. It is by no means necessary that *lamentations* should form the subject of the elegy, still less that it should be the lamentation of *love;* but *emotion* is always essential to it. Excited by events or circumstances of the

---

[1] The flute is described as used at the Comus in the passage of Hesiod cited above, p. 29 (ch. III. § 5).

[2] Thus, in the first lines of the *Iliad* and the *Odyssey*, by omitting the thesis of the third and sixth feet, a perfect elegiac pentameter is obtained.

Μῆνιν ἄειδε θεὰ|Πη|ληϊάδεω 'Αχιλῆ|ος|

'Ανδρα μοι ἔννεπε Μοῦ|σα πο|λυτρόπον ὃς μάλα πολ|λά.

present time and place, the poet in the circle of his friends and countrymen pours forth his heart in a copious description of his experience, in the unreserved expression of his fears and hopes, in censure and advice. And as the commonwealth was in early times the first thought of every Greek, his feelings naturally gave rise to the political and warlike character of the elegy, which we first meet with in the poems of Callinus.

The age of CALLINUS OF EPHESUS is chiefly fixed by the allusions to the expeditions of the Cimmerians and Treres, which occurred in his poems. The history of these incursions is, according to the best ancient authorities, as follows:—The nation of the Cimmerians, driven out by the Scythians, appeared at the time of Gyges in Asia Minor; in the reign of Ardys (Olymp. 25, 3—37, 4; or 678—29 B.C.) they took Sardis, the capital of the Lydian kings, with the exception of the citadel, and then, under the command of Lygdamis, moved against Ionia; where in particular the temple of the Ephesian Artemis was threatened by them. Lygdamis perished in Cilicia. The tribe of the Treres, who appear to have followed the Cimmerians on their expedition, captured Sardis for the second time in union with the Lycians, and destroyed Magnesia on the Mæander, which had hitherto been a flourishing city, and, with occasional reverses, had on the whole come off superior in its wars with the Ephesians. These Treres, however, under their chieftain Cobus, were (according to Strabo) soon driven back by the Cimmerians under the guidance of Madys. Halyattes, the second successor of Ardys, at last succeeded in driving the Cimmerians out of the country, after they had so long occupied it. (Olymp. 40, 4—55, 1; 617—560 B.C.) Now the lifetime of Callinus stands in relation to these events thus: he mentioned the advance of the formidable Cimmerians and the destruction of Sardis by them, but described Magnesia as still flourishing and as victorious against Ephesus, although he also knew of the approach of the Treres.[1] In such perilous

---

[1] Two fragments of Callinus prove this—

νῦν δ' ἐπὶ Κιμμερίων στρατὸς ἔρχεται ὀβριμοεργῶν,

and

Τρήρεας ἄνδρας ἄγων.

Everything else stated in the text is taken from the precise accounts of Herodotus and Strabo. Pliny's story of the picture of Bularchus 'Magnetum excidium,'

times, when the Ephesians were not only threatened with sub-jugation by their countrymen in Magnesia, but with a still worse fate from the Cimmerians and Treres, there was doubt-less no lack of unwonted inducements for the exertion of every nerve. But the Ionians were already so softened by their long intercourse with the Lydians, a people accustomed to all the luxury of Asia, and by the delights of their beautiful country, that even on such an occasion as this they would not break through the indolence of their usual life of enjoyment. It is easy to see how deep and painful the emotion must have been with which Callinus thus addresses his countrymen : ' How long will you lie in sloth ? when will you, youths, show a courageous heart ? are you not ashamed that the neighbouring nations should see you sunk in this lethargy ? You think in-deed that you are living in peace; but war overspreads the whole earth.'[1]

The fragment which begins with the expressions just cited, the only considerable remnant of Callinus, and even that an imperfect one,[2] is highly interesting as the first specimen of a kind of poetry in which so much was afterwards composed both by Greeks and Romans. In general the character of the elegy may be recognized, as it was determined by the metre, and as it remained throughout the entire literature of antiquity. The elegy is honest and straightforward in its expression; it marks all the parts of its picture with strong touches, and is fond of heightening the effect of its images by contrast. Thus in the verses just quoted Callinus opposes the renown of the brave to the obscurity of cowards. The pentameter itself, being a subordinate part of the metre, naturally leads to an expansion of the original thought by supplementary or explana-tory clauses. This diffuseness of expression, combined with the excited tone of the sentiment, always gives the elegy a certain degree of feebleness which is perceptible even in the martial

---

being bought for an equal weight of gold by Candaules, the predecessor of Gyges, must be erroneous. Probably some other Lydian named Candaules is confounded with the old king.

[1] Gaisford, *Poetæ Minores*, vol. I. p. 426.

[2] It is even doubtful whether the part of this elegiac fragment in Stobæus which follows the hiatus, in fact belongs to Callinus, or whether the name of Tyrtæus has not fallen out.

songs of Callinus and Tyrtæus. On the other hand, it is to be observed that the elegy of Callinus still retains much of the fuller tone of the epic style; it does not, like the shorter breath of later elegies, confine itself within the narrow limits of a distich, and require a pause at the end of every pentameter; but Callinus in many cases comprehends several hexameters and pentameters in one period, without caring for the limits of the verses: in which respect the earlier elegiac poets of Greece generally imitated him.

§ 5. With Callinus we will connect his contemporary TYRTÆUS, probably a few years younger than himself. The age of Tyrtæus is determined by the second Messenian war, in which he bore a part. If with Pausanias this war is placed between Olymp. 23, 4, and 28, 1 (685 and 668 B.C.), Tyrtæus would fall at the same time as, or even earlier than, the circumstances of the Cimmerian invasion mentioned by Callinus; and we should then expect to find that Tyrtæus, and not Callinus, was considered by the ancients as the originator of the elegy. As the reverse is the fact, this reason may be added to others for thinking that the second Messenian war did not take place till after the 30th Olympiad (660 B.C.), which must be considered as the period at which Callinus flourished.

We certainly do not give implicit credit to the story of later writers that Tyrtæus was a lame schoolmaster at Athens, sent out of insolence by the Athenians to the Spartans, who at the command of an oracle had applied to them for a leader in the Messenian war. So much of this account may, however, be received as true, that Tyrtæus came from Attica to the Lacedæmonians; the place of his abode being, according to a precise statement, Aphidnæ, an Athenian town, which is placed by the legends about the Dioscuri in very early connexion with Laconia. If Tyrtæus came from Attica, it is easy to understand how the elegiac metre which had its origin in Ionia should have been used by him, and that in the very style of Callinus. Athens was so closely connected with her Ionic colonies, that this new kind of poetry must have been soon known in the mother city. This circumstance would be far more inexplicable if Tyrtæus had been a Lacedæmonian by birth, as was stated vaguely by some ancient authors. For although Sparta was not at this period a stranger to the efforts of the other Greeks in poetry and music, yet the Spartans with their peculiar modes of thinking would not have been very ready to appropriate the new invention of the Ionians.

Tyrtæus came to the Lacedæmonians at a time when they were not only brought into great straits from without by the boldness of Aristomenes, and the desperate courage of the Messenians, but the state was also rent with internal discord. The dissensions were caused by those Spartans who had owned lands in the conquered Messenia: now that the Messenians had risen against their conquerors, these lands were either in the hands of the enemy, or were left untilled from fear that the enemy would reap their produce; and hence the proprietors of them demanded with vehemence a new division of lands— the most dangerous and dreadful of all measures in the ancient republics. In this condition of the Spartan commonwealth Tyrtæus composed the most celebrated of his elegies, which, from its subject, was called *Eunomia*, that is, ' Justice,' or ' Good Government,' (also *Politeia*, or ' The Constitution'). It is not difficult, on considering attentively the character of the early Greek elegy, to form an idea of the manner in which Tyrtæus probably handled this subject. He doubtless began with remarking the anarchical movement among the Spartan citizens, and by expressing the concern with which he viewed it. But as in general the elegy seeks to pass from an excited state of the mind through sentiments and images of a miscellaneous description to a state of calmness and tranquillity, it may be conjectured that the poet in the *Eunomia* made this transition by drawing a picture of the well-regulated constitution of Sparta, and the legal existence of its citizens, which, founded with the divine assistance, ought not to be destroyed by the threatened innovations; and that at the same time he reminded the Spartans, who had been deprived of their lands by the Messenian war, that on their courage would depend the recovery of their possessions and the restoration of the former prosperity of the state. This view is entirely confirmed by the fragments of Tyrtæus, some of which are distinctly stated to belong to the *Eunomia*. In these the constitution of Sparta is extolled, as being founded by the power of the gods; Zeus himself having given the country to the Heracleids, and the power having been distributed in the justest manner, according to the oracles of the Pythian Apollo, among the kings, the gerons in the council, and the men of the commonalty in the popular assembly.

§ 6. But the *Eunomia* was neither the only nor yet the first elegy in which Tyrtæus stimulated the Lacedæmonians to a bold defence against the Messenians.   Exhortation to bravery was the theme which this poet took for many elegies,[1] and wrote on it with unceasing spirit and ever-new invention. Never was the duty and the honour of bravery impressed on the youth of a nation with so much beauty and force of language, by such natural and touching motives.   In this we perceive the talent of the Greeks for giving to an idea the outward and visible form most befitting it.   In the poems of Tyrtæus we see before us the determined hoplite firmly fixed to the earth, with feet apart, pressing his lips with his teeth, holding his large shield against the darts of the distant enemy, and stretching out his spear with a strong hand against the nearer combatant.   That the young, and even the old, rise up and yield their places to the brave ; that it beseems the youthful warrior to fall in the thick of the fight, as his form is beautiful even in death, while the aged man who is slain in the first ranks is a disgrace to his younger companion from the unseemly appearance of his body : these and similar topics are incentives to valour which could not fail to make a profound impression on a people of fresh feeling and simple character, such as the Spartans then were.

That these poems (although the author of them was a foreigner) breathed a truly Spartan spirit, and that the Spartans knew how to value them, is proved by the constant use made of them in the military expeditions.   When the Spartans were on a campaign, it was their custom, after the evening meal, when the pæan had been sung in honour of the Gods, to recite these elegies.   On these occasions the whole mess did not join in the chant, but individuals vied with each other in repeating the verses in a manner worthy of their subject.   The successful

---

[1] Called Ὑποθῆκαι δι' ἐλεγείας (Suidas); *i. e.* Lessons and exhortations in elegiac verse.

competitor then received from the polemarch or commander a larger portion of meat than the others, a distinction suitable to the simple taste of the Spartans.   This kind of recitation was so well adapted to the elegy, that it is highly probable that Tyrtæus himself first published his elegies in this manner.   The moderation and chastened enjoyment of a Spartan banquet were indeed requisite, in order to enable the guests to take pleasure in so serious and masculine a style of poetry : among guests of other races the elegy placed in analogous circum- stances naturally assumed a very different tone.   The elegies of Tyrtæus were, however, never sung on the march of the army and in the battle itself; for these a strain of another kind was composed by the same poet, viz., the anapæstic marches, to which we shall incidentally revert hereafter.

§ 7. After these two ancient masters of the warlike elegy, we shall pass to two other nearly contemporary poets, who have this characteristic in common, that they distinguished them- selves still more in *iambic* than in *elegiac* poetry. Henceforward this union often appears : the same poet who employs the elegy to express his joyous and melancholy emotions, has recourse to the iambus where his cool sense prompts him to censure the follies of mankind.   This relation of the two metres in question is perceptible in the two earliest iambic poets, ARCHILOCHUS and SIMONIDES OF AMORGUS.   The elegies of Archilochus (of which considerable fragments are extant, while of Simonides we only know that he composed elegies) had nothing of that bitter spirit of which his iambics were full, but they contain the frank expression of a mind powerfully affected by outward circumstances.   Probably these circumstances were in great part connected with the migration of Archilochus from Paros to Thasos, which by no means fulfilled his expectations, as his iambics show.   Nor are his elegies quite wanting in the war- like spirit of Callinus.   Archilochus calls himself the servant of the God of War and the disciple of the Muses;[1] and praises the mode of fighting of the brave Abantes in Eubœa, who en- gaged man to man with spear and sword, and not from afar

---

[1] Εἰμὶ δ' ἐγὼ θεράπων μὲν 'Ενυαλίοιο ἄνακτος
    Καὶ Μουσέων ἐρατὸν δῶρον ἐπιστάμενος.

with arrows and slings; perhaps, from its contrast with the practice of their Thracian neighbours who, probably, greatly annoyed the colonists in Thasos by their wild and tumultuary mode of warfare.[1] But on the other hand, Archilochus avows, without much sense of shame, and with an indifference which first throws a light on this part of the Ionic character, that one of the Saians (a Thracian tribe, with whom the Thasians were often at war) may pride himself in his shield, which he had left behind him in some bushes; he has saved his life, and will get a shield quite as good some other time.[2] In other fragments, Archilochus seeks to banish the recollections of his misfortunes by an appeal to steady patience, and by the conviction that all men are equal sufferers; and praises wine as the best antidote to care.[3] It was evidently very natural that from the custom already noticed among the Spartans, of singing elegies after drinking parties (συμπόσια), there should arise a connexion between the subject of the poem and the occasion on which it was sung; and thus wine and the pleasures of the feast became the subject of the elegy. Symposiac elegies of this kind were, at least in later times, after the Persian war, also sung at Sparta, in which, with all respect for the gods and heroes, the guests were invited to drinking and merriment, to the dance and the song; and, in the genuine Spartan feeling, the man was congratulated who had a fair wife at home.[4] Among the Ionians the elegy naturally took this turn at a much earlier period, and all the various feelings excited by the use of wine, in sadness or in mirth, were doubtless first expressed in an elegiac form. It is natural to expect that the praise of wine was not dissociated from the other ornament of Ionic symposia, the Hetæræ (who, according to Greek manners, were chiefly distinguished from virgins or matrons by their

---

[1] Gaisford, *Poet. Gr. Min.* frag. 4.   [2] *Ib.* frag. 3.   [3] Frag. 1. v. 5; and frag. 7.

[4] It is clear that the elegy of Ion of Chios, the contemporary of Pericles, of which Athen. XI. p. 463, has preserved five distichs, was sung in Sparta or in the Spartan camp: and moreover, at the royal table (called by Xenophon the δαμοσία). For Spartans alone could have been exhorted to make libations to Hercules, to Alcmene, to Procles, and to the Perseids. The reason why Procles alone is mentioned, without Eurysthenes (the other ancestor of the kings of Sparta), can only be that the king saluted in the poem (χαιρέτω ἡμέτερος βασιλεὺς σωτήρ τε πατήρ τε) was a Proclid—that is, from the date, probably, Archidamus.

participation in the banquets of men); and there is extant a distich of a symposiac elegy of Archilochus, in which ' the hospitable Pasiphile, who kindly receives all strangers, as a wild fig-tree feeds many crows,' is ironically praised; in relation to which an anecdote is preserved by Athenæus.[1] This convivial elegy was allowed to collect all the images fitted to drive away the cares of life, and to pour a serene hilarity over the mind. Hence it is probable that some beautiful verses of the Ionic poet Asius of Samos (already mentioned among the epic poets), belonged to a poem of this kind; in which a parasite, forcing himself upon a marriage feast, is described with Homeric solemnity and ironical seriousness, as the maimed, scarred, and gray-haired adorer of the fragrancy of the kitchen, who comes unbidden, and suddenly appears among the guests a hero rising from the mud.[2]

§ 8. This joyous tone of the elegy, which sounded in the verses of Archilochus, did not however hinder this poet from also employing the same metre for strains of lamentation. This application of the elegy is so closely connected with its origin from the Asiatic elegies, that it probably occurred in the verses of Callinus; it must have come from the Ionic coast to the islands, not from the islands to the Ionic coast. An elegy of this kind, however, was not a threnos, or lament for the dead, sung by the persons who accompanied the corpse to its burial place: more probably it was chanted at the meal (called περίδειπνον) given to the kinsmen after the funeral, in the same manner as elegies at other banquets. In Sparta also an elegy was recited at the solemnities in honour of warriors who had fallen for their country. A distich from a poem of this kind, preserved by Plutarch, speaks of those whose only happiness either in life or death consisted in fulfilling the duties of both. Archilochus was induced by the death of his sister's husband, who had perished at sea, to compose an elegy of this description, in which he expressed the sentiment that he would feel less sorrow at the event if Hephæstus had performed his office upon the head and the fair limbs of the dead man, wrapt up in white

---

[1] Fragm. 44.

[2] Athen. III. 125. The earliest certain example of parody, to which we will return in the next chapter. On Asius, see above, ch. IX.

linen; that is to say, if he had died on land, and had been burnt on a funeral pile.[1]

§ 9. Even in the ruins in which the Greek elegy lies before us, it is still the best picture of the race among which it chiefly flourished, viz., the Ionian. In proportion as this race of the Greeks became more unwarlike and effeminate, the elegy was diverted from subjects relating to public affairs and to struggles for national independence. The elegies of MIMNERMUS were indeed in great part political; full of allusions to the origin and early history of his native city, and not devoid of the expression of noble feelings of military honour; but these patriotic and martial sentiments were mingled with vain regrets and melancholy, caused by the subjection of a large part of Ionia, and especially of the native city of Mimnermus, to the Lydian yoke. Mimnermus flourished from about the 37th Olympiad (634 B.C.) until the age of the Seven Wise Men, about Olymp. 45 (600 B.C.): as it cannot be doubted that Solon, in an extant fragment of his poems, addresses Mimnermus, as living—' But if you will, even now, take my advice, erase this; nor bear me any ill-will for having thought on this subject better than you; alter the words, Ligyastades, and sing—May the fate of death reach me in my *sixtieth* year' (and not as Mimnermus wished, in his *eightieth*[2]). Consequently the lifetime of Mimnermus, compared with the reigns of the Lydian kings, falls in the short reign of Sadyattes and the first part of the long reign of Halyattes, which begins in Olym. 40, 4, B.C. 617. The native city of Mimnermus was Smyrna, which had at that time long been a colony of the Ionic city Colophon.[3] Mimnermus, in an extant fragment of his elegy *Nanno*, calls himself one of the colonists of Smyrna, who came from Colophon, and whose ancestors at a still earlier period came from the Nelean Pylos. Now Herodotus, in his accounts of the enterprises of the Lydian kings,

---

[1] Fragm. 6.

[2] 'Αλλ' εἴ μοι καὶ νῦν ἔτι πείσεαι, ἔξελε τοῦτο, μηδὲ μέγαιρ', ὅτι σεῦ λώϊον ἐφρασάμην, καὶ μεταποίησον, Λιγυαστάδη, ὧδε δ' ἄειδε, &c. The emendation of Λιγυαστάδη for ἀγυιασταδὶ is due to a young German philologist. It is rendered highly probable by the comparison of Suidas in Μίμνερμος. This familiar address completes the proof that Mimnermus was then still living.

[3] On the relations of Colophon and Smyrna; see above, ch. V. § 2.

states that Gyges made war upon Smyrna, but did not succeed
in taking it, as he did with Colophon.   Halyattes, however, at
length overcame Smyrna in the early part of his reign.[1] Smyrna,
therefore, together with a considerable part of Ionia, lost its independence during the lifetime of Mimnermus, and lost it for
ever, unless we consider the title of allies, which Athens gave
to its subjects, or the nominal *libertas* with which Rome
honoured many cities in this region, as marks of independent
sovereignty.   It is important to form a clear conception of this
time, when a people of a noble nature, capable of great resolutions and endued with a lively and susceptible temperament, but
wanting in the power of steady resistance and resolute union,
bids a half melancholy, half indifferent, farewell to liberty; it is
important, I repeat, to form a clear conception of this time and
this people, in order to gain a correct understanding of the
poetical character of Mimnermus.   He too could take joy in
valorous deeds, and wrote an elegy in honour of the early battle
of the Smyrnæans against Gyges and the Lydians, whose attack
was then (as we have already stated) successfully repulsed.
Pausanias, who had himself read this elegy,[2] evidently quotes
from it[3] a particular event of this war in question, viz., that the
Lydians had, on this occasion, actually made an entrance into
the town, but that they were driven out of it by the bravery of
the Smyrnæans.   To this elegy also doubtless belongs the fragment (preserved by Stobæus), in which an Ionian warrior is
praised, who drove before him the light squadrons of the mounted
Lydians on the plain of the Hermus (that is in the neighbourhood of Smyrna), and in whose firm valour Pallas Athenè herself could find nothing to blame when he broke through the
first ranks on the bloody battle-field.   As in these lines the poet
refers to what he had heard from his predecessors, who had
themselves witnessed the hero's exploits, it is probable that this

---

[1] This appears first, because Herodotus, I. 16, mentions this conquest immediately after the battle with Cyaxares (who died 594 B.C.) and the expulsion of the
Cimmerians; secondly, because, according to Strabo, XIV. p. 646, Smyrna,
having been divided into separate villages by the Lydians, remained in that state
for 400 years, until the time of Antigonus.   From this it seems that Smyrna fell
into the hands of the Lydians before 600 B.C.; even in that case the period cannot
have amounted to more than 300 years.

[2] IX. 29.   [3] IV. 21.

brave Smyrnæan lived about two generations before the period at which Mimnermus flourished—that is, precisely in the time of Gyges. As the poet, at the outset of this fragment, says— ' *Not such,* as I hear, was the courage and spirit of that warrior,' &c.,[1] we may conjecture that the bravery of this ancient Smyrnæan was contrasted with the effeminacy and softness of the actual generation. It seems, however, that Mimnermus sought rather to work upon his countrymen by a melancholy retrospect of this kind, than to stimulate them to energetic deeds of valour by inspiriting appeals after the manner of Callinus and Tyrtæus : nothing of this kind is cited from his poems.

§ 10. On the other hand, both the statements of the ancients and the extant fragments, show that Mimnermus recommended, as the only consolation in all these calamities and reverses, the enjoyment of the best part of life, and particularly love, which the gods had given as the only compensation for human ills. These sentiments were expressed in his celebrated elegy of *Nanno,* the most ancient erotic elegy of antiquity, which took its name from a beautiful and much-loved flute-player. Yet even this elegy had contained allusions to political events : thus it lamented how Smyrna had always been an apple of discord to the neighbouring nations, and then proceeded with the verses already cited on the taking of the city by the Colophonians :[2] the founder of Colophon, Andræmon of Pylos, was also mentioned in it. But all these reflections on the past and present fortunes of the city were evidently intended only to recommend the enjoyment of the passing hour, as life was only worth having while it could be devoted to love, before unseemly and anxious old age comes on.[3] These ideas, which have since been so often repeated, are expressed by Mimnermus with almost irresistible grace. The beauty of youth and love appears with the greater charm when accompanied with the impression of its caducity,

---

[1] Fragm. 11. Gaisford.   [2] Fragm. 9.
[3] That the subject of the elegy should not be contest and war, but the gifts of the Muses and Aphrodite for the embellishment of the banquet, is a sentiment also expressed by an Ionian later by two generations (Anacreon of Teos), who himself also composed elegies : Οὐ φιλέω ὃς κρητῆρι παρὰ πλέῳ οἰνοποτάζων, Νείκεα καὶ πόλεμον δακρυόεντα λέγει. (Athen. XI. p. 463.)

and the images of joy stand out in the more vivid light as contrasted with the shadows of deep-seated melancholy.[1]

§ 11. With this soft Ionian, who even compassionates the God of the Sun for the toils which he must endure in order to illuminate the earth,[2] SOLON the Athenian forms an interesting contrast. Solon was a man of the genuine Athenian stamp, and for that reason fitted to produce by his laws a permanent influence on the public and private life of his countrymen. In his character were combined the freedom and susceptibility of the Asiatic Ionian, with the energy and firmness of purpose which marked the Athenian. By the former amiable and liberal tendencies he was led to favour a system of ' live and let live,' which so strongly distinguishes his legislation from the severe discipline of the Spartan constitutions : by the latter he was enabled to pursue his proposed ends with unremitting constancy. Hence, too, the elegy of Solon was dedicated to the service of Mars as well as of the Muses ; and under the combined influence of a patriotic disposition like that of Callinus, and of a more enlarged view of human nature, there arose poems of which the loss cannot be sufficiently lamented. But even the extant fragments of them enable us to follow this great and noble-minded man through all the chief epochs of his life.

The *Elegy of Salamis,* which Solon composed about Olymp. 44 (604 B.C.) had evidently more of the fire of youth in it than any other of his poems. The remarkable circumstances under which it was written are related by the ancients, from Demosthenes downwards, with tolerable agreement, in the following manner. The Athenians had from an early period contested the possession of Salamis with the Megarians, and the great power of Athens was then so completely in its infancy, that they were not able to wrest this island from their Doric neighbours, small as was the Megarian territory. The Athenians had suffered so many losses in the attempt, that they not only gave up all propositions in the popular assembly for the reconquest of Salamis, but even made it penal to bring forward such a motion. Under these circumstances, Solon one day

---

[1] Fragg. 1—5. [2] Fragm. 8.

suddenly appeared in the costume of a herald, with the proper cap (πιλίον) upon his head, having previously spread a report that he was mad ; sprang in the place of the popular assembly upon the stone where the heralds were wont to stand, and sang in an impassioned tone an elegy, which began with these words :—
' I myself come as a herald from the lovely island of Salamis, using song, the ornament of words, and not simple speech, to the people.' It is manifest that the poet feigned himself to be a herald sent to Salamis, and returned from his mission ; by which fiction he was enabled to paint in far livelier colours than he could otherwise have done the hated dominion of the Megarians over the island, and the reproaches which many Salaminian partisans of Athens vented in secret against the Athenians. He described the disgrace which would fall upon the Athenians, if they did not reconquer the island, as intolerable. ' In that case (he said) I would rather be an inhabitant of the meanest island than of Athens ; for wherever I might live, the saying would quickly circulate—' This is one of the Athenians who have abandoned Salamis in so cowardly a manner.' '[1] And when Solon concluded with the words ' Let us go to Salamis, to conquer the lovely island, and to wipe out our shame,' the youths of Athens are said to have been seized with so eager a desire of fighting, that an expedition against the Megarians of Salamis was undertaken on the spot, which put the Athenians into possession of the island, though they did not retain it without interruption.

§ 12. A character in many respects similar belongs to the elegy of which Demosthenes cites a long passage in his contest with Æschines on the embassy. This, too, is composed in the form of an exhortation to the people. ' My feelings prompt me (says the poet) to declare to the Athenians how much mischief injustice brings over the city, and that justice everywhere restores a perfect and harmonious order of things.' In this elegy Solon laments with bitter regret the evils in the political state of the commonwealth, the insolence and rapacity of the leaders of the people, i. e. of the popular party, and the misery of the poor, many of whom were sold into slavery by the rich,

---

[1] Fragm. 8.

and carried to foreign countries. Hence it is clear that this elegy is anterior to Solon's legislation, which, as is well known, abolished slavery for debt, and made it impossible to deprive an insolvent debtor of his liberty. These verses give us a livelier picture of this unhappy period of Athens than any historical description. ' The misery of the people (says Solon) forces itself into every man's house : the doors of the court-yard are no longer able to keep it out ; it springs over the lofty wall, and finds out the wretch, even if he has fled into the most secret part of his dwelling.'

But in other of Solon's elegies there is the expression of a subdued and tranquil joy at the ameliorations brought about in Athens by his legislative measures (Olymp. 46, 3. 594 B.C.), by which the holders of property and the commonalty had each received their due share of consideration and power, and both were protected by a firm shield.[1] But this feeling of calm satisfaction was not of long continuance, as Solon observed and soon expressed his opinion in elegies, ' that the people, in its ignorance, was bringing itself under the yoke of a monarch (Pisistratus),' and that it was not the gods, but the thoughtlessness with which the people put the means of obtaining the sovereign power into the hands of Pisistratus, which had destroyed the liberties of Athens.[2]

Solon's elegies were therefore the pure expression of his political feelings; a mirror of his patriotic sympathies with the weal and woe of his country. They moreover exhibit an excited tone of sentiment in the poet, called forth by the warm interest which he takes in the affairs of the community, and by the dangers which threaten its welfare. The prevailing sentiment is a wide and comprehensive humanity. When Solon had occasion to express feelings of a different cast—when he placed himself in a hostile attitude towards his countrymen and contemporaries, and used sarcasm and rebuke, he employed not elegiac, but iambic and trochaic metres. The elegies of Solon are not indeed quite free from complaints and reproaches; but these flow from the regard for the public interests which

---

[1] Fragm. 20.
[2] Fragg. 18, 19. The fragm. 18 has received an additional distich from Diod. Exc. I. VII.—X. in Mai, *Script. vit. Nov. Coll.* vol. II. p. 21.

animated his poetry. The repose which always follows an excited state of the mind, and of which Solon's elegies would naturally present the reflection, was found in the expression of hopes for the future, of a calm reliance on the gods who had taken Athens into their protection, and a serious contemplation of the consequences of good or evil acts. From his habits of reflection, and of reliance on his understanding, rather than his feelings, his elegies contained more general remarks on human affairs than those of any of his predecessors. Some considerable passages of this kind have been preserved; one in which he divides human life into periods of seven years, and assigns to each its proper physical and mental occupations;[1] another in which the multifarious pursuits of men are described, and their inability to command success; for fate brings good and ill to mortals, and man cannot escape from the destiny allotted to him by the gods.[2] Many maxims of a worldly wisdom from Solon's elegies are likewise preserved, in which wealth, and comfort, and sensual enjoyment are recommended, but only so far as was, according to Greek notions, consistent with justice and fear of the gods. On account of these general maxims, which are called γνῶμαι, sayings or apophthegms, Solon has been reckoned among the *gnomic* poets, and his poems have been denominated *gnomic elegies*. This appellation is so far correct, that the gnomic character predominates in Solon's poetry; nevertheless it is to be borne in mind that this calm contemplation of mankind cannot alone constitute an elegy. For the unimpassioned enunciation of moral sentences, the hexameter remained the most suitable form : hence the sayings of PHOCYLIDES of Miletus (about Olymp. 60, B.C. 540), with the perpetually recurring introduction, ' This, too, is a saying of Phocylides,' appear, from the genuine remnants of them, to have consisted only of hexameters.[3]

---

[1] Fragm. 14.   [2] Fragm. 5.

[3] Two distichs cited under the name of Phocylides, in which in the first person he expresses warmth and fidelity to friends, are probably the fragment of an elegy. On the other hand, there is a distich which has the appearance of a jocular appendix to the γνῶμαι, almost of a self-parody:—

Καὶ τόδε Φωκυλίδεω· Λέριοι κακοί· οὐχ ὁ μὲν, ὃς δ' οὔ·
Πάντες, πλὴν Προκλέους, καὶ Προκλέης Λέριος.

(Gaisford, fragm. 5.)

§ 13. The remains of THEOGNIS, on the other hand, belong both in matter and form to the elegy properly so called, although in all that respects their connexion and their character as works of art, they have come down to us in so unintelligible a shape, that at first sight the most copious remains of any Greek elegiac poet that we possess—for more than 1400 verses are preserved under the name of Theognis—would seem to throw less light on the character of the Greek elegy than the much scantier fragments of Solon and Tyrtæus. It appears that from the time of Xenophon, Theognis was considered chiefly as a teacher of wisdom and virtue, and that those parts of his writings which had a general application were far more prized than those which referred to some particular occasion. When, therefore, in later times it became the fashion to extract the general remarks and apophthegms from the poets, everything was rejected from Theognis, by which his elegies were limited to particular situations, or obtained an individual colouring; and the *gnomology* or collection of apophthegms was formed, which, after various revisions and the interpolation of some fragments of other elegiac poets, is still extant. We know, however, that Theognis composed complete elegies, especially one to the Sicilian Megarians, who escaped with their lives at the siege of Megara by Gelon (Olymp. 74, 2. 483 B.C.); and the gnomic fragments themselves exhibit in numerous places the traces of poems which were composed for particular objects, and which on the whole could not have been very different from the elegies of Tyrtæus, Archilochus, and Solon. As in these poems of Theognis there is a perpetual reference to political subjects, it will be necessary first to cast a glance at the condition of Megara in his time.

§ 14. Megara, the Doric neighbour of Athens, had, after its separation from Corinth, remained for a long time under the undisturbed dominion of a Doric nobility, which founded its claim to the exercise of the sovereign power both on its descent, and its possession of large landed estates. But before the legislation of Solon, Theagenes had raised himself to absolute power over the Megarians by pretending to espouse the popular cause. After he had been overthrown, the aristocracy was restored, but only for a short period, as the commons rose with violence against the nobles, and founded a democracy, which however led to such a state of anarchy, that the expelled nobles found the means of regaining their lost power. Now the poetry of Theognis, so far as its political character extends, evidently falls in the beginning of this democracy, probably nearer to the 70th (500 B.C.) than the 60th Olympiad (540 B.C.) : for Theognis, although according to the ancient accounts he was born before the 60th Olympiad, yet from his own verses appears to have lived to the Persian war (Olymp. 75. 480 B.C.). Revolutions of this kind were in the ancient Greek states usually accompanied with divisions of the large landed estates among the commons ; and by a fresh partition of the Megarian territory, made by the democratic party, Theognis, who happened to be absent on a voyage, was deprived of the rich heritage of his ancestors. Hence he longs for vengeance on the men who had spoiled him of his property, while he himself had only escaped with his life ; like a dog who throws everything away in order to cross a torrent,[1] and the cry of the crane, which gives warning of the season of tillage, reminds him of his fertile fields now in other men's hands.[2] These fragments are therefore full of allusions to the violent political measures which in Greece usually accompanied the accession of the democratic party to power. One of the principal changes on such occasions was commonly the adoption into the sovereign community of *Periœci*, that is, cultivators who were before excluded from all share in the government. Of this Theognis says,[3] ' Cyrnus, this city is still the city, but a different people are in it, who formerly knew nothing of courts of justice and laws, but wore their country dress of goat-skins at their work, and like timid deer dwelt at a distance from the town. And now they are the better class ; and those who were formerly noble are now the mean : who can endure to see these things ?' The expressions *good* and *bad* men (ἀγαθοὶ, ἐσθλοὶ and κακοὶ, δειλοὶ), which in later times bore a purely moral signification, are evidently used by Theognis in a political sense for nobles and commons ; or rather his use of these words rests in fact upon the supposition that a brave spirit and honourable conduct can be expected only

---

[1] v. 345, *seq.* ed. Bekker.   [2] v. 1297, *seq.*   [3] 53, *seq.*

of men descended from a family long tried in peace and war.
Hence his chief complaint is, that the good man, that is, the
noble, is now of no account as compared with the rich man;
and that wealth is the only object of all. 'They honour
riches, and thus the good marries the daughter of the bad, and
the bad marries the daughter of the good : wealth corrupts the
blood.'[1] Hence, son of Polypas, do not wonder if the race of
the citizens loses its brightness, for good and bad are confounded
together.'[2] Theognis doubtless made this complaint on the
debasement of the Megarian nobility with the stronger feeling
of bitterness, as he himself had been rejected by the parents of
a young woman, whom he had desired to marry, and a far
worse man, that is, a man of plebeian blood, had been preferred
to him.[3] Yet the girl herself was captivated with the noble
descent of Theognis : she hated her ignoble husband, and came
disguised to the poet, ' with the lightness of a little bird,'
as he says.[4]

With regard to the union of these fragments into entire
elegies, it is important to remark that all the complaints, warn-
ings, and lessons having a political reference, appear to be addressed to a *single* young friend of the poet, Cyrnus, the son of
Polypas.[5] Wherever other names occur, either the subject is
quite different, or it is at least treated in a different manner.
Thus there is a considerable fragment of an elegy addressed by
Theognis to a friend named Simonides, at the time of the
revolution, which in the poems addressed to Cyrnus is described as passed by. In this passage the insurrection is
described under the favourite image of a ship tossed about
by winds and waves, while the crew have deposed the skilful
steersman, and entrusted the guidance of the helm to the
common working sailor. ' Let this (the poet adds) be revealed to the good in enigmatic language ; yet a bad man

---

[1] πλοῦτος ἔμιξε γένος.

[2] v. 189, *seq.*   [3] v. 261, *seq.*   [4] v. 1091.

[5] Elmsley has remarked that Πολυπαΐδη is to be read as a patronymic. The
remark is certain, as Πολυπαΐδη never occurs before a consonant, but nine times
before a vowel, and moreover in passages where the verse requires a dactyl. The
exhortations with the addresses Κύρνε and Πολυπαΐδη are also closely connected.
Πολύπας (with the long α) has the same meaning as πολυπάμων, a rich proprietor.

may understand it, if he has sense.'[1] It is manifest that this poem was composed during a reign of terror, which checked the freedom of speech; on the other hand, in the poems addressed to Cyrnus, Theognis openly displays all his opinions and feelings. So far is he from concealing his hatred of the popular party, that he wishes that he could drink the blood of those who had deprived him of his property.[2]

§ 15. On attempting to ascertain more precisely the relation of Cyrnus to Theognis, it appears that the son of Polypas was a youth of noble family, to whom Theognis bore a tender, but at the same time paternal, regard, and whom he desires to see a 'good' citizen, in his sense of the word. The interest felt by the poet in Cyrnus probably appeared much more clearly in the complete elegies than in the gnomic extracts now preserved, in which the address to Cyrnus might appear a mere superfluity. Several passages have, however, been preserved, in which the true state of his relation to Theognis is apparent. 'Cyrnus (says the poet) when evil befals you, we all weep; but grief for others is with you only a transient feeling.'[3] 'I have given you wings, with which you will fly over sea and land, and will be present at all banquets, as young men will sing of you to the flute. Even in future times your name will be dear to all the lovers of song, so long as the earth and sun endure. But to me you show but little respect, deceiving me with words like a little boy.'[4] It is plain that Cyrnus did not place in Theognis that entire confidence which the poet desired. It cannot, however, be doubted that these affectionate appeals and tender reproaches are to be taken in the sense of the earlier and pure Doric custom, and that no connexion of a criminal nature is to be understood, with which it would be inconsistent that the poet recommends a married life to the youth.[5] Cyrnus also is sufficiently old to be sent as a sacred envoy ($\theta\epsilon\omega\rho\grave{o}\varsigma$) to Delphi, in order to bring back an oracle to

---

[1] In v. 667—82 there is a manifest allusion to the $\gamma\hat{\eta}s$ $\dot{\alpha}\nu\alpha\delta\alpha\sigma\mu\grave{o}s$ in the verses
Χρήματα δ' ἁρπάζουσι βίῃ, κόσμος δ' ἀπόλωλεν,
Δασμὸς δ' οὐκέτ' ἴσος γίγνεται ἐς τὸ μέσον.

[2] v. 349.   [3] v. 655, seq.   [4] v. 237, seq.   [5] v. 1225.

the city.   The poet exhorts him to preserve it faithfully, and not to add or to omit a word.[1]

The poems of Theognis, even in the form in which they are extant, place us in the middle of a circle of friends, who formed a kind of eating society, like the philitia of Sparta, and like the ancient public tables of Megara itself.   The Spartan public tables are described to us as a kind of aristocratic clubs; and these societies in Megara might serve to awaken and keep alive an aristocratic disposition.   Theognis himself thinks that those who, according to the original constitution of Megara, possessed the chief power, were the only persons with whom any one ought to eat and drink, and to sit, and whom he should strive to please.[2]   It is therefore manifest that all the friends whom Theognis names, not only Cyrnus and Simonides, but also Onomacritus, Clearistus, Democles, Demonax, and Timagoras, belonged to the class of the 'good,' although the political maxims are only addressed to Cyrnus.   Various events in the lives of these friends, or the qualities which each showed at their convivial meetings, furnished occasions for separate, but probably short elegies.   In one the poet laments that Clearistus should have made an unfortunate voyage, and promises him the assistance which is due to one connected with his family by ancient ties of hospitality :[3] in another he wishes a happy voyage to the same or another friend.[4]   To Simonides, as being the chief of the society, he addresses a farewell elegy, exhorting him to leave to every guest his liberty, not to detain any one desirous to depart, or to waken the sleeping, &c.;[5] and to Onomacritus the poet laments over the consequences of inordinate drinking.[6]   Few of the persons whom he addresses appear to have been without this circle of friends, although his fame had even in his lifetime spread far beyond Megara, by means of his travels as well as of his poetry ; and his elegies were sung in many symposia.[7]

---

[1] v. 805, *seq.*   [2] v. 36, *seq.*   [3] v. 511, *seq.*   [4] v. 691, *seq.*
[5] v. 469, *seq.*   [6] v. 305, *seq.*

[7] Theognis himself mentions that he had been in Sicily, Eubœa, and Sparta, v. 387, *seq.* In Sicily he composed the elegy for his countrymen, which has been mentioned in the text, the colonists from Megara of Megara Hyblæa. The verses 891—4 must have been written in Eubœa. Many allusions to Sparta occur, and

The poetry of Theognis is full of allusions to symposia: so that from it a clear conception of the outward accompaniments of the elegy may be formed. When the guests were satisfied with eating, the cups were filled with the solemn libation ; and at this ceremony a prayer was offered to the gods, especially to Apollo, which in many districts of Greece was expanded into a pœan. Here began the more joyous and noisy part of the banquet, which Theognis (as well as Pindar) calls in general κῶμος, although this word in a narrower sense also signified the tumultuous throng of the guests departing from the feast.[1] Now the Comos was usually accompanied with the flute :[2] hence Theognis speaks in so many places of the accompaniment of the fluteplayer to the poems sung in the intervals of drinking ;[3] while the lyre and cithara (or phorminx) are rarely mentioned, and then chiefly in reference to the song at the libation.[4] And this was the appropriate occasion for the elegy, which was sung by one of the guests to the sound of a flute, being either addressed to the company at large, or (as is always the case in Theognis) to a single guest.

§ 16. We have next to speak of the poems of a man different in his character from any of the elegiac poets hitherto treated of ; a philosopher, whose metaphysical speculations will be considered in a future chapter. XENOPHANES of Colophon, who about the 68th Olympiad (508 B.C.) founded the celebrated school of Elea, at an earlier period, while he was still living at Colophon, gave vent to his thoughts and feelings on the circumstances surrounding him, in the form of elegies.[5] These elegies, like those of Archilochus, Solon, Theognis, &c., were symposiac : there is preserved in Athenæus a considerable fragment, in which the beginning of a symposion is described with much distinctness and elegance, and the guests are exhorted,

---

the passage v. 880—4 is probably from an elegy written by Theognis for a Spartan friend, who had a vineyard on Taygetus. The most difficult of explanation are v. 1200 and 1211, *seq.*, which can scarcely be reconciled with the circumstances of the life of Theognis.

[1] See Theogn. v. 829, 940, 1046, 1065, 1207.   [2] See above, § 2.

[3] v. 241, 761, 825, 941, 975, 1041, 1056, 1065.   [4] v. 534, 761, 791.

[5] There are, however, in Diogenes Laërtius elegiac verses of Xenophanes, in which he states himself to be ninety-two years old, and speaks of his wanderings in Greece.

after the libation and song of praise to the gods, to celebrate over their cups brave deeds and the exploits of youths (*i.e.* in elegiac strains) ; and not to sing the fictions of ancient poets on the battles of Titans, or giants, or centaurs, and such like stories. From this it is evident that Xenophanes took no pleasure in the ordinary amusements at the banquets of his countrymen ; and from other fragments of the same writer, it also appears that he viewed the life of the Greeks with the eye of a philosopher. Not only does he blame the luxury of the Colophonians, which they had learnt from the Lydians,[1] but also the folly of the Greeks in valuing an athlete who had been victorious at Olympia in running or wrestling, higher than the wise man ; a judgment which, however reasonable in our eyes, must have seemed exceedingly perverse to the Greeks of his days.

§ 17. As we intend in this chapter to bring down the history of the elegy to the Persian war, we must also mention SIMO-NIDES of Ceos, the renowned lyric poet, the early contemporary of Pindar and Æschylus, and so distinguished in elegy that he must be included among the great masters of the elegiac song. Simonides is stated to have been victorious at Athens over Æschylus himself, in an elegy in honour of those who fell at Marathon (Olymp. 72, 3 ; 490 B.C.), the Athenians having in-stituted a contest of the chief poets. The ancient biographer of Æschylus, who gives this account, adds in explanation, that the elegy requires a tenderness of feeling which was foreign to the character of Æschylus. To what a degree Simonides pos-sessed this quality, and in general how great a master he was of the pathetic is proved by his celebrated lyric piece con-taining the lament of Danae, and by other remains of his poetry. Probably, also, in the elegies upon those who died at Marathon and at Platæa, he did not omit to bewail the death of so many brave men, and to introduce the sorrows of the widows and orphans, which was quite consistent with a lofty

---

[1] The thousand persons clothed in purple, who, *before the time of the Tyrants*, were, according to Xenophanes (in Athen. XII. p. 526), together in the market-place, formed an aristocratic body among the citizens (τὸ πολίτευμα) ; such as, at this time of transition from the ancient hereditary aristocracies to democracy, also existed in Rhegium, Locri, Croton, Agrigentum, and Cyme in Æolis.

patriotic tone, particularly at the end of the poem.   Simonides likewise, like Archilochus and others, used the elegy as a plaintive song for the deaths of individuals; at least the Greek *Anthology* contains several pieces of Simonides, which appear not to be entire epigrams, but fragments of longer elegies lamenting with heartfelt pathos the death of persons dear to the poet.   Among these are the verses concerning Gorgo, who dying, utters these words to her mother:—'Remain here with my father, and become with a happier fate the mother of another daughter, who may tend you in your old age.'

From this example we again see how the elegy in the hands of different masters sometimes obtained a softer and more pathetic, and sometimes a more manly and robust tone.   Nevertheless there is no reason for dividing the elegy into different kinds, such as the military, political, symposiac, erotic, threnetic, and gnomic; inasmuch as some of these characters are at times combined in the same poem.   Thus the elegy was usually, as we have seen, sung at the symposion; and, in most cases, its main subject is political; after which it assumes either an amatory, a plaintive, or a sententious tone.   At the same time the elegy always retains its appropriate character, from which it never departs.   The feelings of the poet, excited by outward circumstances, seek a vent at the symposion, either amidst his friends or sometimes in a larger assembly, and assume a poetical form. A free and full expression of the poet's sentiments is of the essence of the Greek elegy.   This giving a vent to the feelings is in itself tranquillizing; and as the mind disburdens itself of its alarms and anxieties a more composed state naturally ensued, with which the poem closed.   When the Greek nation arrived at the period at which men began to express in a proverbial form general maxims of conduct,—a period beginning with the age of the Seven Wise Men, these maxims, or γνῶμαι, were the means by which the elegiac poets subsided from emotion into calmness.   So far the elegy of Solon, Theognis, and Xenophanes, may be considered as gnomic, although it did not therefore assume an essentially new character.   That in the Alexandrine period of literature the elegy assumed a different tone, which was, *in part*, borrowed by the Roman poets, will be shown in a future chapter.

§ 18. This place is the most convenient for mentioning a subordinate kind of poetry, the *epigram*, as the elegiac form was the best suited to it; although there are also epigrams composed in hexameters and other metres. The epigram was originally (as its name purports) an inscription on a tombstone, on a votive offering in a temple, or on any other object which required explanation. Afterwards, from the analogy of these real epigrams, thoughts, excited by the view of any object, and which *might* have served as an inscription, were called epigrams, and expressed in the same form. That this form was the elegiac may have arisen from the circumstance that epitaphs appeared closely allied with laments for the dead, which (as has been already shown) were at an early period composed in this metre. However, as this elegy comprehended all the events of life which caused a strong emotion, so the epigram might be equally in place on a monument of war, and on the sepulchral pillar of a beloved kinsman or friend. It is true that the mere statement of the purpose and meaning of the object,—for example, in a sacred offering, the person who gave it, the god to whom it was dedicated, and the subject which it represented— was much prized, if made with conciseness and elegance; and epigrams of this kind were often ascribed to renowned poets, in which there is no excellence besides the brevity and complete- ness of these statements, and the perfect adaptation of the metrical form to the thought. Nevertheless, in general, the object of the Greek epigram is to ennoble a subject by eleva- tion of thought and beauty of language. The unexpected turn of the thought and the pointedness of expression, which the moderns consider as the essence of this species of composition, were not required in the ancient Greek epigram; in which nothing more is requisite than that the entire thought should be conveyed within the limits of a few distichs : and thus in the hands of the early poets the epigram was remarkable for the conciseness and expressiveness of its language; differing in this respect from the elegy, in which a full vent was given to the feelings of the poet.

Epigrams were probably composed in an elegiac form, shortly after the time when the elegy first arose ; and the *Anthology* contains some under the celebrated names of Archilochus,

Sappho, and Anacreon. No peculiar character, however, is to be observed in the genuine epigrams of this early period. It was Simonides, with whom we have closed the series of elegiac poets, who first gave to the epigram the perfection of which, consistently with its purpose, it was capable. In this respect Simonides was favoured by the circumstances of his time ; for on account of the high consideration which he enjoyed both in Athens and Peloponnesus, he was frequently employed by the states which fought against the Persians to adorn with inscriptions the tombs of their fallen warriors. The best and most celebrated of these epitaphs is the inimitable inscription on the Spartans who died at Thermopylæ, which actually existed on the spot : ' Foreigner, tell the Lacedæmonians that we are lying here in obedience to their laws.'[1] Never was heroic courage expressed with such calm and unadorned grandeur. In all these epigrams of Simonides the characteristic peculiarity of the battle in which the warriors fell is seized. Thus in the epigram on the Athenians who died at Marathon—' Fighting in the van of the Greeks, the Athenians at Marathon destroyed the power of the glittering Medians.'[2] There are besides not a few epigrams of Simonides which were intended for the tombstones of individuals : among these we will only mention one which differs from the others in being a sarcasm in the form of an epitaph. It is that on the Rhodian lyric poet and athlete Timocreon, an opponent of Simonides in his art : ' Having eaten much, and drunk much, and said much evil of other men, here I lie, Timocreon the Rhodian.'[3] With the epitaphs are naturally connected the inscriptions on sacred offerings, especially where both refer to the Persian war ; the former being the discharge of a debt to the dead, the latter a thanksgiving of the survivors to the gods. Among these one of the best refers to the battle of Marathon, which, from the neatness and elegance of the expression, loses its chief beauty in a prose translation.[4] It was inscribed on the statue of Pan, which the Athenians had set up in a grotto under their acropolis, because the Arcadian

---

[1] Simonides, fr. 27. ed. Gaisford.   [2] In Lycurgus and Aristides.
[3] Fr. 58.   [4] The words are these (fr. 25)—

Τὸν τραγόπουν ἐμὲ Πᾶνα, τὸν Ἀρκάδα, τὸν κατὰ Μήδων,
Τὸν μετ' Ἀθηναίων στήσατο Μιλτιάδης.

god had, according to the popular belief, assisted them at Marathon. ' Miltiades set up me, the cloven-footed Pan, the Arcadian, who took part against the Medians, and with the Athenians.' But Simonides sometimes condescended to express sentiments which he could not have shared, as in the inscription on the tripod consecrated at Delphi, which the Greeks after-wards caused to be erased : ' Pausanias, the commander of the Greeks, having destroyed the army of the Medes, dedicated this monument to Phœbus.' [1] These verses express the arrogance of the Spartan general, which the good sense and moderation of the poet would never have approved. The form of nearly all these epigrams of Simonides is the elegiac. Simonides usually ad-hered to it except when a name (on account of a short between two long syllables) could not be adapted to the dactylic metre ; [2] in which cases he employed trochaic measures. The character of the language, and especially the dialect, also remained on the whole true to the elegiac type, except that in inscriptions for monuments designed for Doric tribes, traces of the Doric dialect sometimes occur.

---

[1] Fr. 40.   [2] As Ἀρχεναύτης, Ἱππόνικος.

CHAPTER XI.

IAMBIC POETRY.

§ 1. Striking contrast of the Iambic and other contemporaneous Poetry. § 2. Poetry in reference to the bad and the vulgar. § 3. Different treatment of it in Homer and Hesiod. § 4. Homeric Comic Poems, *Margites*, &c. § 5. Scurrilous songs at meals, at the worship of Demeter; the Festival of Demeter of Paros the cradle of the Iambic poetry of Archilochus. § 6. Date and Public Life of Archilochus. § 7. His Private Life; subject of his Iambics. § 8. Metrical form of his iambic and trochaic verses, and different application of the two asynartetes; epodes. § 9. Inventions and innovations in the musical recitation. § 10. Innovations in Language. § 11. Simonides of Amorgus; his *Satirical Poems against Women.* § 12. Solon's iambics and trochaics. § 13. Iambic Poems of Hipponax; invention of choliambics; Ananias. § 14. The Fable; its application among the Greeks, especially in Iambic poetry. § 15. Kinds of the Fable, named after different races and cities. § 16. Æsop, his Life, and the Character of his Fables. § 17. Parody, burlesques in an epic form, by Hipponax. § 18. *Batrachomyomachia.*

§ 1. THE kind of poetry distinguished among the ancients by the name Iambic, was created by the Parian poet Archilochus, at the same time as the elegy. In entering on the consideration of this sort of poetry, and in endeavouring by the same process as we have heretofore employed to trace its origin to the character of the Grecian people, and to estimate its poetical and moral value, we are met at the first glance by facts more difficult, and apparently more impossible of comprehension, than any we have hitherto encountered. At a time when the Greeks, accustomed only to the calm unimpassioned tone of the Epos, had but just found a temperate expression of livelier emotions in the elegy, this kind of poetry, which has nothing in common with the Epos, either in form or in matter, arose. It was a light tripping measure, sometimes loosely constructed or purposely halting and broken, and well adapted to vituperation, unrestrained by any regard to morality or decency.[1]

---

[1] Λυσσῶντες ἴαμβοι, *raging iambics,* says the Emperor Hadrian. (Brunck, *Anal.* II. p. 286.)

'In celeres iambos misit furentem.'—Horace.

The ancients drew a lively image of this bitter and unscrupulous spirit of slanderous attack in the well-known story of the daughters of Lycambes, who hanged themselves from shame and vexation.   Yet this sarcastic Archilochus, this venomous libeller, was esteemed by antiquity not only an unrivalled master in his peculiar line, but, generally, the first poet after Homer.[1]   Where, we are compelled to ask, is the soaring flight of the soul which distinguishes the true poet?   Where that beauty of delineation which confers grace and dignity even on the most ordinary details?

§ 2. But Poetry has not only lent herself, in every age, to the descriptions of a beautiful and magnificent world, in which the natural powers revealed to us by our own experience are invested with a might and a perfection surpassing truth : she has also turned back her glance upon the reality by which she was surrounded, with all its wants and its weaknesses; and the more she was filled with the beauty and the majestic grace of her own ideal world, the more deeply did she feel, the more vividly express, the evils and the deficiencies attendant on man's condition.   The modes in which Poetry has accomplished this have been various; as various as the tempers and the characters of those whom she has inspired.

A man of a serene and cheerful cast of mind, satisfied with the order of the universe, regarding the great and the beautiful in nature and in human things with love and admiration, though he distinctly perceives the defective and the bad, does not suffer his perception of them to disturb his enjoyment of the whole : he contemplates it as the shade in a picture, which serves but to bring out, not to obscure, the brilliancy of the principal parts.   A light jest drops from the poet's tongue, a pitying smile plays on his lip; but they do not darken or deform the lofty beauty of his creations.

The thoughts, the occupations, of another are more intimately blended with the incidents and the conditions of social and civil life; and as a more painful experience of all the errors and perversities of man is thus forced upon him, his voice, even in poetry, will assume a more angry and vehement tone.   And

---

[1] Maximus poeta aut certe summo proximus; as he is called in Valerius Maximus.

yet even this voice of harsh rebuke may be poetical, when it is accompanied by a pure and noble conception of things as they ought to be.

Yet more, the poet may himself suffer from the assaults of human passions. He may himself be stained with the vices and the weaknesses of human nature, and his voice may be poured forth from amidst the whirl and the conflict of the passions, and may be troubled, not only by disgust at the sight of interruptions to the moral order of the world, but by personal resentments and hatreds. The ancients in their day, and we in ours, have bestowed admiring sympathy on such a poet, if the expressions of his scorn and his hate did but betray an unusual vehemence of feeling and vigour of thought; and if, through all the passionate confusion of his spirit, gleams of a nature susceptible of noble sentiments were apparent; for the impotent rage of a vulgar mind will never rise to the dignity of poetry, even though it be adorned with all the graces of language.

§ 3. Here, as in many other places, it will be useful to recur to the two epic poets of antiquity, the authors of all the principles of Greek literature. Homer, spite of the solemnity and loftiness of epic poetry, is full of archness and humour; but it is of that cheerful and good-natured character which tends rather to increase than to disturb enjoyment. Thersites is treated with unqualified severity; and we perceive the peculiar disgust of the monarchically disposed poet at such inciters of the people, who slander everything distinguished and exalted, merely because they are below it. But it must be remarked that Thersites is a very subordinate figure in the group of heroes, and serves only as a foil to those who, like Ulysses, predominate over the people as guides and rulers. When, however, persons of a nobler sort are exhibited in a comic light, as, for instance, Agamemnon, blinded by Zeus and confident in his delusion and in his supposed wisdom,[1] it is done with such a delicacy of handling that the hero hardly loses any of his dignity in our eyes. In this way the comedy of Homer (if we may use the expression) dared even to touch the gods, and in the loftiest regions found subjects for humorous descriptions :

---

[1] See ch. V. § 8.

for, as the gods presided over the moral order of the universe
only as a body, and no individual god could exercise his special
functions without regard to the prerogatives of others, Ares,
Aphrodite, and Hermes might serve as types of the perfection
of quarrelsome violence, of female weakness, and of finished
cunning, without ceasing to have their due share of the honours
paid to divinity.

Of a totally different kind is the wit of Hesiod; especially as
it is employed in the *Theogony* against the daughters of Pandora, the female sex. This has its source in a strong feeling of
disgust and indignation, which leads the poet, in the bitterness
of his mood, to overstep the bounds of justice, and to deny all
virtue to women.

In the *Works and Days*, too, which afford him frequent opportunities for censure, Hesiod is not deficient in a kind of wit
which exhibits the bad and the contemptible with striking
vigour; but his wit is never that gay humour which characterizes the Homeric poetry, of which it is the singular property
to reconcile the frail and the faulty with the grand and the
elevated, and to blend both in one harmonious idea.

§ 4. Before, however, we come to the consideration of the
third stage of the poetical representation of the bad and the
despicable, the existence of which we have hinted at in our
mention of Archilochus, we must remark that even the early
epic poetry contained not only scattered traits of pleasantry
and satire, but also entire pictures in the same tone, which
formed small epics. On this head we have great reason to
lament the loss of the *Margites*, which Aristotle, in his *Poetics*,
ascribes, according to the opinion current among the Greeks, to
Homer himself, and regards as the ground-work of comedy, in
like manner as he regards the *Iliad* and the *Odyssey* as the
precursors of tragedy. He likewise places the *Margites* in the
same class with poems written in the iambic metre; but he
seems to mean that the iambus was not employed for this class
of poetry till subsequently to this poem. Hence it is extremely
probable that the iambic verses which, according to the ancient
grammarians, were introduced irregularly into the *Margites*,
were interpolated in a later version, perhaps by Pigres the Hali-

carnassian, the brother of Artemisia, who is also called the author of this poem.[1]

From the few fragments and notices relative to the Homeric *Margites* which have come down to us, we can gather that it was a representation of a stupid man, who had a high opinion of his own cleverness, for he was said ' to know many works, but know all badly ;'[2] and we discover from a story preserved by Eustathius that it was necessary to hold out to him very subtle reasons to induce him to do things which required but a very small portion of intellect.[3]

There were several other facetious small epics which bore the name of Homer; such as the poem of the *Cercopes*, those malicious, and yet merry elves whom Hercules takes prisoners after they have played him many mischievous tricks, and drags them about till they escape from him by fresh stratagems; the *Batrachomyomachia*, which we shall have occasion to mention hereafter as an example of parody; the *Seven times shorn Goat* (αἴξ ἑπτάπεκτος), and the *Song of the Fieldfares* (ἐπικιχλίδες), which Homer is said to have sung to the boys for fieldfares. Some few such pleasantries have come down to us, particularly the poem of the *Pot-kiln* (κάμινος ἢ κεραμὶς), which applies the imagination and mythological machinery of the epic style to the business of pottery.

§ 5. These humorous poems are too innocuous and too free from personal attacks to have much resemblance to the caustic iambics of Archilochus. More akin to them undoubtedly were the satirical songs which, according to the Homeric hymn to Hermes, the young men sang extemporaneously in a sort of wanton mutual defiance.[4] At the public tables of Sparta, also, keen and pointed raillery was permitted, and conversation sea-

---

[1] Thus the beginning of the *Margites* was as follows:—

Ἦλθέ τις εἰς Κολοφῶνα γέρων καὶ θεῖος ἀοιδός,
Μουσάων θεράπων καὶ ἐκηβόλου Ἀπόλλωνος,
Φίλης ἔχων ἐν χερσὶν εὔφθογγον λύρην.

Concerning Pigres, see below, § 18. He also interpolated the *Iliad* with pentameters.

[2] Πόλλ' ἠπίστατο ἔργα, κακῶς δ' ἠπίστατο πάντα.

[3] Eustath. ad *Od.* X. 552, p. 1669, ed. Rom.

[4] v. 55, *seq.*, ἐξ αὐτοσχεδίης . . . . ἠὕτε κοῦροι
ἡβηταῖ θαλίῃσι παραιβόλα κερτομέουσιν.

soned with Spartan salt was not held to afford any reasonable
ground of offence to those who took part in it. But an occasion
for yet more audacious and unsparing jest was afforded to the
Greeks by some of the most venerable and sacred of their religious rites—the permission, or rather encouragément to wanton
and unrestrained jokes on everything affording matter for such
ebullitions of mirth, connected with certain festivals of Demeter,
and the deities allied to her. It was a law at these festivals
that the persons engaged in their celebration should, on certain
days, banter all who came in their way, and assail them with
keen and licentious raillery.[1] This was the case at the mystic
festival of Demeter at Eleusis, among others. Hence, also,
Aristophanes in the *Frogs* introduces a chorus of the initiated,
who lead a blissful life in the infernal regions, and makes
them pray to Demeter that she would grant them to sport
and dance securely the livelong day, and have much jocose
and much serious talk; and, if the festival had been worthily
honoured by jest and merriment, that they might be crowned
as victors. The chorus also, after inviting the jolly god
Iacchus to take part in its dances, immediately proceeds
to exercise its wit in satirical verses on various Athenian
demagogues and cowards. This raillery was so ancient and
inveterate a custom that it had given rise to a peculiar
word, which originally denoted nothing but the jests and banter
used at the festivals of Demeter, namely, *Iambus*.[2] This was
soon converted into a mythological person, the maid Iambe,

---

[1] Concerning the legality of this religious license there is an important passage in Aristotle, *Pol.* VII. 15. We will set down the entire passage as we understand it :—' As we banish from the state the speaking of indecent things, it is
clear that we also prohibit indecent pictures and representations. The magistrate
must therefore provide that no statue or picture of this kind exist, except for certain
deities, of the class to which the law allows scurrilous jesting (οἷς καὶ τὸν τωθασμὸν
ἀποδίδωσιν ὁ νόμος). At temples of this kind the law also permits all persons of a
mature age to pray to the gods for themselves, their children and wives. But
younger persons ought to be prohibited from being present at the recitation of
iambic verses, or at comedies, until they have reached the age at which they may
sit at table and drink to intoxication.'

[2] It is vain to seek an etymology for the word *iambus:* the most probable supposition is, that it originated in exclamations, ὀλολυγμοί, expressive of joy. Similar in form are θρίαμβος, the Bacchic festival procession; διθύραμβος, a Bacchic
hymn, and ἴθυμβος, also a kind of Bacchic song.

who by some jest first drew a smile from Demeter bewailing her lost daughter, and induced her to take the barley drink of the cyceon; a legend native to Eleusis, which the Homerid who composed the hymn to Demeter has worked up into an epic form.   If we consider that according to the testimony of the same hymn, the island of Paros, the birth-place of Archilochus, was regarded as, next to Eleusis, the peculiar seat of Demeter and Cora; that the Parian colony Thasos, in the settlement of which Archilochus himself had a share, embraced the mystic rites of Demeter as the most important worship;[1] that Archilochus himself obtained the prize of victory over many competitors for a hymn to Demeter, and that one whole division of his songs, called the Io-bacchi, were consecrated to the service of Demeter and the allied worship of Bacchus;[2] we shall entertain no doubt that these festal customs afforded Archilochus an occasion of producing his unbridled iambics, for which the manners of the Greeks furnished no other time or place; and that with his wit and talent he created a new kind of poetry out of the raillery which had hitherto been uttered extempore.   All the wanton extravagance which was elsewhere repressed and held in check by law and custom, here, under the protection of religion, burst forth with boundless license; and these scurrilous effusions were at length reduced by Archilochus into the systematic form of iambic metre.

§ 6. The time at which this took place was the same with that in which the elegy arose, or but little later. ARCHILOCHUS was a son of Telesicles, who, in obedience to a Delphic oracle, led a colony from Paros to Thasos.   The establishment of this colony is fixed by the ancients at the 15th or 18th Olympiad (720 or 708 B.C.); with which it perfectly agrees, that the date at which Archilochus flourished is, according to the chronologists of antiquity, the 23d Olympiad (688 B.C.); though it is often placed lower.   According to this calculation, Archilochus

---

[1] The great painter Polygnotus, a native of Thasos, contemporary with Cimon, in the painting of the infernal regions, which he executed at Delphi, represented in the boat of Charon the Parian priestess Cleobœa, who had brought this mystic worship to Thasos.

[2] Δήμητρος ἀγνῆς καὶ Κόρης τὴν πανήγυριν σέβων,

is from a verse from these poems preserved by Hephæstion, fragm. 68, Gaisford.

began his poetical career in the latter years of the Lydian king Gyges, whose wealth he mentions in a verse still extant;[1] but is mainly to be regarded as the contemporary of Ardys (from Olymp. 25, 3 to 37, 4. B.C. 678—29). In another verse[2] he mentions the calamities of Magnesia, which befel that city through the Treres, and, as we have seen, not in the earliest part of Ardys' reign.[3] Archilochus draws a comparison between the misery of Magnesia and the melancholy condition of Thasos, whither he was led by his family, and was disappointed in his hopes of finding the mountains of gold they had expected. The Thasians seem, indeed, never to have been contented with their island, though its fertility and its mines might have yielded a considerable revenue, and to have tried to get possession of the opposite coast of Thrace, abounding in gold and in wine; an attempt which involved them in wars not only with the natives of that country—for example the Saians[4]—but also with the early Greek colonists. We find in fragments of Archilochus that they had, even in his time, extended their incursions so far eastward as to come into conflict with the inhabitants of Maronea for the possession of Stryme,[5] which at a later period, during the Persian war, was regarded as a city of the Thasians. Dissatisfied with the posture of affairs, which the poet often represents as desperate, (in such expressions as, that the calamities of all Hellas were found combined in Thasos, that the stone of Tantalus was hanging over their heads, &c.,)[6] Archilochus must have quitted Thasos and returned to Paros, since we are informed by credible writers that he lost his life in a war between the Parians and the inhabitants of the neighbouring island of Naxos.

§ 7. From these facts it appears, that the public life of Archilochus was agitated and unsettled ; but his private life was still more exposed to the conflict of contending passions. He had courted a Parian girl, Neobule, the daughter of Lycambes, and his trochaic poems expressed the violent passion with which she had inspired him.[7] Lycambes had actually promised him his daughter,[8] and we are ignorant what induced him to with-

---

[1] Fragm. 10.   [2] Fragm. 71. The reading Θασίων in this fragment is conjectural.   [3] Comp. ch. X. § 4.   [4] Ch. X. § 7.
[5] See Harpocration in Στρύμη.   [6] Fragm. 21, 43.   [7] Fragm. 25, 26.
[8] This is evident from fr. 83, Ὅρκον δ' ἐνοσφίσθης μέγαν, ἅλας τε καὶ τράπεζαν.

draw his consent.   The rage with which Archilochus assailed
the family, now knew no bounds; and he not only accused
Lycambes of perjury, but Neobule and her sisters of the most
abandoned lives.   It is unintelligible how the Parians could
suffer the exasperated poet to heap such virulent abuse on persons with whom he had shortly before so earnestly desired to
connect himself, had not these iambics first appeared at a festival whose solemnization gave impunity to every license; and
had it not been regarded as a privilege of this kind of poetry to
exaggerate at will the evil reports for which any ground existed,
and in the delineation of offences which deserved some reproof
to give the reins to the fancy.   The ostensible object of Archilochus's iambics, like that of the later comedy, was to give
reality to caricatures, every hideous feature of which was made
more striking by being magnified.   But that these pictures, like
caricatures from the hand of a master, had a striking truth, may
be inferred from the impression which Archilochus's iambics
produced, both upon contemporaries and posterity.   Mere
calumnies could never have driven the daughters of Lycambes
to hang themselves, if, indeed, this story is to be believed, and
is not a gross exaggeration.   But we have no need of it; the
universal admiration which was awarded to Archilochus's iambics, proves the existence of a foundation of truth; for when
had a satire which was not based on truth universal reputation
for excellence?   When Plato produced his first dialogues
against the sophists, Gorgias is said to have exclaimed, ' Athens
has given birth to a new Archilochus.'   This comparison, made
by a man not unacquainted with art, shows at all events that
Archilochus must have possessed somewhat of the keen and delicate satire which in Plato is most severe where a dull listener
would be least sensible of it.

§ 8. Unluckily, however, we can form but an imperfect idea
of the general character and tone of Archilochus's poetry; and
we can only lament a loss such as has perhaps hardly been sustained in the works of any other Greek poet.   Horace's *Epodes*
are, as he himself says, formed on the model of Archilochus, as
to form and spirit,[1] but not as to subject; and we can

---

[1]   Parios ego primus iambos
Ostendi Latio, numeros animosque secutus
Archilochi, non res et agentia verba Lycamben.   (Horat. *Ep.* I. 19, 23.)

but rarely detect or divine a direct imitation of the Parian poet.[1]

All that we can now hope to obtain is the knowledge of the external form, especially the metrical structure of Archilochus's poems; and if we look to this alone, we must regard Archilochus as one of those creative minds which discover the aptest expression for new directions of human thought. While the metrical form of the epos was founded upon the dactyl, which, from the equality of the arsis and thesis, has a character of repose and steadiness, Archilochus constructed his metres out of that sort of rhythm which the ancient writers called the double (γένος διπλάσιον), because the arsis has twice the length of the thesis. Hence arose, according as the thesis is at the beginning or the end, the iambus or the trochee, which have the common character of lightness and rapidity. At the same time there is this difference, that the iambus, by proceeding from the short to the long syllable, acquires a tone of strength, and appears peculiarly adapted to impetuous diction and bold invective, while the trochee, which falls from the long to the short, has a feebler character. Its light tripping movement appeared peculiarly suited to dancing songs; and hence, besides the name of trochæus, *the runner*, it also obtained the name of choreius, *the dancer :*[2] occasionally, however, its march was languid and feeble. Archilochus formed long verses of both kinds of feet, and in so doing, with the purpose of giving more strength and body to these short and weak rhythms, he united iambic and trochaic feet in pairs. In every such pair of feet (called *dipodia*), he left the extreme thesis of the dipodia doubtful (that is, in the iambic dipodia the first, in the trochaic the last thesis); so that these short syllables might be replaced by long ones. Archilochus, however, in order not to deprive the metre of its proper rapidity, did not introduce these long syllables so often as Æschylus, for example, who sought, by means of them, to

---

[1] The complaint about perjury (*Epod.* XV.) agrees well with the relations of Archilochus to the family of Lycambes. The proposal to go to the islands of the blessed, in order to escape all misery, in *Epod.* XVI., would be more natural in the mouth of Archilochus, directed to the Thasian colony, than in that of Horace. The Neobule of Horace is Canidia, but with great alterations.

[2] According to Aristot. *Poet.* 4, the trochaic tetrameter is suited to an ὀρχηστικὴ ποίησις, but the iambic verse is most λεκτικός.

give more solemnity and dignity to his verses. Moreover, Archilochus did not admit resolutions of the long syllables, like the comic poets, who thus made the course of the metre more rapid and various. He then united three iambic dipodias (by making the same words common to more than one pair of feet) into a compact whole, the *iambic trimeter :* and four trochaic dipodias, two of which, however, were divided from the other two by a fixed pause (called *diæresis*), into the *trochaic tetra-meter.* Without going more minutely into the structure of the verses, it is sufficiently evident from what has been said, that these metres were in their way as elaborate productions of Greek taste and genius as the Parthenon or the statue of the Olympic Jupiter. Nor can there be any stronger proof of their perfection than that metres, said to have been invented by Archilochus,[1] retained their currency through all ages of the Greek poetry ; and that although their application was varied in many ways, no material improvement was made in their structure.

The distinction observed by Archilochus in the use of them was, that he employed the iambic for the expression of his wrath and bitterness, (whence nearly all the iambic fragments of Archilochus have a hostile bearing), and that he employed the trochaic as a medium between the iambic and the elegiac, of which latter style Archilochus was, as we have already seen, one of the earliest cultivators. As compared with the elegy, the trochaic metre has less rapidity and elevation of sentiment, and approaches more to the tone of common life; as in the passage[2] in which the poet declares that ' he is not fond of a tall general walking with his legs apart, with his hair carefully arranged, and his chin well shorn; but he prefers a short man, with his legs bent in, treading firmly on his feet, and full of spirit and resource.' A personal description of this kind, with a serious intent, but verging on the comic in its tone, would not have suited the elegy ; and although reflections on the mis-fortunes of life occur in trochaic as well as in elegiac verses, yet an attentive reader can distinguish between the languid tone of the latter and the lively tone of the former, which would natu-

---

[1] See Plutarch, *de Musicâ,* c. 28, the chief passage on the numerous inventions of Archilochus in rhythm and music.　　　　[2] Fragm. 9.

rally be accompanied in the delivery with appropriate gesticulation.   Trochaics were also recited by Archilochus at the banquet ;
but while the elegy was an outpouring of feelings in which the
guests were called on to participate, Archilochus selects the
trochaic tetrameter in order to reprove a friend for having
shamelessly obtruded himself upon a feast prepared at the common expense of the guests, without contributing his share, and
without having been invited.[1]

Other forms of the poetry of Archilochus may be pointed out,
with a view of showing the connexion between their metrical
and poetical characters.   Among these are the verses called by
the metrical writers *asynartetes*, or unconnected, and by them
said to have been invented by Archilochus : they are considered
by Plutarch as forming the transition to another class of
rhythms.   Of these difficult metres we will only say, that they
consist of two metrical clauses or members of different kinds ;
for example, dactylic or anapæstic, and trochaic, which are
loosely joined into one verse, the last syllable of the first member
retaining the license of the final syllable of a verse.[2]   This
kind of metre, which passed from the ancient iambic to the
comic poets, has a feeble and languid expression, though
capable at times of a careless grace ; nor was it ever employed
for any grave or dignified subject.   This character especially
appears in the member consisting of three pure trochees, with
which the asynartetes often close ; which was named *Ithyphal-
licus*, because the verses sung at the Phallagogia of Dionysus,
the scene of the wildest revelry in the worship of this god,
were chiefly composed in this metre.[3]   It seems as if the inten-

---

[1] Fragm. 88.   The person reproved is the same Pericles who, in the elegies, is
addressed as an intimate friend.   (See fragm. 1, and 131.)

[2] Archilochus, as well as his imitator Horace, did not allow these two clauses to
run into one another ; but as the comic poets used this liberty (Hephæstion, p. 84.
Gaisf.) it is certain that in Archilochus, 'Ερασμονίδη Χαρίλαε, | χρῆμά τοι γελοῖον,
for example, is to be considered as one verse.

[3] A remarkable example of this class of songs is the poem in which the Athenians
saluted Demetrius, the son of Antigonus, as a new Bacchus, and which is called by
Athenæus ἰθύφαλλος.   It begins as follows (VI. p. 253) :—

'Ως οἱ μέγιστοι τῶν θεῶν καὶ φίλτατοι
τῇ πόλει πάρεισιν.

This poem, by its relaxed and creeping but at the same time elegant and graceful
tone, characterizes the Athens of that time far better than many declamations of
rhetorical historians.

tion had been that after the effort required in the anapæstic or
dactylic member, the voice should find repose in the trochaic
clause, and that the verse should thus proceed with agreeable
slowness. Hence the soft plaintive tone, which may easily be
recognised in the fragments of the asynartetes of Archilochus,
as well as in the corresponding imitations of Horace.[1]

Another metrical invention of Archilochus was a prelude to
the formation of strophes, such as we find them in the remains
of the Æolic lyric poets. This was the *epodes*, which, however, are here to be considered not as separate strophes, but
only as verses ; that is, as shorter verses subjoined to longer
ones. Thus an iambic dimeter forms an epode to a trimeter,
an iambic dimeter or trimeter to a dactylic hexameter, a short
dactylic verse to an iambic trimeter, an iambic verse to an
asynartete ; the object often being to give force and energy to the
languid fall of the rhythm. In general, however, the purposes
of these epodic combinations are as numerous as their kinds;
and if it appears at first sight that Archilochus was guided by
no principle in the formation of them, yet on close examination
it will be found that each has its appropriate excellence.[2]

§ 9. As to the manner in which these metres were recited,
so important a constituent in their effect, we know thus much,
—that the uniformity of the rhapsodists' method of recitation was
broken, and that a freer and bolder style was introduced, which
sometimes passed into the grotesque and whimsical; although, in
general, iambic verses (as we have already seen[3]) were in strictness not sung but rhapsodised. There was, however, a mode

[1] See especially fragm. 24, where Archilochus describes, in asynartetes with
iambic epodes, the violent love which has consumed his heart, darkened his sight,
and deprived him of reason ; probably in reference to his former love for Neobule,
which he had then given up. Horace's eleventh *Epode* is similar in many respects.

[2] When *one* epode follows *two* verses there is a small strophe, as fragm. 38 :—

Αἶνός τις ἀνθρώπων ὅδε,
ὡς ἄρ' ἀλώπηξ κἀετὸς
ξυνωνίην ἔμιξαν.

If the two last verses are here united into one, a proöde is formed, which is the
reverse of the epode; it often occurs in Horace. Another example of a kind of
strophe is the short strain of victory which Archilochus is said to have composed
for the Olympic festival to Hercules and Iolaus (fragm. 60) ; two trimeters with
the ephymnion Τήνελλα καλλίνικε.

[3] Chap. IV. § 3.

of reciting iambics introduced by Archilochus, by which some poems were repeated to the time of a musical instrument, and others were sung.[1] The *paracataloge*, which consisted in the interpolation of a passage recited without strict rhythm and fixed melody, into a piece composed according to certain rules, was also ascribed to Archilochus. Lastly, many entertain the opinion (which, however, seems doubtful,) that Archilochus introduced the separation of instrumental music from singing, to this extent,—that the instrument left the voice, and did not fall in with it till the end, while the early musicians accompanied it, syllable for syllable, with the same notes on the instrument.[2] A peculiar kind of three-cornered stringed instrument, called *iambyce*, was also used to accompany iambics, and probably dated from the time of Archilochus.[3]

§ 10. It was necessary to lay these dry details before the reader in order to give an idea of the inventive genius which places Archilochus next, in point of originality, to Homer, among the Greek poets. There is, however, another remarkable part of the poetical character of Archilochus, viz., his *language*. If we can imagine ourselves living at a time when only the epic style, with its unchanging solemnity, its abundance of graphic epithets, and its diffuse and vivid descriptions, was cultivated by poets, with no other exception than the recent and slight deviation of the elegy, we shall perceive the boldness of introducing into poetry a language which, surrendering all these advantages, attempted to express ideas as they were conceived by a sober and clear understanding. In this diction there are no ornamental epithets, intended only to fill out the image; but every adjective denotes the quality appropriate to the sub-

---

[1] τὰ μὲν ἰαμβεῖα λέγεσθαι παρὰ τὴν κροῦσιν, τὰ δ᾽ ᾄδεσθαι, Plutarch ubi sup. Probably this was connected with the epodic composition; though, according to Plutarch, it also occurred in the tragedians.

[2] In Plutarch the latter is called πρόσχορδα κρούειν, the former ἡ ὑπὸ τὴν ᾠδὴν κροῦσις, which Archilochus is said to have invented. The meaning is made clear by a comparison of Aristot. *Problem.* XIX. 39, and Plato *Leg.* VII. p. 812. Κρούειν denotes the playing on any musical instrument, the flute as well as the cithara.

[3] See Athen. XIV. p. 646. Hesychius and Photius in ἰαμβύκη. The instrument κλεψίαμβοι, mentioned by Athenæus, appears to have been specially destined for the ὑπὸ τὴν ᾠδὴν κροῦσις.

ject, as conceived in the given place.[1] There are no antiquated
words or forms deriving dignity from their antiquity, but it is
the plain language of common life; and if it seem to contain
still many rare and difficult words, it is because the Ionic dialect retained words which afterwards fell into disuse. We
likewise find in it the article,[2] unknown to the epic language;
and many particles used in a manner having a far closer affinity
with a prose than with an epic style. In short, the whole diction is often such as might occur in an Attic comic poet, and,
without the metre, even in a prose writer: nothing but the
liveliness and energy with which all ideas are conceived and expressed, and the pleasing and graceful arrangement of the
thoughts, distinguishes this language from that of common life.[3]

As we have laboured to place the great merit of Archilochus
in its true light, we may give a shorter account of the works of
his followers in iambic poetry. His writings will also furnish
a standard of comparison for the others.

§ 11. SIMONIDES OF AMORGUS follows Archilochus so closely
that they may be considered as contemporaries. He is said to
have flourished in the period following Ol. 29 (664 B.C.). The
principal events of his life, as of that of Archilochus, are connected with the foundation of a colony: he is said to have led
.the Samians to the neighbouring island of Amorgus, and to

---

[1] Of this kind are such adjectives as (fragm. 27)

$$Οὐκ ἔθ' ὁμῶς θάλλεις ἁπαλὸν χρόα, κάρφεται γὰρ ἤδη,$$

where the skin is not called tender generally, but in reference to the former bloom of
the person addressed; and as (fragm. 55)

$$ἀμυδρὰν χοιράδ' ἐξαλευάμενος,$$

where the rock is not called dark generally, but in reference to the difficulty of
avoiding a rock beneath the surface of the water. Such epic epithets as παῖδ' Ἄρεω
μιηφόνου (fragm. 116) are very rare.

[2] E. g. fragm. 58: τοιάνδε δ' ὦ πίθηκε, τὴν πυγὴν ἔχεις, where the article separates
τοιάνδε from πυγήν: 'such are the posteriors which you have.'

[3] We may cite, as instances of the simple language of Archilochus, two fragments
evidently belonging to a poem which had some resemblance to Horace's 6th epode.
In the beginning was fragment 122, πόλλ' οἶδ' ἀλώπηξ, ἀλλ' ἐχῖνος ἕν μέγα; 'the
fox uses many arts, but the hedgehog has one great one,' viz. to roll himself up and
resist his enemy. And towards the end (fragm. 118) ἕν δ' ἐπίσταμαι μέγα, Τὸν
κακῶς τι δρῶντα δεινοῖς ἀνταμείβεσθαι κακοῖς, by which words the poet applied to
himself the image of the hedgehog: he had the art of retaliating on those who ill
treated him. Consequently the first fragment would be an incomplete trochaic
tetrameter.

have there founded three cities. One of these was Minoa, where he settled. Like Archilochus, Simonides composed iambics and trochaic tetrameters; and in the former metre he also attacked individuals with the lash of his invective and ridicule. What the family of Lycambes were to Archilochus, a certain Orodœcides was to Simonides. More remarkable, however, is the peculiar application which Simonides made of the iambic metre: that is to say, he took not individuals, but whole classes of persons, as the object of his satire. The iambics of Simonides thus acquire a certain resemblance to the satire interwoven into Hesiod's epic poems; and the more so, as it is on women that he vents his displeasure in the largest of his extant pieces. For this purpose he makes use of a contrivance which, at a later time, also occurs in the gnomes of Phocylides; that is, he derives the various, though generally bad, qualities of women from the variety of their origin; by which fiction he gives a much livelier image of female characters than he could have done by a mere enumeration of their qualities. The uncleanly woman is formed from the swine, the cunning woman, equally versed in good and evil, from the fox, the talkative woman from the dog, the lazy woman from the earth, the unequal and changeable from the sea, the woman who takes pleasure only in eating and sensual delights from the ass, the perverse woman from the weasel, the woman fond of dress from the horse, the ugly and malicious woman from the ape. There is only one race created for the benefit of men, the woman sprung from the bee, who is fond of her work and keeps faithful watch over her house.

§ 12. From the coarse and somewhat rude manner of Simonides, we turn with satisfaction to the contemplation of SOLON's iambic style. Even in his hands the iambic retains a character of passion and warmth, but it is only used for self-defence in a just cause. After Solon had introduced his new constitution, he soon found that although he had attempted to satisfy the claims of all parties, or rather to give to each party and order its due share of power, he had not succeeded in satisfying any. In order to shame his opponents, he wrote some iambics, in which he calls on his censors to consider of how many citizens the state would have been bereaved, if he had listened to the

demands of the contending factions.　As a witness of the goodness of his plans, Solon, calls the great goddess Earth, the
mother of Cronus, whose surface had before his time been
covered with numerous boundary stones, in sign of the ground
being mortgaged: these he had succeeded in removing, and in
restoring the land in full property to the mortgagers.　This
fragment is well worth reading,[1] since it gives as clear an idea
of the political situation of Athens at that time, as it does of
Solon's iambic style.　It shows a truly Attic energy and address in defending a favourite cause, while it contains the first
germs of that power of speech,[2] which afterwards came to maturity in the dialogue of the Athenian stage, and in the oratory
of the popular assembly and of the courts of justice.　In the
dialect and expressions, the poetry of Solon retains more of the
Ionic cast.

In like manner the few remnants of Solon's trochaics enable
us to form some judgment of his mode of handling this metre.
Solon wrote his trochaics at nearly the same time as his iambics;
when, notwithstanding his legislation, the struggle of parties
again broke out between their ambitious leaders, and some
thoughtless citizens reproached Solon, because he, the true pa-
triot, the friend of the whole community, had not seized the
reins with a firm hand, and made himself monarch: ' Solon was
not a man of deep sense or prudent counsel; for when the god
offered him blessings, he refused to take them: but when he
had caught the prey, he was struck with awe, and drew not up
the great net, failing at once in courage and sense: for else he
would have been willing, having gained dominion and obtained
unstinted wealth, and having been tyrant of Athens only for a
single day, afterwards to be flayed, and his skin made a leathern
bottle, and that his race should become extinct.'[3]　The other
fragments of Solon's trochaics agree with the same subject; so
that Solon probably only composed *one* poem in this metre.

§ 13.　Far more nearly akin to the primitive spirit of the
iambic verse was the style of HIPPONAX, who flourished about
the 60th Olympiad (540 B.C.).　He was born at Ephesus, and
was compelled by the tyrants Athenagoras and Comas to quit

---

[1] Solon, No. 28, Gaisford.　　[2] δεινότης.　　[3] Fragment 25, Gaisford.

his home, and to establish himself in another Ionian city, Clazomenæ. This political persecution (which affords a presumption of his vehement love of liberty) probably laid the foundation for some of the bitterness and disgust with which he regarded mankind. Precisely the same fierce and indignant scorn which found an utterance in the iambics of Archilochus, is ascribed to Hipponax. What the family of Lycambes was to Archilochus, Bupalus and Athenis (two sculptors of a family of Chios, which had produced several generations of artists) were to Hipponax. They had made his small, meagre, and ugly person the subject of a caricature; an insult Hipponax avenged in the bitterest and most pungent iambics, of which some remains are extant. In this instance, also, the satirist is said to have caused his enemy to hang himself. The satire of Hipponax, however, was not concentrated so entirely on certain individuals; from existing fragments it appears rather to have been founded on a general view of life, taken, however, on its ridiculous and grotesque side. The luxury of the Greeks of Lesser Asia, which had already risen to a high pitch, is a favourite object of his sarcasms. In one of the longest fragments he says,[1] 'For one of you had very quietly swallowed a continued stream of thunny with dainty sauces, like a Lampsacenian eunuch, and had devoured the inheritance of his father; therefore he must now break rocks with a mattock, and gnaw a few figs and a little black barley bread, the food of slaves.'

His language is filled with words taken from common life, such as the names of articles of food and clothing, and of ordinary utensils, current among the working people. He evidently strives to make his iambics local pictures full of freshness, nature, and homely truth. For this purpose, the change which Hipponax devised in the iambic metre was as felicitous as it was bold; he crippled the rapid agile gait of the iambic by transforming the last foot from a pure iambus into a spondee, contrary to the fundamental principle of the whole mode of versification. The metre thus maimed and stripped of its beauty and regularity,[2] was a perfectly appropriate rhythmical form

---

[1] Ap. Athen. VII. p. 304. B.   [2] τὸ ἄῤῥυθμον.

for the delineation of such pictures of intellectual deformity as
Hipponax delighted in. Iambics of this kind (called choliambics
or trimeter scazons) are still more cumbrous and halting when
the fifth foot is also a spondee; which, indeed, according to
the original structure, is not forbidden. These were called
broken-backed iambics (ischiorrhogics), and a grammarian[1]
settles the dispute (which, according to ancient testimony, was
so hard to decide), how far the invention of this kind of verse
ought to be ascribed to Hipponax, and how far to another
iambographer, Ananius, by pronouncing that Ananius invented
the ischiorrhogic variety, Hipponax the common scazon. It appears, however, from the fragments attributed to him, that
Hipponax sometimes used the spondee in the fifth foot. In the
same manner and with the same effect these poets also changed
the trochaic tetrameter by regularly lengthening the penulti-
mate short syllable. Some remains of this kind are extant.
Hipponax likewise composed pure trimeters in the style of
Archilochus; but there is no conclusive evidence that he mixed
them with scazons.

ANANIUS has hardly any individual character in literary history distinct from that of Hipponax. In Alexandria their
poems seem to have been regarded as forming one collection ;
and thus the criterion by which to determine whether a particular passage belonged to the one or to the other, was often
lost or never existed. Hence in the uncertainty which is the
true author, the same verse is occasionally ascribed to both.[2]
The few fragments which are attributed with certainty to
Ananius are so completely in the tone of Hipponax, that it
would be a vain labour to attempt to point out any characteristic difference.[3]

§ 14. Akin to the iambic are two sorts of poetry, which,
though differing widely from each other, have both their source
in the turn for the delineation of the ludicrous, and both stand
in a close historical relation to the iambic :—the *Fable* (origi-

---

[1] In Tyrwhitt, *Dissert. de Babrio*, p. 17.

[2] As in Athen. XIV. p. 625 C.

[3] There is no sufficient ground for supposing that Herondas, who is sometimes
mentioned as a choliambic poet, lived in this age. The *mimiambic* poetry ascribed
to him will be treated of in connexion with the Mimes of Sophron.

nally called αἶνος, and afterwards, less precisely, μῦθος and λόγος), and the *Parody*.

With regard to the *fable*, it is not improbable that in other countries, particularly in the north of Europe, it may have arisen from a child-like playful view of the character and habits of animals, which frequently suggest a comparison with the nature and incidents of human life. In Greece, however, it originated in an intentional travestie of human affairs. The αἶνος is, as its name denotes, an admonition,[1] or rather a reproof, veiled, either from fear of an excess of frankness or from love of fun and jest, beneath the fiction of an occurrence happening among beasts. Such is the character of the ainos, at its very first appearance in Hesiod.[2] ' Now I will tell the kings a fable, which they will understand of themselves. Thus spake the hawk to the nightingale, whom he was carrying in his talons aloft in the air, while she, torn by his sharp claws, bitterly lamented—Foolish creature, why dost thou cry out ? One much stronger than thou hast seized thee ; thou must go whithersoever I carry thee, though thou art a songstress ; I can tear thee in pieces or I can let thee go at my pleasure.'

Archilochus employed the ainos in a similar manner in his iambics against Lycambes.[3] He tells how the fox and the eagle had contracted an alliance, but (as the fable, according to other sources, goes on to tell)[4] the eagle was so regardless of her engagement, that she ate the fox's cubs. The fox could only call down the vengeance of the gods, and this shortly overtook her ; for the eagle stole the flesh from an altar, and did not observe that she bore with it sparks which set fire to her nest, and consumed both that and her young ones.

It is clear that Archilochus meant to intimate to Lycambes, that though he was too powerless to call him to account for the breach of his engagement, he could bring down upon him the chastisement of the gods.

Another of Archilochus's fables was pointed at absurd pride of rank.[5]

---

[1] παραίνεσις. See *Philological Museum*, vol. I. p. 281.

[2] *Op. et D.* v. 202, *seq.*   [3] Fr. 38, ed. Gaisford ; see note on fr. 39.

[4] Coraes Μύθων Αἰσωπείων συναγωγὴ, c. I. Aristoph. *Av.* 651, ascribes the fable to Æsop.   [5] See Gaisford, fr. 39.

In like manner Stesichorus cautioned his countrymen, the
Himeræans, against Phalaris, by the fable of the horse, who, to
revenge himself on the stag, took the man on his back, and
thus became his slave.[1]   And wherever we have any ancient
and authentic account of the origin of the Æsopian fable, we
find it to be the same.   It is always some action, some project,
and commonly some absurd one, of the Samians, or Delphians,
or Athenians, whose nature and consequences Æsop describes
in a fable, and thus often exhibits the posture of affairs in
a more lucid, just, and striking manner than could have been
done by elaborate argument.   But from the very circumstance,
that in the Greek fable the actions and business of men are the
real and prominent object, while beasts are merely introduced
as a veil or disguise, it has nothing in common with popular
legendary stories of beasts, nor has it any connexion with
mythological stories of the metamorphoses of animals.   It is
exclusively the invention of those who detected in the social
habits of the lower animals points of resemblance with those
of man; and while they retained the real character in some
respects, found means, by the introduction of reason and speech,
to place them in the light required for their purpose.

§ 15. It is probable that the taste for fables of beasts and
numerous similar inventions, found their way into Greece from
the East; since this sort of symbolical and veiled narrative is
more in harmony with the Oriental than with the Greek character.   Thus, for example, the Old Testament contains a fable
completely in the style of Æsop (Judges, ix. 8).   But not to
deviate into regions foreign to our purpose, we may confine
ourselves to the avowal of the Greeks themselves, contained in
the very names given by them to the fable.   One kind of fable
was called the *Libyan*, which we may, therefore, infer was of
African origin, and was introduced into Greece through Cyrene.
To this class belongs, according to Æschylus,[2] the beautiful
fable of the wounded eagle, who, looking at the feathering of
the arrow with which he was pierced, exclaimed, ' I perish by

---

[1] Arist. *Rhet.* II. 20. The fable of Menenius Agrippa is similarly applied ; but
it is difficult to believe that the *ainos*, so applied, was known in Latium at that
time, and it seems probable that the story was transferred from Greece to Rome.
[2] Fragment of the *Myrmidons*.

feathers drawn from my own wing.' From this example we see that the Libyan fable belonged to the class of fables of animals. So also did the sorts to which later teachers of rhetoric[1] give the names of the *Cyprian* and the *Cilician;* these writers also mention the names of some fabulists among the barbarians, as Cybissus the Libyan and Connis the Cilician. The contest between the olive and the laurel on mount Tmolus, is cited as a fable of the ancient *Lydians.*[2]

The Carian stories or fables, however, were taken from human life, as, for instance, that quoted by the Greek lyric poets, Timocreon and Simonides. A Carian fisherman, in the winter, sees a sea polypus, and he says to himself, 'If I dive to catch it, I shall be frozen to death; if I don't catch it, my children must starve.'[3] The Sybaritic fables mentioned by Aristophanes have a similar character. Some pointed saying of a man or woman of Sybaris, with the particular circumstances which called it forth, is related.[4] The large population of the wealthy Ionian Sybaris appears to have been much given to such repartees, and to have caught them up and preserved them with great eagerness. Doubtless, therefore, the Sicilian poet Epicharmus means, by Sybaritic apophthegms,[5] what others call Sybaritic fables. The Sybaritic fables, nevertheless, occasionally invested not only the lower animals, but even inanimate objects, with life and speech, as in the one quoted by Aristophanes. A woman in Sybaris broke an earthen pot; the pot screamed out, and called witnesses to see how ill she had been treated. Then the woman said, 'By Cora, if you were to leave off calling out for witnesses, and were to make haste and buy a copper ring to bind yourself together, you would show more wisdom.' This fable is used by a saucy merry old man, in ridicule of one whom he has ill treated, and who threatens to lay a complaint against him. Both the Sybaritic and Æsopian fables are represented by Aristophanes as jests, or ludicrous stories (γελοῖα).

---

[1] Theon, and in part also Aphthonius. A fragment of a Cyprian fable, about the doves of Aphrodite, is published in the excerpts from the Codex Angelicus in Walz, *Rhetor. Grec.* vol. II. p. 12.

[2] Callim. fr. 93. Bentl.

[3] From the Codex Angelicus in Walz, *Rhet. Gr.* vol. II. p. 11, and the Proverbs of Macarius in Walz, *Arsenii Violetum,* p. 318.

[4] Aristoph. *Vesp.* 1259, 1427, 1437.   [5] Suidas in v.

§ 16. To return to Æsop: Bentley has shown that he was
very far from being regarded by the Greeks as one of their poets,
and still less as a writer.   They considered him merely as an
ingenious fabulist, under whose name a number of fables, often
applicable to human affairs, were current, and to whom, at a
later period, nearly all that were either invented or derived
from any other source, were attributed.   His history has
been dressed out by the later Greeks, with all manner of
droll and whimsical incidents.   What can be collected from
the ancient writers down to Aristotle is, however, confined
to the following.

Æsop was a slave of the Samian Iadmon, the son of He-
phæstopolis, who lived in the time of the Egyptian king
Amasis.   (The reign of Amasis begins Olymp. 52. 3, 570
B.C.)   According to the statement of Eugeon, an old Samian
historian,[1] he was a native of the Thracian city Mesembria,
which existed long before it was peopled by a colony of
Byzantines in the reign of Darius.[2]   According to a less
authentic account he was from Cotyæon in Phrygia.   It
seems that his wit and pleasantry procured him his freedom;
for though he remained in Iadmon's family, it must have
been as a freedman, or he could not, as Aristotle relates,
have appeared publicly as the defender of a demagogue, on
which occasion he told a fable in support of his client.   It
is generally received as certain that Æsop perished in Delphi;
the Delphians, exasperated by his sarcastic fables, having put
him to death on a charge of robbing the temple.   Aristophanes alludes to a fable which Æsop told to the Delphians,
of the beetle who found means to revenge himself on the
eagle.[3]

The character of the Æsopian fable is precisely that of
the genuine beast-fable, such as we find it among the Greeks.
The condition and habits of the lower animals are turned to
account in the same manner, and, by means of the poetical
introduction of reason and speech, are placed in such a light

---

[1] Εὐγέων, or Εὐγείων, falsely written Εὐγείτων, in Suidas in v. Αἴσωπος.
[2] Mesembria, Pattymbria, and Selymbria, are Thracian names, and mean the
cities of Meses, Pattys, and Selys.
[3] Aristoph. *Vesp.* 1448. cf. *Pac.* 129. Coraes, *Æsop.* c. 2.

as to produce a striking resemblance to the incidents and relations of human life.

Attempts were probably early made to give a poetical form to the Æsopian fable. Socrates is said to have beguiled his imprisonment thus. The iambic would of course suggest itself as the most appropriate form (as at a later period it did to Phædrus), or the scazon, which was adopted by Callimachus and Babrius.[1] But no metrical versions of these fables are known to have existed in early times. The ainos was generally regarded as a mode of other sorts of poetry, particularly the iambic, and not as a distinct class.

§ 17. The other kind of poetry whose origin we are now about to trace, is the *Parody*. This was understood by the ancients, as well as by ourselves, to mean an adoption of the form of some celebrated poem, with such changes in the matter as to produce a totally different effect; and, generally, to substitute mean and ridiculous for elevated and poetical sentiments. The contrast between the grand and sublime images suggested to the memory, and the comic ones introduced in their stead, renders parody peculiarly fitted to place any subject in a ludicrous, grotesque, and trivial light. The purpose of it, however, was not in general to detract from the reverence due to the ancient poet (who, in most cases was Homer), by this travestie, but only to add fresh zest and pungency to satire. Perhaps, too, some persons sporting with the austere and stately forms of the epos, (like playful children dressing themselves in gorgeous and flowing robes of state), might have fallen upon the device of parody.

We have already alluded to a fragment of Asius[2] in elegiac measure, which is not indeed a genuine parody, but which approaches to it. It is a comic description of a beggarly parasite, rendered more ludicrous by a tone of epic solemnity. But, according to the learned Polemon,[3] the real author of parody was the iambographer Hipponax, of whose productions in this kind a hexametrical fragment is still extant.

§ 18. The *Batrachomyomachia, or Battle of the Frogs and*

---

[1] A distich of an Æsopian fable is, however, attributed by Diogenes Laërtius to Socrates. Fragments of fables in hexameters also occur.

[2] Ch. X. § 7.   [3] Ap. Athen. XV. p. 698, B.

the Mice (which has come down to us among the lesser Homeric poems), is totally devoid of sarcastic tendency. All attempts to discover a satirical meaning in this little comic epos have been abortive. It is nothing more than the story of a war between the frogs and the mice, which, from the high-sounding names of the combatants, the detailed genealogies of the principal persons, the declamatory speeches, the interference of the gods of Olympus, and all the pomp and circumstance of the epos, has completely the external character of an epic heroic poem; a character ludicrously in contrast with the subject. Notwithstanding many ingenious conceits, it is not, on the whole, remarkable for vigour of poetical conception, and the introduction falls far short of the genuine tone of the Homeric epos, so that everything tends to show that the *Batrachomyomachia* is a production of the close of this era. This supposition is confirmed by the tradition that Pigres, the brother of the Halicarnassian tyrant Artemisia, and consequently a contemporary of the Persian war, was the author of this poem,[1] although at a later period of antiquity, in the time of the Romans, the *Batrachomyomachia* was ascribed without hesitation to Homer himself.

---

[1] The passage of Plutarch *de Malign. Herod.* c. 43, ought to be written as follows :—Τέλος δὲ καθημένους ἐν Πλαταιαῖς ἀγνοῆσαι μέχρι τέλους τὸν ἀγῶνα τοὺς Ἕλληνας, ὥσπερ βατραχομυομαχίας γινομένης (ἣν Πίγρης ὁ Ἀρτεμισίας ἐν ἔπεσι παίζων καὶ φλυαρῶν ἔγραψεν) ἢ σιωπῇ διαγωνίσασθαι συνθεμένων, ἵνα λάθωσι τοὺς ἄλλους.

Concerning Pigres see Suidas, who, however, confounds the later with the earlier Artemisia.

CHAPTER XII.

PROGRESS OF THE GREEK MUSIC.

§ 1. Transition from the Epos, through the Elegy and Iambus, to Lyric Poetry connexion of Lyric Poetry with Music. § 2. Founders of Greek Music : Terpander, his descent and date. § 3. Terpander's invention of the seven-stringed Cithara. § 4. Musical scales and styles. § 5. Nomes of Terpander for singing to the Cithara; their rhythmical form. § 6. Olympus, descended from an ancient Phrygian family of flute-players. § 7. His influence upon the development of the music of the flute and rhythm among the Greeks. § 8. His influence confined to music. § 9. Thaletas, his age. § 10. His connexion with ancient Cretan worships. Pæans and hyporchemes of Thaletas. § 11. Musicians of the succeeding period—Clonas, Hierax, Xenodamus, Xenocritus, Polymnestus, Sacadas. § 12. State of Greek Music at this period.

§ 1. WHEN the epic, elegiac, and iambic styles had been perfected in Greece, the forms of poetry seemed to have become so various, as scarcely to admit of further increase. The epic style, raised above the ordinary range of human life, had, by the exclusive sway which it exercised for centuries, and the high place which it occupied in general opinion, laid a broad foundation for all future Greek poetry, and had so far influenced its progress that, even in those later styles which differed the most widely from it, we may, to a certain extent, trace an epic and Homeric tone. Thus the lyric and dramatic poets developed the characters of the heroes celebrated in the ancient epic poetry; so that their descriptions appeared rather to be the portraits of real persons than the conceptions of the individual poet. It was not till the minds of the Greeks had been elevated by the productions of the epic muse, that the genius of original poets broke loose from the dominion of the epic style, and invented new forms for expressing the emotions of a mind profoundly agitated by passing events, with fewer innovations in the elegy, but with greater boldness and novelty in the iambic metre. In these two styles of poetry,—the former suited to the expression of grief, the latter to the expression of anger, hatred, and contempt—Greek poetry entered the domain of real life.

Yet a great variety of new forms of poetry was reserved for the invention of future poets. The elegy and the iambus contained the germs of the lyric style, though they do not themselves come under that head. The principal characteristic of lyric poetry is its connexion with *music*, vocal as well as instrumental. This connexion, indeed, existed, to a certain extent, in epic, and still more in elegiac and iambic poetry; but singing was not essential in those styles. Such a recitation by a rhapsodist, as was usual for epic poetry, also served, at least in the beginning, for elegiac, and in great part for iambic verses. Singing and a continued instrumental accompaniment are appropriate, where the expression of feeling or passion is inconsistent with a more measured and equable mode of recitation. In the attempt to express these impulses, the alternation of high and low tones would naturally give rise to singing. Hence, with the fine sense of harmony possessed by the Greeks, there was produced a rising and falling in the *rhythm*, which led to a greater variety and a more skilful arrangement of metrical forms. Moreover, as the expression of strong feeling required more pauses and resting-places, the verses in lyric poetry naturally fell into *strophes*, of greater or less length; each of which comprised several varieties of metre, and admitted of an appropriate termination. This arrangement of the strophes was, at the same time, connected with *dancing;* which was naturally, though not necessarily, associated with lyric poetry. The more lively the expression, the more animated will be the gestures of the reciter; and animated and expressive movements, which follow the rhythm of a poem, and correspond to its metrical structure, are, in fact, dancing.

The Greek lyric poetry, therefore, was characterized by the expression of deeper and more impassioned feeling, and a more swelling and impetuous tone, than the elegy or iambus; and, at the same time, the effect was heightened by appropriate vocal and instrumental music, and often by the movements and figures of the dance. In this union of the sister arts, poetry was indeed predominant; and music and dancing were only employed to enforce and elevate the conceptions of the higher art. Yet music, in its turn, exercised a reciprocal influence on poetry; so that, as it became more cultivated, the choice of the musical measure decided the tone of the whole poem. In order, therefore, that the character of the Greek lyric poetry may be fully understood, we will prefix an account of the scientific cultivation of music. Consistently with this purpose we should limit our attention to the general character of the music of the ancient Greeks, even if the technical details of the art, notwithstanding many able attempts to explain them, were not still enveloped in great obscurity.

§ 2. The mythical traditions of Orpheus, Philammon, Chrysothemis, and other minstrels of the early times being set aside, the history of Greek music begins with TERPANDER the Lesbian. Terpander appears to have been properly the founder of Greek music. He first reduced to rule the different modes of singing which prevailed in different countries, and formed, out of these rude strains, a connected system, from which the Greek music never departed throughout all the improvements and refinements of later ages. Though endowed with an inventive mind, and the commencer of a new era of music, he attempted no more than to systematize the musical styles which existed in the tunes of Greece and Asia Minor. It is probable that Terpander himself belonged to a family who derived their practice of music from the ancient Pierian bards of Bœotia; such an inheritance of musical skill is quite conformable to the manners and institutions of the early Greeks.[1] The Æolians of Lesbos had their origin in Bœotia,[2] the country to which the worship of the Muses and the Thracian hymns belonged;[3] and they probably brought with them the first rudiments of poetry. This migration of the art of the Muses is ingeniously expressed by the legend that, after the murder of Orpheus by the Thracian Mænads, his head and lyre were thrown into the sea, and borne upon its waves to the

---

[1] There were in several of the Greek states, houses or *gentes*, γένη, in which the performance of musical exhibitions, especially at festivals, descended as an hereditary privilege. Thus, at Athens, the playing of the cithara at processions belonged to the Eunids. The Eumolpids of Eleusis were originally, as the name proves, a *gens* of singers of hymns (see above, p. 34, ch. III. § 7). The flute-players of Sparta continued their art and their rights in families. Stesichorus and Simonides also belonged to musical families, as we will show below.

[2] Ch. I. § 5 (p. 12).   [3] Chap. II. § 8.

island of Lesbos ; whence singing and the music of the cithara
flourished in this, the most musical of islands.[1]   The grave
supposed to contain the head of Orpheus was shown in Antissa,
a small town of Lesbos ; and it was thought that in that spot
the nightingales sang most sweetly.[2]   In Antissa also, according
to the testimony of several ancient writers, Terpander was born.
In this way, the domestic impressions and the occupations of
his youth may have prepared Terpander for the great undertaking which he afterwards performed.

The date of Terpander is determined by his appearance in
the mother country of Greece : of his early life in Lesbos
nothing is known.   The first account of him describes him in
Peloponnesus, which at that time surpassed the rest of Greece
in political power, in well-ordered governments, and probably
also in mental cultivation.   It is one of the most certain dates
of ancient chronology, that in the 26th Olympiad (B.C. 676)
musical contests were first introduced at the feast of Apollo
Carneius, and at their first celebration Terpander was crowned
victor.   Terpander was also victor four successive times in the
musical contests at the Pythian temple of Delphi, which were
celebrated there long before the establishment of the gymnastic
games and chariot races (Ol. 47), but which then recurred every
eight, and not every four years.[3]   These Pythian victories
ought probably to be placed in the period from the 27th to
the 33rd Olympiad.   For the 4th year of the 33rd Olympiad
(645 B.C.) is the time at which Terpander introduced among
the Lacedæmonians his nomes for singing to the cithara, and
generally reduced music to a system.[4]   At this time, therefore,
he had acquired the greatest renown in his art by his most
important inventions.   In Lacedæmon, whose citizens had
from the earliest times been distinguished for their love of
music and dancing, the first scientific cultivation of music

---

[1] πασέων δ’ ἐστὶν ἀοιδοτάτη, says Phanocles, the elegiac poet, who gives the most
elegant version of this legend (Stob. tit. LXII. p. 399).

[2] Myrsilus of Lesbos, in Antigon. Caryst. *Hist. Mirab.* c. 5.   In the account in
Nicomachus Geræs. *Enchir. Harm.* II. p. 29. ed. Meibom. Antissa is mentioned
on the same occasion.

[3] Müller's *Dorians*, b. IV. ch. VI. § 2.

[4] Marmor Parium, ep. XXXIV. l. 49, compared with Plutarch *de Musicâ*, c. 9.

was ascribed to Terpander ;[1] and a record of the precise time
had been preserved, probably in the registers of the public
games. Hence it appears that Terpander was a younger contemporary of Callinus and Archilochus ; so that the dispute
among the ancients, whether Terpander or Archilochus were
the elder, must probably be decided by supposing them to
have lived about the same time.

§ 3. At the head of all the inventions of Terpander stands
the seven-stringed cithara. The only accompaniment for the
voice used by the early Greeks was a four-stringed cithara, the
tetrachord; and this instrument had been so generally used,
and held in such repute, that the whole system of music was
always founded upon the tetrachord. Terpander was the first
who added three strings to this instrument; as he himself
testifies in two extant verses.[2] ' Disdaining the four-stringed
song, we shall sound new hymns on the seven-stringed phorminx.' The tetrachord was strung so that the two extreme
strings stood to one another in the relation called by the ancients
diatessaron, and by the moderns a *fourth ;* that is to say, the
lower one made three vibrations in the time that the upper one
made four. Between these two strings, which formed the principal harmony of this simple instrument, there were two others ;
and in the most ancient arrangement of the gamut, called the
diatonic, these two were strung so that the three intervals between these four strings produced twice a whole tone, and in
the third place a semitone. Terpander enlarged this instrument by adding one tetrachord to another : he did not however
make the highest tone of the lower tetrachord the lowest of
the upper, but he left an interval of one tone between the two
tetrachords. By this arrangement the cithara would have had
eight strings, if Terpander had not left out the third string,
which must have appeared to him to be of less importance.
The heptachord of Terpander thus acquired the compass of an
octave, or, according to the Greek expression, a diapason ; be-

---

[1] ἡ πρώτη κατάστασις τῶν περὶ τὴν μουσικὴν, says Plutarch, *de Musicâ,* c. 9.

[2] In Euclid, *Introd. Harm.* p. 19. Partly also in Strabo, XIII. p. 618;
Clemens Alex. *Strom.* VI. p. 814, Potter. The verses are—

'Ημεῖς τοι τετράγηρυν ἀποστέρξαντες ἀοιδὴν
'Επτατόνῳ φόρμιγγι νέους κελαδήσομεν ὕμνους.

cause the highest tone of the upper and the lowest of the lower tetrachord stood in this relation, which is the simplest of all, as it rests upon the ratio of 1 to 2 ; and which was soon acknowledged by the Greeks as the fundamental concord. At the same time the highest tone of the upper tetrachord stands to the highest of the lower in the relation of the fifth, the arithmetical expression of which is 2 to 3 ; and in general the tones were doubtless so arranged that the simplest consonances after the octave—that is to say, the fourth and fifth—governed the whole.[1] Hence the heptachord of Terpander long remained in high repute, and was employed by Pindar; although in his time the deficient string of the lower tetrachord had been supplied, and an octachord produced.[2]

§ 4. It will be convenient in this place to explain the difference between the *scales* (γένη), and the *styles* or *harmonies* (τρόποι, ἁρμονίαι) of Greek music, since it is probable that they were regulated by Terpander. The musical scales are determined by the intervals between the four tones of the tetrachord. The Greek musicians describe three musical scales, viz., the diatonic, the chromatic, and the enharmonic. In the diatonic, the intervals were two tones and a semitone; and hence the diatonic was considered the simplest and most natural, and was the most extensively used. In the chromatic scale the interval is a tone and a semitone, combined with two other semitones.[3] This arrangement of the tetrachord was also very ancient, but it was much less used, because a feeble and languid, though pleasing character, was ascribed to it. The third scale, the enharmonic, was produced by a tetrachord, which, besides an interval of two tones, had also two minor ones of quarter-tones. This was the latest of all, and was invented by Olympus, who must have flourished a short time after Terpander.[4] The

---

[1] The strings of the heptachord of Terpander were called, beginning from the highest, Νήτη, παρανήτη, παραμέση, μέση, λιχανὸς, παρυπάτη, ὑπάτη. The intervals were 1, 1, 1½, 1, 1, ½, if the heptachord was strung, according to the diatonic scale, in the Doric style.

[2] In proof of the account of the heptachord given in the text, see Boeckh, *de Metris Pindari*, III. 7, p. 205, *seq*.

[3] Of these short intervals, however, the one is greater than the other, the former being more, the latter less, than a semitone. The first is called *apotome*, the other *leimma*.

[4] See Plutarch, *de Musica*, 7, 11, 20, 29, 33 ; a treatise full of valuable notices, but written with so little care that the author often contradicts himself.

ancients greatly preferred the enharmonic scale, especially on account of its liveliness and force. But from the small intervals of quarter tones, the execution of it required great skill and practice in singing and playing. These musical scales were further determined by the *styles* or *harmonies*, because on them depended, first, the position or succession of the intervals belonging to the several scales,[1] and, secondly, the height and depth of the whole gamut. Three styles were known in very early times,—the Doric, which was the lowest, the Phrygian, the middle one, and the Lydian, the highest. Of these, the Doric alone is named from a Greek race; the two others are called after nations of Asia Minor, whose love for music, and particularly the flute, is well known. It is probable that national tunes were current among these tribes, whose peculiar character was the origin of these styles. Yet their fixed and systematic relation to the Doric style must have been the work of a Greek musician, probably of Terpander himself, who, in his native island of Lesbos, had frequent opportunities of becoming acquainted with the different musical styles of his neighbours of Asia Minor. Thus a fragment of Pindar relates, that Terpander, at the Lydian feasts, had heard the tone of the pectis, (a Lydian instrument, with a compass of two octaves,) and had formed from it the kind of lyre which was called *Barbiton*.[2] The Lesbians likewise used a particular sort of cithara, called the Asiatic ('Ασιάς); and this was by many held to be the invention of Terpander, by others to be the work of his disciple Cepion.[3] It is manifest that the Lesbian musicians, with Terpander at their head, were the means of uniting the music of Asia Minor with that of the ancient Greeks (which was best preserved among the Dorians in Peloponnesus), and that they founded on it a system, in which each style had its appropriate character. To the establishment of this character

---

[1] For example, whether the intervals of the diatonon are ½, 1, 1, as in the Doric style, or 1, ½, 1, as in the Phrygian, or 1, 1 ½, as in the Lydian.

[2] In Athenæus, XVI. p. 635. There are great difficulties as to the sense of this much-contested passage. Pindar's meaning probably is, that Terpander formed the deep-resounding barbiton by taking the lower octave from the pectis (or magadis). Among the Greek poets, Sappho is said to have first used the pectis or magadis, then Anacreon.

[3] Plutarch, *de Mus.* 6. *Anecd.* Bekker, vol. I. p. 452. Compare Aristoph. *Thesm.* 120, with the *Scholia*.

the *nomes* (νόμοι) contributed, musical compositions of great simplicity and severity, something resembling the most ancient melodies of our church music. The Doric style appears from the statements of all the witnesses to have had a character of great seriousness and gravity, peculiarly calculated to produce a calm, firm, collected frame of mind. 'With regard to the Doric style (says Aristotle), all are agreed that it is the most sedate, and has the most manly character.' The Phrygian style was evidently derived from the loud vehement styles of music employed by the Phrygians in the worship of the Great Mother of the gods and the Corybantes.[1] In Greece, too, it was used in orgiastic worships, especially in that of Dionysus. It was peculiarly adapted to the expression of enthusiasm. The Lydian had the highest notes of any of the three ancient styles, and therefore approached nearer to the female voice; its character was thus softer and feebler than either of the others. Yet it admitted of considerable variety of expression, as the melodies of the Lydian style had sometimes a painful and melancholy, sometimes a calm and pleasing character. Aristotle (who, in his *Politics*, has given some judicious precepts on the use of music in education) considers the Lydian style peculiarly adapted to the musical cultivation of early youth.

In order to complete our view of this subject, we will here give an account of the other styles of Greek music, although they were invented after the time of Terpander. Between the Doric and Phrygian styles—with respect to the height and lowness of the tones,—the Ionic was interpolated; and between the Phrygian and Lydian, the Æolic. The former is said to have had a languid and soft, but pathetic tone; it was particularly adapted to laments. The latter was fitted for the expression of lively, and even impassioned feelings; it is best known from its use in the remains of the Lesbian poets and of Pindar. To these five styles were then added an equal number with higher and lower tones, which were annexed, at their respective extremes, to the original system. The former were called Hyperdorian, Hyperiastian, Hyperphrygian, &c.; the others Hypolydian, Hypoæolian, Hypophrygian, &c. Of these styles none belong to this period except those which approximate

---

[1] See ch. III. § 8.

closely to the first five, viz., the Hyperlydian, and the Hyperdorian, which was also called Mixolydian, as bordering upon
the Lydian. The invention of the former is ascribed to Polymnestus,[1] that of the latter to the poetess Sappho; this latter
was peculiarly used for laments of a pathetic and tender cast.
But the entire system of the fifteen styles was only brought
gradually to perfection by the musicians who lived after the
times of Pindar.

§ 5. Another proof that Terpander reduced to a regular
system the styles used in his time is, that he was the first who
marked the different tones in music. It is stated that Terpander first added musical notes to poems.[2] Of his mode of
notation, indeed, we know nothing; that subsequently used by
the Greeks was introduced in the time of Pythagoras. Hence,
in later times, there existed written tunes by Terpander, of the
kind called *nomes*,[3] whereas the nomes of the ancient bards,
Olen, Philammon, &c., were only preserved by tradition, and
must therefore have undergone many changes. These nomes
of Terpander were arranged for singing and playing upon the
cithara. It cannot, indeed, be doubted that Terpander made use
of the flute, an instrument generally known among the Greeks
in his time; Archilochus, the contemporary of Terpander, even
speaks of Lesbian pæans being sung to the flute;[4] although the
cithara was the most usual accompaniment for songs of this
kind. But it appears, on the whole, from the accounts of the
ancients, that the cithara was the principal instrument in the
Lesbian music. The Lesbian school of singers to the cithara
maintained its pre-eminence in the contests, especially at the
Carnean festival at Sparta, up to Pericleitus, the last Lesbian
who was victorious on the cithara, and who lived before Hipponax (Olym. 60.)[5] Probably some of these nomes of Terpander

---

[1] See § 11.

[2] Μέλος πρῶτος περιέθηκε τοῖς ποιήμασι, says Clemens Alex. *Strom.* I. p. 364, B.
Τὸν Τέρπανδρον . . . . . κιθαρωδικῶν ποιητὴν ὄντα νόμων κατὰ νόμον ἕκαστον τοῖς
ἔπεσι τοῖς ἑαυτοῦ καὶ τοῖς Ὁμήρου μέλη περίθεντα ᾅδειν ἐν τοῖς ἀγωσιν. Plutarch *de
Mus.* 3, after Heraclides. [3] Above, ch. III. § 7.

[4] Αὐτὸς ἐξάρχων πρὸς αὐλὸν Λεσβιὸν παιήονα, Archilochus in Athen. V. p. 180, E,
fr. 58. Gaisford. It may also be conjectured from the mutilated passage of the
Parian marble, Ep. 35, that Terpander practised flute-playing.

[5] Hence in Sappho, fr. 52, Blomf. (69, Neue), the Lesbian singer is called
πέρροχος ἀλλοδαποῖσιν.

were improvements on ancient tunes used in religious rites; and this appears to be the meaning of the statement that some of the nomes noted down by Terpander were invented by the ancient Delphic bard Philammon.   Others seem to have grown out of popular songs, to which the names of Æolic and Bœotian nomes allude.[1]   The greater number were probably invented by Terpander himself. These nomes of Terpander were finished compositions, in which a certain musical idea was systematically worked out; as is proved by the different parts which belonged to one of them.[2]

The rhythmical form of Terpander's compositions was very simple. He is said to have added musical notes to hexameters.[3] In particular he arranged passages of the Homeric poems (which hitherto had only been recited by rhapsodists) to a musical accompaniment on the cithara; he also composed hymns in the same metre, which probably resembled the Homeric hymns, though with somewhat of the lyric character.[4] But the nomes of Terpander can scarcely all have had the simple uniform rhythm of the heroic hexameter. That they had not, is proved by the names of two of Terpander's nomes, the *Orthian* and the *Trochaic;* so called (according to the testimony of Pollux and other grammarians) from the rhythms. The latter was, therefore, composed in trochaic metre; the former in those orthian rhythms, the peculiarity of which consists in a great extension of certain feet.   There is likewise a fragment of Terpander, consisting entirely of long syllables, in which the thought is as weighty and elevated as the metre is solemn and dignified. ' Zeus, first cause of all, leader of all; Zeus, to thee I send this beginning of hymns.'[5] Metres composed exclusively

---

[1] Plutarch, *de Mus.* 4, Pollux, IV. 9. 65.

[2] These, according to Pollux, IV. 9, 66, were ἔπαρχα, μέταρχα, κατάτροπα, μετακατάτροπα, ὀμφαλος, σφραγὶς, ἐπίλογος.

[3] See, particularly, Plutarch, *de Mus.* 3 ; cf. 4. 6. ; Proclus in Photius, *Biblioth.* p. 523.

[4] It is, however, possible that some of the smaller Homeric hymns may have been proems of this kind by Terpander. For example, that to Athene (XXVIII.) appears to be peculiarly fitted for singing to the cithara.

[5] Ζεῦ, πάντων ἀρχὰ, πάντων ἀγήτωρ,
    Ζεῦ, σοι πέμπω ταύταν ὕμνων ἀρχάν.

In Clemens Alex. *Strom.* VI. p. 784, who also states that this hymn to Zeus was set in the Doric style.

of long syllables were employed for religious ceremonies of the greatest solemnity. The name of the *spondaic* foot, which consisted of two long syllables, was derived from the libation (σπονδή), at which a sacred silence was observed.[1] Hymns of this kind were often sung to Zeus in his ancient sanctuary of Dodona, on the borders of Thesprotia and Molossia; and hence is explained the name of the Molossian foot, consisting of three long syllables, by which the fragment of Terpander ought probably to be measured.

§ 6. The accounts of Terpander's inventions, and the extant remains of his nomes, however meagre and scanty, give some notion of his merits as the father of Grecian music. Another ancient master, however, the Phrygian musician OLYMPUS, so much enlarged the system of the Greek music, that Plutarch considers him, and not Terpander, as the founder of it.

The date, and indeed the whole history of this Olympus, are involved in obscurity by a confusion between him (who is certainly as historical as Terpander) and a mythological Olympus, who is connected with the first founders of the Phrygian religion and worship. Even Plutarch, who in his learned treatise upon music has marked the distinction between the earlier and the later Olympus, has still attributed inventions to the fabulous Olympus which properly belong to the historical one. The ancient Olympus is quite lost in the dawn of mythical legends; he is the favourite and disciple of the Phrygian Silenus, Marsyas, who invented the flute, and used it in his unfortunate contest with the cithara of the Hellenic god Apollo. The invention of nomes could only be ascribed to this fabulous Olympus, and to the still more ancient Hyagnis, as certain nomes were attributed by the Greeks to Olen and Philammon; that is to say, certain tunes were sung at festivals, which tradition assigned to these nomes. There was also in Phrygia a family said to be descended from the mythical Olympus, the members of which, probably, played sacred tunes on the flute at the festivals of the Magna Mater: to this family, according to Plutarch, the later Olympus belonged.

§ 7. This later Olympus stands midway between his native

---

[1] εὐφημία.

country Phrygia and the Greek nation. Phrygia, which had in general little connexion with the Greek religion, and was remarkable only for its enthusiastic rites and its boisterous music, obtained, by means of Olympus, an important influence upon the music, and thus upon the poetry, of Greece. But Olympus would not have been able to exercise this influence, if he had not, by a long residence in Greece, become acquainted with the Greek civilization. It is stated that he produced new tunes in the Greek sanctuary of Pytho; and that he had disciples who were Greeks, such as Crates and Hierax the Argive.[1] It was by means of Olympus that the flute attained an equal place in Greek music with the cithara; by which change music gained a much greater compass than before. It was much easier to multiply the tones of the flute than those of the cithara; especially as the ancient flute-players were accustomed to play upon two flutes at once. Hence the severe censors of music in antiquity disapproved of the flute on moral grounds, since they considered the variety of its tones as calculated to seduce the player into an unchaste and florid style of music. Olympus also invented and cultivated the third musical scale, the enharmonic; the powerful effects of which, as well as its difficulties, have been already mentioned. His nomes were accordingly *auletic*, that is, intended for the flute, and belonged to the enharmonic scale.

Among the different names which have been preserved, that of the *Harmateios Nomos* may be particularly mentioned, as we are able to form a tolerably correct idea of its nature. In the *Orestes* of Euripides, a Phrygian Eunuch in the service of Helen, who has just escaped the murderous hands of Orestes and Pylades, describes his dangers in a monody, in which the liveliest expression of pain and terror is blended with a character of Asiatic softness. This song, of which the musical accompaniment was doubtless composed with as much art as the rhythmical structure, was set to the harmatian nome, as Euripides makes his Phrygian say. This mournful and pas-

---

[1] The former is mentioned by Plutarch, *de Mus.* 7; the latter by the same writer, c. 26, and Pollux, IV. 10. 79. Accordingly it is not probable that this second Olympus was a mythical personage, or a collective appellation of the Phrygian music in its improved state.

sionate music appears to have been particularly adapted to the talent and taste of Olympus. At Delphi, where the solemnities of the Pythian games turned principally upon the fight of Apollo with the Python, Olympus is said to have played a dirge in honour of the slain Python upon the flute and in the Lydian style.[1] A nome of Olympus played upon several flutes (ξυναυλία) was well known at Athens. Aristophanes, in the beginning of his *Knights*, describes the two slaves of Demus as giving utterance to their griefs in this tune. But from the esteem in which Olympus was held by the ancients, it seems improbable that all his compositions were of this gloomy character; and we may therefore fairly attribute a greater variety to his genius. His nome to Athene probably had the energetic and serene tone which suited the worship of this goddess. Olympus also shows great richness of invention in his rhythmical forms, and particularly in such as seemed to the Greeks expressive of enthusiasm and emotion. It appears probable from a statement in Plutarch, that he introduced the rhythm of the songs to the Magna Mater, or *Galliambi*.[2] The *Atys* of Catullus shows what an impression of melancholy, beauty, and tenderness this metre was capable of producing, when handled by a skilful artist.

A more important fact, however, is, that Olympus introduced not only the third scale of music, but also a third class of rhythms. All the early rhythmical forms are of two kinds,[3] the *equal* (ἴσον), in which the arsis is equal to the thesis; and the *double* (διπλάσιον), in which the arsis is twice as long as the thesis. The former is the basis of the hexameter, the latter of the chief part of the poetry of Archilochus. The equal rhythm is most appropriate, when a calm composed state of mind is to be expressed, as there is a perfect balance of the arsis and thesis. The double rhythm has a rapid and easy

---

[1] With this is connected the account that Olympus the Mysian cultivated the Lydian style, ἐφιλοτέχνησεν. Clem. Alex. *Strom.* I. p. 363. Potter.

[2] The passage of Plutarch, *de Musica*, c. XXIX., καὶ τὸν χορεῖον (ῥυθμὸν), ᾧ πόλλῳ κέχρηνται ἐν τοῖς Μητρῴοις, probably refers to the Ἰωνικὸς ἀνακλώμενος, which, on account of the prevalence of trochees in it might probably be considered as belonging to the χορεῖος ῥυθμός.

[3] Above, chap. XI. § 8.

march, and is therefore adapted to the expression of passion, but not of great or elevated sentiments, the double arsis requiring no great energy to carry forward the light thesis. Now, besides these, there is a third kind of rhythm, called, from the relation of the arsis to the thesis, *one and a half* (ἡμιόλιον); in which an arsis of two times answers to a thesis of three. The Cretan foot (‿∪‿), and the multifarious class of .pæons belong to this head (‿∪∪∪, ∪∪∪‿, &c.), to which last the theoretical writers of antiquity ascribe much life and energy, and, at the same time, loftiness of expression. That the poets and musicians considered it in the same light may be inferred from the use which they made of it. Olympus was the first who cultivated this rhythm, as we learn from Plutarch, and it is almost needless to remark that this extension of the rhythms agrees with the other inventions of Olympus.[1]

§ 8. It appears, therefore, that Olympus exercised an important influence in developing the rhythms, the instrumental music, and the musical scales of the Greeks, as well as in the composition of numerous nomes. Yet if we inquire to what words his compositions were arranged, we can find no trace of a verse written by him. Olympus is never, like Terpander, mentioned as a poet; he is simply a musician.[2] His nomes, indeed, seem to have been originally executed on the flute alone, without singing; and he himself, in the tradition of the Greeks, was celebrated as a flute-player. It was a universal custom at this time to select the flute-players for the musical performances in Greek cities from among the Phrygians: of this nation, according to the testimony of Athenæus, were Iambus, Adon, and Telos mentioned by the Lacedæmonian lyric poet Alcman, and Cion, Codalus, and Babys, mentioned by Hipponax. Hence, for example, Plutarch says, that Thaletas took the Cretan rhythm from the flute-playing of Olympus,[3] and thus acquired

---

[1] According to Plutarch, *de Mus.* c. 29. Some also ascribe to Olympus the Βακχεῖος ῥυθμός (∪‿‿), which belongs to the same family, though its form makes a less pleasing impression.

[2] Suidas attributes to him μέλη and ἐλεγεῖαι, which may be a confusion between compositions in the lyric and elegiac style and poetical texts.

[3] ἐκ τῆς Ὀλύμπου αὐλήσεως, Plutarch, *de Mus.* c. 10; cf. c. 17. Hence also, in c. 7, *auletic* nomes are ascribed to Olympus; but in c. 3 the first *aulodic* nomes are ascribed to Clonas.

the fame of a good poet. Since Olympus did not properly belong to the Greek literature, and did not enter the lists with the poets of Greece, it is natural that his precise date should not have been recorded. His date, however, is sufficiently marked by the advances of the Greek music and rhythm due to his efforts; and the generation to which he belonged can thus be determined. For, as it appears both from the nature of his inventions and from express testimony that music had made some progress in his time, he must be later than Terpander; on the other hand, he must be prior to Thaletas, according to the statement just mentioned; so that he must be placed between the 30th and 40th Olympiads (B.C. 660—20.)[1]

§ 9. THALETAS makes the third epoch in the history of Greek music. A native of Crete, he found means to express in a musical form the spirit which pervaded the religious institutions of his country, by which he produced a strong impression upon the other Greeks. He seems to have been partly a priest and partly an artist; and from this circumstance his history is veiled in obscurity. He is called a Gortynian, but is also said to have been born at Elyrus; the latter tradition may perhaps allude to the belief that the mythical expiatory priest Carmanor (who was supposed to have purified Apollo himself from the slaughter of the Python, and to have been the father of the bard Chrysothemis) lived at Tarrha, near Elyrus, in the mountains on the west of Crete. It is at any rate certain that Thaletas was connected with this ancient seat of religious poetry and music, the object of which was to appease passion and emotion. Thaletas was in the height of his fame invited to Sparta, that he might restore peace and order to the city, at that time torn by intestine commotions. In this attempt he is supposed to have completely succeeded; and his political influence on this occasion gave rise to the report that Lycurgus had been instructed by him.[2] In fact, however, Thaletas lived several centuries later

---

[1] According to Suidas, Olympus was contemporary with a king Midas, the son of Gordius; but this is no argument against the assumed date, as the Phrygian kings, down to the time of Crœsus, were alternately named Midas and Gordius.

[2] Nevertheless Strabo, X. p. 481, justly calls Thaletas a legislative man. Like the Cretan training in general (Ælian, *V. H.* II. 39), he doubtless combined poetry and music with a measured and well-ordered conduct.

than Lycurgus, having been one of the musicians who assisted
in perfecting Terpander's musical system at Sparta, and giving
it a new and fixed form.   The musicians named by Plutarch,
as the arrangers of this second system, are Thaletas of Gortyna,
Xenodamus of Cythera, Xenocritus the Locrian, Polymnestus of
Colophon, Sacadas of Argos.   Among these, however, the last
named are later than the former; as Polymnestus composed for
the Lacedæmonians a poem in honour of Thaletas, which is
mentioned by Pausanias.   If, therefore, Sacadas was a victor in
the Pythian games in Olymp. 47. 3 (B.C. 590), and if this may
be taken as the time when the most recent of these musicians
flourished, the first of them, Thaletas, may be fixed not later
than the 40th Olympiad (B.C. 620); which places him in the
right relation to Terpander and Olympus.[1]

§ 10. We now return to the musical and poetical productions
of Thaletas, which were connected with the ancient religious
rites of his country.   In Crete, at the time of Thaletas, the
predominating worship was that of Apollo; the character of
which was a solemn elevation of mind, a firm reliance in the
power of the god, and a calm acquiescence in the order of things
proclaimed by him.   But it cannot be doubted that the ancient
Cretan worship of Zeus was also practised, with the wild war-
dances of the Curetes, like the Phrygian worship of the Magna
Mater.[2]   The musical and poetical works of Thaletas fall under
two heads—*pæans* and *hyporchemes*.   In many respects these
two resembled each other; inasmuch as the pæan originally belonged exclusively to the worship of Apollo, and the hyporcheme
was also performed at an early date in temples of Apollo, as at
Delos.[3]   Hence pæans and hyporchemes were sometimes confounded.   Their main features, however, were quite different.
The pæan displayed the calm and serious feeling which prevailed
in the worship of Apollo, without excluding the expression of
an earnest desire for his protection, or of gratitude for aid already

---

[1] Clinton, who, in *Fast. Hellen.* vol. I. p. 199, *sq.*, places Thaletas before Terpander, rejects the most authentic testimony, that concerning the κατάστασις of
music at Sparta ; and moreover, does not allow sufficient weight to the far more
artificial character of the music and rhythms of Thaletas.

[2] Κουρῆτές τε θεοὶ φιλοπαίγμονες ὀρχηστῆρες. Hesiod, fr. 94. Goettling.

[3] Above, ch. III. § 6.

vouchsafed. The hyporcheme, on the other hand, was a dance of a mimic character, which sometimes passed into the playful and the comic. Accordingly the hyporchematic dance is considered as a peculiar species of the lyric dances, and, among dramatic styles of dancing, it is compared with the cordax of comedy, on account of its merry and sportive tone.[1] The rhythms of the hyporcheme, if we may judge from the fragments of Pindar, were peculiarly light, and had an imitative and graphic character.

These musical and poetical styles were improved by Thaletas, who employed both the orchestic productions of his native country, and the impassioned music and rhythms of Olympus. It has already been remarked that he borrowed the Cretan rhythm from Olympus, which doubtless acquired this name from its having been made known by Thaletas of Crete. The entire class of feet to which the Cretan foot belongs, were called *Pæons*, from being used in pæans (or pæons). Thaletas doubtless gave a more rapid march to the pæan by this animated and vigorous rhythm.[2] But the hyporchematic productions of Thaletas must have been still gayer and more energetic. And Sparta was the country which at this time was best suited to the music of dancing. The Gymnopædia, the festival of 'naked youths,' one of the chief solemnities of the Spartans, was well calculated to encourage the love of gymnastic exercises and dances among the youth. The boys in these dances first imitated the movements of wrestling and the pancration; and then passed into the wild gestures of the worship of Bacchus.[3] There was also much jesting and merriment in these dances;[4] a fact which points to mimic representations in the style of the hyporcheme, especially as the establishment of dances and musical entertainments at the gymnopædia is ascribed by Plutarch to

---

[1] Athen. XIV. p. 630, E.

[2] Fragments of a pæan in pæons are preserved in Aristotle, *Rhet.* III. 8—viz., Δαλογενὲς, εἴτε Λυκίαν, and Χρυσεοκόμα ῞Εκατε, παῖ Διός.

[3] These gymnopædic dances, described by Athenæus, XIV. p. 631, XV. p. 678, were evidently different from the γυμνοπαιδικὴ ὄρχησις, which, according to the same Athenæus, was the most solemn kind of lyric dance, and corresponded to the emmeleia among the dramatic dances.

[4] Pollux IV. 14, 104.

the musicians, at the head of whom was Thaletas.[1] The Pyrrhic,
or war-dance, was also formed by the musicians of this school,
particularly by Thaletas.   It was a favourite spectacle of the
Cretans and Lacedæmonians ; and both these nations derived it
from their ancestors, the former from the Curetes, the latter
from the Dioscuri.   It was accompanied by the flute, which
could only have been the case after the music of the flute had
been scientifically cultivated by the Greeks ; although there was
a legend that Athene herself played the war-dance upon the
flute to the Dioscuri.[2]   It was a natural transition from the
simple war-dance to imitations of different modes of fighting,
offensive and defensive, and to the regular representation of
mock fights with several Pyrrhicists.   According to Plato, the
Pyrrhic dance was thus practised in Crete ; and Thaletas, in
improving the national music of Crete, composed hyporchemes
for the Pyrrhic dance.   The rhythms which were chosen for
the expression of the hurried and vehement movements of the
combat were of course quick and changeable, as was usually the
case in the hyporchematic poems ; the names of some of the
metrical feet have been derived from the rhythms employed in
the Pyrrhic dance.[3]

§ 11. Terpander, Olympus, and Thaletas are distinguished
by the salient peculiarities which belong to inventive genius.
But it is difficult to find any individual characteristics in the
numerous masters who followed them between the 40th and
50th Olympiads.   It may, however, be useful to mention some
of their names, in order to give an idea of the zeal with which
the Greek music was cultivated, after it had passed out of the
hands of its first founders and improvers.

The first name we will mention is Clonas, of Thebes, or Tegea,
not much later than Terpander, celebrated as a composer of
aulodic nomes, one of which was called Elegos, on account of
its plaintive tone.   The poetry, which was set to his composi-

---

[1] Plutarch, *de Mus.* 9.   The ancient chronologists place the first introduction of
the gymnopædia somewhat earlier, viz. Olymp. 28. 4 (B.C. 665.)

[2] See Müller's *Dorians*, book IV. ch. 6, § 6 and 7.

[3] Not only the Pyrrhic (ᴗ ᴗ) but also the proceleusmatic, or challenging, foot
(ᴗ ᴗ ᴗ ᴗ), refers to the Pyrrhic dance. The latter ought probably to be considered
a resolved anapæst ; and so the ἐνόπλιος ῥυθμός is removed to the anapæstic measure.

tions and sung to the flute, chiefly consisted of hexameters and
elegiac distichs, without any artificial rhythmical construction.
Secondly, Hierax, of Argos, a scholar of Olympus, was a master
of flute-playing; he invented the music to which the Argive
maidens performed the ceremony of the *Flower-carrying* (ἀνθεσ-
φορία), in the temple of Here; and another in which the
youths represented the graceful exercises of the Pentathlon.
We will next enumerate the masters who, after Thaletas, contributed the most towards the new arrangement of music in
Sparta. These were Xenodamus, a Lacedæmonian of Cythera,
a poet and composer of pæans and hyporchemes, like Thaletas;
Xenocritus, from Locri Epizephyrii in Italy, a town noted for
its taste in music and poetry. To this Xenocritus is attributed
a peculiar Locrian, or Italian measure, which was a modification of the Æolic;[1] as the Locrian love-songs[2] approached closely
to the Æolic poetry of Sappho and Erinna. Erotic poems,
however, are not attributed to Xenocritus, but dithyrambs, the
subjects of which were taken from the heroic mythology; a
peculiar kind of poetry, the origin and style of which we will
endeavour to describe hereafter. Lastly, there are to be mentioned Polymnestus, of Colophon,[3] and Sacadas, of Argos; the
former was an early contemporary of Alcman, who improved
upon the aulodia of Clonas, and exceeded the limits of the five
styles.[4] He appears, in general, to have enlarged the art of
music, and was particularly distinguished in the loud and spirited Orthian nome. Sacadas was celebrated as having been
victorious in flute-playing, at the first three Pythian games, at
which the Amphictyons presided (Olymp. 47. 3; 49. 3; 50. 3;
B.C. 590, 582, 578). He first played the flute in the Pythian
style, but without singing. He left this branch of the art to
Echembrotus, an Arcadian musician, who, in the first Pythiad,
gained the prize for accompanying the voice with the flute.
But, according to Pausanias, this connexion of flute-playing and

---

[1] Boeckh, *de Metris Pind.* p. 212, 225, 241, 279.

[2] Λοκρικὰ ᾄσματα.

[3] The son of Meles, a name derived from Smyrna, which seems to have been
often adopted in families of musicians and poets. (See above, ch. V. § 2).

[4] By the ὑπολύδιος τόνος, Plutarch, *de Mus.* c. 29, although c. 8 does not agree
with this statement. (See above, § 4.)

singing seemed, from its mournful and gloomy expression, so un-
suited to the Pythian festival—a joyful celebration of victory,—
that the Amphictyons abolished this contest after the first time.
With regard to Sacadas, and the state of music in his time, he
is stated to have been the inventor of the tripartite nome (τρι-
μερὴς νόμος), in which one strophe was set in the Doric, the
second in the Phrygian, the third in the Lydian style; the
entire character of the music and poetry being, doubtless,
changed with the change of the style.

§ 12. By the efforts of these masters, music appears to have
been brought to the degree of excellence at which we find it in
Pindar's time; it was then perfectly adapted to express the
general course of any feeling, to which the poet could give a
more definite character and meaning.   For however imperfect
the management of instrumental music and the harmonious
combination of different voices and instruments may have been
among the ancient Greeks, nevertheless the Greek musicians of
this time had solved the great problem of their art, viz., that of
giving an appropriate expression to the different shades of feeling.   It was in Greece the constant endeavour of the great
poets, the best thinkers, and even of statesmen who interested
themselves in the education of youth, to give a good direction
to music; they all dreaded the increasing prevalence of a
luxuriant style of instrumental music, and an unrestricted flight
in the boundless realms of harmony.   But these efforts could
only for a while resist the inclinations and turbulent demands
of the theatrical audiences;[1] and the new style of music was
established about the end of the Peloponnesian war.   It will be
hereafter shown how strong an influence it exercised upon the
poetry of Greece at that time.   At the courts of the Macedonian kings, from Alexander downwards, symphonies were
performed by hundreds of instruments; and from the statements of the ancients it would seem that instrumental music,
particularly as regards wind instruments, was at that time
scarcely inferior in force or number to our own.   Yet amidst
all these grand and brilliant productions, the best judges were
forced to confess that the ancient melodies of Olympus, which

---

[1] The θεατροκρατία of Plato.

were arranged for the simplest instruments, possessed a beauty to which the modern art, with all its appliances, could never attain.[1]

We now turn to lyric poetry, which, assisted by the musical improvements of Terpander, Olympus, and Thaletas, began in the 40th Olympiad (620 B.C.) a course, which, in a century and a half, brought it to the highest perfection.

---

[1] Plutarch, *de Mus.* c. 18.

CHAPTER XIII.

THE ÆOLIC SCHOOL OF LYRIC POETRY.

§ 1. THE lyric poetry of the Greeks is of two kinds, which were cultivated by different schools of poets ; the name which is commonly given to poets living in the same country, and following the same rules of composition. Of these two schools, one is called the *Æolic,* as it flourished among the Æolians of Asia Minor, and particularly in the island of Lesbos ; the other the *Doric,* because, although it was diffused over the whole of Greece, yet it was first and principally cultivated by the Dorians in Peloponnesus and Sicily. The difference of origin appears also in the dialect of these two schools. The Lesbian school wrote in the Æolic dialect, as it is still to be found upon inscriptions in that island, while the Doric employed almost indifferently either a mitigated Dorism, or the epic dialect, the dignity and solemnity of which was heightened by a limited use of Doric forms. These two schools differ essentially in every respect, as much in the subject, as in the form and style of their poems ; and as in the Greek poetry generally, so here in particular, we may perceive that between the subject, form, and style, there is the closest connexion. To begin with the mode of recitation, the Doric lyric poetry was intended to be executed by choruses, and to be sung to choral dances, whence it is sometimes called choral poetry : on the other hand, the Æolic is never called choral, because it was meant to be recited by a single person, who accompanied his recitation with a stringed instrument, generally the lyre, and with suitable gestures. The structure of the Doric lyric strophe is comprehensive, and often very artificial ; inasmuch as the ear, which might perhaps be unable to detect the recurring rhythms, was assisted by the eye, which could follow the different movements of the chorus, and thus the spectator was able to understand the intricate and artificial plan of the composition. The Æolic lyric poetry, on the other hand, was much more limited, and either consisted of verses joined together (τὸ κατὰ στίχον), or was formed of a few short verses, strophes in which the same verse is frequently repeated, and the conclusion is effected by a change in the versification, or by the addition of a short final verse. The strophes of the Doric lyric poetry were also often combined by annexing to two strophes corresponding with one another, a third and different one called an *epode*. The origin of this, according to the ancients, is, that the chorus, having performed one movement during the strophe, return to their former position during the antistrophe ; and they then remain motionless for a time, during which the epode is sung. The short strophes of the Æolic lyric poetry, on the other hand, follow each other in equal measure, and without being interrupted by epodes. The rhythmical structure of the choral strophes of the Doric lyric poetry is likewise capable of much variety, assuming sometimes a more elevated, sometimes a more cheerful character ; whilst in the Æolic, light and lively metres, peculiarly adapted to express the passionate emotion of an excitable mind, are frequently repeated.

Choral poetry required an object of public and general interest, as the choruses were combined with religious festivals ; and if they were celebrated in private, they always needed a solemn occasion and celebration. Thoughts and feelings peculiar to an individual could not, with propriety, be sung by a numerous chorus. Hence the choral lyric poetry was closely connected with the interests of the Greek states, either by celebrating their gods and heroes, and imparting a charm and dignity to the festal recreations of the people, or by extolling citizens who had acquired high renown in the eyes of their

countrymen.   It was also sometimes used at marriages or
funerals;—occasions in which the events of private life are
brought into public notice.   On the other hand, the Æolic
lyric poetry frequently expresses thoughts and feelings in which
only *one* mind can sympathize, and expresses them with such
tenderness as to display the inmost workings of the heart.
How would such impressions be destroyed by the singing of a
chorus of many voices!   Even when political events and other
matters of public interest were touched upon in the Æolic lyric
poetry, they were not mentioned in such a manner as to invite
general sympathy.   Instead of seeking, by wise admonitions, to
settle the disorders of the state, the poet gives expression to
his own party feelings.   Nevertheless, it is probable that the
Æolic poets sometimes composed poems for choral exhibition,
for choruses were undoubtedly performed in Lesbos, as well as
in other parts of Greece; and although some ancient festival
songs might have existed, yet there would naturally be a wish
to obtain new poetry, for which purpose the labour of the poets
in the island would be put in requisition.   Several of the
Lesbian lyric poems, of which we have fragments and accounts,
appear to have been composed for choral recitation.[1]   But the
characteristic excellence of this lyric poetry was the expression
of individual ideas and sentiments, with warmth and frankness.
These sentiments found a natural expression in the native
dialect of these poets, the ancient Æolic, which has a character
of simplicity and fondness; the epic dialect, the general language of Greek poetry, was only used sparingly, in order to
soften and elevate this popular dialect.   Unhappily the works
of these poets were allowed to perish at a time when they had
become unintelligible from the singularity of their dialect and
the condensation of their thoughts.   To this cause, and not to

---

[1] Especially the hymenæus of Sappho, from which the poem of Catullus, 62, is
imitated; it was recited by choruses of young men and women ; see below, § 9.
Choral dances had been usual, in connexion with the hymenæus, from the earliest
times ; see above ch. II. § 5. So likewise the fragment of Sappho, Κρῆσσαί νυ ποθ'
ὧδ', &c., No. 83, ed. Blomfield, No. 46, ed. Neue, alludes to some imitation of a
Cretan dance round the altar ; and dances of this kind were, perhaps, often combined with the hymns of the Æolians ; see *Anthol. Palat.* I, 189. Anacreon's
poems were also sung by female choruses at nocturnal festivals, according to Critias
ap. Athen. XIII. p. 600 D.

the warmth of their descriptions of the passion of love, is to be attributed the oblivion to which they were consigned. For if literary works had been condemned on moral grounds of this kind, the writings of Martial and Petronius, and many poems of the *Anthology,* would not exist; while Alcæus and Sappho would probably be extant. As, however, the productions of these two poets have not been preserved, we must attempt to form as perfect an idea of them as can be obtained from the sources of information which are open to us.

§ 2. The circumstances of the life of ALCÆUS are closely connected with the political circumstances of his native city Mytilene, in the island of Lesbos. Alcæus belonged to a noble family, and a great part of his public life was employed in asserting the privileges of his order. These were then endangered by democratic factions, which appear to have placed ambitious men at their head, and to have given them powerful support, as happened about the same time in Peloponnesus. In many cases the demagogues obtained absolute, or (as the Greeks called it) *tyrannical* power. A tyrant of this kind in Mytilene was Melanchrus, who was opposed by the brothers of Alcæus, Antimenidas and Cicis, in conjunction with Pittacus, the wisest statesman of the time in Lesbos, and was slain by them in the 42nd Olympiad, 612 B.C. At this time the Mytileneans were at war with foreign enemies, the Athenians, who, under Phrynon, had conquered and retained possession of Sigeum, a maritime town of Troas. The Mytileneans, among whom was Alcæus, were defeated in this war; but Pittacus slew Phrynon in single combat, Olymp. 43. 3, 606 B.C. Mytilene henceforth was divided into parties, from the heads of which new tyrants arose, such as (according to Strabo) Myrsilus, Megalagyrus, and the Cleanactids. The aristocratic party, to which Alcæus and Antimenidas belonged, was driven out of Mytilene, and the two brothers then wandered about the world. Alcæus, being exiled, made long sea voyages, which led him to Egypt; and Antimenidas served in the Babylonian army, probably in the war which Nebuchadnezzar waged in Upper Asia with the Egyptian Pharaoh Necho, and the states of Syria, Phœnicia, and Judæa, in the years from B.C. 606 (Ol. 43. 3) to

584 (Ol. 49. 1), and longer.[1]   Some time after this we again
find the brothers in the neighbourhood of their native city, at
the head of the exiled nobles, and trying to effect their return
by force.   Pittacus was then unanimously elected dictator by
the people, to defend the constitution (αἰσυμνήτης).   The administration of Pittacus lasted, according to the accounts of
ancient chronologers, from Olymp. 47. 3 (B.C. 590), to 50. 1
(B.C. 580).   He was so fortunate as to overcome the exiled
party, and to gain them over by his clemency and moderation.
He also (according to a well-authenticated statement) was
reconciled with Alcæus; and it is probable that the poet, after
many wanderings, passed his latter days in the quiet enjoyment
of his home.

§ 3. In the midst of these troubles and perils, Alcæus struck
the lyre, not, like Solon, with a spirit of calm and imparial
patriotism, to bewail the evils of the state, and to show the
way to improvement, but to give utterance to the passionate
emotions of his mind.   When Myrsilus was about to establish
a tyrannical government in Mytilene, Alcæus composed the
beautiful ode, in which he compares the state to a ship tossed
about by the waves, while the sea has washed into the hold,
and the sail is torn by the wind.   A considerable fragment of
this ode has been preserved;[2] and we may also form some idea
of its contents from the fine imitation of it by Horace, which,
however, probably falls short of the original.[3]   When Myrsilus
dies, the joy of the poet knows no bounds.   ‘ Now is the time
for carousing, now is the time for challenging the guests to
drink, for Myrsilus is dead.’[4]   Horace has also taken the
beginning of this ode for one of his finest poems.[5]   After the
death of Myrsilus, we find Alcæus aiming the shafts of his
poetry at Megalagyrus and the Cleanactids, on account of their
attempts to obtain illegal power ; although, according to Strabo,

---

[1] The battle of Carchemish, or Cirgesium, appears from Berosus to fall in 604 B.C.,
the year of Nabopolassar's death ; but 606 B.C., the date of the biblical chronology,
is probably right.

[2] Fragm. 2. Blomf. 2. Matth. cf. 3.

[3] *Carm.* I. 14. O navis referent—

[4] Fragm. 4. Blomf. 4. Matth.

[5] *Carm.* I. 37. Nunc est bibendum—

Alcæus himself was not entirely guiltless of attempts against the constitution of Mytilene. Even when Pittacus was chosen dictator by the people, the discontent of the poet with the political state of his country did not cease; on the contrary, Pittacus (who was esteemed by all a wise, moderate, and patriotic statesman, and who had clearly shown his republican virtue by resigning his power after a ten years' administration) now became the prime object of the vehement attacks of Alcæus. He reproaches the people for having unanimously chosen the ignoble[1] Pittacus to be tyrant over the ill-fated city; and he assails the dictator with vituperative epithets which appear fitter for iambic than for lyric poetry. Thus he taunts him in words of the boldest formation, sometimes with his mean appearance, sometimes with his low and vulgar mode of life.[2] As compared with Pittacus, it seems that the poet now deemed the former tyrant Melanchrus, 'worthy of the respect of the city.'[3]

In this class of his poems (called by the ancients his *party poems*, διχοστασιαστικά), Alcæus gave a lively picture of the political state of Mytilene, as it appeared to his partial view. His war-songs express a stirring martial spirit, though they do not breathe the strict principles of military honour which prevailed among the Dorians, particularly in Sparta. He describes with joy his armoury, the walls of which glittered with helmets, coats of mail, and other pieces of armour, ' which must now be thought upon, as the work of war is begun.'[4] He speaks of war with courage and confidence to his companions in arms; there is no need of walls (he says), ' men are the best rampart of the city;'[5] nor does he fear the shining weapons of the enemy. ' Emblems on shields make no wounds.'[6] He celebrates the battles of his adventurous brother, who had, in the service of

---

[1] τὸν κακοπάτριδα Πιττακόν. Fragm. 23. Blomf. 5. Matth.

[2] In Diog. Laërt. I. 81. Fragm. 6. Matth. Thus he calls Pittacus ζοφοδορπίδας, that is, who sups in the dark, and not in a room lighted with lamps and torches.

[3] Fragm. 7. Blomf. 7. Matth.

[4] Fragm. 24. Blomf. 1. Matth. comp. below § 5.

[5] Fragm. 9. Blomf. 11, 12. Matth.

[6] Fragm. 13. Matth.

the Babylonians, slain a gigantic champion;[1] and speaks of the ivory sword-handle which this brother had brought from the extremity of the earth, probably the present of some oriental prince.[2] Yet the pleasure he seems to have felt in deeds of arms did not prevent him from relating in one of his poems, how in a battle with the Athenians he had escaped indeed with his life, but the victors had hung up his castaway arms as trophies, in the temple of Pallas at Sigeum.[3]

§ 4. A noble nature, accompanied with strong passions, a variety of character frequent among the Æolians, appears in all the poetry of Alcæus, especially in the numerous poems which sing the praises of love and wine. The frequent mention of wine in the fragments of Alcæus shows how highly he prized the gift of Bacchus, and how ingenious he was in the invention of inducements to drinking. Now it is the cold storms of winter which drive him to drink by the flame of the hearth, as in a beautiful poem imitated by Horace;[4] now the heat of the dog-star, which parches all nature, and invites to moisten the tongue with wine.[5] Another time it is the cares and sorrows of life for which wine is the best medicine;[6] and then again, it is joy for the death of the tyrant which must be celebrated by a drinking-bout. Alcæus however does not consider wine-drinking as a mere sensual excitement. Thus he calls wine the drowner of cares;[7] and, as opening the heart, it is a mirror for mankind.[8] Still it may be doubted whether Alcæus composed a separate class of drinking-songs (συμποτικά). From the fragments which remain, and the imitations by Horace, it is more probable that Alcæus connected every exhortation to

---

[1] The fragment in Strabo, XIII. p. 617 (86. Blomf. 8. Matth.), has been thus emended by the author in Niebuhr's *Rheinisches Museum*, vol. I. p. 287.—Καὶ τὸν ἀδελφὸν Ἀντιμενίδαν, ὅν φησιν Ἀλκαῖος Βαβυλωνίοις συμμαχοῦντα τελέσαι μέγαν ἆθλον, καὶ ἐκ πόνων αὐτοὺς ῥύσασθαι κτείναντα ἄνδρα μαχατὰν, ὥς φησι, βασιλήιον, παλαιστὰν ἀπολείποντα μόνον μίαν πάχεων ἀπὸ πέμπων, (Æol. for πέντε) : that is, this royal champion only wanted a palm of five Greek cubits.

[2] Fragm. 32. Blomf. 67. Matth.

[3] Fragm. 56. Blomf. 9. Matth.

[4] Fragm. 1. Blomf. 27. Matth. Horat. *Carm.* I. 9. Vides ut alta.

[5] Fragm. 18. Blomf. 28. Matth.   [6] Fragm. 3. Blomf. 29. Matth.

[7] λαθικηδής, Fragm. 20. Blomf. 31. Matth.

[8] Fr. 16. Blomf. 36, 37. Matth.

drink with some reflection, either upon the particular circumstances of the time or upon man's destiny in general.

It is much to be regretted that so little of the erotic poetry
of Alcæus has reached our time. What could be more interesting than the relations between Alcæus and Sappho? of
the poet with the poetess? whilst on the part of Alcæus love
and respect for the noble and renowned maiden were in conflict.
He salutes her in a poem, ' Violet-crowned, pure, sweetly smiling
Sappho;' and confesses to her in another that he wishes to express more, but shame prevents him. Sappho understands his
meaning, and answers with maiden indignation, ' If thy wishes
were fair and noble, and thy tongue designed not to utter what
is base, shame would not cloud thy eyes, but thou wouldst
freely speak thy just desires.'[1]   That his poems to beautiful
youths breathed feelings of the tenderest love may be conjectured from the well-known anecdote that he attributed a
peculiar beauty to a small blemish in his beloved.[2]   The
amatory poems, like the passages in praise of wine, are free
from a tone of Sybaritic effeminacy, or merely sensual passion.
Throughout his poems, we see the active restless man; and the
tumult of war, the strife of politics, the sufferings of exile,
and of distant wanderings, serve by contrast to heighten the
effect of scenes of tranquil enjoyment. ' The Lesbian citizen
sang of war amidst the din of arms; or, when he had bound the
storm-tossed ship to the shore, he sang of Bacchus and the
Muses, of Venus and her son, and Lycus, beautiful from his
black hair and black eyes.'[3]   It is evident that poetry was not
a mere pastime, or exercise of skill to Alcæus, but a means of
pouring out the inmost feelings of his soul.   How superior are
these poems to the odes of Horace! which, admirable as they
are for the refinement of the ideas and the beauty of the execution, yet are wanting in that which characterized the Æolic
lyric poetry, the expression of vehement passion.

There is little characteristic in the religious poetry of
Alcæus, which consisted of hymns to different deities.   These

---

[1] Fragm. 38. Blomf. and Sappho, Fragm. 30. In Matthiæ, Fragm. 41, 42.
[2] Cicero, de Nat. D. I. 28. The cod. Glogau. has *in Pericle puero.*
[3] Horat. Carm. I. 32. 5. *sqq.* Cf. Schol. Pind. Olymp. X. 15.

poems (judging from a few specimens of them) had so much of
the epic style, and contained so much diffuse and graphic
narrative, that their whole structure must have been different
from that of the poems designed for the expression of opinions
and feelings.   In a hymn to Apollo, Alcæus related the beautiful Delphic legend, that the youthful god, adorned by Zeus
with a golden fillet, and holding the lyre, is carried in a car
drawn by swans to the pious Hyperboreans, and remains with
them for a year; when, it being the time for the Delphic tripods
to sound, the god about the middle of summer goes in his car
to Delphi, while choruses of youths invoke him with poems, and
nightingales and cicadæ salute him with their songs.[1]   Another
hymn, that to Hermes, had manifestly a close resemblance to
the epic hymn of the Homeric poet:[2] both relate the birth of
Hermes, and his driving away the oxen of Apollo, as also the
wrath of the god against the thief, which however is changed
into laughter, when he finds that, in the midst of his threats,
Hermes has contrived to steal the quiver from his shoulder.[3]
In another hymn the birth of Hephæstus was related.   It
appears from a few extant fragments that Alcæus used the same
metres and the same kind of strophes in the composition of
these hymns, as for his other poems.   The flow of the narrative
must, however, have been checked by these short verses and
strophes.   Still Alcæus (as Horace also does sometimes) was
able to carry the same ideas and the same sentence through
several strophes.   It is moreover probable, from the extraordinary taste displayed by the ancient poets, and by Alcæus in
particular, in the choice and management of metrical forms,
that he would in his hymns have brought the verse and the
subject into perfect harmony.

§ 5. The metrical forms used by Alcæus are mostly light and
lively; sometimes with a softer, sometimes with a more vehement character.   They consist principally of Æolic dactyls,
which, though apparently resembling the dactyls of epic poetry,

---

[1] Fragm. 17. Matth.   [2] Above, ch. VII. § 5.
[3] Fragm. 21. Matth. Horace, *Carm.* I. 10. 9, has borrowed the last incident from
Alcæus: but the hymn of Alcæus, which related at length the story of the theft,
was on the whole different from the ode of Horace, which touches on many adventures of Hermes, without dwelling on any.

yet are essentially unlike. Instead of depending upon the perfect balance of the Arsis and Thesis,[1] they admit the shortening of the former ; whence arises an irregularity which was distinguished by the ancient writers on metre by the name of *disproportioned dactyls* (ἄλογοι δάκτυλοι). These dactyls begin with the undetermined foot of two syllables, which is called *basis*, and they flow on lightly and swiftly, without alternating with heavy spondees. The choriambics of the Æolic lyric poets are composed on the same plan, as they have also the preceding basis ; yet this metre always retains something of the stately tone which belongs to it. Hence Alcæus, and also Horace, whose metres are for the most part borrowed from him, composed poems of choriambic verses by simple repetition, without dividing them into strophes ; these poems have a somewhat loftier and more solemn tone than the rest. The Logaœdic metre also belongs peculiarly to the Æolic lyric poets ; it is produced by the immediate junction of dactylic and trochaic feet, so that a rapid movement passes into a feebler one. This lengthened and various kind of metre was peculiarly adapted to express the softer emotions, such as tenderness, melancholy, and longing. Hence this metre was frequently used by the Æolians, and their strophes were principally formed by connecting logaœdic rhythms with trochees, iambi, and Æolic dactyls. Of this kind is the Sapphic strophe, the softest and sweetest metre in the Greek lyric poetry, and which Alcæus seems to have sometimes employed, as in his hymn to Hermes.[2] But the firmer and more vigorous tone of the metre, called after him the Alcaic, was better suited to the temper of his mind. The logaœdic elements[3] of this metre have but little of their characteristic

---

[1] Above, ch. IV. § 4.

[2] That is to say, if the verse in fragm. 37. Blomf. 22. Matth. was the beginning of this hymn. According to Apollonius, *de pronom.* p. 90. ed. Bekker. it runs thus : χαῖρε, Κυλλάνας ὀ μέδεις (as participle, with the Æolic accent, for μεδείς), σὲ γάρ μοι.

[3] In these remarks it is assumed that the second part of the alcaic verse is not choriambic, or dactylic, but logaœdic ; and that the whole ought thus to be arranged :

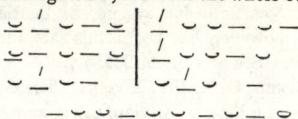

Thus it appears that the third verse of the strophe is a prolongation of the first

softness, and they receive an impulse from the iambic dipodies which precede them. Hence the Alcaic strophe is generally employed by these poets in political and warlike poems, and in all in which manly passions predominate. Alcæus likewise formed longer verses of logaœdic feet, and joined them in an unbroken series, after the manner of choriambic and many dactylic verses. In this way he obtained a beautiful measure for the description of his armoury.[1] Among the various metres used by Alcæus, the last which we shall mention is the Ionic metre (Ionici a minori), which he used to express the emotions of his passionate nature.[2]

§ 6. We come now to the other leader of the Lesbian school of poetry, SAPPHO, the object of the admiration of all antiquity. There is no doubt that she belonged to the island of Lesbos; and the question whether she was born in Eresos or Mytilene is best resolved by supposing that she went from the lesser city to the greater, at the time of her greatest celebrity. She was nearly contemporaneous with her countryman Alcæus, although she must have been younger, as she was still alive in Ol. 53. 568 B.C. About Ol. 46. 596 B.C. she sailed from Mytilene in order to take refuge in Sicily,[3] but the cause of her flight is unknown; she must at that time have been in the bloom of her life. At a much later period she produced the ode mentioned by Herodotus, in which she reproached her brother Charaxus

---

half of the two first verses; and that the fourth verse is a similar prolongation of the second half. The entire strophe is therefore formed of a combination of the two elements, the iambic and the logaœdic.

[1] *Fragm.* 24. Blomf. 1. Matth. The metre ought probably to be arranged as follows (the basis being marked x ⏑):

$$\times\ \underline{}\,\underline{/}\ \smile\smile\underline{}\ \smile\underline{}\,|\ \times\ \underline{}\,\underline{/}\ \smile\smile\underline{}\ \smile\ \ \underline{}\,|\ \underline{/}\,\underline{}\smile$$

Verses 3 and 4 ought to be read thus: χάλκεαι δὲ πασσάλοις κρύπτοισιν περικείμεναι λαμπραὶ κνάμιδες, *i. e.* 'and brazen shining greaves conceal the pegs, to which they are suspended.' πασσάλοις is the Æolic accusative; the dative in this dialect is always πασσάλοισι.

[2] *Fragm.* 36. Blomf. 69. Matth.

ἐμὲ δειλὰν, ἐμὲ πασᾶν κακοτάτων πεδέχοισαν.

Every ten of these Ionic feet formed a system, as Bentley has arranged Horat. *Carm.* III. 12. Horace, however, has not in this ode succeeded in catching the genuine tone of the metre. See above, ch. XI. § 7.

[3] *Marm. Par.* ep. 36. comp. Ovid, *Her.* XV. 51. The date of the Parian marble is lost; but it must have been between Olymp. 44. 1, and 47. 2.

for having purchased Rhodopis[1] the courtesan from her master, and for having been induced by his love to emancipate her. This Rhodopis dwelt at Naucratis, and the event falls at a time when a frequent intercourse with Egypt had already been established by the Greeks. Now the government of Amasis (who permitted the Greeks in Egypt to dwell in Naucratis) began in Olymp. 52. 4, 569 B.C., and the return of Charaxus from the journey to Mytilene, where his sister received him with this reproachful and satirical ode, must have happened some years later.

The severity with which Sappho censured her brother for his love for a courtesan enables us to form some judgment of the principles by which she guided her own conduct. For although at the time when she wrote this ode to Charaxus, the fire of youthful passion had been quenched in her breast; yet she never could have reproached her brother with his love for a courtesan, if she had herself been a courtesan in her youth; and Charaxus might have retaliated upon her with additional strength. Besides we may plainly discern the feeling of unimpeached honour due to a freeborn and well educated maiden, in the verses already quoted, which refer to the relation of Alcæus and Sappho. Alcæus testifies that the attractions and loveliness of Sappho did not derogate from her moral worth, when he calls her ' violet-crowned, pure, sweetly smiling Sappho.'[2] These genuine testimonies are indeed opposed to the accounts of many later writers, who represent Sappho as a courtesan. To refute this opinion, we will not resort to the expedient employed by some ancient writers, who have attempted to distinguish a courtesan of Eresos named Sappho from the poetess. A more probable cause of this false imputation seems to be, that later generations, and especially the refined Athenians, were incapable of conceiving and appreciating the frank simplicity with which Sappho pours forth her feelings, and therefore confounded them with the unblushing immodesty of a courtesan. In Sappho's time, there still existed among the Greeks much of that primi-

---

[1] II. 135, and see Athen. XIII. p. 596. Rhodopis or Doricha was the fellow slave of Æsop, who flourished at the same time (Olymp. 52).

[2] Ἰόπλοχ᾽, ἀγνὰ, μειλιχόμειδε Σαπφοῖ. See above, § 4.

tive simplicity which appears in the wish of Nausicaa in Homer
that she had such a husband as Ulysses. That complete separation between sensual and sentimental love had not yet taken
place which we find in the writings of later times, especially in
those of the Attic comic poets. Moreover the life of women in
Lesbos was doubtless very different from the life of women at
Athens and among the Ionians. In the Ionian States the
female sex lived in the greatest retirement, and were exclusively
employed in household concerns. Hence, while the men of
Athens were distinguished by their perfection in every branch
of art, none of their women emerged from the obscurity of domestic life. The secluded and depressed condition of the female
sex among the Ionians of Asia Minor, originating in circumstances connected with the history of their race, had also become
universal in Athens, where the principle on which the education
of women rested was that just so much mental culture was expedient for women as would enable them to manage the household, provide for the bodily wants of the children, and overlook
the female slaves; for the rest, says Pericles in Thucydides,[1]
' that woman is the best of whom the least is said among men,
whether for evil or for good.' But the Æolians had in some
degree preserved the ancient Greek manners, such as we find
them depicted in their epic poetry and mythology, where the
women are represented as taking an active share not only in
social domestic life, but in public amusements; and they thus
enjoyed a distinct individual existence and moral character.
There can be no doubt that they, as well as the women of the
Dorian states of Peloponnesus and Magna Grecia, shared in the
advantages of the general high state of civilization, which not
only fostered poetical talents of a high order among women,
but, as in the time of the Pythagorean league, even produced
in them a turn for philosophical reflections on human life. But
as such a state of the education and intellect of women was
utterly inconsistent with Athenian manners, it is natural that
women should be the objects of scurrilous jests and slanderous
imputations. We cannot therefore wonder that women who
had in any degree overstepped the bounds prescribed to their

---

[1] II. 45.

sex by the manners of Athens, should be represented by the licentious pen of the Athenian comic writers, as lost to every sentiment of shame or decency.[1]

§ 7. It is certain that Sappho, in her odes, made frequent mention of a youth, to whom she gave her whole heart, while he requited her passion with cold indifference. But there is no trace whatever of her having named the object of her passion, or sought to win his favour by her beautiful verses. The pretended name of this youth, Phaon, although frequently mentioned in the Attic comedies,[2] appears not to have occurred in the poetry of Sappho. If Phaon had been named in her poetry, the opinion could not have arisen that it was the courtesan Sappho, and not the poetess, who was in love with Phaon.[3] Moreover, the marvellous stories of the beauty of Phaon and the love of the goddess Aphrodite for him, have manifestly been borrowed from the mythus of Adonis.[4] Hesiod mentions Phaethon, a son of Eos and Cephalus, who when a child was carried off by Aphrodite, and brought up as the guardian of the sanctuary in her temples.[5] This is evidently founded on the Cyprian legend of Adonis; the Greeks, adopting this legend, appear to have given the name of Phaethon or Phaon to the favourite of Aphrodite; and this Phaon, by various mistakes and misinterpretations, at length became the beloved of Sappho. Perhaps also the poetess may, in an ode to Adonis, have celebrated the beautiful Phaon in such a manner that the verses may have been supposed to refer to a lover of her own.

---

[1] There were Attic comedies with the title of *Sappho*, by Amphis, Antiphanes, Ephippus, Timocles, and Diphilus ; and a comedy by Plato entitled *Phaon*.

[2] As in the verses of Menander in Strabo, X. p. 452.

οὗ δὴ λέγεται πρώτη Σαπφώ
τὸν ὑπέρκομπον θηρῶσα Φάων'
οἰστρῶντι πόθῳ ῥῖψαι πέτρας
ἀπὸ τηλεφανοῦς.

[3] In Athen. XIII. p. 596 E, and several ancient lexicographers.

[4] Cratinus, the comic poet, in an unknown play in Athen. II. p. 69. D. relates that Aphrodite had concealed Phaon ἐν θριδακίναις, *among the lettuce*. The same legend is also related of Adonis by others, in Athenæus ; and it refers to the use of the *horti Adonidis*. Concerning Phaon-Adonis, see also Ælian, *V. H.* XII. 18. Lucian *Dial. Mort.* 9. Plin. *N. H.* XXII. 8. Servius ad Virg. *Æn.* III. 279, not to mention inferior authorities for this legend.

[5] Hesiod, *Theog.* 986. *sq.* νηοπόλον μύχιον, according to the reading of Aristarchus.

According to the ordinary account, Sappho, despised by Phaon, took the leap from the Leucadian rock, in the hope of finding a cure for the pains of unrequited love. But even this is rather a poetical image, than a real event in the life of Sappho. The Leucadian leap was a religious rite, belonging to the expiatory festivals of Apollo, which was celebrated in this as in other parts of Greece. At appointed times, criminals, selected as expiatory victims, were thrown from the high overhanging rock into the sea; they were however sometimes caught at the bottom, and, if saved, they were sent away from Leucadia.[1] This custom was applied in various ways by the poets of the time to the description of lovers. Stesichorus, in his poetical novel named *Calyce*, spoke of the love of a virtuous maiden for a youth who despised her passion; and in despair she threw herself from the Leucadian rock. The effect of the leap in the story of Sappho (viz. the curing her of her intolerable passion) must therefore have been unknown to Stesichorus. Some years later, Anacreon says in an ode, ' again casting myself from the Leucadian rock, I plunge into the grey sea, drunk with love.'[2] The poet can scarcely by these words be supposed to say that he cures himself of a vehement passion, but rather means to describe the delirious intoxication of violent love. The story of Sappho's leap probably originated in some poetical images and relations of this kind; a similar story is told of Aphrodite in regard to her lament for Adonis.[3] Nevertheless it is not unlikely that the leap from the Leucadian rock may really have been made, in ancient times, by desperate and frantic men. Another proof of the fictitious character of the story is that it leaves the principal point in uncertainty, namely, whether Sappho survived the leap or perished in it.

From what has been said, it follows that a true conception of the erotic poetry of Sappho, and of the feelings expressed in it, can only be drawn from fragments of her odes, which, though numerous, are for the most part very short. The most considerable and the best known of Sappho's remains is the com-

---

[1] Concerning the connexion of this custom with the worship of Apollo, see Müller's *Dorians*, B. XI. ch. 11. § 10.

[2] In Hephæstion, p. 130.

[3] See Ptolem. Hephæstion (in Phot. *Bibliothec.*) βιβλίον ζ.

plete ode,[1] in which she implores Aphrodite not to allow the torments and agitations of love to destroy her mind, but to come to her assistance, as she had formerly descended from heaven in her golden car drawn by sparrows, and with radiant smiles on her divine face had asked her what had befallen her, and what her unquiet heart desired, and who was the author of her pain. She promised that if he fled her now, he soon would follow her ; if he did not now accept her presents, he would soon offer presents to her; if he did not love her now, he would soon love her, even were she coy and reluctant. Sappho then implores Aphrodite to come to her again and assist her. Although, in this ode, Sappho describes her love in glowing language, and even speaks of her own frantic heart,[2] yet the indelicacy of such an avowal of passionate love is much diminished by the manner in which it is made. The poetess does not importune her lover with her complaints, nor address her poem to him, but confides her passion to the goddess and pours out to her all the tumult and the anguish of her heart. There is great delicacy in her not venturing to give utterance in her own person to the expectation that the coy and indifferent object of her affection would be transformed into an impatient lover ; an expectation little likely to find a place in a heart so stricken and oppressed as that of the poetess ; she only recalls to her mind, that the goddess had in former and similar situations vouchsafed her support and consolation. In other fragments Sappho's passionate excitable temper is expressed with frankness quite foreign to our manners, but which possesses a simple grace. Thus she says, ' I request that the charming Menon be invited, if the feast is to bring enjoyment to me ;'[3] and she addresses a distinguished youth in these words : ' Come opposite to me, oh friend, and let the sweetness which dwells in thine eyes beam upon me.'[4] Yet we can nowhere find grounds for reproaching her with having tried to please men or met their advances when

---

[1] Fragm. 1. Blomf. 1. Neue.

[2] μαινόλᾳ θυμῷ.

[3] Fragm. 33. Neue, from Hephæst. p. 41 ; it is not, however, quite certain, that the verses belong to Sappho. Compare fragm. 10. Blomf. 5. Neue (ἐλθὲ, Κύπρι).

[4] Fragm. 13. Blomf. 62. Neue. Compare fragm. 24. Blomf. 32. Neue. (γλυκεῖα μᾶτερ, οὔτοι—), and 28 Blomf. 55. Neue, (δέδυκε μὲν ἀ σελάνα—).

past the season of youth.   On the contrary, she says, ' Thou art my friend, I therefore advise thee to seek a younger wife, I cannot bring myself to share thy house as an elder.'[1]

§ 8. It is far more difficult to discover and to judge the nature of Sappho's intimacies with women.   It is, however, certain that the life and education of the female sex in Lesbos was not, as in Athens, confined *within* the house; and that girls were not entrusted exclusively to the care of mothers and nurses.   There were women distinguished by their attainments, who assisted in instructing a circle of young girls, in the same manner as Socrates afterwards did at Athens young men of promising talents.   There were also among the Dorians of Sparta noble and cultivated women, who assembled young girls about them, to whom they devoted themselves with great zeal and affection; and these girls formed associations which, in all probability, were under the direction of the elder women.[2] Such associations as these existed in Lesbos in the time of Sappho ; but they were completely voluntary, and were formed by girls who were studying to attain that proficiency in music or other elegant arts, that refinement and grace of manners, which distinguished the women around whom they congregated. Music and poetry no doubt formed the basis of these societies, and instruction and exercise in these arts were their immediate object.   Though poetry was a part of Sappho's inmost nature, a genuine expression of the feelings by which she was really agitated, it is probable that with her, as with the ancient poets, it was the business and study of life; and as technical perfection in it could be taught, it might, by persevering instructions, be imparted to the young.[3]   Not only Sappho, but many other women in Lesbos, devoted themselves to this mode of life.   In the songs of this poetess, frequent mention was made of Gorgo and Andromeda as her rivals.[4]   A great number of her young

---

[1] Fragm. 12. Blomf. 20. Neue (according to the reading of the latter).

[2] Müller's *Dorians*, B. IV. chap. IV. § 8. ch. V. § 2.

[3] Hence Sappho calls her house, ' the house of the servant of the Muses,' μουσοπόλω οἰκίαν, from which mourning must be excluded : Fragm. 71. Blomf. 28. Neue.

[4] From the passage on the relations of Sappho in Maxim. Tyrius, *Dissert.* XXIV.

friends were from distant countries,[1] as Anactoria of Miletus, Gongyla of Colophon, Eunica of Salamis, Gyrinna, Atthis, Mnasidica. A great number of the poems of Sappho related to these female friendships, and reveal the familiar intercourse of the woman's chamber, the Gynæconitis; where the tender refined sensibility of the female mind was cultivated and impressed with every attractive form. Among these accomplishments, music and a graceful demeanour were the most valued. The poetess says to a rich but uncultivated woman, ' Where thou diest, there wilt thou lie, and no one will remember thy name in times to come, because thou hast no share in the roses of Pieria. Inglorious wilt thou wander about in the abode of Hades, and flit among its dark shades.'[2] She derides one of her rivals, Andromeda, for her manner of dressing, from which it is well known the Greeks were wont to infer much more of the native disposition and character than we do. ' What woman,' says she to a young female friend, ' ever charmed thy mind who wore a vulgar and graceless dress, or did not know how to draw her garments close around her ankles ?'[3] She reproaches one of her friends, Mnasidica, because, though her form was beautiful as that of the young Gyrinna, yet her temper was gloomy.[4] To another, Atthis, to whom she had shown particular marks of affection, and who had grieved her by preferring her rival Andromeda, she says, ' Again does the strength-dissolving Eros, that bitter-sweet, resistless monster agitate me; but to thee, O Atthis, the

---

[1] In Suidas in Σαπφώ the ἑταῖραι and μαθήτριαι of Sappho are distinguished : but the ἑταῖραι were, at least originally, μαθήτριαι. Thus Maximus Tyrius mentions Anactoria as being loved by Sappho ; but it is probable that'Αναγόρα Μιλησία, mentioned by Suidas among her μαθήτριαι, is the same person, and that the name ought to be written 'Ανακτορία Μιλησία. This emendation is confirmed by the fact, that the ancient name of Miletus was Anactoria ; Stephan. Byzant. in voc. Μίλητος, Eustath. ad. Il. II. 8, p. 21, ed. Rom. ; Schol. Apoll. Rhod. I. 187.

[2] Fragm. 11. Blomf. 19. Neue.

[3] Fragm. 35. Blomf. 23. Neue. This passage is illustrated by ancient works of sculpture, on which women are represented as walking with the upper garment drawn close to the leg above the ankle. See, for example, the relief in Mus. Capitol. T. IV. tab. 43.

[4] Fragm. 26, 27. Blomf. 42. Neue. The reading, however, is not quite certain.

thought of me is importunate; thou fliest to Andromeda.'[1]   It is obvious that this attachment bears less the character of maternal interest than of passionate love; as among the Dorians in Sparta and Crete, analogous connexions between men and youths, in which the latter were trained to noble and manly deeds, were carried on in a language of high-wrought and passionate feeling which had all the character of an attachment between persons of different sexes.   This mixture of feelings, which among nations of a calmer temperament have always been perfectly distinct, is an essential feature of the Greek character.

The most remarkable example of this impassioned strain of Sappho in relation to a female friend is that considerable fragment preserved by Longinus, which has often been incorrectly interpreted, because the beginning of it led to the erroneous idea that the object of the passion expressed in it was a man. But the poem says, 'That man seems to me equal to the gods who sits opposite to thee, and watches thy sweet speech and charming smile.   My heart loses its force: for when I look at thee, my tongue ceases to utter; my voice is broken, a subtle fire glides through my veins, my eyes grow dim, and a rushing sound fills my ears.'   In these, and even stronger terms, the poetess expresses nothing more than a friendly attachment to a young girl, but which, from the extreme excitability of feeling, assumes all the tone of the most ardent passion.[2]

§ 9. From the class of Sapphic odes which we have just described, we must distinguish the Epithalamia or Hymeneals, which were peculiarly adapted to the genius of the poetess from the exquisite perception she seems to have had of whatever was attractive in either sex.   These poems appear, from the numerous fragments which remain, to have had great beauty, and much of that mode of expression which the simple, natural manners of those times allowed, and the warm and sensitive

---

[1] Fragm. 31. Blomf. 37. Neue. cf. 32. Blomf. 14. Neue. 'Ηράμαν μὲν ἐγὼ σέθεν, 'Ατθί, πάλαι πότα.

[2] Catullus, who imitates this poem in *Carm.* 51, gives it an ironical termination, (Otium, Catulle, tibi molestum est, &c.,) which is certainly not borrowed from Sappho.

heart of the poetess suggested. The Epithalamium of Catullus, not that playful one on the marriage of Manlius Torquatus, but the charming, tender poem, *Vesper adest, juvenes, consurgite*, is an evident imitation of a Sapphic Epithalamium, which was composed in the same hexameter verse. It appears that in this, as in Catullus, the trains of youths and of maidens advanced to meet; these reproached, those praised the evening star, because he led the bride to the youth. Then comes the verse of Sappho which has been preserved, ' Hesperus, who bringest together all that the rosy morning's light has scattered abroad.'[1] The beautiful images of the gathered flowers and of the vine twining about the elm, by which Catullus alternately dissuades and recommends the marriage of the maiden, have quite the character of Sapphic similes. These mostly turn upon flowers and plants, which the poetess seems to have regarded with fond delight and sympathy.[2] In a fragment lately discovered, which bears a strong impression of the simple language of Sappho, she compares the freshness of youth and the unsullied beauty of a maiden's face to an apple of some peculiar kind, which, when all the rest of the fruit is gathered from the tree, remains alone at an unattainable height, and drinks in the whole vigour of vegetation; or rather (to give the simple words of the poetess in which the thought is placed before us and gradually heightened with great beauty and nature) ' like the sweet apple which ripens at the top of the bough, on the topmost point of the bough, forgotten by the gatherers—no, not quite forgotten, but beyond their reach.'[3] A fragment written in a similar tone, speaks of a hyacinth, which growing among the mountains is trodden underfoot by the shepherds, and its purple flower is pressed to the ground;[4]

---

[1] Fragm. 45. Blomf. 68. Neue.

[2] Concerning the love of Sappho for the rose, see Philostrat. *Epist.* 73, comp. Neue, fragm. 132.

[3] Οἶον τὸ γλυκύμαλον ἐρεύθεται ἄκρῳ ἐπ' ὅσδῳ.

Ὄσδῳ ἐπ' ἀκροτάτῳ, λελάθοντο δὲ μαλοδροπῆες.

Οὐ μὴν ἐκλελάθοντ', ἀλλ' οὐκ ἐδύναντ' ἐφίκεσθαι.

The fragment is in Walz, *Rhetores Græci*, vol. VIII. p. 883. Himerius, *Orat.* I. 4. § 16. cites something similar from a hymenæus of Sappho.

[4] Οἴαν τὰν ὑάκινθον ἐν οὔρεσι ποίμενες ἄνδρες

ποσσὶ καταστείβουσι· χαμαὶ δέ τε πόρφυρον ἄνθος.

Demetrius, *de Elocut.* c. 106, quotes these verses without a name; but it can

thus obviously comparing the maiden who has no husband to
protect her, with the flower which grows in the field, as contrasted with that which blooms in the shelter of a garden.   In
another hymeneal, Sappho compares the bridegroom to a young
and slender sapling.[1] But she does not dwell upon such images
as these alone; she also compares him to Ares,[2] and his deeds
to those of Achilles;[3] and here her lyre may have assumed a
loftier tone than that which usually characterized it.   But there
was another kind of hymeneal among the songs of Sappho, which
furnished occasion to a sort of petulant pleasantry.   In this
the maidens try to snatch away the bride as she is led to the
bridegroom, and vent their mockery on his friend who stands
before the door, and is thence called the Porter.[4]

Sappho also composed hymns to the gods, in which she
invoked them to come from their favourite abodes in different
countries; but there is little information extant respecting their
contents.

§ 10. The poems of Sappho are little susceptible of division
into distinct classes.   Hence the ancient critics divided them
into books, merely according to the metre, the first containing
the odes in the Sapphic metre, and so on.   The hymeneals
were thus placed in different books.   The rhythmical construction of her odes was essentially the same as that of Alcæus,
yet with many variations, in harmony with the softer character
of her poetry, and easily perceptible upon a careful comparison
of the several metres.

How great was Sappho's fame among the Greeks, and how
rapidly it spread throughout Greece, may be seen in the history of Solon,[5] who was a contemporary of the Lesbian poetess.
Hearing his nephew recite one of her poems, he is said to
have exclaimed, that he would not willingly die till he had
learned it by heart.   Indeed the whole voice of antiquity has

---

scarcely be doubted that they are Sappho's.   In Catullus, the young women use
the same image as the young men in Sappho.

[1] Fragm. 42. Blomf. 34. Neue.

[2] Fragm. 39. Blomf. 73. Neue.

[3] Himerius, *Orat.* I. 4. § 16.

[4] Fragm. 43. Blomf. 38. Neue.   It is worthy of remark, that Demetrius, *de
Elocut.* c. 167, expressly mentions the *chorus* in relation to this fragment.

[5] In Stobæus, *Serm.* XXIX. 28.

declared that the poetry of Sappho was unrivalled in grace and sweetness.

And doubtless from that circle of accomplished. women, of whom she formed the brilliant centre, a flood of poetic warmth and light was poured forth on every side. A friend of hers, Damophila the Pamphylian, composed a hymn on the worship of the Pergæan Artemis (which was solemnized in her native land after the Asiatic fashion); in this the Æolic style was blended with the peculiarities of the Pamphylian manner.[1] Another poetess of far higher renown was Erinna, who died in early youth, when chained by her mother to the spinning-wheel; she had as yet known the charm of existence in imagination alone. Her poem, called *The Spindle* ('Ηλακάτη), containing only 300 hexameter verses, in which she probably expressed the restless and aspiring thoughts which crowded on her youthful mind, as she pursued her monotonous work, has been deemed by many of the ancients of such high poetic merit as to entitle it to a place beside the epics of Homer.[2]

§ 11. We now come to ANACREON, whose poetry may be considered as akin to that of Alcæus and Sappho, although he was an Ionian from Teos, and his genius had an entirely different tone and bent. In respect also of the external circumstances in which he was placed, he belonged to a different period; inasmuch as the splendour and luxury of living had, in his time, much increased among the Greeks, and even poetry had contributed to adorn the court of a tyrant. The spirit of the Ionic race was, in Callinus, united with manly daring and a high feeling of honour, and in Mimnermus with a tender melancholy, seeking relief from care in sensual enjoyment; but in Anacreon it is bereft of all these deeper and more serious feelings; and he seems to consider life as valuable only in so far as it can be spent in love, music, wine, and social enjoyments. And even these feelings are not animated with the glow of the Æolic poets; Anacreon, with his Ionic disposition, cares only for the enjoyment of the passing moment, and no feeling takes such deep hold of his heart that it is not always ready to give way to fresh impressions.

---

[1] Philostrat. *Vit. Apollon.* I. 30, p. 37. ed. Olear.
[2] The chief authority is *Anthol. Palat.* IX. 190.

Anacreon had already arrived at manhood, when his native city Teos was, after some resistance, taken by Harpagus, the general of Cyrus.   In consequence of this capture, the inhabitants all took ship, and sailed for Thrace, where they founded Abdera, or rather they took possession of a Greek colony already existing on the spot, and enlarged the town.   This event happened about the 6oth Olymp. 540 B.C.   Anacreon was among these Teian exiles; and, according to ancient testimony, he himself called Abdera 'The fair settlement of the Teians.'[1] About this time, or at least not long after, Polycrates became tyrant of Samos; for Thucydides places the height of his power under Cambyses, who began to reign in Olymp. 62. 4, B.C. 529.   Polycrates was, according to the testimony of Herodotus, the most enterprising and magnificent of all the Grecian tyrants.   His wide dominion over the islands of the Ægean Sea, and his intercourse with the rulers of foreign countries (as with Amasis, king of Egypt), supplied him with the means of adorning his island of Samos, and his immediate retinue, with all that art and riches could at that time effect.   He embellished Samos with extensive buildings, kept court like an oriental prince, and was surrounded by beautiful boys for various menial services; and he appears to have considered the productions of such poets as Ibycus, and especially Anacreon, as the highest ornament of a life of luxurious enjoyment.   Anacreon, according to the well-known story of Herodotus, was still at the court of Polycrates, when death was impending over him; and he had probably just left Samos, when his host and patron was murdered by the treacherous and sanguinary Oroetes. (Olympiad 64. 3, B.C. 522).   At this time Hippias, the son of Pisistratus, ruled in Athens; and his brother Hipparchus shared the government with him.   The latter had more taste for poetry than any of his family, and he is particularly named in connexion with institutions relating to the cultivation of poetry among the Athenians.   Hipparchus, according to a Platonic dialogue which bears his name, sent out a ship with fifty

---

[1] In Strabo, XIV. p. 644.   A fragment in Schol. *Odyss.* VIII. 293. (fragment 132. ed. Bergk,) also refers to the Sintians in Thrace, as likewise does an epigram of Anacreon (*Anthol. Palat.* VIII. 226) to a brave warrior, who had fallen in the defence of his native city Abdera.

oars, to bring Anacreon to Athens; and here Anacreon found several other poets, who had then come to Athens in order to adorn the festivals of the city, and, in particular, of the royal family. Meanwhile Anacreon devoted his muse to other distinguished families in Athens; among others he is supposed to have loved the young Critias, the son of Dropides, and to have extolled this house distinguished in the annals of Athens.[1] At this time the fame of Anacreon appears to have reached its highest point; he must also have been advanced in years, as his name was, among the ancients, always connected with the idea of an old man, whose grey hairs did not interfere with his gaiety and pursuit of pleasure. It is, indeed, stated, that Anacreon was still alive at the revolt of the Ionians, caused by Histiæus, and that being driven from Teos, he took refuge in Abdera.[2] But as this event happened in Olympiad 71. 3, B.C. 494, about 35 years after Anacreon's residence with Polycrates, the statement must be incorrect; and it appears to have arisen from a confusion between the subjugation of the Ionians by Cyrus, and the suppression of their revolt under Darius. From an inscription for the tomb of Anacreon in Teos, attributed to Simonides,[3] it is inferred that he returned in his old age to Teos, which had been again peopled under the Persian government. But the monuments which were erected to celebrated men in their own country were often merely cenotaphs; and this epitaph may perhaps, like many others bearing the

---

[1] Plato, *Charmid.* p. 157 E. Schol. Æschyl. *Prom.* 128. This Critias was at that time (Olymp. 64) about sixteen years old; for he was born in Olymp. 60; and this agrees with the fact, that his grandson Critias, the statesman, one of the thirty tyrants of Athens, was, according to Plato, *Tim.* p. 216, eighty years younger than his grandfather. Consequently, the birth of the younger Critias falls in Olymp. 80, which agrees perfectly with the recorded events of his life. The Critias born in Olymp. 60, is however called a son of the Dropides, who is stated to have been a friend of Solon, and to have succeeded him in the office of Archon in Olymp. 46. 4. B.C. 593. It seems impossible to escape from these chronological difficulties, except by distinguishing this Dropides, and his son Critias, to whom Solon's verses refer (Εἰπέμεναι Κριτίῃ πυρρότριχι πατρὸς ἀκούειν, &c.), from the Dropides and Critias in Anacreon's time. Upon this supposition the dates of the persons of this family would stand thus: Dropides, born about Olymp. 36; Critias πυρρόθριξ Olymp. 44; Dropides, the grandson, Olymp. 52; Critias, the grandson, Olymp. 60; Callæschrus, Olymp. 70; Critias the tyrant, Olymp. 80.

[2] In Suidas in v. 'Ανακρέων, Τέως.

[3] *Anthol. Pal.* VII. 25. fragm. 52. ed. Gaisford.

name of Simonides, have been composed centuries after the
time of that poet.[1] It is probable that Anacreon, when he
had once become known as the welcome guest of the richest
and most powerful men of Greece, and when his social qualities
had acquired general fame, was courted and invited by princes
in other parts of Greece. It is intimated in an epigram that
he was intimately connected with the Aleuads, the ruling family
in Thessaly, who at that time added great zeal for art and literature to the hospitable and convivial qualities of their nation.
This epigram refers to a votive offering of the Thessalian prince
Echecratides, doubtless the person whose son Orestes, in Olympiad 81. 2, B.C. 454, applied to the Athenians to reinstate him
in the government which had belonged to his father.[2]

§ 12. Anacreon seems to have laid the foundation of his poetical fame in his native town of Teos; but the most productive
period of his poetry was during his residence in Samos. The
whole of Anacreon's poetry (says the geographer Strabo, in
speaking of the history of Samos) is filled with allusions to
Polycrates. His poems, therefore, are not to be considered as
the careless outpourings of a mind in the stillness of retirement,
but as the work of a person living in the midst of the splendour
of the Samian tyrant. Accordingly, his notions of a life of
enjoyment are not formed on the Greek model, but on the
luxurious manners of the Lydians,[3] introduced by Polycrates
into his court. The beautiful youths, who play a principal part
in the genuine poems of Anacreon, are not individuals distinguished from the mass of their contemporaries by the poet,
but young men chosen for their beauty, whom Polycrates kept
about his person, and of whom some had been procured from a
distance; as, for example, Smerdies, from the country of the
Thracian Ciconians. Some of these youths enlivened the meals
of Polycrates by music; as Bathyllus, whose flute-playing and
Ionic singing are extolled by a later rhetorician, and of whom
a bronze statue was shown in the Temple of Juno at Samos, in
the dress and attitude of a player on the cithara; but which,

---

[1] The fragment Αἰνοπαθῆ πατρίδ' ἐπόψομαι (Schol. Harl. Od. M. 313, fragm. 33.
Bergk) appears to refer to a journey to this country.

[2] Compare *Anthol. Pal.* VI. 142, with Thucyd. I. 111.

[3] ἡ τῶν Λυδῶν τροφή.

according to the description of Apuleius, appears to have been only an Apollo Citharœdus, in the ancient style. Other youths were perhaps more distinguished as dancers. Anacreon offers his homage to all these youths, and divides his affection and admiration between Smerdies with the flowing locks, Cleobulus with the beautiful eyes, the bright and playful Lycaspis, the charming Megistes, Bathyllus, Simalus, and doubtless many others whose names have not been preserved. He wishes them to sport with him in drunken merriment;[1] and if the youth will take no part in his joy, he threatens to fly upon light wings up to Olympus, there to make his complaints, and to induce Eros to chastise him for his scorn.[2] Or he implores Dionysus, the god with whom Eros, and the dark-eyed nymphs, and the purple Aphrodite, play,—to turn Cleobulus, by the aid of wine, to the love of Anacreon.[3] Or he laments, in verses full of careless grace, that the fair Bathyllus favours him so little.[4] He knows that his head and temples are grey ; but he hopes to obtain the affection of the youths by his pleasing song and speech.[5] In short, he pays his homage to these youths, in language combining passion and playfulness.

§ 13. Anacreon, however, did not on this account withhold his admiration from female beauty. ' Again (he says, in an extant fragment) golden-haired Eros strikes me with a purple ball, and challenges me to sport and play with a maiden with many-coloured sandals. But she, a native of the well-built Lesbos,[6] despises my grey hairs, and prefers another man.' His amatory poetry chiefly consists of complaints of the indifference of women to his love ; which, however, are expressed in so light and playful a manner, that they do not seem to

---

[1] Anacreon has a peculiar term to express this idea, viz. ἡβᾶν or συνηβᾶν. One of the amusements of this kind of life is *gambling*, of which the fragment in Schol. Hom. *Il.* XXIII. 88, fragment 44. Bergk. speaks : ' Dice are the vehement passion and the conflict of Eros.'

[2] Fragm. in Hephæst. p. 52. (22. Bergk.), explained by Julian, *Epist.* 18, p. 386 B.

[3] Fragm. in Dio Chrysost. *Or.* II. p. 31, fr. 2. Bergk.

[4] Horat. *Ep.* XIV. 9. *sq.*

[5] Fragm. in Maxim. Tyr. VIII. p. 96, fr. 42. Bergk.

[6] In Athen. XIII. p. 599. C. fr. 15. Bergk. That it does not refer to Sappho is proved by the dates of her lifetime, and of that of Anacreon.

proceed from genuine regret.   Thus, in the beautiful ode, imitated in many places by Horace :[1] ' Thracian filly, why do you
look at me askance, and avoid me without pity, and will not
allow me any skill in my art ?   Know, then, that I could soon
find means of curbing your spirit, and, holding the reins, could
guide you in the course round the goal.   Still you wander
about the pastures, and bound lightly round them, for there has
been no dexterous hand to tame you.'   But such loves as these
are far different from the deep seriousness with which Sappho
confesses her passion, and they can only be judged by those relations between the sexes which were universally established
among the Ionians at that time.   In the Ionic states of Asia
Minor, as at Athens, a freeborn maiden was brought up within
the strict limits of the family circle, and was never allowed to
enter the society of men.   Thence it happened that a separate
class of women devoted themselves to all those arts which
qualified them to enhance the charm of social life—the Hetæræ,
most of them foreigners or freed women, without the civic
rights which belonged to the daughter of a citizen, but often
highly distinguished by the elegance of their demeanour and by
their accomplishments.   Whenever, therefore, women are mentioned by Ionic and Attic writers, as taking part in the feasts
and symposia of the men, and as receiving at their dwelling
the salutations of the joyous band of revellers,—the Comus,—
there can be no doubt that they were Hetæræ.   Even at the
time of the orators,[2] an Athenian woman of genuine free blood
would have lost the privileges of her birth, if she had so
demeaned herself.   Hence it follows, that the women with
whom Anacreon offers to dance and sing, and to whom, after a
plenteous repast, he addresses a song on the Pectis,[3] are
Hetæræ, like all those beauties whose charms are celebrated by
Horace.   Anacreon's most serious love appears to have been
for the ' fair Eurypyle ;' since jealousy of her moved him to
write a satirical poem, in which Artemon, the favourite of
Eurypyle, who was then passing an effeminate and luxurious life,

---

[1] In Heraclid. *Allegor. Hom.* p. 16. ed. Schow. fr. 79. Bergk.
[2] Demosth. *Neœr.* p. 1352, Reiske, and elsewhere ; Isæus, *de Pyrrhi Hered.*
p. 30. § 14.
[3] In Hephæst. p. 59. fr. 16. Bergk.

is described in the mean and necessitous condition in which he had formerly lived.[1] Anacreon here shows a strength and bitterness of satirical expression resembling the tone of Archilochus; a style which he has successfully imitated in other poems. But Anacreon is content with describing the mere surface, that is, the outward marks of disgrace, the slavish attire, the low-bred demeanour, the degrading treatment to which Artemon had been exposed; without (as it appears) touching upon the intrinsic merit or demerit of the person attacked. Thus, if we compare Anacreon with the Æolic lyric poets, he appears less reflective, and more occupied with external objects. For instance, wine, the effects of which are described by Alcæus with much depth of feeling, is only extolled by Anacreon as a means of social hilarity. Yet he recommends moderation in the use of it, and disapproves of the excessive carousings of the Scythians, which led to riot and brawling.[2] The ancients, indeed (probably with justice), considered the drunkenness of Anacreon as rather poetical than real. In Anacreon we see plainly how the spirit of the Ionic race, notwithstanding the elegance and refinement of Ionian manners, had lost its energy, its warmth of moral feeling, and its power of serious reflection, and was reduced to a light play of pleasing thoughts and sentiments. So far as we are able to judge of the poetry of Anacreon, it seems to have had the same character as that attributed by Aristotle to the later Ionic school of painting of Zeuxis, that ' it had elegance of design and brilliancy of colouring, but was wanting in moral character ($\tau\grave{o}$ $\mathring{\eta}\theta o\varsigma$.)'

§ 14. The Ionic softness, and departure from strict rule, which characterizes the poetry of Anacreon, may also be perceived in his versification. His language approached much nearer to the style of common conversation than that of the Æolic lyric poets, so as frequently to seem like prose embellished with ornamental epithets; and his rhythm is also softer and less bounding than that of the Æolians, and has an easy and graceful negligence, which Horace has endeavoured to imitate. Sometimes he makes use of logœdic metres, as in

---

[1] In Athen. XII. p. 533 E. fr. 19. Bergk.
[2] In Athen. X. p. 427. A. fr. 62. Bergk. Similarly Horace I. 27. 1. *sq.*

the Glyconean verses, which he combines into strophes by sub-
joining a Pherecratean verse to a number of Glyconeans.   In
this metre he shows his love for variety and novelty by mixing
strophes of different lengths with several Glyconean verses, yet
so as to preserve a certain symmetry in the whole.[1]   Anacreon
also, like the Æolic lyric poets, sometimes used long choriambic
verses, particularly when he intended to express energy of feeling, as in the poem against Artemon, already mentioned.
This metre also exhibits a peculiarity in the rhythm of the
Ionic poets, viz., an alternation of different metres, producing a
freer and more varied, but also a more careless, flow of the
rhythm.   In the present poem this peculiarity consists in the
alternation of choriambics with iambic dipodies.[2]   The same
character is still more strongly shown in the Ionic metre (Ionic
a minori) which was much used by Anacreon.   At the same
time he changed its expression (probably after the example of
the musician Olympus),[3] by combining two Ionic feet, so that
the last long syllable of the first foot was shortened and the
first short syllable of the second foot was lengthened; by which
change the second foot became a trochaic dipody.[4]   By this
process, called by the ancients a *bending*, or *refraction*
(ἀνάκλασις), the metre obtained a less uniform, and at the
same time a softer, expression; and thus, when distributed into

---

[1] So in the long fragment in Schol. Hephæst. p. 125. fr. 1. Bergk.

γουνοῦμαί σ᾽ ἐλαφηβόλε
ξανθὴ παῖ Διὸς, ἀγρίων
δέσποιν᾽ Ἄρτεμι θηρῶν.

This is followed by a second strophe, with four glyconeans and a pherecratean ;
and both strophes together form a larger whole. This hymn of Anacreon, the only
composition of its kind which is known, is evidently intended for the inhabitants of
Magnesia, on the Mæander and Lethæus, rebuilt after its destruction (ch. IX.
§ 4), where Artemis was worshipped under the title of Leucophryne.

[2] So that the metre is

$$\acute{} \cup \cup \_ | \ \acute{} \cup \cup \_ | \ \acute{\cup} \ \underset{\cup}{} \cup \_ | \ \underset{\cup}{\cup} \ \acute{} \ \cup \_$$

πολλὰ μὲν ἐν δουρὶ τιθεὶς αὐχένα πολλὰ δ᾽ ἐν τρόχῳ,
πολλὰ δὲ νῶτον σκυτίνῃ μάστιγι θωμιχθεὶς, κόμην—

Two such verses as these are then followed by an iambic dimeter, as an epode :

πώγωνά τ᾽ ἐκτετιλμένος.

[3] See ch. XII. § 7.

[4] So that $\cup \cup \acute{} \_ | \ \cup \cup \_ \_ -$ is changed into $\cup \cup \acute{} \cup | \ \acute{} \cup \_ \ -$

short verses, it became peculiarly suited to erotic poetry. The only traces of this metre, before Anacreon's time, occur in two fragments of Sappho. Anacreon, however, formed upon this plan a great variety of metres, particularly the short Anacreontic verse (a *dimeter Ionicus*), which occurs so frequently, both in his genuine fragments and in the later odes imitated from his style. Anacreon used the trochaic and iambic verses in the same manner as Archilochus, with whom he has as much in common, in the technical part of his poetry, as with the Æolic lyric poets. The composition of verses in strophes is less frequent with Anacreon than with the Lesbian poets ; and when he forms strophes, it often happens that their conclusion is not marked by a verse different from those that precede ; but the division is only made by the juxtaposition of a definite number of short verses (for example, four Ionic dimeters), relating to a common subject.

§ 15. It is scarcely possible to treat of the genuine remains of the poetry of Anacreon, without adverting to the collection of odes, preserved under his name. Indeed, these graceful little poems have so much influenced the notion formed of Anacreon, that even now the admiration bestowed upon him is almost entirely founded upon these productions of poets much later than him in date, and very different from him in poetical character. It has long since been proved that these Anacreontics are not the work of Anacreon ; and no further evidence of their spuriousness is needed than the fact, that out of about 150 citations of passages and expressions of Anacreon, which occur in the ancient writers, only one (and that of recent date) refers to a poem in this collection. But their subject and form furnish even stronger evidence. The peculiar circumstances under which Anacreon wrote his poetry never appear in these odes. The persons named in them (as, for example, Bathyllus) lose their individual reality ; the truth and vigour of life give place to a shadowy and ideal existence. Many of the commonplaces of poetry, as an old age of pleasure, the praise of love and wine, the power and subtlety of love, &c., are unquestionably treated in them with an easy grace and a charming simplicity. But generalities of this kind, without any reference to particular events or persons, do not consist with the character of Ana-

creon's poetry, which was drawn fresh from the life. Moreover, the principal topics in these poems have an epigrammatic
and antithetical turn : the strength of the weaker sex, the
power of little Eros, the happiness of dreams, the freshness of
age, are subjects for epigrams ; and for epigrams like those
composed in the first century before Christ (especially by
Meleager), and not like those of Simonides. Throughout these
odes love is represented as a little boy, who carries on a sort of
mischievous sport with mankind; a conception unknown to
ancient art, and closely akin to the epigrammatic sports which
belonged to the literature of a later period, and to the analogous
representations of Cupid in works of art, especially on gems,
where he appears, in various compositions, as a froward mischievous child. None of these works are more ancient than
the time of Lysippus or Alexander. The Eros of the genuine
Anacreon, who ' strikes at the poet with a great hatchet, like a
smith, and then bathes in the wintry torrent,'[1] is evidently a
being different both in body and mind. The language of these
odes is also prosaic and mean, and the versification monotonous,
inartificial, and sometimes faulty.[2]

These objections apply to the entire collection; nevertheless,
there is a great difference between the several odes, some of
which are excellent in their way, and highly pleasing from their
simplicity ;[3] while others are feeble in their conception and
barbarous in their language and versification. The former may,
perhaps, belong to the Alexandrian period ; in which (notwithstanding its refined civilization) some poets attempted to express
the simplicity of childish dispositions, as appears from the
Idylls of Theocritus. Those of inferior stamp may be ascribed to the later period of declining paganism, and to un-

---

[1] Fragm. in Hephæst. p. 68. Gais. fr. 45. Bergk.

[2] The prevailing metre in these Anacreontics $\smile - \smile - \smile - \smile$ (a dimeter
iambic catalectic) does not occur in the fragments, except in Hephæst. p. 30, Schol.
Aristoph. *Plut.* 302. (fr. 92. Bergk.) The verses there quoted are imitated in
one of the Anacreontics, *od.* 38. Hephæstion calls this metre, the ' so called
'Ἀνακρεόντειον.'

[3] One of the best, viz., Anacreon's advice to the toreutes, who is to make him a
cup, (No. 17 in the collection,) is cited by Gellius, *N.A.* XIX. 9, as a work of Anacreon himself ; but it has completely the tone and character of the common Anacreontics.

cultivated writers, who imitated a hackneyed style of poetical composition. However, many even of the better Anacreontics may have been written at as late a period as that of the national migrations. There can be no doubt that the century which produced the epic poetry of Nonnus, and so many ingenious and well-expressed epigrams, possessed sufficient talent and knowledge for Anacreontics of this kind.

§ 16. With Anacreon ceased the species of lyric poetry, in which he excelled : indeed he stands alone in it, and the tender softness of his song was drowned by the louder tones of the choral poetry. The poem (or melos) destined to be sung by a single person, never, among the Greeks, acquired so much extent as it has since attained in the modern English and German poetry. By modern poets it has been used as the vehicle for expressing almost every variety of thought and feeling. The ancients, however, drew a more precise distinction between the different feelings to be expressed in different forms of poetry ; and reserved the Æolic melos for lively emotions of the mind in joy or sorrow, or for impassioned overflowings of an oppressed heart. Anacreon's poetry contains rather the play of a graceful imagination than deep emotion ; and among the other Greeks there is no instance of the employment of lyric poetry for the expression of strong feeling : so that this kind of poetry was confined to a short period of time, and to a small portion of the Greek territory. One kind of lyric poems nearly resembling the Æolic, was, however, cultivated in the whole of Greece, and especially at Athens, viz., the *Scolion.*

Scolia were songs, which were sung at social meals during drinking, when the spirit was raised by wine and conversation to a lyrical pitch. But this term was not applied to all drinking songs. The scolion was a particular kind of drinking song, and is distinguished from other *parœnia*. It was only sung by particular guests, who were skilled in music and poetry ; and it is stated that the lyre, or a sprig of myrtle, was handed round the table, and presented to any one who possessed the power of amusing the company with a beautiful song, or even a good sentence in the lyric form. This custom really existed ;[1]

---

[1] See particularly the scene described in Aristoph. *Vesp.* 1219. *sq.* where the Scolion is caught up from one by the other.

although the notion that the name of the song arose from its irregular course round the table (σκολιόν, *crooked*) · is not probable. It is much more likely (according to the opinion of other ancient writers), that in the melody, to which the scolia were sung, certain liberties and irregularities were permitted, by which the extempore execution of the song was facilitated; and that on this account the song was said to be *bent*. The rhythms of the extant scolia are very various, though, on the whole, they resemble those of the Æolic lyric poetry; only that the course of the strophes is broken by an accelerated rhythm, and is in general more animated.[1] The Lesbians were the principal composers of Scolia. Terpander, who (according to Pindar) invented this kind of song, was followed by Alcæus and Sappho, and afterwards by Anacreon and Praxilla of Sicyon;[2] besides many others celebrated for choral poetry, as Simonides and Pindar. We will not include in this number the seven wise men; for although Diogenes Laërtius, the historian of ancient philosophy, cites popular verses of Thales, Solon, Chilon, Pittacus, and Bias, which are somewhat in the style of scolia;[3] yet the genuineness of these sententious songs is very questionable. With respect to language and metre, they all appear formed upon the same model; so that we must suppose the seven wise men to have agreed to write in an uniform style, and moreover in a kind of rhythm which did not become common until the time of the

---

[1] This is particularly true of the apt and elegant metre, which occurs in eight Scolia (one of them the Harmodius), and of which there is a comic imitation in Aristoph. *Eccl.* 938.

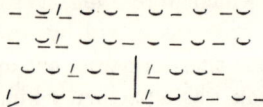

Here the hendecasyllables begin with a composed and feeble tone; but a more rapid rhythm is introduced by the anapæstic beginning of the third verse; and the two expressions are reconciled by the logaœdic members in the last verse.

[2] Praxilla (who, according to Eusebius, flourished in Olymp. 81. 2, B.C. 451, and is mentioned as a composer of odes of an erotic character) is stated to be the author of the Scolion Ὑπὸ παντὶ λίθῳ, which was in the παροίνια Πραξίλλης. (Schol. Rav. in Aristoph. *Thesm.* 528), and of the Scolion, Οὐκ ἔστιν ἀλωπεκίζειν, (Schol. *Vesp.* 1279. [1232.])

[3] Diogenes generally introduces them with some such expression as this: τῶν δ' ᾀδομένων αὐτοῦ μάλιστα εὐδοκίμησεν ἐκεῖνο.

tragedians.[1] Nevertheless they appear, in substance, to be as early as the age to which they are assigned, as their tone has a great resemblance to that of the scolia in the Æolic manner. For example, one of the latter contains these thoughts : ' Would that we could open the heart of every man, and ascertain his true character ; then close it again, and live with him sincerely as a friend ;' the scolion, in Doric rhythms, ascribed to Chilon, has a similar tone : ' Gold is rubbed on the touchstone, and thus tried ; but the minds of men are tried by gold, whether they are good or bad.' Hence it is probable that these scolia were framed at Athens, in the time of the tragedians, from traditional sayings of the ancient philosophers.

§ 17. Although scolia were mostly composed of moral maxims or of short invocations to the gods, or panegyrics upon heroes, there exist two, of greater length and interest, the authors of which are not otherwise known as poets. The one beginning, ' My great wealth is my spear and sword,' and written by Hybrias, a Cretan, in the Doric measure, expresses all the pride of the dominant Dorian, whose right rested upon his arms ; inasmuch as through them he maintained his sway over bondmen, who were forced to plough and gather in the harvest, and press out the grapes for him.[2] The other beginning, ' In the myrtle-bough will I bear my sword,' is the work of an Athenian, named Callistratus, and was written probably not long after the Persian war, as it was a favourite song in the time of Aristophanes. It celebrates the liberators of the Athenian people,

---

[1] They are all in Doric rhythms (which consist of dactylic members and trochaic dipodies), but with an ithyphallic (_ . ᴗ _ ᴗ _ ᴗ) at the close. This composite kind of rhythm never occurs in Pindar, occurs only once in Simonides, but occurs regularly in the Doric choruses of Euripides. The following scolion of Solon may serve as an example :

Πεφυλαγμένος ἄνδρα ἕκαστον ὅρα,
Μὴ κρυπτὸν ἔγχος ἔχων κραδίη φαιδρῷ προσεννέπῃ προσώπῳ,
Γλῶσσα δέ οἱ διχόμυθος ἐκ μελαί-
νας φρενὸς γεγωνῇ.

Also the following one of Pittacus :

Ἔχοντα δεῖ τόξα καὶ ἰοδόκον φαρέτρην στείχειν ποτὶ φῶτα κακόν.
Πιστὸν γὰρ οὐδὲν γλῶσσα διὰ στόματος λαλεῖ, διχόμυθον ἔχουσα
Καρδίῃ νόημα.

In that of Thales (Diog. Laërt. I. i. 35), the ithyphallic is *before* the last verse.

[2] See Müller's *Dorians*, B. III. ch. 4. § 1.

Harmodius and Aristogiton, for having, at the festival of Athene, slain the tyrant Hipparchus, and restored equal rights to the Athenians ; for this they lived for ever in the islands of the blest, in community with the most exalted heroes, and on earth their fame was immortal.[1] This patriotic scolion does not indeed rest on an historical foundation ; for it is known from Herodotus and Thucydides, that, though Hipparchus, the younger brother of the tyrant, was slain by Harmodius and Aristogiton, this act only served to make the government of Hippias, the elder brother, more cruel and suspicious ; and it was Cleomenes the Spartan, who, three years later, really drove the Pisistratids from Athens.   But the patriotic delusion in which the scolion was composed was universal at Athens. Even before the Persian war, statues of Harmodius and Aristogiton had been erected, as of heroes ; which statues, when carried away by Xerxes, were afterwards replaced by others. Supposing the mind of the Athenian poet possessed with this belief, we cannot but sympathize in the enthusiasm with which he celebrates his national heroes, and desires to imitate their costume at the Panathenaic festival, when they concealed their swords in boughs of myrtle.   The simplicity of the thoughts, and the frequent repetition of the same burden, ' for they slew the tyrant,' is quite in conformity with the frank and open tone of the scolion : and we may perhaps conjecture that this poem was a real impromptu, the product of a rapid and transient inspiration of its author.

---

[1] These, and most of the other scolia, are in Athenæus, XV. p. 694. *sq.*

CHAPTER XIV.

CHORAL LYRIC POETRY.

§ 1. THE characteristic features of the Doric lyric poetry have been already described, for the purpose of distinguishing it from the Æolic. These were; recitation by choruses, the artificial structure of long strophes, the Doric dialect, and its reference to public affairs, especially to the celebration of divine worship. The origin of this kind of lyric poetry can be traced to the earliest times of Greece : for (as has been already shown) choruses were generally used in Greece before the time of Homer; although the dancers in the ancient choruses did not also sing, and therefore an exact correspondence of all their motions with the words of the song was not requisite. At that period, however, the joint singing of several persons was practised, who either sat, stood, or moved onwards; as in pæans and hymenæals; sometimes the mimic movements of the dancer were explained by the singing, which was executed by other persons, as in the hyporchemes. And thus nearly every variety of the choral poetry, which was afterwards so elaborately and so brilliantly developed, existed, even at that remote period, though in a rude and unfinished state. The production of those polished forms in which the style of singing and the movements of the dance were brought into perfect harmony, coincides with the last advance in musical art; the improvements in which, made by Terpander, Olympus, and Thaletas, have formed the subject of a particular notice.

Thaletas is remarkable for having cultivated the art of dancing as much as that of music; while his rhythms seem to have been nearly as various as those afterwards employed in choral poetry. The union of song and dance, which was transferred from the lyric to the dramatic choruses,[1] must also have been introduced at that time; since the complicated structure of the strophes and antistrophes is founded, not on singing alone, but on the union of that art with dancing. In the first century subsequent to the epoch of these musicians, choral poetry does not, however, appear in its full perfection and individuality; but approaches either to the Lesbian lyric poetry, or to the epos; thus the line which separated these two kinds (between which the choral songs occupy a middle place) gradually became more distinct. Among the lyric poets whom the Alexandrians placed in their canon, Alcman and Stesichorus belong to this period of progress; while finished lyric poetry is represented by Ibycus, Simonides with his disciple Bacchylides, and Pindar.

We shall now proceed to take a view of these poets separately; classing among the former the dithyrambic poet Arion, and among the latter Pindar's instructor Lasus, and a few others who have sufficient individuality of character to distinguish them from the crowd.

We must first, however, notice the erroneous opinion that choral poetry existed among the Greeks in the works of these great poets only; they are, on the contrary, to be regarded merely as the eminent points arising out of a widely extended mass: as the most perfect representatives of that poetical fervour which, at the religious festivals, inspired all classes. Choral dances were so frequent among the Greeks at this period,

---

[1] Πάλαι μὲν γὰρ οἱ αὐτοὶ καὶ ᾖδον καὶ ὡρχοῦντο, says Lucian, de Saltat. 30, comparing the modern pantomimic style of dancing with the ancient lyric and dramatic style.

among the Dorians in particular, and were performed by the whole people, especially in Crete and Sparta, with such ardour and enthusiasm, that the demand for songs to be sung as an accompaniment to them must have been very great. It is true that, in many places, even at the great festivals, people contented themselves with the old traditionary songs, consisting of a few simple verses in which the principal thoughts and fundamental tone of feeling were rather touched than worked out. Thus, at the festival of Dionysus, the women of Elis sang, instead of an elaborate dithyramb, the simple ditty, full of antique symbolic language : ' Come, hero Dionysus, to thy holy sea-temple, accompanied by the Graces, and rushing on, oxen-hoofed ; holy ox ! holy ox !' [1]

At Olympia too, long before the existence of Pindar's skilfully composed Epinikia, the little song ascribed to Archilochus[2] was sung in honour of the victors at the games. This consisted of two iambic verses :

' Hail, Hercules, victorious prince, all hail !
Thyself and Iolaus, warriors bold,'

with the burden ' Tenella ! victorious !' to which a third verse, in praise of the victor of the moment, was probably added extempore. So also the three Spartan choruses, composed of old men, adults, and boys, sang at the festivals the three iambic trimeters :

' Once we were young, and strong as other youths.
We are so still ; if you list, try our strength.
We shall be stronger far than all of you.' [3]

But from the time that the Greeks had learned the charm of perfect lyric poetry, in which not merely a single chord of feeling was struck by the passing hand of the bard, but an entire melody of thoughts and sentiments was executed, their choruses did not persist in the mere repetition of verses like these ; songs were universally demanded, distinguished for a more artificial metre, and for an ingenious combination of ideas. Hence every considerable town, particularly in the Doric Pelo-

---

[1] Plutarch, *Quæst. Græc.* 36.　　　[2] See above, p. 184, note 2.
[3] Plutarch, *Lycurg.* 21. These triple choruses are called τριχόρια in Pollux, IV. 107, where the establishment of them is attributed to Tyrtæus.

ponnesus, had its poet who devoted his whole life to the training and execution of choruses—in short to the business, so important to the whole history of Greek poetry, of the Chorodidascalus.   How many such choral poets there were, whose fame did not extend beyond their native place, may be gathered from the fact that Pindar, while celebrating a pugilist of Ægina, incidentally mentions two lyric poets of the same family, the Theandrids, Timocritus and Euphanes.   Sparta also possessed seven lyric poets besides Alcman, in these early times.[1]   There too, as in other Doric states, women, even in the time of Alcman, contributed to the cultivation of poetry; as, for example, the maiden whom Alcman himself celebrates in these words,[2] ' This gift of the sweet Muses hath the fair-haired Megalostrata, favoured among virgins, displayed among us.'   From this we see how widely diffused, and how deeply rooted, were the feeling and the talent for such poetical productions in Sparta; and that Alcman, with his beautiful choral songs, introduced nothing new into that country, and only employed, combined, and perfected elements already existing.   But neither Alcman, nor the somewhat earlier Terpander, were the first who awakened this spirit among the Spartans.   Even the latter found the love for arts of this description already in existence, where, according to an extant verse of his, ' The spear of the young men, and the clear-sounding muse, and justice in the wide market-place, flourish.'

§ 2. According to a well-known and sufficiently accredited account, ALCMAN was a Lydian of Sardis, who grew up as a slave in the house of Agesidas, a Spartan; but was emancipated, and obtained rights of citizenship, though of a subordinate kind.[3] A learned poet of the Alexandrian age, Alexander the Ætolian, says of Alcman, (or rather makes him say of himself,) ' Sardis, ancient home of my fathers, had I been reared within thy walls,

---

[1] Their names are Spendon, Dionysodotus, Xenodamus (see chap. XII. § 11), Gitiadas, Areius, Eurytus, and Zarex.

[2] Fragm. 27. ed. Welcker.

[3] According to Suidas he was ἀπὸ Μεσόας, and Mesoa was one of the phylæ of Sparta, which were founded on divisions of the city. Perhaps, however, this statement only means that Alcman dwelt in Mesoa, where the family of his former master and subsequent patron may have resided.

I were now a cymbal-bearer,[1] or a eunuch-dancer in the service of the Great Mother, decked with gold, and whirling the beau-ful tambourine in my hands. But now I am called Alcman, and belong to Sparta, the city rich in sacred tripods; and I have become acquainted with the Heliconian Muses, who have made me greater than the despots Daskyles and Gyges.' Alcman however, in his own poems, does not speak so contemptuously of the home of his forefathers, but puts into the mouth of a chorus of virgins, words wherein he himself is celebrated as being 'no man of rude unpolished manners, no Thessalian or Ætolian, but sprung from the lofty Sardis.'[2] This Lydian ex-traction had doubtless an influence on Alcman's style and taste in music. The date at which he lived is usually placed at so remote a period as to render it unintelligble how lyric poetry could have already attained to such variety as is to be found in his works. It may indeed be true that he lived in the reign of the Lydian king Ardys; but it does not thence follow that he lived at the beginning of it; on the contrary, his childhood was contemporary with the close of that reign. (Ol. 37. 4. B.C. 629.) Alcman, in one of his poems, mentioned the musi-cian Polymnastus, who, in his turn composed a poem to Thale-tas.[3] According to this, he must have flourished about Ol. 42. (B.C. 612), which is the date assigned to him by ancient chrono-logists. His mention of the island Pityusæ[4] near the Balearic islands, points to this age; since, according to Herodotus, the western parts of the Mediterranean were first known to the Greeks by the voyages of the Phocæans, from the 35th Olym-piad downwards; and then became a subject of geographical knowledge, not, as heretofore, of fabulous legends. Alcman had thus before him music in that maturity which it had at-tained, not only by the labours of Terpander, but also by those of Thaletas; he lived at a time when the Spartans, after the termination of the Messenian wars, had full leisure to devote themselves to the arts and pleasures of life; for their ambition

---

[1] Κερνᾶς is equivalent to κερνοφόρος, the bearer of the dish, κέρνος, used in the worship of Cybele. See the epigram in *Anthol. Pal.* VII. 709.

[2] Fragm. 11. ed. Welcker, according to Welcker's explanation.

[3] See ch. XII. § 9.   [4] Steph. Byz. in Πιτνοῦσαι.

was not as yet directed to distinguishing themselves from the other Greeks by rude unpolished manners. Alcman devoted himself entirely to the cultivation of art; and we find in him one of the earliest examples of a poet who consciously and purposely strove to embellish his works with new artistical forms. In the ode which is regarded by the ancients as the first, he says, ' Come, Muse, clear-voiced Muse, sing to the maidens a melodious song in a new fashion ;'[1] and he elsewhere frequently mentions the originality and the ingenuity of his poetical forms. He ought always to be imagined as at the head of a chorus, by means of which, and together with which, he seeks to please.

.' Arise, Muse,' exclaims he, ' Calliope, daughter of Jove, sing us pleasant songs, give charm to the hymn, and grace to the chorus.'[2] And again, ' May my chorus please the house of Zeus, and thee, oh lord !'[3] Alcman is regarded by some as the true inventor of choral poetry, although others assign this reputation to his predecessor Terpander, or to his successor Stesichorus. He composed more especially for choruses of virgins, as several of the fragments quoted above show ; as well as the title of a considerable portion of his songs, Parthenia. The word Parthenia is, indeed, not always employed in the same sense ; but in its proper technical signification it denotes choral songs sung by virgins, not erotic poems addressed to them. On the contrary, the music and the rhythm of these songs are of a solemn and lofty character ; many of those of Alcman and the succeeding lyric poets were in the Doric harmony. The subjects were very various : according to Proclus, gods and men were celebrated in them, and the passage of Alcman, in which the virgins, with Homeric simplicity, exclaim, ' Oh father Zeus, were he but my husband !'[4] was doubtless in a Parthenion. If we inquire more minutely into the relation of the poet to his

---

[1] This is the meaning of fragm. I, which probably ought to be written and distributed (with a slight alteration) as follows :

Μῶσ' ἄγε, Μῶσα λιγαῖα, πολυμελὲς μέλος
Νεοχμὸν ἄρχε παρθένοις ἀείδειν.

The first verse is logaœdic, the second iambic.

[2] Fragm. 4.   [3] Fragm. 68.
[4] Schol. Hom. Od. VI. 244.

chorus, we shall not find, at least not invariably, that it as yet possessed that character to which Pindar strictly adhered. The chorus was not the mere organ of the poet, and all the thoughts and feelings to which it gave utterance, those of the poet.[1] In Alcman, the virgins more frequently speak in their own persons; and many Parthenia contain a dialogue between the chorus and the poet, who was at the same time the instructor and the leader of the chorus. We find sometimes addresses of the chorus of virgins to the poet, such as has just been mentioned; sometimes of the poet to the virgins associated with him; as in that beautiful fragment in hexameters, ' No more, ye honey-voiced, holy-singing virgins, no more do my limbs suffice to bear me; oh that I were a Cerylus, which with the halcyons skims the foam of the waves with fearless heart, the sea-blue bird of spring.'[2]

But, doubtless, Alcman composed and directed other choruses, since the Parthenia were only a part of his poetical works, besides which Hymns to the Gods, Pæans, Prosodia,[3] Hymeneals, and love-songs, are attributed to him. These poems were generally recited or represented by choruses of youths. The love-songs were probably sung by a single performer to the cithara. The clepsiambic poems, consisting partly of singing, partly of common discourse, and for which a peculiar instrument, bearing the same name, was used, also occurred among the works of Alcman, who appears to have borrowed them, as well as many other things, from Archilochus.[4] Alcman blends the sentiments and the style of Archilochus, Terpander, and Thaletas, and, perhaps, even those of the Æolian lyric poets: hence his works exhibit a great variety of metre, of dialect, and of general poetical tone. Stately hexameters are followed by the iambic and trochaic verse of Archilochus, by the ionics and cretics of Olympus and Thaletas, and by various sorts of

---

[1] There are only a few passages in Pindar, in which it has been thought that there was a separation of the persons of the chorus and the poet—viz. *Pyth.* V. 68. (96.) IX. 98. (174.) *Nem.* I. 19. (29.) VII. 85. (125.); and these have, by an accurate interpretation, been reduced to the above-mentioned rule.

[2] Fragm. 12. See Müller's *Dorians*, b. IV. ch. VII. § 11.

[3] Προσόδια, songs to be sung during a procession to a temple, before the sacrifice.

[4] Above, p. 185, note 3, with Aristoxenus ap. Hesych. in v. Κλεψίαμβος.

logaœdic rhythms. His strophes consisted partly of verses of different kinds, partly of repetitions of the same, as in the ode which opened with the invocation to Calliope above mentioned.[1] The connexion of two corresponding strophes with a third of a different kind, called an epode, did not occur in Alcman. He made strophes of the same measure succeed each other in an indefinite number, like the Æolic lyric poets : there were, however, odes of his, consisting of fourteen strophes, with an alteration (μεταβολή) in the metre after the seventh;[2] which was of course accompanied with a marked change in the ideas and in the whole tone of the poem.

It ought also to be mentioned that the Laconic metre, a kind of anapæstic verse, used as a march (ἐμβατήριον), which the Spartan troops sang as they advanced to attack the enemy, is attributed to Alcman;[3] whence it may be conjectured that Alcman imitated Tyrtæus, and composed war-songs similar to his, consisting not of strophes, but of a repetition of the same sort of verse. The authority for such a supposition is, however slight. There is not a trace extant of any marches composed by Alcman, nor is there any similarity between their form and character and any of his poetry with which we are acquainted. It is true that Alcman frequently employed the anapæstic metre, but not in the same way as Tyrtæus,[4] and never unconnected with other rhythms. Thus Tyrtæus, who was Alcman's predecessor by one generation, and whom we have already described as an elegiac poet, appears to have been the only notable composer of Embateria. These were sung to the flute in the Castorean measure by the whole army ; and, as is proved by a few extant verses, contained simple, but vigorous and manly exhortations to bravery. The measure in which they were written was also called the Messenian, because the second Mes-

---

[1] Μῶσ' ἄγε, Καλλίοπα, θύγατερ Διος. Dactylic tetrameters of this kind were combined into strophes, without hiatus and *syllaba anceps*, that is, after the manner of systems.

[2] Hephæst. p. 134. ed. Gaisford.

[3] The metrical scholia to Eurip. *Hec.* 59.

[4] According to the Latin metrical writers, Servius and Marius Victorinus, the dimeter hypercatalectos, the trimeter catalecticus, and the tetrameter brachycatalectos were called *Alcmanica metra*. The embateria were partly in the dimeter catalecticus, partly in the tetrameter catalecticus.

senian war had given occasion to the composition of war-songs of peculiar force and fervour.

§ 3. Alcman is generally regarded as the poet who success-fully overcame the difficulties presented by the rough and in-tractable dialect of Sparta, and invested it with a certain grace. And, doubtless, independent of their general Doric form, many Spartan idioms are found in his poems,[1] though by no means all the peculiarities of that dialect.[2] Alcman's language, there-fore, agrees with the other poetical dialects of Greece, in not representing a popular dialect in its genuine state, but in elevating and refining it by an admixture with the language of epic poetry, which may be regarded as the mother and nurse of every variety of poetry among the Greeks.

We may also observe that this tinge of popular Laconian idioms is by no means equally strong in all the varieties of Alcman's poetry ; they are most abundant in certain fragments of a hearty, simple character,[3] in which Alcman depicts his own way of life, his eating and drinking, of which, without being absolutely a glutton, he was a great lover.[4]

But even here we may trace the admixture with the Æolic character,[5] which ancient grammarians attribute to Alcman. It is explained by the fact that Peloponnesus was indebted for the first perfect specimen of lyric poetry to an Æolian of Lesbos, Terpander. In other fragments the dialect approximates more nearly to the epic, and has retained only a faint tinge of Dorism ; especially in all the poems in hexameters, and, indeed, wherever the poetry assumes a dignified, majestic character.[6]

Alcman is one of the poets whose image is most effaced by

---

[1] As σ for θ (σάλλεν for θάλλεν, &c.), the rough termination ρς in μάκαρς, Περίηρς.

[2] For example, not Μῶα, Τιμόθεορ, ἄκκορ (for ἄσκος), &c.

[3] Fragm. 24. 28.

[4] ὁ πάμφαγος 'Αλκμάν.

[5] Especially in the sound ΟΙΣ for an original ΟΝΣ, as in φέροιαα. It appears, however, that the pure Doric form Μῶσα ought to be introduced everywhere for Μοῖσα. In the third person plural, Alcman probably had, like Pindar, either αἰνέοντι (fr. 73), or εὔδοισιν. The σδ in τράπεσδα, κιθαρίσδεν, is also Æolic ; the pure Doric form was κιθαρίδδεν, &c.

[6] As in the beautiful fragment, No. 10, in Welcker's collection, which contains a description of the repose of night.

time, and of whom we can the least hope to obtain any accurate knowledge. The admiration awarded to him by antiquity is scarcely justified by the extant remains of his poetry ; but, doubtless, this is because they are extremely short, or are cited only in illustration of trifles. A true and lively conception of nature pervades the whole, elevated by that power of quickening the inanimate which descended from remote antiquity : thus, for instance, the poet calls the dew, Hersa, a daughter of Zeus and Selene, of the God of the Heavens and the Moon.[1]

He is also remarkable for simple and cheerful views of human life, connected with an intense enthusiasm for the beautiful in whatsoever age or sex, especially for the grace of virgins, the objects of Alcman's most ardent homage. The only evidence that his erotic poetry is somewhat voluptuous[2] is to be found in the innocence and simplicity with which, in the true Spartan fashion, he regarded the relation between the sexes. A corrupt, refined sensuality neither belongs to the age in which he lived, nor to the character of his poetry ; and although, perhaps, he is chiefly conversant with sensual existence, yet indications are not wanting of a quick and profound conception of the spiritual.[3]

§ 4. The second great choral poet, STESICHORUS, has so little in common with Alcman, that he can in no respect be regarded as successor to the Laconian poet, in his endeavours to bring that branch of poetry to perfection. We must consider him as starting from the same point, but led by the originality of his genius into a totally different path. Stesichorus is of rather a later date than Alcman. He was born, indeed, just at the period when the first steps towards the development of lyric poetry were made by Terpander (Olympiad 33. 4. 643 B.C. ; according to others, Olympiad 37. B.C. 632), but his life was protracted above eighty years (to Olympiad 55. 1. 560 B.C. ; according to others 56. B.C. 556) ; so that he might be a contemporary of the Agrigentine tyrant Phalaris, against whose ambitious

---

[1] Fr. 47.

[2] ἀκόλαστον, Archytas (ὁ ἁρμονικός) in Athen. XIII. p. 600. F.

[3] Alcman called the memory, the μνήμη, by the name φρασίδορκον, 'that which sees in the mind :' as should be written in *Etym. Gud.* p. 395. 52. for φασὶ δόρκον. Φρασὶ is a well-known Doric form for φρεσί.

projects he is said by Aristotle to have warned his fellow-citizens in an ingenious fable.[1] According to common tradition, Stesichorus was a native of Himera, a city containing a mixed population, half Ionic, half Doric, the Himeræans having come partly from the Chalcidian colony Zancle, partly from Syracuse. But at the time Stesichorus was born, Himera was but just founded, and his family could have been settled there but a few years. His ancestors, however, were neither Zanclæans nor Syracusans, but dwelt at Mataurus, or Metaurus, a city on the south of Italy, founded by the Locrians.[2] This circumstance throws a very welcome light on the otherwise strange tradition, which Aristotle[3] thought worthy of recording, that Stesichorus was a son of Hesiod, by a virgin named Ctimene, of Œneon, a place in the country of the Ozolian Locrians. If we abstract from this what belongs to the ancient mode of expression, which generally clothes in the simplest forms all relationships of blood, the following will result from the first mentioned facts. There was, as we saw above,[4] a line of epic bards in the style of Hesiod, who inhabited Œneon, and the neighbouring Naupactus, in the country of the Locrians. A family in which a similar practice of the poetical art was hereditary came through the colony of Locri in Italy, in which the Ozolian Locrians took peculiar interest, to these parts, and settled in Mataurus. From this family sprang Stesichorus.

Stesichorus lived at a time when the serene tone of the epos and an exclusive devotion to a mythical subject no longer sufficed; the predominant tendency of the Greek mind was towards lyric poetry. He himself was powerfully affected by this taste, and consecrated his life to the transplantation of all the rich materials, and the mighty and imposing shapes, which had hitherto been the exclusive property of the epos, to the choral poem. His special business was the training and direction of choruses, and he assumed the name of *Stesichorus,* or leader of choruses, his original name being Tisias. This occupation must have remained hereditary in his family in Himera;

---

[1] Above, ch. XI. § 14.

[2] Steph. Byz. in Μάταυρος, Στησίχορος, Ματαυρῖνος γένος. See Klein, Fragmenta Stesichori, p. 9.

[3] In Proclus and Tzetzes, Proleg. to Hesiod.   [4] Ch. VIII. § 4.

a younger Stesichorus of Himera came, in Olympiad 73. 1.
B.C. 485, to Greece as a poet;[1] a third Stesichorus of Himera
was victor at Athens, doubtless as chorus-leader, in Olympiad
102. 3. B.C. 370.[2] The eldest of them, Stesichorus Tisias,
made a great change in the artistical form of the chorus. He
it was who first broke the monotonous alternation of the strophe
and antistrophe through a whole poem, by the introduction of
the epode, differing in measure, and by this means made the
chorus stand still.[3] During the strophe, the chorus moved in a
certain evolution, which again during the antistrophe was made
back to its original station, where it remained while the epode
was sung. The chorus of Stesichorus seems to have consisted
of a combination of several rows or members of eight dancers;
the number eight appears indeed from various traditions to have
been, as it were, consecrated by him.[4] The musical accompaniment was the cithara. The strophes of Stesichorus were
of great extent, and composed of different verses, like those of
Pindar, though of a simpler character. In many poems they
consisted of dactylic series, which were sometimes broken
shorter, sometimes extended longer, as it were variations of the
hexameter. With these Stesichorus combined trochaic dipodies,[5]
by which the gravity of the dactyls was somewhat tempered;
the metres used by Pindar, and generally for all odes in the
Dorian style of music, thus arose. Although Stesichorus also
mainly employed this grave and solemn harmony, yet he himself mentions on one occasion the use of the Phrygian, which is
characterized by a deeper pathos, and a more passionate expression.[6] It appears from this fragment that the poet chose, as

---

[1] *Marm. Par.* ep. 50.　　　　[2] *Ibid.* ep. 73.

[3] See several grammarians and compilers in τρία Στησιχόρου, or Οὐδὲ τρία Στησιχόρου γιγνώσκεις.

[4] Several grammarians at the explanation of πάντα ὀκτώ.

[5] / ‿ — ‿. Several verses of greater or less length, formed of dipodies of
this kind, are called by the grammarians Stesichorean verses.

[6] Fragm. 12. *Mus. Crit. Cantab.* Fasc. VI. Fragm. 39. ed. Klein:

> τοιάδε χρὴ Χαρίτων δα-
> μώματα καλλικόμων ὑμ-
> νεῖν Φρύγιον μέλος ἐξευ-
> ρόντας,
> Ἁβρῶς ἦρος ἐπερχομένου.

Stesichorus, also, according to Plutarch, used the ἁρμάτιος νόμος, which had been
set by Olympus in the Phrygian ἁρμονία; above, ch. XII. § 7.

its metrical form, dactylic systems (*i. e.* combinations of similar series without any close or break), to which ponderous trochees were attached.[1] Elsewhere, Stesichorus used also anapæsts and choriambics, which correspond in their character to the dactylic verses just mentioned. Occasionally, however, he used the lighter and rather pleasing than solemn logaœdic measure.

§ 5. As the metres of Stesichorus approach much more nearly to the epos than those of Alcman, as his dialect also is founded on the epic, to which he gave a different tone only by the most frequent and most current Dorisms, so also with regard to the matter and contents of his poems, Stesichorus makes, of all lyric poets, the nearest approach to the epic. ‘ Stesichorus,’ says Quintilian elegantly, ‘ sustained the weight of epic poetry with the lyre.’ We know the epic subjects which he treated in this manner ; they have a great resemblance to the subjects of the shorter epic poems of the Hesiodean school, of which we have spoken above. Many of them were borrowed from the great mythic cycle of Hercules (whom he, like Pisander, invariably represented with the lion's skin, club, and bow) ; such as his expedition against the triple giant of the west, Geryon (Γηρυονίς) ; Scylla (Σκύλλα), whom, in the same expedition, Hercules subdued ; the combat with Cycnus (Κύκνος),[2] the son of Ares, and the dragging of Cerberus (Κέρβερος) from the infernal regions. Others related to the mythic cycle of Troy ; such as the destruction of Ilium (Ἰλίου πέρσις), the returns of the heroes (Νόστοι), and the story of Orestes (Ὀρεστεία). Other mythical subjects were, the prizes which Acastus, King of Iolcus, distributed at the funeral games of his father Pelias (ἐπὶ Πελίᾳ ἆθλα) ; Eriphyle, who seduced her husband Amphiaraus to join in the expedition against Thebes (Ἐριφύλα) ; the hunters of the Calydonian boar (συοθῆραι, according to the most probable interpretation) ; lastly, a poem called Europeia (a title also borne by the epos of Eumelus), which, from the little we know of it, seems to have treated of the traditional stories of Cadmus, with which that of Europa was interwoven.

A question here arises, how these epic subjects could be treated in a lyric form. It is manifest that these poems could

---

[1] τροχαιοὶ σημαντοί.   [2] Ch. VIII. (p. 131-2.)

not have had the perfect repose, the vivid and diffuse descriptions, in short all the characteristics of the epos. To connect with these qualities the accompaniment of many voices and instruments, a varied rhythmical structure, and choral dancing, would have seemed to the Greeks, with their fine sense of harmony and congruity, a monstrous misunion. There must, therefore, have been something which induced Stesichorus, or his fellow-citizens, to take an interest in these heroes and their exploits. Thus in Pindar all the mythological narratives have reference to some recent event.[1] In Stesichorus, however, the mythical subject must have been treated at greater length, and have occupied nearly the entire poem; otherwise the names of these poems would not have been like those of epic compositions. One of them, the Oresteia, was so long, that it was divided into two books; and it contained so much mythical matter, that in the Iliac table, a well known ancient bas-relief, the destruction of Troy is represented in a number of scenes from this poem. The most probable supposition, therefore, is that these poems were intended to be represented at the mortuary sacrifices and festivals, which were frequently celebrated in Magna Græcia to the Greek heroes, especially to those of the Trojan cycle.[2]

The entire tone in which Stesichorus treated these mythic narratives was also quite different from the epic. It is evident from the fragments that he dwelt upon a few brilliant adventures, in which the force and the glory of the heroes was, as it were, concentrated; and that he gave the reins to his fancy. Thus, in an extant fragment, Hercules is described as returning to the god of the sun (Helios), on the goblet on which he had swum to the island of Geryoneus; 'Helios, the Hyperionid, stepped into the golden goblet, in order to go, over the ocean, to the sacred depths of the dark night to his mother, and wife, and dear children;' while the son of Zeus (Hercules) entered into the laurel grove.'[3] In another, the dream of Clytæmnestra, in the night before she was killed, is described: 'A serpent

---

[1] Below, ch. XV. § 1.

[2] Thus in Tarentum ἐναγισμοί were offered to the Atrids, Tydids, Alcids, Laertiads (Pseud-Aristot. *Mirab. Ausc.* 114); in Metapontum to the Nelids (Strabo VI. p. 263), &c.

[3] Fragm. 3. (10. ed. Klein).

seemed to approach her, its crest covered with blood; but, of a sudden, the king of Pleisthenes' race (Agamemnon) came out of it.'[1] In general, a lyric poet like Stesichorus was more inclined than an epic poet to alter the current legend : since his object was not so much mere narration, as the praise of individual heroes, and the mythus was always introduced with a view to its application. As a proof of this assertion, it is sufficient to refer to the story, celebrated in antiquity, of Stesichorus having, in a poem (probably the destruction of Troy), attributed all the sufferings of the Trojan war to Helen ;[2] but the deified heroine having, as it was supposed, deprived him of his sight, as a punishment for this insult, he composed his famous Palinodia, in which he said that the Helen who had been seen in Troy, and for whom the Greeks and Trojans fought during so many years, was a mere shadow ($\phi\acute{a}\sigma\mu a$, $\epsilon\emph{i}\delta\omega\lambda o\nu$) ; while the true Helen had never embarked from Greece. Even this, however, is not to be considered as pure invention ; there were in Laconia popular legends of Helen's having appeared as a shade long after her death,[3] like her brothers Castor and Pollux ; and it is possible that Stesichorus may have met with some similar story. Stesichorus simply conceived Helen to have remained in Greece ; he did not suppose her to have gone to Egypt.[4]

The language of Stesichorus likewise accorded with the tone of his poetry. Quintilian, and other ancient critics, state that

---

[1] Fragm. inc. 1. (43. Klein). This fragment too is in a lyric metre, and ought not to be forced into an elegiac distich.

[2] Hence in the Iliac table, Menelaus is represented as attempting to stab Helen whom he has just recovered; while she flies for protection to the temple of Aphrodite.

[3] Herod. VI. 61.

[4] Others supposed that Proteus, the marine demigod skilled in metamorphoses, went to the island of Pharos, and there formed a false Helen with which he deceived Paris; a version of the story which even the ancient Scholiasts have confounded with that of Stesichorus. As this Proteus was converted by the Egyptian interpreters ($\dot{\epsilon}\rho\mu\eta\nu\epsilon\hat{\iota}s$) into a king of Egypt, this king was said to have taken Helen from Paris, and to have kept her for Menelaus. This was the story which Herodotus heard in Egypt, II. 112. Euripides, in his Helen, gives quite a new turn to the tale. In this play, the gods form a false Helen, whom Paris takes to Troy; the true Helen is carried by Hermes to the Egyptian king Proteus. In this manner, Proteus completely loses the character which he bears in the ancient Greek mythus ; but the events tend to situations which suited the pathetic tragedy of Euripides.

it corresponded with the dignity of the persons described by him ; and that he might have stood next to Homer, if he had restrained the copiousness of his diction. It is possible that, in expressing this opinion, Quintilian did not sufficiently advert to the distinction between the epic and lyric styles.

§ 6. We have subjoined these remarks to the longer lyric poems of Stesichorus, which were nearest to the epos, as it was in these that the peculiar character of his poetry was most clearly displayed. Stesichorus, however, also composed poems in praise of the gods, especially pæans and hymns ; not in an epic, but in a lyric form. There were also erotic poems of Stesichorus, differing as much as his other productions from the amatory lyric poems of the Lesbians. They consisted of love-stories ; as the *Calyce,* which described the pure but unhappy love of a maiden of that name ; and the *Rhadina,* which related the melancholy adventures of a Samian brother and sister, whom a Corinthian tyrant put to death out of love for the sister, and jealousy of the brother.[1] These are the earliest instances in Greek literature of love-stories forming the basis of romantic poetry ; the stories themselves probably having been derived from the tales with which the inmates of the Greek gynæcea amused themselves. These stories (which were afterwards collected by Parthenius, Plutarch, and others) usually belonged, not to the purely mythical period, but either to historical times, or to the transition period between fable and history. In this manner the story involved the ordinary circumstances of life, while extraordinary situations could be introduced, serving to show the fidelity of the lovers. Of a similar character was the bucolic poem, which Stesichorus first raised from a rude strain of merely local interest, to a classical branch of Greek poetry. The first bucolic poem is said to have been sung by Diomus, a cowherd in Sicily, a country abounding in cattle.[2] The hero of this pastoral poetry was the shepherd Daphnis (celebrated in Theocritus), who had been beloved by a nymph, and deprived

---

[1] Compare Strab. VIII. p. 347. D. with Pausan. VII. 5. 6. The chief authority for these love-stories is the long excursus in Athenæus on the popular songs of the Greeks, XIV. p. 618. *sqq.*

[2] Βουκολιασμός, Epicharmus ap. Athen. XIV. p. 619. The song of Eriphanis, Μακραὶ δρύες, ὦ μέγαλαι, appears to have been of native Sicilian origin.

by her, out of jealousy, of his sight; and with whose laments all nature sympathized. This legend was current in the native country of Stesichorus, near the river Himeras, where Daphnis is said to have uttered his laments; and near Cephalœdium, where a stone resembling a man's form was said to have once been Daphnis. Himera was the only one among the ancient Greek colonies in Sicily, which lay on the northern coast of the island; it was entirely surrounded by the aboriginal inhabitants, the Siculians; and it is therefore probable that the hero Daphnis, and the original form of the pastoral song, belonged to the Siculian peasantry.[1]

From what precedes, it appears that the poetry of Stesichorus was not employed in expressing his own feelings, or describing the events of his own life, but that he preferred the past to the present. This character seems to have been common to all the poems of Stesichorus. Thus he did not, like Sappho, compose Epithalamia having an immediate reference to the present, but he took some of his materials from mythology. The beautiful Epithalamium of Theocritus,[2] supposed to have been sung by the Laconian virgins before the chamber of Menelaus and Helen, is, in part, imitated from a poem of Stesichorus.

§ 7. Thus much for the peculiarities of this choral poet, not less remarkable in himself, than as a precursor of the perfect lyric poetry of Pindar. Our information respecting ARION is far less complete and satisfactory; yet the little that we know of him proves the wide extension of lyric poetry in the time of Alcman and Stesichorus. Arion was the contemporary of Stesichorus; he is called the disciple of Alcman, and (according to the testimony of Herodotus) flourished during the reign of Periander at Corinth, between Olymp. 38. 1. and 48. 4. (628 and 585 B. C.), probably nearer the end than the beginning of this period. He was a native of

---

[1] It appears from Ælian *V. H.*, X. 18. that the legend of Daphnis was given in Stesichorus, not as it is expanded in Theocrit. *Id.* I., but as it is touched upon in *Id.* VII. 73. The pastoral legend of the Goatherd Comatas, who was inclosed in a box by the king's command, and fed by a swarm of bees, sent by the Muses (Theocrit. VII. 78. *sq.*) has all the appearance of a story embellished by Stesichorus.

[2] *Id.* XVIII.

Methymna in Lesbos; a district in which the worship of Bacchus, introduced by the Bœotians, was celebrated with orgiastic rites, and with music. Arion was chiefly known in Greece as the perfecter of the dithyramb. The dithyramb, as a song of Bacchanalian festivals, is doubtless of great antiquity; its name is too obscure to have arisen at a late period of the Greek language, and probably originated in the earliest times of the worship of Bacchus.[1] Its character was always, like that of the worship to which it belonged, impassioned and enthusiastic; the extremes of feeling, rapturous pleasure, and wild lamentation, were both expressed in it. Concerning the mode of its representation we are but imperfectly informed. Archilochus says, that 'he is able, when his mind is inflamed with wine, to sing the dithyramb, the beautiful strain of Dionysus:'[2] from which expressions it is probable that in the time of Archilochus, one of a band of revellers sometimes sang the dithyramb, while the others joined him with their voices. There is, however, no trace of a *choral* performance of the dithyramb at this time. Choruses had been already introduced in Greece, but in connexion with the worship of Apollo, and they danced to the cithara (φόρμιγξ), the instrument used in this worship. In the worship of Dionysus, on the other hand, an irregular band of revellers, led by a flute-player, was the prominent feature.[3] Arion, according to the concurrent testimonies of the historians and grammarians of antiquity, was the first who practised a chorus in the representation of a dithyramb, and therefore gave a regular and dignified character to this song, which before had probably consisted of irregular expressions of excited feeling, and of inarticulate ejaculations. This improvement was made at Corinth, the rich and flourishing city of Periander; hence Pindar in his eulogy of Corinth exclaims: ' Whence, but from Corinth, arose the pleasing festivals of Dionysus, with the dithyramb, of which the prize is an ox?'[4] The choruses which

---

[1] On the formation of διθύραμβος, see p. 177, note 2.

[2] 'Ως Διωνύσου ἄνακτος καλὸν ἐξάρξαι μέλος
    Οἶδα διθύραμβον οἴνῳ συγκεραυνωθεὶς φρένας.

ap. Athen. XIV. p. 628.   [3] See ch. III. § 5.

[4] Pind. *Ol.* XIII. 18. (25.), where the recent editors give a full and accurate explanation of the matter.

sang the dithyramb were *circular choruses* (κύκλιοι χοροί); so called, because they danced in a circle round the altar on which the sacrifice was burning. Accordingly, in the time of Aristophanes, the expressions 'dithyrambic poet,' and 'teacher of cyclian choruses' (κυκλιοδιδάσκαλος), were nearly synonymous.[1] With regard to the subjects of the dithyrambs of Arion we know nothing, except that he introduced the *tragic style* into them.[2] This proves that he had distinguished a choral song of a gloomy character, which referred to the dangers and sufferings of Dionysus, from the ordinary dithyramb of the joyous kind; as will be shown in a subsequent chapter.[3] With regard to the musical accompaniment of the dithyrambs of Arion, it may be remarked, that the cithara was the principal instrument used in it, and not the flute, as in the boisterous comus. Arion was himself the first cithara-player of his time : and the exclusive fame of the Lesbian musicians from Terpander downwards was maintained by him. Arion also, according to the well known fable,[4] played the orthian nome,[5] when he was compelled to throw himself from a ship into the sea, and was miraculously saved by a dolphin.[6] Arion is also stated, as well as Terpander, to have composed proœmia, that is, hymns to the gods, which served as an introduction to festivals.[7]

---

[1] Hence Arion is said to have been the son of *Cycleus*.

[2] Τραγικὸς τρόπος, Suidas in ᾽Αρίων. Concerning the satyrs whom Arion is said to have used on this occasion, see below, chap. XXI.

[3] Chap. XXI. The finest specimen of a dithyramb of the joyful kind is the fragment of a dithyramb by Pindar, in Dion. Hal. *de Comp. Verb.* 22. This dithyramb was intended for the great Dionysia (τὰ μεγάλα or τὰ ἄστει Διονύσια), which are described in it as a great vernal festival, at the season ' when the chamber of the Hours opens, and the nectarian plants feel the approach of the fragrant spring.'

[4] Herod. I. 23. This fable probably arose from a sacred offering in a temple at Tænarum, which represented *Taras* sitting on a dolphin, as he appears on the coins of Tarentum. Plutarch, *Conv. Sept. Sap.* c. 18. mentions the Pythian instead of the orthian nome.

[5] The orthian nome was mentioned above, chap. XII. § 15, in connexion with Polymnestus.

[6] The nomos orthios was sung to the cithara (Herod. I. 24. Aristoph. *Eq.* 1279. *Ran.* 1308, et Schol.), but also to the Phrygian flute (Lucian 4).

[7] Suidas in *v.* The ode to Neptune which Ælian, *H. A.*, XII. 45, ascribes to Arion, is copious in words, but poor in ideas, and is quite unworthy of such a poet as Arion. It also presupposes the truth of the fable that Arion was saved by a dolphin.

§ 8. In descending to the choral poets who lived nearer the time of the Persian war, we meet with two poets of very peculiar characters; the vehement Ibycus, and the tender and refined Simonides.

IBYCUS was a native of Rhegium, the city near the southern-most point of Italy, which was closely connected with Sicily, the country of Stesichorus. Rhegium was peopled partly by Ionians from Chalcis, partly by Dorians from Peloponnesus; the latter of whom were a superior class. The peculiar dialect formed in Rhegium had some influence on the poems of Ibycus; although these were in general written in an epic dialect with a Doric tinge, like the poems of Stesichorus.[1] Ibycus was a wandering poet, as is intimated in the story of his death having been attested and revenged by cranes; but his travels were not, like those of Stesichorus, confined to Sicily. He passed a part of his time in Samos with Polycrates; whence the flourishing period of Ibycus may be placed at Olymp. 63 (B.C. 528).[2] We have already explained the style of poetry which was admired at the court of Polycrates. Ibycus could not here compose solemn hymns to the gods, but must accommodate his Doric cithara, as he was best able, to the strains of Anacreon. Accordingly, it is probable that the poetry of Ibycus was first turned mainly to erotic subjects during his residence in the court of Polycrates; and that his glowing love-songs (especially to beautiful youths), which formed his chief title to fame in antiquity, were composed at this time.

But that the poetical style of Ibycus resembled that of Stesichorus is proved by the fact that the ancient critics often doubted to which of the two a particular idea or expression belonged.[3] It may indeed be conjectured that this doubt arose from the works of these two poets being united in the

---

[1] A peculiarity of the Rheginian dialect in Stesichorus was the formation of the third persons of barytone verbs in ησι; φέρησι, λέγησι, &c.

[2] Above, ch. XIII. § 12.

[3] Citations of Stesichorus *or* Ibycus, or (for the same expression) of Stesichorus *and* Ibycus, occur in Athen. IV. p. 172 D., Schol. Ven. ad *Il.* XXIV. 259. III. 114. Hesych. in βρυαλίκται, vol. I. p. 774. ed. Alb., Schol. Aristoph. *Av.* 1302, Schol. Vratislav. ad Pind. *Ol.* IX. 128. (οἱ περὶ Ἴβυκον καὶ Στησίχορον), *Etymol. Gud.* in ἄτερπνος, p. 98. 31,

same collection, like those of Hipponax and Ananius, or of Simo-nides and Bacchylides; but their works would not have been so united by the ancient editors if there had not been a close affinity between them. The metres of Ibycus also resemble those of Stesichorus, being in general dactylic series, connected together into verses of different lengths, but sometimes so long, that they are rather to be called systems than verses. Besides these, Ibycus frequently uses logaœdic verses of a soft or languid character: and in general his rhythms are less stately and dignified, and more suited to the expression of passion, than those of Stesichorus. Hence the effeminate poet Agathon is represented by Aristophanes as appealing to Ibycus with Ana-creon and Alcæus, who had made music more sweet, and worn many-coloured fillets (in the oriental fashion), and had led the wanton Ionic dance.[1]

§ 9. The subjects of the poems of Ibycus appear also to have a strong affinity with those of the poems of Stesichorus. For although no poems with such names as *Cycnus* or the *Orestea* are attributed to Ibycus; yet so many peculiar accounts of mythological stories, especially relating to the heroic period, are cited from his poems, that it seems as if he too had written long poems on the Trojan war, the expedition of the Argonauts, and other similar subjects. That, like Stesichorus, he dwelt upon the marvellous in the heroic mythology, is proved by a fragment in which Hercules is introduced as saying: 'I also slew the youths on white horses, the sons of Molione, the twins with like heads and connected limbs, both born in the silver egg.'[2]

The *erotic* poetry of Ibycus is however more celebrated. We know that it consisted of odes to youths, and that these breathed a fervour of passion far exceeding that expressed in any similar productions of Greek literature. Doubtless the poet gave ut-terance to his own feelings in these odes; as indeed appears from the extant fragments. Nevertheless the length of the strophes and the artificial structure of the verses prove that these odes were performed by choruses. Birth-days or other

---

[1] *Thesm.* 161.
[2] Ap. Athen. p. 57 F. (Fr. 27. coll. Schneidewin).

family festivals, or distinctions in the gymnasia, may have afforded the poet an opportunity of coming with a chorus into the court-yard of the house, and offering his congratulations in the most imposing and brilliant manner. The occasions of these poetical congratulations were doubtless the same as those which gave rise to the painted vases in Magna Græcia, with the inscription 'the boy is beautiful' (καλὸς ὁ παῖς), and scenes from gymnastic exercises and social life. But that in the poems of Ibycus, as well as of Pindar, the chorus was the organ of the poet's thoughts and feelings, is sufficiently proved (as has been already remarked) by the extant fragments. In a very beautiful fragment, the versification of which expresses the course of the feeling with peculiar art, Ibycus says :[1] 'In the spring the Cydonian apple-trees flourish, watered by rivulets from the brooks in the untrodden garden of the virgins, and the grapes which grow under the shady tendrils of the vine. But Eros gives me peace at no season; like a Thracian tempest, gleaming with lightning, he rushes from Cypris, and, full of fury, he stirs up my heart from the bottom.' In some other extant verses he says :[2] 'Again Eros looks at me from beneath his black eyelashes with melting glances, and drives me with blandishments of all kinds into the endless nets of Cypris. I tremble at his attack; as a harnessed steed which contends for the prize in the sacred games, when he approaches old age, unwillingly enters the race-course with the rapid chariot.'

These amatory odes of Ibycus did not however consist merely of descriptions of his passion, which could scarcely have afforded sufficient materials for choral representation. He likewise called in the assistance of mythology in order to elevate, by a comparison with divine or heroic natures, the beauty of the youth or his own passion. Thus in a poem of this kind, addressed to Gorgias, Ibycus told the story of Ganymedes and Tithonus, both Trojans and favourites of the gods; who were described as contemporary,[3] and were associated in the narrative.

---

[1] Fragm. 1. coll. Schneidewin. The end of the fragment is very difficult; the translation is made from the following alteration of the text : ἀτέμβησι κραταιῶς πεδόθεν σαλάσσων ἡμετέρας φρένας.

[2] Schol. Plat. Parm. p. 137. A. (Fragm. 2. coll. Schneidewin).

[3] After the Little Iliad, in which Ganymedes is the son of Laomedon : Schol. Vat. ad Eurip. Troad. 822. Elsewhere Tithonus is his son.

Ganymedes is carried off by Zeus in the form of an eagle, in order to become his favourite and cup-bearer in Olympus; and, at the same timè, Eros incites the rising Aurora to bear away from Ida, Tithonus, a Trojan shepherd and prince.[1] The perpetual youth of Ganymedes, the short manhood and the melancholy old age of Tithonus, probably gave the poet occasion to compare the different passions which they excited, and to represent that of Zeus as the more noble, that of Aurora the less praise-worthy.

§ 10. Leaving Ibycus in the obscurity which envelopes all the Greek lyric poets anterior to Pindar, we come to a brighter point in SIMONIDES. This poet has been already described as one of the greatest masters of the elegy and the epigram; but a full account of him has been reserved for this place.

Simonides was born at Julis in the island of Ceos, which was inhabited by Ionians; according to his own testimony,[2] about Olymp. 56. 1. B.C. 556. He lived, according to a precise account, 89 years, and died in 78. 1. B.C. 468. He belonged to a family which sedulously cultivated the musical arts; his grandfather on the paternal side had been a poet;[3] Bacchylides, the lyric poet, was his nephew: and Simonides the younger, known by the name of 'the genealogist,' on account of a work on genealogies (περὶ γενεαλογιῶν), was his grandson. He him-self exercised the functions of a chorus-teacher in the town of Carthæa in Ceos; and the house of the chorus (χορηγεῖον) near the temple of Apollo was his customary abode.[4] This occupa-tion was to him, as to Stesichorus, the origin of his poetical efforts. The small island of Ceos at this time contained many things which were likely to give a good direction to a youthful mind. The lively genius of the Ionic race was here restrained by severe principles of moderation (σωφροσύνη); the laws of Ceos are celebrated for their excellence;[5] and although Prodicus

---

[1] This account of the poem of Stesichorus is taken from Schol. Apollon. Rhod. III. 158. compared with Nonnus *Dionys.* XV. 278. ed. Graefe.

[2] In the epigram in Planudes, Jacobs *Anthol. Palat.* Append. *Epigr.* 79. (203 Schneidewin).

[3] *Marm. Par.* ep. 49. according to Boeckh's explanation, *Corp. Inscrip.* vol. II. p. 319.

[4] Chamæleon ap. Ath. X. p. 456. E.

[5] Muller's *Æginetica*, p. 132, note u.

of Ceos is named among the sophists attacked by Socrates, yet
he was considered as a man of probity, and the friend of
a beneficent philosophy.   Simonides, also, appears throughout
his whole life to have been attached to philosophy; and his
poetical genius is characterized rather by versatility and purity
of taste than by fervid enthusiasm.   Many ingenious apophthegms and wise sayings are attributed to him, nearly resembling those of the seven sages; for example, the evasive
answer to the question, what is God? is attributed both to
Simonides and Thales: in the one anecdote the questioner is
Hiero, in the other Crœsus.   Simonides himself is sometimes
reckoned among the philosophers, and the sophists considered
him as a predecessor in their art.   The 'moderation of Simonides' became proverbial;[1] a modest consciousness of human
weakness, and a recognition of a superior power, are everywhere traceable in his poetry.   It is likewise recorded that
Simonides used, and perfected, the contrivances which are
known by the name of the Mnemonic art.

It must be admitted, that, in depth and novelty of ideas,
and in the fervour of poetical feeling, Simonides was far inferior to his contemporary Pindar.   But the practical tendency
of his poetry, the worldly wisdom, guided by a noble disposition,
which appeared in it, and the delicacy with which he treated all
the relations of states and rulers, made him the friend of the most
powerful and distinguished men of his age.   Scarcely any poet
of antiquity enjoyed so much consideration in his lifetime, or
exercised so much influence upon political events, as Simonides.
He was one of the poets entertained by Hipparchus the Pisis-
tratid (Olymp. 63. 2.—66. 3. B.C. 527—14.), and was highly
esteemed by him.   He was much honoured by the families of
the Aleuads and Scopads, who at that time ruled in Thessaly, as
powerful and wealthy nobles, in their cities of Larissa and Cran-
non, and partly as kings of the entire country.   These families attempted, by their hospitality and liberality to the poets and wise
men whom they entertained, either to soften the rough nature of
the Thessalians, or, at least, to cover it with a varnish of civiliza-

---

[1] Ἡ Σιμωνίδου σωφροσύνη.   Aristides περὶ τοῦ παραφθ. III. 645 A. Canter. II.
p. 510. Dindorf. Simonidis reliquiæ ed. Schneidewin, p. xxxiii.

tion. That, however, they were not always equally liberal to Simonides, appears from the anecdote that Scopas once refused to give him more than half the promised reward, and referred him for the other half to the Dioscuri, whom he had also praised in his ode ; and that, in consequence, the Dioscuri saved Simonides when the house fell upon the impious Scopas.[1] Simonides appears to have passed much of the latter part of his life in Sicily, chiefly with the tyrant of Syracuse. That he was in high honour at this court is proved by the well attested story, that when, after Gelo's death, a discord arose between the allied and closely connected families of the tyrants of Syracuse and Agrigentum, Hiero of Syracuse and Thero of Agrigentum, with their armies, were standing opposite to each other on the river Gelas, and would have decided their dispute with arms, if Simonides (who, like Pindar, was the friend of both tyrants) had not restored peace between them (Olymp. 76. 1. B.C. 476). But the high reputation of Simonides among the Greeks is chiefly apparent in the time of the Persian war. He was in friendly intercourse both with Themistocles and the Spartan general Pausanias ; the Corinthians sought to obtain his testimony to their exploits in the Persian war ; and he, more than any other poet, partly at the wish of others, and partly of his own accord, undertook the celebration of the great deeds of that period. The poems which he wrote for this purpose were for the most part epigrams ; but some were lyric compositions, as the panegyric of those who had fallen at Thermopylæ, and the odes on the sea-fights of Artemisium and Salamis. Others were elegiac, as the elegy to those who fought at Marathon, already mentioned.

§ 11. The versatility of mind and variety of knowledge, which Simonides appears from these accounts to have possessed, are connected with his facility of poetical composition. Simonides was probably the most prolific lyric poet whom Greece had seen, although all his productions did not descend to posterity. He gained (according to the inscription of a votive

---

[1] That the ancients themselves had difficulties in ascertaining the true version of this story, appears from Quintilian, *Inst.* XI. 2. 11 ; it is however certain that the family of the Scopads at that time suffered some great misfortune which Simonides lamented in a threne : Phavorin. ap. Stob. *Serm.* CV. 62.

tablet, written by himself)[1] 56 oxen and tripods in poetical contests ; and yet prizes of this kind could only be gained at public
festivals, such as the festival of Bacchus at Athens.   Simonides,
according to his own testimony, conquered at this latter festival
in Olymp. 75. 4. B.C. 476, with a cyclian chorus of 50 men.
The muse of Simonides was, however, far oftener in the pay
of private men ; he was the first who sold his poems for money,
according to the frequent reproach of the ancients.   Thus
Socrates in Plato[2] says that Simonides was often forced to
praise a tyrant or other powerful man, without being convinced
of the justice of his praises.

Among the poems which Simonides composed for public
festivals, were hymns and prayers (κατευχαὶ) to various gods,
pæans to Apollo, hyporchemes, dithyrambs, and parthenia.   In
the hyporchemes Simonides seemed to have excelled himself ;
so great a master was he of the art of painting, by apt rhythms
and words, the acts which he wished to describe ; he says of
himself that he knows how to combine the plastic movements
of the feet with the voice.[3]   His dithyrambs were not, according to their original purpose, dedicated to Dionysus, but admitted subjects of the heroic mythology ; thus a dithyramb of
Simonides bore the title of *Memnon*.[4]   This transfer to heroes,
of poems properly belonging to Dionysus will be considered
more fully in connexion with the subject of tragedy.   Moreover the odes just mentioned, which celebrated those who fell
at Thermopylæ and in the sea-fights against the Persians, were
doubtless intended to be performed at public festivals in honour
of victories.

Among the poems which Simonides composed for private
persons, the Epinikia and Threnes are worthy of especial notice.
At this period the Epinikia—songs which were performed at a
feast in honour of a victor in public and sacred games, either
on the scene of the conflict, or at his return home—first received the polish of art from the hands of the choral poets.
At an earlier age, a few verses, like those of Archilochus,
had answered the same purpose.   The Epinikia of Simonides

---

[1] *Anthol. Palat.* VI. 213.   [2] *Protag.* p. 346. B.
[3] Plutarch, *Sympos.* IX. 15. 2.   [4] Strabo XV. p. 728. B.

and Pindar are nearly contemporaneous with the erection of statues in honour of victorious combatants, which first became common about Olymp. 60, and, especially in the time of the Persian war, employed the most eminent artists of the schools of Ægina and Sicyon. A general idea of the structure of the epinikia of Simonides may be formed from those of Pindar (of which a copious analysis will be found in the next chapter). In these odes, too, the celebration of mythical heroes (as of the Dioscuri in the epinikion of Scopas) was closely connected with the praise of the victor. General reflections and apophthegms were also applied to his peculiar circumstances. Thus in the same ode, the general maxim was stated, that the gods alone could be always good: that no man could be invariably good or bad, but could only act virtuously by the grace of the gods, and upon this principle the saying of Pittacus, ' it is difficult to be good,' was censured as requiring too much, and probably was applied for the purpose of extenuating some faults in the life of the victorious prince.[1]

We should be guilty of injustice to Simonides were we to conclude that he did violence to his own convictions, and offered mercenary and bespoken homage; we rather discover a trace of the mild and humane, though somewhat lax and commodious, opinions on morals, prevalent among the Ionians. Among the Dorians, and in part also among the Æolians, law and custom were more rigorous in their demands upon the constancy and the virtue of mankind.

The epinikia of Simonides appear to have been distinguished from those of Pindar mainly in this; that the former dwelt more upon the particular victory which gave occasion to his song, and described all its details with greater minuteness; while Pindar, as we shall see, passes lightly over the incident, and immediately soars into higher regions. In an epinikion which Simonides composed for Leophron the son of the tyrant Anaxilas and his vicegerent in Rhegium,[2] and

---

[1] See this long fragment from the odes of Simonides in Plato, *Protag.* p. 339. *sq.*

[2] As the historical relations are difficult of comprehension, I remark briefly, that Anaxilas was tyrant of Rhegium, and, from about Ol. 71. 3. (B.C. 494), of Messene; and that he dwelt in the latter city, leaving Leophron to administer the government of Rhegium. On the death of Anaxilas in Olymp. 76. 1. (B.C. 476), Leophron, as his eldest son, succeeded him in the city of Messene: and the freedman Micythus

in which he had to celebrate a victory obtained with a chariot
drawn by mules (ἀπήνη), the poet congratulated the victorious
animals, dexterously passing in silence over the meaner, and
directing attention to the nobler, side of their parentage : ' Hail,
ye daughters of storm-footed steeds !' Simonides, too, in these
songs of victory more frequently indulged in pleasantry than
befitted a poem destined to be recited at a sacred feast ; as, for
example, in the epinikion composed in honour of an Athenian
who had conquered Crios of Ægina in wrestling at Olympia ;
where he plays upon the name of the defeated combatant : ' Not
ill has the ram (ὁ Κρῖος) got himself shorn by venturing into
the magnificent grove, the sanctuary of Zeus.' [1]

But the merits of Simonides were still more remarkable (as
we have already seen in treating of the elegy) in dirges (θρῆνοι).
His style, as an ancient critic observes, was not as lofty as that
of Pindar ; but what he lost in sublimity he gained in pathos.[2]
While Pindar's soaring flights extolled the happiness of the
dead who had finished their earthly course with honour, and
enjoyed the glories allotted to them in another existence,
Simonides gave himself up to the genuine feelings of human
nature ; he expressed grief for the life that was extinguished ;
the fond regret of the survivors ; and sought consolation rather
after the manner of the Ionian elegiac poets, in the perishable-
ness and weariness of human life. The dirges of Simonides on
the hapless Scopad, and the Aleuad Antiochus, son of Echecratides,[3] were remarkable examples of this style ; and doubtless the celebrated lament of Danae was part of a threne. En-

---

was to administer Rhegium for the younger sons, but he was soon compelled to
abandon his office. For these facts, see Herod. VII. 170. Diod. XI. 48. 66. Heraclid.
Pont. *pol.* 25. Dionys. Hal. *Exc.* p. 539. Vales. Dionys. Hal. XIX. 4. Mai. Athen.
I. p. 3. Pausan. V. 26. 3. Schol. Pind. *Pyth.* II. 34. Justin. IV. 2. XXI. 3. Macrob.
Sat. I. 11. The Olympic victory of Leophron (by some writers ascribed to Anaxi-
las) must have taken place before Olymp. 76. 1. B.C. 476.

[1] That the words Ἐπέξαθ' ὁ Κρῖος οὐκ ἀεικέως &c. are to be understood as is indicated
in the text, is proved by the manner in which Aristoph. *Nub.* 1355. gives the substance of the song, which was sung at Athens at meals, from a patriotic interest,
like a scolion. The contest must be placed about Olymp. 70. B.C. 500.

[2] Τὸ οἰκτίζεσθαι μὴ μεγαλοπρεπῶς ὡς Πίνδαρος, ἀλλὰ παθητικῶς. Dion. Hal. *Cens.
Vet. Script.* II. 6. p. 420. Reiske.

[3] The son of the Echecratides, who was mentioned in ch. XIII. § 11. in connexion
with Anacreon, and the elder brother of Orestes.

closed with her infant Perseus in a chest, and exposed to the raging of the storm, she extols the happiness of the unconscious sleeping babe, in expressions full of the charm of maternal tenderness and devotion.[1]

§ 12. Simonides did not, like Pindar, in the overflowing riches of his genius, touch briefly on thoughts and feelings; he wrought out everything in detail with care and finish;[2] his verses are like a diamond which throws a sparkling light from each of its many polished faces. If we analyze a passage, like the fragment from the eulogy on the heroes of Thermopylæ, we are struck with the skill and grace with which the hand of the master plays with a single thought; the glory of a great action before which all sorrow disappears; and the various lights under which he presents it.

' Those who fell at Thermopylæ have an illustrious fate, a noble destiny: their tomb is an altar, their dirge a song of triumph. And neither eating rust, nor all-subduing time, shall obliterate this epitaph of the brave. Their subterranean chamber has received the glory of Hellas as its inhabitant. Of this, Leonidas, the king of Sparta, bears witness, by the fair and undying renown of virtue which he left behind him.'[3] Some idea may be formed of this same kind of description naturally leading to a light and agreeable tissue of thoughts; of this easy graceful style of Simonides, so extremely dissimilar to that of Pindar, from a feeble prosaic translation of another fragment taken from an ode to a conqueror in the Pentathlon, which treats of Orpheus:—

' Countless birds flew around his head; fishes sprang out of the dark waters at his beautiful song. Not a breath of wind arose to rustle the leaves of the trees, or to interrupt the honied voice which was wafted to the ears of mortals. As when, in the wintry moon, Zeus appoints fourteen days as the sacred brooding time of the gay-plumed halcyons, which the earth-dwellers call the sleep of the winds.'[4] With this smooth and highly polished style of composition everything in the poetry of

---

[1] Dionys. Hal. de Verb. Comp. 26. Fr. 7. Gaisford. 50. Schneidewin.
[2] Simonides said that poetry was vocal painting. Plutarch, de Glor. Ath. 3.
[3] Diod. XI. 11. Fr. 16. Gaisf. 9. Schneid.
[4] Fr. 18. Schneidewin.

Simonides is in the most perfect harmony ; the choice of words, which seeks, indeed, the noble and the graceful, yet departs less widely from the language of ordinary life than that of Pindar ; and the treatment of the rhythms which is distinguished from that of the Theban poet by a stronger preference for light and flowing measures (more especially the logaœdic) and by less rigorous rules of metre.

§ 13. BACCHYLIDES, the nephew of Simonides, adhered closely to the system and the example of his uncle. He flourished towards the close of the life of Simonides, with whom he lived at the court of Hiero in Syracuse ; little more of his history is known. That his poetry was but an imitation of one branch of that of Simonides, cultivated with great delicacy and finish, is proved by the opinions of ancient critics; among whom Dionysius adduces perfect correctness and uniform elegance as the characteristics of Bacchylides. His genius and art were chiefly devoted to the pleasures of private life, love and wine ; and, when compared with those of Simonides, appear marked by greater sensual grace and less moral elevation. Among the kinds of choral poetry which he employed, besides those of which he had examples in Simonides and Pindar, we find erotic songs : such, for example, as that in which a beautiful maiden is represented, in the game of the Cottabus, as raising her white arm and pouring out the wine for the youths ;[1] a description which could apply only to a Hetæra partaking of the banquets of men.

In other odes, which were probably sung to cheer the feast, and which were transformed into choral odes from scolia, the praise of wine is celebrated as follows :[2] ‘A sweet compulsion flows from the wine cups and subdues the spirit, while the

---

[1] Athen. XI. p. 782. XVI. p. 667. Fr. 23. ed. Neue.

[2] Athen. II. p. 39. Fr. 26. Neue. The ode consists of short strophes in the Doric measure, which are to be reduced to the following metre.

This arrangement necessitates no other alterations than those which have been made for other reasons : except that αὐτόθε, ‘straightways,’ should be written for αὐτὸς in v. 6.

wishes of love, which are mingled with the gifts of Dionysus, agitate the heart. The thoughts of men take a lofty flight; they overthrow the embattled walls of cities, and believe themselves monarchs of the world. The houses glitter with gold and ivory; corn-bearing ships bring hither from Egypt, across the glancing deep, the abundance of wealth. To such heights soars the spirit of the drinker.' Here too we remark that elaborate and brilliant execution which is peculiar to the school of Simonides; and the same is shown in all the longer fragments of Bacchylides, among which we shall only quote the praise of peace:

'To mortals belong lofty peace, riches, and the blossoms of honey-voiced song. On altars of fair workmanship burn thighs of oxen and thick-fleeced sheep in golden flames to the gods. The cares of the youths are, gymnastic exercises, flute-playing, and joyous revelry (αὐλοὶ καὶ κῶμοι). But the black spiders ply their looms in the iron-bound edges of the shields, and the rust corrodes the barbed spear-head, and the two-edged sword. No more is heard the clang of brazen trumpets; and beneficent sleep, the nurse and soother of our souls, is no longer scared from our eyelids. The streets are thronged with joyous guests, and songs of praise to beautiful youths resound.'[1]

We recognise here a mind which dwells lovingly on the description of these gay and pleasing scenes, and paints itself in every feature, but without penetrating deeper than the ordinary observation of men reaches. Bacchylides, like Simonides, transfers the diffuseness of the elegy to the choral lyric poem; although he himself composed no elegies, and followed the traces of his uncle only as an epigrammatist. The reflections scattered through his lyrics, on the toils of human life, the instability of fortune, on resignation to inevitable evils, and the rejection of vain cares, have much of the tone of the Ionic elegy. The structure of Bacchylides' verse is generally very simple; nine-tenths of his odes, to judge from the fragments, consisted of dactylic series and trochaic dipodias, as we find in those odes of Pindar which were written in the Doric mode. Bacchylides, however, gave a lighter character to this measure; inasmuch as

---

[1] Stobæus, *Serm.* LIII. p. 209. Grot. Fr. 12. Neue.

in the places where the syllable might be either long or short, he often preferred the latter.

We find, in his poems, trochaic verses of great elegance; as, for example, a fragment, preserved by Athenæus, of a religious poem in which the Dioscuri are invited to a feast.[1] But its character is feeble and languid; and how different from the hymn of Pindar, the third among the Olympian odes, in celebration of a similar feast of the Dioscuri, held by Theron in Agrigentum!

§ 14. The universal esteem in which Simonides and Bacchylides were held in Greece, and their acknowledged excellence in their art, did not prevent some of their contemporaries from striking into various other paths, and adopting other styles of treating lyric poetry. LASOS OF HERMIONE was a rival of Simonides during his residence in Athens, and likewise enjoyed high favour at the court of Hipparchus.[2] It is however difficult to ascertain, from the very scanty accounts we possess of this poet, wherein consisted the point of contrast between him and his competitor. He was more peculiarly a dithyrambic poet, and was the first who introduced contests in dithyrambs at Athens,[3] probably in Olymp. 68. 1. B.C. 508.[4] This style predominated so much in his works, that he gave to the general rhythms of his odes a dithyrambic turn, and a free movement, in which he was aided by the variety and flexibility of tone of the flute, his favourite instrument.[5] He was also a theorist in his art, and investigated the laws of music (i.e. the relation of musical intervals to rapidity of movement), of which later musicians retained much. He was the instructor of Pindar in lyric poetry. It is also very possible that these studies led him to attach excessive value to art; for he was guilty of over-refinement in the rhythm and the sound of words, as, for example, in his odes written without the letter σ

---

[1] Athen. XI. p. 500 B.　Fr. 27. Neue.

[2] Aristoph. *Vesp.* 1410. comp. Herod. VII. 6.

[3] Schol. Aristoph. ubi sup.

[4] The statement of the Parian marble, ep. 46. appears to refer to the cyclic choruses.

[5] Plutarch *de Mus.* 39. The fragment of a hymn by Lasus to Demeter, in Athen. XIV. p. 624 E, agrees very well with this account.

($\ddot{a}\sigma\iota\gamma\mu o\iota$ $\dot{\wp}\delta ai$), the hissing sound of which is entirely avoided as dissonant.

TIMOCREON THE RHODIAN was a genius of an entirely peculiar character. Powerful both as an athlete and a poet, he transferred the pugnacity of the Palæstra to poetry. To the hate which he bore in political life to Themistocles, and, on the field of poetry, to Simonides, he owes his chief celebrity among the ancients. In an extant fragment[1] he bitterly reproaches the Athenian statesman for the arbitrary manner in which he settled the affairs of the island, recalling exiles, and banishing others, of which Timocreon himself was one of the victims. He attacks his enemy with the heavy pompous measure of the Dorian mode, as with the shock of a catapulta, though on other occasions he composed in elegiac distichs and measures of the Æolic kind; and it cannot be denied that his vituperation receives singular force from the stateliness of the expression, and the grandeur of the form. Timocreon seems to have ridiculed and parodied Simonides on account of some tricks of his art, as where Simonides expresses the same thought in the same words only transposed, first in an hexameter, then in a trochaic tetrameter.[2]

The opposition in which we find Pindar with Simonides and Bacchylides is of a much nobler character. For though the desire to stand highest in the favour of the Syracusan tyrant, Hiero, and Thero of Agrigentum stimulated the jealousy between these two poets, yet the real cause lies deeper; it is to be found in the spirit and temper of the men; and the contest which necessarily arose out of this diversity, does no dishonour to either party.

The ancient commentators on Pindar refer a considerable number of passages to this hostility:[3] and in general these are in praise of genuine wisdom as a gift of nature, a deep rooted power of the mind, and in depreciation of acquired knowledge

---

[1] Plutarch, *Themist.* 21.

[2] *Anthol. Pal.* XIII. 30. Concerning this enmity, see also Diog. Laërt. II. 46, and Suidas in Τιμοκρέων. The citation from Simonides and Timocreon in Walz. *Rhet. Græc.* vol. II. p. 10, is probably connected with their quarrel.

[3] *Ol.* II. 86. (154.) IX. 48 (74). *Pyth.* II. 52. (97.) and passim *Nem.* III. 80. (143). IV. 37. (60). *Isthm.* II. 6 (10).

in the comparison; or the poet represents genial invention as the highest of qualities, and demands novelties even in mythic narratives. On the contrary, Simonides and Bacchylides thought themselves bound to adhere faithfully to tradition, and reproved any attempt to give a new form to the stories of antiquity.[1]

---

[1] See Plutarch, *Num.* 4. Fr. 37. Neue, and Clem. *Strom.* V. p. 687. Pott. Fr. 13. Neue.

CHAPTER XV.

PINDAR.

§ 1. Pindar's descent; his early training in poetry and music. § 2. Exercise of his art; his independent position with respect to the Greek princes and republics. § 3. Kinds of poetry cultivated by him. § 4. His Epinikia; their origin and objects. § 5. Their two main elements, general remarks, and mythical narrations. § 6. Connexion of these two elements; peculiarities of the structure of Pindar's odes. § 7. Variety of tone in his odes, according to the different musical styles.

§ 1. PINDAR was born in the spring of 522 B.C. (Olymp. 64. 3); and, according to a probable statement, he died at the age of eighty.[1] He was therefore nearly in the prime of his life at the time when Xerxes invaded Greece, and the battles of Thermopylæ and Salamis were fought. He thus belongs to that period of the Greek nation, when its great qualities were first distinctly unfolded; and when it exhibited an energy of action, and a spirit of enterprise, never afterwards surpassed, together with a love of poetry, art, and philosophy, which produced much, and promised to produce more. The modes of thought, and style of art, which arose in Athens after the Persian war, must have been unknown to him. He was indeed the contemporary of Æschylus, and he admired the rapid rise of Athens in the Persian war; calling it 'The Pillar of Greece, brilliant Athens, the worthy theme of poets.' But the causes which determined his poetical character are to be sought in an earlier period, and in the Doric and Æolic parts of Greece; and hence we shall divide Pindar from his contemporary Æschylus, by placing the former at the close of the early period, the latter at the head of the new period of literature.

---

[1] For Pindar's life, see Boeckh's Pindar, tom. III. p. 12. To the authorities there mentioned, may be added the Introduction of Eustathius to his Commentary on Pindar in Eustathii Opuscula, p. 32. ed. Tafel. 1832. (Eustath. *Proœm. Comment. Pindar.* ed. Schneidewin. 1837).

Pindar's native place was Cynocephalæ, a village in the territory of Thebes, the most considerable city of Bœotia. Although in his time the voices of Pierian bards, and of epic poets of the Hesiodean school had long been mute in Bœotia, yet there was still much love for music and poetry, which had taken the prevailing form of lyric and choral compositions. That these arts were widely cultivated in Bœotia is proved by the fact that two women, Myrtis and Corinna, had attained great celebrity in them during the youth of Pindar. Both were competitors with Pindar in poetry. Myrtis strove with him for a prize at public games: and although Corinna said, ' It is not meet that the clear toned Myrtis, a woman born, should enter the lists with Pindar :'[1] yet she is said (perhaps from jealousy of his growing fame) to have often contended against him in the agones, and to have gained the victory over him five times.[2] Pausanias, in his travels, saw at Tanagra, the native city of Corinna, a picture in which she was represented as binding her head with a fillet of victory which she had gained in a contest with Pindar. He supposes that she was less indebted for this victory to the excellence of her poetry than to her Bœotian dialect, which was more familiar to the ears of the judges at the games, and to her extraordinary beauty. Corinna also assisted the young poet with her advice; it is related of her that she recommended him to ornament his poems with mythical narrations, but that when he had composed a hymn, in the first six verses of which (still extant) almost the whole of the Theban mythology was introduced, she smiled and said, ' We should sow with the hand, not with the whole sack.' Too little of the poetry of Corinna has been preserved to allow of our forming a safe judgment of her style of composition. The extant fragments refer mostly to mythological subjects, particularly to heroines of the Bœotian legends; this, and her rivalry with Pindar, show that she must be classed not in the Lesbian school of lyric poets, but among the masters of choral poetry.

---

[1] The following is the passage in Corinna's dialect :

μέμφομη δὲ κὴ λιγούραν Μούρτιδ' ἰώνγα
ὅτι βάνα φοῦσ ' ἔβα Πινδάροιο ποτ' ἔριν.

Apollon. *de Pronom.* p. 924. B.

[2] Ælian, *V. H.* XIII. 24.

The family of Pindar seems to have been skilled in music; we learn from the ancient biographies of him that his father, or his uncle, was a flute-player. Flute-playing (as we have more than once remarked) was brought from Asia Minor into Greece; its Phrygian origin may perhaps be indicated by the fact that Pindar had in his house at Thebes a small temple of the Mother of the gods and Pan, the Phrygian deities, to whom the first hymns to the flute were supposed to have been sung.[1] The music of the flute had moreover been introduced into Bœotia at a very early period; the Copaic lake produced excellent reeds for flutes, and the worship of Dionysus, which was supposed to have originated at Thebes, required the varied and loud music of the flute. Accordingly the Bœotians were early celebrated for their skill in flute-playing; whilst at Athens the music of the flute did not become common till after the Persian war, when the desire for novelty in art had greatly increased.[2]

§ 2. But Pindar very early in his life soared far beyond the sphere of a flute-player at festivals, or even a lyric poet of merely local celebrity. He placed himself under the tuition of Lasus of Hermione, a distinguished poet, already mentioned, but probably better versed in the theory than the practice of poetry and music. Since Pindar made these arts the whole business of his life,[3] and was nothing but a poet and a musician, he soon extended the boundaries of his art to the whole Greek nation, and composed poems of the choral lyric kind for persons in all parts of Greece. At the age of twenty he composed a song of victory in honour of a Thessalian youth belonging to the *gens* of the Aleuads.[4] We find him employed soon afterwards for the Sicilian rulers, Hiero of Syracuse, and Thero of Agrigentum; for Arcesilaus, king of Cyrene, and Amyntas, king of Macedonia, as well as for the free cities of Greece. He made no distinction according to the race of the persons whom he celebrated: he was honoured and loved by the Ionian states, for himself as well as for his art; the Athenians made him their public guest (πρόξενος); and the inhabitants of Ceos

---

[1] *Marm. Par.* ep. 10. [2] Aristot. *Polit.* VIII. 7.
[3] Like Sappho, he is called μουσοποιός.
[4] *Pyth.* X. composed in Olymp. 69. 3. B.C. 502.

employed him to compose a processional song (προσόδιον), although they had their own poets, Simonides and Bacchylides. Pindar, however, was not a common mercenary poet, always ready to sing the praises of him whose bread he ate. He received indeed money and presents for his poems, according to the general usage previously introduced by Simonides; yet his poems are the genuine expression of his thoughts and feelings. In his praises of virtue and good fortune, the colours which he employs are not too vivid; nor does he avoid the darker shades of his subject; he often suggests topics of consolation for past and present evil, and sometimes warns and exhorts to avoid future calamity. Thus he ventures to speak freely to the powerful Hiero, whose many great and noble qualities were alloyed by insatiable cupidity and ambition, which his courtiers well knew how to turn to a bad account. Pindar exhorts him to tranquillity and contentedness of mind, to calm cheerfulness, and to clemency, saying to him :[1] ' Be as thou knowest how to be; the ape in the boy's story is indeed fair, very fair; but Rhadamanthus was happy because he plucked the genuine fruits of the mind, and did not take delight in the delusions which follow the arts of the whisperer. The venom of calumny is an evil hard to be avoided, whether by him who hears or by him who is the object of it; for the ways of calumniators are like those of foxes.' Pindar speaks in the same free and manly tone to Arcesilaus IV., king of Cyrene, who afterwards brought on the ruin of his dynasty by his tyrannical severity, and who at that time kept Damophilus, one of the noblest of the Cyreneans, in unjust banishment. ' Now understand the enigmatic wisdom of Œdipus. If any one lops with a sharp axe the branches of a large oak, and spoils her stately form, she loses indeed her verdure, but she gives proof of her strength, when she is consumed in the winter fire, or when, torn from her place in the forest, she performs the melancholy office of a pillar in the palace of a foreign prince.[2] Thy office is to be the physician

---

[1] *Pyth.* II. 72. (131.) This ode was composed by Pindar at Thebes, but doubtless not till after he had contracted a personal acquaintance with Hiero.

[2] In this allegory, the oak is the state of Cyrene; the branches are the banished nobles; the winter fire is insurrection; the foreign palace is a foreign conquering power, especially Persia.

of the country: Pæan honours thee; therefore thou must treat with a gentle hand its festering wounds. It is easy for a fool to shake the stability of a city; but it is hard to place it again on its foundations, unless a god direct the rulers. Gratitude for these good deeds is already in store for thee. Deign therefore to bestow all thy care upon the wealthy Cyrene.'[1]

Thus lofty and dignified was the position which Pindar assumed with regard to these princes; and he remained true to the principle which he so frequently proclaims, that frankness and sincerity are always laudable. But his intercourse with the princes of his time appears to have been limited to poetry. We do not find him, like Simonides, the daily associate, counsellor, and friend of kings and statesmen; he plays no part in the public events of his time, either as a politician or a courtier. Neither was his name, like that of Simonides, distinguished in the Persian war; partly because his fellow-citizens, the Thebans, were, together with half of the Grecian nation, on the Persian side, whilst the spirit of independence and victory were with the other half. Nevertheless, the lofty character of Pindar's muse rises superior to these unfavourable circumstances. He did not indeed make the vain attempt of gaining over the Thebans to the cause of Greece; but he sought to appease the internal dissensions which threatened to destroy Thebes during the war, by admonishing his fellow-citizens to union and concord:[2] and after the war was ended, he openly proclaims, in odes intended for the Æginetans and Athenians, his admiration of the heroism of the victors. In an ode, composed a few months after the surrender of Thebes to the allied army of the Greeks[3] (the seventh Isthmian), his feelings appear to be deeply moved by the misfortunes of his native city; but he returns to the cultivation of poetry as the Greeks were now delivered from their great peril, and a god had removed the stone of Tantalus from their heads. He expresses a hope that freedom will repair all misfortunes: and he turns with a friendly confidence to the city of Ægina, which, according to ancient legends, was closely allied with Thebes, and whose good offices with the Pelopon-

---

[1] *Pyth.* IV.
[2] Polyb. IV. 31. 5. Fr. incert. 125. ed. Boeckh.
[3] In the winter of Olymp. 75. 2. B.C. 479.

nesians might perhaps raise once more the humbled head of Bœotia.

§ 3. Having mentioned nearly all that is known of the events of Pindar's life, and his relations to his contemporaries, we proceed to consider him more closely as a poet, and to examine the character and form of his poetical productions.

The only class of poems which enable us to judge of Pindar's general style are the *epinikia* or *triumphal odes*. Pindar, indeed, excelled in all the known varieties of choral poetry ; viz., hymns to the gods, pæans and dithyrambs appropriate to the worship of particular divinities, odes for processions ($\pi\rho o\sigma\acute{o}\delta\iota a$), songs of maidens ($\pi a\rho\theta\acute{\epsilon}\nu\epsilon\iota a$), mimic dancing songs ($\acute{v}\pi o\rho$-$\chi\acute{\eta}\mu a\tau a$), drinking songs ($\sigma\kappa o\lambda\iota\grave{a}$), dirges ($\theta\rho\tilde{\eta}\nu o\iota$), and encomiastic odes to princes ($\acute{\epsilon}\gamma\kappa\acute{\omega}\mu\iota a$) which last approached most nearly to the epinikia. The poems of Pindar in these various styles were nearly as renowned among the ancients as the triumphal odes; which is proved by the numerous quotations of them. Horace too, in enumerating the different styles of Pindar's poetry, puts the dithyrambs first, then the hymns, and afterwards the epinikia and the threnes. Nevertheless, there must have been some decided superiority in the epinikia, which caused them to be more frequently transcribed in the later period of antiquity, and thus rescued them from perishing with the rest of the Greek lyric poetry. At any rate, these odes, from the vast variety of their subjects and style, and their refined and elaborate structure,—some approaching to hymns and pæans, others to scolia and hyporchemes,—serve to indemnify us for the loss of the other sorts of lyric poetry.

We will now explain, as precisely as possible, the occasion of an epinikian ode, and the mode of its execution. A victory has been gained in a contest at a festival, particularly at one of the four great games most prized by the Greek people,[1] either by the speed of horses, the strength and dexterity of the human body, or

---

[1] Olympia, Pythia, Nemea, Isthmia. Some of the epinikia, however, belong to other games. For example, the second Pythian is not a Pythian ode, but probably belongs to games of Iolaus at Thebes. The ninth Nemean celebrates a victory in the Pythia at Sicyon, (not at Delphi ;) the tenth Nemean celebrates a victory in the Hecatombæa at Argos ; the eleventh Nemean is not an epinikion, but was sung at the installation of a prytanis at Tenedos. Probably the Nemean odes were

by skill in music.[1] Such a victory as this, which shed a lustre not only on the victor himself, but on his family, and even on his native city, demanded a solemn celebration.   This celebration might be performed by the victor's friends upon the spot where the victory was gained ; as, for example, at Olympia, when in the evening after the termination of the contests, by the light of the moon, the whole sanctuary resounded with joyful songs after the manner of encomia.[2]   Or it might be deferred till after the victor's solemn return to his native city, where it was sometimes repeated, in following years, in commemoration of his success.[3]   A celebration of this kind always had a religious character ; it often began with a procession to an altar or temple, in the place of the games or in the native city ; a sacrifice, followed by a banquet, was then offered at the temple, or in the house of the victor ; and the whole solemnity concluded with the merry and boisterous revel called by the Greeks κῶμος.   At this sacred, and at the same time joyous, solemnity, (a mingled character frequent among the Greeks,) appeared the chorus, trained by the poet, or some other skilled person,[4] for the purpose of reciting the triumphal hymn, which was considered the fairest ornament of the festival.   It was during either the procession or the banquet that the hymn was recited ; as it was not properly a religious hymn, which could be combined with the sacrifice.   The form of the poem must, to a certain extent, have been determined by the occasion on which it was to be recited.   From expressions which occur in several epinikian odes, it is probable that all odes consisting of strophes without epodes[5] were sung during a pro-

---

placed at the end of the collection, after the Isthmian ; so that a miscellaneous supplement could be appended to them.

[1] For example, *Pyth.* XII., which celebrates the victory of Midas, a flute-player of Agrigentum.

[2] Pindar's words in *Olymp.* XI. 76. (93), where this usage is transferred to the mythical establishment of the Olympia by Hercules.   The 4th and 8th Olympian, the 6th, and probably also the 7th Pythian, were sung at the place of the games.

[3] The 9th Olympian, the 3rd Nemean, and the 2nd Isthmian, were produced at a memorial celebration of this kind.

[4] Such as Æneas the Stymphalian in *Olymp.* VI. 88. (150), whom Pindar calls ' a just messenger, a scytala of the fair-haired Muses, a sweet goblet of loud-sounding songs,' because he was to receive the ode from Pindar in person, to carry it to Stymphalus, and there to instruct a chorus in the dancing, music, and text.

[5] *Ol.* XIV. *Pyth.* VI. XII. *Nem.* II. IV. IX. *Isthm.* VII.

cession to a temple or to the house of the victor; although
there are others which contain expressions denoting movement,
and which yet have epodes.[1] It is possible that the epodes in
the latter odes may have been sung at certain intervals when the
procession was not advancing; for an epode, according to the
statements of the ancients, always required that the chorus
should be at rest.   But by far the greater number of the odes
of Pindar were sung at the Comus, at the jovial termination of
the feast : and hence Pindar himself more frequently names
his odes from the Comus than from the victory.[2]

§ 4. The occasion of an epinikian ode,—a victory in the
sacred games,—and its end,—the ennobling of a solemnity connected with the worship of the gods,—required that it should be
composed in a lofty and dignified style.   But, on the other
hand, the boisterous mirth of the feast did not admit the
severity of the antique poetical style, like that of the hymns
and nomes; it demanded a free and lively expression of feeling,
in harmony with the occasion of the festival, and suggesting the
noblest ideas connected with the victor.   Pindar, however,
gives no detailed description of the victory, as this would have
been only a repetition of the spectacle which had already been
beheld with enthusiasm by the assembled Greeks at Olympia
or Pytho; nay, he often bestows only a few words on the
victory, recording its place and the sort of contest in which it
was won.[3]   Nevertheless he does not (as many writers have
supposed) treat the victory as a merely secondary object; which
he despatches quickly, in order to pass on to subjects of greater
interest.   The victory, in truth, is always the point upon which
the whole of the ode turns: only he regards it, not simply as
an incident, but as connected with the whole life of the victor.
Pindar establishes this connexion by forming a high conception
of the fortunes and character of the victor, and by representing

---

[1] *Ol.* VIII. XIII. The expression τόνδε κῶμον δέξαι doubtless means, 'Receive
this band of persons who have combined for a sacrificial meal and feast.' Hence
too it appears that the band went into the temple.

[2] ἐπικώμιος ὕμνος, ἐγκώμιον μέλος. The grammarians, however, distinguish the
encomia, as being laudatory poems strictly so called, from the epinikia.

[3] On the other hand, we often find a precise enumeration of all the victories, not
only of the actual victor, but of his entire family: this must evidently have been
required of the poet.

the victory as the result of them. And as the Greeks were
less accustomed to consider a man in his individual capacity,
than as a member of his state, and his family; so Pindar considers the renown of the victor in connexion with the past and
present condition of the race and state to which he belongs.
Now there are two different points from which the poet might
view the life of the victor; viz. *destiny* or *merit;*[1] in other
words, he might celebrate his good fortune or his skill. In
the victory with horses, external advantages were the chief
consideration; inasmuch as it required excellent horses and an
excellent driver, both of which were attainable only by the
rich. The skill of the victor was more conspicuous in gymnastic feats, although even in these, good luck and the favour
of the gods might be considered as the main causes of success;
especially as it was a favourite opinion of Pindar's, that all excellence is a gift of nature.[2] The good fortune or skill of the
victor could not however be treated abstractedly; but must be
individualized by a description of his peculiar lot. This individual colouring might be given by representing the good
fortune of the victor as a compensation for past ill fortune; or,
generally, by describing the alternations of fortune in his lot
and in that of his family.[3] Another theme for an ode might
be, that success in gymnastic contests was obtained by a family
in alternate generations; that is, by the grandfathers and
grandsons, but not by the intermediate generation.[4] If, however, the good fortune of the victor had been invariable, con-
gratulation at such rare happiness was accompanied with moral
reflections, especially on the right manner of estimating or
enduring good fortune, or on the best mode of turning it to
account. According to the notions of the Greeks, an extraordinary share of the gifts of fortune suggested a dread of the
Nemesis which delighted in humbling the pride of man; and
hence the warning to be prudent, and not to strive after further
victories.[5] The admonitions which Pindar addresses to Hiero

---

[1] ὄλβος and ἀρετή.

[2] τὸ δὲ φυᾷ κράτιστον ἅπαν, *Ol.* IX. 100 (151), which ode is a development of
this general idea. Compare above, ch. XV. near the end.

[3] *Ol.* II. Also *Isthm.* III.　　　　　　　　　　　[4] *Nem.* VI.

[5] μηκέτι πάπταινε πόρσιον.

are to cultivate a calm serenity of mind, after the cares and toils by which he had founded and extended his empire, and to purify and ennoble by poetry a spirit which had been ruffled by unworthy passions. Even when the skill of the victor is put in the foreground, Pindar in general does not content himself with celebrating this bodily prowess alone, but he usually adds some moral virtue which the victor has shown, or which he recommends and extols. This virtue is sometimes moderation, sometimes wisdom, sometimes filial love, sometimes piety to the gods. The latter is frequently represented as the main cause of the victory : the victor having thereby obtained the protection of the deities who preside over gymnastic contests ; as Hermes, or the Dioscuri. It is evident that, with Pindar, this mode of accounting for success in the games was not the mere fiction of a poet; he sincerely thought that he had found the true cause, when he had traced the victory to the favour of a god who took an especial interest in the family of the victor, and at the same time presided over the games.[1] Generally, indeed, in extolling both the skill and fortune of the victor, Pindar appears to adhere to the truth as faithfully as he declares himself to do; nor is he ever betrayed into a high-flown style of panegyric. A republican dread of incurring the censure of his fellow citizens, as well as an awe of the divine Nemesis, induced him to moderate his praises, and to keep in view the instability of human fortune and the narrow limits of human strength.

Thus far the poet seems to wear the character of a sage who expounds to the victor his destiny, by showing him the dependence of his exploit upon a higher order of things. Nevertheless, it is not to be supposed that the poet placed himself on an eminence remote from ordinary life, and that he spoke like a priest to the people, unmoved by personal feelings. The Epinikia of Pindar, although they were delivered by a chorus, were, nevertheless, the expression of his individual feelings and opinions,[2] and are full of allusions to his personal relations to the victor. Sometimes, indeed, when his relations of this

---

[1] As e.g. Ol. VI. 77. (130). sqq. In the above remarks I have chiefly followed Dissen's Dissertation De Ratione poeticâ Carminum Pindaricorum, in his edition of Pindar, sect. i. p. xi.   [2] See above, ch. XIV. § 2.

kind were peculiarly interesting to him, he made them the main subject of the ode; several of his odes, and some among the most difficult, are to be explained in this manner. In one of his odes,[1] Pindar justifies the sincerity of his poetry against the charges which had been brought against it; and represents his muse as a just and impartial dispenser of fame, as well among the victors at the games, as among the heroes of antiquity. In another,[2] he reminds the victor that he had predicted the victory to him in the public games, and had encouraged him to become a competitor for it;[3] and he extols him for having employed his wealth for so noble an object. In another, he excuses himself for having delayed the composition of an ode which he had promised to a wrestler among the youths, until the victor had attained his manhood; and, as if to incite himself to the fulfilment of his promise, he points out the hallowed antiquity of these triumphal hymns, connecting their origin with the first establishment of the Olympic games.[4]

§ 5. Whatever might be the theme of one of Pindar's epinikian odes, it would naturally not be developed with the systematic completeness of a philosophical treatise. Pindar, however, has undoubtedly much of that sententious wisdom which began to show itself among the Greeks at the time of the Seven Wise Men, and which formed an important element of elegiac and choral lyric poetry before the time of Pindar. The apophthegms of Pindar sometimes assume the form of general maxims, sometimes of direct admonitions to the victor. At other times, when he wishes to impress some principle of morals or prudence upon the victor, he gives it in the form of an opinion entertained by himself: ' I like not to keep much riches hoarded in an inner room; but I like to live well by my possessions, and to procure myself a good name by making large gifts to my friends.'[5]

The other element of Pindar's poetry, his mythical narra-

---

[1] *Nem.* VII.   [2] *Nem.* I.

[3] I refer to this the sentiment in v. 27 (40); 'The mind showed itself in the counsels of those persons to whom nature has given the power of foreseeing the future;' and also the account of the prophecy of Tiresias, when the serpents were killed by the young Hercules.

[4] *Ol.* XI.   [5] *Nem.* I. 31 (45).

tives, occupies, however, far more space in most of his odes.
That these are not mere digressions for the sake of ornament
has been completely proved by modern commentators.   At the
same time, he would sometimes seem to wish it to be believed
that he had been carried away by his poetical fervour, when he
returns to his theme from a long mythical narration, or when
he annexes a mythical story to a proverbial saying; as, for
example, when he subjoins to the figurative expression, ' Neither
by sea nor by land canst thou find the way to the Hyperboreans,'
the history of Perseus' visit to that fabulous people.[1]   But even
in such cases as these, it will be found, on close examination,
that the fable belongs to the subject.   Indeed, it may be
observed generally of those Greek writers who aimed at the
production of works of art, whether in prose or in poetry, that
they often conceal their real purpose ; and affect to leave in
vague uncertainty that which had been composed studiously
and on a preconceived plan.   Thus Plato often seems to allow
the dialogue to deviate into a wrong course, when this very
course was required by the plan of the investigation.   In
other passages, Pindar himself remarks that intelligence and
reflection are required to discover the hidden meaning of his
mythical episodes.   Thus, after a description of the Islands of
the Blessed, and the heroes who dwell there, he says, ' I have
many swift arrows in my quiver, which speak to the wise, but
need an interpreter for the multitude.'[2]   Again, after the story
of Ixion, which he relates in an ode to Hiero, he continues—
' I must, however, have a care lest I fall into the biting violence
of the evil speakers ; for, though distant in time, I have seen
that the slanderous Archilochus, who fed upon loud-tongued
wrath, passed the greater part of his life in difficulties and distress.'[3]   It is not easy to understand in this passage what
moves the poet to express so much anxiety ; until we advert to
the lessons which the history of Ixion contains for the rapa-
cious Hiero.

The reference of these mythical narratives to the main theme
of the ode may be either *historical* or *ideal*.   In the first case,
the mythical personages alluded to are the heroes at the head

---

[1] *Pyth.* X. 29. (46).   [2] *Ol.* II. 83. (150).
[3] *Pyth.* II. 54. (99).

of the family or state to which the victor belongs, or the founders of the games in which he has conquered. Among the many odes of Pindar to victors from Ægina, there is none in which he does not extol the heroic race of the Æacids. ' It is,' he says, ' to me an invariable law, when I turn towards this island, to scatter praise upon you, O Æacids, masters of golden chariots.'[1] In the second case, events of the heroic age are described, which resemble the events of the victor's life, or which contain lessons and admonitions for him to reflect upon. Thus two mythical personages may be introduced, of whom one may typify the victor in his praiseworthy, the other in his blameable acts ; so that the one example may serve to deter, the other to encourage.[2] In general, Pindar contrives to unite both these modes of allusion, by representing the national or family heroes as allied in character and spirit to the victor. Their extraordinary strength and felicity are continued in their descendants ; the same mixture of good and evil destiny,[3] and even the same faults,[4] recur in their posterity. It is to be observed that, in Pindar's time, the faith of the Greeks in the connexion of the heroes of antiquity with passing events was unshaken. The origin of historical events was sought in a remote age ; conquests and settlements in barbarian countries were justified by corresponding enterprises of heroes ; the Persian war was looked upon as an act of the same great drama, of which the expedition of the Argonauts and the Trojan war formed the earlier parts. At the same time, the mythical past was considered as invested with a splendour and sublimity of which even a faint reflection was sufficient to embellish the present. This is the cause of the historical and political allusions of the Greek tragedy, particularly in Æschylus. Even the history of Herodotus rests on the same foundation ; but it is seen most distinctly in the copious mythology which Pindar has pressed into the service of his lyric poetry. The manner in which mythical subjects were treated by the lyric poets was of course different from that in which they had been treated by the epic poets. In epic poetry, the mythical narrative is interesting in

---

[1] *Isthm.* V. [VI.] 19. (27).   [2] As Pelops and Tantalus, *Ol.* I.
[3] As the fate of the ancient Cadmeans in Theron, *Ol.* II.
[4] As the errors (ἀμπλακίαι) of the Rhodian heroes in Diagoras, *Ol.* VII.

itself, and all parts of it are developed with equal fulness.   In
lyric poetry, it serves to exemplify some particular idea, which
is usually stated in the middle or at the end of the ode; and
those points only of the story are brought into relief, which
serve to illustrate this idea.   Accordingly, the longest
mythical narrative in Pindar (viz., the description of the
voyage of the Argonauts, in the Pythian ode to Arcesilaus,
king of Cyrene, which is continued through twenty-five strophes)
falls far short of the sustained diffuseness of the epos.   Consistently with the purpose of the ode, it is intended to set forth
the descent of the kings of Cyrene from the Argonauts, and
the poet only dwells on the relation of Jason with Pelias—of
the noble exile with the jealous tyrant—because it contains a
serious admonition to Arcesilaus in his above-mentioned relation
with Damophilus.

§ 6. The mixture of apophthegmatic maxims and typical
narratives would alone render it difficult to follow the thread of
Pindar's meaning; but, in addition to this cause of obscurity,
the entire plan of his poetry is so intricate, that a modern
reader often fails to understand the connexion of the parts,
even where he thinks he has found a clue.   Pindar begins
an ode full of the lofty conception which he has formed
of the glorious destiny of the victor ; and he seems, as it were,
carried away by the flood of images which this conception pours
forth.   He does not attempt to express directly the general
idea, but follows the train of thought which it suggests into its
details, though without losing sight of their reference to the
main object.   Accordingly, when he has pursued a train of
thought, either in an apophthegmatic or mythical form, up to a
certain point, he breaks off, before he has gone far enough to
make the application to the victor sufficiently clear; he then
takes up another thread, which is perhaps soon dropped for a
fresh one: and at the end of the ode he gathers up all these
different threads, and weaves them together into one web, in
which the general idea predominates.   By reserving the explanation of his allusions until the end, Pindar contrives that
his odes should consist of parts which are not complete or intelligible in themselves ; and thus the curiosity of the reader is
kept on the stretch throughout the entire ode.   Thus, for

example, the ode upon the Pythian victory, which was gained by Hiero, as a citizen of Ætna, a city founded by himself,[1] proceeds upon a general idea of the repose and serenity of mind which Hiero at last enjoys, after a laborious public life, and to which Pindar strives to contribute by the influence of music and poetry. Full of this idea, Pindar begins by describing the effects of music upon the gods in Olympus, how it delights, inspires, and soothes them, although it increases the anguish of Typhos, the enemy of the gods, who lies bound under Ætna. Thence, by a sudden transition, he passes to the new town of Ætna, under the mountain of the name; extols the happy auspices under which it was founded; and lauds Hiero for his great deeds in war, and for the wise constitution he has given to the new state; to which Pindar wishes exemption from foreign enemies and internal discord. Thus far it does not appear how the praises of music are connected with the exploits of Hiero as a warrior and a statesman. But the connexion becomes evident when Pindar addresses to Hiero a series of moral sentences, the object of which is to advise him to subdue all unworthy passions, to refresh his mind with the contemplation of art, and thus to obtain from the poets a good name, which will descend to posterity.

§ 7. The characteristics of Pindar's poetry, which have been just explained, may be discerned in all his epinikian odes. Their agreement, however, in this respect is quite consistent with the extraordinary variety of style and expression which has been already stated to belong to this class of poems. Every epinikian ode of Pindar has its peculiar tone, depending upon the course of the ideas and the consequent choice of the expressions. The principal differences are connected with the choice of the rhythms, which again is regulated by the musical style. According to the last distinction, the epinikia of Pindar are of three sorts, Doric, Æolic, and Lydian; which can be easily distinguished, although each admits of innumerable varieties. In respect of metre, every ode of Pindar has an individual character; no two odes having the same metrical structure. In the Doric ode the same metrical forms occur as those which prevailed in the choral lyric poetry of Stesichorus,

---

[1] *Pyth.* I.

viz., systems of dactyls and trochaic dipodies,[1] which most nearly approach the stateliness of the hexameter. Accordingly, a serene dignity pervades these odes; the mythical narrations are developed with greater fulness, and the ideas are limited to the subject, and are free from personal feeling; in short, their general character is that of calmness and elevation. The language is epic, with a slight Doric tinge, which adds to its brilliancy and dignity. The rhythms of the Æolic odes resemble those of the Lesbian poetry, in which light dactylic, trochaic, or logaœdic metres prevailed; these rhythms, however, when applied to choral lyric poetry, were rendered far more various, and thus often acquired a character of greater volubility and liveliness. The poet's mind also moves with greater rapidity; and sometimes he stops himself in the midst of narrations which seem to him impious or arrogant.[2] A larger scope is likewise given to his personal feelings; and in the addresses to the victor there is a gayer tone, which at times even takes a jocular turn.[3] The poet introduces his relations to the victor, and to his poetical rivals; he extols his own style, and decries that of others.[4] The Æolic odes, from the rapidity and variety of their movement, have a less uniform character than the Doric odes; for example, the first Olympic, with its joyous and glowing images, is very different from the second, in which a lofty melancholy is expressed, and from the ninth, which has an expression of proud and complacent self-reliance. The language of the Æolic epinikia is also bolder, more difficult in its syntax, and marked by rarer dialectical forms. Lastly, there are the Lydian odes, the number of which is inconsiderable; their metre is mostly trochaic, and of a particularly soft character, agreeing with the tone of the poetry. Pindar appears to have preferred the Lydian rhythms for odes which were destined to be sung during a procession to a temple or at the altar, and in which the favour of the deity was implored in a humble spirit.

---

[1] The ancient writers on music explain how those trochaic dipodies were reduced to an uniform rhythm with the dactylic series. These writers state that the trochaic dipody was considered as a rhythmical foot, having the entire first trochee as its arsis, the second as its thesis; so that, if the syllables were measured shortly, it might be taken as equivalent to a dactyl.

[2] *Ol.* I. 52. (82). IX. 35.   [3] *Ol.* IV. 26. (40). *Pyth.* II. 72. (131).

[4] *Ol.* II. 86. (155). IX. 100. (151). *Pyth.* II. 79. (145).

CHAPTER XVI.

THEOLOGICAL AND PHILOSOPHICAL POETRY.

§ 1. Moral improvement of Greek poetry after Homer especially evident in the notions as to the state of man after death. § 2. Influence of the mysteries and of the Orphic doctrines on these notions. § 3. First traces of Orphic ideas in Hesiod and other epic poets. § 4. Sacerdotal enthusiasts in the age of the Seven Sages ; Epimenides, Abaris, Aristeas, and Pherecydes. § 5. An Orphic literature arises after the destruction of the Pythagorean league. § 6. Subjects of the Orphic poetry ; at first cosmogonic, § 7, afterwards prophetic, in reference to Dionysus.

§ 1. WE have now traced the progress of Greek poetry from Homer to Pindar, and observed it through its different stages, from the simple epic song to the artificial and elaborate form of the choral ode. Fortunately the works of Homer and Pindar, the two extreme points of this long series, have been preserved nearly entire. Of the intermediate stages we can only form an imperfect judgment from isolated fragments and the statements of later writers.

The interval between Homer and Pindar is an important period in the history of Greek civilization. Its advance was so great in this time that the latter poet may seem to belong to a different state of the human race from the former. In Homer we perceive that infancy of the mind which lives entirely in seeing and imagining, whose chief enjoyment consists in vivid conceptions of external acts and objects, without caring much for causes and effects, and whose moral judgments are determined rather by impulses of feeling than by distinctly-conceived rules of conduct. In Pindar the Greek mind appears far more serious and mature. Fondly as he may contemplate the images of beauty and splendour which he raises up, and glorious as are the forms of ancient heroes and modern athletes which he exhibits, yet the chief effort of his genius is to discover a standard of moral government ; and when he has distinctly conceived it, he applies it to the fair and living forms which the fancy of former times had created. There is too much truth in Pindar's poetry, it is too much the expression of his genuine feelings, for him to attempt to conceal its difference from the ancient style, as the later poets did. He says[1] that the fame of Ulysses has become greater through the sweet songs of Homer than from his real adventures, because there is something ennobling in the illusions and soaring flights of Homer's fancy; and he frequently rejects the narratives of former poets, particularly when they do not accord with his own purer conceptions of the power and moral excellence of the gods.[2]

But there is nothing in which Pindar differs so widely from Homer as in his notions respecting *the state of man after death*. According to the description in the *Odyssey*, all the dead, even the most renowned heroes, lead a shadowy existence in the infernal regions (Aides), where, like phantoms, they continue the same pursuits as on earth, though without will or understanding. On the other hand, Pindar, in his sublime ode of consolation to Theron,[3] says that all misdeeds of this world are severely judged in the infernal regions, but that a happy life in eternal sunshine, without care for subsistence, is the portion of the good; 'while those who, through a threefold existence in the upper and lower worlds, have kept their souls pure from all sin, ascend the path of Zeus to the citadel of Cronus,[4] where the Islands of the Blessed are refreshed by the breezes of Ocean, and golden flowers glitter.' In this passage the Islands of the Blessed are described as a reward for the highest virtue, whilst in Homer only a few favourites of the gods (Menelaus, for example, because his wife was a daughter of Zeus) reach the Elysian Field on the border of the ocean. In his threnes, or laments for the dead, Pindar more distinctly developed his ideas about immortality, and spoke of the tranquil life of the blessed, in perpetual sunshine, among fragrant groves, at festal games and sacrifices; and of the torments of the

---

[1] *Nem.* VII. 20 (29).

[2] See, for example, *Ol.* I. 52 (82); IX. 35 (54).

[3] *Ol.* II. 57 (105).

[4] That is, the way which Zeus himself takes when he visits his dethroned father Cronus (now reconciled with him, and become the ruler of the departed spirits in bliss), in order to advise with him on the destiny of mankind.

wretched in eternal night. In these, too, he explained himself more fully as to the existence alternating between the upper and lower world, by which lofty spirits rise to a still higher state. He says[1]—' Those from whom Persephone receives an atonement for their former guilt, their souls she sends, in the ninth year, to the sun of heaven. From them spring great kings and men mighty in power and renowned for wisdom, whom posterity calls sacred heroes among men.'[2]

§ 2. It is manifest that between the periods of Homer and Pindar a great change of opinions took place, which could not have been effected at once, but must have been produced by the efforts of many sages and poets. All the Greek religious poetry treating of death and the world beyond the grave refers to the deities whose influence was supposed to be exercised in the dark region at the centre of the earth, and who were thought to have little connexion with the political and social relations of human life. These deities formed a class apart from the gods of Olympus, and were comprehended under the name of the *Chthonian gods.*[3] The mysteries of the Greeks were connected with the worship of these gods alone. That the love of immortality first found a support in a belief in these deities appears from the fable of Persephone, the daughter of Demeter. Every year, at the time of harvest, Persephone was supposed to be carried from the world above to the dark dominions of the invisible King of Shadows ('Αΐδης), but to return every spring, in youthful beauty, to the arms of her mother. It was thus that the ancient Greeks described the disappearance and return of vegetable life in the alternations of the seasons. The changes of nature, however, must have been considered as typifying the changes in the lot of man ; otherwise Persephone would have been merely a symbol of the seed committed to the ground, and would not have become the queen of the dead. But when the goddess of inanimate nature

---

[1] *Thren.* fr. 4, ed. Boeckh.

[2] In order to understand this passage it is to be observed that, according to the ancient law, a person who had committed homicide must expiate his offence by an exile or even servitude of eight years before his guilt was removed.

[3] Concerning this distinction, the most important in the Greek religious system, see ch. II. § 5.

had become the queen of the dead, it was a natural analogy which must have early suggested itself, that the return of Persephone to the world of light also denoted a renovation of life and a new birth to men. Hence the *Mysteries of Demeter*, and especially those celebrated at Eleusis (which at an early period acquired great renown among all the Greeks), inspired the most elevating and animating hopes with regard to the condition of the soul after death. 'Happy' (says Pindar of these mysteries)[1] 'is he who has beheld them, and descends beneath the hollow earth; he knows the end, he knows the divine origin of life;' and this praise is repeated by all the most distinguished writers of antiquity who mention the Eleusinian mysteries.

But neither the Eleusinian nor any other of the established mysteries of Greece obtained any influence upon the literature of the nation, since the hymns sung and the prayers recited at them were only intended for particular parts of the imposing ceremony, and were not imparted to the public. On the other hand, there was a society of persons who performed the rites of a mystical worship, but were not exclusively attached to a particular temple and festival, and who did not confine their notions to the initiated, but published them to others, and committed them to literary works. These were the *followers of Orpheus* (οἱ Ὀρφικοί); that is to say, associations of persons, who, under the guidance of the ancient mystical poet Orpheus, dedicated themselves to the worship of Bacchus, in which they hoped to find satisfaction for an ardent longing after the soothing and elevating influences of religion. The Dionysus to whose worship these Orphic and Bacchic rites were annexed,[2] was the Chthonian deity, Dionysus Zagreus, closely connected with Demeter and Cora, who was the personified expression not only of the most rapturous pleasure, but also of a deep sorrow for the miseries of human life. The Orphic legends and poems related in great part to this Dionysus, who was combined, as an infernal deity, with Hades; (a doctrine given by the philosopher Heraclitus as the opinion of a particular sect);[3] and upon

---

[1] *Thren.* fr. 8, ed. Boeckh.
[2] Τὰ Ὀρφικὰ καλεόμενα καὶ Βακχικά. Herod. II. 81.
[3] Ap. Clem. Alex. *Protr.* p. 30, Potter.

whom the Orphic theologers founded their hopes of the purification and ultimate immortality of the soul. But their mode
of celebrating this worship was very different from the popular
rites of Bacchus. The Orphic worshippers of Bacchus did
not indulge in unrestrained pleasure and frantic enthusiasm,
but rather aimed at an ascetic purity of life and manners.[1]
The followers of Orpheus, when they had tasted the mystic
sacrificial feast of raw flesh torn from the ox of Dionysus
(ὠμοφαγία), partook of no other animal food. They wore
white linen garments, like Oriental and Egyptian priests, from
whom, as Herodotus remarks, much may have been borrowed
in the ritual of the Orphic worship.

§ 3. It is difficult to determine the time when the Orphic
association was formed in Greece, and when hymns and other
religious songs were first composed in the Orphic spirit.
But, if we content ourselves with seeking to ascertain the
beginning of higher and more hopeful views of death than
those presented by Homer, we find them in the poetry of
Hesiod. In Hesiod's *Works and Days*, at least, all the heroes
are described as collected by Zeus in the Islands of the Blessed
near the ocean ; according indeed to one verse (which, however,
is not recognised by all critics), they are subject to the dominion of Cronus.[2] In this we may see the marks of a great
change in opinion. It became repugnant to men's feelings to
conceive divine beings, like the gods of Olympus and the
Titans, in a state of eternal dissension ; the former selfishly
enjoying undisturbed felicity, and the latter abandoned to all the
horrors of Tartarus. A humaner spirit required a reign of
peace after the rupture of the divine dynasties. Hence the
belief, entertained by Pindar, that Zeus had released the Titans
from their chains ;[3] and that Cronus, the god of the golden
age, reconciled with his son Zeus, still continued to reign, in
the islands of the ocean, over the blessed of a former generation.
In Orphic poems, Zeus calls on Cronus, released from his

---

[1] On this and other points mentioned in the text see Lobeck, *Aglaophamus*,
p. 244.

[2] According to v. 169 : τηλοῦ ἀπ' ἀθανάτων τοῖσιν Κρόνος ἐμβασιλεύει, (concerning this reading see Goettling's edition) ; which verse is wanting in some manuscripts.

[3] Ζεὺς ἔλυσε Τιτᾶνας.

chains, to assist him in laying the foundation of the world. There is also, in other epic poets after Homer, a similar tendency to lofty and tranquillizing notions. Eugammon, the author of the *Telegonia*,[1] is supposed to have borrowed the part of his poem which treated of Thesprotia, from Musæus, the poet of the mysteries. Thesprotia was a country in which the worship of the gods of death was peculiarly cultivated. In the *Alcmæonis*, which celebrated Alcmæon, the son of Amphiaraus, Zagreus was invoked as the highest of all the gods.[2] The deity meant in this passage was the god of the infernal regions, but in a much more elevated sense than that in which Hades is usually employed. Another poem of this period, the *Minyas*, gave an ample description of the infernal regions; the spirit of which may be inferred from the fact that this part (which was called by the name of ' The Descent to Hades ') is attributed, among other authors, to Cecrops, an Orphic poet, or even to Orpheus himself.[3]

§ 4. At the time when the first philosophers appeared in Greece, poems must have existed which diffused, in mythical forms, conceptions of the origin of the world and the destiny of the soul, differing from those in Homer. The endeavour to attain to a knowledge of divine and human things was in Greece slowly and with difficulty evolved from the religious notions of a sacerdotal fanaticism; and it was for a long period confined to the refining and rationalizing of the traditional mythology, before it ventured to explore the paths of independent inquiry. In the age of the Seven Sages several persons appeared, who, (being mainly under the influence of the ideas and rites of the worship of Apollo,) partly by a pure and holy mode of life, and partly by a fanatical temper of mind, surrounded themselves with a sort of supernatural halo, which makes it difficult for us to discern their true character. Among these persons was Epimenides of Crete, an early contemporary of Solon, who was sent for to Athens, in his character of expiatory priest, to free it from the curse which had rested upon it since the Cylonian massacre (about Olymp. 42. B.C. 612). Epimenides

---

[1] See above, ch. VI. § 6.
[2] Πότνια Γῆ, Ζαγρεῦ τε θεῶν πανυπέρτατε πάντων.   *Etym. Gud.* in v. Ζαγρεύς.
[3] ἡ ἐς Ἀιδου κατάβασις.

was a man of a sacred and marvellous nature, who was brought up by the nymphs, and whose soul quitted his body, as long and as often as it pleased ; according to the opinion of Plato and other ancients, his mind had a prophetic and inspired sense of divine things.[1] Another and more extraordinary individual of this class was Abaris, who, about a generation later, appeared in Greece as an expiatory priest, with rites of purification and holy songs. In order to give more importance to his mission, he called himself a Hyperborean; that is, one of the nation which Apollo most loved, and in which he manifested himself in person; and, as a proof of his origin, he carried with him an arrow which Apollo had given him in the country of the Hyperboreans.[2] Together with Abaris may be mentioned Aristeas of Proconnesus, on the Propontis ; who took the opposite direction, and, inspired by Apollo, travelled to the far north, in search of the Hyperboreans. He described this marvellous journey in a poem, called *Arimaspea,* which was read by Herodotus, and Greeks of still later date. It consisted of ethnographical accounts and stories about the northern nations, mixed with notions belonging to the worship of Apollo. In this poem, however, Aristeas so far checked his imagination, that he only represented himself to have penetrated northwards from the Scythians as far as the Issedones ; and he gave as mere reports the marvellous tales of the one-eyed Arimaspians, of the griffins which guarded the gold, and of the happy Hyperboreans beyond the northern mountains. Aristeas became quite a marvellous personage : he is said to have accompanied Apollo, at the founding of Metapontum, in the form of a raven, and to have appeared centuries afterwards, (viz., when he really lived, about the time of Pythagoras,) in the same city ef Magna Græcia.

---

[1] Whether the oracles, expiatory verses, and poems (as the origin of the Curetes and Corybantes) attributed to him are his genuine productions cannot now be determined. Damascius, *De Princip.* p. 383, ascribes to him (after Eudemus) a cosmogony, in which the mundane egg plays an important part, as in the Orphic cosmogonies.

[2] This is the ancient form of the story in Herod. IV. 36, the orator Lycurgus, &c. According to the later version, which is derived from Heraclides Ponticus, Abaris was himself carried by the marvellous arrow through the air round the world. Some expiatory verses and oracles were likewise ascribed to Abaris ; also an epic poem, called ' the Arrival of Apollo among the Hyperboreans.'

Pherecydes, of the island of Syros, one of the heads of the
Ionic school, belongs to this class of the sacerdotal sages, inasmuch as he gave a mythical form to his notions about the
nature of things and their internal principles.   There are
extant some fragments of a theogony composed by him, which
bear a strange character, and have a much closer resemblance
to the Orphic poems than to those of Hesiod.[1]   They show
that by this time the character of the theogonic poetry had been
changed, and that Orphic ideas were in vogue.

§ 5. No name of any literary production of an Orphic poet
before Pherecydes is known; probably because the hymns and
religious songs composed by the Orphic poets of that time
were destined only for their mystical assemblies, and were in-
dissolubly connected with the rites performed at them.   An
extensive Orphic literature first appeared about the time of the
Persian war, when the remains of the Pythagorean order in
Magna Græcia united themselves to the Orphic associations.
The philosophy of Pythagoras had in itself no analogy with the
spirit of the Orphic mysteries; nor did the life, education, and
manners of the followers of Orpheus at all resemble those of the
Pythagorean league in lower Italy.   Among the Orphic theologers, the worship of Dionysus was the centre of all religious
ideas, and the starting-point of all speculations upon the world
and human nature.   The worship of Dionysus, however, appears
not to have been held in honour in the cities of the Pythagorean league; these philosophers preferred the worship of Apollo
and the Muses, which best suited the spirit of their social and
political institutions.   This junction was evidently not formed
till after the dissolution of the Pythagorean league in Magna
Græcia, and the sanguinary persecution of its members, by the
popular party (about Olymp. 69. 1. B.C. 504).   It was natural
that many Pythagoreans, having contracted a fondness for
exclusive associations, should seek a refuge in these Orphic con-
venticles, sanctified, as they were, by religion.   Several persons

---

[1] Sturz, *De Pherecyde* p. 40. sqq. The mixture of divine beings (θεοκρασία), the
god Ophioneus, the unity of Zeus and Eros, and several other things in the Theogony of Pherecydes also occur in Orphic poems. The Cosmogony of Acusilaus
(Damascius, p. 313, after Eudemus), in which Æther, Eros, and Metis, are made
the children of Erebos and Night, also has an Orphic colour. See below, § 6.

who are called Pythagoreans, and who were known as the
authors of Orphic poems, belong to this period; as Cercops,
Brontinus, and Arignote. To Cercops was attributed the great
poem called the 'Sacred Legends' (ἱεροὶ λόγοι), a complete
system of Orphic theology, in twenty-four rhapsodies; probably
the work of several persons, as a certain Diognetus was also
called the author of it. Brontinus, likewise a Pythagorean,
was said to be the author of an Orphic poem upon nature
(φυσικὰ), and of a poem called 'The Mantle and the Net'
(πέπλος καὶ δίκτυον), Orphic expressions symbolical of the
creation. Arignote, who is called a pupil, and even a daughter,
of Pythagoras, wrote a poem called *Bacchica*. Other Orphic
poets were Persinus of Miletus, Timocles of Syracuse, Zopyrus
of Heraclea, or Tarentum.

The Orphic poet of whom we know the most is Onomacritus,
who, however, was not connected with the Pythagoreans, having
lived with Pisistratus and the Pisistratids, and been held in high
estimation by them, before the dissolution of the Pythagorean
league. He collected the oracles of Musæus for the Pisistratids;
in which work, the poet Lasus is said (according to Herodotus)
to have detected him in a forgery. He also composed songs for
Bacchic initiations; in which he connected the Titans with the
mythology of Dionysus, by describing them as the intended mur-
derers of the young god;[1] which shows how far the Orphic
mythology departed from the *Theogony* of Hesiod. In the time
of Plato, a considerable number of poems, under the names of
Orpheus and Musæus, had been composed by these persons, and
were recited by rhapsodists at the public games, like the epics
of Homer and Hesiod.[2] The Orpheotelests, likewise, an obscure set of mystagogues derived from the Orphic associations,
used to come before the doors of the rich, and promise to release
them from their own sins, and those of their forefathers, by
sacrifices and expiatory songs; and they produced at this ceremony a heap of books of Orpheus and Musæus, upon which they
founded their promises.[3]

§ 6. In treating of the subjects of this early Orphic poetry,

---

[1] This is the meaning of the important passage of Pausan. VIII. 37. 3.
[2] Plato, *Ion*, p. 536 B.   [3] Plato, *Rep.* II. p. 364.

we may remark, first, that there is much difficulty in distinguishing it from Orphic productions of the decline of paganism;
and, secondly, that a detailed explanation of it would involve us
in the mazes of ancient mythology and religion. We will,
therefore, only mention the principal contents of these compositions; which will suffice to give an idea of their spirit and
character. We shall take them chiefly from the Orphic cosmogony, which later writers designate as the common one (ἡ
συνήθης),—for there were others still more wild and extravagant,
—and which probably formed a part of the long poetical collection of 'Sacred Legends,' which has been already mentioned.

We see, at the very outset of the Orphic theogony, an attempt
to refine upon the theogony of Hesiod, and to arrive at higher
abstractions than his chaos. The Orphic theogony placed
Chronos, Time, at the head of all things, and conferred upon it
life and creative power. Chronos was then described as spon-
taneously producing chaos and æther, and forming from chaos,
within the æther, a mundane egg, of brilliant white. The
mundane egg is a notion which the Orphic poets had in common with many Oriental systems; traces of it also occur in
ancient Greek legends, as in that of the Dioscuri; but the Orphic
poets first developed it among the Greeks. The whole essence
of the world was supposed to be contained in this egg, and to
grow from it, like the life of a bird. The mundane egg, which
included the matter of chaos, was impregnated by the winds,
that is, by the æther in motion; and thence arose the golden-
winged Eros.[1] The notion of Eros, as a cosmogonic being, is
carried much further by the Orphic poets than by Hesiod. They
also called him Metis, the mind of the world. The name of
Phanes first became common in Orphic poetry of a later date.
The Orphic poets conceived this Eros-Phanes as a pantheistic
being; the parts of the world forming, as it were, the limbs of
his body, and being thus united into an organic whole. The
heaven was his head, the earth his foot, the sun and moon his

---

[1] This feature is also in the burlesque Orphic cosmogony in Aristoph. *Av.* 694;
according to which the Orphic verse in Schol. Apoll. Rhod. III. 26. should be thus
understood:

Αὐτὰρ ἔρωτα χρόνος (not Κρόνος) καὶ πνεύματα πάντα (in the nominative case)
ἐτέκνωσεν.

eyes, the rising and setting of the heavenly bodies his horns.
An Orphic poet addresses Phanes in the following poetical language : ' Thy tears are the hapless race of men ; by thy laugh
thou hast raised up the sacred race of the gods.' Eros then
gives birth to a long series of gods, similar to that in Hesiod.
By his daughter, Night, he produces Heaven and Earth ; these
then bring forth the Titans, among whom Cronus and Rhea become the parents of Zeus. The Orphic poets, as well as Hesiod,
made Zeus the supreme god at this period of the world. He
was, therefore, supposed to supplant Eros-Phanes, and to unite
this being with himself. Hence arose the fable of Zeus having
swallowed Phanes ; which is evidently taken from the story in
Hesiod, that Zeus swallowed Metis, the goddess of wisdom.
Hesiod, however, merely meant to imply that Zeus knows all
things that concern our weal or woe ; while the Orphic poets go
further, and endow their Zeus with the *anima mundi*. Accordingly, they represent Zeus as now being the first and last ; the
beginning, middle, and end ; man and woman ; and, in fine,
everything. Nevertheless, the universe was conceived to stand
in different relations to Zeus and to Eros. The Orphic poets
also described Zeus as uniting the jarring elements into one
harmonious structure ; and thus restoring, by his wisdom, the
unity which existed in Phanes, but which had afterwards been
destroyed, and replaced by confusion and strife. Here we meet
with the idea of a *creation*, which was quite unknown to the
most ancient Greek poets. While the Greeks of the time of
Homer and Hesiod considered the world as an organic being,
which was constantly growing into a state of greater perfection ;
the Orphic poets conceived the world as having been formed by
the Deity out of pre-existing matter, and upon a predetermined
plan. Hence, in describing creation, they usually employed the
image of a ' crater,' in which the different elements were supposed to be mixed in certain proportions ; and also of a ' peplos,'
or garment, in which the different threads are united into one
web. Hence ' Crater,' and ' Peplos,' occur as the titles of Orphic
poems.

§ 7. Another great difference between the notions of the
Orphic poets and those of the early Greeks concerning the order
of the world was, that the former did not limit their views to

the *present* state of mankind; still less did they acquiesce in Hesiod's melancholy doctrine of successive ages, each one worse than the preceding; but they looked for a cessation of strife, a holy peace, a state of the highest happiness and beatitude of souls at the end of all things. Their firm hopes of this result were founded upon Dionysus, from the worship of whom all their peculiar religious ideas were derived. According to them, Dionysus-Zagreus was a son of Zeus, whom he had begotten, in the form of a dragon, upon his daughter Cora-Persephone, before she was carried off to the kingdom of shadows. The young god was supposed to pass through great perils. This was always an essential part of the mythology of Dionysus, especially as it was related in the neighbourhood of Delphi; but it was converted by the Orphic poets, and especially by Onomacritus, into the marvellous legend which is preserved by later writers. According to this legend, Zeus destined Dionysus for king, set him upon the throne of heaven, and gave him Apollo and the Curetes to protect him. But the Titans, instigated by the jealous Here, attacked him by surprise, having disguised themselves under a coating of plaster (a rite of the Bacchic festivals), while Dionysus, whose attention was engaged with various playthings, particularly a splendid mirror, did not perceive their approach. After a long and fearful conflict the Titans overcame Dionysus, and tore him into seven pieces,[1] one piece for each of themselves. Pallas, however, succeeded in saving his palpitating heart,[2] which was swallowed by Zeus in a drink. As the ancients considered the heart as the seat of life, Dionysus was again contained in Zeus, and again begotten by him. Zeus at the same time avenges the slaughter of his son by striking and consuming the Titans with his thunderbolts. From their ashes, according to this Orphic legend, proceeded the race of men. This Dionysus, torn in pieces and born again, is destined to succeed Zeus in the government of the world, and to restore the golden age. In the same system Dionysus was also the god from whom the liberation of souls was expected; for, according to an Orphic notion, more than once alluded to by Plato, human

---

[1] The Orphic poets added Phorcys and Dione to the Titans and Titanides of Hesiod.

[2] Κραδίην παλλομένην, an etymological fable.

souls are punished by being confined in the body, as in a prison. The sufferings of the soul in its prison, the steps and transitions by which it passes to a higher state of existence, and its gradual purification and enlightenment, were all fully described in these poems; and Dionysus and Cora were represented as the deities who performed the task of guiding and purifying the souls of men.

Thus, in the poetry of the first five centuries of Greek literature, especially at the close of this period, we find, instead of the calm enjoyment of outward nature which characterized the early epic poetry, a profound sense of the misery of human life and an ardent longing for a condition of greater happiness. This feeling, indeed, was not so extended as to become common to the whole Greek nation; but it took deep root in individual minds, and was connected with more serious and spiritual views of human nature.

We will now turn our attention to the progress made by the Greeks, in the last century of this period, in *prose composition*.

CHAPTER XVII.

THE EARLY GREEK PHILOSOPHERS.

§ 1. Opposition of philosophy and poetry among the Greeks; causes of the introduction of prose writings. § 2. The Ionians give the main impulse; tendency
of philosophical speculation among the Ionians. § 3. Retrospect of the theological speculations of Pherecydes. § 4. Thales; he combines practical talents
with bold ideas concerning the nature of things. § 5. Anaximander, a writer
and inquirer on the nature of things. § 6. Anaximenes pursues the physical
inquiries of his predecessors. § 7. Heraclitus; profound character of his
natural philosophy. § 8. Changes introduced by Anaxagoras; new direction
of the physical speculations of the Ionians. § 9. Diogenes continues the early
doctrine. Archelaus, an Anaxagorean, carries the Ionic philosophy to Athens.
§ 10. Doctrines of the Eleatics, founded by Xenophanes; their enthusiastic
character is expressed in a poetic form. § 11. Parmenides gives a logical form
to the doctrines of Xenophanes; plan of his poem. § 12. Further development
of the Eleatic doctrine by Melissus and Zeno. § 13. Empedocles, akin to
Anaxagoras and the Eleatics, but conceives lofty ideas of his own. § 14. Italic
school; receives its impulse from an Ionian, which is modified by the Doric
character of the inhabitants. Coincidence of its practical tendency with its
philosophical principle.

§ 1. AS the design of this work is to give a history, not of
the philosophy, but of the literature of Greece, we
shall limit ourselves to such a view of the early Greek philosophers as will illustrate the literary progress of the Greek nation.
Philosophy occupies a peculiar province of the human mind;
and it has its origin in habits of thought which are confined to
a few. It is necessary not only to possess these habits of
thought, but also to be singularly free from the shackles of any
particular system, in order fully to comprehend the speculations
of the ancient Greek philosophers, as preserved in the fragments
and accounts of their writings. Even if a history of physical
and metaphysical speculation among the early Greek philosophers were likely to interest the reader, yet it would be foreign
to the object of the present work, which is intended to illustrate

the intellectual progress and character of the entire Greek nation. Philosophy, for some time after its origin in Greece, was
as far removed from the ordinary thoughts, occupations, and
amusements of the people, as poetry was intimately connected
with them. Poetry ennobles and elevates all that is most
characteristic of a nation ; its religion, mythology, political and
social institutions, and manners. Philosophy, on the other
hand, begins by detaching the mind from the opinions and
habits in which it has been bred up ; from the national conceptions of the gods and the universe; and from the traditionary
maxims of ethics and politics. The philosopher attempts as far
as possible to think for himself; and hence he is led to disparage all that is handed down from antiquity. Hence, too, the
Greek philosophers from the beginning renounced the ornaments of verse ; that is, of the vehicle which had previously been
used for the expression of every elevated feeling. Philosophical
writings were nearly the earliest compositions in the unadorned
language of common life. It is not probable that they would
have been composed in this form, if they had been intended for
recital to a multitude assembled at games and festivals. It
would have required great courage to break in upon the rhythmical flow of the euphonious hexameter and lyric measures, with
a discourse uttered in the language of ordinary conversation.
The most ancient writings of Greek philosophers were however
only brief records of their principal doctrines, designed to be
imparted to a few persons. There was no reason why the form
of common speech should not be used for these, as it had been
long before used for laws, treaties, and the like. In fact, prose
composition and writing are so intimately connected, that we
may venture to assert that, if writing had become common
among the Greeks at an earlier period, poetry would not have
so long retained its ascendency. We shall indeed find that
philosophy, as it advanced, sought the aid of poetry, in order to
strike the mind more forcibly. And if we had aimed at minute
precision in the division of our subject, we should have passed
from theological to philosophical poetry. But it is more convenient to observe, as far as possible, the chronological order of
the different branches of literature, and the dependence of one
upon another ; and we shall therefore classify this philosophical

poetry with prose compositions, as being a limited and peculiar deviation from the usual practice with regard to philosophical writings.

§ 2. However the Greek philosophers may have sought after originality and independence of thought, they could not avoid being influenced in their speculations by the peculiar circumstances of their own position. Hence the earliest philosophers may be classed according to the *races* and *countries* to which they belonged; the idea of a *school* (that is, of a transmission of doctrines through an unbroken series of teachers and disciples) not being applicable to this period.

The earliest attempts at philosophical speculation were made by the Ionians; that race of the Greeks, which not only had, in common life, shown the greatest desire for new and various kinds of knowledge, but had also displayed the most decided taste for scientific researches into the phenomena of external nature. From this direction of their inquiries, the Ionic philosophers were called by the ancients, ‘physical philosophers,’ or ‘physiologers.’ With a boldness characteristic of inexperience and ignorance, they began by directing their inquiries to the most abstruse subjects; and, unaided by any experiments which were not within the reach of a common man, and unacquainted with the first elements of mathematics, they endeavoured to determine the origin and principle of the existence of all things. If we are tempted to smile at the temerity with which these Ionians at once ventured upon the solution of the highest problems, we are, on the other hand, astonished at the sagacity with which many of them conjectured the connexion of appearances, which they could not fully comprehend without a much greater progress in the study of nature. The scope of these Ionian speculations proves that they were not founded on *à priori* reasonings, independent of experience. The Greeks were always distinguished by their curiosity, and their powers of delicate observation. Yet this gifted nation, even when it had accumulated a large stock of knowledge concerning natural objects, seems never to have attempted more than the observation of phenomena which presented themselves unsought; and never to have made experiments devised by the investigator.

§ 3. Before we pass from these general remarks to an account of the individual philosophers of the Ionic school, (taking the term in its most extended sense,) we must mention a man who is important as forming an intermediate link between the sacerdotal enthusiasts, Epimenides, Abaris, and others, noticed in the last chapter, and the Ionic physiologers. PHERECYDES, a native of the island of Syros, one of the Cyclades, is the earliest Greek of whose prose writings we possess any remains,[1] and was certainly one of the first who, after the manner of the Ionians (before they had obtained any papyrus from Egypt), wrote down their unpolished wisdom upon sheep-skins.[2] But his prose is only so far prose that it has cast off the fetters of verse, and not because it expresses the ideas of the writer in a simple and perspicuous manner. His book began thus : ' Zeus and Time (Chronos), and Chthonia existed from eternity. Chthonia was called Earth (γῆ), since Zeus endowed her with honour.' Pherecydes next relates how Zeus transformed himself into Eros, the god of love, wishing to form the world from the original materials made by Chronos and Chthonia. ' Zeus makes (Pherecydes goes on to say) a large and beautiful garment ; upon it he paints Earth and Ogenos (ocean), and the houses of Ogenos ; and he spreads the garment over a winged oak.'[3] It is manifest, without attempting a complete explanation of these images, that the ideas and language of Pherecydes closely resembled those of the Orphic theologers, and that he ought rather to be classed with them than with the Ionic philosophers.

§ 4. Pherecydes lived in the age of the Seven Sages ; one of whom, THALES OF MILETUS, was the first in the series of the Ionic physical philosophers. The Seven Sages, as we have already had occasion to observe, were not solitary thinkers, whose renown for wisdom was acquired by speculations unintelligible to the mass of the people. Their fame, which ex-

---

[1] See chap. XVIII. § 3.

[2] Herod. V. 58. The expression Φερεκύδου διφθέρα probably gave rise to the fable that Pherecydes was flayed as a punishment for his atheism ; a charge which was made against most of the early philosophers.

[3] See Sturz, Commentatio de Pherecyde utroque, in his *Phcrecydis Fragmenta*, ed. alt. 1824. The genuineness of the fragments is especially proved by the rare ancient Ionic forms, cited from them by the learned grammarians, Apollonius and Herodian.

tended over all Greece, was founded solely on their acts as statesmen, counsellors of the people in public affairs, and practical men. This is also true of Thales, whose sagacity in affairs of state and public economy appears from many anecdotes. In particular, Herodotus relates that, at the time when the Ionians were threatened by the great Persian power of Cyrus, after the fall of Crœsus, Thales, who was then very old, advised them to establish an Ionian capital in the middle of their coast, somewhere near Teos, where all the affairs of their race might be debated, and to which all the other Ionic cities might stand in the same relation as the Attic demi to Athens. At an earlier age, Thales is said to have foretold to the Ionians the total eclipse of the sun, which (either in 610 or 603 B.C.) separated the Medes from the Lydians in the battle which was fought by Cyaxares against Halyattes.[1] For this purpose, he doubtless employed astronomical formulæ, which he had obtained, through Asia Minor, from the Chaldeans, the fathers of Grecian, and indeed of all ancient astronomy; for his own knowledge of mathematics could not have reached as far as the Pythagorean theorem. He is said to have been the first teacher of such problems as that of the equality of the angles at the base of an isosceles triangle. In the main, the tendency of Thales was practical; and, where his own knowledge was insufficient, he applied the discoveries of nations more advanced than his own in natural science. Thus he was the first who advised his countrymen, when at sea, not to steer by the Great Bear, which forms a considerable circle round the Pole; but to follow the example of the Phœnicians (from whom, according to Herodotus, the family of Thales was descended), and to take the Lesser Bear for their Polar star.[2]

Thales was not a poet, nor indeed the author of any written work, and, consequently, the accounts of his doctrine rest only upon the testimony of his contemporaries and immediate suc-

---

[1] If Thales was (as is stated by Eusebius) born in Olymp. 35. 2. B.C. 639, he was then either twenty-nine or thirty-six years old.

[2] This constellation was hence called Φοινίκη. See Schol. Arat. *Phœn.* 39. Probably some traditions of this kind served as the basis, of the ναυτικὴ ἀστρολογία, which was attributed to Thales by the ancients, but, according to a more precise account, was the work of a later writer, Phocius of Samos.

cessors ; so that it would be vain to attempt to construct from them a system of natural philosophy according to his notions. It may, however, be collected from these traditions that he considered all nature as endowed with life : ' Everything (he said) is full of gods ;'[1] and he cited, as proofs of this opinion, the magnet and amber, on account of their magnetic and electric properties. It also appears that he considered water as a general principle or cause ;[2] probably because it sometimes assumes a vapoury, sometimes a liquid form; and therefore affords a remarkable example of a change of outward appearance. This is sufficient to show that Thales broke through the common prejudices produced by the impressions of the senses ; and sought to discover the principle of external forms in moving powers which lie beneath the surface of appearances.

§ 5. ANAXIMANDER, also a Milesian, is next after Thales. It seems pretty certain that his little work ' upon nature,' (περὶ φύσεως),—as the books of the Ionic physiologers were mostly called,—was written in Olymp. 58. 2, B.C. 547, when he was sixty-four years old.[3] This may be said to be the earliest philosophical work in the Greek language ; for we can scarcely give that name to the mysterious revelations of Pherecydes. It was probably written in a style of extreme conciseness, and in language more befitting poetry than prose, as indeed appears from the few extant fragments. The astronomical and geographical explanations attributed to Anaximander were probably contained in this work. Anaximander possessed a gnomon, or sun-dial, which he had doubtless obtained from Babylon ;[4] and, being at Sparta (which was still the focus of Greek civilization), he made observations by which he determined exactly the

---

[1] In the passage of Aristotle, de Animâ, I. 5. the words πάντα πλήρη θεῶν εἶναι, alone express the traditional account of the doctrine of Thales ; the words ἐν ὅλῳ τὴν ψυχὴν μεμῖχθαι are the gloss of Aristotle.

[2] Ἀρχὴ, αἰτία. The expression ἀρχὴ was first used by Anaximander.

[3] From the statement of Apollodorus, that Anaximander was sixty-four years old in Olymp. 58. 2. (Diog. Laërt. II. 2), and of Pliny (N. H. II. 8.), that the obliquity of the ecliptic was discovered in Olymp. 58, it may be inferred that Anaximander mentioned this year in his work. Who else could, at that time, have registered such discoveries ?

[4] Herod. II. 109. Concerning Anaximander's gnomon, see Diog. Laërt. II. 1, and others.

solstices and equinoxes, and calculated the obliquity of the ecliptic.[1] According to Eratosthenes, he was the first who attempted to draw a map; in which his object probably was rather to make a mathematical division of the whole earth, than to lay down the forms of the different countries composing it. According to Aristotle, Anaximander thought that there were innumerable worlds, which he called gods; supposing these worlds to be beings endowed with an independent power of motion. He also thought that existing worlds were always perishing, and that new worlds were always springing into being; so that motion was perpetual. According to his views, these worlds arose out of the eternal, or rather indeterminable, substance, which he called τὸ ἄπειρον; he arrived at the idea of an original substance, out of which all things arose, and to which all things return, by excluding all attributes and limitations. ' All existing things (he says in an extant fragment) must, in justice, perish in that in which they had their origin. For one thing is always punished by another for its injustice (*i.e.*, its injustice in setting itself in the place of another), according to the order of time.'[2]

§ 6. ANAXIMENES, another Milesian, according to the general tradition of antiquity, followed Anaximander, and must, therefore, have flourished not long before the Persian war.[3] With him the Ionic philosophy began to approach closer to the language of argumentative discussion; his work was composed in the plain simple dialect of the Ionians. Anaximenes, in seeking to discover some sensible substance, from which outward objects could have been formed, thought that *air* best fulfilled the conditions of his problem; and he showed much ingenuity in collecting instances of the rarefaction and condensation of bodies from air. This elementary principle of the Ionians was always considered as having an independent power of

---

[1] The obliquity of the ecliptic (that is, the distance of the sun's course from the equator) must have been evident to any one who observed it with attention; but Anaximander found the means of measuring it, in a certain manner, with the gnomon.

[2] Simplicius ad Aristot. *Phys.* fol. 6.

[3] The more precise statements respecting his date are so confused, that it is difficult to unravel them. See Clinton in the *Philological Museum*, vol. I. p. 91.

motion; and as endowed with certain attributes of the divine essence. ' As the soul in us (says Anaximenes in an extant fragment),[1] which is air, holds us together, so breath and air surround the whole world.'

§ 7. A person of far greater importance in the history of Greek philosophy, and especially of Greek prose, is HERACLITUS OF EPHESUS. The time when he flourished is ascertained to be about the 69th Olympiad, or B.C. 505. He is said to have dedicated his work, which was entitled ' Upon Nature' (though titles of this kind were usually not added to books till later times), to the native goddess of Ephesus, the great Artemis— as if such a destination were alone worthy of it, and he did not consider it worth his while to give it to the public. The con-current tradition of antiquity describes Heraclitus as a proud and reserved man, who disliked all interchange of ideas with others. He thought that the profound cogitations on the nature of things which he had made in solitude, were far more valu-able than all the information which he could gain from others. ' Much learning (he said) does not produce wisdom; otherwise it would have made Hesiod wise, and Pythagoras, and again Xenophanes and Hecatæus.'[2] He dealt rather in intimations of important truths than in popular expositions of them, such as the other Ionians preferred. His language was prose only in-asmuch as it was free from metrical shackles; but its expres-sions were bolder and its tone more animated than those of many poems. The cardinal doctrine of his natural philosophy seems to have been, that everything is in perpetual motion, that nothing has any stable or permanent existence, but that everything is assuming a new form or perishing. ' We step (he says, in his symbolical language) into the same rivers and we do not step into them' (because in a moment the water is changed). 'We are and are not' (because no point in our ex-istence remains fixed).[3] Thus every sensible object appeared to

---

[1] Stobæus, *Eclog.*, p. 296.

[2] In Diog. Laërt. X. 1 : πολυμαθίη νόον οὐ διδάσκει (better than φύει). 'Ησίοδον γὰρ ἂν ἐδίδαξε καὶ Πυθαγόρην, αὖθίς τε Ξενοφάνεά τε καὶ 'Εκαταῖον. An important passage on the first appearance of *learning* among the Greeks.

[3] Ποταμοῖς τοῖς αὐτοῖς ἐμβαίνομεν τε καὶ οὐκ ἐμβαίνομεν, εἶμεν τε καὶ οὐκ εἶμεν, Heraclit. *Alleg. Hom.* c. XXIV. p. 84. The image of a stream, into which a person

him, not as something individual, but only as another form of something else; ' Fire (he says) lives the death of the earth; air lives the death of fire; water lives the death of air; and the earth that of water;[1] by which he meant that individual things were only different forms of a universal substance, which mutually destroy each other. In like manner he said of men and gods, ' Our life is their death; their life is our death;'[2] that is, he thought that men were gods who had died, and that gods were men raised to life.

Seeking in natural phenomena for the principle of this perpetual motion, Heraclitus supposed it to be *fire*, though he probably meant, not the fire perceptible by the senses, but a higher and more universal agent. For, as we have already seen, he conceived the sensible fire as living and dying, like the other elements; but of the igneous principle of life he speaks thus: ' The unchanging order of all things was made neither by a god nor a man, but it has always been, is, and will be, the living fire, which is kindled and extinguished in regular succession.'[3] Nevertheless, Heraclitus conceived this continual motion not to be the mere work of chance, but to be directed by some power, which he called εἱμαρμένη, or fate, and which guided ' the way upwards and downwards' (his expression for production and destruction). ' The sun (he said) will not overstep its path; if it did, the Erinnyes, the allies of justice, would find it out.'[4] He recognised in motion an eternal law, which was maintained by the supreme powers of the universe. In this respect the followers of Heraclitus appear to have departed from the wise example of their teacher; for the exaggerated Heracliteans

---

cannot step twice, as it is always different, was used by Heraclitus in several parts of his work, in order to show that all existing things are in a constant state of flux.

[1] Ζῇ πῦρ τὸν γῆς θάνατον, καὶ ἀὴρ ζῇ τὸν πυρὸς θάνατον, ὕδωρ ζῇ τὸν ἀέρος θάνατον, γῆ τὸν ὕδατος. Maxim. Tyr. *Diss.* XXV. p. 260. The expression that one thing lives the death of another is frequent in the fragments of Heraclitus, and generally he appears often to use certain fixed phrases.

[2] Ζῶμεν τὸν ἐκείνων θάνατον, τεθνήκαμεν δὲ τὸν ἐκείνων βίον. Philo. *Alleg. leg.* p. 60. Heracl. *Alleg. Hom.* c. XXIV.

[3] Κόσμον τὸν αὐτὸν ἁπάντων οὔτε τις θεῶν οὔτ' ἀνθρώπων ἐποίησεν, ἀλλ' ἦν ἀεὶ καὶ ἔστιν καὶ ἔσται πῦρ ἀείζωον ἀπτόμενον μέτρα καὶ ἀποσβεννύμενον μέτρα. Clemens Alex. *Strom.* V. p. 599.

[4] Ἥλιος οὐχ ὑπερβήσεται μέτρα· εἰ δὲ μὴ, Ἐρίννυες μὲν Δίκης ἐπίκουροι ἐξευρήσουσιν. Plutarch, *De Exil.* c. XI. p. 604.

(whom Plato in joke calls οἱ ῥέοντες, ' the runners') aimed at proving a perpetual change and motion in all things.

Heraclitus, like nearly all the other philosophers, despised the popular religion. Their object was, by arguments derived from their immediate experience, to emancipate themselves from all traditional opinions, which included not only superstition and prejudices, but also some of the most valuable truths. Heraclitus boldly rejected the whole ceremonial of the Greek religion. ' They worship images (he said of his countrymen) : just as if any one were to converse with houses.'[1] Nevertheless, the opinions of Heraclitus on the important question of the relation between mind and body agreed with the popular religion and with the prevailing notions of the Greeks. The primitive beings of the world were, in the popular creed, both spiritual powers and material substances; and Heraclitus conceived the original matter of the world to be the source of life. On the other hand, one of the most important changes in the history of the human mind was produced by Anaxagoras after the time of Heraclitus, inasmuch as he rejected all the popular notions on religion and struck into a new path of speculation on sacred things. Similar opinions had indeed been previously entertained in the East, and, in particular, the Mosaic conceptions of the Deity and the world belong to the same class of religious views. But among the Greeks these views (which the Christian religion has made so familiar in modern times) were first introduced by Anaxagoras, and were presented by him in a philosophical form; and having been, from the beginning, much more opposed than the doctrines of former philosophers to the popular mythological religion, they tended powerfully, by their rapid diffusion, to undermine the principles upon which the entire worship of the ancient gods rested, and therefore prepared the way for the subsequent triumph of Christianity.

§ 8. ANAXAGORAS, though he is called a disciple of Anaximenes, followed him at some interval of time; he flourished at a period when not only the opinions of the Ionic physical philosophers, but those of the Pythagoreans and even of the

---

[1] Καὶ ἀγάλμασι τουτέοισι εὔχονται, ὁκοῖον εἴ τις δόμοις λεσχηνεύοιτο. Clemens Alex. *Cohort.* p. 33.

Eleatics, had been diffused in Greece, and had produced some influence upon speculation.   But since it is impossible to arrange together the contemporaneous advances of the different schools or series of philosophers, and since Anaxagoras resembled his Ionic predecessors both in the object of his researches and his mode of expounding them, we will finish the series of the Ionic philosophers before we proceed to the Eleatics and Pythagoreans.

The main events of the life of Anaxagoras are known with tolerable certainty from concurrent chronological accounts.   He was born at Clazomenæ, in Ionia, in Olymp. 70. 1, B.C. 500, and came to Athens in Olymp. 81. 1, B.C. 456.[1]   There he lived for twenty-five years (which is also called thirty in round numbers), till about the beginning of the Peloponnesian war. At this time there was a faction in the Athenian state whose object it was to shake the power of the great statesman Pericles, and to lower his credit with the people; but before they ventured to make a direct attack upon him, they began by attacking his friends and familiars.   Among these was Anaxagoras, at that time far advanced in age; and the freedom of his inquiries into Nature had afforded sufficient ground for accusing him of unbelief in the gods adored by the people.   The discrepancy of the testimony makes it difficult to ascertain the result of this accusation; but thus much is certain, that in consequence of it Anaxagoras left Athens in Olymp. 87. 2, B.C. 431. He died three years afterwards at Lampsacus, in Olymp. 88. 1, B.C. 428, at the age of seventy-two.

The treatise on Nature by Anaxagoras (which was written late in his life, and therefore at Athens)[2] was in the Ionic dialect, and in prose, after the example of Anaximenes.   The copious fragments extant[3] exhibit short sentences connected by particles (*as, and, but, for*) without long periods.   But though

---

[1] In the archonship of Callias, who has been confounded with Callias or Calliades, archon in Olymp. 75. 1.   This time, in the midst of the terrors of the Persian war, was little favourable to the philosophical studies of Anaxagoras.

[2] After Empedocles was known as a philosopher, Aristot. *Metaph.* I. 3, where ἔργα expresses the entire philosophical performances.

[3] The longest is in Simplicius ad Aristot. *Phys.* p. 336.   *Anaxagoræ Fragmenta Illustrata*, ab E. Schaubach, Lipsiæ, 1827 ; fragm. 8.

his style was loose, his reasoning was compact and well arranged. His demonstrations were synthetic, not analytic; that is to say, he subjoined the proof to the proposition to be proved, instead of arriving at his result by a process of inquiry.[1]

The philosophy of Anaxagoras began with his doctrine of atoms, which, contrary to the opinion of all his predecessors, he considered as limited in number. He was the first to exclude the idea of creation from his explanation of nature. 'The Greeks (he said) were mistaken in their doctrine of creation and destruction; for nothing is either created or destroyed, but it is only produced from existing things by mixture, or it is dissolved by separation. They should therefore rather call creation a conjunction, and destruction a dissolution.'[2] It is easy to imagine that Anaxagoras, with this opinion, must have arrived at the doctrine of atoms which were unchangeable and imperishable, and which were mixed and united in bodies in different ways. But since, from the want of chemical knowledge, he was unable to determine the component parts of bodies, he supposed that each separate body (as bone, flesh, wood, stone) consisted of corresponding particles, which are the celebrated ὁμοιομέρειαι of Anaxagoras. Nevertheless, to explain the production of one thing from another he was obliged to assume that all things contained a portion of all other things, and that the particular form of each body depended upon the preponderating ingredient. Now, as Anaxagoras maintained the doctrine that bodies are mere matter, without any spontaneous power of change, he also required a principle of life and motion beyond the material world. This he called *spirit* (νοῦς), which, he says, is 'the purest and most subtle of all things, having the most knowledge and the greatest strength.'[3] Spirit does not obey the universal law of the ὁμοιομέρειαι, viz. that of mixing with every thing; it exists in animate beings, but not so closely combined with the material atoms as these are with each

---

[1] Hence, for example, the passage concerning production quoted lower down was not at the beginning, but followed the propositions about ὁμοιομέρειαι, νοῦς, and motion.

[2] Simplicius ad *Phys.* p. 346, fragm. 22, Schaubach. Concerning the position see Panzerbieter, *de Fragm. Anaxag. Ordine*, p. 9, 21.

[3] Ἔστι γὰρ λεπτότατόν τε πάντων χρημάτων καὶ καθαρώτατον, καὶ γνώμην γε περὶ παντὸς πᾶσαν ἴσχει, καὶ ἰσχύει μεγίστον. Simplicius, ubi sup. Fragm. 8, Schaub.

other. This spirit gave to all those material atoms, which in the beginning of the world lay in disorder, the impulse by which they took the forms of individual things and beings. Anaxagoras considered this impulse as having been given by the νοῦς in a circular direction; according to his opinion, not only the sun, moon, and stars, but even the air and the æther, are constantly moving in a circle.[1] He thought that the power of this circular motion kept all these heavenly bodies (which he supposed to be masses of stone) in their courses. No doctrine of Anaxagoras gave so much offence, or was considered so clear a proof of his atheism, as his opinion that the sun, the bountiful god Helios, who shines upon both mortals and immortals, was a mass of red-hot iron.[2] How startling must these opinions have appeared at a time when the people were accustomed to consider nature as pervaded by a thousand divine powers! And yet these new doctrines rapidly gained the ascendency, in spite of all the opposition of religion, poetry, and even the laws which were intended to protect the ancient customs and opinions. A hundred years later Anaxagoras, with his doctrine of νοῦς, appeared to Aristotle a sober inquirer, as compared with the wild speculators who preceded him;[3] although Aristotle was aware that his applications of his doctrines were unsatisfactory and defective. For as Anaxagoras endeavoured to explain natural phenomena, and in this endeavour he, like other natural philosophers, extended the influence of natural causes to its utmost limits, he of course attempted to explain as much as possible by his doctrine of circular motion, and to have recourse as rarely as possible to the agency of νοῦς. Indeed, it appears that he only introduced the latter, like a *deus ex machinâ*, when all other means of explanation failed.

---

[1] The mathematical studies of Anaxagoras appear likewise to have referred chiefly to the *circle*. He attempted a solution of the problem of the quadrature of the circle, and, according to Vitruvius, he instituted some inquiries concerning the optical arrangement of the stage and theatre, which also depended on properties of the circle.

[2] μυδρὸς διάπυρος. This opinion concerning the substance of the heavenly bodies was in great measure founded upon the great meteoric stone which fell at Ægos Potami, on the Hellespont, in Olymp. 78. 1; Anaxagoras and Diogenes of Apollonia both spoke of this phenomenon. Boeckh, *Corp. Inscript. Gr.* vol. II. p. 320.

[3] Aristot. *Met.* A. III. p. 984, ed. Berol.: οἷον νήφων ἐφάνη παρ᾽ εἰκῇ λέγοντας τοὺς πρότερον.

§ 9. Although DIOGENES OF APOLLONIA (in Crete) is not equal in importance, as a philosopher, to his contemporary Anaxagoras, he is yet too considerable a writer upon physical subjects to be here passed over in silence. Without being either the disciple or the teacher, he was a contemporary, of Anaxagoras; and in the direction of his studies he closely followed Anaximenes, expanding the main doctrines of this philosopher rather than establishing new principles of his own. He began his treatise (which was written in the Ionic dialect) with the laudable principle, ' It appears to me that every one who begins a discourse ought to state the subject with distinctness, and to make the style simple and dignified.' [1] He then laid down the principle maintained by all the physical philosophers who preceded Anaxagoras, viz., that all things are different forms of the same elementary substance; which principle he proved by saying that otherwise one thing could not proceed out of another and be nourished by it. Diogenes, like Anaximenes, supposed this elementary substance to be *air*, and, as he conceived it endowed with animation, he found proofs of his doctrine not only in natural phenomena, but also in the human soul, which, according to the popular notions of the ancient Greeks, was *breath* (ψυχή), and therefore *air*. In his explanations of natural appearances Diogenes went into great detail, especially with regard to the structure of the human body; and he exhibited not only acquirements which are very respectable for his time, but also a spirit of inquiry and discussion, and a habit of analytical investigation, which are not to be found even in Anaxagoras. The language of Diogenes also shows an attempt at a closer connexion of ideas by means of periodic sentences, although the difficulty of taking a general philosophical view is very apparent in his style. [2]

Diogenes, like Anaxagoras, lived at Athens, and is said to have been exposed to similar dangers. A third Ionic physical philosopher of this time, Archelaus of Miletus, who followed the

---

[1] Λόγου παντὸς ἀρχόμενον δοκέει μοι χρεὼν εἶναι τὴν ἀρχὴν ἀναμφισβήτητον παρέχεσθαι, τὴν δὲ ἑρμηνηίην ἁπλῆν καὶ σέμνην. Diog. Laërt. VI. 81, IX. 57. Diogen. *Apolloniat. Fragm.*, ed. F. Panzerbieter (Lipsiæ, 1830), Fragm. 1.

[2] Especially in the fragment in Simplicius ad Aristot. *Phys.* p. 32. 6 ; Fragm. 2. ed. Panzerbieter.

manner of Anaxagoras, is chiefly important from having established himself permanently at Athens.   It is evident that these
men were not drawn to Athens by any prospect of benefit to
their philosophical pursuits ; for the Athenians at this time
showed a disinclination to such studies, which they ridiculed
under the name of *meteorosophy*, and even made the subject of
persecution.   It was undoubtedly the power which Athens had
acquired as the head of the confederates against Persia, and the
oppression of the states of Asia Minor, which drove these
philosophers from Clazomenæ and Miletus to the independent,
wealthy, and flourishing Athens.   And thus these political
events contributed to transfer to Athens the last efforts of Ionic
philosophy, which the Athenians at first rejected as foreign to
their modes of thinking, but which they afterwards understood
and appreciated, and used as a foundation for more extensive
and accurate investigations of their own.

§ 10. But before Athens had reached this pre-eminence in
philosophy, the spirit of speculation was awakened in other parts
of Greece, and had struck into new paths of inquiry.   The
Eleatics afford a remarkable instance of independent philosophical
research at this period ; for, although Ionians by descent, they
departed very widely from their countrymen on the coast of
Asia Minor.   Elea, (afterwards Velia, according to the Roman
pronunciation,) was a colony founded in Italy by the Phocæans,
when, from a noble love of freedom, they had delivered up their
country in Asia Minor to the Persians, and had been forced by
the enmity of the Etruscans and Carthaginians to abandon their
first settlement in Corsica; which happened about the 61st
Olympiad, B.C. 536.   It is probable that XENOPHANES, a native
of Colophon, was concerned in the colonizing of Elea ; he wrote
an epic poem of two thousand verses upon this settlement, as
he had sung the foundation of Colophon ; he has been before
mentioned as an elegiac poet.[1]   It appears that poetry was the
main employment of his earlier years, and that he did not attach
himself to philosophy until he had settled at Elea : for there is
no trace of the influence of his Ionic countrymen in his philosophy ; and again his philosophy was established only in Elea, and

---

[1] Chap. X. § 16.   The verse of Xenophanes, Πηλίκος ἦσθ' ὅθ' ὁ Μῆδος ἀφίκετο,
Athen. II. p. 54. E., probably refers to the arrival of the army of Cyrus in Ionia.

never gained a footing among the Ionians in Asia Minor. All the chronological statements are consistent with the supposition that he flourished in Elea as a philosopher between the 65th and 70th Olympiads.[1] But, even as a philosopher, Xenophanes retained the poetic form of composition; his work upon nature was written in epic language and metre, and he himself recited it at public festivals after the manner of a rhapsodist.[2] This deviation from the practice of the Ionic physical philosophers, (of whom, at least, Anaximander and Anaximenes must have been known to him,) can hardly be explained by the fact that he had, upon other subjects, accustomed himself to a poetical form. Some other and weightier cause must have induced him to deliver his thoughts upon the nature of things in a more dignified and pretending manner than his predecessors. This cause, doubtless, was the elevation and enthusiasm of mind, which were connected with the fundamental principles of the Eleatic philosophy.

Xenophanes, from the first, adopted a different principle from that of the Ionic physical philosophers; for he proceeded upon an ideal system, while their system was exclusively founded upon experience. Xenophanes began with the idea of the god-head, and showed the necessity of conceiving it as an eternal and unchanging existence.[3] The lofty idea of an everlasting and immutable God, who is all spirit and mind,[4] was described in his poem as the only true knowledge. 'Wherever (he says) I might direct my thoughts, they always returned to the one and unchanging being; everything, however I examined it, resolved itself into the self-same nature.'[5] How he reconciled

---

[1] Especially that *he* mentioned Pythagoras, and that Heraclitus and Epicharmus mentioned *him*. Xenophanes lived at Zancle (Diog. Laërt. IX. 18); evidently not till after it had become Ionian, that is, after Olymp. 70. 4, B.C. 497. He is also said to have been alive in the reign of Hiero, Olymp. 75. 3, B.C. 478. (See Clinton, *F. H.* ad a. 477).

[2] αὐτὸς ἐρραψῴδει τὰ ἑαυτοῦ.

[3] See principally the treatise of Aristotle (or Theophrastus) *de Xenophane, Zenone, et Gorgiâ.*

[4] This idea is expressed in the verse: οὖλος ὁρᾷ, οὖλος δὲ νοεῖ, οὖλος δέ τ' ἀκούει. See *Xenophanis Colophonii carminum reliquiæ,* ed. S. Karsten. Brux. 1830.

[5] This is the meaning of the passage in Sext. Empir. *Hypot.* I. 224.

ὅππη γὰρ ἐμὸν νόον εἰρύσαιμι
εἰς ἓν ταὐτό τε πᾶν ἀνελύετο, πᾶν δὲ ὂν [οἱ?] αἰεὶ
πάντῃ ἀνελκόμενον μίαν εἰς φύσιν ἵσταθ' ὁμοίαν.

The first metaphor is taken from a journey, the second from the balance.

these doctrines with the evidence of the senses, we are not
sufficiently informed; but he does not appear to have worked
out the pantheistic doctrine of one God comprehending all
things with the logical consistency and definiteness of ideas
which we shall find in his successor. Probably, however, he
considered all experience and tradition as mere opinion and
apparent truth. Xenophanes did not hesitate to represent openly
the anthropomorphic conceptions of the Greeks concerning
their gods as mere prejudices. ' If (said he) oxen and lions
had hands wherewith to paint and execute works as men do,
they would paint gods with forms and bodies like their own;
horses like horses, oxen like oxen.'[1] Homer and Hesiod, the
poets who developed and established these anthropomorphic
conceptions, were considered by Xenophanes as corruptors of
genuine religion. ' These poets are not contented with ascribing
human qualities and virtues to the gods, but have attributed to
them everything which is a shame and reproach among men,
as thieving, adultery, and deceit.'[2] This is the first decided
manifestation of that discord which henceforth reigned between
poets and philosophers, and, as is well known, was still carried
on with much vehemence in the time of Plato.

§ 11. Xenophanes was followed by PARMENIDES OF ELEA,
who, as we know from Plato, was born about Olymp. 66. 2, and
passed some time at Athens, when he was about 65 years old.[3]
It is therefore possible that in his youth he may have conversed
with Xenophanes, although Aristotle mentions with doubt the
tradition that he was the disciple of the latter philosopher. It
is, however, certain that the philosophy of Parmenides has
much of the spirit of that of Xenophanes, and differs from it
chiefly in having reached a maturer state. The all-comprehen-
siveness of the Deity, which appeared to Xenophanes a refuge

---

[1] Clem. Alex. *Strom.* V. p. 601. fragm. 6. Karsten.

[2] Sext. Empir. *ad Mathem.* IX. p. 193. fr. 7. Karsten.

[3] Parmenides came, at the age of 65, with Zeno, who was at the age of 40, to
great Panathenæa. (See Plato *Parmen.* p. 127). Socrates (born in Olymp. 77.
3 or 4) was then σφόδρα νέος, but yet old enough to take a part in philosophical discussions, and therefore probably about the age of 20. Accordingly this philosophical meeting (unless it be a pure invention of Plato) cannot be placed before
Olymp. 82. 3 ; from which date the rest follows.

from the difficulties of metaphysical speculation, was demon-
strated by Parmenides by arguments derived from the idea of
existence. This mode of deductive reasoning from certain
simple fundamental principles (analogous to mathematical reasoning) was first employed to a great extent by Parmenides.
His whole philosophy rests upon the idea of *existence*, which,
strictly understood, excludes the ideas of creation and annihilation. For, as he says himself, in some sonorous verses,[1]
' How could that which exists, first will to exist? how could it
become what it is not? If it becomes what it is not, it no
longer exists; and the same, if it begins to exist. Thus all
idea of creation is extinguished; and annihilation is incredible.' Although in this and other passages the expression of
such abstract ideas in epic metre and language may excite surprise, yet there is great harmony between the matter of Parmenides and the form in which he has clothed it. His pantheistic doctrine of existence, which he pursued into all its
logical consequences, and to which he sacrificed all the evidence
of the senses, appeared to him a great and holy revelation. His
whole poem on nature was composed in this spirit ; and he
expressed (though in figurative language) his genuine sentiments, when he related that ' the coursers which carry men as
far as thought can reach, accompanied by the virgins of the
Sun, brought him to the gates of day and night ; that here
Justice, who keeps the key of the gate, took him by the hand,
addressed him in a friendly manner, and announced to him
that he was destined to know everything, the fearless spirit of
convincing truth, and the opinions of mortals in which no sure
trust is to be placed, &c.'[2] And accordingly his poem, in pur-
suance of the subject mentioned in these verses, began with the
doctrine of pure existence, and then proceeded to an explanation
of the phenomena of external nature. It was given in the form
of a revelation by the goddess Justice, who was described as
passing from the first to the second branch of the subject in the
following manner : ' Here I conclude my sure discourse and
thoughts upon truth ; henceforward hear human opinions, and

---

[1] Ap. Simplic. ad Aristot. *Phys.* f. 31. b. V. 80. sqq. in Brandis *Commentationes
Eleaticæ.*

[2] Sext. Empir. *adv. Mathem.* VII. 111. *Comm. Eleat.* V. 1 sqq.

listen to the deceitful ornaments of my speech.' Here however
Parmenides evidently disparages his own labours; for, although
in this second part he departed from his fundamental principle,
still it is clear, from the fragments which exist, that he never
lost sight of his object of bringing the opinions founded on external perceptions, into closer accordance with the knowledge of
pure intellect.

§ 12. As compared with this great luminary of philosophical
pantheism, his successors (whose youth, at least, falls in the
time of which we are treating) appear as lesser lights. It will
be sufficient for our purpose to explain the philosophical character of MELISSUS and ZENO. The first was a native of Samos,
and was distinguished as being the general who resolutely de-
fended his city against the Athenians, in the war of Olymp. 85.
1, B.C. 440, and even defeated the Athenian fleet, in the absence
of Pericles. He followed close upon Parmenides, whose doctrines he appears to have transferred into Ionic prose; and thus
gave greater perspicuity and order to the arguments which the
former had veiled in poetic forms.[1] The other, Zeno of Elea,
a friend and disciple of Parmenides, also developed the doctrines
of Parmenides in a prose work, in which his chief object was
to justify the disjunction of philosophical speculation from the
ordinary modes of thought (δόξα). This he did by showing
the absurdities involved in the doctrines of variety, of motion,
and of creation, opposed to that of an all-comprehending substance. Yet the sophisms seriously advanced by him show how
easily the mind is caught in its own snares, when it mistakes
its own abstractions for realities;[2] and it only depended upon

---

[1] In order to give an example of his manner, we translate a fragment of
Melissus in Simplic. ad *Phys.* f. 22 b. 'If nothing exists, what can be predicated
of it as of something existing? But if something exists, it is either produced or
eternal. If it is produced, it is produced either from something which exists, or
from something which does not exist. But it is impossible that anything should
be produced from that which does not exist; for, since nothing which exists is produced from that which does not exist, much less can abstract existence (τὸ ἁπλῶς
ἐὸν) be so produced. In like manner, that which exists cannot be produced from
that which does not exist; for in that case it would exist without having been produced. That which exists cannot therefore change. It is, therefore, eternal.'

[2] Thus Zeno, in order to disprove the existence of space (which he sought to
disprove, for the purpose of disproving the existence of motion), argued as follows:
'If space exists, it must be in something; there must, therefore, be a space con-

these Eleatics to argue with the same subtlety against the doctrine of existence and unity, in order to make it appear equally absurd with those which they strove to confute.

§ 13. Before we turn from the Eleatics to those other philosophers of Italy, to whom the name of *Italic* has been appropriated, we must notice a Sicilian, who is so peculiar both in his personal qualities and his philosophical doctrines, that he cannot be classed with any sect, although his opinions were influenced by those of the Ionians, the Eleatics, and the Pythagoreans. EMPEDOCLES OF AGRIGENTUM does not belong to so early a period as might be inferred from the accounts of his character and actions, which represent him as akin to Epimenides or Abaris. It is known that this Empedocles, the son of Meton,[1] flourished about the eighty-fourth Olympiad, B.C. 444, when he was concerned in the colony of Thurii, which was established by nearly all the Hellenic races, with unanimous enthusiasm and great hopes of success, upon the site of the ruined Sybaris. Aristotle considers him as a contemporary of Anaxagoras, but as having preceded him in the publication of his writings. Empedocles was held in high honour by his countrymen of Agrigentum, and also apparently by the other Doric states of Sicily. He reformed the constitution of his native city by abolishing the oligarchical council of the Thousand ; which measure gave such general satisfaction, that the people are said to have offered him the regal authority. The fame of Empedocles was, however, principally acquired by improvements which he made in the physical condition of large tracts of country. He destroyed the pestiferous exhalations of the marshes about Selinus by carrying two small streams through the swampy grounds, and thus draining off the water. This act is recorded on some beautiful coins of Selinus, which are still extant.[2] In other places he blocked up some narrow valleys with large constructions, and thus screened a town

---

taining space.' He did not consider that the idea of space is only conceived, in order to answer the question, In what ? not the question, What ?

[1] There was an earlier Empedocles, the father of Meton, who gained the prize with the race-horse in Olymp. 71.

[2] Concerning these coins, see *Annali dell' Instituto di corrisp. archeologica*, 1835, p. 265.

from the noxious winds which blew into it; by which he earned to himself the title of ' wind averter' (κωλυσανέμας).[1] It is probable that Empedocles did not conceal his consciousness of possessing extraordinary intellectual powers, and of rising above the limited capacities of the mass of mankind; so that we need not wonder at his having been considered by his countrymen in Sicily as a person endowed with supernatural and prophetic gifts. Among the sharpsighted and sceptical Ionians, who were always seeking to penetrate into the natural causes of appearances, such an opinion could scarcely have gained ground at this time. But the Dorians in Sicily were as yet accustomed to connect all new events with their ancient belief in the gods, and to conceive them in the spirit of their religious traditions.

The poem of Empedocles upon nature also bears the mark of enthusiasm, both in its epic language and the nature of its contents. At the beginning of it he said, that fate and the divine will had decreed that, if one of the gods should be betrayed into defiling his hands with blood, he should be condemned to wander about for thirty thousand years, far removed from the immortals. He then described himself to have been exiled from heaven, for having engaged in deadly conflict, and committed murder.[2] As, therefore, since the heroic times of Greece, a fugitive murderer required an expiation and purification; so a god ejected from heaven, and condemned to appear in the likeness of a man, required some purification that might enable him to resume his original high estate. This purification was supposed to be in part accomplished by the lofty contemplations of the poem, which was hence—either wholly or in part—called a song of expiation (καθαρμοί). According to the idea of the transmigration of souls, Empedocles supposed that, since his exile from heaven, he had been a shrub, a fish, a bird, a boy, and a girl. For the present, ' the powers which conduct souls' had borne him to the dark cavern of the earth;[3] and from

---

[1] Empedocles Agrigentinus, de vitâ et philosophiâ ejus exposuit, carminum reliquias collegit Sturz. Lipsiæ. 1805, T. I. p. 49.

[2] Fragment ap. Plutarch. de exilio. c. 17. (p. 607). ap. Sturz. v. 3. sqq.

[3] V. 362. and v. 9. in Sturz (from Diog. Laërt. VIII. 77. and Porphyr. de antro nymph. c. 8), ought evidently to be connected in the manner indicated in the text.

hence the return to divine honours was open to him, as to seers and poets, and other benefactors of mankind. The great doctrine, that *Love* is the power which formed the world, was probably announced to him by the Muse whom he invoked, as the secret by the contemplation of which he was to emancipate himself from all the baneful effects of discord.[1]

The physical philosophy of Empedocles has much in common with that of the Eleatics; and hence Zeno is said to have commented on his poem, that is, probably, he reduced it to the strict principles of the Eleatic school. It has also much in common with the philosophy of Anaxagoras; which would itself scarcely have arisen, if the Eleatic doctrine of eternal existence had not been already opposed to that of Heraclitus concerning the flux of things. Empedocles also denied the possibility of creation and destruction, and saw in the processes so called nothing more than combination and separation of parts; like the Eleatics, he held the doctrine of an eternal and imperishable existence. But he considered this existence as having different natures; inasmuch as he supposed that there are four elements of things. To these he gave mythological names, calling fire *the all-penetrating Zeus,* air, *the life-giving Here;* earth (as being the gloomy abode of exiled spirits), *Aidoneus;* and water, by a name of his own, *Nestis.* These four elements he supposed to be governed by two principles, one positive and one negative, that is to say, connecting, creating love, and dissolving, destroying discord. By the working of discord the world was disturbed from its original condition, when all things were at rest in the form of a globe, ' the divine sphærus ;' and a series of changes began, from which the existing world gradually arose. Empedocles described and explained, with much ingenuity, the beautiful structure of the universe, and treated of the nature of the earth's surface and its produc-

---

[1] This is proved by the passage in Simplic. ad *Phys.* f. 34. v. 52. sq. Sturz. :

Καὶ φιλότης ἐν τοῖσιν, ἴση μῆκός τε πλάτος τε.

τὴν σὺ νόῳ δέρκευ, μηδ' ὄμμασιν ἧσο τεθηπώς, &c.

In like manner the Muse says to the poet :

σὺ οὖν ἐπεὶ ὧδ' ἐλιάσθης,

πεύσεαι· οὐ πλεῖόν γε βροτείη μῆτις ὄρωρεν.

v. 331. from Sext. Empir. *adv. math.* VII. 122. sq. The invocation of the Muse is in Sext. Empir. *adv. Math.* VII. 124. v. 341. sq.

tions. In these inquiries he appears to have anticipated some of the discoveries of modern science. Thus, for example, his doctrine that mountains and rocks had been raised by a sub-terranean fire[1] is an anticipation of the theory of elevation esta-blished by recent geologists; and his descriptions of the rude and grotesque forms of the earliest animals seem almost to show that he was acquainted with the fossil remains of extinct races.[2]

§ 14. We now turn to that class of ancient philosophers which in Greece itself was called the Italic;[3] the most obscure region of the Greek philosophy, as we have no accounts of in-dividual writings, and scarcely even of individual writers, belonging to it. Nevertheless, the personal history of PYTHA-GORAS, the most conspicuous name among the Italic philosophers, is not so obscure as to compel us to resort to the hypothesis of an antehistorical Pythagoras, from whom a sort of Pythagorean religion, together with the primitive constitution of the Italian cities, was derived, and who had been celebrated in very early legends as the instructor of Numa and the author of an ancient civilization and philosophy in Italy.[4] The Greeks who first made mention of Pythagoras (viz., Heraclitus and Xenophanes) do not speak of him as a fabulous person. Heraclitus, in particular, mentions him as a rival whose method of seeking wisdom differed from his own. There are, moreover, good grounds for believing the general tradition of antiquity, that Pythagoras, the son of Mnesarchus, was not a native of the country in which he acquired such extraordinary honour, but of the Ionic island of Samos, and that he migrated to Italy when Samos fell under the tyrannical dominion of Polycrates; which migration is placed, with much probability, in Olymp. 62. 4. B.C. 529.[5] Considering the different characters and dis-

---

[1] Plutarch, de primo frig. c. 19. (p. 953).
[2] See Ælian, Hist. An. XVI. 29. ap. Sturz. v. 14 sq.
[3] This appellative is an instance of the limited sense of the name Italia, accord-ing to which it only comprehends the later Bruttii and Calabria. Otherwise the Eleatics could not be distinguished from the Italic school.
[4] Niebuhr's hypothesis. See his Hist. of Rome, vol. I. p. 165. 244. ed. 2. [p. 158. Eng. transl. last ed.].
[5] That the ancient chronologists in Cicero de Republ. II. 15, fixed Ol. 62. 4, as the year of the arrival of Pythagoras in Italy, is proved by the context. Ol. 62. 1, is given as the first year of the reign of Polycrates. Comp. Ch. XIII. § 11.

positions of the Hellenic races, it was natural that philosophy, which seeks to give independence to the mind, and to free it from prejudices and traditions, should always receive its first impulse from Ionians. The notion of gaining wisdom by one's own efforts was exclusively Ionic; the Dorians laid greater stress on the traditions of their fathers, and their hereditary religion and morality, than on their own speculations. It is probable that Pythagoras, before he left the Ionic Samos, and came to Italy, was not very different from such men as Thales and Anaximander. He had doubtless an inquiring mind, and habits of careful observation; and he probably combined with mathematical studies (which made their first steps among the Ionians) a knowledge of natural history and of other subjects, which he increased by travelling.[1] Thus Heraclitus not only includes him among persons of much knowledge,[2] but says of him as follows: ' Pythagoras, the son of Mnesarchus, has made more inquiries than any other man; he has acquired wisdom, knowledge, and mischievous refinement.'[3] But since this Ionic philosopher found himself, on his arrival at Croton, among a mixed population of Dorians and Achæans; and since his adherents in the neighbouring Doric states were constantly increasing; it is difficult to say whether the opinions and dispositions which he had brought with him from Samos, or the opinions and dispositions of the citizens of Croton and the neighbouring cities, who received his doctrines, exercised the greater influence upon him. Thus much, however, is evident, that speculations upon nature, prompted by the mere love of truth, could not be in question; so that the principal efforts of Pythagoras and his adherents were directed to practical life, especially to the regulation of political institutions according to general views of the order of human society. There is no doubt that Croton, Caulonia, Metapontum, and other cities in Lower Italy, were long governed, under the superintendence of

---

[1] That Pythagoras acquired his wisdom in Egypt cannot be safely inferred from Isocrat. *Busir.* § 30; the Busiris being a mere rhetorical and sophistical exercise, in which little regard would be paid to historical truth.

[2] See above, § 7.

[3] Πυθαγόρης Μνησάρχου ἱστορίην ἤσκησεν ἀνθρώπων μάλιστα πάντων . . . ἐποιήσατο ἑαυτοῦ σοφίην, πολυμαθίην, κακοτεχνίην. Diog. Laërt. VIII. 6. ἱστορίη, according to the Ionic meaning of the word, is an inquiry founded upon interrogation.

Pythagorean societies, upon aristocratic principles; and that they enjoyed prosperity at home, and were formidable, from their strength, to foreign states. And even when, after the destruction of Sybaris by the Crotoniats (Olymp. 67. 3. B.C. 510.), dissensions between the nobles and the people concerning the division of the territory had led to a furious persecution of the Pythagoreans ; yet the times returned when Pythagoreans were again at the head of Italian cities ; for instance, Archytas, the contemporary of Socrates and Plato, administered the affairs of Tarentum with great renown.[1] It appears that the individual influence of Pythagoras was exercised by means of lectures, or of sayings uttered in a compressed and symbolical form, which he communicated only to his friends, or by means of the establishment and direction of the Pythagorean associations and their peculiar mode of life. For there is no authentic account of a single writing of Pythagoras, and no fragment which appears to be genuine. The works which have been attributed to Pythagoras, such as ' the Sacred Discourse' (ἱερὸς λόγος), are chiefly forgeries of those Orphic theologers who imitated the Pythagorean manner, and whose relation to the genuine Pythagoreans has been explained in a former chapter.[2] The fundamental doctrines of the Pythagorean philosophy ; viz., that the essence of all things rests upon a numerical relation ; that the world subsists by the harmony, or conformity, of its different elements; that *numbers* are the principle of all that exists ;—all these must have originated with the master of the school. But the scientific development of these doctrines, in works composed in the Doric dialect (as we find them in the extant fragments of Philolaus, who lived about the 90th Olympiad, B.C. 420), belongs to a later period. The doctrines so developed are, that the essence of things consists, not, according to the ancient Ionians, in an animate substance, nor,

---

[1] It appears that there was a second expulsion of the Pythagoreans from Italy after the time of Archytas. Lysis, the Pythagorean, seems to have gone, in consequence of it, to Thebes, where he became the teacher of Epaminondas. The jokes about the Pythagoreans and the Πυθαγορίζοντες, with their strange and singular mode of life, are not earlier than the middle and new comedy, that is, than the 100th Olympiad ; this sort of philosophers did not previously exist in Greece. Meineke, *Quæst. Scen.* I. p. 24. See Theocrit. *Id.* XIV. 5.

[2] Ch. XVI. § 5.

according to the more recent Ionians, in a union of mind and matter, but in a form dependent upon fixed proportions ; and that the regularity of these proportions is itself a principle of production. The doctrines in question derived much support from mathematical studies, which were introduced by Pythagoras into Italy, and, as is well-known, were much advanced by him, until they were there first made an important part of education. The study of music also promoted the Pythagorean opinions, in two ways ; *theoretically,* because the effects of the relations of numbers were clearly seen in the power of the notes ; and *practically,* because singing to the cithara, as used by the Pythagoreans, seemed best fitted to produce that mental repose and harmony of soul which the Pythagoreans considered the highest object of education.

CHAPTER XVIII.

THE EARLY GREEK HISTORIANS.

§ 1. High antiquity of history in Asia; causes of its comparative lateness among the Greeks. § 2. Origin of history among the Greeks. The Ionians, particularly the Milesians, took the lead. § 3. Mythological historians; Cadmus, Acusilaus. § 4. Extensive geographical knowledge of Hecatæus; his freer treatment of native traditions. § 5. Pherecydes; his genealogical arrangement of traditions and history. § 6. Charon; his chronicles of general and special history. § 7. Hellanicus; a learned inquirer into mythical and true history. Beginning of chronological researches. § 8. Xanthus, an acute observer. Dionysius of Miletus, the historian of the Persian wars. § 9. General remarks on the composition and style of the logographers.

§ 1. IT is a remarkable fact, that a nation so intellectual and cultivated as the Greeks, should have been so long without feeling the want of a correct record of its transactions in war and peace.

From the earliest times the East had its annals and chronicles. That Egypt possessed a history ascending to a very remote antiquity, not formed of mythological materials, but based upon accurate chronological records, is proved by the extant remains of the work of Manetho.[1] The sculptures on buildings, with their explanatory inscriptions, afforded a history of the priests and kings, authenticated by names and numbers; and we have still hopes that this will hereafter be completely deciphered. The kingdom of Babylon also possessed a very ancient history of its princes; which Berosus imparted to the Greeks,[2] as Manetho did the Egyptian history. Ahasuerus is described, in the book of Esther, as causing the benefactors of

---

[1] Manetho, high-priest at Heliopolis in Egypt, wrote under Ptolemy Philadelphus (284 B.C). three books of *Ægyptiaca*.

[2] Berosus of Chaldæa wrote under Antiochus Theos (262 B.C.) a work called *Babylonica* or *Chaldaica*.

his throne to be registered in his chronicle,[1] which was read to him in nights when he could not sleep. Similar registers were perhaps kept many centuries earlier at the courts of Ecbatana and Babylon. The ancient sculptures of central Asia have likewise the same historical character as those of Egypt: they record military expeditions, treaties, pacifications of kingdoms, and the tributes of subject provinces. From the discoveries which have been recently made, it may be expected that many more sculptures of this description will be found in different parts of the ancient kingdom of Assyria. The early concentration of vast masses of men in enormous cities; the despotic form of the government; and the great influence exercised by the events of the court upon the weal and woe of the entire population, directed the attention of millions to *one* point, and imparted a deep and extensive interest to the journal of the monarch's life. Even, however, without these incentives, which are peculiar to a despotic form of government, the people of Israel, from the early union of its tribes around one sanctuary, and under one law, (for the custody of which a numerous priesthood was appointed,) recorded and preserved very ancient and venerable historical traditions.

The difference between these Oriental nations and the Greeks, with respect to their care in recording their history, is very great. The Greeks evinced a careless and almost infantine indifference about the registering of passing events, almost to the time when they became one of the great nations of the world, and waged mighty wars with the ancient kingdoms of the East. The celebration of a bygone age, which imagination had decked with all its charms, engrossed the attention of the Greeks, and prevented it from dwelling on more recent events. The division of the nation into numerous small states, and the republican form of the governments, prevented a concentration of interest on particular events and persons; the attention to domestic affairs was confined within a narrow circle, the objects of which changed with every generation. No action, no event, before the great conflict between Greece and Persia, could be compared in interest with

---

[1] Βασιλικαὶ διφθέραι; from which Ctesias derived information. Diod. II. 32.

those great exploits of the mythical age, in which heroes from all parts of Greece were supposed to have borne a part; certainly none made so pleasing an impression upon all hearers. The Greeks required that a work read in public, and designed for general instruction and entertainment, should impart unmixed pleasure to the mind; but, owing to the dissensions between the Greek republics, their historical traditions could not but offend some, if they flattered others. In short, it was not till a late period that the Greeks outgrew their poetical mythology, and considered contemporary events as worthy of being thought of and written about. From this cause, the history of many transactions prior to the Persian war has perished; but, without its influence, Greek literature could never have become what it was. Greek poetry, by its purely fictitious character, and its freedom from the shackles of particular truth, acquired that general probability, on account of which Aristotle considers poetry as more philosophical than history.[1] Greek art, likewise, from the lateness of the period at which it descended from the ideal representation of gods and heroes to the portraits of real men, acquired a nobleness and beauty of form which it could never have otherwise attained. And, in fine, the intellectual culture of the Greeks in general would not have taken its liberal and elevated turn, if it had not rested on a poetical basis.

§ 2. Writing was probably known in Greece some centuries before the time of Cadmus of Miletus[2], the earliest Greek historian; but it had not been employed for the purpose of preserving any detailed historical record. The lists of the Olympic victors, and of the kings of Sparta and the prytanes of Corinth, which the Alexandrian critics considered sufficiently authentic to serve as the foundation of the early Greek chronology; ancient treaties and other contracts, which it was important to perpetuate in precise terms; determinations of boundaries, and other records of a like description, formed the first rudiments of a documentary history. Yet this was still very remote from a detailed chronicle of contemporary events.

---

[1] Aristot. *Poet.* 9.   [2] See above, ch. IV. § 5.

And even when, towards the end of the age of the Seven Sages, some writers of historical narratives in prose began to appear among the Ionians and the other Greeks, they did not select domestic and recent events. Instead of this, they began with accounts of distant times and countries, and gradually narrowed their view to a history of the Greeks of recent times. So entirely did the ancient Greeks believe that the daily discussion of common life and oral tradition were sufficient records of the events of their own time and country.

The Ionians, who throughout this period were the daring innovators and indefatigable discoverers in the field of intellect, took the lead in history. They were also the first, who, satiated with the childish amusement of mythology, began to turn their keen and restless eyes on all sides, and to seek new matter for thought and composition. The Ionians had a peculiar delight in varied and continuous narration. Nor is it to be overlooked, that the first Ionian who is mentioned as a *historian*, was a *Milesian*. Miletus, the birth-place of the earliest philosophers; flourishing by its industry and commerce; the centre of the political movements produced by the spirit of Ionian independence; and the spot in which the native dialect was first formed into written Greek prose; was evidently fitted to be the cradle of historical composition in Greece. If the Milesians had not, together with their neighbours of Asia Minor, led a life of too luxurious enjoyment; if they had known how to retain the severe manners and manly character of the ancient Greeks, in the midst of the refinements and excitements of later times; it is probable that Miletus, and not Athens, would have been the teacher of the world.

§ 3. CADMUS OF MILETUS is mentioned as the earliest historian, and, together with Pherecydes of Syros, as the earliest writer of prose. His date cannot be placed much before the 60th Olympiad, B.C. 540;[1] he wrote a history of the foundation of Miletus (Κτίσις Μιλήτου), which embraced the whole of Ionia. The subject of this history lay in the dim period, from which only a few oral traditions of an historical kind, but intimately connected with mythical notions, had been

---

[1] See Clinton, *F. H.* Vol. II. p. 368, sqq.

preserved. The genuine work of Cadmus seems to have been early lost; the book which bore his name in the time of Dionysius (that is, the Augustan age) was considered a forgery.[1]

The next historian, in order of time, to Cadmus, was ACUSILAUS OF ARGOS. Although by descent a Dorian, he wrote his history in the Ionic dialect, because the Ionians were the founders of the historical style: a practice universally followed in Greek literature. Acusilaus confined his attention to the mythical period. His object was to collect into a short and connected narrative all the events from the formation of chaos to the end of the Trojan war. It was said of him that he translated Hesiod into prose:[2] an expression which serves to characterise his work. He appears, however, to have related many legends differently from Hesiod, and in the tone of the Orphic theologers of his own time.[3] He seems to have written nothing which can properly be called history.

§ 4. HECATÆUS OF MILETUS, the Ionian, was of a very different character of mind. With regard to his date, we know that he was a man of great consideration at the time when the Ionians wished to attempt a revolt against the Persians under Darius (Olymp. 69. 2. B.C. 503). At that time he came forward in the council of Aristagoras, and dissuaded the undertaking, enumerating the nations which were subject to the Persian king, and all his warlike forces. But if they determined to revolt, he advised them to endeavour, above all things, to maintain the sea by a large fleet, and for this purpose to take the treasures from the temple of Branchidæ.[4] This advice proves Hecatæus to have been a prudent and sagacious man, who understood the true situation of things. Hecatæus did not share the prevalent interest about the primitive history of

---

[1] Concerning Xanthus and all the following historians, see the paper 'On certain early Greek historians mentioned by Dionysius of Halicarnassus,' in the *Museum Criticum*, Vol. I. p. 80, 216; Vol. II. p. 90.

[2] Clem. Alex. *Strom.* VI. p. 629 A.

[3] Ch. XVI. § 4, note. For the fragments of Acusilaus see Sturz's edition of Pherecydes.

[4] Herod. V. 36, who calls him Ἑκαταῖος ὁ λογοποιός. The times of the birth and death of Hecatæus are fixed with less certainty at Olymp. 57, and Olymp. 75. 4.

his nation, and still less had he the infantine and undoubting faith which was exhibited by the Argive Acusilaus. He says, in an extant fragment[1]—'Thus says Hecatæus the Milesian: these things I write, as they seem to me to be true; for the stories of the Greeks are manifold and ludicrous, as it appears to me.' He also shows traces of that perverse system of interpretation which seeks to transmute the marvels of fable into natural events; as, for example, he explained Cerberus as a serpent which inhabited the promontory of Tænarum. But his attention was peculiarly directed to passing events and the nature of the countries and kingdoms with which Greece began to entertain intimate relations. He had travelled much, like Herodotus, and had in particular collected much information about Egypt. Herodotus often corrects his statements; but by so doing he recognises Hecatæus as the most important of his predecessors. Hecatæus perpetuated the results of his geographical and ethnographical researches in a work entitled 'Travels round the Earth' ($\Pi\epsilon\rho\acute{\iota}o\delta o\varsigma$ $\gamma\tilde{\eta}\varsigma$), by which a description of the coasts of the Mediterranean Sea and of southern Asia as far as India was understood. The author began with Greece, proceeding in a book, entitled 'Europe,' to the west, and in another, entitled ' Asia,' to the east.[2] Hecatæus also improved and completed the map of the earth sketched by Anaximander;[3] it must have been this map which Aristagoras of Miletus brought to Sparta before the Ionian revolt, and upon which he showed the king of Sparta the countries, rivers, and principal cities of the East. Besides this work, another is ascribed to Hecatæus, which is sometimes called ' Histories,' sometimes ' Genealogies,' and of which four books are cited. Into this work, Hecatæus admitted many of the genealogical legends of the Greeks; and, notwithstanding his contempt for old fables, he laid great stress

---

[1] See Demetr. de Elocut. § 12. Historicorum Græc. Antiq. Fragmenta, coll. F. Creuzer, p. 15.

[2] Three hundred and thirty-one fragments of this work are collected in Hecatæi Milesii fragmenta ed. R. H. Klausen. Berolini, 1830. It appears in some cases to have received additions since its first publication, as was commonly the case with manuals of this kind. Thus Hecatæus Fr. 27 mentions Capua, which name, according to Livy, was given to Vulturnum in A.U.C. 315 (B.C. 447).

[3] This is certain from Agathemerus I. 1.

upon genealogies ascending to the mythological period; thus he made a pedigree for himself, in which his sixteenth ancestor was a god.[1] Genealogies would afford opportunities for introducing accounts of different periods; and Hecatæus certainly narrated many historical events in this work,[2] although he did not write a connected history of the period comprised in it. Hecatæus wrote in the pure Ionic dialect; his style had great simplicity, and was sometimes animated, from the vividness of his descriptions.[3]

§ 5. PHERECYDES also wrote on genealogies and mythical history, but did not extend his labours to geography and ethnography. He was born at Leros, a small island near Miletus, and afterwards went to Athens; whence he is sometimes called a Lerian, sometimes an Athenian. He flourished about the time of the Persian war. His writings comprehended a great portion of the mythical traditions; and, in particular, he gave a copious account, in a separate work, of the ancient times of Athens. He was much consulted by the later mythographers, and his numerous fragments must still serve as the basis of many mythological inquiries.[4] By following a genealogical line he was led from Philæus, the son of Ajax, down to Miltiades, the founder of the sovereignty in the Chersonesus; he thus found an opportunity of describing the campaign of Darius against the Scythians; concerning which we have a valuable fragment of his history.

§ 6. CHARON, a native of Lampsacus, a Milesian colony, also belongs to this generation,[5] although he mentioned some events which fell in the beginning of the reign of Artaxerxes, Olymp. 78. 4. B.C. 465.[6] Charon continued the researches of Hecatæus

---

[1] Herod. II. 143.   [2] As that in Herod. VI. 137.

[3] As in the fragment from Longinus *de Sublim.* 27. Creuzer. *Hist. Ant.* fr. p. 54.

[4] Sturz *Pherecydis fragmenta,* ed. altera. Lips. 1824. Whether the ten books cited by the ancients were published by Pherecydes himself in this order, or whether they were not separate short treatises of Pherecydes which had been collected by later editors and arranged as parts of one work, seems doubtful and difficult of investigation.

[5] Dionysius Halic. *de Thucyd. jud.* 5. p. 818. Reiske places Charon with Acusilaus, Hecatæus, and others, among the early; Hellanicus, Xanthus, and others, among the more recent predecessors of Thucydides.

[6] Plutarch. *Themist.* 27.

into eastern ethnography. He wrote (as was the custom of these ancient historians) separate works upon Persia, Lybia, Ethiopia, &c. He also subjoined the history of his own time, and he preceded Herodotus in narrating the events of the Persian war, although Herodotus nowhere mentions him. From the fragments of his writings which remain, it is manifest that his relation to Herodotus was that of a dry chronicler to a historian, under whose hands everything acquires life and character.[1] Charon wrote besides a chronicle[2] of his own country, as several of the early historians did, who were thence called *horographers*. Probably most of the ancient historians, whose names are enumerated by Dionysius of Halicarnassus, belonged to this class.[3]

§ 7. HELLANICUS OF MYTILENE was almost a contemporary of Herodotus; we know that at the beginning of the Peloponnesian war he was 65 years old,[4] and still continued to write. The character of Hellanicus as a mythographer and historian is essentially different from that of the early chroniclers, such as Acusilaus and Pherecydes; he has far more the character of a learned compiler, whose object is, not merely to note down events, but to arrange his materials and to correct the errors of others. Besides a number of writings upon particular legends and local fables, he composed a work entitled ' the Priestesses of Herè of Argos;' in which the women who had filled this priesthood were enumerated up to a very remote period (on no better authority than of certain obscure traditions), and various striking events of the heroic time were arranged in chronological order, according to this series. Hellanicus could hardly have been the first who ventured to make a list of this kind, and to dress it up with chronological dates. Before his time the priests and temple-attendants at Argos had perhaps employed their idle hours in compiling a series of the priestesses of Herè, and in explaining it by monuments supposed to be of great

---

[1] Charon's fragments are collected in Creuzer, *ibid.* p. 89, sq.

[2] Ὧροι, corresponding to the Latin *annales*, ought not to be confounded with ὅροι, *termini, limites.* See Schweighæuser ad. Athen. XI. p. 475 B. XII. 520 D.

[3] Eugeon of Samos (above Ch. XI. § 16), Deiochus of Proconnesus, Eudemus of Paros, Democles of Phigalia, Amelesagoras of Chalcedon (or Athens).

[4] The learned Pamphila in Gellius *N. A.* XV. 23.

antiquity.[1] The *Carneonicæ* of Hellanicus would be of more importance for our immediate purpose, as it contained a list of the victors in the musical and poetical contests of the Carnea at Sparta (from Olymp. 26. B.C. 676),[2] and was therefore one of the first attempts at literary history. The writings of Hellanicus contained a vast mass of matter; since, besides the works already mentioned, he wrote accounts of Phœnicia, Persia, and Egypt, and also a description of a journey to the renowned oracle of Zeus-Ammon in the desert of Libya, (the genuineness of which last work was however doubted). He also descended to the history of his own time, and described some of the events between the Persian and Peloponnesian wars, but briefly, and without chronological accuracy, according to the reproach of Thucydides.

§ 8. Among the contemporaries of Hellanicus was (according to the statement of Dionysius) XANTHUS, the son of Candaules of Sardis, a Lydian, but one who had received a Greek education. His work upon Lydia, written in the Ionic dialect, bears, in the few fragments which remain, the stamp of high excellence. Some valuable remarks upon the nature of the earth's surface in Asia Minor, which pointed partly to volcanic agency, and partly to the extension of the sea; and precise accounts of the distinctions between the Lydian races, are cited from it by Strabo and Dionysius.[3] The passages quoted by these writers bear unquestionable marks of genuineness; in later times, however, some spurious works were attributed to Xanthus. In particular, a work upon magic, which passed current under his name, and which treated of the religion and worship of Zoroaster, was indubitably a recent forgery.

A still greater uncertainty prevails with respect to the writings of DIONYSIUS OF MILETUS, inasmuch as the ancient

---

[1] Instances of similar catalogues of priests (in the concoction of which some pious fraud must have been employed) are the genealogy of the Butads, which was painted up in the temple of Athene Polias(Pausan. I. 26. 6, Plutarch X. *Orat.* 7), and which doubtless ascended to the ancient hero Butes; and the line of the priests of Poseidon at Halicarnassus, which begins with a son of Poseidon himself, in Boeckh, *Corp. Inscript. Gr.* No. 2655.

[2] See Ch. XII. § 2.

[3] The fragments in Creuzer, ubi sup. p. 135, sq.

writer of this name was confounded by the Greek critics themselves with a much later writer on mythology. It is certain that
the Dionysius, whom Diodorus follows in his account of the Greek
heroic age, belongs to the times of learning and historical
systems; he turns the whole heroic mythology into an historical
romance, in which great princes, captains, sages, and benefactors
of mankind take the places of the ancient heroes.[1] Of the works
which appear to belong to the ancient Dionysius, viz., the
Persian histories and the events after Darius (probably a
continuation of the former), nothing precise is known.

§ 9. To the Greek historians before Herodotus modern
scholars have given the common name of *logographers*, which
is applied by Thucydides to his predecessors. This term,
however, had not so limited a meaning among the ancients; as
logos signified any discourse in prose. Accordingly, the
Athenians gave the same name to writers of speeches, *i.e.*
persons who composed speeches for others, to be used in courts
of justice. It is however convenient to comprehend these
ancient Greek chroniclers under a common name, since they had
in many respects a common character. All were alike animated
by a desire of recording, for the instruction and entertainment
of their contemporaries, the accounts which they had heard or
collected. But they did this, without attempting, by ingenuity
of arrangement or beauty of style, to produce such an impression
as had been made by works of poetry. The first Greek to whom
it occurred that fiction was not necessary for this purpose, and
that a narrative of true facts might be made intensely interesting,
was Herodotus, the Homer of history.

---

[1] Whether this Dionysius is the Dionysius of Samos cited by Athenæus, who
wrote concerning the cyclus, or Dionysius Scytobrachion of Mytilene, has not been
completely determined.

CHAPTER XIX.

HERODOTUS.

§ 1. Events of the life of Herodotus. § 2. His travels. § 3. Gradual formation of his work. § 4. Its plan. § 5. Its leading ideas. § 6. Defects and excellencies of his historical researches. § 7. Style of his narrative; character of his language.

§ 1. HERODOTUS, the son of Lyxes, was, according to a statement of good authority,[1] born in Olymp. 74. 1. B.C. 484, in the period between the first and second Persian wars. His family was one of the most distinguished in the Doric colony of Halicarnassus, and thus became involved in the civil commotions of the city. Halicarnassus was at that time governed by the family of Artemisia, the princess who fought so bravely for the Persians in the battle of Salamis, that Xerxes declared that she was the only man among many women. Lygdamis, the son of Pisindelis, and grandson of Artemisia, was hostile to the family of Herodotus. He killed Panyasis, who was probably the maternal uncle of Herodotus, and who will be mentioned hereafter as one of the restorers of epic poetry; and he obliged Herodotus himself to take refuge abroad. His flight must have taken place about the eighty-second Olympiad, B.C. 452.

Herodotus repaired to Samos, the Ionic island, where probably some of his kinsmen resided.[2] Samos must be looked upon as the second home of Herodotus; in many passages of his work he shows a minute acquaintance with this island and its inhabitants, and he seems to take a pleasure in incidentally mentioning the part played by it in events of importance. It must have been in Samos that Herodotus imbibed the Ionic spirit which pervades his history. Herodotus likewise undertook from Samos the liberation of his native city from the yoke of Lygdamis; and he succeeded in the attempt; but the contest

---

[1] Of Pamphila in Gellius N. A. XV. 23.
[2] Panyasis too is called a Samian.

between the nobles and the commons having placed obstacles in the way of his well-intentioned plans, he once more forsook his native city.

Herodotus passed the latter years of his life at Thurii, the great Grecian settlement in Italy, to which so many distinguished men had intrusted their fortunes. It does not however follow from this account that Herodotus was among the first settlers of Thurii; the numbers of the original colonists doubtless received subsequent additions. It is certain that Herodotus did not go to Thurii till after the beginning of the Peloponnesian war; since at the beginning of it he must have been at Athens. He describes a sacred offering, which was on the Acropolis of Athens, by its position with regard to the Propylæa;[1] now the Propylæa were not finished till the year in which the Peloponnesian war began. Herodotus likewise evidently appears to adopt those views of the relations between the Greek states, which were diffused in Athens by the statesmen of the party of Pericles; and he states his opinion that Athens did not deserve, after her great exploits in the Persian war, to be so envied and blamed by the rest of the Greeks; which was the case just at the beginning of the Peloponnesian war.[2]

Herodotus settled quietly in Thurii, and devoted the leisure of his latter years entirely to his work. Hence he is frequently called by the ancients a Thurian, in reference to the composition of his history.

§ 2. In this short review of the life of Herodotus we have taken no notice of his travels, which are intimately connected with his literary labours. Herodotus did not visit different countries from the accidents of commercial business or political missions; his travels were undertaken from the pure spirit of inquiry, and for that age they were very extensive and important. Herodotus visited Egypt as high up as Elephantine, Libya, at least as far as the vicinity of Cyrene, Phœnicia, Babylon, and probably also Persia; the Greek states on the Cimmerian Bosporus, the contiguous country of the Scythians, as well as Colchis; besides which, he had resided in several states of Greece and

---

[1] Herod. V. 77.
[2] Compare Herod. VII. 139 with Thuc. II. 8.

Lower Italy, and had visited many of the temples, even the remote one of Dodona. The circumstance of his being, in his capacity of Halicarnassian, a subject of the king of Persia, must have assisted him materially in these travels ; an Athenian, or a Greek of any of the states which were in open revolt against Persia, would have been treated as an enemy, and sold as a slave. Hence it may be inferred that the travels of Herodotus, at least those to Egypt and Asia, were performed from Halicarnassus in his youth.

Herodotus, of course, made these inquiries with the view of imparting their results to his countrymen. But it is uncertain whether he had at that time formed the plan of connecting his information concerning Asia and Greece with the history of the Persian war, and of uniting the whole into one great work. When we consider that an intricate and extensive plan of this sort had hitherto been unknown in the historical writings of the Greeks, it can scarcely be doubted that the idea occurred to him at an advanced stage of his inquiries, and that in his earlier years he had not raised his mind above the conception of such works as those of Hecatæus, Charon, and others of his predecessors and contemporaries. Even at a later period of his life, when he was composing his great work, he contemplated writing a separate book upon Assyria ('Ασσύριοι λόγοι); and it seems that this book was in existence at the time of Aristotle.[1] In fact, Herodotus might also have made separate books out of the accounts of Egypt, Persia, and Scythia given in his history ; and he would, no doubt, have done so, if he had been content to tread in the footsteps of the logographers who preceded him.

§ 3. It is stated that Herodotus recited his history at different festivals. This statement is, in itself, perfectly credible, as the Greeks of this time, when they had finished a composition with care, and had given it an attractive form, reckoned more upon oral delivery than upon solitary reading. Thucydides, blaming the historians who preceded him, describes them as courting the

---

[1] Aristotle, *Hist. An.* VIII. 18 mentions the account of the siege of Nineveh in Herodotus (for, although the manuscripts generally read *Hesiod*, *Herodotus* is evidently the more suitable name) ; that is, undoubtedly, the siege which Herodotus, I. 106, promises to describe in his separate work on Assyria (comp. I. 184.)

transient applause of an audience.[1] The ancient chronologists have also preserved the exact date of a recitation, which took place at the great Panathenæa at Athens, in Olymp. 83. 3. B.C. 446 (when Herodotus was thirty-eight years old). The collections of Athenian decrees contained a decree proposed by Anytus (ψήφισμα Ἀνύτου), from which it appeared that Herodotus received a reward of ten talents from the public treasury.[2] There is less authority for the story of a recitation at Olympia ; and least authority of all for the well-known anecdote, that Thucydides was present at it as a boy, and that he shed tears, drawn forth by his own intense desire for knowledge, and his deep interest in the narrative. To say nothing of the many intrinsic improbabilities of this story, so many anecdotes were invented by the ancients in order to bring eminent men of the same pursuits into connexion with each other, that it is impossible to give any faith to it, without the testimony of more trustworthy witnesses.

The public readings of Herodotus (such as that at the Panathenaic festival) must have been confined to detached portions of his subject, which he afterwards introduced into his work ; for example, the history and description of Egypt, or the accounts concerning Persia. His great historical work could not have been composed till the time of the Peloponnesian war. Indeed, his history, and particularly the four last books, are so full of references and allusions to events which occurred in the first period of the war,[3] that he appears to have been diligently occupied with the composition or final revision of it at this time. It is however very questionable whether Herodotus lived into the second period of the Peloponnesian war.[4] At all events, he must have been

---

[1] Thucyd. I. 21.

[2] Plutarch de Malign. Herod. 26.

[3] As the expulsion of the Æginetans, the surprise of Platæa, the Archidamian war, and other events. The passages of Herodotus which could not have been written before this time are, III. 160; VI. 91, 98; VII. 137, 233 ; IX. 73.

[4] The passage in IX. 73, which states that the Lacedæmonians, in their devastations of Attica, always spared Decelea and kept at a distance from it (Δεκελέης ἀπέχεσθαι), cannot be reconciled with the siege of Decelea by Agis in Olymp. 91, 3, B.C. 413. The passages VI. 98 and VII. 170, also contain marks of having been written before this time. On the other hand, the passage I. 130 appears to refer to the insurrection of the Medes in Olymp. 93, 1, B.C. 408 (Xen. Hell. I. 2, 19): on this supposition, however, it is strange that Herodotus should have called Darius Nothus by the simple name Darius without any distinctive adjunct.

occupied with his work till his death, for it seems to be in an unfinished state. There is no obvious reason why Herodotus should have carried down the war between the Greeks and Persians to the taking of Sestos, without mentioning any subsequent event of it.[1] Besides, in one place he promises to give the particulars of an occurrence in a future part of his work;[2] a promise which is nowhere fulfilled.

§ 4. The plan of the work of Herodotus is formed upon a notion which, though it cannot in strictness be called true, was very current in his time, and had even been developed, after their fashion, by the learned of Persia and Phœnicia, who were not unacquainted with Greek mythology. The notion is that of an ancient enmity between the Greeks and the nations of Asia. The learned of the East considered the rapes of Io, Medea, and Helen, and the wars which grew out of those events, as single acts of this great conflict; and their main object was to determine which of the two parties had first used violence against the other. Herodotus, however, soon drops these stories of old times, and turns to a prince whom he knows to have been the aggressor in his war against the Greeks. This is Crœsus, king of Lydia. He then proceeds to give a detailed account of the enterprises of Crœsus and the other events of his life; into which are interwoven as episodes, not only the early history of the Lydian kings and of their conflicts with the Greeks, but also some important passages in the history of the Greek states, particularly Athens and Sparta. In this manner Herodotus, in describing the first subjugation of the Greeks by an Asiatic power, at the same time points out the origin and progress of those states by which the Greeks were one day to be liberated. Meanwhile, the attack of Sardis by Cyrus brings the Persian power on the stage in the place of the Lydian; and the narrative proceeds to explain the rise of the Persian from the Median kingdom, and to describe its increase by the subjugation of the nations of Asia Minor

---

[1] It may, however, be urged against this view, that the secession of the Spartans and their allies, the formation of the alliance under the supremacy of Athens, and the change in the character of the war from defensive to offensive, made the taking of Sestos a distinctly marked epoch. See Thucyd. I. 89.

[2] Herod. VII. 213.

and the Babylonians. Whenever the Persians come in contact with other nations, an account, more or less detailed, is given of their history and peculiar usages. Herodotus evidently, as indeed he himself confesses,[1] strives to enlarge his plan by episodes; it is manifestly his object to combine with the history of the conflict between the East and West a vivid picture of the contending nations. Thus to the conquest of Egypt by Cambyses (Book II.) he annexes a description of the country, the people, and their history; the copiousness of which was caused by his fondness for Egypt, on account of its early civilization, and the stability of its peculiar institutions and usages. The history of Cambyses, of the false Smerdis, and of Darius, is continued in the same detailed manner (Book III.); and an account is given of the power of Samos, under Polycrates, and of his tragical end; by which the Persian power began to extend to the islands between Asia and Europe. The institutions established by Darius at the beginning of his reign afford an opportunity of surveying the whole kingdom of Persia, with all its provinces, and their large revenues. With the expedition of Darius against the Scythians (which Herodotus evidently considers as a retaliation for the former incursions of the Scythians into Asia) the Persian power begins to spread over Europe (Book IV.). Herodotus then gives a full account of the north of Europe, of which his knowledge was manifestly much more extensive than that of Hecatæus; and he next relates the great expedition of the Persian army, which, although it did not endanger the freedom of the Scythians, first opened a passage into Europe to the Persians. The kingdom of Persia now stretches on one side to Scythia, on the other over Egypt to Cyrenaica. A Persian army is called in by Queen Pheretime against the Barcæans; which gives Herodotus an opportunity of relating the history of Cyrene, and describing the Libyan nations, as an interesting companion to his description of the nations of northern Europe. While (Book V.) a part of the Persian army, which had

---

[1] Herod. IV. 30. Thus he speaks of the Libyans in the 4th book, only because he thinks that the expedition of the Satrap Aryandes against Barca was in fact directed against all the nations of Libya. See IV. 167.

remained behind after the Scythian expedition, reduces a
portion of the Thracians and the little kingdom of Macedonia
under the power of the great king, the great Ionian revolt
arises from causes connected with the Scythian expedition,
which brings still closer the decisive struggle between Greece
and Persia. Aristagoras, the tyrant of Miletus, seeks aid in
Sparta and Athens for the Ionians; whereupon the historian
takes occasion to continue the history of these and other Greek
states, from the point where he had left it (Book I.); and in
particular to describe the rapid rise of the Athenians, after they
had thrown off the yoke of the Pisistratids. The enterprising
spirit of the young republic of Athens is also shown in the
interest taken by it in the Ionian revolt, which was begun in a
rash and inconsiderate manner, and, having been carried on
without sufficient vigour, terminated in a complete defeat
(Book VI.). Herodotus next pursues the constantly increasing
causes of enmity between Greece and Persia; among which is
the flight of the Spartan king Demaratus to Darius. To this
event he annexes a detailed explanation of the relations and
enmities of the Greek states, in the period just preceding the
first Persian war. The expedition against Eretria and Athens
was the first blow struck by Persia at the mother country of
Greece, and the battle of Marathon was the first glorious
signal that this Asiatic power, hitherto unchecked in its
encroachments, was there at length to find a limit. From
this point the narrative runs in a regular channel, and pursues
to the end the natural course of events; the preparations for
war, the movements of the army, and the campaign against
Greece itself (Book VII.). Even here, however, the narrative
moves at a slow pace; and thus keeps the expectation upon
the stretch. The march and mustering of the Persian army
give full time and opportunity for forming a distinct and
complete notion of its enormous force; and the negotiations of
the Greek states afford an equally clear conception of their
jealousies and dissensions; facts which make the ultimate issue
of the contest appear the more astonishing. After the preliminary and undecisive battles of Thermopylæ and Artemisium
(Book VIII.), comes the decisive battle of Salamis, which is
described with the greatest vividness and animation. This is

followed (in Book IX.) by the battle of Platæa, drawn with the same distinctness, particularly as regards all its antecedents and circumstances ; together with the contemporaneous battle of Mycale and the other measures of the Greeks for turning their victory to account.   Although the work seems unfinished, it concludes with a sentiment which cannot have been placed casually at the end ; viz. that (as the great Cyrus was supposed to have said) ' It is not always the richest and most fertile country which produces the most valiant men.'

§ 5. In this manner Herodotus gives a certain unity to his history ; and, notwithstanding the extent of his subject, which comprehends nearly all the nations of the world at that time known, the narrative is constantly advancing.   The history of Herodotus has an epic character, not only from the equable and uninterrupted flow of the narrative, but also from certain pervading ideas, which give an uniform tone to the whole.   The principal of these is the idea of a fixed destiny, of a wise arrangement of the world, which has prescribed to every being his path ; and which allots ruin and destruction, not only to crime and violence, but to excessive power and riches, and the overweening pride which is their companion.   In this consists *the envy of the Gods* (φθόνος τῶν θεῶν), so often mentioned by Herodotus ; by the other Greeks usually called *the divine Nemesis*.   He constantly adverts, in his narrative, to the influence of this divine power, the *Dæmonion*, as he also calls it.   Thus he shows how the deity visits the sins of the ancestors upon their descendants ; how the human mind is blinded by arrogance and recklessness ; how man rushes, as it were, wilfully upon his own destruction ; and how oracles, which ought to be warning voices against violence and insolence, mislead from their ambiguity, when interpreted by blind passion.   Besides the historical narrative itself, the scattered speeches serve rather to enforce certain general ideas, particularly concerning the envy of the gods and the danger of pride, than to characterize the dispositions, views, and modes of thought of the persons represented as speaking.   In fact, these speeches are rather the lyric than the dramatic part of the history of Herodotus ; and if we compare it with the different parts of a Greek tragedy, they correspond, not to the dialogue, but to the choral songs.

Herodotus lastly shows his awe of the divine Nemesis by his moderation and the firmness with which he keeps down the ebullitions of national pride. For, if the eastern princes by their own rashness bring destruction upon themselves, and the Greeks remain the victors, yet he describes the East, with its early civilization, as highly worthy of respect and admiration; he even points out traits of greatness of character in the hostile kings of Persia; shows his countrymen how they often owed their successes to divine providence and external advantages, rather than to their own valour and ability; and, on the whole, is anything but a panegyrist of the exploits of the Greeks. So little indeed has he this character, that when the rhetorical historians of later times had introduced a more pretending account of these events, the simple, faithful, and impartial Herodotus was reproached with being actuated by a spirit of calumny, and with seeking to detract from the heroic acts of his countrymen.[1]

§ 6. Since Herodotus saw the working of a divine agency in all human events, and considered the exhibition of it as the main object of his history, his aim is entirely different from that of a historian who regards the events of life merely with reference to *man*. Herodotus is, in truth, a theologian and a poet as well as an historian. The individual parts of his work are treated entirely in this spirit. His aim is not merely to give the results of common experience in human life. His mind is turned to the extraordinary and the marvellous. In this respect his work bears an uniform colour. The great events which he relates—the gigantic enterprises of princes, the unexpected turns of fortune, and other marvellous occurrences—harmonize with the accounts of the astonishing buildings and other works of the East, of the multifarious and often singular manners of the different nations, the surprising phenomena of nature, and the rare productions and animals of the remote regions of the world. Herodotus presented a picture of strange and astonishing things to his mobile and curious countrymen. It were vain to deny that Herodotus,

---

[1] Plutarch's Treatise περὶ τῆς Ἡροδότου κακοηθείας, concerning the malignity of Herodotus.

when he does not describe things which he had himself
observed, was often deceived by the misrepresentations of priests,
interpreters, and guides; and, above all, by that propensity to
boasting and that love of the marvellous which are so common
in the East.[1]   Yet, without his singlehearted simplicity, his
disposition to listen to every remarkable account, and his admiration (undisturbed by the national prejudices of a Greek) for
the wonders of the Eastern world, Herodotus would never have
imparted to us many valuable accounts, in which recent
inquirers have discovered substantial truth, though mixed with
fable.   How often have modern travellers, naturalists, and
geographers, had occasion to admire the truth and correctness
of the observations and information which are contained in the
seemingly marvellous narratives of Herodotus !   It is fortunate
that he was guided by the maxim which he mentions in his
account of the circumnavigation of Africa in the reign of Necho.
Having expressed his disbelief of the statement that the sailors
had the sun on their right hand, he adds: 'I must say what
has been told to me ; but I need not therefore believe all, and
this remark applies to my whole work.'

Herodotus must have completely familiarized himself with the
manners and modes of thought of the Oriental nations.   The
character of his mind and his style of composition also resemble
the Oriental type more than those of any other Greek ; and
accordingly his thoughts and expressions often remind us of the
writings of the Old Testament.   It cannot indeed be denied that
he has sometimes attributed to the eastern princes ideas which
were essentially Greek ; as, for example, when he makes the
seven grandees of the Persians deliberate upon the respective
advantages of monarchy, aristocracy, and democracy.[2]   But, on
the whole, Herodotus seizes the character of an Oriental monarch,
like Xerxes, with striking truth ; and transports us into the very
midst of the satellites of a Persian despot.   It would be more

---

[1] Aristotle, in his *Treatise on the Generation of Animals*, III. 5, calls him
'Ηρόδοτος ὁ μυθολόγος, ' Herodotus the story-teller.'

[2] Herod. III. 80. He afterwards (VI. 43) defends himself against the charge of
having represented a Persian as praising democracy, of which the Persians knew
nothing. This passage proves that a part at least of Book III. had been published
before the entire work was completed.

just to reproach Herodotus with a want of that political discernment, in judging the affairs of the Greek states, which had already
been awakened among the Athenian statesmen of his time.
Moreover, in the events arising from the situation and interests
of states, he lays too much stress on the feelings and passions of
particular individuals; and ascribes to Greek statesmen (as, for
instance, the two Cleisthenes of Sicyon and Athens, in reference
to their measures for the division of the people into new tribes)
motives entirely different from those by which they appear, on a
consideration of the case, to have been really actuated. He
likewise relates mere anecdotes and tales, by which the vulgar
explained (and still continue to explain) political affairs; where
politicians, such as Thucydides and Aristotle, exhibit the true
character of the transaction.

§ 7. But no dissertation upon the historical researches or the
style of Herodotus can convey an idea of the impression made
by reading his work. To those who have read it, all description
is superfluous. It is like hearing a person speak who has seen
and lived through an infinite variety of the most remarkable
things; and whose greatest delight consists in recalling the
images of the past, and perpetuating the remembrance of them.
He had eager and unwearied listeners, who were not impatient
to arrive at the end; and he could therefore complete every
separate portion of the history, as if it were an independent
narrative. He knew that he had in store other more attractive
and striking events; yet he did not hurry his course, as he dwelt
with equal pleasure on everything that he had seen or heard.
In this manner, the stream of his Ionic language flows on with
a charming facility. The character of his style (as is natural in
mere narration) is to connect the different sentences loosely together, with many phrases for the purpose of introducing,
recapitulating, or repeating a subject. These phrases are characteristic of oral discourse, which requires such contrivances, in
order to prevent the speaker, or the hearer, from losing the
thread of the story. In this, as in other respects, the language
of Herodotus closely approximates to oral narration; of all
varieties of prose, it is the furthest removed from a written style.
Long sentences, formed of several clauses, are for the most part
confined to speeches, where reasons and objections are compared,

conditions are stated, and their consequences developed.   But it must be confessed that where the logical connexion of different propositions is to be expressed, Herodotus mostly shows a want of skill, and produces no distinct conception of the mutual relations of the several members of the argument.   But, with all these defects, his style must be considered as the perfection of the *unperiodic style* (the λέξις εἰρομένη), the only style employed by his predecessors, the logographers.[1]   To these is to be added the tone of the Ionic dialect,—which Herodotus, although by birth a Dorian, adopted from the historians who preceded him,[2]—with its uncontracted terminations, its accumulated vowels, and its soft forms.   These various elements conspire to render the work of Herodotus a production as harmonious and as perfect in its kind as any human work can be.

---

[1] Demetrius *de Elocutione*, § 12.

[2] Nevertheless, according to Hermogenes, p. 513, the Ionic dialect of Hecatæus is alone quite pure; and the dialect of Herodotus is mixed with other expressions.

SECOND PERIOD OF GREEK LITERATURE.

CHAPTER XX.

LITERARY PREDOMINANCE OF ATHENS.

§ 1. Early formation of a national literature in Greece. § 2. Athens subsequentl takes the lead in literature and art. Her fitness for this purpose. § 3. Concurrence of the political circumstances of Athens to the same end. Solon. The Pisistratids. § 4. Great increase in the power of Athens after the Persian war. § 5. Administration and policy of Pericles, particularly with respect to art and literature. § 6. Seeds of degeneracy in the Athenian Commonwealth at its most flourishing period. § 7. Causes and modes of the degeneracy. § 8. Literature and art were not affected by the causes of moral degeneracy.

§ 1. GREEK literature, so far as we have hitherto followed its progress, was a common property of the different races of the nation; each race cultivating that species of composition which was best suited to its dispositions and capacities, and impressing on it a corresponding character. In this manner the town of Miletus in Ionia, the Æolians in the island of Lesbos, the colonies in Magna Græcia and Sicily, as well as the Greeks of the mother country, created new forms of poetry and eloquence. The various sorts of excellence thus produced, did not, after the age of the Homeric poetry, remain the exclusive property of the race among which they originated; as popular poems composed in a peculiar dialect are known only to the tribe by whom the dialect is spoken. Among the Greeks a *national literature* was early formed; every literary work in the Greek language, in whatever dialect it might be composed, was enjoyed by the whole Greek nation. The songs of the Lesbian Sappho aroused the feelings of Solon in his old age, notwithstanding their foreign Æolian dialect;[1] and the researches

---

[1] Ch. XIII. § 10.

of the philosophers of Elea in Œnotria influenced the thoughts of Anaxagoras when living at Miletus and Athens : [1] whence it may be inferred that the fame of remarkable writers soon spread through Greece at that time. Even in an earlier age, the poets and sages used to visit certain cities, which were considered almost as theatres, where they could bring their powers and acquirements into public notice. Among these, Sparta stood the highest, down to the time of the Persian war ; for the Lacedæmonians, though they produced little themselves, were considered as sagacious and sound judges of art and philosophy.[2] Accordingly, the principal poets, musicians, and philosophers of those times are related to have passed a part of their lives at Sparta.[3]

§ 2. But the literature of Greece necessarily assumed a different form, when Athens, raised as well by her political power and other external circumstances as by the mental qualities of her citizens, acquired the rank of a *capital* of Greece, with respect to literature and art. Not only was her copious native literature received with admiration by all the Greeks, but her judgment and taste were predominant in all things relating to language and the arts, and decided what should be generally recognised as the classical literature of Greece, long before the Alexandrine critics had prepared their canons. There is no more important epoch in the history of the Greek intellect than the time when Athens obtained this pre-eminence over her sister states.

The character of the Athenians peculiarly fitted them to take this lead. The Athenians were Ionians; and, when their brethren separated from them in order to found the twelve cities on the coast of Asia Minor, the foundations of the peculiar character of Ionic civilization had already been laid. The dialect of the Ionians was distinguished from that of the Dorians and Æolians by clear and broad marks : the worship

---

[1] Chap. XVII. § 8.

[2] Aristot., *Polit.* VIII. 5. οἱ Λάκωνες . . . . οὐ μανθάνοντες ὅμως δύνανται κρίνειν ὀρθῶς, ὡς φασί, τὰ χρηστὰ καὶ τὰ μὴ χρηστὰ τῶν μελῶν.

[3] For example, Archilochus, Terpander, Thaletas, Theognis, Pherecydes, Anaximander.

of the gods, which had a peculiarly joyful and serene cast among the Ionians, had been moulded into fixed national festivals:[1] and some steps towards the development of republican feeling had already been taken, before this separation occurred. The boundless resources and mobility of the Ionian spirit are shown by the astonishing productions of the Ionians in Asia and the islands in the two centuries previous to the Persian war; viz., the iambic and elegiac poetry, and the germs of philosophic inquiry and historical composition; not to mention the epic poetry, which belongs to an earlier and different period. The literary works produced during that time by the Ionians who remained behind in Attica, seem poor and meagre, as compared with the luxuriant outburst of literature in Asia Minor: nor did it appear, till a later period, that the progress of the Athenian intellect was the more sound and lasting. The advance of the literature of the Ionians in Asia Minor (which reminds us of the premature growth of a plant taken from a cold climate and barren soil, and carried to a warmer and more fertile region), as compared with that of the Athenians, corresponds with the natural circumstances of the two countries. Ionia had, according to Herodotus, the softest and mildest climate in Greece; and, although he does not assign it the first rank in fertility, yet the valleys of this region (especially that of the Mæander) were of remarkable productiveness. Attica, on the other hand, was rocky, and its soil was shallow;[2] though not barren, it required more skill and care in cultivation than most other parts of Greece: hence, according to the sagacious remark of Thucydides, the warlike races turned by preference to the fertile plains of Argos, Thebes, and Thessaly, and afforded an opportunity for a more secure and peaceable development of social life and industry in Attica. Yet Attica was not deficient in natural beauties. It had (as Sophocles says in the splendid chorus in the *Œdipus at Colonus*) ' green valleys, in which the clear-voiced nightingale poured forth her sweet laments, under

---

[1] Hence the Thargelia and Pyanepsia of Apollo, the Anthesteria and Lenæa of Dionysus, the Apaturia and Eleusinia, and many other festivals and religious rites, were common to the Ionians and Athenians.

[2] τὸ λεπτόγεων.

the shade of the dark ivy, and the sacred foliage of Bacchus, covering abundant fruit, impenetrable to the sun, and unshaken by the blasts of all storms.'[1] Above all, the clear air, refreshed and purified by constant breezes, is celebrated as one of the chief advantages of the climate of Attica, and is described by Euripides as lending a charm to the productions of the Athenian intellect. 'Descendants of Erechtheus (the poet says to the Athenians),[2] happy from ancient times, favourite children of the blessed gods, you pluck from your sacred unconquered country renowned wisdom, as a fruit of the soil, and constantly walk, with graceful step, through the glittering air of your heaven, where the nine sacred Muses of Pieria are said to have once brought up the fair-haired Harmony as their common child. It is also said that the goddess Cypris draws water from the beautifully flowing Cephisus, and breathes over the land mild and refreshing airs; and that, twining her hair with fragrant roses, she sends the gods of love as companions of wisdom, and supporters of virtue.'

§ 3. The political circumstances of Attica contributed, in a remarkable manner, to produce the same effects as its physical condition. When the Ionians settled on the coast of Asia Minor, they soon discovered their superiority in energy and military skill to the native Lydian, Carian, and other tribes. Having obtained possession of the entire coast, they entered into a friendly relation with these tribes, which, owing to the early connexion of Lydia with Babylonia and Nineveh, brought them many luxuries and pleasures from the interior of Asia. The result was, that when the Lydian monarchy was strengthened under the Mermnadæ, and began to aim at foreign conquest, the Ionians were so enfeebled and corrupted, and were so deficient in political unity, that they fell an easy prey to the neighbouring kingdom; and passed, together with the other subjects of Crœsus, under the power of the Persians. The Ionic inhabitants of Attica, on the other hand, encompassed, and often pressed by the manly tribes of Greece, the Æolians, Bœotians, and Dorians, were forced to keep the sword constantly in their hands, and were placed in circumstances which re-

---

[1] Soph. *Œd. Col.* v. 670.   [2] Eurip. *Med.* v. 824.

quired much courage and energy, in addition to the openness and excitability of the Ionic character. Athens, indeed, did not immediately attain to the proud security which the Spartans derived from their possession of half Peloponnesus, and their undisputed mastery of the practice of war. Hence the Athenians were forced to be constantly on the look-out, and to seek for opportunities of extending their empire. At the same time, while the Athenians sought to improve their political constitution, they strove to increase the liberty of the people; and a man like Solon could not have arisen in an Ionian state of Asia Minor, to become the peaceful regulator of the state with the approbation of the community. Solon was able to reconcile the hereditary rights of the aristocracy with the claims of the commonalty grown up to manhood : and to combine moral strictness and order with freedom of action. Few statesmen shine in so bright a light as Solon; his humanity and warm sympathies with all classes of his countrymen appear from the fragments of his elegies and iambics which have been already cited.[1]

After Solon comes the dominion of the Pisistratids, which lasted, with some interruptions, for fifty years (from 560 to 510 B.C). This government was administered with ability and public spirit, so far as was consistent with the interests of the ruling house. Pisistratus was a politic and circumspect prince : he extended his possessions beyond Attica, and established his power in the district of the gold mines on the Strymon,[2] to which the Athenians subsequently attached so much importance. In the interior of the country, he did much to promote agriculture and industry, and he is said to have particularly encouraged the planting of olives, which suited the soil and climate in so remarkable a manner. The Pisistratids also, like other tyrants, showed a fondness for vast works of art; the temple of the Olympian Zeus, built by them, always remained, though only half-finished, the largest building in Athens. In like manner, tyrants were fond of surrounding themselves with all the splendour which poetry and other musical arts could give to their house : and the Pisistratids certainly had the merit of diffusing

---

[1] Ch. X. § 11, 12. ch. XI. § 12.　　　[2] Herod. I. 64.

the taste for poetry among the Athenians, and of naturalizing among them the best literary productions which Greece then possessed. The Pisistratids were unquestionably the first to introduce the recital of the entire *Iliad* and *Odyssey* at the Panathenæa;[1] and the gentle and refined Hipparchus, the son of Pisistratus, was the means of bringing to Athens the most distinguished lyric poets of the time, as Anacreon,[2] Simonides,[3] and Lasus.[4] Some of the collectors and authors of the mystical poetry also found a welcome reception at the court of the Pisistratids, as Onomacritus; whom they took with them, at their expulsion from Athens, to the court of the King of Persia.[5] But, notwithstanding their patronage of literature and art, Herodotus is undoubtedly right in stating that it was not till after the fall of their dynasty, that Athens shot up with the vigour which can only be derived from the consciousness of every citizen that he has a share in the common weal.[6] This statement of Herodotus refers, indeed, principally to the warlike enterprises of Athens, but it is equally true of her intellectual productions. It is, indeed, a remarkable fact that Athens produced her most excellent works in literature and art in the midst of the greatest political convulsions, and of her utmost efforts for self-preservation or conquest. The long dominion of the Pisistratids, notwithstanding the concourse of foreign poets, produced nothing more important than the first rudiments of the tragic drama; for the origin of comedy at the country festivals of Bacchus falls in the time *before* Pisistratus. On the other hand, the thirty years between the expulsion of Hippias and the battle of Salamis (B.C. 510 to 480) was a period marked by great events both in politics and literature. During this period, Athens contended with energy and success against her neighbours in Bœotia and Eubœa, and soon dared to interfere in the affairs of the Ionians in Asia, and to support them in their revolt against Persia; after which, she received and warded off the first powerful attack of the Persians upon Greece. During the same period at Athens, the pathetic tragedies of Phrynichus, and the lofty tragedies of Æschylus, appeared on

---

[1] Ch. V. § 14.
[2] Ch. XIII. § 11.
[3] Ch. XIV. § 10.
[4] Ch. XIV. § 14.
[5] Ch. XVI. § 5.
[6] Herod. V. 78.

the stage ; political eloquence was awakened in Themistocles ; historical researches were commenced by Pherecydes; and everything seemed to give a promise of the greatness to which Athens afterwards attained.   Even sculpture at Athens did not flourish under the encouragement which it doubtless received from the enterprising spirit of the Pisistratids, but first arose under the influence of political freedom.   While, from B.C. 540, considerable masters and whole families and schools of brass-founders, workers in gold and ivory, &c., existed in Argos, Lacedæmon, Sicyon, and elsewhere, the Athens of the Pisis-tratids could not boast of a single sculptor ; nor is it till the time of the battle of Marathon, that Antenor, Critias, and Hegias are mentioned as eminent masters in brass-founding. But the work for which both Antenor and Hegias were chiefly celebrated was the brazen statues of Harmodius and Aristogiton, the tyrannicides and liberators of Athens from the yoke of the Pisistratids, according to the tradition of the Athenian people.[1]

§ 4. The great peril of the Persian war thus came upon a race of high-spirited and enterprising men, and exercised upon it the hardening and elevating influence, by which great dangers, successfully overcome, become the highest benefit to a state. Such a period withdraws the mind from petty, selfish cares, and fixes it on great and public objects.   At the moment when half Greece had quailed before the Persian army, the Athenians, with a fearless spirit of independence, abandon their country to the ravages of the enemy : embarking in their ships, they decide the sea-fights in favour of the Greeks, and again they are in the land-war the steadiest supporters of the Spartans. The wise moderation with which, for the sake of the general good, they submitted to the supreme command of Sparta, com-bined with a bold and enterprising spirit, which Sparta did not possess, is soon rewarded to an extent which must have exceeded the most sanguine hopes of the Athenian statesmen.   The attachment of the Ionians to their metropolis, Athens, which had been awakened before the battle of Marathon, soon led to a closer connexion between nearly all the Greeks of the Asiatic coast and this state.   Shortly afterwards, Sparta withdrew, with

---

[1] Ch. XIII. § 17.

the other Greeks of the mother country, from any further concern in the contest ; and an Athenian alliance was formed for
the termination of the national war, which was changed, by
gradual yet rapid transitions, into a dominion of Athens over
her allies ; so that she became the sovereign of a large and
flourishing empire, comprehending the islands and coasts of the
Ægean, and a part of the Euxine seas.   In this manner, Athens
gained a wide basis for the lofty edifice of political glory which
was raised by her statesmen.

§ 5. The completion of this splendid structure was due to
Pericles, during his administration, which lasted from about
B.C. 464, to his death (B.C. 429).   Pericles changed the allies
of Athens into her subjects, by declaring the common treasure
to be the treasure of the Athenian state; and he resolutely
maintained the supremacy of Athens, by punishing with severity
every attempt at defection.   Through his influence, Athens
became a dominant community, whose chief business it was to
administer the affairs of an extensive empire, flourishing in
agriculture, mechanical industry, and commerce.   Pericles,
however, did not make the acquisition of this power the highest
object of his exertions, nor did he wish the Athenians to consider it as their greatest good.   His aim was to realize in
Athens the idea which he had conceived of human greatness.
He wished that great and noble thoughts should pervade the
whole mass of the ruling people; and this was in fact the case,
so long as his influence lasted, to a greater degree than has
occurred in any other period of history.   Pericles stood among
the citizens of Athens, without any public office which gave
him extensive legal power;[1] and yet he exercised an influence
over the multitude which has been rarely possessed by an hereditary ruler.   The Athenians saw in him, when he spoke to
the people from the bema, an Olympian Zeus, who had the

---

[1] Pericles was indeed treasurer of the administration (ὁ ἐπὶ τῆς διοικήσεως) at
the breaking out of the Peloponnesian war; but, although this office required an
accurate knowledge of the finances of Athens, it did not confer any legal power.
It is assumed that the times are excepted, in which Pericles was strategus, particularly at the beginning of the Peloponnesian war, when the strategus had a very
extensive executive power, because Athens, being in a state of siege, was treated
like a fortified camp.

thunder and lightning in his power.   It was not the volubility of his eloquence, but the irresistible force of his arguments, and the majesty of his whole appearance, which gained him this appellation : hence a comic poet said of him, that he was the only one of the orators who left his sting in the minds of his hearers.[1]

The objects to which Pericles directed the people, and for which he accumulated so much power and wealth at Athens, may be best seen in the still extant works of architecture and sculpture which originated under his administration.   The defence of the state being already provided for, through the instrumentality of Themistocles, Cimon, and Pericles himself, by the fortifications of the city and harbour and the long walls, Pericles induced the Athenian people to expend upon the decoration of Athens, by works of architecture and sculpture, a larger part of its ample revenues than was ever applied to this purpose in any other state, either republican or monarchical.[2] This outlay of public money, which at any other period would have been excessive, was then well-timed ; since the art of sculpture had just reached a pitch of high excellence, after long and toilsome efforts, and persons endowed with its magical powers, such as Phidias, were in close intimacy with Pericles. Of the surpassing skill with which Pericles collected into one focus the rays of artistical genius at Athens, no stronger proof can be afforded, than the fact that no subsequent period, through the patronage either of Macedonian or Roman princes, produced works of equal excellence.   Indeed, it may be said that the creations of the age of Pericles are the only works of art which completely satisfy the most refined and cultivated taste.

---

[1] Μόνος τῶν ῥητόρων Τὸ κέντρον ἐγκατέλειπε τοῖς ἀκρωμένοις.   Eupolis in the *Demi.*

[2] The annual revenue of Athens at the time of Pericles is estimated at 1000 talents (rather more than 200,000*l.*) ; of which sum 600 talents flowed from the tributes of the allies. If we reckon that the Propylæa (with the buildings belonging to it) cost 2012 talents, the expense of all the buildings of this time,—the Odeon, the Parthenon, the Propylæa, the temple at Eleusis, and other contemporary temples in the country, as at Rhamnus and Sunium, together with the sculpture and colouring, statues of gold and ivory, as the Pallas in the Parthenon, carpets, &c.,—cannot have been less than 8000 talents. And yet all these works fell in the last twenty years of the Peloponnesian war.

But it cannot have been the intention of Pericles, or of the Athenians who shared his views, to limit their countrymen to those enjoyments of art which are derived from the eye. It is known that Pericles was on terms of intimacy with Sophocles; and it may be presumed that Pericles thoroughly appreciated such works as the *Antigone* of Sophocles; since (as we shall show hereafter) there was a close analogy between the political principles of Pericles and the poetical character of Sophocles. Pericles, however, lived on a still more intimate footing with Anaxagoras, the first philosopher who proclaimed in Greece the doctrine of a regulating intelligence.[1] The house of Pericles, particularly from the time when the beautiful and accomplished Milesian Aspasia presided over it with a greater freedom of intercourse than Athenian usage allowed to wives, was a point of union for all the men who had conceived the intellectual superiority of Athens. The sentiment attributed by Thucydides to Pericles in the celebrated funeral oration, that ' Athens is the school of Greece,' is doubtless, if not in words, at least in substance, the genuine expression of Pericles.[2]

§ 6. It could not be expected that this brilliant exhibition of human excellence should be without its dark side, or that the flourishing state of Athenian civilization should be exempt from the elements of decay. The political position of Athens soon led to a conflict between the patriotism and moderation of her citizens and their interests and passions. From the earliest times, Athens had stood in an unfriendly relation to the rest of Greece. Even the Ionians, who dwelt in Asia Minor, surrounded by Dorians and Æolians, did not, until their revolt from Persia, receive from the Athenians the sympathy common among the Greeks between members of the same race. Nor did the other states of the mother country ever so far recognise the intellectual supremacy of Athens, as to submit to her in political alliances; and therefore Athens never exercised such an ascendency over the independent states of Greece as

---

[1] The author of the first *Alcibiades* (among the Platonic dialogues), p. 118, unites the philosophical musicians, Pythocleides and Damon, with Anaxagoras, as friends of Pericles. Pericles is also said to have been connected with Zeno the Eleatic and Protagoras the sophist.

[2] Thucyd. II. 41. ξυνελών τε λέγω τὴν πᾶσαν πόλιν τῆς Ἑλλάδος παίδευσιν εἶναι.

was at various times conceded to Sparta. At the very foundation of her political greatness, Athens could not avoid struggling
to free herself from the superintendence of the other Greeks;
and since Attica was not an island,—which would have best
suited the views of the Athenian statesmen,—Athens was, by
means of immense fortifications, as far as possible isolated from
the land and withdrawn from the influence of the dominant
military powers. The eyes of her statesmen were exclusively
turned towards the sea. They thought that the national character of the Ionians of Attica, the situation of this peninsula,
and its internal resources, especially its silver mines, fitted
Athens for maritime sovereignty. Moreover, the Persian war
had given her a powerful impulse in this direction; and by her
large navy she stood at the head of the confederate islanders and
Asiatics, who wished to continue the war against Persia for
their own liberation and security. These confederates had
before been the subjects of the King of Persia; and had long
been more accustomed to slavish obedience than to voluntary
exertion. It was their refusals and delays, which first induced
Athens to draw the reins tighter, and to assume a supremacy
over them. The Athenians were not cruel and sanguinary by
nature; but a reckless severity, when there was a question of
maintaining principles which they thought necessary to their
existence, was implanted deeply in their character; and circumstances too often impelled them to employ it against their
allies. The Athenian policy of compelling so many cities to
contribute their wealth in order to make Athens the focus of
art and cultivation, was indeed accompanied with pride and
selfish patriotism. Yet the Athenians did not reduce millions
to a state of abject servitude, for the purpose of ministering to
the wants of a few thousand persons. The object of their
statesmen, such as Pericles, doubtless was, to make Athens the
pride of the whole confederacy; that their allies should enjoy
in common with them the productions of Athenian art, and
especially should participate in the great festivals, the Panathenæa and Dionysia, on the embellishment of which all the
treasures of wealth and art were lavished.[1]

---

[1] There are many grounds for thinking that these festivals were instituted expressly for the allies, who attended them in large numbers. Prayers were also

§ 7. Energy in action and cleverness in the use of language[1] were the qualities which most distinguished the Athenians in comparison with the other Greeks, and which are most clearly seen in their political conduct and their literature. Both qualities are very liable to abuse. The energy in action degenerated into a restless love of adventure, which was the chief cause of the fall of the Athenian power in the Peloponnesian war, after the conduct of it had ceased to be directed by the clear and composed views of Pericles. The consciousness of dexterity in the use of words, which the Athenians cultivated more than the other Greeks, induced them to subject everything to discussion. Hence too arose a copiousness of speech, very striking as compared with the brevity of the early Greeks, which compressed the results of much reflection in a few words. It is remarkable that, soon after the Persian war, the great Cimon was distinguished from his countrymen by avoiding all Attic eloquence and loquacity.[2] Stesimbrotus, of Thasos, a contemporary, observed of him, that the frank and noble were prominent in his character, and that he had the qualities of a Peloponnesian more than of an Athenian.[3] Yet this fluency of the Athenians was long restrained by the deeply-rooted maxims of traditional morality; nor was it till the beginning of the Peloponnesian war, when a foreign race of teachers, chiefly from the colonies in the east and west, established themselves at Athens, that the Athenians learnt the dangerous art of subjecting the traditional maxims of morality to a scrutinizing examination. For although this examination ultimately led to the establishing of morality on a scientific basis, yet it at first gave a powerful impulse to immoral motives and tendencies, and, at any rate,

---

publicly offered at the Panathenæa for the Plateans (Herod. VI. 111.), and at all great public festivals for the Chians (Theopomp. ap. Schol. Aristoph. *Av.* 880), who were nearly the only faithful allies of the Athenians in the Peloponnesian war, after the defection of the Mytilenæans. Moreover, the colonies of Athens (*i.e.* probably, in general, the cities of the confederacy) offered sacrifices at the Panathenæa.

[1] τὸ δραστήριον καὶ τὸ δεινόν.   [2] δεινότης and στωμυλία.

[3] In Plutarch, *Cimon*, c. IV., indeed, Stesimbrotus is not unjustly censured for his credulity and his fondness for narrating the *chronique scandaleuse* of those times : but statements, such as that in the text, founded upon personal observation of the general state of society, are always very valuable.

destroyed the habits founded on unreasoning faith.   These arts of the *sophists*—for such was the name of the new teachers— were the more pernicious to the Athenians, because the manli- ness of the Athenian character, which shone forth so nobly during the Persian war and the succeeding period, had already fallen off before the Peloponnesian war, under the administra- tion of Pericles.   This degeneracy was owing to the same acci- dental causes, which produced the noble qualities of the Athe- nians.   Plato says that Pericles made the Athenians lazy, cowardly, loquacious, and covetous.[1]   This severe judgment, suggested to Plato by his constant repugnance to the practical statesmen of his time, cannot be considered as just ; yet it must be admitted that the principles of the policy of Pericles were closely connected with the demoralization so bluntly described by Plato.   By founding the power of the Athenians on domi- nion of the sea, he led them to abandon land-war and the mili- tary exercises requisite for it, which had hardened the old warriors of Marathon.   In the ships, the rowers played the chief part, who, except in times of great danger, consisted not of citizens, but of mercenaries ; so that the Corinthians in Thucydides about the beginning of the Peloponnesian war justly describe the power of the Athenians as being rather purchased with money than native.[2]   In the next place, Pericles made the Athenians a dominant people, whose time was chiefly devoted to the business of governing their widely extended empire. Hence it was necessary for him to provide that the common citizens of Athens should be able to gain a livelihood by their attention to public business ; and accordingly it was contrived that a considerable part of the large revenues of Athens should be distributed among the citizens, in the form of wages for attendance in the courts of justice, the public assembly, and the council, and also on less valid grounds, for example, as money for the theatre.   Those payments to the citizens for their share in the public business were quite new in Greece ; and many well-disposed persons considered the sitting and listening in the Pnyx and the courts of justice as an idle life in comparison

---

[1] Plat. *Gorg.* p. 515 E.
[2] Thucyd. I. 121.   Comp. Plutarch, *Pericl.* 9.

with the labour of the ploughman and vinegrower in the country. Nevertheless, a considerable time elapsed before the bad qualities developed by these circumstances so far prevailed as to overcome the noble habits and tendencies of the Athenian character. For a long time the industrious cultivators, the brave warriors, and the men of old-fashioned morality were opposed, among the citizens of Athens, to the loquacious, luxurious, and dissolute generation who passed their whole time in the market-place and courts of justice. The contest between these two parties is the main subject of the early Attic comedy; and accordingly we shall recur to it in connexion with Aristophanes.

§ 8. Literature and art, however, were not, during the Peloponnesian war, affected by the corruption of morals. The works of this period—which the names of Æschylus, Sophocles, and Phidias are sufficient to call to our minds—exhibit not only a perfection of form, but also an elevation of soul and a grandeur of conception, which fill us almost with as much admiration for those whose minds were sufficiently mature and strong to enjoy such works of art, as for those who produced them. Pericles, whose whole administration was evidently intended to diffuse a taste for genuine beauty among the people, could justly use the words attributed to him by Thucydides : ' We are fond of beauty without departing from simplicity, and we seek wisdom without becoming effeminate.'[1] A step farther, and the love of genuine beauty gave place to a desire for evil pleasures, and the love of wisdom degenerated into a habit of idle logomachy.

We now turn to the *drama*, the species of poetry which peculiarly belongs to the Athenians; and we shall here see how the utmost beauty and elegance were gradually developed out of rude, stiff, antique forms.

---

[1] Thucyd. II. 40. φιλοκαλοῦμεν γὰρ μετ' εὐτελείας, καὶ φιλοσοφοῦμεν ἄνευ μαλακίας. The word εὐτέλεια is not to be understood as if the Athenians did not expend large sums of public money upon works of art; what Pericles means is, that the Athenians admired the simple and severe beauty of art alone, without seeking after glitter and magnificence.

CHAPTER XXI.

§ 1. THE spirit of an age is, in general, more completely and faithfully represented by its poetry than by any branch of prose composition ; and, accordingly, we may best trace the character of the three different stages of civilization among the Greeks in the three grand divisions of their poetry. The epic poetry belongs to a period when, during the continuance of monarchical institutions, the minds of the people were impregnated and swayed by legends handed down from antiquity. Elegiac, iambic, and lyric poetry arose in the more stirring and agitated times which accompanied the development of republican governments ; times in which each individual gave vent to his personal aims and wishes, and all the depths of the human breast were unlocked by the inspirations of poetry. And now when, at the summit of Greek civilization, in the very prime of Athenian power and freedom, we see dramatic poetry spring up, as the organ of the prevailing thoughts and feelings of the time, and throwing all other varieties of poetry into the shade, we are naturally led to ask, how it comes that this style of poetry agreed so well with the spirit of the age, and so far outstripped its competitors in the contest for public favour ?

Dramatic poetry, as the Greek name plainly declares, represents *actions ;* which are not (as in the epos) merely narrated, but seem to take place before the eyes of the spectator.   Yet this external appearance cannot constitute the essential difference between dramatic and epic poetry : for, since the events thus represented do not really happen at the moment of their representation ; since the speech and actions of the persons in the drama are only a fiction of the poet, and, when successful, an illusion to the spectator ; it would follow that the whole difference turned upon a mere deception. The essence of this style of poetry has a much deeper source ; viz., the state of the poet's mind, when engaged in the contemplation of his subject. The epic poet seems to regard the events which he relates, from afar, as objects of calm contemplation and admiration, and is always conscious of the great interval between him and them ; while the dramatist plunges, with his entire soul, into the scenes of human life, and seems himself to experience the events which he exhibits to our view. He experiences them in a two-fold manner : first, because in the drama, actions (as they arise out of the depths of the human heart) are represented as completely and as naturally as if they originated in our own breasts ; secondly, because the effect of the actions and fortunes of the personages upon the sympathies of other persons in the drama itself is exhibited with such force, that the listener feels himself constrained to like sympathy, and powerfully attracted within the circle of the drama. This second means, the strong sympathy in the action of the drama, was, at the time when this style of poetry was developing itself, by far the most important ; and hence arose the necessity of the chorus, as a participator in the fortunes of the principal characters in the drama of this period. Another similar fact is that the Greek drama did not originate from the narrative, but from a branch of lyric poetry. The latter point, however, we shall examine hereafter. At present, we merely consider the fact that the drama comprehends and develops the events of human life with a force and depth which no other style of poetry can reach ; and that these admit only of a dramatic treatment, while outward nature is best described in epic and lyric poetry.

§ 2. If we carry ourselves in imagination back to a time when dramatic composition was unknown, we must acknowledge that its creation required great boldness of mind. Hitherto the bard had only sung of gods and heroes, as elevated beings, from ancient traditions; it was, therefore, a great change for the poet himself to come forward all at once in the character of the god or hero; in a nation which, even in its amusements, had always adhered closely to established usage. It is true that there is much in human nature which impels it to dramatic representations; namely, the universal love of imitating other persons, and the childlike liveliness with which a narrator, strongly impressed with his subject, delivers a speech which he has heard, or, perhaps, only imagined. Yet there is a wide step from these disjointed elements to the genuine drama; and it seems that no nation except the Greeks ever made this step. The Old Testament contains narratives interwoven with speeches and dialogues, as the Book of Job; and lyric poems placed in a dramatic connexion, as Solomon's Song; but we nowhere find in this literature any mention of dramas properly so called. The dramatic poetry of the Indians belongs to a time when there had been much intercourse between Greece and India; and the *mysteries* of the Middle Ages were grounded upon a tradition, though a very obscure one, from antiquity. Even in ancient Greece and Italy, dramatic poetry, and especially tragedy, attained to perfection only in Athens; and, even here, it was only exhibited at a few festivals of a single god, Dionysus; while epic rhapsodies and lyric odes were recited on various occasions. All this is incomprehensible, if we suppose dramatic poetry to have originated in causes independent of the peculiar circumstances of the time and place. If a love of imitation, and a delight in disguising the real person under a mask, were the basis upon which this style of poetry was raised, the dramà would have been as natural and as universal among men as these qualities are common to their nature.

§ 3. A more satisfactory explanation of the origin of the Greek drama may be found in its connexion with the worship of the gods, and particularly that of Bacchus. The Greek worship contains a great number of dramatic elements. The gods were supposed to dwell in their temples, and participate in their festivals; and it was not considered presumptuous or unbecoming to represent them as acting like human beings. Thus, Apollo's combat with the dragon, and his consequent flight and expiation, were represented by a noble youth of Delphi; in

Samos the marriage of Zeus and Here was exhibited at the great festival of the goddess. The Eleusinian mysteries were (as an ancient writer expresses it)[1] ' a mystical drama,' in which the history of Demeter and Cora was acted, like a play, by priests and priestesses; though, probably, only with mimic action, illustrated by a few significant sentences of a symbolic nature, and by the singing of hymns. There were also similar mimic representations in the worship of Bacchus; thus, at the Anthesteria at Athens, the wife of the second Archon, who bore the title of Queen, was betrothed to Dionysus in a secret solemnity, and in public processions even the god himself was represented by a man.[2] At the Bœotian festival of the Agrionia, Dionysus was supposed to have disappeared, and to be sought for among the mountains; there was also a maiden (representing one of the nymphs in the train of Dionysus), who was pursued by a priest, carrying a hatchet, and personating a being hostile to the God. This festival rite, which is frequently mentioned by Plutarch, is the origin of the fable, which occurs in Homer, of the pursuit of Dionysus and his nurses by the furious Lycurgus.

But the worship of Bacchus had one quality which was, more than any other, calculated to give birth to the drama, and particularly to tragedy; namely, the *enthusiasm* which formed an essential part of it. This enthusiasm (as we have already remarked)[3] proceeded from an impassioned sympathy with the events of nature, in connexion with the course of the seasons; especially with the struggle which Nature seemed to make in winter, in order that she might break forth in spring with renovated beauty : hence the festivals of Dionysus at Athens and elsewhere were all solemnized in the months which were nearest to the shortest day.[4] The feeling which originally prevailed at

---

[1] Clem. Alex. *Protrept.* p. 12. Potter.

[2] A beautiful slave of Nicias represented Dionysus on an occasion of this kind : Plutarch, *Nic.* 3. Compare the description of the great Bacchic procession under Ptolemy Philadelphus in Athen. V. p. 196, *sq.*

[3] Ch. II. § 4.

[4] In Athens the months succeeded one another in the following order :—Poseideon, Gamelion (formerly Lenæon), Anthesterion, Elaphebolion; these, according to Boeckh's convincing demonstration, contained the Bacchic festivals of the lesser

these festivals was, that the enthusiastic participators in them believed that they perceived the god to be really affected by the changes · of nature ; killed or dying, flying and rescued, reanimated or returning, victorious and dominant; and all who shared in the festival felt these joyful or mournful events, as if they were under the immediate influence of them.   Now the great changes which took place in the religion, as well as in the general cultivation of the Greeks, banished from men's minds the conviction that the happy or unhappy events, which they bewailed or rejoiced in, really occurred in nature before their eyes.   Bacchus, accordingly, was conceived as an individual, anthropomorphic, self-existing being ; but the enthusiastic sympathy with Dionysus and his fortunes, as with real events, always remained.   The swarm of subordinate beings—Satyrs, Panes, and Nymphs—by whom Bacchus was surrounded, and through whom life seemed to pass from the god of outward nature into vegetation and the animal world, and branch off into a variety of beautiful or grotesque forms, were ever present to the fancy of the Greeks; it was not necessary to depart very widely from the ordinary course of ideas, to imagine that dances of fair nymphs and bold satyrs, among the solitary woods and rocks, were visible to human eyes, or even in fancy to take a part in them.   The intense desire felt by every worshipper of Bacchus to fight, to conquer, to suffer, in common with him, made them regard these subordinate beings as a convenient step by which they could approach more nearly to the presence of their divinity.   The custom, so prevalent at the festivals of Bacchus, of taking the disguise of satyrs, doubtless originated in this feeling, and not in the mere desire of concealing excesses under the disguise of a mask ; otherwise, so serious and pathetic a spectacle as tragedy could never have originated in the choruses of these satyrs.   The desire of escaping from *self*, into something new and strange, of living in an imaginary world, breaks forth in a thousand instances in these festivals of Bacchus.   It is seen in the colouring the body with plaster, soot, vermilion, and different sorts of green and red juices of plants, wearing

---

or country Dionysia ; Lenæa, Anthesteria, the greater or city Dionysia.   In Delphi the three winter months were sacred to Dionysus (Plutarch, *de Ei ap. Delphos*, c. 9.), and the great festival of Trieterica was celebrated on Parnassus at the time of the shortest day.

goats' and deer skins round the loins, covering the face with large leaves of different plants; and, lastly, in the wearing masks of wood, bark, and other materials, and of a complete costume belonging to the character.

§ 4. These facts seem to us to explain how the drama might naturally originate from the enthusiasm of the worship of Bacchus, as a part of his festival ceremonies. We now come to consider the direct evidence respecting its origin. The learned writers of antiquity agree in stating that tragedy, as well as comedy, was originally a choral song.[1] It is a most important fact in the history of dramatic poetry, that the lyric portion, the song of the chorus, was the original part of it. The action, the adventure of the god, was pre-supposed, or only symbolically indicated by the sacrifice : the chorus expressed their feelings upon it. This choral song belonged to the class of *dithyrambs* ; Aristotle says that tragedy originated with the singers of the dithyramb.[2] The dithyramb was, as we have already seen,[3] an enthusiastic ode to Bacchus, which had in early time been sung at convivial meetings by the drunken revellers, but, after the time of Arion (about B.C. 620), was regularly executed by a chorus. The dithyramb was capable of expressing every variety of feeling excited by the worship and mythology of Bacchus. There were dithyrambs of a gay and joyous tone, celebrating the commencement of spring ; but tragedy, with its solemn and gloomy character, could not have proceeded from these. The dithyramb, from which tragedy probably took its origin, turned upon the *sorrows of Dionysus*. This appears from the remarkable account of Herodotus, that in Sicyon, in the time of the tyrant Cleisthenes (about 600 B.C.), tragic choruses had been represented, which celebrated the sorrows, not of Dionysus, but of the hero Adrastus; and that Cleisthenes restored these choruses to the worship of Dionysus.[4]

---

[1] One passage will serve for many : Euanthius, *de tragœdiâ et comœdiâ*, c. 2. Comœdia fere vetus, ut ipsa quoque olim tragœdia, simplex fuit carmen, quod chorus circa aras fumantes nunc spatiatus, nunc consistens, nunc revolvens gyros, cum tibicine concinebat.

[2] Aristot. *Poet.* 4. ἀπὸ τῶν ἐξαρχόντων τὸν διθύραμβον.   [3] Ch. XIV. § 7.

[4] Herod. V. 67. τὰ πάθεα αὐτοῦ τραγικοῖσι χοροῖσι ἐγέραιρον, τὸν μὲν Διόνυσον οὐ τιμέωντες, τὸν δὲ Ἄδρηστον. Κλεισθένης δὲ χορους μὲν τῷ Διονύσῳ ἀπέδωκε. Whether ἀπέδωκε is translated, 'He gave them back,' or 'He gave them as something due,' the result is the same.

This shows, not only that there were at that time tragic choruses, but also that the subject of them had been changed from
Dionysus to other heroes, especially those who were distinguished
by their misfortunes and sufferings. The reason why sometimes the dithyramb,[1] and afterwards tragedy, was transferred
from Dionysus to heroes, and not to other gods of the Greek
Olympus, was that the latter were elevated above the chances
of fortune, and the alternations of joy and grief, to which both
Dionysus and the heroes were subject. The date given by
Herodotus agrees well with the statement of the ancient grammarians, that the celebrated dithyrambic poet, Arion (about
580 B.C.), invented the *tragic style* ($\tau\rho\alpha\gamma\iota\kappa\grave{o}\varsigma \tau\rho\acute{o}\pi o\varsigma$); evidently
the same variety of dithyramb as that usual in Sicyon in the
time of Cleisthenes. This narrative also gives some probability
to the tradition of a tragic author of Sicyon, named Epigenes,
who lived before the time of the Athenian dramatists; from
the perplexed and, in part, corrupt notices of him it is conjectured that he was the first who transferred tragedy from
Dionysus to other persons.

§ 5. In attempting to form a more precise conception of the
ancient tragedy, when it still belonged exclusively to the worship of Bacchus, we are led by the statement of Aristotle, ' that
tragedy originated with the chief singers of the dithyramb,' to
suppose that the leaders of the chorus came forward separately.
It may be conjectured that these, either as representatives of
Dionysus himself, or as messengers from his train, narrated the
perils which threatened the god, and his final escape from or
triumph over them; and that the chorus then expressed its
feelings, as at passing events. The chorus thus naturally assumed the character of satellites of Dionysus; whence they
easily fell into the parts of satyrs, who were not only his companions in sportive adventures, but also in combats and misfortunes; and were as well adapted to express terror or fear, as
gaiety or pleasure. It is stated by Aristotle and many grammarians, that the most ancient tragedy bore the character of a
sport of satyrs; and the introduction of satyrs into this species

---

[1] There was a dithyramb, entitled Memnon, composed by Simonides, Strabo,
XV. p. 728. Above, chap. XIV., § 11.

of poetry is ascribed to Arion, who is said to have invented the tragic dithyramb. The name of *tragedy*, or *goat's song*, was even by the ancients derived from the resemblance of the singers, in their character of satyrs, to goats. Yet the slight resemblance in form between satyrs and goats could hardly have given a name to this kind of poetry ; it is far more probable that this species of dithyramb was originally performed at the burnt sacrifice of a goat ; the connexion of which with the subject of the earliest tragedy can only be explained by means of mythological researches foreign to the present subject.[1]

Thus far had tragedy advanced among the Dorians, who therefore considered themselves the inventors of it. All its further development belongs to the Athenians ; while among the Dorians it seems to have been long preserved in its original lyric form. Doubtless tragic dithyrambs of the same kind as those in Sicyon and Corinth continued for a long time to be sung in Athens ; probably at the temple of Bacchus, called Lenæum, and the Lenæan festival, with which all the genuine traditions respecting the origin of tragedy were connected. Moreover, the Lenæan festival was solemnized exactly at the time when, in other parts of Greece, the sorrows of Dionysus were bewailed. Hence in later times, when the dramatic spectacles were celebrated at the three Dionysiac festivals of the year, tragedy preceded comedy at the Lenæa, and followed immediately after the festival procession ; while both at the greater and lesser Dionysia, comedy, which came after a great carousal, was first, and was followed by tragedy.[2] At these festivals, before the innovations

---

[1] We here reject the common account (adopted, among other writers, by Horace) of the invention of comedy at the vintage, the faces smeared with lees of wine, the waggon with which Thespis went round Attica, and so forth ; since all these arise from a confusion between the origin of comedy and tragedy. Comedy really originated at the rural Dionysia, or the vintage festival (see ch. XXVII.). Aristophanes calls the comic poets of his own time *lee-singers* (τρυγῳδοί), but he never gives this name to the tragic poets and actors. The waggon suits not the dithyramb, which was sung by a standing chorus, but a procession, which occurred in the earliest form of comedy ; moreover, in many festivals, there was a custom of throwing out jests and scurrilous abuse from a waggon (σκώμματα ἐξ ἀμαξῶν). It is only by completely avoiding this error (which rests on a very natural confusion) that it is possible to reconcile the earliest history of the drama with the best testimonies, especially that of Aristotle.

[2] According to the very important statements concerning the parts of these fes-

of Thespis, when the chorus had assembled round the altar of Dionysus, an individual from the midst of the chorus is said to have answered the other members of the chorus from the sacrificial table (ἐλεός) near the altar; that is to say, he probably imparted to them in song the subjects which excited and guided the feelings expressed by the chorus in its chants.

§ 6. The ancients, however, are agreed that Thespis first caused tragedy to become a drama, though a very simple one. In the time of Pisistratus (B.C. 536), Thespis made the great step of connecting with the choral representation (which had hitherto at most admitted an interchange of voices) a regular dialogue, which was only distinguished from the language of common life by its metrical form and by a more elevated tone. For this purpose, he joined one person to the chorus, who was the first actor.[1] Now, according to the ideas which we have formed from the finished drama, *one* actor appears to be no better than *none at all*. When however it is borne in mind, that, according to the constant practice of the ancient drama, one actor played several parts in the same piece (for which the linen masks, introduced by Thespis, must have been of great use); and moreover, that the chorus was combined with the actor, and could maintain a dialogue with him, it is easy to see how a dramatic action might be introduced, continued and concluded by the speeches inserted between the choral songs. Let us, for example, from among the pieces whose titles have been preserved,[2] take the *Pentheus*. In this, the single actor might appear successively as Dionysus, Pentheus, a Messenger, and Agave, the mother of Pentheus; and, in these several characters, might announce designs and intentions, or relate events which could not conveniently be represented, as the murder of Pentheus by his unfortunate mother, or express triumphant joy at the deed; by which means he would represent, not without in-

---

tivals, which are in the documents cited in the speech of Demosthenes against Midias. Of the Lenæa it is said, ἡ ἐπὶ Ληναίῳ πομπὴ καὶ οἱ τραγῳδοὶ καὶ οἱ κωμῳδοί; of the greater Dionysia, τοῖς ἐν ἄστει Διονυσίοις ἡ πομπὴ καὶ οἱ παῖδες καὶ ὁ κῶμος καὶ οἱ κωμῳδοὶ καί οἱ τραγῳδοί; of the lesser Dionysia in the Piræus, ἡ πομπὴ τῷ Διονύσῳ ἐν Πειραιεῖ καὶ οἱ κωμῳδοὶ καὶ οἱ τραγῳδοί.

[1] Called ὑποκριτὴς, from ὑποκρίνεσθαι, because he answered the songs of the chorus.

[2] The Funeral Games of Pelias or Phorbas, the Priests, the Youths, Pentheus.

teresting scenes, the substance of the fable, as it is given in the *Bacchæ* of Euripides. Messengers and heralds probably played an important part in this early drama (which, indeed, they retained to a considerable extent in the perfect form of Greek tragedy;) and the speeches were probably short, as compared with the choral songs which they served to explain. In the drama of Thespis, the persons of the chorus frequently represented satyrs, as well as other parts; for, before the satyric drama had acquired a distinctive character, it must have been confounded with tragedy.

The dances of the chorus were still a principal part of the performance; the ancient tragedians in general were teachers of dancing, (or, as we should say, ballet-masters,) as well as poets and musicians.

In the time of Aristophanes, (when plays of Thespis could scarcely be represented upon the stage,) the dances of Thespis were still performed by admirers of the ancient style.[1] Moreover, Aristotle remarks that the earliest tragedians used the long trochaic verse (the trochaic tetrameter) in the dialogue more than the iambic trimeter; now the former was peculiarly adapted to lively, dance-like gesticulations.[2] These metres were not invented by the tragic poets, but were borrowed by them from Archilochus, Solon, and other poets of this class,[3] and invested with the appropriate character and expression. Probably the tragic poets adopted the lively and impassioned trochaic verse, while the comic poets adopted the energetic and rapid iambic verse, formed for jest and wrangling; the latter seems to have only obtained gradually, chiefly through Æschylus, the form in which it seemed a fitting metre for the solemn and dignified language of heroes.[4]

§ 7. In PHRYNICHUS likewise, the son of Polyphradmon, of Athens, who was in great repute on the Athenian stage from Olymp. 67. 1, (B.C. 512), the lyric predominated over the dra-

---

[1] Aristoph. *Vesp.* 1479.

[2] This is also confirmed by the passage of Aristoph. *Pax.* 322.

[3] Ch. XI. § 8.

[4] The fragments preserved under the name of Thespis are indeed iambic trimeters; but they are evidently taken from the pieces composed by Heraclides Ponticus in his name. See Diog. Laërt. V. 92.

matic element. He, like Thespis, had only one actor, at least
until Æschylus had established his innovations; but he used
this actor for different, and especially for female parts. Phrynichus was the first who brought female parts upon the stage
(which, according to the manners of the ancients, could only be
acted by men); a fact which throws a light upon his poetical
character. The chief excellence of Phrynichus lay in dancing
and lyric compositions; if his works were extant, he would
probably seem to us rather a lyric poet of the Æolian school
than a dramatist. His tender, sweet, and often plaintive songs
were still much admired in the time of the Peloponnesian war,
especially by old-fashioned people. The chorus, as may be
naturally supposed, played the chief part in his drama; and
the single actor was present in order to furnish subjects on
which the chorus should express its feelings and thoughts, instead of the chorus being intended to illustrate the action
represented upon the stage. It appears even that the great
dramatic chorus (which originally corresponded to the dithyrambic) was distributed by Phrynichus into subdivisions, with
different parts, in order to produce alternation and contrast
in the long lyric compositions. Thus in the famous play of
Phrynichus, entitled the *Phœnissæ* (which he brought upon the
stage in Olymp. 75. 4, B.C. 476, and in which he celebrated the
exploits of Athens in the Persian war),[1] the chorus consisted in
part, as the name of the drama shows, of Phœnician women
from Sidon and other cities of the neighbourhood, who had
been sent to the Persian court;[2] but another part of it was
formed of noble Persians, who in the king's absence consulted
about the affairs of the kingdom. For we know that at the
beginning of this drama (which had a great resemblance to the
Persians of Æschylus) a royal eunuch and carpet-spreader[3] came

---

[1] It is related that Phrynichus composed a piece in Olymp. 75. 4 (B.C. 477) for
a tragic chorus, which Themistocles had furnished as choregus. Bentley has conjectured with much probability that this piece was the *Phœnissæ,* in which Phrynichus dwelt on the merits of Themistocles. Among the titles of the plays of Phrynichus in Suidas, Σύνθωκοι, 'the consultors or deliberators,' probably designates
the *Phœnissæ,* which would otherwise be wanting.

[2] The chorus of Phœnician women sang at its entrance:—Σιδώνιον ἄστυ λιποῦσα
καὶ δροσερὰν Ἄραδον, as may be seen from the Schol. Aristoph. *Vesp.* 220, and
Hesych. in γλυκερῷ Σιδωνίῳ.   [3] στρώτης.

forward, who prepared the seats for this high council, and announced its meeting. The weighty cares of these aged men, and the passionate laments of the Phœnician damsels who had been deprived of their fathers or brothers by the sea-fight, doubtless made a contrast, in which one of the main charms of the drama consisted. It is remarkable that Phrynichus, in several instances, deviated from mythical subjects to subjects taken from contemporary history. In a former drama, entitled the *Capture of Miletus*, he represented the calamities which had befallen Miletus, the colony and ally of Athens, at the Persian conquest, after the Ionic revolt (B.C. 498). Herodotus relates that the whole theatre was moved by it to tears; notwithstanding which the people afterwards sentenced him to a considerable fine ' for representing to them their own misfortunes;' a remarkable judgment of the Athenians concerning a work of poetry, by which they manifestly expected to be raised into a higher world, not to be reminded of the miseries of the present life.

§ 8. Contemporary with Phrynichus on the tragic stage was CHŒRILUS, a prolific and, for a long time, active poet; since he came forward so early as the 64th Olympiad (B.C. 524), and maintained his ground not only against Æschylus, but even for some years against Sophocles. The most remarkable fact known with regard to this poet is, that he excelled in the satyric drama,[1] which had therefore in his time been separated from tragedy. For as tragedy constantly inclined to heroic fables, in preference to subjects connected with Dionysus, and as the rude style of the old Bacchic sport yielded to a more dignified and serious mode of composition, the chorus of satyrs was no longer an appropriate accompaniment. But it was the custom in Greece to retain and cultivate all the earlier forms of poetry which had anything peculiar and characteristic, together with the newer varieties formed from them. Accordingly a separate *Satyric Drama* was developed, in addition to tragedy; and, for the most part,[2] three tragedies and one satyric drama at the conclusion, were represented together, forming a connected

---

[1] According to the verse : Ἡνίκα μέν βασιλεὺς ἦν Χοίριλος ἐν σατύροις.

[2] For the most part, I say; for we shall see, when we come to the *Alcestis* of Euripides, that tetralogies occur, composed of tragedies alone.

whole. This satyric drama was not a comedy, but (as an ancient author aptly describes it) a playful tragedy.[1] Its subjects were taken from the same class of adventures of Bacchus and the heroes, as tragedy; but they were so treated in connexion with rude objects of outward nature, that the presence and parti-cipation of rustic, petulant satyrs seemed quite appropriate. Accordingly, all scenes from free, untamed nature, adventures of a striking character, where strange monsters or savage tyrants of mythology are overcome by valour or stratagem, belong to this class; and in such scenes as these the satyrs could express various feelings of terror and delight, disgust and desire, with all the openness and unreserve which belong to their character. *All* mythical subjects and characters were not therefore suited to the satyric drama. The character best suited to this drama seems to have been the powerful hero Hercules, an eater and drinker and boon companion, who, when he is in good humour, allows himself to be amused by the petulant sports of satyrs, and other similar elves.

§ 9. The complete separation of the satyric drama from the other dramatic varieties is attributed by ancient grammarians to PRATINAS OF PHLIUS, and therefore a Dorian from Peloponnesus, although he came forward in Athens as a rival of Chœrilus and Æschylus about Olymp. 70 (B.C. 500), and probably still earlier. He also wrote lyric poems of the hyporche-matic kind,[2] which are closely connected with the satyric drama;[3] and he moreover composed tragedies; but he chiefly excelled in the satyric drama, in the perfecting of which he probably followed native masters: for Phlius was a neighbour of Corinth and Sicyon, which produced the tragedy of Arion and Epigenes, represented by satyrs. He bequeathed his art to his son Aristeas, who, like his father, lived at Athens as a privileged alien, and obtained great fame on the Athenian stage in competition with Sophocles. The satyric pieces of these two Phliasians were considered, together with those of Æschylus, as the best of their kind.

We are now come to the point where Æschylus appears on

---

[1] Παίζουσα τραγῳδία, Demetrius, *de Elocut.* § 169. Comp. Hor. *Art. P.* 231.
[2] See ch. XII. § 10.
[3] Perhaps the hyporcheme in Athen. XIV. p. 617, occurred in a satyric drama.

the tragic stage. Tragedy, as he received it, was still an infant, though a vigorous one; when it passed from his hands it had reached a firm and goodly youth. By adding the second actor, he first gave the dramatic element its due development; and at the same time he imparted to the whole piece the dignity and elevation of which it was susceptible.

We should now proceed immediately to this first great master of the tragic art, if it were not first necessary, for the purpose of forming a correct conception of his tragedy, to obtain a distinct idea of the external appearance of this species of dramatic representation, and of the established forms with which every tragic poet must comply. Much may indeed be gathered from the history of the origin of the tragic drama; but this is not sufficient to give a full and lively notion of the manner in which a play of Æschylus was represented on the stage, and of the relation which its several parts bore to each other.

CHAPTER XXII.

FORM AND CHARACTER OF THE GREEK TRAGEDY.

§ 1. Ideal character of the Greek tragedy; splendid costume of the actors.
§ 2. Cothurnus; masks. § 3. Structure of the theatre. § 4. Arrangement of
the orchestra in connexion with the form and position of the chorus. § 5. Form
of the stage, and its meaning in tragedy. § 6. Meaning of the entrances of the
stage. § 7. The actors; limitation of their number. § 8. Meaning of the
protagonist, deuteragonist, tritagonist. § 9. The changes of the scene inconsiderable; ancient tragedy not being a picture of outward acts. § 10. Eccyclema. § 11. Composition of the drama from various parts; songs of the
entire chorus. § 12. Division of a tragedy by the choral songs. § 13. Songs
of single persons of the chorus and of the actors. § 14. Parts of the drama
intermediate between song and speech. § 15. Speech of the actors; arrangement of the dialogue and its metrical form.

§ 1. WE shall now endeavour to arrive at a distinct conception of the peculiar character of ancient tragedy,
as it appeared in those stable forms which the origin and taste
of the Greeks impressed upon it.

The tragedy of antiquity was perfectly different from that
which, in progress of time, arose among other nations;—a
picture of human life agitated by the passions, and corresponding, as accurately as possible, to its original in all its features.
Ancient tragedy departs entirely from ordinary life; its character is in the highest degree ideal.

We must observe, first, that as tragedy, and indeed dramatic
exhibitions generally, were seen only at the festivals of Bacchus,[1]
the character of these festivals exercised a great influence on
the drama. It retained a sort of Bacchic colouring; it appeared

---

[1] In Athens new tragedies were acted at the Lenæa and the great Dionysia; the
latter being a most brilliant festival, at which the allies of Athens and many
foreigners were also present. Old tragedies also were acted at the Lenæa; and
none but old ones were acted at the lesser Dionysia. These facts appear, in great
measure, from the *didascaliæ*; that is, registers of the victories of the lyric and
dramatic poets as teachers of the chorus (χοροδιδάσκαλοι), from which, through the
learned writers of antiquity, much has passed into the commentaries on the remains
of Greek poetry, especially the arguments prefixed to them.

in the character of a Bacchic solemnity and diversion; and the extraordinary excitement of all minds at these festivals, by raising them above the tone of every-day existence, gave both to the tragic and the comic muse unwonted energy and fire.

The *costume* of the persons who represented tragedy was far removed from that free and natural character which we find raised to the perfection of beauty by the Greeks in the arts of design. It was a Bacchic festal costume. Almost all the actors in a tragedy wore long striped garments, reaching to the ground,[1] over which were thrown upper garments[2] of purple or some other brilliant colour, with all sorts of gay trimmings and gold ornaments; the ordinary dress at Bacchic festal processions and choral dances.[3] Nor was the Hercules of the stage represented as the sturdy athletic hero whose huge limbs were only concealed by a lion's hide; he appeared in the rich and gaudy dress we have described, to which his distinctive attributes, the club and the bow, were merely added. The choruses, also, which were furnished by wealthy citizens under the appellation of choregi, in the names of the tribes of Athens, vied with each other in the splendour of their dress and ornaments, as well as in the excellence of their singing and dancing.

§ 2. The chorus, which came from among the people at large, and which always bore a subordinate part in the action of the tragedy, was in no respect distinguished from the stature and appearance of ordinary men.[4] On the other hand, the actor who represented the god or hero, in whose fate the chorus was interested, needed to be raised, even to the outward sense, above the usual dimensions of mortals. A tragic actor was a very strange, and, according to the taste of the ancients themselves at a later period, a very monstrous being.[5] His person

---

[1] χιτῶνες ποδήρεις, στολαί.   [2] ἱμάτια and χλαμύδες.

[3] This is evident from the detailed accounts of Pollux, IV. c. 18, as well as from works of ancient art, representing scenes of tragedies, especially the mosaics in the Vatican, edited by Millin. See Description d'une Mosaïque antique du Musée Pio-Clémentin à Rome, représentant des scènes de tragédies, par A. L. Millin. Paris, 1819.

[4] The opposition of the chorus and the scenic actors is generally that of the Homeric λαοί and ἄνακτες.

[5] Ὡς εἰδεχθὲς καὶ φοβερὸν θέαμα, is the remark of Lucian, de Saltat. c. 27, upon a tragic actor.

was lengthened out considerably beyond the ordinary proportions of the human figure ; in the first place by the very high
soles of the tragic shoe, the cothurnus, and secondly by the
length of the tragic mask, called *onkos ;* and the chest and
body, arms and legs, were stuffed and padded to a corresponding size. It was impossible that the body should not lose
much of its natural flexibility, and that many of those slighter
movements which, though barely perceptible, are very significant
to the attentive observer, should not be suppressed. It followed
that tragic gesticulation (which was regarded by the ancients
themselves as one of the most important parts of the art) necessarily consisted of stiff, angular movements, in which little was
left to the emotion or the inspiration of the moment. The
Greeks, prone to vehement and lively gesticulation, had constructed a system of expressive gesture, founded on their temperament and manners. On the tragic stage this seemed
raised to its highest pitch, corresponding always with the
powerful emotions of the actors.

Masks, also, which originated in the taste for mumming and
disguises of all sorts, prevalent at the Bacchic festivals, had
become an indispensable accompaniment to tragedy. They not
only concealed the individual features of well-known actors, and
enabled the spectators entirely to forget the performer in his
part, but gave to his whole aspect that ideal character which
the tragedy of antiquity demanded. The tragic mask was not,
indeed, intentionally ugly and caricatured, like the comic ; but
the half-open mouth, the large eye-sockets, the sharply-defined
features, in which every characteristic was presented in its
utmost strength, the bright and hard colouring, were calculated
to make the impression of a being agitated by the emotions and
the passions of human nature in a degree far above the standard
of common life. The loss of the usual gesticulation was not felt
in ancient tragedy ; since it would not have been forcible
enough to suit the conception of an ancient hero, nor would it
have been visible to the majority of the spectators in the vast
theatres of antiquity. The unnatural effect which a set and
uniform cast of features would produce in tragedy of varied
passion and action, like ours, was much less striking in ancient
tragedy ; wherein the principal persons, once forcibly possessed

by certain objects and emotions, appeared through the whole remaining piece in a state of mind which was become the habitual and fundamental character of their existence. It is possible to imagine the Orestes of Æschylus, the Ajax of Sophocles, the Medea of Euripides, throughout the whole tragedy with the same countenance, though this would be difficult in the case of Hamlet or Tasso. The masks could, however, be changed between the acts, so as to represent the necessary changes in the state or emotions of the persons. Thus in the tragedy of Sophocles, after King Œdipus knows the extent of his calamity and has executed the bloody punishment on himself, he appeared in a different mask from that which he wore in the confidence of virtue and of happiness.

We shall not enter into the question whether the masks of the ancients were also framed with a view to increase the power of the voice. It is, at least, certain that the voices of the tragic actors had a strength and a metallic resonance, which must have been the result of practice, no less than of natural organization. Various technical expressions of the ancients denote this sort of tone, drawn from the depth of the chest,[1] which filled the vast area of the theatre with a monotonous sort of chant. This, even in the ordinary dialogue, had more resemblance to singing than to the speech of common life; and in its unwearied uniformity and distinctly measured rhythmical cadence, must have seemed like the voice of some more powerful and exalted being than earth could then produce, resounding through the ample space.

§ 3. But before we examine further into the impressions which the ear received from the tragedy of antiquity, we must endeavour to complete the outline of those made upon the eye; and to give such an account of the place of representation and the scenic arrangements as properly belongs to a history of literature. The ancient theatres were stone buildings of enormous size, calculated to accommodate the whole free and adult population of a Greek city at the spectacles and festal games; for example, the 16,000 Athenian citizens, with the educated women and many foreigners. These theatres were not designed exclusively

---

[1] Βομβεῖν, λαρυγγίζειν, especially ληκυθίζειν, περιᾳδειν τὰ ἰαμβεῖα in Lucian.

for dramatic poetry ; choral dances, festal processions, and revels, all sorts of representations of public life and popular assemblies, were held in them. Hence we find theatres in every part of Greece, though dramatic poetry was the peculiar growth of Athens. Much, however, in theatrical architecture, such as it became in Athens, where the forms were determined by fixed rules, can only be explained by the adaptation of those forms to dramatic exhibitions.

The Athenians began to build their stone theatre in the temple of Dionysus on the south side of the citadel,[1] in Olymp. 70. 1, B.C. 500; the wooden scaffolding, from which the people had heretofore witnessed the games, having fallen down in that year. It must very soon have been so far completed as to render it possible for the masterpieces of the three great tragedians to be represented in it; though perhaps the architectural decorations of all the parts were finished later. As early as the Peloponnesian war, singularly beautiful theatres were built in Peloponnesus and Sicily.

§ 4. The whole structure of the theatre, as well as the drama itself, may be traced to the chorus, whose station was the original centre of the whole performance. Around this all the rest was grouped. The orchestra (which occupied a circular level space in the centre, and, at the same time, at the bottom of the whole building) grew out of the chorus, or dancing-place, of the Homeric times ;[2] a level smooth space, large and wide enough for the unrestrained movements of a numerous band of dancers. The altar of Dionysus, around which the dithyrambic chorus danced in a circle, had given rise to a sort of raised platform in the centre of the orchestra, the *Thymele*, which served as resting-place for the chorus when it took up a stationary position. It was used in various ways, according to purposes required by the particular tragedy ; whether as a funeral monument, a terrace with altars, &c.[3] The chorus itself, in its transition from lyric

---

[1] Τὸ ἐν Διονύσου θέατρον or τὸ Διονύσου θέατρον.

[2] Above, ch. III. § 6.

[3] It is sufficient here briefly to remark, that the form of the ancient Attic theatre should not be confounded with that usual in the Macedonian period, in Alexandria, Antiochia, and similar cities. In the latter, the original orchestra was divided into halves, and the half which was nearest the stage, was, by means of a platform

to dramatic poetry, had undergone a total change of form. As a dithyrambic chorus, it moved in a ring around the altar which served as a centre, and had a completely independent character and action. As a dramatic chorus, it was connected with the action of the stage, was interested in what was passing there, and must therefore, of necessity, front the stage. Hence, according to the old grammarians, the chorus of the drama was quadrangular, *i. e.*, arranged so that the dancers, when standing in their regular places in rows and groups (στίχοι and ζυγά), formed right angles. In this form it passed through the wide side-entrances of the orchestra (the πάροδοι) into the centre of it, where it arranged itself between the thymele and the stage in straight lines. The number of dancers in the tragic chorus was probably reduced from fifty, the number of the choreutæ in the dithyrambic chorus, in the following manner. First, a quadrangular chorus, of forty-eight persons, was formed; and this was divided into four parts or sets which met together. This hypothesis will explain many difficulties: for example, how it is that, at the end of the *Eumenides* of Æschylus, two separate choruses, the Furies and the festal train, come on the stage together.[1] The chorus of Æschylus accordingly consisted of twelve persons; at a later period Sophocles increased them to fifteen, which was the regular number in the tragedies of Sophocles and Euripides.[2]

The places occupied by the choral dancers were all determined by established usages, the main object of which was to afford the public the most favourable view of the chorus, and to bring into the foreground the handsomest and best dressed of the

---

of boards, converted into a spacious inferior stage, upon which the mimes or pla-nipedarii, as well as musicians and dancers, played; while the stage, strictly so called, continued to be appropriated to the tragic and comic actors. This division of the orchestra was then called *thymele*, or even *orchestra*, in the limited sense of the word.

[1] The same fact also throws a light on the number of the chorus of comedy, twenty-four. This was half the tragic chorus, since comedies were not acted by fours, but singly.

[2] The accounts of the ancient grammarians respecting the arrangements of the chorus refer to the chorus of *fifteen* persons; as their accounts respecting the arrangements of the stage refer to the *three* actors. The reason was, that the form of the Æschylean tragedy had become obsolete.

choreutæ. The usual movements of the tragic chorus were solemn and stately, as beseemed the dignified venerable persons, such as matrons and old men, who frequently appeared in them. The tragic style of dancing, called *Emmeleia*, is described as the most grave and solemn of the public dances.

§ 5. Although the chorus not only sang alone, when the actors had quitted the stage, but sometimes sang alternately with the persons of the drama, and sometimes entered into dialogue with them, yet it did not, in general, stand on the same level with them, but on a raised stage or platform, considerably higher than the orchestra. But as the orchestra and the stage were not only contiguous, but joined, our information on this point is by no means so clear as might be wished. To the eye of the spectator the relation in which the persons of the drama stood to the chorus was determined by their appearance; the former, heroes of the mythical world, whose whole aspect bespoke something mightier and more sublime than ordinary humanity; the latter, generally composed of men of the people, whose part it was to show the impression made by the incidents of the drama on lower and feebler minds; and thus, as it were, interpret them to the audience, with whom they owned a more kindred nature. The ancient stage was remarkably long, but of little depth. It was but a small segment cut from the circle of the orchestra; but it extended on either side so far that its length was nearly double the diameter of the orchestra.[1] This form of the stage is founded on the artistical taste of the ancients generally; and again, influenced their dramatic representation in a remarkable manner. As ancient sculpture delighted above all things in the long lines of figures which we see in the pediments and friezes, and as even the painting of antiquity placed single figures in perfect outline near each other, but clear and distinct, and rarely so closely grouped as that one inter-

---

[1] Those readers who wish for more precise information about architectural measures and proportions may consult the beautiful plan given by Donaldson, in the supplemental volume to Stuart's *Antiquities of Athens*, London, 1830, p. 33. It should, however, be observed, that the projecting sides of the proscenium, which Donaldson has assumed with Hirt, are not supported by any ancient testimony, nor can they be justified by any requirement of the dramatic representations of the Greeks. The space required for these projections ought rather to be allotted to the side entrances of the orchestra, the πάροδοι.

cepted the view of another; so also the persons on the stage, the
heroes and their attendants (who were often numerous), stood
in long rows on this long and narrow stage. The persons who
came from a distance were never seen advancing from the back
of the stage, but from the side, whence they often had to walk
a considerable distance before they reached the centre where the
principal actors stood. The oblong space which the stage
formed was inclosed on three sides by high walls, the hinder one
of which alone was properly called the *Scene*, the narrow walls
on the right and left were styled *Parascenia*, the stage itself
was called in accurate language, not scene, but *Proscenium*, because it was in front of the scene. *Scene* properly means a tent
or hut, and such was doubtless erected of wood by the earliest
beginners of dramatic performances, to mark the dwelling of the
principal person represented by the actor. Out of this he came
forth into the open space, and into this he retired again.

And although this poor and small hut at length gave place
to the stately scene, enriched with architectural decorations, yet
its purpose and destination remained essentially the same. It
was the dwelling of the principal person or persons; the proscenium was the space in front of it, and the continuation of
this space was the orchestra. Thus the scene might represent
a camp with the tent of the hero, as in the *Ajax* of Sophocles;
a wild region of wood and rock, with a cave for a dwelling-
place, as in the *Philoctetes*; but its usual purport and decoration were the front of a chieftain's palace with its colonnades,
roofs and towers, together with all the accessory buildings which
could be erected on the stage, with more or less of finish and of
adaptation to the special exigencies of the tragedy. Sometimes
also it exhibited a temple, with the buildings and arrangements
appertaining to a Grecian sanctuary. But in every case it is
the front alone of the palace or the temple that is seen, not the
interior.

In the life of antiquity, everything great and important, all
the main actions of family or political interest, passed in the
open air and in the view of men. Even social meetings took
place rather in public halls, in market-places and streets, than
in rooms and chambers; and the habits and actions, which were
confined to the interior of a house, were never regarded as form-

ing subjects for public observation. Accordingly, it was necessary that the action of the drama should come forth from
the interior of the house; and tragic poets were compelled to
comply strictly with this condition in the invention and plan
of their dramatic compositions. The heroic personages, when
about to give utterance to their thoughts and feelings, came
forth into the court in front of their houses. From the other
side came the chorus out of the city or district in which the
principal persons dwelt; they assembled, as friends or neighbours might, to offer their counsel or their sympathy to the
principal actors on the stage, on some open space; often a
market-place, designed for popular meetings; such as, in the
monarchical times of Greece, was commonly attached to the
prince's palace.

Far from shocking received notions, the performance of choral
dances in this place was quite in accordance with Greek usages.
Anciently, these market-places were specially designed for numerous popular choruses; they even themselves bore the name
of *chorus*.[1] When the stage and the whole theatre had been
adapted for this kind of representation, it was necessary that
comedy also should conform to it; even in those productions
which exclusively represented the incidents and passions of private and domestic life. In the imitations of the later Attic
comedy which we owe to Plautus and Terence, the stage represents considerable portions of streets; the houses of the persons
of the drama are distinguishable, interspersed with public buildings and temples; everything is arranged by the poet with the
utmost attention to effect; and generally to nature and probability, so that the actors, in all their goings and comings, their
entrances and exits, their meetings in the streets and at their
doors, may disclose just so much of their sentiments and their
projects as it is necessary or desirable for the spectator to
know.

§ 6. The massive and permanent walls of the stage had certain openings which, although differently decorated for different
pieces, were never changed. Each of these entrances to the
stage had its established and permanent signification, and this

---

[1] Ch. III. § 6.

enabled the spectator to apprehend many things at the first glance, which he must have otherwise gradually made out in the course of the piece; since contrivances similar to our play-bills were unknown to the ancients. On the other hand, the audience came furnished with certain preliminary information concerning what they were about to witness, by means of which the plot was far more clear to them than it can now be by mere reading. Of this kind was the distinct meaning attached to the right and the left side. The theatre at Athens was built on the south side of the Acropolis, in such a manner that a person standing on the stage saw the greater part of the city and the harbour on his left, and the country of Attica on his right. Hence, a man who entered on the right by the parascenia, was invariably understood to come from the country, or from afar; on the left, from the city, or the neighbourhood. The two side-walls always bore the same relation to each other in the arrangements, as to exterior or interior. Of course, the lower side entrance which led into the orchestra, stood in the same relation; but of these, the right one was little used, because the chorus generally consisted of inhabitants of the place, or of the immediate neighbourhood. The main wall, however, or the scene, properly so called, had three doors; the middle, which was called the royal door, represented the principal entrance to the palace, the abode of the prince himself; that on the right was held to be a passage leading without, especially to the apartments of the guests, which in Greek houses were often in a detached building appropriated to that purpose; that on the left, more towards the interior, leading to a part of the house not obvious to the first approach; such as a shrine, a prison, the apartments of the women, &c.

§ 7. But the Greeks carried still further this association of certain localities with certain incidents or appearances. The moment an actor entered, they could decide upon his part and his relation to the whole drama. And here we come to the point in which the Greek drama seems the most fettered by inflexible rules, and forced into forms which appear, to our feelings, stiff and unnatural. Grecian art, however, as we have often had occasion to remark, in all its manifestations, loves distinct and unvarying forms, which take possession of the mind with all the force of habit, and immediately put it into a certain frame and temper. If, on the one hand, these forms appear to cramp the creative genius, to check the free course of the fancy ; on the other, works of art, which have a given measure, a prescribed form, to fill out, acquire, when this form is animated by a corresponding spirit, a peculiar stability which seems to raise them above the capricious and ephemeral productions of the human mind, and to assimilate them to the eternal works of nature, where the most rigorous conformity to laws is combined with boundless variety and beauty.

In the dramatic poetry of Greece, indeed, the outward form to which genius is forced to adapt itself, appears the more rigid, and, we may say arbitrary, since, to the conditions imposed on the choice of thoughts, expression, and metre, are added rules, prescribed by the local and personal character of the representation. With regard to the persons of the drama, the ancients show that historical taste which consists in a singular union of attachment to given forms, with aspiration after further progress. The antique type is never unnecessarily rejected ; but is rendered susceptible of a greater display of creative power by expansions which may be said to lie in its very nature.

We have seen how a single actor was detached from the chorus, and how Thespis and Phrynichus contented themselves with this arrangement, by causing him to represent in succession all the persons of the drama, and either before, or with the chorus, to conduct the whole action of the piece. Æschylus added the second actor, in order to obtain the contrast of two acting persons on the stage, since the general character of the chorus was that of a mere hearer or recipient ; and although capable of expressing its own wishes, hopes, and fears, it was not adapted to independent action. According to this form, only two speaking persons (mutes might be introduced in any number) could appear on the stage at the same time :—they, however, might both enter again in other characters, time only being allowed for change of dress. The appearance of the same actor in different parts of the same play did not strike the ancients as more extraordinary than his appearance in different parts in different plays ; since the persons of the actors were effectually disguised by masks, and their skill enabled them to represent various characters with perfect success. The dramatic art of those times required extraordinary natural gifts; strength of body and of voice, as well as a most careful education and training for the profession.

From the time of the great poets, and even later, in the age of Philip and Alexander, when the interest and character of dramatic performance rested entirely on the actors, the number of actors capable of satisfying the taste and judgment of the public was always very small. Hence, it was an object to turn the talents of the few eminent actors to the greatest possible account; and to prevent that injury to the general effect which the interposition of inferior actors, even in subordinate parts, must ever produce; and, in fact, so often nowadays does produce. Even Sophocles did not venture beyond the introduction of a third actor; this appeared to accomplish all that was necessary to the variety and mobility of action in tragedy, without sacrificing the simplicity and clearness which, in the good ages of antiquity, were always held to be the most essential qualities. Æschylus adopted this third actor in the three connected plays, the *Agamemnon*, *Choëphorœ*, and *Eumenides*; which he seems to have brought out at Athens at the end of his career. His other tragedies, which were performed earlier, are all so constructed that they could be represented by two actors.[1] All the plays of Sophocles and Euripides are adapted for three actors only, excepting one, the *Œdipus in Colonus*, which could not be acted without the introduction of a fourth. The rich and intricate composition of this noble drama would have been impossible without this innovation.[2] But even Sophocles himself does not appear to have dared to introduce it on the stage. It is known that the *Œdipus in Colonus* was not acted till after his death, when it was brought out by Sophocles the younger.

---

[1] The prologue of the *Prometheus* appears, indeed, to require three actors for the parts of Prometheus, Hephæstus, and Cratos; but these might have been so arranged, as not to require a third actor.

[2] Unless we assume that the part of Theseus in this play was partly acted by the person who represented Antigone, and partly by the person who represented Ismene. It is, however, far more difficult for *two* actors to represent *one* part in the same tone and spirit, than for *one* actor to represent *several* parts with the appropriate modifications.

§ 8. But the ancients laid more stress upon the precise number and the mutual relations of these three actors than might be inferred from what has been said.   They distinguished them by the technical names of Protagonistes, Deuteragonistes, and Tritagonistes.   These names are used with different meanings.   Sometimes the actors themselves are designated by their parts; as, for example, when Cleandrus is called the protagonist of Æschylus, and Myniscus his deuteragonist; or when Demosthenes, in his contest with Æschines, says, that to represent such a stern and cruel tyrant as Creon in the *Antigone*, is the peculiar glory and privilege of the tritagonist; Æschines himself having served under more distinguished actors as tritagonist. Sometimes the persons entering the stage are distinguished by these three names: as when Pollux the grammarian says, that the protagonist should always enter from the middle door; that the dwelling of the deuteragonist should be on the right hand, and that of the third person of the drama on the left.   According to a passage in a modern Platonic philosopher,[1] important to the history of the ancient drama, the poet does not create the protagonist, deuteragonist, or tritagonist; he only gives to each of these actors his appropriate part.

This, and other expressions of the ancients have involved the subject in many perplexing difficulties, which it would detain us too long to examine in detail.   Our purpose will be best accomplished by giving such a summary explanation as will enable these distinctions to be understood.

The tragedy of antiquity originated in the delineation of a suffering or passion (πάθος), and remained true to its first destination.   Sometimes it is outward suffering, danger, and injury; sometimes, rather inward; a fierce struggle of the soul, a grievous burthen on the spirit; but it is always *one passion*, in the largest sense of the word, which claims the sympathy of the audience.   The person, then, whose fate excites this sympathy, whose outward or inward wars and conflicts are exhibited, is the *protagonist*.   In the four dramas which require only two actors, the protagonist is easily distinguished: in the *Prometheus*, the

---

[1] Plotin. *Ennead.* II. L. II. p. 268.   Basil. p. 484.   Creuzer.   Compare the note of Creuzer, vol. III. p. 153, ed. Oxon.

chained Titan himself; in the *Persians*, Atossa, torn with anxiety for the fate of the army and the kingdom; in the *Seven against Thebes*, Eteocles driven by his father's curse to fratricide; in the *Suppliants*, Danaus, the fugitive, seeking a new home. The *deuteragonist*, in this form of the drama, is not, in general, the author of the sufferings of the protagonist. This is some external power, which, in these tragedies, is not brought to view. His only function is to call forth the expressions of the various emotions of the protagonist, sometimes by friendly sympathy, sometimes by painful tidings : as for example, in the *Prometheus*, Oceanus, Io, and Hermes, are all parts of the deuteragonist. The protagonist may also appear in other parts; but the tragedian generally sought to concentrate all the force and activity of the piece on one part. When a *tritagonist* is introduced, he generally acts as instigator or cause of the sufferings of the protagonist; although himself the least pathetic or sympathetic person of the drama, he is yet the occasion of situations by which pity and interest for the principal person are powerfully excited. To the deuteragonist fall the parts in which, though distinguished by a lofty ardour of feeling, there is not the vehemence and depth appropriate to the protagonist; feebler characters, with calmer blood and less daring aspiration of mind, whom Sophocles is fond of attaching to his heroes as a sort of foil, to bring out their full force. But even these sometimes display a peculiar beauty and elevation of character. Thus the gradation of these three kinds of parts depends on the degree in which the one part is calculated to excite pity and anxiety, and to command, generally, the sympathy of the audience. If we look over the titles of the plays of the three great tragedians, we shall find that, when they are not derived from the chorus, or the general subject of the piece, they always consist of the names of the persons to whom the chief interest attaches. Antigone, Electra, Œdipus, the king and the exile, Ajax, Philoctetes, Dejanira, Medea, Hecuba, Ion, Hippolytus, &c., are unquestionably all protagonistic parts.[1]

---

[1] A more detailed illustration of this point, which would lead to investigations into the structure of the several tragedies, is not consistent with the plan of the present work. We will, however, state the distribution of the parts in several

It was the great endeavour of Greek art to exhibit the character and rank of the individuals whom it grouped together, and to present to the eye a symmetrical image, corresponding with the idea of the action which was to be represented. The protagonist, as the person whose fate was the centre around which all revolved, must therefore occupy the centre of the stage; the deuteragonist and tritagonist approached him from either side. Hence it was an invariable rule for the protagonist never to leave the stage by either of the side-doors. If, however, he came from abroad, like Agamemnon and Orestes in Æschylus, he passed through the middle door into the interior of the palace, which was his habitation. With regard to the deuteragonist and tritagonist, many difficulties must have arisen from the local meaning attached to the two side doors; but, if space sufficed for such detailed explanations, we might show, from numerous examples, how the tragic poets found means to fulfil all these conditions.

§ 9. Changes of scene were very seldom necessary in ancient tragedy. The Greek tragedies are so constructed that the speeches and actions, of which they are mainly composed, might with perfect propriety pass on one spot, and indeed ought generally to pass in the court in front of the royal house. The actions to which no speech is attached, and which do not serve

---

tragedies, which seems to us the most probable. In the extant trilogy of Æschylus, the problem must be to preserve the same part for the same actor through all the three plays.

Agamemnon . .	Protag. Agamemnon, guard, herald.
	Deuterag. Cassandra, Ægisthus.
	Tritag. Clytæmnestra.
Choëphori . .	Protag. Orestes.
	Deuterag. Electra, Ægisthus, Exangelos.
	Tritag. Clytæmnestra, female attendant.
Eumenides . .	Protag. Orestes.
	Deuterag. Apollo.
	Tritag. Pythias, Clytæmnestra, Athene.

For Sophocles, the *Antigone* and the *Œdipus Tyrannus* may serve as examples.

Antigone . . .	Protag. Antigone, Tiresias, Eurydice, Exangelos.
	Deuterag. Ismene, guard; Hæmon, messenger.
	Tritag. Creon.
Œdipus Tyr. . .	Protag. Œdipus.
	Deuterag. Priest, Jocasta, servant, Exangelos.
	Tritag. Creon, Tiresias, messenger.

to develope thoughts and feelings, (such as Eteocles' combat with his brother ; the murder of Agamemnon ; Antigone's performance of the obsequies of Polynices, &c.), are imagined to pass behind or without the scene, and are only related on the stage. Hence the importance of the parts of messengers and heralds in ancient tragedy. The poet was not influenced only by the reason given by Horace,[1] viz., that bloody spectacles and incredible events excite less horror and doubt when related, and ought therefore not to be produced on the stage : there was also the far deeper general reason, that it is never the outward act with which the interest of ancient tragedy is most intimately bound up. The action which forms the basis of every tragedy of those times is internal and spiritual ; the reflections, resolutions, feelings, the mental or. moral phenomena, which can be expressed in speech, are developed on the stage. For outward action, which is generally mute, or, at all events, cannot be adequately represented by words, the epic form—narration—is the only appropriate vehicle. Battles, single combats, murders, sacrifices, funerals, and the like, whatever in mythology is accomplished by strength of hand, passes behind the scenes ; even when it might, without any considerable difficulty, be performed in front of them. Exceptions, such as the chaining of Prometheus, and the suicide of Ajax, are rather apparent than real, and indeed serve to confirm the general rule ; since it is only on account of the peculiar psychological state of Prometheus when bound, and of Ajax at the time of his suicide, that the outward acts are brought on the stage. Moreover, the costume of tragic actors was calculated for impressive declamation, and not for action. The lengthened and stuffed out figures of the tragic actors would have had an awkward, not to say a ludicrous effect, in combat or other violent action.[2] From the sublime to the ridiculous would here have been but one step, which antique tragedy carefully avoided risking.

Thus it was rather from reasons inherent in its nature, than from obedience to prescribed rules, that Greek tragedy observed,

---

[1] *Art. Poet.* 180 *sq.*
[2] According to Lucian, *Somnium sive Gallus,* c. 26, it was ludicrous to see a person fall with the cothurnus.

with few exceptions, unity of plan; and hence it required no arrangement for a complete change of scenic decorations, which was first introduced in the Roman theatre.[1] In Athens, all the necessary changes were effected by means of the *Periactæ*, erected in the corners of the stage. These were machines of the form of a triangular prism, which turned round rapidly and presented three different surfaces. On the side which was supposed to represent foreign parts, it afforded at each turn a different perspective view, while, on the home side, some single near object alone was changed. For example, the transition from the temple of Delphi to the temple of Pallas on the Acropolis of Athens, in the *Eumenides* of Æschylus, was effected in this manner. No greater change of scene than this takes place in any extant Greek tragedy. Where different but neighbouring places are represented, the great length of the stage sufficed to contain them all, especially as the Greeks required no exact and elaborate imitation of reality : a slight indication was sufficient to set in activity their quick and mobile imaginations. In the *Ajax* of Sophocles, the half of the stage on the left hand represents the Grecian camp; the tent of Ajax, which must be in the centre, terminates the right wing of this camp; on the right, is seen a lonely forest with a distant view of the sea; here Ajax enters when he is about to destroy himself; so that he is visible to the audience, but cannot for a long time be seen by the Chorus, which is in the side space of the orchestra.

§ 10. On the other hand, ancient tragedy was required to fulfil another condition, which could only co-exist with such a conception of the locality as has been just described. It is this: the proscenium or stage represents a space in the open air : what passes here is in public; even in confidential discourse the presence of witnesses is always to be feared. But it was occasionally necessary to place before the spectator a scene which was confined to the interior of the house; for example, when the plan and the idea of the piece required what is called a tragic situation, that is, a living picture, in which a whole series of affecting images are crowded together. Scenes of this tremendous power are that in which Clytæmnestra with the

---

[1] The *scena ductilis* and *versilis*.

bloody sword stands over the bodies of Agamemnon and Cassandra, holding the garment in which she has entangled her unfortunate husband; and, in the succeeding tragedy of the same trilogy, that in which Orestes is seen on precisely the same spot, where the same bathing robe now covers the bodies of Ægisthus and Clytæmnestra. Or, in the tragedy of Sophocles, Ajax, standing among the animals which he has slaughtered in his frenzy, taking them for the princes of the Greek host, and now, sunk in the deepest melancholy, contemplates the effects of his madness. It is easy to perceive that it is not the *acts* themselves in the moment of execution; but the *circumstances*, arising out of those acts when accomplished, which occupied the reflections and the feelings of the chorus and of the audience. To bring on the stage groups like these, (in the choice and disposition of which we recognise the plastic genius of the age that produced a Phidias), and to bring to view the interior of dwellings hidden behind the scenes, machines were used, called *Eccyclema* and *Exostra* (the one being rolled, the other pushed forward). It were presumptuous to attempt to describe the construction of these machines from the slight indications we could gather from the grammarians; but their working may be clearly perceived in the tragedians themselves. The side doors of a palace or tent are thrown open, and in the same moment an inner chamber with its appropriate decorations is distinctly seen on the stage, where it remains as a central point of the dramatic action, till the progress of the drama requires its disappearance in the same manner. We may fairly presume that these local representations were far from rude or tasteless; that they were worthy of the feeling for beauty, and the fancy of the age and nation which produced them; especially in the latter years of Æschylus, and during the whole career of Sophocles, when the mathematicians Anaxagoras and Democritus had begun to study perspective with a view to the stage; while the scene-painting of Agatharchus gave rise to a peculiar branch of that art,[1] which, by means of light and shadow, produced more perfect imitations of real bodies than had been heretofore known.

---

[1] Called σκηνογραφία or σκιαγραφία.

Machinery for raising figures from beneath the stage, or bearing them through the air, for the imitation of thunder and lightning, &c., arrived at sufficient perfection in the time of the three great tragedians to accomplish its end. The tragedies of Æschylus, especially *Prometheus*, prove that he was not unjustly reproached with a great love for fantastic appearances; such as winged cars; and strange hippogryphs, on which deities, like Oceanus and his daughters, were borne on the stage.

§ 11. We believe that we have now brought before our readers the principal features of Greek tragedy, such as it appeared to the spectator when represented in the theatre. But it is equally necessary, before we venture upon an estimate of the several tragedians, to offer some remarks on the combination of the several parts or elements of a Greek tragedy; since this also involves much that is not implied in the general notion of a drama, and can only be elucidated by the peculiar historical origin of the tragic art in Greece.

Ancient Grecian tragedy consists of a union of lyric poetry and dramatic discourse, which may be analysed in different ways. The chorus may be distinguished from the actors, song from dialogue, the lyrical element from the strictly dramatic. But the most convenient distinction, in the first place, is that suggested by Aristotle,[1] between the song of many voices and the song or speech of a single person. The first belongs to the chorus only; the second to the chorus or the actors. The many-voiced songs of the chorus have a peculiar and determinate signification for the whole tragedy. They were called *stasimon* when they were sung by the chorus in its proper place, in the middle of the orchestra, and *parodos* when sung by the chorus while advancing through the side entrance of the orchestra, or otherwise moving towards the place where it arranged itself in its usual order. The difference between the parodos and the stasimon consists mainly in this,—that the former more frequently begins with long series of anapæstic systems, which were peculiarly adapted to a procession or march; or a system of this sort was introduced between the lyrical songs. As to the signification of these songs, the situa-

---

[1] *Poet.* 12.

tion of the actors, and the action itself, form the subjects of reflection, and the emotions which they excite in a sympathizing and benevolent mind are expressed. The parodos chiefly explains the entrance of the chorus and its sympathy in the business of the drama, while the stasima develope this sympathy in the various forms which the progress of the action causes it to assume. As the chorus, generally, represented *the ideal spectator*, whose mode of viewing things was to guide and control the impressions of the assembled people, so it was the peculiar province of the stasimon, amidst the press and tumult of the action, to maintain that composure of mind which the Greeks deemed indispensable to the enjoyment of a work of art; and to divest the action of the accidental and personal, in order to place in a clearer light its inward signification and the thoughts which lay beneath the surface. Stasima, therefore, are only introduced in pauses, when the action has run a certain course; the stage is often perfectly clear, or, if any persons have remained on it, others come on who were not in connexion with them before, in order that they may have time for the change of costume and masks. In this manner the songs of the assembled chorus divide the tragedy into certain parts, which may be compared to the acts of modern plays, and from which the Greeks called the part before the parodos the *prologue*, the parts between the parodos and the stasima, *episodia*, the part after the last stasimon, *exodus*. The chorus appears in this kind of songs in its appropriate character, and is true to its destination, viz., to express the sentiments of a pious, well-ordered mind in beautiful and noble forms. Hence this part of ancient tragedy, both in matter and form, has the greatest resemblance to the choral lyrics of Stesichorus, Pindar, and Simonides. The metrical form consists of strophes and antistrophes, which are connected in simple series, without any artificial interweaving, as in the choral lyric poetry. Instead, however, of the same scheme of strophes and antistrophes being preserved through a whole stasimon, it is changed with each pair. Nor are there epodes after every pair of strophes; but only at the close of the ode.[1] This change of metre (which seems also to have been

---

[1] The epodes, which are apparently in the middle of a long choral song (as in Æsch. *Agam.* 140—59. Dindorf.) form the conclusion of the *parodos*. In the

occasionally connected with an alteration of the musical mode) was used to express a change in the ideas and feelings; and herein the dramatic lyric poetry differs essentially from the Pindaric. For whereas the latter rests on one fundamental thought and is essentially pervaded by one tone of feeling, the dramatic lyric, containing allusions to past and to coming events, and subject to the influence of various leanings to the several interests which are opposed on the stage, undergoes changes which often materially distinguish the beginning from the end. The rhythmical treatment of the several parts, too, is generally less that artificial combination of various elements which we find in the works of the above-mentioned masters of choral lyric poetry, than a working out of one theme, often with few variations. It is as if we heard the passionate song rushing in a mighty torrent right onwards, while the stream of Pindar's verse winds its mazy way through all the deep and delicate intricacies of thought. Without venturing upon the extensive and difficult subject of the difference between the rhythmical structure of lyric and tragic choral verse, we may remark that, as the tragedians used not only the Pindaric measures, but also those of the older Ionic and Æolic lyric poets, they observe very different rules in the combination of series and verses. To make this clear, it would be necessary to go into all the niceties of the theory of the Greek metres.

§ 12. The pauses which the choral songs produced naturally divided tragedy into the parts already mentioned, prologue, episodia, and exodus. The number, length, and arrangement of these parts admit of an astonishing variety. No numerical rule, like that prescribed by Horace,[1] here confines the natural development of the dramatic plan.

The number of choral songs was determined by the number of stages in the action calculated to call forth reflections on the

---

instance just adverted to, this consists of nine anapæstic systems, and a strophe, antistrophe, and epode in dactylic measures, and is immediately followed by the first *stasimon*, which contains five strophes and antistrophes in trochaic and logaœdic metres.

[1] *Art. Poet.* 189.

> Neve minor, neu sit quinto productior actu
> Fabula, quæ posci vult et spectata reponi.

human affections, or the laws of fate which governed the events.
These again depend on the plot, and on the number of persons
necessary to bring it about. Sophocles composed some intricate tragedies, with many stages of the action and many characters, like the *Antigone,* which is divided into seven acts;
and some simple, in which the action passes through few but
carefully worked-out stages, like the *Philoctetes,* which contains
only one stasimon, and therefore consists of three acts, inclusive
of the prologue. Long portions of a tragedy may run on without any such pause, and form an act. In the *Agamemnon* of
Æschylus, the choral song which precedes the predictions of
Cassandra is the last stasimon.[1] These prophecies coincide so
closely with their fulfilment by the death of Agamemnon, and
the emotions which they excite are so little tranquillizing, that
there is no opportunity for another stasimon. In Sophocles'
Œdipus at Colonus, the first general choral song (that is to say,
the parodos, in the meaning above given to it) occurs after the
scene in which Theseus promises to Œdipus shelter and protection in Attica.[2] Hitherto the chorus, vacillating between
horror of the accursed and pity for his woes; first fearing much,
then hoping greatly from him; is in a state of restless agitation,
and can by no means attain to the serenity and composure
which are necessary to enable it to discern the hand of an overruling power.

§ 13. As to the combination of the episodia or acts, the lyric
may here be far more intimately blended with the dramatic than
in the choral songs of which we have hitherto treated. Wherever the discourse does not express subjects of the intellect, but
feelings, or impulses of lively emotion, it becomes lyrical, and
finds utterance in song. Such songs, which do not stand
between the steps or pauses of the action, but enter into the
action itself (inasmuch as they determine the will of the actors),
may belong to the persons of the drama, to the chorus, or to
both; but in no case can they be given to a full chorus. The
third kind of these songs is, in its origin, the most remark-

---

[1] V. 975—1032. Dindorf.
[2] V. 668—719. Dindorf. This ode is called the πάροδος of the *Œdipus Coloneus*
in Plutarch, *An Seni sit ger. Resp.* 3.

able and important, and unquestionably had place in the
early lyrical tragedy. The name of this song, common to the
actors and the chorus, is *commos*, which properly means *planctus*,
' the wailing for the dead.' The wail over the dead is therefore
the primary form from which this species of odes took its rise.
The liveliest sympathy with suffering constantly remains the
main ingredient of the commos; although the endeavour to incite to an action, or to bring a resolution to maturity, may be
connected with it. The commos often occupies a considerable
part of a tragedy, especially those of Æschylus : as for instance,
in the *Persians*[1] and the *Choëphorœ*.[2] Such a picture of grief
and suffering, worked out in detail, was an essential part of the
early tragedies. In a commos, moreover, the long systems of
artfully interwoven strophes and antistrophes had an appropriate place ; since in representation they derived a distinctness
and effect from the corresponding movements of the persons of
the drama and of the chorus, which is necessarily lost to us in
the mere perusal. We find a variety of the commos in scenes
where the one party appears in lyrical excitement, while the
other enounces its thoughts in ordinary language; whence a
contrast arises which produces deeply affecting scenes even in
Æschylus, as in the *Agamemnon*[3] and the *Seven against Thebes*.[4]
But the chorus itself, when agitated by violent and conflicting
emotions, may carry on a lyrical dialogue ; and hence arose a
peculiar kind of choral poetry, in which the various voices are
easily recognized by the broken phrases now repeating, now dis-
puting, what has preceded. Long lyric dialogues of this sort,
in which all or many voices of the chorus are distinguished, are
to be found in Æschylus, and have been noticed by the ancient
commentators.[5] Succeeding tragedians appear to have em-

---

[1] Æsch. *Pers.* 907—1076. The entire exodus is a commos.

[2] Æsch. *Choëph.* 306—478.

[3] Æsch. *Agam.* 1069—1177, where the lyrical excitement gradually passes from
Cassandra to the chorus.

[4] Æsch. *Sept. cont. Theb.* 369—708, through nearly the whole episodion. Comp.
Suppl. 346—437.

[5] See Schol. Æsch. *Eum.* 139, and *Theb.* 94. Instances are furnished by *Eum.*
140—77, 254—75, 777—92, 836—46. *Theb.* 78—181. *Suppl.* 1019—74. The
editions frequently denote these single voices by hemichoria; but the division of
the chorus into two equal parts, called διχόρια in Pollux, only occurred in certain
rare circumstances, as in Æsch. *Theb.* 1052. Soph. *Aj.* 866.

ployed these choral songs, exclusively in connexion with commi, and bring forward only a few single voices out of the whole chorus.[1] When the chorus enters the orchestra, not with a song of many voices, sung in regular rows, but in broken ranks, with a song executed in different parts, the choral ode consists of two portions ; first, one resembling a commos, which accompanies this irregular entrance ; and, secondly, one like a stasimon, which the chorus does not execute till it has fallen into its regular order. Examples are to be found in the *Eumenides* of Æschylus and the *Œdipus Coloneus* of Sophocles.[2] The tragedians have also interspersed separate smaller choral songs, which the ancients expressly distinguish from the stasima,[3] and which are properly designated by the word Hyporchemes ;[4] songs which depict an enthusiastic state of feeling, and were united with expressive animated dances, of a kind very different from the ordinary grave Emmeleia. They are frequently used by Sophocles in suitable places, to mark a strong but transitory sentiment.[5] On the other hand, lyrical parts were sometimes allotted to the persons of the drama : these were in general called ἀπὸ σκηνῆς, and were either distributed into dialogues or delivered by single performers. Long airs of this sort, called *Monodies,* in which one person, generally the protagonist of the drama, abandons himself, without restraint, to his emotions, form a principal feature in the tragedies of Euripides.[6] As the regular return of fixed musical modes and rhythms was not reconcileable with the free utterance and almost uncontrollable current of such passionate outpourings, the antistrophe gradually

---

[1] As in Soph. *Œd. Col.* 117, *sqq.* Eurip. *Ion.* 184, *sqq.*

[2] In the *Eumenides* of Æschylus, the expression χορὸν ἄψωμεν, v. 307, denotes this regular disposition of the chorus.

[3] Schol. Soph. *Trach.* 205. Similar odes in *Aj.* 693. *Phil.* 391, 827.

[4] Which occurs in Tzetzes, περὶ τραγικῆς ποιήσεως, in Cramer *Anecd.* vol. III. p. 346.

[5] The hyporchemes, however, can scarcely be distinguished from the songs resembling the commos, since in the latter the entire chorus could hardly have joined in the song and dance. In the commatic odes in the *Seven against Thebes* of Æschylus, especially in the first, v. 78—181, a dancer named Telestes (probably as leader of the chorus) represented, by means of mimic dances, the scenes of war described in the poetry, Athen. I. p. 22. A.

[6] Aristophanes says of him, that he ἀνέτρεφεν (τὴν τραγῳδίαν) μονῳδίαις, Κηφισοφῶντα μιγνύς ; Cephisophon being his chief actor. *Ran.* 944. cf. 874.

disappeared, and the almost infinitely irregular rhythmical structures (called ἀπολελυμένα), in the style of the later dithyrambics, came into use. The artificial system of regular forms, to which Greek art (and more particularly that of the earlier periods) completely subjected the expression of feeling and passion, was here completely swept away by the torrent of human affections and desires, and a kind of natural freedom was established.

As to what regards the detail of rhythmical forms, it is sufficient for our purpose to remark, that all the earlier lyrical measures might be used for the songs of a single person of the chorus or the stage, as well as for the stasima; but that, generally, grave and solemn forms were applicable only to the songs of the whole chorus; and that lighter and more sprightly measures, more suited to the expression of emotion and affection, prevailed in the monodies. Hence the rhythms of the Doric mode, known from Pindar, are found only in the stasima; not in commi and songs ἀπὸ σκηνῆς, which afford no place where this mode could sustain its peculiar character.[1] On the other hand, dochmia[2] are admirably fitted, by their rapid movement and the apparent antipathy of their elements, to depict the most violent excitement of the human mind; while the great variety of form which may be developed from them, lends itself equally to the expression of stormy passion and of deep melancholy. Tragedy has no form more peculiarly her own, nor more characteristic of her entire being and essence. A fixed difference in the metrical forms of the commos and the ἀπὸ σκηνῆς is not perceptible; we only know from Aristotle, that certain modes were peculiar to certain persons of the drama, in consequence of the peculiar energy or pathos of the character, which appeared suited to the acting or suffering heroes or heroines of the drama, but not to the merely sympathizing chorus.[3]

---

[1] Plutarch *de Musicâ* 17, indeed, says that even τραγικοὶ οἶκτοι, *i. e.* commoi, were originally set in the Doric mode; but this must refer to the tragedians before Æschylus.

[2] The main form is ‿ / ‿ ‿ / ; an antispastic composition, in which the arsis of the iambic and that of the trochaic part coincided.

[3] Aristot. *Probl.* XIX. 48.

§ 14. All the odes we have hitherto described are properly of a musical nature, called *mele* by the ancients ; they were sung to an accompaniment of instruments, among which sometimes the cithara and lyre, sometimes the flute predominated. Other pieces belong to that middle kind, between song and speech, of which we have spoken in treating of the rhapsodic recitation of the epos, the elegy, and the iambus.[1] The anapæstic systems, which were chanted sometimes by the chorus, sometimes by the actors, but properly as an accompaniment to a marching move-ment, either of entrance or exit, escort or salutation, recall the Spartan marching songs.[2] We can hardly imagine them as set to regular melodies, nor yet as delivered in common speech. In the early tragedy they are allotted, in long systems, as a portion of the parodos, to the chorus when entering in rank and file. Hexameters were sometimes recited by the actors in announcing important tidings, or uttering serious reflections ; where the peculiar dignity and gravity of this majestic measure produced great effect.[3] The usual trochaic verses which were allied to dialogue admitted of a higher-toned recitation, and espe-cially of a more lively gesticulation, like that used in dancing ; as we have already had occasion to remark.

§ 15. We now come to the Epeisodia, where the predomi-nant character is not, as in the parts we have hitherto consi-dered, the feeling, but the intellect, which, by directing the will, seeks to render external things subject to itself, and the opinions of others conformable to its own. This was originally the least important element. The variety of forms of discourse which tragedy exhibits grew by degrees out of mere narration. Here also the chorus forms no contrast to the persons of the drama. It is itself, as it were, an actor. The dialogues which it holds with the persons on the stage are, however, necessarily carried on, except in a few cases,[4] not by all its members, but by its leader. Rare examples, and those only in Æschylus, are to be found, in which the members of the chorus converse among

---

[1] Ch. IV. § 3. ch. X. § 2. [2] Ch. XIV. § 2.
[3] See Soph. *Phil.* 839. Eurip. *Phaethon*, fragm. e cod. Paris. v. 65. (fragm. 2. ed. Dindorf.)
[4] As Æsch. *Pers.* 154. χρεὼν αὐτὴν πάντας μύθοισι προσαυδᾶν.

themselves; as in the *Agamemnon*, where the twelve choreutæ deliver their thoughts as twelve actors might do;[1] others, in which they express their opinions individually, in the form of dialogue with a person on the stage.[2] The arrangement of the dialogue is remarkable for that studious attention to regularity and symmetry which distinguishes Greek art. The opinions and desires which come into conflict are, as it were, poised in a balance throughout the whole dialogue; till at length some weightier reason or decision is thrown into one of the scales. Hence the frequent scenes so artfully contrived in which verse answers to verse, like stroke to stroke;[3] and again, others in which two, and sometimes more, verses are opposed to each other in the same manner. Even whole scenes, consisting of dialogue and lyrical parts, are sometimes thus symmetrically contrasted, like strophes and antistrophes.[4]

The metre generally used in this portion of ancient tragedy was, as we have already remarked, in early times the Trochaic tetrameter, which, in the extant tragedies, is found only in dialogues full of lively emotion, and in many does not occur at all. The *Persians* of Æschylus,—probably the earliest tragedy we possess,—contains the greatest number of trochaic passages. On the other hand, the Iambic trimeter, which Archilochus had fashioned into a weapon of scorn and ridicule, was converted, by judicious alterations in the treatment, leaving its fundamental character unchanged, into the best metrical form for a vigorous, animated, and yet serious conversation. But in the works of Æschylus it maintained a greater elevation above ordinary prose than in those of his predecessors; not only from the stately sound of the reiterated long syllables, but also from the regular accordance of the pauses in the sense with the ends of verses, by which the several verses stand out distinct. The later tragedians not only made the construction of the verses more varied, light, and voluble, but also divided and connected them more frequently according to the endings and beginnings

---

[1] Æsch. *Agam.* 1346—71. The three preceding trochaic verses, by which the consultation is introduced, are spoken by the three first persons of the chorus alone.

[2] Æsch. *Agam.* 1047—1113.

[3] These single verses were called στιχομύθια.

[4] As in the *Electra* of Sophocles, v. 1398—1421, and v. 1422—41, correspond.

of sentences; whereby the dialogue acquired an expression of freer and more natural movement.

After having thus investigated and analyzed in detail the forms in which the tragic poet had to embody the creations of his genius, we should naturally proceed to investigate the essence of a Greek tragedy, following the track indicated by the celebrated definition of Aristotle, ' Tragedy is the imitation of some action that is serious, entire, and of a proper magnitude; effecting through pity and terror the refinement of these and similar affections of the soul.' [1]

But this cannot be done till we have examined more closely the plan and contents of separate tragedies of Æschylus and Sophocles. We shall therefore best accomplish our aim by proceeding to consider the peculiar character of Æschylus as presented to us by his life and works.

---

[1] Aristot. *Poet.* 6. μίμησις πράξεως σπουδαίας καὶ τελείας, μέγεθος ἐχούσης . . . δι' ἐλέου καὶ φόβου περαίνουσα τὴν τῶν τοιούτων παθημάτων κάθαρσιν.

CHAPTER XXIII.

ÆSCHYLUS.

§ 1.   ÆSCHYLUS, the son of Euphorion, an Athenian, from the hamlet of Eleusis, was, according to the most authentic record, born in Olymp. 63. 4. B.C. 525.[1] He was therefore thirty-five years old at the time of the battle of Marathon, and forty-five years old at the time of the battle of Salamis. Accordingly, he was among the Greeks who were contemporary, in the fullest sense of the word, with these great events, and who had felt them with all the emotions of a patriotic spirit. His epitaph speaks only of his fame in the battle of Marathon, not of his glories in poetic contests.[2] Æschylus belonged completely to the race of the warriors of Marathon, in the sense which this appellation bore in the time of Aristophanes; those patriotic and heroic Athenians, of the ancient stamp, from whose manly and honourable character sprang all the glory and greatness which were so rapidly developed in Athens after the Persian war.

Æschylus, like almost all the great masters of poetry in ancient Greece, was a poet by profession; he had chosen the

---

[1] The celebrated chronological inscription of the island of Paros states the year of his death and his age, whence the year of his birth can be determined.

[2] Cynægeirus, the enthusiastic fighter of Marathon, is called the brother of Æschylus: it is certain that his father was named Euphorion, Herod. VI. 114, with Valckenaer's note. On the other hand, Ameinias, who began the battle of Salamis, cannot well have been a brother of Æschylus, since he belonged to the deme of Pallene, while Æschylus belonged to the deme of Eleusis.

exercise of the tragic art as the business of his life.   This exercise of art was combined with the training of choruses for religious solemnities.   The tragic, like the comic, poets were essentially *chorus teachers*.   When Æschylus desired to represent a tragic poem, he was obliged to repair, at the proper time, to the Archon, who presided over the festivals of Bacchus,[1] and obtain a chorus from him.   If this public functionary had the requisite confidence in the poet, he granted him the chorus; that is to say, he assigned him one of the choruses which were raised, maintained, and fitted out by the wealthy and ambitious citizens, as choregi, in the name of the tribes or Phylæ of the people.   The principal business of Æschylus then was to practise this chorus in all the dances and songs which were to be performed in his tragedy ; and it is stated that Æschylus employed no assistant for this purpose, but arranged and conducted the whole himself.

Thus far the tragic was upon the same footing as the lyric, especially the dithyrambic, poet, since the latter received his dithyrambic chorus in the same manner, and was likewise required to instruct it.   The tragic poet, however, also required actors, who were paid, not by the choregus, but by the state, and who were assigned by lot to the poet, in case he was not already provided.   For some poets had actors, who were attached to them, and who were peculiarly practised in their pieces ; thus Cleandrus and Myniscus acted for Æschylus.   The practising or rehearsal of the piece was always considered the most important, because the public and official part of the business.   Whoever thus brought out upon the stage a piece which had not been performed before, obtained the rewards offered by the state for it, or the prize, if the play was successful.   The poet, who merely composed it in the solitude of his study, could lay no claim to the rewards due for its public exhibition.

§ 2. These statements show that the exercise of the tragic art was the sole occupation of a man's life, and (from the great fertility of the ancient poets) absorbed every faculty of his mind. There were extant in antiquity seventy dramas of Æschylus ;

---

[1] This was for the great Dionysia, the first Archon, ὁ ἄρχων κατ' ἐξοχήν ; for the Lenea, the second, the basileus.

and among these the satyric dramas do not appear to be included.[1] All these plays fall in the period between Olymp. 70. 1. B.C. 500, and Olymp. 81. 1. B.C. 456. In the former of these years, Æschylus, then in his twenty-fifth year, first strove with Pratinas for the prize of tragedy, (upon which occasion the ancient scaffolding is said to have given way), and in the latter year the poet died in Sicily. Accordingly he produced seventy tragedies in a period of forty-four years. That the excellence of these works was generally recognized is proved by the fact of Æschylus having obtained the prize for tragedy thirteen times.[2] For, since at every contest he produced three tragedies, it follows that more than half his works were preferred to those of his competitors, among whom there were such eminent poets as Phrynichus, Chœrilus, ·Pratinas, and Sophocles;[3] the latter of whom had, at his first representation, in Olymp. 77. 4. B.C. 493, obtained the prize from Æschylus.

It has been already stated that Æschylus composed three tragedies for every tragic contest in which he appeared as a competitor; and to these, as was also remarked, a satyric drama was annexed. In making this combination, Æschylus followed a custom which had probably grown up before his time, and which was retained as long as tragedy continued to flourish in Athens. But Æschylus differed from his successors in this, that his three tragedies formed a whole, connected in subject and plan; while Sophocles began to oppose three separate tragedies to an equal number produced by his rivals.[4] We

---

[1] In the much contested passage at the end of the *Vita Æschyli*, should probably be written, ἐποίησε δράματα ἑβδομήκοντα καὶ ἐπὶ τούτοις σατυρικά ἀμφίβολα πέντε. ' He composed 70 dramas, and also satyric dramas; five are ascribed to him on doubtful authority.' The extant titles of dramas of Æschylus are, including the satyric dramas, about 38.

[2] According to the life. First in Olymp. 73, 4. according to the Parian marble.

[3] The calculation is indeed rendered somewhat uncertain by the fact that Euphorion, the son of Æschylus, gained the prize four times after his father's death, with dramas which had been bequeathed to him by his father, and which had not been before represented: Suidas in Εὐφορίων. Accordingly, 12 of the 70 tragedies probably fall after Olymp. 81. 1. The four prizes ought not, however, to be deducted from the 13 gained by Æschylus, since Euphorion was publicly proclaimed victor, although it was well known that the tragedies were composed by Æschylus.

[4] This is the meaning of the words, δρᾶμα πρὸς δρᾶμα ἀγωνίζεσθαι, ἀλλὰ μὴ τριλογίαν. Suidas in Σοφοκλῆς.

should be at a loss to understand by what means the three pieces composing the trilogy were formed into a connected series, without depriving each piece of its individual character, if we were not so fortunate as to possess a trilogy of Æschylus, in his *Agamemnon, Choëphorœ,* and *Eumenides.* The best illustration of the nature of a trilogy will therefore be a short analysis of these dramas, and accordingly we proceed to give an account of his extant works.

§ 3. Of the early part of the career of Æschylus we do not possess a single work. All his extant dramas are of a later date than the battle of Salamis. Probably his early works contained little to attract the taste of the later Greeks.

The earliest of the extant works of Æschylus is probably the *Persians,* which was performed in Olymp. 76. 4. B.C. 472 ; a piece unique in its kind, which appears, at a first glance, more like a lament over the misfortunes of the Persians than a tragic drama. But we are led to modify this opinion, on considering the connexion of the parts of the trilogy, which is apparent in the drama itself.

We will give an outline of the plan of the *Persians* of Æschylus. The chorus (consisting of the most distinguished men of the Persian empire, into whose hands Xerxes, at his departure, had committed the government of the country) proclaim in their opening song the numbers and power of the Persian army ; but, at the same time, express a fear of its destruction ; for ' what mortal man may elude the insidious deceit of the gods ?' The first *stasimon,* which immediately follows the opening choral song, describes, in a more agitated manner, the grief of the country in case the army should not return. The chorus is preparing for a deliberation, when Atossa appears, the mother of Xerxes, and widow of Darius ; she relates an ominous dream which has filled her with anxious forebodings. The chorus advise her to implore the gods to avert the impending evil, and especially to propitiate the spirit of Darius by libations, and to pray for blessing and protection. To her questions concerning Athens and Greece they answer with characteristic descriptions of the distinctions of the different nations ; when a messenger from Greece arrives, and, after the first announcements of mishap and laments of the chorus, he presents a magnificent picture of the battle of Salamis, with its terrific consequences for the Persian army. Atossa resolves, though everything is lost, to follow the advice of the chorus, in case any benefit may be obtained from it. In the second stasimon the chorus dwell upon the desolation of Asia, to which is added a fear that the subject nations will no longer endure their servitude. In the second episodion the libations for the dead change into an evocation of the spirit of Darius. The chorus, during the libations of Atossa, call upon Darius, in songs resembling a commos, full of warmth and feeling, as the wise and happy ruler, the good father of his people, who now alone can help them, to appear on the summit of the tomb. Darius appears, and learns from Atossa (for fear and respect tie the tongue of the chorus) the destruction of the kingdom. He immediately recognizes in the event the 'too speedy fulfilment of oracles,' which might have been long delayed, had not the arrogance of Xerxes hastened their accomplishment. 'But when any man, of his own accord, hurries on to his ruin, the deity seconds his efforts.' He regards the crossing of the Hellespont as an enterprise contrary to the will of the gods, and as the main cause of their wrath; and, on the authority of oracles known to him, which are now to be completely fulfilled, especially on account of the violation of the Greek temples, he announces that the remains of the invading Persian army will be destroyed at the battle of Platæa. The annihilation of its power in Europe is a warning given by Zeus to the Persians, that they should be satisfied with their possessions in Asia. The third stasimon, which concludes this act, describes the power which Darius had gained without himself invading Greece or crossing the Halys; contrasted with the misfortunes sent by the gods upon Persia for infringing these principles. In the third act Xerxes himself appears as a fugitive, in torn and ragged kingly garments, and the whole concludes with a long commos, or orchestic and musical representation of the despair of Xerxes, in which the chorus takes a part.

§ 4. It appears from this outline, that the evocation and appearance of Darius, and not the description of the victory, form the main subject of this drama. The arrogance and folly of Xerxes have brought about the accomplishment of the ancient oracles, and caused the fate which was hanging over Asia and Greece to be fulfilled in the destruction of the Persian power. The oracles alluded to in general terms by Darius are known to us from Herodotus. They were predictions attributed to Bacis, Musæus, and others, and they had been made known, though in a garbled form, by Onomacritus, the companion of the Pisistratids at the Persian court.[1] They contained allusions to the bridging of the Hellespont, the destruction of the Grecian temples, and the invasion of Greece by a barbarian army. They referred, indeed, in part, to mythical events, but they were then (as has been often the case with other predictions) applied to the events of the time.[2] Now we know from a didascalia that the *Persians* was, at its representation, preceded by a piece entitled the *Phineus*. It is sufficient to observe that Phineus, according to the mythologists, received the Argonauts on their voyage to Colchis, and, at the same time, foretold to them the adventures which were yet to befal them.

We have shown in a former chapter[3] that the notion of an ancient conflict between Asia and Europe, leading, by successive stages, to events constantly increasing in magnitude, was one of the prevailing ideas of that time. It is probable that Æschylus took this idea as the basis of the prophecies of Phineus, and that he represented the expedition of the Argonauts as a type of the greater conflicts between Asia and Europe which succeeded it. We will not follow out the mythical combinations which the poet might have employed, inasmuch as what we have said is sufficient to explain the connexion and subject of the entire trilogy.

The same purpose is likewise perceptible in the third piece, the *Glaucus Pontius*.[4] The extant fragments show that this marine demigod (of whose wanderings and appearances on various coasts strange tales were told in Greece) described in this tragedy a voyage which he had made from Anthedon

---

[1] See ch. XVI. § 5.   [2] Herod. VII. 6. IX. 42, 43.
[3] Ch. XIX. §. 4.

[4] The argument of the *Persians* mentions the Γλαῦκος Ποτνιεύς. But as the two plays of Æschylus, the *Glaucus Pontius* and *Glaucus Potnieus* are confounded in other passages, we may safely adopt the conjecture of Welcker, that the *Glaucus Pontius* is the play meant in the argument just cited.

through the Eubœan and Ægean seas to Italy and Sicily. In this narrative a prominent place was filled by Himera, the city in which the power of the Sicilian Greeks had crushed the attempts of the Carthaginian invaders, at the time of the battle of Salamis. In this manner Æschylus had an opportunity of bringing this event (which was considered as the second great exploit by which Greece was saved from the yoke of the barbarians) into close connexion with the battle of Platæa; since the scene of the drama was Anthedon in Bœotia, where Glaucus was supposed to have lived as a fisherman. It may likewise be conjectured that in the tragedy of *Phineus*, the Phœnicians, as well as the Persians, may have been introduced into the predictions respecting the conflicts between Asia and Greece.[1]

§ 5. Accordingly in this trilogy, Æschylus shows himself a friend of the Sicilian Greeks, as well as of his countrymen at Athens. His connexion with the princes and republics of Sicily must be here considered, since it exercised some influence upon his poetry. The later grammarians (who have filled the history of literature with numerous stories founded upon mere conjecture) have assigned the most various motives for the residence of Æschylus in Sicily, which was an ascertained fact, by enumerating all the circumstances in his life at Athens, which could have induced him to become a voluntary exile. Some accounts of a different character have, however, been preserved, on which we may safely rely.[2] Æschylus was in Sicily with Hiero, just after this ruler of Syracuse had built the town of Ætna, at the

---

[1] [The explanation given in § 4 of the trilogy referred to is exceedingly doubtful. The main subject of the *Persians* is evidently the discomfiture of the invading Persians by the Greeks. The evocation of Darius is merely a device to introduce the battle of Platæa, which consummated their defeat, as well as the battle of Salamis. The notion that the *Phineus, Persians,* and *Glaucus* formed a trilogy in which the subjects of the three pieces were connected, is highly improbable; and the conjecture that the third piece was the *Glaucus Pontius,* and not the *Potnieus,* as the didascalia tells us, is gratuitous. It cannot be doubted that *many* of the plays of Æschylus were written in connected trilogies; but it is impossible to prove that they *all* were, and that the introduction of disconnected pieces was an innovation of Sophocles, as is asserted below, chap. XXIV. § 4. p. 450. The very trilogy in question will be, to many persons, a sufficient proof of the contrary.—EDITOR.]

[2] Eratosth. ap. Schol. Aristoph. *Ran.* 1055 (1060), and the *Vita Æschyli,* with the *additam. e cod. Guelferbytano.*

foot of the mountain, and in the place of the ancient Catana. At this time he composed his tragedy of the *Women of Ætna*, in which he announced the prosperity of the new colony. The subject of it, as its name, borrowed from the chorus, betokens, must have been taken from the events of the day. At the same time he reproduced the *Persians* at the court of Hiero; but whether with alterations, or as it had been acted at Athens, was a matter of controversy among the ancient scholars. Hence it appears that Æschylus, soon after the appearance of the *Persians*, went to Sicily, about the year 471 B.C., four years after the time when Ætna was founded, and when it was not quite finished. Hiero died four years afterwards, in 467 B.C., (Olymp. 78. 2.); but Æschylus must have left Sicily before this event, as in the beginning of the year 468 B.C. (Olymp. 77. 4.) we find him again at Athens, and engaged in a poetical contest with Sophocles. According to the ancients, his acquaintance with the Pythagorean philosophy and his use of certain rare Doric expressions then used in Sicily, may be traced to his residence in that island.

§ 6. The tragedy of the *Seven against Thebes* falls in the next time. It is known to have been acted after the *Persians*, and before the death of Aristides (which occurred about 462 B.C.)[1] In this drama the ancients peculiarly admired the warlike spirit exhibited by the poet; and, in fact, a fire burns throughout it which could only have been kindled in a brave and heroic breast. Eteocles appears as a wise and resolute general and hero, as well in the manner in which he recommends tranquillity to the women of the chorus, as in the answers which he makes to the tidings of the messengers, and in his opposing to each of the seven haughty leaders of the hostile army (who come like giants to storm the walls of Thebes) a brave Theban hero; until at length Polynices, his own brother, is named, when he declares his resolution to go out himself to meet him. The determination of Polynices to reserve himself for the combat with his brother creates an anxious interest in an attentive hearer; and his announcement of this resolution is the pivot upon which the

---

[1] See Clinton, *F. H.* ad ann. 472. Aristophanes, *Ran.* 1026, appears to consider the *Persians* as *posterior* to the *Seven against Thebes*.

whole piece turns. Nothing can be more striking than the gloomy resoluteness with which Eteocles recognizes the operation of the curse pronounced by Œdipus against his two sons, and yet proceeds to its fulfilment. The stasimon of the chorus which follows plainly recognizes the wrath and curse of Œdipus as the cause of all the calamities which threaten the Thebans. This dark side of the destiny of Thebes had not been revealed in the previous part of the drama, although Eteocles had once before declared his fear of the woes which this curse might bring upon Thebes (v. 70). Soon afterwards arrives the account of the preservation of the city, but with the reciprocal slaughter of the brothers. The two sisters, Antigone and Ismene, now appear upon the stage ; and, with the chorus, sing a lament for the dead ; which is very striking from the blunt ingenuity and melancholy with which Æschylus has contrived to paint in the strongest colours the calamities and perversities of human life.[1] At the conclusion, the two sisters separate from the chorus ; inasmuch as Antigone declares her intention to bury her brother Polynices, against the command of the senate of Thebes, which had just been proclaimed.

§ 7. This concluding scene therefore points as distinctly as the end of the *Choëphorœ* to the subject of a new piece, which was doubtless the *Eleusinians*. This drama appears to have turned upon the burial of the Argive heroes slain before the gates of Thebes ; which burial was carried into execution by Theseus with the Athenians, against the will of the Thebans, and in the territory of Eleusis. It is manifest that the fate of Antigone (who, following her own impulse, had buried her brother, and either suffered or was to suffer death in consequence) was closely connected with this subject. But neither the plan nor the prevailing ideas of this last drama of the trilogy can be gathered from the few fragments of it which remain.

The connexion of the *Seven against Thebes* with a preceding

---

[1] As when the chorus says, 'Their hate is ended: their lives have flowed together on the gory earth; now in truth are they *blood-relations*' (ὅμαιμοι) v. 938-40, or where it is said, that the evil genius of the race has placed the trophies of destruction at the gate where they fell, and never rested till it had overcome *both*. V. 957-60.

piece is less evident, in the same way that the *Choëphorœ* points forward far more distinctly to the *Eumenides* than it points backward to the *Agamemnon*. But since we perceive in the extant trilogy that Æschylus was accustomed to develope completely all the essential parts of a mythological series, it cannot be doubted that the *Seven against Thebes* was preceded by some drama with which it was connected. The subject of this drama should not, however, be sought, with some critics, in the fables respecting the expedition of the Argive heroes; for they do not form the centre about which this tragic composition revolves, but are a vast foreign power breaking in upon the destinies of Thebes. It should rather be sought in the earlier fortunes of the royal family of Thebes. If we consider the great effect produced in the *Seven against Thebes* by the curse of Œdipus, we must conclude that this curse must have been treated as the principal subject of the preceding play; so as to be kept in mind by the spectators during the speeches of Eteocles, and to spread over the whole that feeling of anxious foreboding which is one of the most striking effects of tragedy.[1] It may, therefore, be probably inferred that it was the *Œdipus*, one of the lost plays of Æschylus, with which this trilogy commenced.

The poetry of Æschylus furnishes distinct and certain evidence of his disposition and opinions, particularly with respect to those public occurrences which at that time occupied the mind of every patriotic Greek; and in speaking of the *Seven against Thebes*, our attention has been called to his political principles, which appear still more clearly in the Orestean trilogy. Æschylus was one of those Athenians who strove to moderate the restless struggles of their countrymen after democracy and dominion over other Greeks; and who sought to maintain the ancient severe principles of law and morality,

---

[1] The account of this curse which was given by Æschylus seems to have been in several respects peculiar. Œdipus not only announced that the brothers would not divide their heritage in amity (according to the *Thebaid* in Athen. XI. p. 466), but he also declared that a stranger from Scythia (the steel of the sword) should make the partition as an arbitrator (δατητής, according to the language of the Attic law). If Œdipus had not used these words, the chorus, v. 729 and 944, and the messenger, v. 817, could not express the same idea, in nearly the same terms.

together with the institutions by which these were supported. The just, wise, and moderate Aristides was the statesman approved of by Æschylus, and not Themistocles, who pursued the distant objects of his ambition, through straight and crooked paths, with equal energy. The admiration of Æschylus for Aristides is clearly seen in his description of the battle of Salamis.[1] In the *Seven against Thebes*, the description of the upright Amphiaraus, who wished, not to seem, but to be, the best; the wise general, from whose mind, as from the deep furrows of a well-ploughed field, noble counsels proceed; was universally applied by the Athenian people to Aristides, and was doubtless intended by Æschylus for him. Then the complaint of Eteocles, that this just and temperate man, associated with impetuous companions, must share their ruin, expresses the disapprobation felt by Æschylus of the dispositions of other leaders of the Greeks and Athenians; among the rest, of Themistocles, who at that time had probably gone into exile on account of the part he had taken in the treasonable designs of Pausanias.

§ 8. We come next to the trilogy which may be called the *Danais*, and of which only the middle piece is preserved in the *Suppliants*. An historical and political spirit pervades this trilogy. The extant piece turns upon the reception in Pelasgic Argos of Danaus and his daughters, who had fled from Egypt in order to escape the violence of their suitors, the sons of Ægyptus. They sit as suppliants near a group of altars (κοινοϐωμία), in front of the city of Argos; and the king of the Argives (who is fearful of involving his kingdom in distress and danger) is induced, after many prayers and entreaties, to convene an assembly of the people, in order to deliberate concerning their reception. The assembly, partly from respect for the rights of suppliants, and partly from compassion for the persecuted daughters of Danaus, decrees to receive them. The opportunity soon presents itself of fulfilling the promise of protection and security: for the sons of Ægyptus land upon the coast, and (during the absence of Danaus, who is gone to procure assistance) the Egyptian herald attempts to carry off the

---

[1] Comp. *Persæ*, vv. 447—471, with Herodot. VIII. 95.

deserted maidens, as being the rightful property of his masters. Upon this, the king of the Pelasgians appears in order to protect them, and dismisses the herald, notwithstanding his threats of war. Nevertheless, the danger is averted only for the moment; and the play concludes with prayers to the gods that these forced marriages may be prevented, with which are intermingled doubts concerning the fate determined by the gods.

The want of dramatic interest in this drama partly proceeds from its being the *middle* piece of a trilogy. The third piece, the *Danaides*, doubtless contained the decision of the contest by the death of the suitors, with the exception of Lynceus; while a preceding drama, the *Egyptians*, must have explained the cause and origin of the contest in Egypt. There are other instances, in the middle pieces of the trilogies of Æschylus, of the action standing nearly still, the attention being made to dwell upon the sufferings caused by the elements which have been set in motion. The idea of the timid, afflicted virgins flying from their suitors' violence like doves before the vulture (which is worked out, in lyric strains, with great warmth and intensity of feeling) is evidently the main subject of the drama; it seems, indeed, that the preservation of the play has been due to the beauty of these choral odes. Yet the reception of the Danaides must have been a much more appropriate and important subject for a tragedy, according to the ideas of Æschylus, than according to those of Sophocles and Euripides. What this action wants in moral significance was compensated, in his opinion, by its historical interest. Æschylus belongs to a period when the national legends of Greece were considered, not as mere amusing fictions, but as evidences of the divine power which ruled over Greece. An event like the reception of the Danaides in Argos, on which depended the origin of the families of the Perseids and Heracleids, appeared to him as a great work of the counsels of Zeus; and to record the operation of these on human affairs seemed to him the highest calling of the tragic poet. Contrary to the custom of epic and tragic poets, he ascribes the greatest merit of the act to the Argive people, not to their king, and accordingly, the chorus, in a beautiful song (v. 625—709), invokes blessings upon them, the cause of which is evidently to be found in the relations which then subsisted between Athens and Argos. Æschylus, however, never makes forced allusions to contemporary events ; they arise naturally out of his mode of considering history, which closely resembles that of Pindar. According to this view, it was in the early mythical ages that the Greek states received the lot of their future destinies and were fixed in that position which they occupied in later times. Those passages in the *Suppliants* which so plainly refer to the establishment of a well regulated popular government in Argos and to treaties with foreign states by which war might be avoided,[1] make it evident that this piece was produced about the time when the alliance between Athens and Argos was already in operation, perhaps towards the end of Ol. 79, B.C. 461.[2] Also, the threats of a war with Egypt, which are implied in the plot of this tragedy, furnish the poet with a favourable opportunity for introducing some striking and impressive sayings, which necessarily held out great encouragement to the Athenians for the war with Egypt, which began Olymp. 79. 3. B.C. 462 ; as when we find it said that ' The fruit of the papyrus ' (which was the common food of the Egyptians) ' conquers not the wheat-stalk.'[3]

§ 9. The *Prometheus* was in all probability one of the last efforts of the genius of Æschylus, for the third actor is to a certain extent employed in it (chap. XXII. § 7). It is, beyond all question, one of his greatest works. Historical allusions are not to be expected in this play, as the subject does not comprise the events of any particular state or family, but refers to the condition and relations of the whole human race. Prometheus, as we had occasion to remark when speaking of Hesiod (chap. VIII. § 3, p. 122 note), represents the provident, aspiring understanding of man, which ardently seeks to improve in all ways the condition of our being. He was represented as a Titan, because the Greeks, who considered

---

[1] Thus the chorus says, v. 698—703 : ' May the people, who rule the city, maintain their rights—may they give foreigners their due, before they put weapons into the hands of Ares.'

[2] This alliance is more distinctly mentioned in the *Eumenides* (v. 765, seqq.), which was brought out a few years after.

[3] V. 761, comp. v. 954.

the gods of Olympus as rulers only, not as creators, of the human race, laid the foundation and beginning of man in the time which preceded the kingdom of the Olympian gods. Thus, according to the conception of Æschylus, he is the friend and mediator of man—'the dæmon most friendly to mankind,' in that period of the world when the kingdom of Zeus began. He does not, however, spiritualize him into a mere allegory of foresight and prudence, for in Æschylus a real, lively faith in the existence of mythical beings is harmoniously combined with a consideration of their significance. By teaching men the use of fire, Prometheus has made them acquainted with all the arts which render human life more endurable; in general, he has made them wiser and happier in every respect, especially by taking from them the fear of death. But in this he does not respect the limits which, according to the view of the ancients, the gods, who are alone immortal, have prescribed to the human race; he seeks to acquire for mortals perfections which the gods had reserved for themselves alone; for a mind which is always striving after advancement, and using all means to obtain it, cannot easily, from its very constitution, confine itself within the narrow limits prescribed to it by custom and law. These efforts of Prometheus, which we also learn occasionally from the play that has come down to us, were in all probability depicted with much greater perfection, and in connexion with his stealing the fire, in the first portion of the trilogy, which was called *Prometheus the Fire-bringer* (Προμηθεὺς πυρφόρος).[1]

The extant play, the *Prometheus Bound* (Προμηθεὺς δεσμώτης), begins at once with the fastening of the gigantic Titan to the rocks of Scythia, and the fettered prisoner is the centre of all the action of the piece. The daughters of Oceanus, who constitute the chorus of the tragedy, come to comfort and calm him; he is then visited by the aged Oceanus himself, and afterwards by Hermes, who endeavour, the one by mild arguments, the other by insults and threats, to move him to compliance and

---

[1] This *Prometheus Pyrphorus* must, as Welcker has shown, be distinguished from the *Prometheus Pyrkaëus*, 'the fire-kindler,' a satyric drama which was appended to the trilogy of the *Persæ*, and probably had reference to the festal customs of the *Promethea* in the Cerameicus, which comprised a torch-race.

submission. Meanwhile Prometheus continues to defy the superior power of Zeus, and stoutly declares that, unless his base fetters
are removed, he will not give out an oracle that he has learned
from his mother Themis, respecting the marriage, by means of
which Zeus was destined to lose his sovereign power. He
would rather that Zeus should bury his body in the rocks amid
thunder and lightning. With this the drama concludes, in
order to allow him to come forth again and suffer new torments.
This grand and sublime defiance of Prometheus, by which the
free will of man is perfectly maintained under overwhelming
difficulties from without, is generally considered the great
design of the poem; and in reading the remaining play of the
trilogy, there is no doubt on which side our sympathies should
be enlisted; for Prometheus appears as the just and suffering
martyr; Zeus as the mighty tyrant, jealous of his power. Nevertheless, if we view the subject from the higher ground of the
old poetic associations, we cannot rest content with such a solution as this. Tragedy could not, in conformity with those
associations, consist entirely of the opposition and conflict between the free will of an individual and omnipotent fate; it
must appease contending powers and assign to each of them its
proper place. Contentions may rise higher and higher, the
opposition may be stretched to the utmost, yet the divine guidance
which presides over the whole finds means to restore order and
harmony, and allots to each conflicting power its own peculiar
right.

The contest, with all its attendant miseries, appears even
beneficial in its results. This is the course of the tragedies of
Æschylus, and indeed of Greek tragedy in general, so far as it
remains true to its object. The tragedies of Æschylus uni-
formly require faith in a divine power, which, with steady eye
and firm hand, guides the course of events to the best issue,
though the path through which it leads may be dark and difficult, and fraught with distress and suffering. The poetry of
Æschylus is full of profound and enthusiastic glorifications of
Zeus as this power. How then could Zeus be depicted in this
drama as a tyrant, how could the governor of the world be represented as arbitrary and unjust? It is true that the Greek
divinities are always described as beings who are not what they

were, (above, p. 122,) and hence it is difficult to separate from them the ideas of strife and contention. This also accounts for the severity with which Zeus, at the time described by Æschylus, proceeds against every attempt to limit and circumscribe his newly established sovereignty. But Æschylus, in his own mind, must have felt how this severity, a necessary accompaniment of the transition from the Titanian period to the government of the gods of Olympus, was to be reconciled with the mild wisdom which he makes an attribute of Zeus in the subsequent ages of the world. Consequently the deviation from right, the ἁμαρτία in the tragic action, which, according to Aristotle, should not be considered as depravity, but as the error of a noble nature,[1] would all lie on the side of Prometheus; and even the poet has clearly shown this in the piece itself, when he makes the chorus of Oceanides, who are friendly to Prometheus, and even to the sacrifice of themselves, perpetually recur to the same thoughts. 'Those only are wise who humbly reverence Adrastea,' (the inexorable goddess of Fate.[2])

§ 10. In these remarks upon the *Prometheus Bound* we have passed over one act of the play, which, however, is of the highest importance for an understanding of the whole trilogy, namely, the appearance of Io, who, having won the love of Zeus, has brought upon herself the hatred of Hera. Persecuted by horrid phantoms, she comes in her wanderings to Prometheus, and learns from him the further miseries, all of which she has still to endure. The misfortunes of Io very much resemble those of Prometheus, since Io also might be considered as a victim to the selfish severity of Zeus, and she is so considered by Prometheus. At the same time, however, as Prometheus does not conceal from Io that the thirteenth in descent from her is to release him from all his sufferings; the love of Zeus for her appears in a higher light, and we obtain for the fate of Prometheus also that sort of assuaging tranquillity, which it was always the aim of the ancients to preserve, even in their most impas-

---

[1] That is to say, so far as it is the ἁμαρτία of the *protagonists*, as of Prometheus, Agamemnon, Antigone, Œdipus, and so forth; for the ἁμαρτίαι of the *tritagonists* are of a totally different kind.

[2] V. 936. Οἱ προσκυνοῦντες τὴν Ἀδράστειαν σοφοί.

sioned scenes.   But as Hermes announces that Zeus will never
succeed in overcoming the rebellious Titans till an immortal
shall freely lay down his life for him, the issue remains dark
and doubtful.

The *Prometheus Unbound* (Προμηθεὺς λυόμενος), the loss of
which we lament more almost than that of any other tragedy,
although many considerable fragments of it remain, began at a
totally different period of the world.   Prometheus, however,
still remains bound to the rock in Scythia, and, as Hermes had
prophetically threatened, he is daily torn by the eagle of Zeus.
The chorus, instead of the Oceanides, consists of *Titans* escaped
from durance in Tartarus.   Æschylus, therefore, like Pindar,[1]
adopts the idea, originating with the Orphic poets, that Zeus,
after he had firmly fixed the government of the world,
proclaimed a general amnesty, and restored peace among the
vanquished powers of heaven.   Meanwhile mankind had arrived
at a much higher degree of dignity than even Prometheus had
designed for them, by means of the hero race, and man became,
as it were, ennobled through heroes sprung from the Olympic
gods.   Hercules, the son of Zeus by a distant descendant of Io,
was the greatest benefactor and friend of man among heroes, as
Prometheus was among Titans.   He now appears, and, after
hearing from Prometheus the benefits he has conferred upon
man, and receiving a proof of his good will in the way of pre-
diction and advice with regard to his own future adventures,
releases the sufferer from the torments of the eagle, and from
his chains.   He does this of his own free will, but manifestly
by the permission of Zeus.   Zeus has already fixed upon the
immortal who is ready to resign his immortality.   Cheiron is,
without Hercules' intending it, wounded by one of the poisoned
arrows of the hero, and, in order to escape endless torments, is
willing to descend into the lower world.   We must suppose
that, at the end of the piece, the power and majesty of Zeus
and the profound wisdom of his decrees are so gloriously manifested, that the pride of Prometheus is entirely broken.[2]   Pro-

---

[1] Pindar, *Pyth.* IV. 291.   Comp. above, chap. XVI. § 1.
[2] Even after his liberation from fetters Prometheus had called Hercules ' the
most dear son of a hated father.'   Fragm. 187. Dindorf.

metheus now brings a wreath of *Agnus Castus*, (λύγος,) and probably a ring also, made from the iron of his fetters, mysterious symbols of the dependence and subjection of the human race; and he now willingly proclaims his mother's ancient prophecy, that a son more powerful than the father who begot him should be born of the sea-goddess Thetis; whereupon Zeus resolves to marry the goddess to the mortal Peleus.

It is scarcely possible to conceive a more perfect *katharsis* of a tragedy, according to the requisitions of Aristotle.

The passions of fear, pity, hatred, love, anger, and admiration, as excited and stirred up by the actions and destiny of the individual characters in this middle piece, produce rather a distressing than a pleasing effect; but under the guidance of sublime and significant images they take such a course of development, that an elevated yet softened tone is shed over them, and all is resolved into a feeling of awe and devotion for the decrees of a higher power.

§ 11. The poetical career of Æschylus concludes for us, as for the ancient Athenians, with the only complete trilogy that is extant, the possession of which, after the *Iliad* and *Odyssey*, might be considered the richest treasure of Greek poetry, if it had been better preserved, and had come down to us without the gaps and interpolations by which it is defaced. Æschylus brought this trilogy upon the stage at a moment of great political excitement in his native city, Olymp. 80. 2, B.C. 458; at the time when the democratic party, under the guidance of Pericles, were endeavouring to overthrow the Areopagus, the last of those aristocratic institutions which tended to restrain the innovating spirit of the people in public and private life. He was impelled to make the legend of Orestes the groundwork of a trilogic composition, of which, as we have still the whole before us, we will give only the principal points.

Agamemnon comes on the stage in the tragedy which bears his name, in one scene only, when he is received by his wife Clytæmnestra as a conquering hero, and, after some hesitation, walks over the outspread purple carpets into the interior of his palace. He is, however, the chief person of the piece, for all through it the actors and chorus are almost exclusively occupied with his character and destiny.

Æschylus represents him as a great and glorious monarch, but who, by his enterprise against Troy, has sacrificed to his warlike ambition the lives of many men,[1] and, above all, that of his own daughter Iphigenia;[2] and he has thus involved in a gloomy destiny his house, which is already suffering from wounds inflicted long before his time. Clytæmnestra, on the other hand, is a wife, who, while she pursues her impulses and pleasures with unscrupulous resolution, has power and cunning enough to carry her evil designs into full effect. Agamemnon is completely enveloped in her subtle schemes, even before she throws the traitorous garment over him like a net; and after the deed is done, she has the skill, in her conversation with the chorus, to throw over it a cloak of that sophistry of the passions, which Æschylus so well knew how to paint, by enumerating all the reasons she might have had for it, had the real ground not been sufficient.

The great tragic effect which this play cannot fail to produce on every one who is capable of reading and understanding it, is the contrast between the external splendour of the house of the Atridæ and its real condition. The first scenes are very imposing;—the light of the beacon, the news of the fall of Troy, and the entrance of Agamemnon;—but, amidst these signs of joy, a tone of mournful foreboding resounds from the songs of the chorus, which grows more and more distinct and impressive till the inimitable scene between the chorus and Cassandra, when the whole misfortune of the house bursts forth into view. From this time forth our feelings are wrought to the highest pitch—the murder of Agamemnon follows immediately upon this announcement; while the triumph of Clytæmnestra and Ægisthus—the remorseless cold-bloodedness with which she exults in the deed, and the laments and reproaches of the chorus —leave the mind, sympathizing as it does with the fate of the

---

[1] 'For the gods,' says the chorus (v. 461), 'never lose sight of those who have been the cause of death to many men' (τῶν πολυκτόνων γὰρ οὐκ ἄσκοποι θεοί).

[2] The chorus does not hesitate to censure this sacrifice, (especially in v. 217) and considers it as actually completed, so does Clytæmnestra, v. 1555; though Æschylus does not mean by this to set aside the story of Iphigenia's deliverance. According to his view of the case the sacrificers themselves must have been blinded by Artemis.

house, in an agony of horror and excitement which has not a minute of repose or consolation, except in a sort of feeling that Agamemnon has fallen by means of a divine Nemesis.

§ 12. The *Choëphorœ* contains the mortal revenge of Orestes. The natural steps of the action, the revenge planned and resolved upon by Orestes with the chorus and Electra, the artful intrigues by which Orestes at length arrives at the execution of the deed, the execution itself, the contemplation of it after it is committed, all these points form so many acts of the drama. The first is the longest and the most finished, as the poet evidently makes it his great object to display distinctly the deep distress of Orestes at the necessity he feels of revenging his father's death upon his mother. Thus the whole action takes place at the tomb of Agamemnon, and the chorus consists of Trojan women in the service of the family of the Atridæ; they are sent by Clytæmnestra, who has been terrified by horrid dreams, in order, for the first time, to appease with offerings the spirit of her murdered husband, and, by the advice of Electra, bring the offerings, but not for the purpose for which they were sent. The spirit of Agamemnon is formally conjured to appear from below the earth, and to take an active part in the work of his own revenge, and the guidance of the whole work is repeatedly ascribed to the subterranean gods, especially to Hermes, the leader of the dead, who is also the god of all artful and hidden acts; and the poet has contrived to shed a gloomy and shadowy light over this whole proceeding. The act itself is represented throughout as a sore burthen undertaken by Orestes upon the requisition of the subterranean gods, and by the constraining influence of the Delphic oracle; no mean motive, no trifling indifference mingle with his resolves, and yet, or rather the more on that very account, while Orestes stands beside the corpses of his mother and her paramour upon the same spot where his father was slain, and justifies his own act by proclaiming the heinousness of their crime, even at that moment the furies appear before him, and, visible to the spectators, though unseen by the chorus, torture him with their horrid forms till he rushes away and hastens to beg for atonement and purification from Apollo, who has urged him to the deed. We here perceive that, according to the views of Æschylus and other

Greeks, the furies do not properly betoken the degree of moral guilt or the power of an evil conscience, (in which case they must have appeared in a more terrible shape to Clytæmnestra than to Orestes); but they exhibit the fearful nature of the deed itself, of a mother's murder as such; for this, from whatever motive it may be committed, is a violation of the ordinances of nature which cannot fail to torture and perplex the human mind.

§ 13. This character of the *Erinnyes* is more definitely developed in the concluding play of the trilogy, in the chorus of which Æschylus, combining the artist with the poet, gives an exhibition of these beings, of whom the Greeks had hitherto but a glimmering idea. He bestows upon them a form taken partly from their spiritual qualities and partly from the analogy of the Gorgons. They avenge the matricidal act as a crime in itself, without inquiring into motives or circumstances, and it is therefore pursued with all the inflexibility of a law of nature, and by all the horror and torments as well of the upper as of the lower world. Even the expiation granted by Apollo to Orestes at Delphi has no influence upon them; for all that Apollo can accomplish is to throw them for a short period into a deep sleep, from which they are awakened by the appearance of the ghost of Clytæmnestra, condemned for her crime to wander about the lower world; and this apparition must have produced the greatest effect upon the stage. After the scene in Delphi, we are transported to the sanctuary of Pallas Athena, on the Acropolis, whither Orestes has repaired by the advice of Apollo, and where, in a very regular manner, and with many allusions to the actual usages of the Athenian law, the court of the Areopagus is established by Pallas, who recognizes the claims of both parties, but is unwilling to arrogate to herself the power of arbitrarily deciding the questions between them. Before this court of justice the dispute between Orestes and his advocate Apollo on the one side, and the furies on the other, is formally discussed. In these discussions, it must be owned, there occur many points which belong to the main question, and these are, as it were, summed up; for instance, the command of Apollo; the vengeance for blood which is imposed as a duty upon the son by the ghost of his father; the revolting manner in which Agamemnon was murdered ; nevertheless, the intrinsic difference between the act of Orestes and that of Clytæmnestra is not marked as we should have expected it to be. It is manifest that Æschylus distinctly perceived this difference in feeling, without quite working it out. Apollo concludes his apology with rather a subtle argument, showing why the father is more worthy of honour than the mother, by which he makes interest with Pallas, who had no mother, but proceeded at once out of the head of her father, Zeus. When the judges, of whom there are twelve,[1] come to the vote, it is found the votes on each side are equal ; upon this the goddess gives the casting vote—' the voting pebble of Athena,'—the destination of which she has declared beforehand, and so decides in favour of Orestes. The poet here means to imply that the duty of revenge and the guilt of matricide are equally balanced, and that stern justice has no alternative ; but the gods of Olympus, being of the nature of man, and acquainted and entrusted with the personal condition of individuals, can find and supply a refuge for the unfortunate, who are so by no immediate guilt of their own. Hence the repeated references to the overruling name of Zeus, who always steps in between contending powers as the saviour-god (Ζεὺς σωτήρ),[2] and invariably turns the scale in favour of virtue. After his acquittal, Orestes leaves the stage with blessings and promises of friendly alliance with Athens, but somewhat more hastily than we expected, after the intense interest which his fate has inspired. But the cause of this is seen in the heartfelt love of Æschylus for the Athenians. The goddess of wisdom, who has veiled her power in the mildest and most persuasive form, succeeds in soothing the rage of the furies, which threatens to bring destruction upon Athens, by promising to ensure them for ever the honour and respect of the Athenians ; and thus the whole concludes with a song of blessing by the furies (wherein, on the supposition that their power is duly acknowledged, they assume the character of beneficent deities), and with the establishment of the worship of

---

[1] The number twelve is inferred from the arrangement of the short speeches made by the parties while the voting is going on (v. 710—733).

[2] Vv. 759, 797, 1045.

the Eumenides, who are at once conducted by torchlight to their
sanctuary in the Areopagus with all the pomp with which their
sacrifices at Athens were attended. The Athenians are here
plainly admonished to treat with reverence the Areopagus thus
founded by the gods, and the judicial usages of which are so
closely connected with the worship of the Eumenides; and not
to take from that body its cognizance of charges of murder, as
was about to be done, in order to transfer their functions to the
great jury courts. The *stasima*, too, in which the ideas of the
piece appear still more clearly than in the treatment of the
mythus, utter no sentiment more definitely than this; that it
is above all things necessary to recognize without hesitation a
power which bridles the unruly affections and sinful thoughts of
man.[1]

We may remark in few words, that the satyrical drama
which was appended to this trilogy, the *Proteus,* was in all probability connected with the same mythical subject, and turned
upon the adventure of Menelaus and Helen with Proteus,
the sea-dæmon and keeper of the sea-monsters, an adventure
which is known to us from Homer. The useless wanderings of
Menelaus, who on his return home left his brother behind, and
thereby arrived too late not only to save, but even to avenge
him,[2] might give room for abundant mirth and entertainment,
without disturbing or effacing the impressions which had been
produced by the tragic fate of the house of the Atridæ.

§ 14. These short accounts of those trilogies of Æschylus
which have been preserved, in whole or in part, will suffice,
we conceive, to give as much insight into the mind of that
great poet as can be expected in a work of this kind. It must
be confessed, however, that there is a wide difference between
these cold abstracts of the dramas of Æschylus and the tone
and character of the works themselves, which, even in the
minutest details of execution, show all the power of a mind full
of poetic inspiration, and impressed with the truth and pro-
foundness of its own conceptions. As all the persons brought
on the stage by Æschylus express their feelings and characters

---

[1] Ξυμφέρει σωφρονεῖν ὑπὸ στένει, v. 520.
[2] Compare above, chap. VI. § 5. and *Agam.* 624, 839.

in strong and forcible terms, so also the forms of speech they make use of have a proud and lofty tone; the diction of these plays is like a temple of Ictinus, constructed solely of huge rectangular blocks of polished marble. In the individual expressions, the poetical form predominates over the syntactical; this is brought about by the employment of metaphorical phrases and new compounds :[1] and here the poet's great knowledge and true comprehension of nature and human life give to his expressions a vividness and warmth which only differs from the *naïveté* of the epic style by the greater admixture of acute reflection which it displays, and by which he has contrived to mark at once a feeling of connexion and a consciousness of difference.[2] The forms of syntax are rather those which rest upon a parallel connexion of sentences (consequently, copulative, adversative, and disjunctive sentences) than those which result from the subordination of one sentence to another (as in causal and conditional periods, &c.). The language has little of that oratorical flow which at a later period sprung up in the courts and assemblies, and just as little of a subtle development of complicated connexions of thought. It is throughout better calculated to display powerful impulses of the feelings and desires, and the instinctive actions of prompt and decided character, than the reflection of minds impelled by various motives. Hence in each piece we find some leading thoughts frequently repeated, particularly in the different forms of speech, dialogue, anapæsts, lyric measures, &c. Yet the poet by no means wants the power of adapting his language to the different characters, to say nothing of all those differences which depend upon the metrical forms; and, notwithstanding the general elevation of his style, persons of an inferior grade, such as the watchman in the *Agamemnon*, and the nurse of Orestes in the *Choëphoræ*, are made to descend, as well in the words as in the turn of the expressions, to the use of language more nearly approaching

---

[1] We may also mention his employment of obsolete expressions, especially those borrowed from epic poetry—τὸ γλωσσῶδες τῆς λέξεως. Æschylus is a few degrees more epic in his language than Sophocles or Euripides.

[2] Hence arise the *oxymora* of which Æschylus is so fond : for instance, when he calls dust 'the dumb messenger of the army.'

that of common life, and manifest even in the collocation of
their words a weaker order of mind.

§ 15. To return once more to the Orestean trilogy of
Orestes : the judges of tragic merit adjudged the prize to it
before all the rival pieces.　But this poetic victory seems to
have been no compensation to Æschylus for the failure of the
practical portion of his design, as the Athenians at the same
time deprived the Areopagus of all the honour and power which
the poet had striven to preserve for it.　Æschylus returned a
second time to Sicily, and died in his favourite city of Gela,
three years after the performance of the Orestea.

The Athenians had a feeling that Æschylus would not be
satisfied with the course their public life and their taste for art
and science took in the next generation ; the shadow of the
poet, as he is brought up by Aristophanes from the other world in
the *Frogs*, manifests an angry discontent with the public, who
were so pleased with Euripides, although the latter was no rival
of Æschylus, for he did not appear upon the stage till the year
in which Æschylus died.　Yet this did not prevent the Athenians from recognizing most fully the beauty and sublimity of
his poetry.　' With him his muse died not,' said Aristophanes,
alluding to the fact that his tragedies were allowed to be performed after his death, and might even be brought forward as
new pieces.　The poet who taught his chorus the plays of
Æschylus, was remunerated by the state, and the crown was
dedicated to the poet who had been long dead.[1]　The family of
Æschylus, which continued for a long time, preserved a school
of poetry in his peculiar style, which we will hereafter notice.

---

[1] This is the result of the passages in the *Vita Æschyli ;* Philostrat. *Vita Apollon.*
VI. 11. p. 245, Olear.; Schol. Aristoph. *Acharn.* 10. *Ran.* 892.　The *Vita Æschyli*
says that the poet was crowned after his death ; and this view seems preferable to
Quinctilian's assertion (*Inst.* X. 1), that many other poets obtained the crown by
representing the plays of Æschylus.　We must distinguish from this case the victories of Euphorion (above, § 2 and note) obtained by producing plays of Æschylus
that had not been represented ; the law of Lycurgus, too, with regard to the representation of pieces by the three great tragedians, from copies officially verified, has
nothing to do with the custom alluded to in the text.

CHAPTER XXIV.

SOPHOCLES.

§ 1. THE tragic trilogies of Æschylus had given a dramatic representation of the great cycle of Hellenic legends. In exhibiting the history of whole families, tribes, and states, the poet had contrived to show the influence of supreme wisdom and power shining amidst the greatest difficulty and darkness. Every Greek who witnessed such an exhibition of the dispensations of Providence in the history of his race, must have been filled with mingled emotions of wonder and joyful exultation. A tragedy of this kind was at once political, patriotic, and religious.

How was it possible that, after these mighty creations of so great a genius as Æschylus, a still fairer renown should be in reserve for Sophocles? In what direction could such great advances be made from the point to which Æschylus had brought the tragic art?

We will not indulge ourselves in an *à priori* determination of the way in which this advance *might have been made*, but will rather consider, with history for our guide, how it *really* took place. It will be seen that the change was retrograde as well as progressive; that if something was gained on the one side, it was because something was also given up on the other; and that it was due above all to that moderation and sobriety of character, which was the noblest and most amiable property of the Greek mind.

Before we can solve the great question proposed above, we must give an account of so much of the poet's life as may be necessary for an understanding of his poetical career.

SOPHOCLES, the son of Sophilus, was born at the Attic demus or village of Colonus, in Olymp. 71. 2, B.C. 495.[1] He was, therefore, fifteen years old when the battle of Salamis was fought. He could not, of course, share in the dangers of the fight, but he was the *exarchus*, or leader of the chorus which sang the pæan of victory, and in that capacity appeared naked, according to the rule in gymnastic solemnities, anointed with oil, and holding a lyre in his left hand. The managers of the feast had selected him for this purpose on account of his youthful beauty[2] and the musical education which he had received.

Eleven or twelve years after this, in Olymp. 77. 4,[3] B.C. 468, Sophocles came forward for the first time as a competitor in a dramatic contest, and, indeed, as a rival of the old hero Æschylus. This happened at the great Dionysia, when the first Archon presided ; it was his duty to nominate the judges of the contest. Cimon, who had just conquered the pirates of Scyros, and brought back to Athens the bones of Theseus, happened to come into the theatre along with his colleagues in order to pay the suitable offerings to Bacchus, and Aphepsion the Archon thought it due to the importance of the contest to submit the decision of the poetical victory to these glorious victors in real battle. Cimon, a man of the old school, and of noble moderation of character, who undoubtedly appreciated Æschylus, gave the prize to his young rival, from which we may infer how completely his genius outshone all competition, even at his first coming out. The play with which he gained this victory is said to have been the *Triptolemus*,[4] a patriotic piece, in which

---

[1] This is the statement in the *Vita Sophoclis*. The Parian marble makes him two years older, but this is opposed to the fact mentioned in the note to § 2.

[2] Athenæus I. p. 20. f., in speaking of this occasion, says that Sophocles was καλὸς τὴν ὥραν, which applies best to the age assigned to him above.

[3] All new dramas at Athens were performed at the Lenæa and the great Dionysia, the former of which took place in the month Gamelion, the latter in Elaphebolion, and therefore in the second half of the Attic or Olympian year, after the winter solstice ; consequently, in the history of the drama we must always reckon the year of the Olympiad equal to the year B.C. in which its second half falls.

[4] This appears from a combination of the narrative in the text with a chronological statement in Pliny, *N. H.* XVIII. 12.

this Eleusinian hero was celebrated as promoting the cultivation of corn, and humanizing the manners even of the wildest barbarians.

§ 2. The first piece of Sophocles which has been preserved is twenty-eight years subsequent to this event; it is remarkable as also marking a glorious period in the poet's life. Sophocles brought out the *Antigone* in Olymp. 84. 4, B.C. 440. The goodness of the play, but above all the shrewd reflections and admirable sentiments on public matters which are frequently expressed in it, induced the Athenians to elect him to the office of general for the ensuing year. It must be remembered that the ten *Strategi* were not merely the commanders of the troops, but also very much employed in the administration of affairs at home, and in carrying on negotiations with foreign states. Sophocles was one of the generals, who, in conjunction with Pericles, carried on the war with the aristocrats of Samos, who, after being expelled from Samos by the Athenians, had returned from Anæa on the continent with Persian aid, and stirred up the island to revolt against Athens.[1] This war was carried on in Olymp. 85. 1, B.C. 440, 439.

According to several old anecdotes, Sophocles preserved even in the bustle of war his cheerfulness of temper, and that poetical disposition which delights in a clear and tranquil contemplation of human affairs. It was also on this occasion that Sophocles became acquainted with Herodotus, who about this time was living at Samos (chap. XIX. § 1), and composed a poem for him, no doubt a lyrical one.[2] It is interesting to think of the social intercourse of two such men with one another. They both scrutinized the knowledge of human affairs with calm and comprehensive vision; but the Samian, with a more boyish

---

[1] On this account the *Vita Sophoclis* calls the war, in the management of which Sophocles took a part, τὸν πρὸς ’Αναίαν πόλεμον. The list of generals in this war is preserved to a certain extent complete in a fragment of Androtion, quoted by the Scholiast on Aristides, p. 225 C (p. 182, Ed. Frommel).

[2] See Plutarch, *An seni*, &c. 3., where this story is brought in by the head and shoulders. It is from this poem, of course, that the author of the *Vita Sophoclis* derives his assertion with regard to the age of Sophocles at the time of the Samian war; otherwise, how did he come to make an assertion so unusual with grammarians? We must, therefore, emend the readings in the *Vita Sophoclis* according to the passage in Plutarch, where the text is more to be depended on. This will make Sophocles 55 years old at this period.

disposition, sought out the traditions of many nations and many lands, while the Athenian had applied his riper and more searching intellect to that which was immediately before him, —the secret workings of power and passion in the breast of every man.

It is doubtful whether Sophocles took any further part in public affairs at a later period. On the whole, he was, as his contemporary Ion of Chios tells us,[1] neither very well acquainted with politics nor particularly qualified for public business. In all this, he did not get beyond the ordinary standard of individuals of the better sort. It is clear that, in this case, as in that of Æschylus, poetry was the business of his life. The study and exercise of the art of poetry occupied the whole of his time, as appears at once from the number of his dramas. There existed under his name 130 plays, of which according to the grammarian Aristophanes, seventeen were wrongly ascribed to him. The remaining 113 seem to comprise tragedies and satyrical dramas. In several of the tetralogies, however, the satyrical drama must have been lost or perhaps never existed (as we find to be the case with other poets also), because otherwise the number could not have been so uneven; at the utmost there could only have been twenty-three extant satyrical dramas to ninety tragedies. All these pieces were brought out between Olymp. 77. 4, B.C. 468, when Sophocles first came forward, and Olymp. 93. 2, B.C. 406, when he died; consequently, in a period of sixty-two years, the last of which, comprehending his extreme old age, cannot have added much to the number. The years of the Peloponnesian war must have been the most prolific; for if we may depend upon the tradition[2] that the *Antigone* was the thirty-second play in a chronological arrangement of the dramas of Sophocles, there still remain eighty-one dramas for the second half of his poetical career; or, if we leave out the satyrical dramas, we have about fifty-eight pieces remaining. We arrive at the same result from a date relating to Euripides,

---

[1] Athenæus XIII. p. 603.

[2] See the hypothesis to the *Antigone*, by Aristophanes of Byzantium. If the number thirty-two included the satyrical dramas also, some of the trilogies must have been without this appendage; otherwise the thirty-second piece would have been a satyrical drama.

of whose pieces, said to be ninety-two in number, the *Alcestis* was the sixteenth.[1] Now, according to the same authority, the *Alcestis* was exhibited in Olymp. 85. 2, B.C. 438, the seventeenth year of the poetical life of Euripides, which lasted for forty-nine, from Olymp. 81. 1, B.C. 455, to Olymp. 93. 2, B.C. 406. It may be seen from this, that at first both poets brought out a tetralogy every three or four years, but afterwards every two years at least. A consequence of this more rapid production appears in that slight regard for, or rather the absolute neglect of, the stricter models, which has been remarked in the lyrical parts of tragedy after the 90th or 89th Olympiad.

§ 3. As far as one can judge from internal and external evidence, the remaining tragedies are all subsequent to the *Antigone* : the following is perhaps their chronological order ; *Antigone, Electra, Trachinian Women, King Œdipus, Ajax, Philoctetes, Œdipus at Colonus.* The only definite information we possess is that the *Philoctetes* was acted in Olymp. 92. 3, B.C. 409, and the *Œdipus at Colonus* not till Olymp. 94. 3, B.C. 401, when it was brought out by the younger Sophocles, the author being dead. Taken together, they exhibit the art of Sophocles in its full maturity, in that mild grandeur which Sophocles was the first to appropriate to himself, when, after having (to use a remarkable expression of his own which has been preserved) put away the pomp of Æschylus along with his boyish things, and laid aside a harshness of manner which had sprung up from his own too great art and refinement, he had at length attained to that style which he himself considered to be the *best and the most suited to the representation of the characters of men.*[2] In the *Antigone*, the *Trachinian Women*,

---

[1] See the *didascalia* to the *Alcestis e. cod. Vaticano*, published by Dindorf in the Oxford edition, 1836. The number ιξ' is, in accordance with this view, changed to ιϛ', which suits the reckoning better than ιξ'. We have a third date of this kind in *the Birds* of Aristophanes, which is the thirty-fifth of that poet's comedies.

[2] The important passage, quoted by Plutarch, *De Profectu Virtut. Sent.* p. 79, B., should undoubtedly be written as follows :—ὁ Σοφοκλῆς ἔλεγε, τὸν Αἰσχύλου διαπεπαιχὼς ὄγκον, εἶτα τὸ πικρὸν καὶ κατάτεχνον τῆς αὑτοῦ κατασκευῆς, εἰς τρίτον ἤδη τὸ τῆς λέξεως μεταβάλλειν εἶδος, ὅπερ ἐστὶν ἠθικώτατον καὶ βέλτιστον.

[The κατασκευὴ here opposed to the λέξις means the language or words as opposed to the style or their arrangement. See Plutarch *Comp. Aristoph. et Menandr.* p. 853 C., ἐν τῇ κατασκευῇ τῶν ὀνομάτων.—ED.]

and the *Electra,* we have still, perhaps, a little of that artificial style and studied obscurity which Sophocles objected to in himself; the *Ajax* and *Philoctetes,* as well as the two *Œdipuses,* show, in a manner which cannot be mistaken, an easier flow of language than his earlier plays, and do not require so great an effort on the part of the reader. Nevertheless, the tragic art of Sophocles is fully shown in all of them, and is like nothing but itself; Sophocles must have hit upon the changes which he introduced into the tragedy of Æschylus, long before he wrote any one of those plays, and must have already made, in accordance with his principles, a complete change in the whole constitution of tragedy.

§ 4. We have mentioned these alterations, as far as concerns the details, in the two preceding chapters : we must here consider their connexion with the change of the whole essence and organization of tragedy effected by Sophocles. The foundation and corner-stone of this new edifice, which was erected on the same area as the old building, but according to a different plan, was always this, that, though Sophocles still followed the old usages and laws, and always, or as a general rule, exhibited at one time three tragedies and a satyrical drama, he nevertheless loosened the connexion of these pieces with one another, and presented to the public not *one* great dramatic poem, but four separate poetical works, which might just as well have been brought forward at different festivals.[1] The tragic poet, too, no longer proposed to himself to exhibit a series of mythical actions, the development of the complicated destinies of families and tribes, which was inconsistent with the compass and unity of plan required by separate tragedies ; he was obliged to limit himself to *one* leading fact, and, to take the example of the Orestea, could only oppose to such a trilogy fragments of itself, like the *Electra* of Sophocles or Euripides, in which everything is referred to the murder of Clytæmnestra. The tragedies subsequent to Olymp. 80 had indeed become considerably longer,[2]

---

[1] As *e. g.* Euripides brought out in B.C. 431, the *Medea, Philoctetes, Dictys,* and the satyrical drama the *Reapers* (Θηρισταί) : in B.C. 414, Xenocles exhibited the *Œdipus, Lycaon, Bacchœ,* and the satyrical drama the *Athamas.*

[2] *E. g.* the *Persians,* 1076 ; *Suppliants,* 1074 ; *Seven against Thebes,* 1078 ; *Prometheus,* 1093. On the other hand, the *Agamemnon,* 1673 ; the *Antigone,*

which is said to have originated with Aristarchus, a tragedian who made his appearance in Olymp. 81. 2, B.C. 454.[1] The *Agamemnon* of Æschylus, however, the first piece of his last trilogy, is considerably longer than the others, and nearly of the same length as a play of Sophocles. Still, this extension has not been effected by an increase in the action, which even in Sophocles turns upon a single point, and very seldom, as in the *Antigone*, is divided into several important moments, but is entirely subservient to the development of the events out of the character and passions of actors, and belongs to the delineation of their state of mind. The lyrical element, on the contrary, so far from gaining anything by this extension, was considerably diminished, especially in the part which fell to the chorus, since it is clear that Sophocles did not feel himself so much called upon, as Æschylus did, to represent the impression of the events and circumstances upon those who took no part in them, and to lend his voice to express the feelings of right-minded spectators, which was the chief business of the tragic chorus, but he directed his efforts to express what was going on in the bosoms of the persons whose actions were represented on the stage.

It is sufficiently obvious that the introduction of the third actor (chap. XXII. § 7,) was necessary for this change. The dialogue naturally gains much in variety by the addition of a third interlocutor; for this enables the characters to show themselves on different sides. If it is the property of the *tritagonist*, to produce opposition on the part of the first person by gainsaying him, the *deuteragonist*, on the other hand, may, in friendly conversation, draw from his bosom its gentler feelings and more secret thoughts. It was not till the separation of the *deuteragonist* from the *tritagonist* that we could have persons like Chrysothemis by the side of Electra, and Ismene by the side of Antigone, who elevate the vigour of the chief character by the opposition and contrast of a gentler womanhood.[2]

These outward changes in the stage business of tragedy en-

---

[1]353 ; *King Œdipus*, 1530; *Œdipus at Colonus*, 1780, according to the numbers in Dindorf's edition.

[1] Suidas v. 'Αρίσταρχος . . . . ὃς πρῶτος εἰς τὸ νῦν αὐτῶν μῆκος τὰ δράματα κατέστησεν. Eusebius gives us the year of his first appearance.

[2] Comp. Schol. on the *Electra*, 328.

able us at once to see the point to which Sophocles desired to
bring tragic poetry ; he wished to make it a true mirror of the
impulses, passions, strivings, and struggles of the soul of man.
While he laid aside those great objects of national interest,
which made the Greek look upon the time gone by as a high
and a holy thing, and to keep up the remembrance of which
the art of Æschylus had been for the most part dedicated, the
mythical subjects gained in his hands a general, and therefore
a lasting significance.   The rules of Greek art obliged him to
depict strong and great characters, and the shocks to which
they are exposed are exceedingly violent ; they are drawn, however, with such intrinsic truth that every man may recognize in
them in some points a likeness of himself ; the corrections and
limitations of the exercise of man's will, and the requirements
and laws of morality are expressed in the most forcible manner.
There has hardly been any poet whose works can be compared
with those of Sophocles for the universality and durability of
their moral significance.

§ 5. We cannot here attempt to submit the plan of the different tragedies of Sophocles to a circumstantial analysis (to
which the remarks in chap. XXII. furnish a sort of introduction) ; it will, however, be in accordance with the object of this
work to take a nearer view of the particular situations which
form the turning-points of the different plays, and of the ethical
ideas which are asserted in them.

The *Antigone* turns entirely on the contest between the interests and requirements of the *state* and the rights and duties
of the *family*.   Thebes has successfully repulsed the attack of
the Argive army ; but Polyneices, one of her citizens, and a
member of the Theban royal family, lies dead before the walls
among the enemies who had threatened Thebes with fire and
sword.   Creon, the king of Thebes, only follows a custom of
the Greeks, the object of which was to preserve a state from the
attacks of its own citizens, when he leaves the enemy of his
native land unburied as a prey to dogs and vultures ; yet the
manner in which he keeps up this political principle, the excessive severity of the punishment denounced against those who
wished to bury the corpse, the terrible threats addressed to those
who watched it, and, still more the boastful and violent strain

in which he sets forth and extols his own principles—all this
gives us a proof of that infatuation of a narrow mind, unen-
lightened by gentleness of a higher nature, which appeared to
the Greeks to contain in itself a foreboding of approaching misfortune.   But what was to be done by the relations of the dead
man, the females of his family, on whom the care of the corpse
was imposed as a religious duty by the universal law of the
Greeks?   That they should feel their duty to the family in all
its force, and not comprehend what they owed to the state, is
in accordance with the natural character of women; but while
the one sister, Ismene, only sees the impossibility of performing
the former duty, the great soul of Antigone fires with the occasion, and forms resolves of the greatest boldness. ⟨Defiance
begets defiance: Creon's harsh decree calls forth in her breast
the most obstinate, inflexible self-will, which disregards all consequences, and despises all gentler means.   In this consists her
guilt, which Sophocles does not conceal; on the contrary, he
brings it prominently before us, and especially in the choruses;[1]
but the very reason why Antigone is so highly tragical a character is this, that, notwithstanding the crime she has committed,
she appears to us so great and so amiable.   The sentinel's description of her, how she came to the corpse in the burning
heat of the sun, while a scorching whirlwind (τυφὼς) was throwing all nature into confusion, and how she raised a shrill cry of
woe when she saw that the earth she had scattered over it had
been taken away, is a picture of a being, who, possessed by an
ethical idea as by an irresistible law of nature, blindly follows
her own noble impulses.

It must, however, be insisted on that it is not the tragical
end of this great and noble creature, but the disclosure of Creon's
infatuation, which forms the general object of the tragedy; and
that, although Sophocles considers Antigone's act as going
beyond what women should dare, he lays much more stress on the
truth; *that there is something holy without and above the state, to
which the state should pay respect and reverence:* a doctrine which
Antigone declares with such irresistible truth and sublimity.[2]

---

[1] See particularly v. 853 Dindorf: προβᾶσ' ἐπ' ἔσχατον θράσους.

[2] V. 450.   οὐ γάρ τί μοι Ζεὺς ἦν—

Every movement in the course of this piece which could shake
Creon in the midst of his madness, and open his eyes to his
own situation, turns upon this and is especially directed to him :
—the noble security with which Antigone relies on the holiness
of her deed ; the sisterly affection of Ismene, who would willingly share the consequences of the act; the loving zeal of
Hæmon, who is at first prudent and then desperate ; the warn-
ings of Teiresias ;—all are in vain, till the latter breaks out into
those prophetic threatenings of misfortune which at last, when
it is too late, penetrate Creon's hardened heart.   Hæmon slays
himself on the body of Antigone, the death of the mother follows that of her son, and Creon is compelled to acknowledge
that there are blessings in one's family for which no political
wisdom is an adequate substitute.

§ 6. The characteristics of the art of Sophocles are most prominently shown in the *Electra*, because we have here an opportunity of making a direct comparison with the Orestea of
Æschylus, and in particular with the *Choëphoræ*. Sophocles
takes an entirely different view of this mythological subject, as
well by representing the punishment of Clytæmnestra without
the connexion of a trilogy, as by making Electra the chief
character and protagonist.   This was impracticable in the case
of Æschylus, for he was obliged to make Orestes, who was the
chief person in the legend, also the chief character in the drama.
But for Sophocles' finer delineation of character, and for his
psychological views, Electra was a much more suitable heroine.
For while Orestes, a matricide from duty and conscience, an
avenger of blood from his birth, and especially intrusted with
this commission by the Delphic oracle, appears to be urged to it
by a superior power ; Electra, on the contrary, is sustained in her
burning hatred against her mother and her mother's paramour,
by her own feelings,—which are totally different from those of her
sister Chrysothemis,—by her entire devotion to the sublime
image of her murdered father, which is ever present to her mind,
by disgust for her mother's pride and lust, in short by the most
secret impulses of a young maiden's heart : that Ægisthus wears
the robes of Agamemnon, that Clytæmnestra held a feast on the
day of her husband's murder, these are continually recurring
provocations.   Such is the character which Sophocles has made

the central figure in his tragedy, a character in which the warmest feelings are blended with the peculiar shrewdness that distinguished the female character at the time represented, and he has contrived to give such a direction to the plot, that the interest is entirely centred in the actions and feelings of this person. According to Æschylus, Orestes had been driven from the house by Clytæmnestra, and sent to Strophius of Phocis; he appears in the paternal mansion as an expelled and illegally disinherited son. According to Sophocles, Orestes, then a child, was to have been put to death when Agamemnon was murdered, and it was only Electra who rescued him and put him under the care of his father's friend, Strophius,[1] by which she gains the credit of having preserved an avenger of her father, and a deliverer of the whole family.[2] On the other hand, Sophocles is obliged to omit the secret plot between Orestes and Electra, and their conspiracy to effect the murder, which is the leading incident in the play of Æschylus, because Sophocles did not set so much importance on making Electra a participator in the deed, as in exhibiting the mind of the high-souled maiden driven about by a storm of contending emotions. This he effects by some slight modifications of the story, in which he makes all possible use of his predecessor's ideas, but follows them out and works them up with such gentle and delicate touches that they fit exactly with his new plan. Æschylus had already hit upon the contrivance by which Orestes gets into the house of the Atridæ; he appeared as an ally and vassal of the house with the pretended funeral urn of Orestes;[3] but Electra had herself planned this device with him, and speaks in concert with him; consequently, the completion of the scheme commences immediately after the first leading division of the play. In Sophocles, where there is no such concert between him and his

---

[1] It is for this reason that Sophocles considers Strophius of Crisa as the friend of Agamemnon and his children, and therefore he names Phanoteus, the hero of a state hostile to the Crisæans, as the person who sends Clytæmnestra the message about her son, although Strophius had collected and sent the ashes of Orestes.

[2] Euripides, in his *Electra*, gives this incident up again, and supposes that Electra and Orestes were separated from one another as *children*.

[3] Up to v. 548 of the *Choëphorœ*, Orestes wears the common dress of a tra-veller; it is not before v. 652 that he appears in a different costume as δορύξενος of the house.

sister, Electra is herself deceived by the trick, and is cast down and grieved in the same degree as Clytæmnestra, after a transient outbreak of maternal affection, is gladdened and tranquillized by it.[1] The funeral offerings of Orestes at his father's grave, which in Æschylus lead to the recognition, in Sophocles only excite a hope in Chrysothemis, which is at once cast down by Electra, who refuses to take comfort from it. Her desire for revenge becomes only the more urgent when she believes herself deprived of all help from man; her grief reaches its highest point when she holds in her arms the sepulchral urn, which she supposes to contain her only hope. As it is Orestes himself who gives it to her, the recognition scene follows immediately, and this constitutes the revolution, or *peripeteia,* as the ancients called it. The death of Clytæmnestra and Ægisthus is treated by Sophocles more as a necessary consequence of the rest, and less as the chief incident; and while it is the aim of Æschylus to place this action itself in its proper light, Sophocles at once relaxes his efforts as soon as Electra is relieved from her sorrow and disquietude.

§ 7. The *Trachinian Women* of Sophocles has also entirely the plan and object of a delineation of character, and the imperfections with which this play is not altogether unreasonably charged, arise from the conflict between the legend on which the play is founded, and the intentions of Sophocles. The tragical end of Hercules forms the subject of the play; Sophocles, however, has again made the heroine Deianeira, and not Hercules, the chief person in the play. *Sorrow arising from love,* this is the moving theme of the drama, and, treated as the poet wished it to be, it is one possessing the greatest beauties. All Deianeira's thoughts and endeavours are directed towards regaining the love of her husband, on whom her whole dependence is placed, and towards assuring herself of his constant attachment to herself. By pursuing this impulse without sufficient foresight, she brings upon him, as it appears to her, the most frightful misery and ruin. By this her fate is decided;

---

[1] It was a kindly trait in Sophocles, which would never have occurred to Æschylus, that Clytæmnestra's first feeling, when she hears the news, is a natural emotion of love for the child which she had borne with pain and travail, v. 770.

but in the ancient tragedy, even when a person perishes, it is possible, by a justification of his name and memory, to attain to that tranquillizing effect which was required by the feelings of Sophocles as well as by those of Æschylus. It is this, not to speak of the conclusion of the legend itself, which is the object of the best part of the *Trachinian Women*, in which Hercules appears as the chief character, and, after uttering the most violent imprecations against his wife, at last acknowledges that Deianeira, influenced by love alone, had only contributed to bring about the end which fate had destined for him.[1] It is true that Hercules does not, as we might expect, give way to compassionate lamentations for Deianeira, and earnest wishes that she were present to receive his parting forgiveness. The feelings of a Greek would be satisfied by the hero's quitting the world without uttering any reproaches against his unhappy wife, for this removes any real grounds for reprehension.

§ 8. We shall form the clearest idea of the meaning of *King Œdipus*, if we consider what it does *not* mean. It does not contain a history of the crime of Œdipus and its detection ; but this crime, which fate had brought upon him, without his knowledge or his will, forms a dark and gloomy background on which the action of the drama itself is painted with bold and strong colours. The action of the drama has reference throughout to the *discovery* of these horrors, and the moral ideas which are developed in it must be brought out in this discovery, if they are particularly contained in it. Let us consider, then, what changes take place in Œdipus in the course of the tragedy. At the beginning, not only is he praised by the Thebans in the most emphatic terms as the best and wisest of men, but he also shows that he is himself fully conscious of his own worth, and well satisfied with the measures he has set on foot, in the first instance to investigate the cause of the destructive malady, and then to discover the murderer of Laïus ; and in this he is not disturbed by any misgiving, not even by the faintest shadow of a suspicion, that he himself may be this murderer. In this self-reliance, and the confidence which springs from it, we have an explanation of the violence and unjustifiable warmth with

---

[1] Hyllus says of her, v. 1136: ἅπαν τὸ χρῆμ' ἥμαρτε, χρηστὰ μωμένη.

which Œdipus repels the declaration of Teiresias, that he himself by his presence has brought pollution on the land, which
he ought to remove by withdrawing as soon as possible.   Here
an occasion was presented on which Œdipus should have felt
how vain and perishable human greatness is, how weak the
virtue of man ; on which he ought to have examined his heart,
and to have questioned himself whether there was no dark spot
in his life to which this fearful crime might correspond.   Such,
however, is his self-confidence, that where the truth comes so
near to him, he sees only falsehood and treason, and maintains
his fancied security, until, in a conversation with Jocasta, when
she mentions that Laïus was murdered at a place *where three
roads meet,* he is for the first time disturbed by a sudden suspicion,[1] and an entire revolution takes place in his mind.   It
is particularly worthy of remark that the steps which Jocasta
takes to tranquillize her husband, and to banish all the terror
occasioned by the prophecies of Teiresias, are just those which
lead to a discovery of all the horrors; she endeavours to prove
the nothingness of the prophetic art by means of that which
shortly afterwards confirms its authority.   We may recognize
in this, as in many other features of this tragedy, distinct traces
of that sublime *irony,* which expresses the poet's sorrow for the
limitation of human existence by striking contrasts between
the conceptions of the individual and the real state of the case.
It is expressed in many passages of the tragedies of Sophocles,
but is particularly developed in *King Œdipus,* for the theme of
the whole is the infatuation of man in regard to his own destiny, and in this play the idea is echoed even by the words and
turns of expression.[2]   The same sort of *peripeteia* is further
repeated when Œdipus has allowed himself to be calmed by his
queen, and believes that the news he has received of the death
of his parents in Corinth has freed him from all fear of having
committed the horrible crimes denounced by the oracle : it is,
however, by the narrative of this same messenger, with regard
to his discovery on Cithæron, that he is suddenly torn from

---

[1] V. 726: Οἷόν μ' ἀκούσαντ' ἀρτίως ἔχει, γύναι,
ψυχῆς πλάνημα κἀνακίνησις φρενῶν.
[2] See Mr. Thirlwall's excellent essay 'on the Irony of Sophocles,' in the *Philological Museum,* vol. II. No. VI. p. 483.

this state of security, and from that moment, though Jocasta sees at one glance the whole connexion of their horrible fate, he cannot rest or be quiet until he has become fully convinced of his parricidal act, and of his incestuous connexion with his mother. He accordingly inflicts punishment on himself, which is the more terrible, the more confident he was before that he was good and blameless in the eyes of God and man. 'O ye generations of mortals, how unworthy of the name of life I must reckon your existence :' so begins the last stasimon of the chorus, which in this tragedy, as in all those of Sophocles, performs the duty which Aristotle prescribes as its proper vocation ; it gives indication of a humane sympathy, which, although not based upon such deep views as to solve all the knotty points in the action, is guided by such a train of thought as to bring back the violent emotions and the shocks of passion to a certain measure of tranquil contemplation. The chorus of Sophocles, therefore, when in its songs it meddles with the action of the piece, often appears weak, vacillating, and even blinded to the truth : when, on the contrary, it collects its different feelings into a general contemplation of the laws of our being, it peals forth the sublimest hymns, such as that beautiful stasimon, which, after Jocasta's impious speeches, recommends a fear of the gods, and a regard for those ordinances which had their birth in heaven, which the moral nature of man has not brought forth, and which will never be plunged by oblivion into the sleep of death.[1]

§ 9. In the *Ajax* of Sophocles the extraordinary power of the poet is shown in the production of a character, which, though entirely peculiar, and like nothing but itself, is nevertheless a general picture of humanity, applicable to every individual case. Sophocles' *Ajax*, like Homer's, is from first to last a brave and noble character, always ready to exert his unwearying heroism for the benefit of his people. He is a man who relies on himself, and can depend upon his own firmness in every case that occurs. But in the full consciousness of his indomitable courage, he has forgotten that there is a higher power on which man is dependent, even for that which he con-

---

[1] *King Œdip.* v. 863 : εἴ μοι ξυνείη φέροντι.

siders most steadfast and most his own, the practical part of his character. This is the more deeply-rooted guilt of Ajax, which is shown at the very beginning of the play ; but it does not appear in its full compass till afterwards, in the prophecies communicated to Teucer by Calchas, where Ajax's arrogant words —'With the assistance of the gods even the feeble might conquer; that he was confident he could perform his part even without their help ;' are cited as proof of his mode of thinking.[1] Now, by the vote of the Greeks which has awarded the arms of Achilles to Ulysses and not to him, Ajax has suffered that sort of humiliation, which, to a character like his, is always most intolerable, and the gods have chosen this moment for the punishment of his presumption. In the night after the decision, when Ajax has set out in the most ungovernable passion to wreak his vengeance on the Atridæ and Ulysses, Athena distracts his mind so that he mistakes oxen and sheep for his enemies, and gives vent to his wrath against them. In this unworthy condition and performing these unworthy actions, Sophocles shows him at the very beginning of his drama as 'Ajax the whip-bearer' (Αἴας μαστιγοφόρος). When he returns to his senses, his whole soul is possessed with the deepest sense of shame, and the more so as all his pride is shaken to its foundation. The beautiful *Eccyclema* scene[2] is introduced for the purpose of representing Ajax, ashamed and humbled, with all the circumstances of his case. However deeply he feels his disgrace, and however clearly he recognizes the gods as the authors of it, he is as far as possible from being a downcast penitent. His whole character is far too consistent to allow him to live on in humble resignation. He has convinced himself that he can no longer live with honour. It is true that the poet, in the oracle ascribed to Calchas, 'that Athena is persecuting Ajax *only for this day*, and that he will be delivered if he survives it,' suggests the possibility of Ajax having more modest views, of his recognizing the limits of his power. But

---

[1] See the speech of Calchas, v. 758 :—

Τὰ γὰρ περισσὰ κἀνόνητα σώματα
πίπτειν βαρείαις πρὸς θεῶν δυσπραξίαις,
ἔφασχ' ὁ μάντις.

[2] Vv. 346—595. comp. chap. XXXII. § 10.

this, though possible, is never actually the case. Ajax remains as he is. His death, in order to effect which he employs a sort of stratagem, is the only atonement which he offers to the gods.[1] Sophocles, however, would look upon this as only one side of the complete development of the action. Severely as the poet punishes what was worthy of punishment in Ajax, he acknowledges with equal justice the greatness of such a character as his. The opinions of antiquity, which regarded a man's burial as an essential part of the destiny of his life, allowed a continuation of the action after the death of the hero. Teucer, the brother of Ajax, contends, as the champion of his honour, with the Atridæ, who seek to deprive him of the rites of burial; and Ulysses, the very person whom Ajax had hated most bitterly, comes forward on the side of Teucer, openly and distinctly acknowledging the excellences of the deceased warrior.[2] And thus Ajax, the noble hero, whom the Athenians too honoured as a hero of their race,[3] appears as a striking example of the divine Nemesis, and the more so as his heroism was altogether spotless in every other respect.

§ 10. In the *Philoctetes*, which was not represented till Olymp. 92. 3, B.C. 439, when the poet was eighty-five years old, Sophocles had to emulate not only Æschylus, but also Euripides, who had before this time endeavoured to impart novelty to the legend by making great alterations in it, and adding some very strange contrivances of his own.[4] Sophocles needed no such

---

[1] Compare the ambiguous words in the deceitful speech, v. 654:—ἀλλ' εἶμι πρός τε λουτρὰ, &c.

[2] It is not till this incident that we have the *Peripeteia*, which was always a violent change in the direction of the piece (ἡ εἰς τὸ ἐναντίον τῶν πραττομένων μεταβολή, Aristot. *Poet.* 11); the death of Ajax, on the other hand, lay quite *in the direction* which the drama had taken from the very beginning.

[3] It is worthy of remark that Sophocles speaks only of the sword of Eurysaces, and not of Philæus, from whom the family of Miltiades and Cimon derived their descent. He manifestly avoids the appearance of paying intentional homage to distinguished families.

[4] Euripides had feigned that the Trojans also sent an embassy to Philoctetes and offered him the sovereignty in return for his aid, in order (as Dio Chrysostom remarks, *Orat.* 52. p. 549) to give himself an opportunity of introducing the long speeches, pro and con, of which he is so fond. Ulysses, disguised as a Greek whom his countrymen before Troy had ill-used, endeavours to induce him to assist his countrymen, rather than the enemy. The proper solution of the difficulties in this piece is still very doubtful.

means to give a peculiar interest to the subject as treated by himself. He lays the chief stress on a skilful outline and consistent filling up of the characters; it is the object of his drama to depict the results of these characters in the natural, and, to a certain extent, necessary development of their peculiarities. In this piece, however, this psychological development, starting from an hypothesis selected in the first instance and proceeding in accordance with it, leads to results entirely different from those contained in the original legend. In order to avoid this contest between his art and the old mythological story, Sophocles has been obliged for once to avail himself of a resource which he elsewhere despises, though it is frequently employed by Euripides, namely, the *Deus ex machinâ*, as it is called, *i. e.*, the intervention of some deity, whose sudden appearance puts an end to the play of passions and projects among the persons whose actions are represented, and, as it were, cuts the Gordian knot with the sword.

Sophocles having assumed that Ulysses has associated with himself the young hero Neoptolemus, in order to bring to Troy Philoctetes, or his weapons, we have from the beginning of the piece an interesting contrast between the two heroes thus united for a common object. Ulysses relies altogether on the ambition of Neoptolemus, who is destined by fate to be the conqueror of Troy, if he can obtain the aid of the weapons of Philoctetes, and Neoptolemus does, in fact, suffer himself to be prevailed upon to deceive Philoctetes by representing himself as an enemy of the Greeks who are besieging Troy, and is just on the point of carrying him off to their camp, under the pretence of taking him home; meanwhile Neoptolemus is deeply touched, in the first place, by the unsophisticated eloquence of Philoctetes, and then by the sight of his unspeakable sufferings; [1] but it is long before the resolute temper of the young hero can be drawn aside by this from the path he has once entered on. The first time he departs from it is after Philoctetes has given him

---

[1] V. 965: 'Εμοὶ μὲν οἶκτος δεινὸς ἐμπέπτωκέ τις

τοῦδ' ἀνδρὸς, οὐ νῦν πρῶτον ἀλλὰ καὶ πάλαι.

The silence of Neoptolemus in the scene beginning with ΟΔ. ὦ κάκιστ' ἀνδρῶν τί δρᾷς v. 974, and ending with the words ἀκούσομαι μὲν, v. 1074, is just as characteristic as any speech could have been.

his bow to take care of, when he candidly admits the truth, that he is obliged to take him to Troy, and cannot conduct him to his home. Yet he still follows the plans of Ulysses, though much against his own inclination, and this drives Philoctetes into a state of despair, which almost transcends all his bodily sufferings, until Neoptolemus suddenly reappears in violent dispute with Ulysses, *as himself*, as the simple-minded, straightforward, noble young hero, who will not in any case deceive the confidence of Philoctetes; and as Philoctetes cannot and will not overcome his hatred of the Achæans, he throws aside all his ambitious hopes and wishes, and is on the point of escorting the sick hero to his native land, when Hercules, the *Deus ex machinâ*, suddenly makes his appearance, and, by announcing the decrees of fate, produces a complete revolution in the sentiments of Philoctetes and Neoptolemus. This drama, then, is exceedingly simple, for the foundation on which it is built is the relation between three characters, and it consists of two acts only, separated by the *stasimon* before the scene, in which the change in Neoptolemus's views is brought about. But if we consider the consistent and profound development of the characters, it is by far the most artificial and elaborate of all the works of Sophocles. The appearance of Hercules only effects an *outward peripeteia*, or that sort of revolution which bears upon the occurrences in the piece; the intrinsic revolution, the real *peripeteia* in the drama of Sophocles, lies in the previous return of Neoptolemus to his genuine and natural disposition, and this peripeteia is, quite in accordance with the spirit of Sophocies, brought about by means of the characters and the progress of the action itself.

§ 11. In all the pieces of which we have spoken hitherto, the prevailing ideas are *ethical*, but necessarily based on a religious foundation, since it is always by reference to the divinity that the proper bias is given to human actions in every field. There is, however, one drama in which the religious ideas of Sophocles are brought so prominently forward that the whole play may be considered as an exposition of the Greek belief in the gods.

This drama, the *Œdipus at Colonus*, is always connected in the old stories with the last days of the poet. Sophocles attained the age of 89, or thereabouts, for he did not die till

Olymp. 93. 2, B.C. 406,[1] and yet he did not himself bring out
the *Œdipus at Colonus;* it was first brought on the stage in
Olymp. 94. 3, B.C. 401, by his grandson, *the younger Sophocles.*
This younger Sophocles was a son of Ariston, the offspring of
the great poet and Theoris of Sicyon. Sophocles had also a
son Iophon by a free-woman of Athens, and he alone, according
to the Attic law, could be considered as his legitimate son
and rightful heir. Iophon and Sophocles both emulated their
father and grandfather; the former brought tragedies on the
stage during his father's lifetime, the latter after his grandfather's death : the whole family seems, like that of Æschylus,
to have dedicated itself to the tragic muse. But the heart of
the old man yearned towards the offspring of his beloved Theoris ;
and it was said, that he was endeavouring to bestow upon his
grandson during his own lifetime a considerable part of his
means. Iophon, fearing lest his inheritance should be too
much diminished by this, was urged to the undutiful conduct
of proposing to the members of the *phratria* (who had a sort
of family jurisdiction) that his father should not be permitted to have any control over his property, which he was no
longer capable of managing. The only reply which Sophocles
made to this charge was to read to his fellow-tribesmen the
parodos from the *Œdipus at Colonus ;*[2] which must, therefore,
have been just composed, if it were to furnish any proof for the
object he had in view ; and we think it does the greatest honour
to the Athenian judges, that, after such a proof of the poet's

---

[1] The old authorities give Olymp. 93. 3. as the year of Sophocles' death : this
was the year of the Archon Callias, in which Aristophanes' *Frogs* was brought out
at the Lenæa, and the death of Sophocles is presupposed in this comedy as well as
that of Euripides. The *Vita Sophoclis*, however, following Istrus and Neanthes,
places the death of Sophocles at the *Choës ;* and as the Choës, which belonged to
the Anthesteria, were celebrated in the month of Anthesterion, after the Lenæa,
which fell in the month Gamelion, the death of Sophocles must be referred to the
year before the archonship of Callias, consequently to Olymp. 93. 2. If we suppose that some confusion has taken place, and substitute for the Choës the lesser,
or country Dionysia, we should still be very far short of the necessary time for
conceiving, writing, and preparing for the stage such a comedy as the *Frogs*, even
though we should also suppose an intercalary month inserted between Poseideon
and Gamelion.

[2] V. 668. *seq.*—Εὔιππου, ξένε, τᾶσδε χώρας.   Comp. chap. XXII. § 12.

powers of mind, they paid no attention to the proposal of Iophon, even though he was right in a legal point of view. Iophon, it seems, became sensible of his error, and Sophocles afterwards forgave him. The ancients found an allusion to this fact in a passage of the *Œdipus at Colonus*,[1] where Antigone says, by way of apology for Polyneices, 'Other people, too, have had bad children, and a choleric temper, but have been induced by the soothing speeches of their friends to give up their anger.'

§ 12. It was then in the latter years of his life that Sophocles composed this tragedy, which the ancients justly designate as a sweet and charming poem;[2] so wonderfully is it pervaded by gentle and amiable feelings, so deeply tinged with a tone mixed up of sorrow for the miseries of human existence and of comforting and elevating hopes. This drama impresses every susceptible reader with a warmth of sensibility as if it treated of the weal of the poet himself; here, more than in any other poem, one can recognize the immediate language of the heart.[3] In this play the aged Sophocles has plunged into the recollections of his youth, during which the monuments and traditions of his rustic home, the village of Colonus near Athens, had made a deep and lasting impression on his mind: in the whole piece, and especially in the charming *parodos*-song which celebrates the natural beauties and ancient glory of Colonus, he expresses in the most amiable manner his patriotism and his love for his home. At Colonus were hallowed spots of every kind, consecrated by faith in the powers of darkness; a grove of the Erinnyes, who were designated as 'the venerable goddesses' (σεμναί); 'a brazen threshold,' as it was called, which was regarded as the portal of the subterranean world; and, among other things, also an abode where Œdipus was said to dwell beneath the earth as a propitious deity, conferring upon the land peace and bliss, and destroying its enemies,

---

[1] V. 1192. *seq.*: ἀλλ' ἔα αὐτόν· εἰσι χἀτέροις γοναὶ κακαί.

[2] Mollissimum ejus carmen de Œdipode. Cicero, *de Fin.*, V. 1. 3.

[3] Not to touch upon the higher ideas, we may also refer to the complaints of the chorus about the miseries of old age, v. 1211. There is a counterpoise to these laments in the subsequent praises of an easy death, at peace with the gods.

especially the Thebans. The touching thought that this
Œdipus, whom the Erinnyes had so cruelly persecuted in his
life-time, should find rest from his sorrows in their sanctuary,
had been mythically expressed in other places, and was connected with particular localities. That such a sacrifice, however, to the avenging goddesses, one reconciled to them, and
even tranquillized by them, should also possess the power of
conferring blessings, depends upon the fundamental ideas of the
worship of the Chthonian deities among the Greeks, which
directly ascribe to the powers of the earth and the night a
secret and mysterious fulness of life. It was in reference to
these,[1] according to the views of Sophocles, that Œdipus, at the
very commencement of his unhappy career, before his rencontre
with Laïus, received an oracle from the Delphic Apollo, stating
that he would reach the end of his sorrowful journey through
life in that place, where he should obtain an hospitable reception from the Erinnyes. He does not, however, perceive that
he is approaching the fulfilment of the oracle till the beginning
of the drama, when, wandering about as an exile, he unexpectedly learns that he is in the sanctuary of these goddesses.
It is, however, long before the people of Colonus, who hasten to
the spot, are willing to receive him : they are shocked in the
first place by the audacity of the stranger who has so boldly
profaned the grove of the fearful goddesses, and in the next
place by the terrible curse which attaches to his destiny : and
it is the noble and humane disposition of Theseus, the prince of
the country, which first assures him of reception and protection
in Attica. Meanwhile, a second oracle comes to light. It has

---

[1] Sophocles himself says, v. 62, of the temples and monuments of Colonus,

τοιαῦτά σοι ταῦτ' ἐστίν, ὦ ξέν', οὐ λόγοις
τιμῶμεν' ἀλλὰ τῇ ξυνουσίᾳ πλέον,

i. e., not celebrated by poets and orators, but only by local tradition. How far
Æschylus was from conceiving anything of the kind may be seen from several
passages in the *Seven against Thebes* ; according to which Œdipus must have been
dead and buried in Thebes before the war, and this was in accordance with the
more ancient traditions. See v. 976. 1004. It is true that Euripides has the same
tradition in his *Phœnissæ*, v. 1707 ; but this tragedy belongs to a period (about
Olymp. 93) when Sophocles' *Œdipus at Colonus*, though not yet brought out,
might have been known to the lovers of literature at Athens.

been obtained by the parties who are contending for the sovereignty of Thebes, and promises conquest and prosperity to
those who possess Œdipus or his grave. This gives occasion
for a number of scenes in which Creon and Polyneices, both of
whom have grievously offended Œdipus, strive with all their
might to gain his aid for their own purposes ; but they are at
once haughtily rejected by him, assured as he is by the protection of Athens from all outward violence. The real object of
these scenes, which fill up the middle portion of the tragedy,
obviously is to represent the blind and aged Œdipus a miserable
being, bowed down by a curse, disgraced, and banished, yet
raised to a state of honour and majesty by the interposition of
the divinity in his favour ; and in this state he is elevated far
above his enemies, who before ill-treated him in the insolence
of power. There is a sort of majesty even in the anger with
which he sends from him, loaded with a curse, his wicked son
Polyneices, now so deeply humbled ; although, according to our
notions, the Greek Charis may appear somewhat harsh and rude
in this instance. After this exaltation upon earth, the thunder
of Zeus is heard, calling Œdipus to the other world ; and we
learn, partly from what Œdipus said before, and partly from the
messenger who comes back to us, how Œdipus, adorned for
death in festal attire, and summoned by subterraneous thunders
and voices, has vanished in a mysterious manner from the surface of the earth. Theseus puts a stop to the laments of the
daughters with the words, ' One must not complain of the
manner in which the Chthonian powers display their favours :
it were an offence to the gods to do so.'[1]

It cannot have escaped any attentive reader how much in this
mythus, so treated, is applicable not merely to the old hero
Œdipus, but also to the destiny of man in general, and how a
gentle longing for death, as a deliverance from all worldly
troubles and as a clearing up of our existence, runs through
the whole ; and certainly the political references to the position
of Athens at that time in regard to other states, even though

---

[1] V. 1751. παύετε θρήνων, παῖδες· ἐν οἷς γὰρ
Χάρις ἡ Χθονία ξύν' ἀπόκειται,
πενθεῖν οὐ χρή· νέμεσις γάρ.

they are more prominent in this than in other pieces, are quite subordinate in comparison with these leading ideas.[1]

§ 13. Thus the tragedies of Sophocles appear to us as pictures of the mind, as poetical developments of the secrets of our souls and of the laws to which their nature makes them amenable. Of all the poets of antiquity, Sophocles has penetrated most deeply into the recesses of the human heart. He bestows very little attention on facts; he regards them as little more than vehicles to give an outward manifestation to the workings of the mind. For the representation of this world of thought, Sophocles has contrived a peculiar poetical language. If the general distinction between the language of poetry and prose is that the former gives the *ideas* with greater clearness and vividness, and the *feelings* with greater strength and warmth; the style of Sophocles is not poetical in the same degree as that of Æschylus, because it does not strive after the same vivid description of sensible impressions, and because his art is based upon a delineation of the manifold delicate shades of feeling, and not on an exhibition of the strong and uncontrollable emotions. Accordingly, the style of Sophocles comes a good deal nearer to prose than that of Æschylus, and is distinguished from it less by the *choice* of words than by their *use* and *connexion*, and by a sort of boldness and subtilty in the employment of ordinary expressions. Sophocles seeks to make his words imply something which people in general would not expect in them: he employs them according to their derivation

---

[1] It is true that the whole piece is full of references to the Peloponnesian war and to the devastations to which Attica was subjected, though they spared the country about Colonus and the Academy, and the holy olive-trees. Difficulties, too, are occasioned by the tone of commendation in which Theseus speaks of the character of Thebes in general (v. 919), for Thebes was certainly at this period one of the foes of Athens; and it might be supposed that this passage was added by the younger Sophocles after Thrasybulus had liberated Athens with the aid of the Thebans. The drama, however, is too much of one character to give any room for such a surmise; and we must therefore conclude, that Sophocles knew there existed among the people of Thebes a disposition favourable to Athens, whereas the aristocrats who had the upper hand in the government were hostile to that city. After the termination of the Peloponnesian war, the democratic party at Thebes showed themselves more and more in favour of Athens and opposed to Sparta.

rather than according to their actual use; and thus his expressions have a peculiar pregnancy and obscurity[1] which easily degenerates into a sort of play with words and significations. With regard to this, it must be remarked that, at the period when he wrote, the spirit of the Greek nation was in a state of progressive development, in which it entered upon speculations beyond its own impulses and their utterance by means of words and sentences, and in which the reflecting powers were every day gaining more and more the mastery over the powers of perception.   In such a period as this, an observation of and attention to words in themselves is perfectly natural.   Besides, at this time of vehement excitement, the Athenians had an especial fondness for a certain difficulty of expression.[2]   An orator would please them less by telling them everything plainly than by leaving them something to guess, and so giving them the satisfaction of acquiring a sort of respect for their own sagacity and discernment.   Thus Sophocles often plays at hide and seek with the significations of words, in order that the mind, having exerted itself to find out his meaning, may comprehend it more vividly and distinctly when it is once arrived at.   In the syntactical combinations, too, Sophocles is very expressive, and to a certain extent artificial, while he strives with great precision to mark all the subordinate relations of thought.   Perspicuity and fluency are incompatible with such a style as this; and, indeed, these properties were not generally characteristic of the rhetoric of the time.   The style of Sophocles moves on with a judicious and accurate observation of all incidental circumstances, and does not hurry forwards with inconsiderate haste; though in this very particular there is a difference between the *older* and the more *recent* tragedies of Sophocles, for several speeches in the *Ajax,* the *Philoctetes,* and the *Œdipus at*

---

[1] Especially also one, of which the speakers themselves are unconscious; so that, without knowing it, they often describe the real state of the case. This belongs essentially to the tragical irony of Sophocles, of which we have spoken above (§ 8).

[2] Cleon says (in Thucydides, III. 38) that the Athenians may easily be deceived by novelties of style; that they despise what is common, admire what is strange, and, though they speak not themselves, are nevertheless so far rivals of the speaker that they follow close upon him with their thoughts, and even outrun him.

Colonus have the same oratorical flow which we find in Euripides.[1]   In the lyrical parts, this distinct exhibition and clear illustration of the thoughts are combined with an extraordinary grace and sweetness : several of the choral odes are, even taken by themselves, masterpieces of a sort of lyric poetry which rivals that of Sappho in beauty of description and grace of conception.   Sophocles, too, has with singular good taste cultivated the Glyconian metre, which is so admirably calculated for the expression of gentle and kindly emotions.

------

[1] See the speeches of Menelaus, Agamemnon, and Teucer, in the second part of the *Ajax*, and Œdipus' defence in v. 960 of the *Œdipus at Colonus*.

CHAPTER XXV.

EURIPIDES.

§ 1. Difference between Sophocles and Euripides. The latter essentially speculative. Tragedy a subject ill-suited for his genius. § 2. Intrusion of tragedy
into the interests of the private and, § 3, public life of the time. § 4. Alterations in the plan of tragedy introduced by Euripides. Prologue and, § 5,
Deus ex machinâ. § 6. Comparative insignificance of the chorus. Prevalence
of monodies. § 7. Style of Euripides. § 8. Outline of his plays : the *Alcestis;*
§ 9. the *Medea;* § 10. the *Hippolytus;* § 11. the *Hecuba.* § 12. Epochs in the
mode of treating his subject : the *Heracleidæ;* § 13. the *Suppliants;* § 14. the
Ion; § 15. the *Raging Heracles;* § 16. the *Andromache;* § 17. the *Trojan
Women;* § 18. the *Electra;* § 19. the *Helena;* § 20. the *Iphigenia at Tauri;*
§ 21. the *Orestes;* § 22. the *Phœnician Women;* § 23. the *Bacchanalians;* § 24.
the *Iphigenia at Aulis.* § 25. Lost pieces : the *Cyclops.*

§ 1. THE tragedies of Sophocles are a beautiful flower of
Attic genius, which could only have sprung up on the
boundary line between two ages differing widely in their opinions
and mode of thinking.[1] Sophocles possessed in perfection that
free Attic training which rests upon an unprejudiced observation of human affairs ; his thoughts had entire freedom, and
the power of mastering outward impressions ; yet with all this,
Sophocles admits a something which cannot be moved and
must not be touched, which is deeply rooted in our conscience,
and which a voice from within warns us not to bring into the
whirlpool of speculation. He is, of all the Greeks, at once
the most pious and most enlightened. In treating of the
positive objects of the popular religion of his country, he has hit
upon the right mean between a superstitious adherence to outward forms and a sceptical opposition to the traditionary belief.
He has always the skill to call attention to that side of his

---

[1] Comp. chap. XX. § 7.

religion which must have produced devotional feelings even in a reflecting and educated mind of that time.[1]

The position of Euripides, in reference to his own time, was totally different. Although he was only eleven years younger than Sophocles, and died about half a year before him, he seems to belong to an entirely different generation, in which the tendencies, still united in Sophocles and presided over by the noblest perception of beauty, had become irreconcileably opposed to one another. Euripides was naturally a serious character, with a decided bias towards nice and speculative inquiries into the nature of things human and divine. In comparison with the cheerful Sophocles, whose spirit without any effort comprehended life in all its significance, Euripides appeared to be morose and peevish.[2] Although he had applied himself to the philosophy of the time, and had entered deeply into Anaxagoras' ideas with regard to matters relating principally to physical science in general, while in regard to moral studies he had manifestly allowed himself to be allured by some of the views of the sophists; nevertheless, the philosophy of Socrates, the opponent and conqueror of the sophists, had, on the whole, gained the upper hand in his estimation. We do not know what induced a person with such tendencies to devote himself to tragic poetry, which he did, as is well known, in the twenty-sixth year of his age, and in the very same year in which Æschylus died (Olymp. 81. 1, B.C. 455).[3] Suffice it to say,

---

[1] The respect which Sophocles everywhere evinces for the prophetic art is highly worthy of remark, and to a modern reader must be particularly surprising. It does not, however, appear in his dramas as an inexplicable guessing at accidental occurrences, but as a thorough initiation into the great and just dispensations of providence. In the *Ajax*, the *Philoctetes*, the *Trachinian Women*, the *Antigone*, the two *Œdipuses*, the prophecies express profound ideas though enveloped occasionally in a mystical phraseology. Euripides has no sympathy with this reverence for the prophetic art.

[2] He is called στρυφνὸς and μισογέλως by Alexander Ætolus, in the verses quoted by Gellius, *N. A.* XV. 20. 8.

[3] This is in accordance with the *Vita Euripidis*, which Elmsley published from a MS. in the Ambrosian Library, and which, with several alterations and additions, is also found in a Paris and Vienna MS. According to Eratosthenes, who gives the age of 26 for his first appearance and of 75 for his death, he must have been born in Olymp. 74. 3, B.C. 482-1, although the Parian marble places his birth at Olymp. 73. 4. It is clearly only a legend that he was born on the day of the battle of Salamis.

that tragic poetry became the business of his life, and he had no other means of giving to the world the results of his meditations. With respect to the mythical traditions, however, which the tragic muse had selected as her subjects, he stood upon an entirely different footing from Æschylus, who recognized in them the sublime dispensations of providence, and from Sophocles, who regarded them as containing a profound solution of the problem of human existence. He found himself placed in a strange, distorted position with regard to the objects of his poetry, which were fully as disagreeable as they were attractive to him. He could not bring his philosophical convictions with regard to the nature of God and his relation to mankind into harmony with the contents of these legends, nor could he pass over in silence their incongruities. Hence it is that he is driven to the strange necessity of carrying on a sort of polemical discussion with the very materials and subjects of which he had to treat. He does this in two ways : sometimes, he rejects as false those mythical narratives which are opposed to purer conceptions about the gods ; at other times, he admits the legends as true, but endeavours to give a base or contemptible appearance to characters and actions which they have represented as great and noble. Thus, the two favourite themes of Euripides are, to represent Helen, whom Homer has had the skill, notwithstanding her failings, to clothe with dignity as well as loveliness, as a common prostitute, and Menelaus as a great simpleton, who, in order to get back his worthless wife, has brought so many brave men into distress and danger—and distinctly to blame and misrepresent the deed of Orestes as a crime to which he had been urged by the Delphic oracle ; whereas Æschylus has striven to exhibit it as an unavoidable though a dreadful deed.

§ 2. Although Euripides, as an enlightened philosopher, might have found pleasure in showing the Athenians the folly of many of the traditions which they believed in and considered as holy, yet it is somewhat strange that he all along kept close to these mythical subjects, and did not attempt to substitute for them subjects of his own invention, as his contemporary Agathon did, according to Aristotle, in his piece called the *Flower* (ἄνθος). It is certain that Euripides regarded these mythological traditions as merely the substratum, the canvas, on which he paints his great moral pictures without the restraint of any rules.   He avails himself of the old stories in order to produce situations in which he may exhibit the men *of his own time* influenced by mental excitement and passionate emotion.   There is great truth in the distinction which Sophocles, according to Aristotle, made between the characters of his plays and those of Euripides, when he said that he represented men as they ought to be, Euripides men as they are :[1] for, while Sophocles' persons have all something noble and great in their composition, and even the less noble are in a measure justified and ennobled by the sentiments of which they are the vehicle,[2] Euripides, on the other hand, strips his of the ideal greatness which they claimed as heroes and heroines, and allows them to appear with all the petty passions and weaknesses of people of his own time [3]—properties which often make a singular contrast to the grave and measured speeches and the outward pomp which the tragic cothurnus carries with it.   All the characters of Euripides have that loquacity and dexterity in the use of words [4] which distinguished the Athenians of his day, and that vehemence of passion which, formerly restrained by the conventions of morality, was now appearing with less desire for concealment every day.   They have all an extraordinary fondness for arguing, and consequently are on the watch for every opportunity of reasoning on their views of things human and divine.   Along with this, objects of common life are treated with the minutest attention to petty circumstances of daily occurrence,[5] as when Medea makes a detailed complaint of the

---

[1] Arist. *Poet.* 25.

[2] Like the Atridæ in the *Ajax*, Creon in the *Antigone*, Ulysses in the *Philoctetes*. There are no absolute villains in Sophocles ; but in Euripides, Polymestor in the *Hecuba*, Menelaus in the *Orestes*, and the Achæan princes in the *Troades*, very nearly deserve that appellation.   In general every person in ancient tragedy is, to a certain extent, right in his way of thinking : the absolutely insignificant and contemptible occupy by no means so much space in ancient tragedy as in our own.

[3] Thus Euripides represents heroes, like Bellerophon and Ixion, as mere *misers.* With similar caprice, he turns the seven heroes warring against Thebes into so many characters from common life, interesting enough, it is true, but not elevated above the ordinary standard.

[4] στωμυλία, δεινότης.   Comp. chap. XX. § 7.

[5] οἰκεῖα πράγματα, οἷς χρώμεθ', οἷς ξύνεσμεν, says Aristophanes, *Frogs*, 959.

unhappy lot of women, who are obliged to bring a quantity of money as dowry in order to purchase for themselves a lord and master ;[1] and as Hermione, in the *Andromache*, enlarges on the topic, that a prudent husband will not allow his wife to be visited by strange women, because they would corrupt her mind with all sorts of bad speeches.[2] Euripides must have bestowed the greatest pains on his study of the female character. Almost all his tragedies are full of vivid sketches and ingenious remarks referring to the life and habits of women. The deeds of passion, bold undertakings, fine-spun plans, as a general rule, always originate with the female characters, and the men often play a very dependent and subordinate part in their execution. One may easily conceive what a shock would be given by thus bringing forward the women from the domestic restraint and retirement in which they lived at Athens. But it would be doing Euripides great injustice if we were, like Aristophanes, to make this a ground for calling him a woman-hater. The honour which his mode of treating the subject confers on the female sex is quite equal to any reproaches which he puts upon women. Euripides also brings children on the stage more frequently than his predecessors ; perhaps he did this for the same reason that made people, when brought before the criminal courts on charges involving severe punishment, produce their children to the judges in order to touch their hearts by the sight of their innocence and helplessness. He brings them on in situations which must have moved the heart of every affectionate father and mother among his audience,[3] although they were seldom introduced as speaking or singing, because this was not possible without making some tedious arrangements.[4]

---

[1] Euripides, *Medea*, 235. [2] Eurip., *Androm.*, 944.

[3] As when Peleus holds up the little Molossus to untie the cords with which his mother is bound (*Androm.* 724). Astyanax, in the *Troades*, is first embraced by his mother in the midst of her bitter grief, and afterwards brought in dead upon a shield. The infant Orestes must coax Agamemnon, so as to make him listen to the prayers of Iphigenia.

[4] As in the scenes in the *Alcestis* and the *Andromache* (for the children of Medea are heard crying out from behind the scenes). One of the chorus then stood behind the scenes and sang the part which the child acted, and which was called παρασκήνιον, also παραχορήγημα, a name which comprehended all the chorus did besides their proper part.

§ 3. Euripides also avails himself of every opportunity of touching upon public events, in order to give weight to his opinions on political subjects, whether favourable or unfavourable. He expresses himself against the dominion of the multitude, especially when it consisted chiefly of the sea-faring people who were so numerous among the Athenians.[1] He inveighs severely against the demagogues who, by their unbridled audacity, were hurrying the people to destruction.[2] He shows himself, however, no friend to the aristocrats of the time, but represents their pride in their riches and high descent as utter folly. When he declares his political creed more directly,[3] he makes the well-being of the state and the preservation of good order depend on the middle class.[4] Euripides has an especial affection for the agriculturists who till the land with their own hands : he regards them as the real patriots and the protectors of the state.[5] Thus we may select from the works of Euripides sentences and sentiments for every situation of human life; for Euripides is fond of taking a general and abstract view of all relations of things : and it is just because it is so easy to extract sententious passages from his plays, and collect them in *anthologies,* that the later writers of antiquity, who were better able to appreciate the part than the whole—the pretty and clever passages than the general plan of the work—have so greatly liked and admired this poet. Euripides takes such liberties with his dialogue, and allows himself such an arbitrary extension of it, that he has a place in it even for indirect poetical criticisms, which he turns against his predecessors, especially Æschylus. There are distinct passages in the *Electra* and the *Phœnissœ,* which every one at Athens must have understood as

---

[1] The ναυτικὴ ἀναρχία is mentioned in the *Hec.* 607, and again in the *Iphig. at Aul.* 914.

[2] The demagogue of Argos mentioned in the *Orestes,* 904, 'an Argive and no Argive,' seems to be an allusion to Cleophon, who had great influence towards the end of the Peloponnesian war, but was said to be a Thracian, and therefore not a genuine citizen of Athens.

[3] As in the remarkable passage of the *Suppliants,* 238 : τρεῖς γὰρ πολιτῶν μερίδες, &c.

[4] *Suppl.* 244. τριῶν δὲ μοιρῶν, ἡ 'ν μέσῳ σώζει πόλιν.

[5] The αὐτουργοί : see *Electra,* 389, *Orest.* 910. He has a great antipathy to the heralds, whom he attacks on every occasion.

objecting, the former to the recognition scenes in the *Choëphoræ*, the latter to the descriptions of the besieging warriors, *before* the decision of the battle, as stiff and unnatural.[1] Euripides never expresses himself against Sophocles in this manner. Although the contemporary and rival of Sophocles, he always appears, even in the *Frogs* of Aristophanes, in hostile opposition to Æschylus, whose manner he despised as rough and uncultivated, Æschylus being the favourite of the old honest Athenians of the race of those who fought at Marathon, and Euripides the hero of the more modern youth, brought up in sophistical opinions and rhetorical studies. Sophocles stands superior to this clash of parties, for he had actually found the means of reconciling and uniting in himself the old deep-rooted morality and the more enlightened views of the age. That the Athenians were conscious of this, and that in his life-time Euripides had not so many partisans as we might have supposed, may be seen in the fact that, although he wrote a great number of plays (in all ninety-two),[2] he did not gain nearly so many tragic victories as Sophocles.[3]

§ 4. We may connect with these remarks on the development of the thoughts in the tragedies of Euripides, some observations on their *form* or outward arrangement, since it may easily be shown how nearly this is connected with his mode of treating the subjects. There are two elements in the outward form of tragedy which are almost entirely due to Euripides— the *prologue* and the *deus ex machinâ*, as it is called. In the prologue, some personage, a god or a hero, tells in a monologue who he is, how the action is going on, what has happened up to the present moment, to what point the business has come, nay more, if the prologuer is a god, also to what point it is destined to be carried.[4] Every unprejudiced judge must look upon

---

[1] Eurip. *Electra*, 523, *Phœniss.*, 751. *After* the battle, however, Euripides finds this description quite appropriate.

[2] Of which seventy-five are spoken of as extant; and of these three were not considered genuine.

[3] Euripides did not gain a victory till Olymp. 84. 3, B.C. 441. His victories amounted on the whole to five; according to some writers, to fifteen. Sophocles gained eighteen, twenty, or twenty-four victories.

[4] For example, in the *Ion*, the *Hippolytus*, and the *Bacchæ*; in the *Hecuba*, too, the shade of Polydorus appears with the divine power of foretelling the future. In

these prologues as a retrograde step from a more perfect form to one comparatively defective. It is doubtless much easier to show the state of affairs by a detached narrative of this kind than by speeches and dialogues which proceed from the action of the piece; but the very fact that these narratives have nothing to do with the context of the drama, but are only a make-shift of the poet, is also a reason why the form of the drama should suffer from them. That Euripides himself probably felt this appears from the manner in which he has been at the pains of justifying, or at least excusing, this sort of prologue in the *Medea,* one of the oldest of his remaining plays. The nurse of Medea there says, after having recounted the hard fate of her mistress and the resentment which it has excited in her, that she has herself been so overcome with grief on Medea's account, that she is possessed with a longing to proclaim to earth and heaven her mistress's unhappy lot.[1] Euripides, however, with his peculiar tendencies, could not well have dispensed with these prologues. As it is his sole object to represent men under the influence of passion, he found it necessary to lay before the spectator a concise statement of the circumstances which had brought them to that point, in order that he might be able, as soon as the piece actually began, to paint the particular passion in all its strength.[2] Besides, so complicated are the situations into which he brings his characters, in order to have an opportunity of thoroughly developing a varied play of affections and passions, that it would be difficult to make them intelligible to the spectators otherwise than by a circumstantial narration, especially when Euripides, in his arbitrary treatment of the old stories, ventures to give a different turn to the incidents from that with which the Athenians were already familiar from their traditions and poetry.[3]

§ 5. With regard to the *deus ex machinâ,* it is much the

---

the *Alcestis,* however, the whole form of the prologue is different. In the *Troades* the prologue, included in the dialogue between Poseidon and Athena, goes a good way beyond the action of the piece. Comp. § 16.

[1] Eurip. *Med.* 56. *seq.*

[2] As in the *Medea,* the *Hippolytus,* and other plays.

[3] Examples confirmatory of these views may be derived from the *Orestes,* the *Helena,* and the *Electra.*

same sort of contrivance for the end of a play of Euripides that the monologues we have mentioned are for the beginning. It is a symptom that dramatic action had already lost the principle of its natural development, and was no longer capable of producing, in a satisfactory manner, from its own resources, a connexion of beginning, middle, and end. When the poet had by means of the prologue pointed out the situation, from which resulted an effect on the passions of the chief character and a contest with opposing exertions, he introduced all sorts of complications, which rendered the contest hotter and hotter, and the play of passions more and more involved, till at last he can hardly find any side on which he may bring the impassioned actions of the characters to a definite end, whether it be a decided victory of one of the parties, or peace and a reconciliation of the contending interests. Upon this, some divinity appears in the sky, supported by machinery, announces the decrees of fate, and makes a just and peaceable arrangement of the affair. Euripides, however, by degrees only, became bolder in employing this sort of denouement. He winds up his earliest plays without any *deus ex machinâ*; then follow pieces in which the action is brought to its proper end by the persons themselves, the deity being introduced only to remove any remaining doubt and to complete the work of tranquillizing the minds of those who might be discontented; and it was not till the end of his career that Euripides ventured to lay all the weight on the *deus ex machinâ*, so that it is left to this power alone, not to undo, but to cut asunder the complicated knot of human passions, which otherwise would be inextricable.[1] The poet attempted to make up for any want of satisfaction which this might occasion to the mind, by endeavouring to gratify the bodily eye: he often introduced the divinity in such a manner as to surprise, or even, in the first instance, to terrify the spectator, by exhibiting him in all his greatness and power, and surrounding him with a halo of light; in some cases he combined with this other startling appearances, which could not have

---

[1] This applies to the *Orestes*. Besides this, we find the *Deus ex machinâ* in the *Hippolytus*, the *Ion*, the *Iphigenia at Tauri*, the *Suppliants*, the *Andromache*, the *Helena*, the *Electra*, and the *Bacchœ*.

been brought forward without some acquaintance with the
science of optics.[1]

§ 6. The position of the chorus also was essentially perverted
by the changes which Euripides allowed himself to make in the
outward form of tragedy. The chorus fulfils its proper office
when it comes forward to mediate between, to advise, and to
tranquillize opposing parties, who are actuated by different views
of the case, and who have, or at least for the time appear to
have, each of them the right on their own side. The special
object of the *stasima* is, by reference to higher ideas, to which
the contending powers ought to submit, to introduce a sort of
equilibrium into the irregularities of the action. The chorus
fulfils this office in very few of the plays of Euripides;[2] it is
generally but little suited for so dignified a position. Euripides likes to make his chorus the confidant and accomplice of
the person whom he represents as under the influence of passion; the chorus receives his wicked proposals, and even lets itself be bound by an oath not to betray them, so that, however
much it may wish to hinder the bad consequences resulting
from them, it is no longer capable of doing so.[3] As a chorus
so related to the actors is seldom qualified to pronounce weighty
and authoritative opinions, by which a restraint may be
placed on the unbridled passions of the actors, it generally fills up the pauses, in which its songs take place, with
lyrical narrations of events which happened before, but have
some reference to the action of the piece. How many of the
choral songs of Euripides consist of descriptions of the Grecian

---

[1] In the *Helena* it is clear that, while the Dioscuri are speaking, we see Helen
escape from the shore (v. 1662) ; so also in the *Iphig. Taur.* v. 1445, we see the
ship with the fugitives out at sea. In the *Orestes*, v. 1631, Helen appears hovering
in the air. It is clear that these were images, which must have been prepared
and lighted up in some peculiar manner so as to produce the desired impression.
For this purpose, no doubt, they used the ἡμικύκλιον, of which Pollux says (IV.
§ 131) that distant objects were represented by means of it, such as heroes swim-
ming in the sea or carried up to heaven.

[2] Most of all perhaps in the *Medea*, where the *stasima*, altogether or in part composed in the lively rhythms of the Doric mode, are sometimes designed to represent
the justice of Medea's wrath and hatred against Jason, at other times to mitigate
her revenge which is hurrying her to extremes.

[3] Thus in the *Hippolytus*, v. 904.

hosts which sailed for Troy and of the terrible destruction of
that city ! In the *Phœnissæ*, the subject of which is the contest of the hostile brothers at Thebes, the choral songs tell all
the terrible and shocking stories connected with the house of
Cadmus. We might almost class these *stasima* with the species
of choral songs mentioned by Aristotle, and called *embolima*,
because they were arbitrarily inserted as a lyrical and musical
interlude between the acts, without any reference to the subject
of the play ; much in the same way as those pauses are now-a-
days filled up with instrumental music *ad libitum*. We are
told that these *embolima* were first introduced by Agathon, a
friend and contemporary of Euripides.[1]

The tragedy of Euripides did not, however, on this account
lose its lyrical element ; it only came more and more into the
hands of the actors, in the same proportion as it was taken from
the chorus. The songs of persons on the stage form a considerable part of the tragedies of Euripides, and especially the
prolix airs or monodies, in which one of the chief persons declares his emotions or his sorrows in passionate outpourings.[2]
These monodies were among the most brilliant parts of the
pieces of Euripides : his chief actor, Cephisophon, who was nearly
connected with the poet, showed all his power in them. A
lively expression of the emotions, called forth by certain outward acts, was their chief business ; we must not expect here
that elevation of soul which is nurtured by great thoughts.
With Euripides in particular, this species of lyric poetry lost
more and more in real, sterling value ; and these descriptions
of pain, sorrow, and despair degenerated into a trifling play
with words and melodies, to which the abrupt short sentences,
tumbling topsy-turvy, as it were, the questions and exclamations, the frequent repetitions, the juxtaposition of words of

---

[1] A Latin critic of some weight, the tragedian and reviewer Accius, who in his
Didascaliæ imitated the similar labours of the Alexandrine grammarians, says in a
fragment quoted by Nonius, p. 178. ed. Mercer., *Euripides, qui choros temerarius
in fabulis.*—Former critics have supposed that a choral song in the *Helena* of
Euripides (v. 1301) has been interpolated from another tragedy ; and indeed some
things in it would be more intelligible if the choral song had originally belonged
to the *Protesilaus*.

[2] See above, chap. XXII. § 13.

the same sound, and other artifices, imparted a sort of outward
charm, but could not make up for the want of meaning in
them.   There is a feeble, childish, affected tone in these parts
of the later pieces of Euripides, which Aristophanes, who never
spares him, not only felt himself, but rendered obvious to others
by means of striking parodies.[1]

The laxity and shallowness of these lyrical pieces is also shown
in the *metrical form*, which is always growing looser and more
irregular in several ways, especially in the accumulation of
short syllables.   In the Glyconic system, in particular, Euripides, after Olymp. 89 (about B.C. 424), allowed himself to
take some liberties by virtue of which the peculiar charms of
this beautiful metre degenerated more and more into voluptuous
weakness.[2]

§ 7. The style of Euripides in the dialogue cannot be distinguished in any marked manner from the mode of speaking
then common in the public assemblies and law courts.   The
comedian calls him a poet of law speeches; conversely, he
asserts, it is necessary to speak ' *in a spruce Euripidean style*' [3]
in the public exhibitions.   The perspicuity, facility, and energetic adroitness of this style made the greatest impression at the
time.   Aristophanes, who was reproached with having learned
much from the poet to whom he was so constantly opposed,
admits that he had adopted his condensation of speech, but
adds, sarcastically, that he takes his thoughts less from the
daily intercourse of the market-place.[4]   Aristotle remarks,[5] that
Euripides was the first to produce a poetical illusion by borrowing his expressions from ordinary language; that his audience
needed not for illusion's sake to transport themselves into a
strange world, raised far above themselves, but remained at
Athens in the midst of the Athenian orators and philosophers.

---

[1] See Aristophan. *Frogs*, v. 1331 *seq.*

[2] G. Hermann has in several places called attention to the revolution which
occurred in Olymp. 90 in the mode of treating several metres.

[3] κομψευριπικῶς: *Knights*, v. 18.

[4]   χρῶμαι γὰρ αὐτοῦ τοῦ στόματος τῷ στρογγύλῳ,
        τοὺς νοῦς δ' ἀγοραίους ἧττον ἢ κεῖνος ποιῶ.

—Fragment in the Scholia to Plato's *Apology*, p. 93, 8. Fragm. No. 397. Dindorf.

[5] *Rhetor.* III. 2. § 5.

Euripides was incontestably the first who proved on the stage
the power which a fluent style, drawing the listener along with
it by means of its beautiful periods and harmonious falls, must
exert upon the public mind; nay more, he even produced a re-
action on Sophocles by means of it. But it cannot be denied
that he gave himself up too much to this facility also, and his
characters sometimes display quite as much garrulity as eloquence : the attentive reader often misses the stronger nourishment of thoughts and feelings furnished by the style of Sophocles,
which, though more difficult, is at the same time more expressive. Euripides, too, descends so low to common life in his
choice of expressions that he actually uses words of a nobler
meaning in the sense which they bore in the common colloquial
language.[1] Finally, it must be remarked, though the establishment of this position belongs to the history of the Greek language, that we find traces in Euripides of an impaired feeling
for the laws of his own language. In the lyrical passages he
uses forms of inflexion, and in the dialogue compound words,
which offend against the well-founded analogy of the Greek
language ; and he is perhaps the first of all the Greek authors
who can be charged with this.

§ 8. In these considerations of the poetry of Euripides in
general we have often referred to the distinction which subsists
between the earlier and later plays of this poet; in the following remarks on some of the separate plays we shall endeavour
to make this distinction still clearer and more definite.

The first, in point of time, of the extant plays of Euripides
is, as it happens, not adapted to serve as a striking example of
the style of his tragedies at that time. The same authority[2]
that has made known to us the year in which the *Alcestis* was
brought out (Olymp. 85. 2, B.C. 438), also informs us that this
drama was the last of four pieces, consequently, that it was
added *instead of a satyric drama* to a trilogy of tragedies.
This one notice places us at once on the right footing with

---

[1] Thus he used σεμνὸς in a bad sense, as signifying 'proud,' 'arrogant;'
Medea, 216, see Elmsley; *Hippolyt.* 93, 1064 ; παλαιότης as signifying 'simplicity,' 'foolishness;' *Helena*, 1056.

[2] A *didascalia* of the *Alcestis, e cod. Vaticano*, published by Dindorf in the
Oxford Edition of 1834.

regard to it, and sets us free from a number of difficulties which would otherwise interfere with our forming a right judgment of the piece.   When we consider all the singularities of this play —its hero, Admetus, allowing his wife to die for him, and reproaching his father with not having made this sacrifice ; the toper Hercules making a most unmusical uproar in the house of mourning as he feasts like a glutton and drinks potations pottle-deep ; and especially the farcical concluding scene, in which Admetus, the sorrowing widower, strives long not to be obliged to receive Alcestis, who has been won back from death and is introduced to him as a stranger, because he is afraid of his continence—we must admit that this piece deserves the name of a tragi-comedy rather than that of a tragedy proper. We cannot get rid of the comicality of these situations by an excuse derived from the rude *naïveté* of the ancient poetry. The shortness of the drama, in comparison with the other plays of this poet, and the simplicity of the plan, which requires only two actors,[1] all this convinces us that we must not include this play in the list of the regular tragedies of Euripides.   As it is, however, it perfectly fulfils its destination of furnishing a cheerful conclusion to a series of real tragedies, and thus relieving the mind from the stress of tragic feeling which they had occasioned.

§ 9. The *Medea*, on the contrary, which was brought out Olymp. 87. 1, B.C. 431, is unquestionably a model of the tragedies of Euripides, a great and impressive picture of human passion.   In this piece Euripides takes on himself the risk, and it was certainly no slight risk in those days, of representing in all her fearfulness a divorced and slighted wife : he has done this in the character of Medea with such vigour, that all our feelings are enlisted on the side of the incensed wife, and we follow with the most eager sympathy her crafty plan for obtaining, by dissimulation, time and opportunity for the destruction of all that is dear to the faithless Jason ; and, though we cannot regard this denouement without horror, we even consider the murder of her children as a deed necessary under the

---

[1] For Alcestis, when she returns to the stage as delivered from the power of death, is represented by a mute.   The part of Eumelus is a *parachoregema*, as it was called.   See above, § 2 note.

circumstances. The exasperation of Medea against her husband and those who have deprived her of his love certainly contains nothing grand : but the irresistible strength of this feeling, and the resolution with which she casts aside all and every of her own interests, and even rages against her own heart, produces a really great and tragic effect. The scene which paints the struggle in Medea's breast between her plans of revenge and her love for her children, will always be one of the most touching and impressive ever represented on the stage. The judgment of Aristotle that Euripides, although he does not manage everything for the best, is nevertheless *the most tragical* of the poets,[1] is particularly true of this piece. Euripides is said to have based his *Medea* on a play by Neophron, an older or contemporary tragedian, in which Medea was also represented as murdering her own children.[2] Others, on the contrary, maintain that Euripides was the first who represented Medea as the murderess of her children, whereas the Corinthian tradition attributed their death to the Corinthians,—but certainly he did not make this change in the story because the Corinthians had bribed him to take the imputation of guilt from them, but because it was only in this way that the plot would receive its full tragical significance.

§ 10. The *Hippolytus Crowned*,[3] brought out Olymp. 87. 4, B.C. 428, is related to the *Medea* in several points, but is far behind it in unity of plan and harmony of action. The unconquerable love of Phædra for her step-son, which, when scorned, is turned into a desire to make him share her own ruin, is a passion of much the same kind as that of Medea. These women, loving and terrible in their love, were new appearances on the Attic stage, and scandalized many a champion of the old morality ; at any rate, Aristophanes often affects to believe that the morals of the Athenian women were corrupted by such representations on the stage. The passion of Phædra, however, is not so completely the main subject of the whole play as Medea's is : the chief character from first to last is the young

---

[1] *Poet.* c. 13.   [2] According to the fragments of Neophron in the Scholia.
[3] As distinguished from an older play, the *Veiled Hippolytus*, which appeared in an altered and improved form in the *Hippolytus Crowned*.

Hippolytus, the model of continence, the companion and friend of the chaste Artemis, whom Euripides, in consequence of his tendency to attribute to the past the customs of his own age, has made an adherent of the ascetic doctrines of the Orphic school;[1] the destruction of this young man through the anger of Aphrodite, whom he has despised, is the general subject of the play, the proper action of the piece; and the love of Phædra is, in reference to this action, only a lever set in motion by the goddess hostile to Hippolytus. It cannot be denied that this plot, as it turns upon the selfish and cruel hatred of a deity, can give but little satisfaction, notwithstanding the great beauties of the piece, especially the representation of Phædra's passion.

§ 11. The *Hecuba* also, although a little more recent,[2] belongs to this class of tragedies, in which the emotion of passion, a *pathos* in the Greek sense of the word, is set forth in all its might and energy. The piece has been much censured, because it is deficient in unity of action, which is certainly much more important to tragedy than the unity of time or place. The censure, however, is unjust. It is only necessary that the chief character, Hecuba, should be made the centre-figure throughout the piece, and that all that happens should be referred to her, in order to bring the seemingly inconsistent action to one harmonious ending. Hecuba, the afflicted queen and mother, learns at the very beginning of the piece a new sorrow; it is announced to her that the Greeks demand the sacrifice of her daughter Polyxena at the tomb of Achilles. The daughter is torn from her mother's arms, and it is only in the willing resignation and noble resolution with which the young maiden meets her fate that we have any alleviation of the pain which we feel in common with Hecuba. Upon this, the female servant, who was sent to fetch water to bathe the dead body of Polyxena, finds on the sea-shore, washed up by the breakers, the corpse of Polydorus, the only remaining hope of his mother's declining age. The revolution or *peripeteia* of the piece con-

---

[1] Comp. chap. XVI. § 3.

[2] Aristophanes ridicules the play in the *Clouds*, consequently in Olymp. 89. 1, B.C. 423. The passage v. 649 seems to refer to the misfortunes of the Spartans at Pylos in B.C. 425.

sists in this, that Hecuba, though now cast down into the lowest abyss of misery, no longer gives way to fruitless wailings; she complains now much less than she did before of this last and worst of misfortunes; but she, a weak, aged woman, a captive, and deprived of all help, nevertheless finds means in her own powerful and active mind (for the Hecuba of Euripides is from first to last a woman of extraordinary boldness and freedom of mind[1]) to take fearful vengeance on her perfidious and cruel enemy, the Thracian king, Polymestor. With all the craft of a woman, and by sagaciously availing herself of the weak as well as of the good side of Agamemnon's character, she is enabled not merely to entice the barbarian to the destruction prepared for him, but also to make an honourable defence of her deed before the leader of the Greek host.

§ 12. It seems as if Euripides had exhausted at rather an early period the materials most suited to his style of poetry: no one of his later pieces paints a passion of such energy as the jealousy of Medea or the revengeful feelings of Hecuba. It is possible too that his method generally may not have had such capabilities as the manner in which Sophocles has been able to make the old legends applicable to the development of characters and moral tendencies. Euripides endeavours to find a substitute for the interest, which he could no longer excite by a representation of the effects of passion, in the introduction of a greater number of incidents on the stage and in a greater complication of the plot. He calls up the most surprising occurrences in order to keep the attention on the stretch; and the action is designed to represent the proper development of a great destiny, notwithstanding the accidents which may thwart and oppose it. The pieces of this period are also particularly rich in allusions to the events of the day and the relative position of the parties which were formed in the Greek states, and calculated in many ways to flatter the patriotic vanity of the

---

[1] She is also a sort of free-thinker. She says (*Hecuba*, 799) 'that law and custom (νόμος) rule over the gods; for it is in conformity with custom that we believe in the gods.' And in the *Troades* (v. 884) she prays to Zeus, whoever he may be in his inscrutable power, whether he is *the necessity of nature or the mind of men;* upon which Menelaus justly remarks that she has 'innovated' the prayers to the gods (εὐχὰς ἐκαίνισας).

Athenians.   But on this it must be remarked, that he does not,
like Æschylus, consider the mythical events in any real connexion with the historical, and treat the legends as the foundation, type, and prophecy of the destinies of the time being,
but only seeks out and eagerly lays hold of an opportunity of
pleasing the Athenians by exalting their national heroes and
debasing the heroes of their enemies.

The *Heracleidæ* can afford us no satisfaction unless we pay
attention to these political views.   This play narrates with
much circumstantial detail and exactness like a pragmatical
history, how the Heracleidæ, as poor persecuted fugitives, find
protection in Athens, and how by the valour of their own and
the Athenian heroes they gain the victory over their oppressor,
Eurystheus; it does not, however, create much tragic interest.
The episode in which Macaria with surprising fortitude volun-
tarily offers herself as a sacrifice, is designed to put a little
spirit into the drama; only it must be allowed that Euripides
makes rather too much use of the touching representation of a
noble, amiable maiden yielding herself up as a sacrifice, either of
her own accord or at least with singular resolution.[1]   All the
weight, however, in this piece is laid upon the political allusions.
The generosity of the Athenians to the Heracleidæ is celebrated
in order to charge with ingratitude their descendants, the
Dorians of the Peloponnese, who were such bitter enemies to
Athens, and the oracle which Eurystheus makes known at the
end of the play, that his corpse should be a protection to the
land of Attica against the descendants of the Heracleidæ when
they should invade Attica as enemies, was obviously designed to
strengthen the confidence of the less enlightened portion of the
audience in regard to the issue of this struggle.   The drama
was probably brought out at the time when the Argives stood
at the head of the Peloponnesian confederacy, and it was thought
probable that they would join the Spartans and Bœotians in
their march against Athens, about Olymp. 89. 3, B.C. 421.

§ 13. The *Suppliants* has a considerable affinity to the *Heracleidæ*.   In this play also a great political action is represented
with circumstantial detail and with an ostentatious display of

---

[1] Polyxena, Macaria, Iphigenia at Aulis.

patriotic speeches and stories.   The whole turns on the interment of the fallen Argive heroes, which was refused by the
Thebans, but brought about by Theseus.   It is highly probable
that Euripides had in view the dispute between the Athenians
and Bœotians after the battle of Delium, on which occasion the
latter refused to give up the dead bodies for sepulture (Olymp.
89. 2, B.C. 424).   The alliance which Euripides makes the
Argive ruler contract with Athens on behalf of all his descendants, refers unquestionably to the alliance which actually took
place between Athens and Argos about this time (Olymp. 89. 4,
B.C. 421).   The piece has, however, besides this political bearing, some independent beauties, especially in the songs of the
chorus, which is composed of the mothers of the seven heroes
and their attendants; to which are added, later in the piece,
seven youths, the sons of the fallen warriors.   The temple of
Demeter at Eleusis, where the scene is laid, forms an imposing
background to the whole piece.   The burning of the dead
bodies, which is seen on the stage, the urns with the bones of
the dead which are carried by the seven youths, are scenes
which must have produced a great outward effect; and the
frantic conduct of Evadne, who of her own accord throws herself
on the blazing funeral pile of her husband Capaneus, must have
created emotions of terror and surprise in the minds of the spectators.   It is clear that in this play Euripides summoned to his
aid all the resources which might contribute to make its representation splendid and effective.

§ 14. The *Ion* of Euripides possesses great beauties, but is
defective in the very same points as those which we have just
described.   No great character, no violent passion predominates
in the poem; the only motive by which the characters are
actuated is a consideration of their own advantage; all the interest lies in the ingenuity of the plot, which is so involved that,
while on the one hand it keeps our expectation on the stretch
and agreeably surprises us, on the other hand the result is
highly flattering to the patriotic wishes of the Athenians.
Apollo is desirous of advancing Ion, his son by Creusa, the
daughter of Erechtheus, to the sovereignty of Athens, but without acknowledging that he is his father.   With this view he
delivers an ambiguous oracle, which induces Xuthus, the hus-

band of Creusa, to believe that Ion is his own son, begotten before his marriage with the Athenian princess. The violence of Creusa, however, hinders the success of this plan. She endeavours to poison him whom she considers as her husband's bastard and as an intruder into the ancient royalty of the Erechtheidæ, and Ion, protected by the gods from her attempt upon his life, is about to take a bloody revenge on the authoress of the murderous design. Upon this, the woman who took care of Ion in his infancy appears with the tokens which prove his origin, and Ion at once embraces as his mother the enemy whom he was about to punish. The worthy Xuthus, however, whom gods and men leave in his error, undoubtingly receives the stranger youth into his house and kingdom as his son and heir. It is clear that the general object of this play is to maintain undimmed and undiminished the pride of the Athenians, their *autochthony*, their pure descent from their old earth-born patriarchs and national kings. The common ancestor of the Ionians who ruled in Attica must not be the son of a stranger settled in the country, an Achæan chieftain, like Xuthus, but must belong to the pure old Attic stock of the Erechtheidæ.

§ 15. The *Raging Hercules* contains very definite indications that the poet composed it at a time when he began to feel the inconvenience of old age, which might easily be the case from Olymp. 89. 3, B.C. 422.[1] This piece is also constructed so as to produce a great effect in the way of surprise, and contains scenes—such as the appearance of the goddess *Lyssa* (Madness), and the representation, by means of an *eccyclema*, of Hercules, bound and recovering from his madness—which must have produced a powerful effect on the stage. But it is altogether wanting in the real satisfaction which nothing but a unity of ideas pervading the drama could produce. It is hardly possible to conceive that the poet should have combined in one piece two actions so totally different as the deliverance of the children of Hercules from the persecutions of the bloodthirsty Lycus, and their murder by the hands of their frantic father, merely

---

[1] In the choral song, v. 639 *seq.*: ἁ νεότας μοι φίλον—especially in the words ἔτι τοι γέρων ἀοιδὸς κελαδεῖ μναμοσύναν. Compare with this *Cresphontes*, frag. 15, ed. Matthiæ.

because he wished to surprise the audience by a sudden and unexpected change to the precise contrary of what had gone before.
We believe that the afflictions of Hercules and his family are
over, when suddenly the goddess of madness appears to bring
about a new and greater sorrow, and to destroy the children by
the hands of the very person who had delivered them from
death in the first part of the play, and that too with no apparent ground, except that Hera will give no rest to Hercules,
although he has got over all the labours hitherto imposed upon
him.

§ 16. We have assigned the two last pieces to this epoch
not from any external grounds, but on the evidence of their
contents. Other pieces, the date of which may be definitely
assigned, show still more clearly the form which the tragedy of
Euripides assumed from after Olymp. 90, B.C. 420. It became
more and more his object to represent the wayward and confused impulses of human passion, in which, by sudden and surprising changes, now the one side, now the other, gains the
mastery; the plans of the wicked fail, but even the just suffer
adversity and affliction, without our being able to perceive any
solid foundation on which those varied destinies of the individual actors are based.

This is particularly applicable to the *Andromache*, in which,
at first, the helpless wife of Hector, who is represented in the
play as the slave of Neoptolemus, is persecuted to the utter-
most by his wife Hermione and her father Menelaus; then, by
the opportune intervention of Peleus, Andromache is set free,
Menelaus compelled to retire, and Hermione plunged into the
most desperate sorrow; upon this Orestes appears, carries off
Hermione, who was betrothed to him before, and contrives
plans for the destruction of her husband, Neoptolemus; the
news soon arrives that Neoptolemus has been slain at Delphi
in consequence of the intrigues of Orestes; and Thetis, who
comes forward as the *deus ex machinâ*, brings consolation and
tranquillity, not from the past but from the future, by promising
to the descendants of Andromache the sovereignty of the Molossi,
and to Peleus immortality among the deities of the sea. If
we must seek in this play for a subject which goes all through
the piece, it is the mischief which a bad wife may, in many

ways, direct and indirect, bring upon a family. Hermione causes mischief in the family of Neoptolemus, as well by the jealous cruelty which she exercises in the house as by faithlessly leaving her husband for a stranger. The political references bear a very prominent part in the piece. The bad characters are throughout Peloponnesians, and especially Spartans ; and Euripides embraces, with a delight which cannot be mistaken, this opportunity of giving vent to all the ill-will that he felt towards the cruel and crafty men and the dissolute women of Sparta. The want of honour and sincerity with which he charges the Spartans [1] appears to refer particularly to the transactions of the year 420, Olymp. 89. 4,[2] so that the play seems to have been brought out in the course of the 90th Olympiad.

§ 17. The *Troades* or *Trojan Women,* of which we know with certainty that it was brought out Olymp. 91. 1, B.C. 415,[3] is the most irregular of all the extant pieces of Euripides. It is nothing more than a picture of the horrors which befall a conquered city and of the cruelties exercised by arrogant conquerors, though it is continually hinted that the victors are in reality more unhappy than the vanquished. The distribution of the Trojan women among the Achæans ; the selection of the prophetic maiden, Cassandra, to be the mistress of Agamemnon, whose death she prophesies ; the sacrifice of Polyxena at the tomb of Achilles, Astyanax torn from his mother's arms in order that he may be thrown from the battlements of the city walls ; then the strange contest between Hecuba and Helen before Menelaus, in which he pretends to desire to bring the authoress of all the calamities to a severe account, but is clearly in his heart actuated by different motives, and is willing

---

[1] See v. 445 *seq.*, especially the words λέγοντες ἄλλα μὲν γλώσσῃ, φρονοῦντες δ' ἄλλα.

[2] When Alcibiades, by his intrigues, had got the Spartan ambassadors to say before the people something different from what they had intended and wished to speak—a deceit *which no one saw through at the time.*—Thucyd. V. 45.

[3] In conjunction with two other pieces, the *Alexander* and the *Palamedes,* which likewise referred to the Trojan war, and followed in chronological order (for the *Alexander* referred to the discovery of Paris before the Trojan war, and the *Palamedes* to the earlier part of the war itself), without, however, constituting a trilogy according to the views of *Æschylus.*

to take his faithless wife home with him; lastly, the burning of the city, which forms the grand finale of the piece; what are all these but a series of significant pictures, unfolded one after the other and submitted to the contemplation of the reflective spectator? The remarkable feature, however, in this play is, that the *prologue* goes a good way beyond the drama itself, and contains the proper conclusion of the whole; for in it the deities, Athena and Poseidon, determine between themselves to raise a tempest as the Greeks are returning home and so make them pay for all the sins they have committed at Troy. In order to gain an end which will satisfy the intentions of the poet, we must suppose that this compact is really fulfilled at the end of the piece. We almost feel ourselves compelled to conjecture that we have lost the epilogue, in which some deity, Poseidon or Athena, appeared as the *deus ex machinâ*, and described the destruction of the fleet as in the act of taking place; there might also have been a perspective view, such as that which we have pointed out in several other pieces (§ 5 note), representing the sea raging and the fleet foundering; and thus there would be contrasted with the burning city another picture necessary to give a suitable conclusion to the ideas developed in the drama and to satisfy the moral requisitions suggested by it.

§ 18. We must next speak of the *Electra*, which must obviously be assigned to the period of the Sicilian expedition.[1] In this piece Euripides goes farther than in any other in his endeavour to reduce the old mythical stories to the level of every-day life. He has invented an incident, not altogether improbable—that Ægisthus married Electra to a common countryman, in order that her children might never gain power or influence enough to endanger his life—and this enables the poet to put together a set of scenes representing domestic arrangements of the most limited and trifling kind. The king's daughter spends her time in labours of housewifery, not so much from need, as in a spirit

---

[1] The passage (v. 1347) in which the Dioscuri propose to themselves to protect the ships in the Sicilian sea, clearly refers to the fleet which sailed from Athens to Sicily; and the following lines possibly refer to the charge of impiety under which Alcibiades then laboured.

of defiance, in order to show how ill she is treated by her mother; she represents an economical manager, who scolds her husband for bringing into their poor cottage guests of too great expectations; she tells him he must go out and get something to eat from an old friend of his, for it is impossible to obtain anything from her father's house. Euripides considers the murder of Ægisthus and Clytemnestra as proceeding from the vindictive spirit of the brother and sister; they bitterly regret it as soon as done, and even the Dioscuri, who appear as *dii ex machinâ,* censure it as the *unwise* act of the wise god Apollo.

§ 19. In the concluding scene of the *Electra,*[1] Euripides hints at an alteration in the story of Helen, which he worked out shortly after (Olymp. 91. 4, B.C. 412) in a separate play, the *Helena,*[2] in which this personage, so often abused by Euripides, is on a sudden represented as a most faithful wife, a pattern of female virtue, a most noble and elevated character. This is effected by assuming and arbitrarily adapting to his own purpose an idea started by Stesichorus,[3] that the Trojans and Achæans fought for a mere shadow of Helen. Of course it is not to be imagined that Euripides was in earnest when he adopted this idea, and that he considered this form of the tradition as the true and genuine one; he uses it merely for this tragedy, and, as we may see in the *Orestes,* soon returns to the easier and more congenial representation of Helen as a worthless runaway wife. The *Helena* turns entirely on the escape of this heroine from Egypt, where the young king wishes to compel her to marry him. Her deliverance is effected entirely by her own cunning plans, and Menelaus is only a subordinate instrument

---

[1] V. 1292.

[2] The *Helena* was performed along with the *Andromeda* (*Schol. Ravenn.* on Aristoph. *Thesm.* 1012); and the *Andromeda* came out in the eighth year before the *Frogs* of Aristophanes (*Schol.* on the *Frogs,* 53), which appeared in Olymp. 93. 3, B.C. 405. The *Andromeda* is parodied in the *Thesmophoriazusæ* (Olymp. 92. 1, B.C. 411), as a piece brought out the year before; and in several passages of the same play, Aristophanes also ridicules the *Helena:* consequently, the *Helena* must have been brought out Olymp. 91. 4, B.C. 412. This applies very well to the violent invectives against the soothsayers (v. 744 *seq.*), probably occasioned by the recent failure of the Sicilian expedition, which (according to Thucydides and Aristophanes) the soothsayers of Athens had especially urged the people to undertake.

[3] On this, see chap. XIV. § 5.

in carrying them into execution. The country and people of Egypt, who are in most points represented under a Greek type, form a very interesting background to the drama. The king's sister, Theonoe, a virgin priestess skilled in the future, but full of sympathy for the troubles of mankind, and presiding like a protecting goddess over the plans of Helen and her husband, is a grand and beautiful conception of the poet.

§ 20. From the manner in which Euripides has treated the story of Helen in the piece we have just spoken of, it bears a strong resemblance to the action in the *Iphigenia at Tauri*, except that the ancient poet has made no use of the incentive of love in this latter play, for Thoas is sufficiently constrained by religious motives to prevent the escape of the priestess of the Tauric Artemis and of the strangers destined to be sacrificed at her altar. From an argument, too, derivable from the metrical form of the choral songs, we should feel obliged to place the *Tauric Iphigenia* about this time (Olymp. 92). The efforts of the poet in this piece are chiefly directed to construct an artificial plot, to introduce, in a surprising but at the same time natural manner, the recognition of Orestes by his sister Iphigenia, and to form a plan of flight, possible under the circumstances, and taking into the account all the difficulties and dangers of the case. The drama, however, has other beauties —of a kind, too, rather uncommon in Euripides—in the noble bearing and moral worth of the characters. Iphigenia appears as a pure-minded young maiden, who has inspired even the barbarians with reverence; her love for her home, and the conviction that she is doing the will of the gods, are her only incentives to flight, and these are sufficient excuses, according to the views of the Greeks, for the imposition which she practises upon the good Thoas. The poet, too, has taken care not to spoil the pleasure with which we contemplate this noble picture, by representing Iphigenia as a priestess who slays human victims on the altar. Her duty is only to consecrate the victims by sprinkling them with water outside the temple; others take them into the temple and put them to death.[1] Fate, too, has contrived that hitherto no Greek has been driven to this coast.[2]

---

[1] V. 617 *seq.*   [2] V. 244 *seq.*

When she flies, however, a symbolical representation is substituted for the rites of an actual sacrifice,[1] whereby the humanity of the Greeks triumphs over the religious fanaticism of the barbarians. Still more attractive and touching is the connexion of Orestes and Pylades, whose friendship is exalted in this more than in any other play. The scene in which the two friends strive which of them shall be sacrificed as a victim and which shall return home, is very affecting, without any design on the part of the poet to call forth the tears of the spectators. According to our ideas, it must be confessed, Pylades yields too soon to the pressing entreaties of his friend, partly because the arguments of Orestes actually convince him, partly because, as having more faith in the Delphic Apollo, he still retains the hope that the oracle of the god will in the end deliver them both; whereas we desire, even in such cases, an enthusiastic resignation of all thoughts to the *one* idea, in which no thought can arise except the deliverance of our friend. The feelings of the people of antiquity, however, were made of sterner stuff; their hardihood and simplicity of character would not allow them to be so easily thrown off their balance, and while they preserved the truth of friendship, they could keep their eyes open for all the other duties and advantages of life.

§ 21. We have a remarkable contrast to the *Iphigenia at Tauri* in the *Orestes*, which was produced Olymp. 92. 4, B.C. 408, and consequently was not far removed in point of time from the last-mentioned drama. The old grammarians remark that the piece produced a great effect on the stage, though all the characters in it are bad, with the exception of Pylades;[2] and that the catastrophe inclines to the comic. It seems to have been the design of Euripides to represent a wild chaos of selfish passions, from which there is absolutely no means of escape. Orestes is about to be put to death for matricide by virtue of the decree of an Argive tribunal, while Menelaus, on whom he had placed his dependence, deserts him out of pure cowardice

---

[1] V. 1462 *seq.*

[2] The old critics have also remarked upon the references to the state of affairs at the time in the character of Menelaus, who may be considered as a representative of the vacillating and uncertain policy of Sparta at that period. See Schol. on v. 371, 772, 903.

and selfishness. Enraged at this abandonment, he determines not to die till he has taken vengeance on Helen, the cause of all the mischief, who has hidden herself in the palace through fear of the Argives; and when she, in a surprising manner, vanishes to heaven, he threatens to slay her daughter Hermione, unless Menelaus will pardon and rescue him. Upon this the Dioscuri appear, bid him take to wife the damsel at whose throat he is holding the drawn sword, and promise him deliverance from the curse of the matricidal act. In this manner the knot is outwardly untied, or rather cut asunder, without any attempt or hint at unravelling the real intricacies, the moral questions to which the tragedy leads, or purifying the passions by means of themselves, which is the object of tragedy, in the proper sense of the word. So far from attaining to this object, the only impression produced by such a drama as the *Orestes* is a feeling of the comfortless confusion of human exertions and relations.

§ 22. The *Phœnissæ*, or *Phœnician Women,* was not much later than the *Orestes.* We know on sure testimony that it was one of the last pieces which Euripides brought out at Athens,[1] but it is certainly by no means one of the least valuable of his works. In general, it would be very difficult to discern in the last pieces of Euripides any marks of the feebleness of age, which seems, on the whole, to have had little effect on the poets of antiquity. There are great beauties in the *Phœnissæ,* such as the splendid scene at the beginning,—in which Antigone, attended by an aged domestic, surveys the army of the seven heroes from a tower of the palace,—and the entrance of Polyneices into the hostile city; we might add the episode about Menœceus, were it not a mere repetition of the scene about Macaria in the *Heracleidæ;* besides, Euripides has made too much use of these voluntary self-sacrifices to produce any striking effect by means of them. Notwithstanding, however, all the beauties of the details and all the abundance of the materials (for the piece contains, in addition to the fall of the hostile brother, also the expulsion of Œdipus and Antigone's two heroic resolves to perform the funeral rites for her brother and

---

[1] *Schol.* on Aristoph. *Frogs,* 53.

to accompany her banished father),[1] we miss in this play, too, that real unity and harmony of action which can result only from an idea springing from the depths of the heart and ripened by the genial warmth of the feelings.

§ 23. Three pieces, of which two are still extant, were brought out by the *younger* Euripides, a son, or more probably a nephew, of the celebrated tragedian, and were performed, after the death of the author, as new plays at the great Dionysia. These were the *Iphigenia at Aulis*, the *Alcmæon*, a lost play,[2] and the *Bacchæ*. Of these three plays the *Bacchæ* was, as far as we can see, completed by the author himself; not, however, immediately for Athens, but for representation in Macedonia. Euripides spent the last years of his life, when Athens was groaning under the weight of the Peloponnesian war, at the court of the Macedonian king, Archelaus, who was not a man of exalted moral character, but a politic ruler who had taken great pains in civilizing his country, and for that object had collected around himself a considerable circle of Greek poets and musicians. It is the common tradition of antiquity that Euripides died here. The worship of Bacchus was very prevalent in Macedonia, especially in Pieria near Olympus, where, at a later period, Olympias, the mother of Alexander, roamed about with the Mimallones and Clodones; Archelaus may have celebrated the feast of Bacchus here with dramatic spectacles,[3] at which the *Bacchæ* was performed for the first time. To this there is an allusion in the words of the chorus [4]—' Happy Pieria, thee Bacchus honours, and he will come in order to dance in thee with Bacchic revelry; he will conduct his Mænads over the swift flowing Axius and the Lydias, whose streams pour forth blessings.' Euripides would hardly have celebrated these rivers in such a manner had not Pella, the residence of the Macedonian kings, been situated between them, and had not the

---

[1] One does not see, however, how Antigone could find it possible to carry both her resolutions into effect at once.

[2] This was the 'Αλκμαίων διὰ Κορίνθου, for the 'Αλκμαίων διὰ Ψωφῖδος was brought out by Euripides along with the *Alcestis*.

[3] As he also instituted dramatic contests at Dion in Pieria in honour of Zeus and the Muses. Diodor. Sic. XVII. 16. Wesseling on XVI. 56.

[4] V. 565.

court of the king come to Pieria in order to bear a part in the dramatic festival celebrated there.

The *Bacchæ*, or *Bacchanalians*, developes the story of Pentheus, who was so fearfully punished for his attempt to keep the Dionysian rites from being introduced into Thebes, and gives a lively and comprehensive picture of the impassioned and enthusiastic nature of this worship; at the same time, this tragedy furnishes us with remarkable conclusions in regard to the religious opinions of Euripides at the close of his life. In this play he appears, as it were, converted into a positive believer, or, in other words, convinced that religion should not be exposed to the subtilties of reasoning; that the understanding of man cannot subvert ancestral traditions which are as old as time; that the philosophy which attacks religion is but a poor philosophy, and so forth;[1] doctrines which are sometimes set forth with peculiar impressiveness in the speeches of the old men, Cadmus and Teiresias, or, on the other hand, form the foundation of the whole piece : although it must be owned that Euripides, with the vacillation which he always displays in such matters, ventures, on the other hand, to explain the offensive story about the second birth of Bacchus from the thigh of Zeus, by a very frigid pun on a word which he assumes to have been misunderstood in the first instance.[2]

§ 24. The case is different with the *Iphigenia at Aulis*, which has obviously not come down to us in so perfect a state from the hands of the author. In its really genuine and original parts, this *Iphigenia* is one of the most admirable of this poet's tragedies, and it is based upon such a noble idea that we might put it on the same footing with the works of his better days, such as the *Medea* or the *Hecuba*. This idea is, that a pure and elevated mind, like that of *Iphigenia*, can alone find a way out of all the intricacies and entanglements caused by the passions and efforts of powerful, wise, and brave men, contending with and running counter to one another. In this play Euripides has had the skill to invest the subject with such intense

---

[1] See v. 200, οὐδὲν σοφιζόμεσθα τοῖσι δαίμοσιν, and the following verses: v. 1257, μὴ σοφοῖς χαίρειν κακοῖς.

[2] By an interchange of μηρὸς and ὅμηρος, v. 292.

interest by depicting the fruitless efforts of Agamemnon to save
his child, the too late compunction of Menelaus, the pride and
courage with which Achilles offers himself for the rescue of his
affianced bride and for her defence against the whole army, that
the willingness of Iphigenia to sacrifice herself appears as the
solution of a very complicated knot, such as generally requires
a *deus ex machinâ* in Euripides, and shines with the brightest
lustre as an act of the highest sublimity.   Unfortunately, however, this admirable work is disfigured by the interpolation of a
number of passages, poor and paltry both in matter and in form.[1]
We know not if we judge too harshly of the younger Euripides,
when we regard these as additions by which he sought to complete the piece for representation ; if so, we must conclude that
the art of tragedy sunk altogether soon after the death of the
great poets.   The question is the more difficult to answer from
the fact that in ancient times there was a totally different epilogue to the *Iphigenia at Aulis*.[2]   It is possible, or rather probable, that this was the ending added by the younger Euripides,
while in other copies the genuine parts alone were transcribed,
and that at a later period, after the decline of poetry, these
copies were completed as we have them now.

§ 25. The still extant dramas of Euripides are so numerous
and varied that we have not found it necessary to our judgment
of his works to take into account his lost pieces, though, if we
are to believe the hostile criticisms in Aristophanes and the remarks of other ancient writers, there were several of these
pieces which presented even more glaring specimens of the poet's
faulty mannerism than those which we still have ; for instance,
he attempted in the beggar-hero *Telephus* to produce a touching effect by the outward appearance, by ragged clothes, and so
forth ;[3] the *Andromeda* abounded in showy fooleries in the lyrical

---

[1] The worst addition is the epilogue ; the *parodos* of the chorus is also liable to
strong suspicions.   The prologue, together with the anapests, differs from the customary style of Euripides; but it has beauties of its own, and, moreover, this part
of the play has been imitated by Ennius.

[2] According to the well-known passage in Ælian's *Hist. Animal*. VII. 39.

[3] Euripides subsequently introduced many alterations into this piece, but not
on account of the jokes in the *Frogs* of Aristophanes, as we might infer from
Eustath. on the *Iliad*, XVI. p. 1084 ; for it is well known that he was not living

parts; and the *wise Melanippe* was full of the enlightened reasonings of the new philosophy. The *Chrysippus* and the *Peirithous* were especially rich in speculations about nature and the soul, the *Sisyphus* in sophistical arguments about the origin of religions; the two last pieces, however, were more correctly ascribed to *Critias*, the pupil of Socrates and the sophists, and well known as one of the Thirty Tyrants.[1]

The predilection of antiquity for Euripides has also preserved us one of his satyric dramas, the *Cyclops* (the only specimen we have of this sort of play), though Euripides had not distinguished himself particularly in this branch of dramatic poetry. As a specimen of the satyric drama, for which the story of *Polyphemus* is peculiarly adapted, the play possesses some interest, but it wants that genial originality which we should have been warranted in expecting in a satyrical drama by Æschylus.

Euripides probably died in Olymp. 93. 2, B.C. 407, though the ancients also assign the following year for his death.[2] Sophocles mourned for him in common with the rest of Athens, and brought his actors uncrowned to the tragic contest. This must have happened at the dramatic contests in the winter of B.C. 407 and 406; Sophocles himself died soon after, about the spring of B.C. 406 (Olymp. 93. 2), if we may give credit to the old stories which place his death in connexion with the feast of the Anthesteria.

---

when that comedy was produced. In general, Euripides frequently altered his plays to suit the public taste, as we are told he did the *Hippolytus*. In the first edition of this play, Phædra was a much more importunate lover.

[1] We have entirely passed over the *Rhesus;* for although there was a play of Euripides with this name, which Attius seems to have imitated in the *Nyctegersis*, the extant piece bears no mark of the pen of Euripides, and must rather be considered as an imitation of Æschylus or Sophocles. It probably belongs to the later Athenian tragedy, perhaps to the school of *Philocles*, for it is clear from v. 944 that it comes from Athens. The scene in which Paris appears the instant that Diomedes and Ulysses have left the stage, while Athena is still there, requires four actors; and this may also be used as an argument to prove that it was composed at a later period.

[2] See chap. XXIV. § 11 note.

CHAPTER XXVI.

THE OTHER TRAGIC POETS.

§ 1. Inferiority of the other tragic poets. § 2. Contemporaries of Sophocles and Euripides: Neophron, Ion, Aristarchus, Achæus, Carcinus, Xenocles. § 3. Tragedians somewhat more recent: Agathon; the anonymous son of Cleomachus. Tragedy grows effeminate. § 4. Men of education employ tragedy as a vehicle of their opinions on the social relations of the age. § 5. The families of the great tragedians: the Æschyleans, Sophocleans, and the younger Euripides. § 6. Influence of other branches of literature; tragedy is treated by Chæremon in the spirit of lax and effeminate lyric poetry. § 7. Tragedy is subordinated to rhetoric in the dramas of Theodectes.

§ 1. WE may consider ourselves fortunate in possessing, as specimens of Greek tragedy, masterpieces by those poets whom their contemporaries and all antiquity unanimously regarded as the heroes of the tragic stage. Æschylus, Sophocles, and Euripides are the names which continually recur whenever the ancients speak of the height which tragic poetry attained at Athens; the state itself distinguished them by founding institutions the object of which was to preserve their works pure and unadulterated, and to protect them from being interpolated at the caprice of the actors;[1] and soon afterwards they were rather read in the closet than heard in the theatre, and became identified with the existence of the later Greeks and Romans.

Their contemporaries among the tragedians must be regarded as, for the most part, far from insignificant poets, inasmuch as they maintained their place on the stage beside them, and not unfrequently gained the tragic prize in competition with them.

---

[1] According to a law, proposed by the orator Lycurgus, authentic copies of the works of the three poets were kept in the archives of Athens, and it was the duty of the public secretary (γραμματεὺς τῆς πόλεως) to see that the actors delivered this text only. See the life of Lycurgus in Plutarch's *Vitæ decem Oratorum*, where the words, οὐκ ἐξεῖναι γὰρ αὐτὰς ἄλλως ὑποκρίνεσθαι have been properly added.

Yet, though their *separate* productions may have been in part happy enough to merit most fully the approbation of the public, the *general* character of these poets must have been deficient in that depth and peculiar force of genius by which the great tragedians were distinguished. If this had not been the case, their works would assuredly have attracted greater attention and have been read more frequently in later times.

§ 2. NEOPHRON of Sicyon must have been one of the most ancient of these poets, if the *Medea* of Euripides was really in part an imitation of one of his plays :[1] in that case he must be distinguished from a younger Neophron, who was a contemporary of Alexander the Great.

ION, of Chios, lived at Athens in the time of Æschylus and Cimon, and in the fragments of his writings speaks of the events of their day as from personal knowledge. He was a very comprehensive writer, and what was very uncommon in ancient times, a prose author as well as a poet. He wrote history in the dialect and after the manner of Herodotus, except that he paid more attention to the private life of distinguished individuals : he also composed elegies[2] and lyrical poems of various sorts. He did not come forward as a tragedian till after the death of Æschylus (Olymp. 82), whose place, it seems, he expected to fill on the stage. The materials of his dramas were in a great measure taken from Homer ; they may have been connected in trilogies like those of Æschylus ; the few remains,[3] however, hardly allow us to trace the connexion of these trilogical compositions. Although correct and careful in the execution, his productions were deficient in that higher energy which is remarkable in the more genial poets.[4]

ARISTARCHUS, of Tegea, came forward in Olymp. 81. 2, B.C. 454, and, as we have mentioned above,[5] was the first to

---

[1] See the *didascalia* to the *Medea* of Euripides (where it would be best to change γενναιοφρόνως διασκευάσας into τὴν Νεόφρονος δ.), and Diog. Laërt. II. 134. But a good deal might be said against this account, and perhaps the relation between the two plays was precisely the converse.

[2] See chap. X. § 7, p. 152, notes.

[3] Ionis Chii fragmenta collegit Nieverding. Lipsiæ, 1836.

[4] According to the judgment of the critic Longinus, *de Sublim.* 33.

[5] Chap. XXI. § 4.

produce tragedies, according to the standard of greater length, which was subsequently observed by Sophocles and Euripides. Some of his tragedies, especially the *Achilles*, gained some reputation at a later period, from being imitated by Ennius.

ACHÆUS, of Eretria, brought out many dramas at Athens after Olymp. 83, but only once obtained the prize. A sort of artificial manner was peculiar to him; the fragments of his dramas[1] contain much strange mythology, and we learn that his expressions were often forced and obscure. Nevertheless, with such peculiarities he may easily have merited the favourable opinion of some ancient critics, who considered him the best writer of satyric dramas next to Æschylus. In constructing such dramas he could hardly have avoided making some strange combinations and indulging in some far-fetched witticisms.

CARCINUS, with his sons, forms a family of tragedians, known to us chiefly from the jokes and mockeries of Aristophanes. The father was a tragedian, and the sons appeared as choral-dancers in his plays; only one of them, Xenocles, also devoted himself to the profession of poetry. As far as we can judge from a few hints, both father and son were distinguished by a sort of antiquated harshness in their mode of expression. Yet Xenocles, with his tragic trilogy, *Œdipus, Lycaon, Bacchæ*, and the satyrical drama *Athamas*, gained the prize over the trilogy of Euripides to which the *Troades* belonged. From the Athenian Carcinus we must distinguish a later tragedian of the same name, who was of Agrigentum.

§ 3. AGATHON was a very singular character. He came before the public with his first tragedy in Olymp. 90. 4, B.C. 416, when he was still a young man, and spent his riper years at the court of Archelaus, King of Macedon, where he died about Olymp. 94. 4, B.C. 400. His strange demeanour and habits have enabled Aristophanes (especially in the *Thesmophoriazusæ*) and Plato (in the *Symposium*) to give us some sketches of him, which bring the man before our eyes in the most vivid and striking manner. Naturally delicate and effeminate, as well in body as in mind, he gave himself up entirely to this mood, and coquetted with a sort of grace and charm with which

---

[1] Achæi Eretriensis fragmenta collegit Urlichs. Bonn. 1834.

he endeavoured to invest everything that he took in hand.
The lyrical part of his tragedies was an amiable and insinuating
display of cheerful thoughts and kindly images, but did not
penetrate deeply into the feelings. In accordance with these
views, Agathon had devoted himself to the new arts, by which
the sophists of the time, and especially Gorgias, had produced
such an effect on the Athenian public. He borrowed from
Gorgias his novel and ingenious combinations of thought, which
deluded the hearer into the idea that he had really gained an
entirely new insight into the subject, and also the figures of opposition and parallelism (*Antitheta*, *Parisa*), which gratified the
prevailing taste of the age by giving the structure of the sentence an appearance of symmetry and regularity.[1] We should,
however, have prized very much the possession of such an
original work as Agathon's *Flower* (ἄνθος) must have been.

Still more effeminate must have been the poetry of an author
whom Cratinus the comedian designates only as *the Son of Cleomachus*.[2] The Archon, he tells us, gave this poetaster a chorus
in preference to Sophocles, although he was not worthy to provide songs for a chorus at the wanton female festival of the
Adonia. He compares the chorus of this poet, which expressed,
in soft Lydian melodies, corresponding thoughts and feelings, to
licentious women from Lydia, who were ready for all sorts of
harlotry. It seems that the same poet, who was probably
named Cleomenes, composed erotic poems in a lyrical form, and
transferred their characteristics to his tragedies.

§ 4. About this time the tragic stage received a great influx
of poets, which, however, does not prove that a great advance
had taken place in the art of tragic poetry. Aristophanes
speaks of thousands of tragedy-making prattlers, more garrulous

---

[1] As in the example quoted by Aristotle, *Rhetor.* II. 24, 10 : 'We might call
that *probable*, that many things not *probable* would occur among men.'

[2] In the difficult passage quoted by Athenæus, XIV. p. 638, where, after ὁ Κλεομάχου, we must write also τῷ Κλεομάχου ; at all events, the converse alteration is
less probable. Gnesippus can hardly be this son of Cleomachus, as Athenæus
expressly calls him a writer of jocular songs only. We must, at any rate, suppose
with Casaubon that something has fallen out before σκώπτει, and it is almost
probable that *Cleomenes*, who is mentioned in connexion with Gnesippus, is more
precisely referred to in the lost passage.

by a good deal. than Euripides: he calls their poems muses' groves for swallows, comparing their trifling and insignificant attempts at polite literature with the chirping of birds;[1] happily these dilettanti were generally satisfied with presenting themselves *once* before the people as tragic poets. There was such a taste for the composition of tragedies that we find among those who wrote for the stage men of the most different pursuits and dispositions, such as CRITIAS, the head of the oligarchical party at Athens, and DIONYSIUS THE FIRST, tyrant of Syracuse, who often came forward as a competitor for the tragic prize, and had the satisfaction of receiving the crown once before he died. Such men were fond of availing themselves of tragedy, in the same way that Euripides did, as a vehicle for bringing before the public in a less suspicious manner their speculations on the political and social interests of their auditors. In the drama called *Sisyphus* (which is perhaps more rightly ascribed to Critias than to Euripides[2]), there was a development of the pernicious doctrine of the sophists, that religion was an ancient political institution, designed to sanction the restraints of law by superadding the fear of the gods; and we are told that Dionysius wrote a drama against Plato's theory of the state, which was called a tragedy, but had rather the character of a comedy. It is well known, too, that *Plato* also composed a tragic tetralogy in his younger days, which he committed to the flames when he had convinced himself that dramatic poetry was not his vocation. In the opposite party, among the accusers of Socrates, *Meletus* was not a philosopher, but a tragedian by profession; we are told, however, that his poetry was as frigid and tedious as his character appears hateful to us from his persecution of the illustrious sage.

§ 5. The families of the great poets contributed in a considerable degree to continue the tragic art after their deaths. As the great poets not only felt themselves called upon by their own taste to devote themselves to dramatic poetry, and to bring out plays and teach the chorus year after year, but really practised this art as an ostensible profession, we cannot wonder

---

[1] Aristophanes' *Frogs*, v. 89 *seq.*: χελιδόνων μουσεῖα.
[2] See above, chap. XXV. § 25.

that this, like other employments and trades, was transmitted by a regular descent to their sons and grandsons. *Æschylus* was followed by a succession of tragedians, who flourished through several generations;[1] his son Euphorion sometimes brought out plays of his father's which had not been represented before, sometimes pieces of his own, and he gained the tragic prize in competition with both Sophocles and Euripides; similarly, Æschylus' nephew, *Philocles*, gained the prize against the *King Œdipus* of Sophocles, a piece which, in our opinion, is not to be surpassed. Philocles must have had a good deal of his uncle's manner; his tetralogy the *Pandionis*, probably developed the destinies of Procne and Philomela in a connected series of dramas quite according to the Æschylean model, and the hardness and harshness [2] with which he is reproached may have followed naturally from his imitation of the style of the old tragedy. Morsimus, the son of Philocles, seems to have done but little honour to the family; but after the Peloponnesian war the Æschyleans gained new lustre from Astydamas, who brought out 240 pieces and gained fifteen victories. From these numbers we see that Astydamas in his time supplied the Athenian public with new tetralogies almost every year at the Lenæa and great Dionysia, and that, on an average, he gained the prize once every four contests.[3]

---

[1] To make this clearer, we subjoin the pedigree of the whole family, chiefly derived from Boeckh., *Tragœd. Græc. principes*, p. 32. and Clinton, *Fast. Hellen.* II. p. xxxiii.

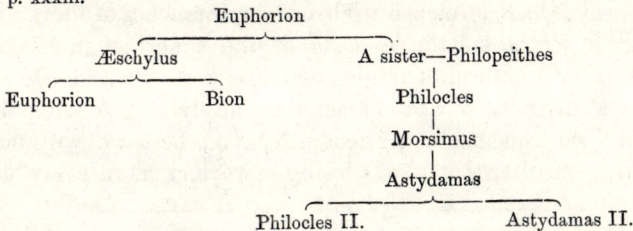

```
                        Euphorion
        ┌───────────────────┴────────────────────┐
     Æschylus                        A sister—Philopeithes
   ┌─────┴─────┐                               │
Euphorion    Bion                          Philocles
                                               │
                                           Morsimus
                                               │
                                           Astydamas
                             ┌─────────────────┴──────────────────┐
                       Philocles II.                        Astydamas II.
```

According to Suidas, Bion was also a tragedian. Philocles must have flourished even before the Peloponnesian war, for his son Morsimus is ridiculed as a tragic poet in the *Knights* (Olymp. 88. 4, B.C. 424), and *Peace* (Olymp. 90. 1, B.C. 419), of Aristophanes; and Astydamas came out as a tragedian in Olymp. 95. 2, B.C. 398.

[2] Πικρία, Schol. Aristoph. *Av.*; Suidas, v. Φιλοκλῆς. He gained from this the epithets Ἁλμίων and Χολή, 'salt-pickle' and 'gall.'

[3] He was the first of the family of Æschylus who was honoured by the Athenians

With regard to the family of *Sophocles*, *Iophon* was an active and popular tragedian in his father's life-time, and Aristophanes considers him as the only support of the tragic stage after the death of the two great poets. We do not, however, know how a later age answered the comedian's doubtful question, whether Iophon would be able to do as much by himself now that he was deprived of the benefit of his father's counsel and guidance. Some years later the *younger Sophocles*, the grandson of the great poet, came forward, at first with the legacy of unpublished dramas which his grandfather had left him, and soon after with plays of his own. As he gained the prize twelve times, he must have been one of the most prolific poets of the day ; he was undoubtedly the most considerable rival of the Æschylean Astydamas.

A younger *Euripides* also gained some reputation by the side of these descendants of the two other tragedians. He stands on the same footing in relation to his uncle as Euphorion to Æschylus, and the younger Sophocles to his grandfather ; he first brought out plays by his renowned kinsman, and then tried the success of his own productions.

§ 6. By the side of these successors of the great tragedians others from time to time made their appearance, and in them we may see more distinct traces of those tendencies of the age which were not without their influence on the others. In them tragic poetry appears no longer as independent and as following its own object and its own laws, but as subordinated to the spirit which had developed itself in other branches of literature. The *lyric poetry* and the *rhetoric* of the time had an especial influence on the form of tragic poetry.

We shall endeavour to characterize the lyric poetry of this age in a subsequent chapter (chap. XXX.) ; here we will only remark generally, that it was losing more and more every day

---

with a statue of bronze ('Αστυδάμαντα πρῶτον τῶν περὶ Αἰσχύλον ἐτίμησαν εἰκόνι χαλκῇ), which is mentioned by *Diog. Laërt.* II. 5. 43, as an instance of the unjust distribution of distinctions. He is not quite right, however ; for Astydamas lived at the time when the use of honorary statues first came into vogue. The statues of the older poets, which were shown at Athens at a later period, were erected subsequently and by way of supplement. The passage quoted above has been wrongly suspected and needlessly altered.

the predominance of ideas and feelings, and that the minor accessories of composition, which were formerly subjected to the ruling conceptions, were now, as it were, gradually becoming independent of them. It hunts about for stray charms to gratify the senses, and consequently loses sight of its true object, to elevate the thoughts and ennoble the sensibilities.

How much CHÆREMON, who flourished about Olymp. 100, B.C. 380, was possessed with the spirit of the lyrical poetry of his time, is clear from all that is related of him. The contemporary dithyrambic poets were continually making sudden transitions in their songs from one species of tones and rhythms to another, and sacrificed the unity of character to a striving after metrical variety of expression. But nobody went farther in this than Chæremon, who, according to Aristotle, mixed up all kinds of metres in his *Centaur*, which seems to have been a most extraordinary compound of epic, lyric, and dramatic poetry.[1] His dramatic productions were rich in descriptions, which did not, like all those of the old tragedians, belong to the pieces, and contribute to place in a clearer light the condition, the relations, the deeds of some person engaged in the action, but sprung altogether from a fondness for delineating subjects which produce a pleasing impression on the senses. No tragedian could be compared with Chæremon in the number of his charming pictures of female beauty, in which the serious muse of the great tragedians is exceedingly chaste and retiring; the only counterpoise to this is his passion for the multifarious perfumes and colours of flowers. With this mixture of foreign ingredients, tragedy ceases to be a *drama*, in the proper sense of the word, in which everything depends on the causes and developments of actions and on manifestations of the will of man. Accordingly, Aristotle calls this Chæremon in connexion with the dithyrambic poet Licymnius, *poets to be read*,[2] and says, of the former in particular, that he is exact, *i.e.* careful and accurate in detail, like a professed writer, whose sole object is the satisfaction of his readers.

---

[1] Aristotle (*Poet.* 1.) calls it a μικτὴ ῥαψῳδία, so that the epic element must have been the foundation of the whole. Athenæus, XIII. p. 608, calls it a δρᾶμα πολύμετρον.

[2] ἀναγνωστικοί. Aristotle, *Rhetor.* III. 12.

§ 7. But this later tragedy was still more powerfully affected by the *rhetoric* of the time, that is, the art of speaking as taught in the school. Dramatic poetry and oratory were so near one another from the beginning, that they often seem to join hands over the gap which separates poetry from prose. The object of oratory is to determine by means of argument the convictions and the will of other men ; but dramatic poetry leaves the actions of the persons represented to be determined by the development of their own views and the expression of the opinions of others. The Athenians were so habituated to hear long public speeches in their courts and assemblies, and had such a passion for them, that their tragedy, even in its better days, admitted a greater proportion of speeches on opposite sides of a question than would have been the case had their public life taken another direction. But, in process of time, this element was continually gaining upon the others, and soon transcended its proper limits, as we see even in Euripides, and still more in his successors. The excess consists in this, that the speeches, which in a drama should only serve as a means of explaining the changes in the thoughts and frame of mind of the actors and of influencing their convictions and resolves, became, on their own account, the chief business of the play, so that the situations and all the labour of the poet were directed towards affording opportunities for the display of rhetorical sparring. And as the practical object of real life was, naturally enough, wanting to this stage-oratory, and as it depended on the poet alone how he should put the point of dispute, it is easy to conceive that this theatrical rhetoric would, in most cases, make a display of the more artificial forms, which in practical life were thrown aside as useless, and would approximate rather to the scholastic oratory of the sophists than to the eloquence of a Demosthenes, which, possessed by the great events of the time, raised itself far above the trammels of a scholastic art.

THEODECTES, of Phaselis, the chief specimen of this class of writers, flourished about Olymp. 106, B.C. 356, in the time of Philip of Macedon. Rhetoric was his chief study, though he also applied himself to philosophy ; he belongs to the scholars of Isocrates, another of whom, a son of Aphareus, also left the rhetorical school for the tragic stage. Theodectes never gave up his original pursuits, but came forward both as orator and tragedian. At the splendid funeral feast, which the Carian queen, Artemisia, instituted in honour of Mausolus, the husband whom she mourned for so ostentatiously (Olymp. 106. 4, B.C. 353), Theodectes, in competition with Theopompus and other orators, delivered a panegyric on the deceased, and at the same time produced a tragedy, the *Mausolus*, the materials for which were probably borrowed from the mythical traditions or early history of Caria; but the author certainly had also in view the exaltation of the prince of the same name just dead.[1] Theodectes had so hit the taste of the age in his tragedies that he obtained eight victories in thirteen contests.[2] Aristotle, who was his friend, and, according to some, also his teacher, made use of his tragedies, as furnishing him with examples of rhetoric. Thus Theodectes, in his *Orestes*, makes the murderer of Clytæmnestra rest the justification of his deed on two points; first, that the wife who has murdered her husband ought to be put to death; and then, that it is the duty of a son to avenge his father; but, with sophistical address, he leaves out the third point to be proved, that the son must murder his mother. In his *Lynceus*, Danaus and Lynceus contend before an Argive tribunal. The former has discovered the secret marriage of his daughters with the sons of Ægyptus, and brings the latter bound before the tribunal in order to have him condemned and executed; but Lynceus unexpectedly gains the victory in the court, and Danaus is condemned to death. Affecting speeches, based on skilful argumentation, recognition scenes ingeniously introduced, and paradoxical assertions cleverly maintained, formed the chief part of the tragedies of this time, as we may see from the quotations in Aristotle's *Rhetoric* and *Poetic*. The subjects were taken from a very circumscribed set of fables, which furnished the sophistical ingenuity of the poet with an

---

[1] The *Archelaus* of Euripides is similarly related to the Macedonian king, of the name in whose honour it was composed. The name Mausolus was an old one in Caria. See Herod. V. 118.

[2] According to the epigram quoted by Steph. Byzant. v. Φασηλίς. According to Suidas, he composed fifty dramas; if this number is correct, he contended eleven times with tetralogies and twice with trilogies only.

inexhaustible fund of materials. The style approximated more and more to prose;[1] for a high poetical tone, or an antique majesty of diction, would have been altogether ill-suited to the subtle niceties of reasoning with which the speeches were pervaded.

---

[1] See particularly Aristot. *Rhetor.* III. 1. 9; and compare *Poetic.* 6. The *Cleophon*, whom Aristotle often mentions as having painted characters from everyday life, people who are quite commonplace in all their thoughts and words, probably also belongs to the times of Theodectes.

END OF VOL. I.